The Value of Work since the 18th Century

The Value of Work since the 18th Century

Custom, Conflict, Measurement and Theory

Edited by
Massimo Asta and Pedro Ramos Pinto

BLOOMSBURY ACADEMIC
LONDON • NEW YORK • OXFORD • NEW DELHI • SYDNEY

BLOOMSBURY ACADEMIC
Bloomsbury Publishing Plc, 50 Bedford Square, London, WC1B 3DP, UK
Bloomsbury Publishing Inc, 1385 Broadway, New York, NY 10018, USA
Bloomsbury Publishing Ireland, 29 Earlsfort Terrace, Dublin 2, D02 AY28, Ireland

BLOOMSBURY, BLOOMSBURY ACADEMIC and the Diana logo are trademarks of Bloomsbury Publishing Plc

First published in Great Britain 2023
This paperback edtion published in 2025

Copyright © Massimo Asta and Pedro Ramos Pinto, 2023

Massimo Asta and Pedro Ramos Pinto have asserted their right under the Copyright, Designs and Patents Act, 1988, to be identified as Editors of this work.

For legal purposes the Acknowledgements on p. xiii constitute an extension of this copyright page.

Cover design: Terry Woodley
Cover image © Kazimir Malevich, *Portrait of a record-setter in work productivity*, 1932. Artefact/Alamy Stock Photo.

All rights reserved. No part of this publication may be: i) reproduced or transmitted in any form, electronic or mechanical, including photocopying, recording or by means of any information storage or retrieval system without prior permission in writing from the publishers; or ii) used or reproduced in any way for the training, development or operation of artificial intelligence (AI) technologies, including generative AI technologies. The rights holders expressly reserve this publication from the text and data mining exception as per Article 4(3) of the Digital Single Market Directive (EU) 2019/790.

Bloomsbury Publishing Plc does not have any control over, or responsibility for, any third-party websites referred to or in this book. All internet addresses given in this book were correct at the time of going to press. The author and publisher regret any inconvenience caused if addresses have changed or sites have ceased to exist, but can accept no responsibility for any such changes.

A catalogue record for this book is available from the British Library.

A catalog record for this book is available from the Library of Congress.

Library of Congress Cataloging-in-Publication Data

Names: Ramos Pinto, Pedro, editor. | Asta, Massimo, editor.
Title: The value of work since the 18th century : custom, conflict, measurement and theory / edited by Massimo Asta and Pedro Ramos Pinto.
Description: London ; New York : Bloomsbury Academic, 2023. | Includes bibliographical references and index.
Identifiers: LCCN 2023019433 (print) | LCCN 2023019434 (ebook) | ISBN 9781350332072 (hardback) | ISBN 9781350332089 (ebook) | ISBN 9781350332096 (epub)
Subjects: LCSH: Wages–History. | Employees–Economic conditions.
Classification: LCC HD4909 .V357 2023 (print) | LCC HD4909 (ebook) | DDC 331.2/973–dc23/eng/20230606
LC record available at https://lccn.loc.gov/2023019433
LC ebook record available at https://lccn.loc.gov/2023019434

ISBN:	HB:	978-1-3503-3207-2
	PB:	978-1-3503-3210-2
	ePDF:	978-1-3503-3208-9
	eBook:	978-1-3503-3209-6

Typeset by RefineCatch Limited, Bungay, Suffolk

For product safety related questions contact productsafety@bloomsbury.com.

To find out more about our authors and books visit www.bloomsbury.com and sign up for our newsletters.

Contents

List of Illustrations	vii
List of Contributors	ix
Acknowledgements	xiii

Introduction: Exploring the Political Economy of Wages
    Massimo Asta and Pedro Ramos Pinto   1

Part One Custom and Conflict

1. Conceptualizing the Earnings of Wool Spinners in England before Industrialization *Craig Muldrew*   37
2. Wage Practices at a Red Bread Factory (Ghent, 1880–1914) *Peter Scholliers*   67
3. Papers and Wages: Identity Documents and Work in Habsburg Austria During the Late Nineteenth and Early Twentieth Century *Sigrid Wadauer*   83
4. Custom, Wages, and Hobsbawm's 'Rules of the Game': New Perspectives on Eighteenth-Century Wages *Judy Z. Stephenson*   105
5. Regulating Wage, Realizing Rights: Domestic Workers in India *Samita Sen*   121
6. Enumerating Fairness: Wages and Labour Contractors in Pre-1949 China *Limin Teh*   145
7. Everywhere but in the Strike Statistics? Wage Systems and Work Stoppages in Sweden, 1863–1927 *Tobias Karlsson*   163

Part Two Measurement and Theory

8. From Poverty Lines to Equal Pay for Equal Work: Commensuration Struggles in Apartheid South Africa *Grace Davie*   185
9. Wages Measurement in the Belgian Congo and French Sub-Saharan Africa from 1919 to Independence: a Challenge? *Béatrice Touchelay*   207
10. Down with the *Caro-vita*! A Social and Intellectual History of the Cost-of-Living Statistics in Italy, 1910s–1930s *Massimo Asta*   227

11	Adam Smith on Wages and Labour: Social Norms and Institutions as Necessary Limits to Competition *Antonella Stirati*	249
12	Devaluing Labour and Radical Theories of Worker Discrimination in North America in the Late Twentieth Century *Tiago Mata*	265
13	Rethinking the Concept of the Living Wage: Ontological Presuppositions of Emancipatory Action *Zoe Adams*	281

Selected Bibliography	303
Index	329

Illustrations

Figures

1.1 Thomas Griggs' Ballingdon Spinning Book, The National Archives (TNA), TNA, C104/19, Book 31 — 44
1.2 Thomas Griggs' Payment Book from 1758, TNA, C104/19, Book 30 — 45
1.3 Cloth Making Book of Thomas Long of Melksham 1700–10, Wiltshire and Swindon History Centre, WRO 947, 803-2 — 47
1.4 Cloth Making Book of Thomas Long of Melksham 1700–10, Wiltshire and Swindon History Centre, WRO 947, 803-1 — 47
1.5 Cloth Making Book of John Jeffries and John Usher of Wiltshire, 1721–45 — 48
1.6 Spinning Account Book of Jonathan Akroyd of Halifax, 1770s, Leeds University Library Archives, Ackroyd Accounts, 158-1 — 49

Graphs

2.1 Weekly wages of bakers at Vooruit, and cost-of-living index (1913=10), 1880–1913 — 79
3.1 Labour booklets issued in Vienna, 1861–1913 — 87
3.2 Formal charges (*Anzeigen*) filed by trade inspectors concerning labour booklets, 1894–1916 — 94
3.3 Issues at trade courts in Vienna, 1898–1914 — 101
3.4 Workers' concerns brought forward to trade inspectors, 1894–1900 — 101
4.1 Gin men's tide work at Bridge House April 1755 to April 1756. Team 1 — 116
4.2 Gin men's tide work at Bridge House April 1755 to April 1756. Team 2 — 116
4.3 Gin men's tide work at Bridge House April 1755 to April 1756. Team 3 — 117
7.1 Strikes in Sweden, 1859–1938 — 167
7.2 Proportions of work stoppages on wage levels, other issues and multiple issues in Sweden, 1903–27 — 173
7.3 Mentions of terms related to specific wage systems in relation to all work stoppages with stated causes in Sweden, 1903–27 — 173

Tables

1.1 Deductions in Pence per lb. From Spinning Rates for Market Conditions in Sussex over Time — 53

1.2	Probate Accounts from National Probate Account Database: 1600–1710	63
4.1	Number of days worked by labourers, St Paul's Cathedral, 1676–1709	115
5.1	Rise in average monthly wages of day domestic workers in Kolkata from 2006–07 to 2013–14	133
6.1	Workers' earnings of shipping companies in Shanghai, Gu Zhanran, 1932	160
7.1	List of work stoppages where the workers' stated purpose indicates a conflict over piece work in Sweden, 1859–1902	171
7.2	Nature of workers' demands in work stoppages related to wage systems in Sweden, 1903–27	174

Contributors

Zoe Adams, University of Cambridge

Zoe Adams is Fellow and Admissions Tutor at King's College Cambridge, and Affiliated Lecturer in Law at the University of Cambridge, UK, and teaches tort law, labour law, and law and economics. Zoe completed a Junior Research Fellowship at King's College Cambridge, and has recently published her second monograph, *The Legal Concept of Work*. Her first monograph, *Labour and the Wage: A Critical Perspective* (2020) was shortlisted for the SLSA-Hart Book prize, and the SLSA-Hart Early Career Academics Prize, 2021. Her academic interests lie primarily in the realm of labour law, political economy, and legal methodology.

Massimo Asta, Contemporary History Institute, Nova University of Lisbon, University of Cambridge

Massimo Asta is Research Fellow at the Contemporary History Institute (FCSH/IN2PAST) of Nova University of Lisbon, Portugal, Affiliated Lecturer at the Faculty of History of the University of Cambridge, and PDRA at Robinson College, UK. Massimo is an historian of modern and contemporary European history. His research interests include history of economic thought, intellectuals, labour history and left politics. He taught in Paris (Sciences Po) and Cambridge. He published in 2017 *Girolamo Li Causi, un rivoluzionario del Novecento (1896-1977)*.

Grace Davie, Queens College, CUNY

Grace Davie is Associate Professor of History at Queens College, CUNY, USA. Grace has received fellowships and awards from the Woodrow Wilson Center, the Social Science Research Council, and the Fulbright Scholars Program. Her first book was *Poverty Knowledge in South Africa: A Social History of Human Science, 1855–2005* (2015). Her current book, *Webs of Power: Labor Union Corporate Campaigns in the United States, 1960 2015* (forthcoming), tells the story of civil rights activists, New Left radicals, and activist-researchers who used power mapping to develop strategies and tactics for struggling labour unions in a period of rapid transformation, financialization, and anti-union repression.

Tobias Karlsson, Lund University

Tobias Karlsson is Associate Professor at the Department of Economic History, Lund University, Sweden. Tobias's research has focused on the history of labour markets and employment relationships in the nineteenth and twentieth centuries, often combining quantitative and qualitative methods. In previous projects he has addressed issues such as the gender gap in earnings, absenteeism and intergenerational transmission of occupations. Among his recent publications is 'More Power to the People: Electricity Adoption, Technological Change, and Labor Conflict' published in *The Journal of Economic History*, 81, no. 2 (2021), 481–512, co-written with Jakob Molinder and Kerstin Enflo.

Tiago Mata, University College of London

Tiago Mata is Associate Professor in Science and Technology Studies at UCL, UK. The main focus of his research has been the history of political economy. He worked both on the study of the economics discipline in the twentieth century paying attention to economists' modes of public advocacy and their engagement with social movements, and on media representations of economic knowledge and expertise. His latest research seeks to describe the corporate management of scientific research in the context of the neoliberal political economy. He has recently co-edited 'Symposium on 50 years of the Union for Radical Political Economics', *Research in the History of Economic Thought and Methodology*, 37 (A), 3–100.

Craig Muldrew, University of Cambridge

Craig Muldrew is Professor of Early Modern Economic and Social History at the University of Cambridge and Fellow of Queens' College, UK. Craig's research mainly focuses on two areas. The first is the investigation of the economic and social role of trust in the development of the market economy in England between 1500–1700. The second is the living standards and work of agricultural labourers in the early modern English economy, published as a monograph entitled, *Food, Energy and the Industrious Revolution: Work and Material Culture in Agrarian England, 1550–1780* (2011). He has also written articles in the field of legal history, on the cultural nature of money, and wages in the early modern period.

Pedro Ramos Pinto, University of Cambridge

Pedro Ramos Pinto is Associate Professor in International Economic History and Fellow of Trinity Hall at the University of Cambridge, UK, where he has taught since 2013. His work focuses on the historical origins and reproduction of inequality, with a particular focus on the history and politics of measurement. Between 2014 and 2018 he directed a research project on the History of Measurement of Inequality. He is also interested in the history and political economy of welfare, and in social movements and protest, both historical and contemporary perspective. He is the co-editor of *The History of Universal Basic Income* (2021) and *Inequality: A Global History*, forthcoming.

Peter Scholliers, Vrije Universiteit Brussel

After working for over forty years in Academia, Peter Scholliers gladly retired in 2018 but continues conducting research (actually, more than ever). Peter's interests include the history of food in Europe since the eighteenth century, material culture, development of wages, prices and purchasing power, and social inequality (these all, of course, converge). He recently published 'L'écart salarial entre femmes et hommes dans un tissage de coton gantois au XIXe siècle', in *Le Mouvement social* N° 276, no. 3 (2021):

93–106 and a book on the history of bread and bakers in Belgium since the late eighteenth century (in Dutch). The following project will be on food recommendations.

Samita Sen, University of Cambridge

Samita Sen is Vere Harmsworth Professor of Imperial and Naval History at the University of Cambridge, and fellow of Trinity College, UK. Her monograph, *Women and Labour in Late Colonial India* (1999) won the Trevor Reese Prize in Commonwealth History. She has published extensively on gender and labour, particularly on trade union movements, transport workers, domestic workers, domesticity, slavery and indenture. Her specialization is colonial South Asia but she has also done contemporary and interdisciplinary research on issues such as domestic violence and labour in the informal sector. She has co-written *Domestic Days: Women, Work and Politics in Contemporary Kolkata* (2016).

Judy Z. Stephenson, University College of London

Judy Z. Stephenson is Associate Professor in Economic History of the Built Environment at UCL, UK. Her first monograph *Contracts and Pay, Work in London Construction 1660–1785* was published by Palgrave in 2020. Judy's second monograph *Wages before Machines*, a history of wage formation and bargaining in the two centuries before industrialization, is under contract at Princeton University Press. She is currently researching different topics, such as imperfect competition in labour markets in London before industrialization, carbon, materials and finance in the preindustrial construction industry, financing of the reconstruction of London after the Great Fire, female building contractors before 1800, and literacy in the services industries in London 1550–1700.

Antonella Stirati, University of Rome 3

Antonella Stirati is Professor of Political Economy at University of Rome 3, Italy. Antonella's research primarily focuses on macroeconomics and the role of effective demand, functional distribution of income from a theoretical, applied (Italy, Europe, United States) and history of economic thought perspectives, job market, as well as on employment theory, the relationship between unemployment and inflation, and the macroeconomic effects of technological innovation. She co-edited *Sraffa and the Reconstruction of Economic Theory*, 3 vols (2013), and recently published *Lavoro e salari. Un punto di vista alternativo sulla crisi* (2020).

Limin Teh, Leiden University

Limin Teh is Lecturer in Modern Chinese History at the University of Leiden, Netherlands. Limin's research interests include social history of twentieth-century China, urban history, labour history, Japanese imperialism and the co-evolution of states and markets. She has recently published 'Geopolitics, Coal Production, and Labor Processes in the Fushun Coalmine, 1946-1948' in Christine Moll-Murata (ed.), *Northeast Asia in focus: life, work and industry between the Steppe and the Metropoles*,

1900-2020: essays in commemoration of Flemming Christiansen's retirement: Festschrift, no. 131 (2022): 45–52.

Béatrice Touchelay, University of Lille

Béatrice Touchelay is Professor in Modern and Contemporary History at the University of Lille, France. Béatrice's research focuses on the history of quantification. She is interested in the production, uses and effects of statistics on the societies that use them. Starting from the field, that of the producers and their accountants or that of the investigators of the statistical and tax services, including the institutions that centralize and transform these data to disseminate and control, she seeks to illuminate the process of the making these figures and the way they transform their environment. She has recently co-edited *Chiffres privés, chiffres publics, XVII-XXIe siècle. Entre hybridations et conflits* (2023), and edited *Fraudes, Frontières et Territoires (XIIIe-XXIe Siècle)* (2020).

Sigrid Wadauer, University of Vienna

Sigrid Wadauer is Senior Researcher in Economic and Social History at the University of Vienna, Austria. Her research focuses on topics like work and mobility, crafts and trades, autobiography and life course, and street level bureaucracy from the late eighteenth to the early twentieth century, with a regional focus on Central Europe. She has received various research grants, including an ERC-Starting grant for the project 'The Production of Work' (2008–13). Currently she is working on a project funded by the Austrian Science fund, 'Co-Producing and Using Identity Documents: Habsburg Monarchy/Austria ca. 1850-1938'. She co-edited *The History of Labour Intermediation: Institutions and Finding Employment in the Nineteenth and Early Twentieth Centuries* (2015), and recently published *Der Arbeit nachgehen? Auseinandersetzungen um Lebensunterhalt und Mobilität (Österreich 1880–1938)* (2021).

Acknowledgements

This project has received funding from the European Union's Horizon 2020 research and innovation programme under the Marie Sklodowska-Curie grant agreement no. 837524, and from Isaac Newton Trust, University of Cambridge.

Introduction: Exploring the Political Economy of Wages[1]

Massimo Asta and Pedro Ramos Pinto

I

The spectacular increase of wealth and income inequality across the globe in the last forty years has given new vigour to the debate over the determinants of the rewards of work. The expansion of the role of a dynastic, patrimonial rentier class taking advantage over those who rely on only work for their income has fuelled criticism of the relationship between capital and labour, and of the value of different forms of work.[2] This intellectual conjuncture has led to a lively global debate and demands for urgent solutions. In labour economics, it has led to a different and more complex understanding of the functioning of the labour market, and a more pluralistic approach has prevailed, even if the ontological conceptions within mainstream economics may appear substantially unchanged.[3] Interpretations of changes in wage levels have moved from demand-based explanations between sectors and within groups to approaches that take into account the role of politics, and ideology, including the demise of the social democratic tripartite arrangement, the neoliberal turn in economic policy, and the role of sharp declines in union membership.[4] The idea that employers have a determinant market power and act as a monopsonist in setting wages of their employees, even if only on account of market frictions that make it costly for workers to change jobs, has triggered a flourishing research area.[5] This view has been confirmed

---

[1] This introductory chapter is the result of a mutual enriching discussion between the two authors. Massimo Asta wrote the first four sections, Pedro Ramos Pinto the last two sections.
[2] See works of leading scholars in the field such as Branko Milanovic, *Global Inequality: A New Approach for the Age of Globalization* (Cambridge: Harvard University Press, 2016) and Thomas Piketty, *Capital in the Twenty-First Century* (Cambridge: Harvard University Press, 2016).
[3] This is the stance taken in David Spencer, *The Political Economy of Work* (London: Routledge, 2008).
[4] See for a more than anecdotal insight on the economists' mood about the topic, Paul Krugman, 'Thomas Piketty Turns Marx on His Head', *The New York Times*, 8 March 2020.
[5] Monopsony is not a new concept in labour economics. It was present in classicals as Adam Smith, Karl Marx, and Thomas Malthus. Joan Robinson re-elaborated and contributed to popularizing it. Current discussions often start from William M. Boal and Michael R. Ransom, 'Monopsony in the Labour Market', *Journal of Economic Literature*, 35, no. 1 (1997): 86–112 and Alan Manning, *Monopsony in Motion. Imperfect Competition in Labor Markets* (Princeton: Princeton University Press, 2003).

by recent studies of labour relations, which note common patterns across countries resulting 'first and foremost as an increase in employer discretion everywhere'.[6] In short, the political dimensions of work have become an important explanatory factor for wage levels, alongside the role of globalization and technological change. Unexpectedly, a similar debate on the meaning and the value of work and its remuneration has been raised by the COVID-19 pandemic, in particular concerning the role of key workers.

This broader focus on the political economy of work suggests reaching beyond the utilitarian and neoclassical concepts of marginal productivity and subjective theory of value (work-leisure trade off) and implies the inclusion of the role of institutional factors, culture and power relations.[7] What is valuable in labour, how social norms organize it and determine wages, are becoming key issues for the humanities and social sciences. In short, the question of the value of labour as it emerged in the eighteenth century is coming back into fashion.[8]

It is not only the ineffectiveness of neoclassical labour economics in explaining the incredible wage gap in recent decades that has motivated this volume. The discipline of economic history has been part of this movement, witnessing a renewed attention to the questions of wages. Nonetheless, the focus of much of this scholarship has remained predominantly the study of long-term movements in nominal and real wages, and the appreciation of the standards of living they afforded, with often the aim of comparing data across centuries, countries and continents. For the most part, these works adopt a purely quantitative approach, and the cultural, social and political determinants of wages have attracted less interest.[9] We argue that despite the huge contribution of this genre of studies to the field, long-run quantitative perspectives can also lead to an analytical and methodological narrowing of the topic,[10] and in some cases have favoured a misunderstanding of how the labour markets worked in the past (and in the present). Our intention is to provide a fresh look into the political economy of wages in history and highlight questions that may inform new studies. The contributions gathered in

---

[6] See Lucio Baccaro and Chris Howell, *Trajectories of Neoliberal Transformation: European Industrial Relations Since the 1970s* (Cambridge: Cambridge University Press, 2017), 198.

[7] Heterodox economic approaches to the labour market, Marxist, institutional, neo-Ricardian (Sraffian), post-Keynesians all stress the critical role of bargaining in shaping wage. From the perspective of the sociology of labour relations, see for example the insights brought by the supporters of the Power Resources Approach opened by Erik Olin Wright, 'Working-class Power, Capitalist-class Interests and Class Compromise', *American Journal of Sociology*, 105, no. 4 (2000): 957–1002, and Beverly Silver, *Forces of Labor. Workers' Movements and Globalization since 1870*, (Cambridge: Cambridge University Press, 2003).

[8] See for example David Graeber, *Bullshit Jobs. A Theory* (London: Penguin, 2018) and Mariana Mazzucato, *The Value of Everything. Making and Taking in the Global Economy* (London: Allen Lane, 2018), which re engaged with and enriched this debate.

[9] For a different historical institutional perspective see Michel Margairaz and Michel Pigenet (eds), *Le Prix du Travail, France et espaces coloniaux, XIXe XXIe siècle*, Paris: Éditions de la Sorbonne, 2019 and Michel-Pierre Chélini, *Histoire des salaires en France des années 1940 aux années 1960 (1944-67). Analyse historique et économique d'un système salarial avancé* (Bern : Peter Lang, 2021).

[10] For recent similar conclusions see Emma Griffin, 'Diets, Hunger and Living Standards During the British Industrial Revolution', *Past & Present*, 239, no. 1 (2018): 71–111 and Thomas Max Safley, 'The Economy of work', in *A Cultural History of Work in the Early Modern Age*, eds Thomas Max Safley and Bert De Munck (London: Bloomsbury, 2022), chapter 1.

this volume address cases across four centuries, from the eighteenth century to the present day, focusing on four key dimensions, custom, conflict, theory and measurement, which we consider essential to think about how workers were remunerated for the value their labour produces.

The eighteenth century represented a turning point in labour history as work encountered an industrializing modernity. Wage work came to be increasingly important, and people began working longer days and more days per year, as well as more years over their lives.[11] Economic and political changes triggered new ideas and practices about work. Popular conceptions emerged that viewed work as a source of political identity,[12] and later of popular sovereignty.[13] Poverty and unemployment became the subjects of reformist discourse and a policy problem.[14] Economic thought emerged as discipline, focusing on the question of labour, and theorized its economic value, originating arguments which have been, and still are, debated and contribute to shape how we look at it. 'Virtually all known forms of wage struggles and their repertoire of actions are as old as the existence of labourers'[15], but the eighteenth century saw the emergence of the first trade unions and the intensification of strikes in the repertoire of collective action.

However, the global turn in labour history invites us to question the linearity of this reading and modify this narrative by looking for transnational connected dynamics, but also by recognizing the specificities of each historical path. Looking beyond Europe implies taking into account the lasting permanence of forms of coerced and informal labour, a differentiation which cannot be explained solely by the impact of colonial domination on the forms of labour relations. It asks us to recognize the importance of recurrent (and sometimes successful) labour conflicts without the presence of large and centralized trade unions. It highlights other forms of wage setting, whether or not they involve state actors. Finally, it contributes to undermining the modernization theory and stress both diachronically and synchronically the porosity between preindustrial and industrial labour relations, and by then has re-proposed the problem of unity and comparability in different and new terms.[16]

---

[11] Jan de Vries, *The Industrious Revolution: Consumer Demand and the Household Economy, 1650 to the Present* (Cambridge: Cambridge University Press, 2008).
[12] See the chapter by Carmen Sarasúa in Deborah Simonton and Anne Montenach (eds), *A Cultural History of Work in the Age of Enlightenment* (London: Bloomsbury, 2018).
[13] William H. Sewell, *Work and Revolution in France: The Language of Labor from the Old Regime to 1848* (Cambridge: Cambridge University Press, 1980).
[14] Martin Ravallion, *The Economics of Poverty: History, Measurement, and Policy* (Oxford: Oxford University Press, 2016).
[15] Catharina Lis, Jan Lucassen and Hugo Soly, 'Introduction', in 'Before the Unions: Wage Earners and Collective Action in Europe, 1300-1850', ed. Id. *International Review of Social History*, 39 no. 2 supplement (1994): 8.
[16] Marcel Van der Linden, *Workers of the World. Essays toward a Global Labor History* (Leiden: Brill, 2008); Id., 'The Promise and Challenges of Global Labor History', *International Labor and Working-Class History*, 82, Fortieth Anniversary Issue, (2012): 57–76; id. and Karin Hofmeester (eds), *Handbook The Global History of Work* (Berlin: Degruyter, 2018); Van der Linden, Andreas Eckert, 'New Perspectives on Workers and the History of Work: Global Labor History', in *Global History Globally*, eds Sven Beckert and Dominic Sachsenmaier (London: Bloomsbury, 2018); Jan Lucassen (ed.), *Global Labour History A State of the Art. International and Comparative Social History* (Oxford: Blackwell, 2008); Lucassen and Sabyasachi Bhattacharya (eds), *Workers In The Informal Sector: Studies In Labour History 1800–2000* (Delhi: MacMillan, 2006).

By exploring the history of wage earners in Europe, United States, Africa, China and India, this book questions the traditional Europe-centred view. As Jan Lucassen has written, the history of wages, certainly, as history of work 'which is performed on the basis of a contract between a worker and an employer, and which the employer remunerates in the form of a wage', is part of the universal history of humanity, spread across different continents and regions over centuries and millennia.[17] If this represents the broad historical framework,[18] we chiefly aim to trace the complexity and the diversity of different labour historical contexts while starting from common questions which link across epochs and regions of the world. The purpose is an effort to appreciate wages as the result of complex social relations and understanding how they were perceived, theorized and contested over and regulated in specific times and spaces. We adopt agency, institutions, theory, culture and power relations as focuses to analyse how they interact with the economic factors, such as scarcity, productivity, technology, organization of labour, and so on. By including the modern and contemporary periods, intellectual and social history, economics, law, politics and policy, the aim is also to overcome the chronological, disciplinary and sub-disciplinary separations which often shape wages studies.

II

Quantitative inquiries on historical wage trends date back to the end of the nineteenth century and early twentieth century. They were triggered by the interest aroused by the rise of the labour movement, the spread of the practice of strikes and the pressing questions addressed to the state for its involvement in the functioning of the labour market. Statisticians, economists and sociologists such as Émile Levasseur and François Simiand in France, Luigi Bodio and Giuseppe Ricca Salerno in Italy, Gustav Schmoller and Robert Kuczynski in Germany, James E. T. Rogers, Arthur Bowley and George Wood in the United Kingdom, and Wesley C. Mitchell, Edith Abbott, Scott Nearing and Paul H. Douglas in the United States were the pioneers of these studies, collecting data for the production of statistical wages series from the mid-nineteenth century onwards (and in the case of Simiand even from the French Revolution) attempting to elaborate an experimental and coherent economic wage theory. These studies encouraged an international debate on the nature and measurement of wages, of which the states were in part promoters through the figures provided by their national bureaus of labour and statistics. This scholarship influenced and in turn was inspired by the public discourse of trade unions, intellectuals, experts and politicians. The impact on historiography was considerable, so much so that it was at the origin of a long well-established field of research in economic history.

---

[17] Jan Lucassen, *The Story of Work: A New History of Humankind* (New Haven: Yale University Press, 2021).
[18] See the outcomes of the fascinating research project based at the International Institute of Social History of Amsterdam, 'Global Collaboratory on the History of Labour Relations in the period 1500–2000', https://datasets.iisg.amsterdam/dataverse/labourrelations (accessed 4 August 2022).

Over time, the rationale of these studies shifted, moving from the issues of the distribution of capital and the related question of wage setting, to the measurement of past standards of living and the effect of the industrial revolution – a question that since at least the 1950s has divided scholars into 'optimists' and 'pessimists'. In addition, the increasing use of wage rates as a proxy of economic performances has been used to date and explain the unequal emergence and spread of capitalism in different regions and countries of the world, as in the debate on the Great Divergence and the European Little Divergence. Such research pursues different goals than the early nineteenth-century interest on the history of wages and appears much more interpretatively ambitious. A turning point was the publication in the 1950s of the work by Henry Phelps Brown and Sheila Hopkins which provided data on the daily wage rates for building craftsmen and labourers and the movement of prices of essential consumer goods over seven centuries.[19] Since then, historians and economists have developed approaches to wage rates in the very long run by aggregating increasingly large amounts of data and creating complex econometric models. Often, like in the works of scholars such as Robert Allen, Stephen Broadberry and Jan Luiten van Zanden, this is integrated into large scale global comparisons.[20] An important advance of studies such as these has been the inclusion of previously neglected aspects, such as the earnings and annual contracts of male and female farm servants, which allow a better appreciation of agricultural labour force;[21] the consideration of living standards across the life-cycle; the contribution of children and women to household incomes;[22] as well as the role of contractors in labour markets.[23]

Nevertheless, purely quantitative studies of wages may encounter some intrinsic limits. As John Hatcher and Judy Stephenson have recently argued, questions remain about the reliability of some long-run statistical series. The charge consists in pointing the tendency of this scholarship to create a 'false narrative' and the illusion of 'continuity

---

[19] E. Henry Phelps Brown and Sheila V. Hopkins, 'Seven Centuries of Building Wages', *Economica*, 87, (1955): 195–206; Id., 'Seven centuries of the prices of consumables, compared with builders' wage-rates', *Economica*, 23 (1956): 296–314; Id., 'Wage-rates and prices: evidence for population pressure in the sixteenth century', *Economica*, 24 (1957): 289–306, reprinted in Id, *A Perspective of Wages and Prices* (London: Routledge, 2013).

[20] Robert Allen, 'The Great Divergence in European Wages and Prices from the Middle Ages to the First World War', *Explorations in Economic History*, 38, no. 4 (2001): 411–47; Id. et al., 'Wages, Prices and Living Standards in China 1738-1925 in comparison with Europe, Japan and India', *The Economic History Review*, 64, no. S1 (2011): 8–38; Stephen Broadberry and Gupta Bishnupriya, 'The Early Modern Great Divergence: Wages, Prices and Economic Development in Europe and Asia, 1500-1800', *The Economic History Review*, 59, no. 1, (2006): 2–31; Jan Lun Van Zanden, 'Wages and Standards of Living in Europe, 1500-1800', *European Review of Economic History*, 3, no. 2 (1999): 175–98.

[21] Jane Humphries and Jacob Weisdorf, 'Wages of Women in England, 1260-1850', *The Journal of Economic History*, 75, no. 2 (2015): 405–47; id., 'Unreal Wages? Real Income and Economic Growth in England, 1260-1850', The Economic Journal, 623, October (2019): 2867–87.

[22] Sara Horrell, Jane Humphries, Jacob Weisdorf, 'Beyond the male breadwinner: Life-cycle living standards of intact and disrupted English working families, 1260-1850', *The Economic History Review*, 75 no. 2 (2022): 530–60.

[23] See the contributions of Judy Stephenson in *Seven Centuries of Unreal Wages. The Unreliable Data, Sources and Methods that have been used for Measuring Standards of Living in the Past*, eds Id., John Hatcher (London: Palgrave, 2018), chapters 5 and 6.

across the centuries that disregards the long succession of profound changes that occurred in occupational structures, the distribution of income and wealth, the importance of wage labour, the availability and continuity of employment, the level of supplementary incomes and much more'.[24] In short, they are not always able to satisfactorily overcome the difficulties posed by the extreme rarefaction of sources about wages before the nineteenth century, by the interpretation of often ambiguous records in the available sources and by the questionable representativeness of the data collected, especially if these are meant as indices capable of measuring the well-being of the entire population of workers and the economic development of nations over centuries.

This volume does not propose a critique of the tools used by purely quantitative studies and of their results. Instead, it brings forward questions not often addressed by them in order to contribute to a renewal of interest in the study of wages in their full economic, political, social, cultural and intellectual dimensions. Most macro quantitative works on the historical determinants of labour market in the long run could not avoid using the daily wage as unit of measure (which is in most cases a statistical artefact), or to adopt more or less simplified labour market models in order to make the data intelligible and comparable across place and time. The assumption is often that the forces of supply and demand regulate labour, essentially in the same way as they regulate the exchange of any other type of commodity, and all that remains is to find its information (i.e. prices) to empirically explain its historical dynamics. In this view nominal and real prices, of wages and other types of earnings, would contain all the essential information required to understand the scarcity of labour per sector and as a whole, the working of human capital in setting the levels of wages for different skills, labour productivity and so on. The point is not only that the fragmentary figures provided by the few accounting records that have come down to us are used for a heuristic task that is hard to achieve, but that often the mention of the labour market and the role of supply and demand works as shorthand for the assumption of an ahistorical neoclassical perfect competitive market model which is adopted even when knowledge about the substitution elasticities, i.e. the degree of competition in those markets, is quite vague. Different assumptions about what we interpret as constitutive factors of the determination of wages or conversely residual and temporary imperfections have important methodological and interpretative consequences. Quantitative wage studies in the long run can tell us little about how working people in a specific historical conjunctures, towns, sectors, or places of work perceived their earnings, on how income and work depended on and influenced their social status, which in turn influenced their propensity to supply their work. The welfare ratio method widely used since Allen, whether it is based on the caloric computation of a 'subsistence' basket or a 'respectability' basket,[25] remains a tool conceived to serve cliometric purposes. Without necessarily claiming, as Edward Thompson did in his

---

[24] John Hatcher, *Seven Centuries of Unreal Wages*, Ibid., 16.
[25] Robert Allen, *The British Industrial Revolution in Global Perspective* (Cambridge: Cambridge University Press, 2009), 35–8.

invective against the 'science of average', that 'is quite possible for statistical averages and human experiences to run in opposite directions',[26] it illuminates very little about what workers considered a decent or respectable wage and life. Finally, they tell us nothing about agency. Without adopting an adequate observation scale, we can learn little on situated bargaining position and power relations between capital and labour, and to what extent workers were able to bargain through individual disputes, negotiations and collective actions to maintain, restore or improve the level of wages they considered as necessary and fair. They tell us only a one-sided story about the relationship between workers' freedom and wages. Both Karl Marx and Lionel Robbins could agree that on the long run the level of wages are rigidly determined, though for very different reasons and potentially with very different outcomes. For the former it implied that 'between equal rights' of the employees and the employers, 'force decides'; for the latter it implied an imperative obligation to laissez-faire market policies.[27]

III

Economic history studies of wages are hardly impervious to the contemporary evolution of economics. When Eric Hobsbawm wrote in 1960 the seminal article 'Custom, Wages, and Workload in Nineteenth-Century Industry'[28] on the change of attitude from labourers and employers towards the rules of the market game between the middle and end of nineteenth century, he was also addressing contemporary debates in labour economics. Maybe he turned (again?) his attention to Maurice Dobb's volume *Wages*,[29] whose last revised edition of 1959 maintained the author's scepticism about the opportunity and the reliability of a general theory of wages, together with his belief about the centrality of workers' and employers' bargaining power in wage setting. Hobsbawm may have been thinking, and if this is true surely with significant disappointment, of the recent success of neoclassical labour economic theories and the beginning of the decline of Marshallian and institutionalist theories of wages.[30] Hobsbawm's article mentioned the lack of realism of marginal productivity distribution theory. It emphasized that 'even the workers most open to wage-incentives are so only up to a point: social security, comfort at work, leisure, etc., compete with money'; and that 'economic behaviour' is not based 'on long-term rational analysis, but on custom, empiricism, or short-term calculation'.[31] For Hobsbawm, this was as much the case for

---

[26] Edward P. Thompson, *The Making of the English Working Class* (London: V. Gollancz, 1963), 211.
[27] Karl Marx, *Capital. A Critique of Political Economy*, Vol. I (Hamburg: Verlag von Otto Meissner,1867); Lionel Robbins, *Wages: An Introductory Analysis of the Wage System under Modern Capitalism* (London: Jarrolds, 1926).
[28] Eric J. Hobsbawm, 'Custom, Wages and Work Load in Nineteenth-Century Industry', in *Essays in Labour History in Memory of G. D. H. Cole, 25 September 1889 -14 January 1959*, eds Asa Briggs and John Saville (London: Macmillan, 1967), reprinted in E. J. Hobsbawm, *Labouring Men: Studies in the History of Labour* (London: Anchor Books, 1968), chapter 17.
[29] Maurice H. Dobb, *Wages* (London: Nisbet and Co and Cambridge University Press, 1959)
[30] See George Boyer and Robert Smith, 'The Neoclassical Tradition in Labor Economics', *Industrial and Labor Relations Review*, 54, no. 2 (2001): 199–223.
[31] Hobsbawm, *Labouring Men*, 406.

preindustrial societies as for the present, although in different degrees. The turning point in the second half of the nineteenth century was full of consequences, but the watershed should not be interpreted in a markedly dichotomous way, as a full superseding of the preindustrial customary economy by a market-oriented capitalist economy. It is clear that a teleological perspective and a Marxist-based modernization theory bias informed Hobsbawm's take. For him, workers learned to look at labour as a commodity to sell in the labour market, and 'where they had any choice, to measure effort by payment'.[32] Nevertheless, this implies that monopsony by employers prevailed in many other cases. Conversely, employers learned through scientific management to squeeze effort and extract more output per unit of time beyond previous social constraints, that is beyond what was previously considered as customary. The evolution of the strategy of trade unions showed since the mid-nineteenth century the partial adaptation to free market bargaining and in the first decade of the twentieth century short-lived opposition to the new organization of labour.

Hobsbawm's insights inspired scholars interested in studying the 'social history of wages', as Peter Scholliers and Leonard Schwarz stressed,[33] those who considered it worthwhile analysing the standpoint of the dimensions of experience and culture of workers and employers and taking into account multiple social factors beyond of scarcity and productivity. Hobsbawm did not deny the operation of a labour market in preindustrial society. The changes he described were largely inside what in Marxian terms are relations of production. Rather he claimed that an efficient labour market arbitrage, or a self-regulating competitive market has never existed. Custom, which evolved also, but not exclusively, in relation to the mode of production, instead somewhat 'distorts' market forces in the sense that it contributes to explaining the supply side of the problem: 'The important thing to bear in mind is that the worker's wage calculation remained for long, and still to some extent remains, largely a customary and not a market calculation.'[34] This has an impact on the setting of wages but cannot by itself determine wages as other economic and social factors intervene. This kind of approach can be interpreted as an invitation to beware historical visions that try to solve the puzzle of wage determination too rapidly by opposing the economic and political spheres, and supply and demand forces to custom. This represents one of the important conceptual intuitions upon which this volume builds.

In *The Making of the English Working Class* (1963) E. P. Thompson largely took up Hobsbawm's approach. Thompson's work remains unavoidable in labour history, even if many commentaries have rightly highlighted how it failed to take into account central factors such as gender, race and the role of the empire.[35] Thompson argued that, until the beginning of the nineteenth century skilled craftsman saw their wages as regulated by custom or by their own face-to-face bargaining rather than by the rules of

---

[32] Ibid.
[33] Peter Scholliers and Leonard Schwarz (eds), *Experiencing Wages. Social and Cultural Aspects of Wage Forms in Europe since 1500*, (New York, Oxford: Berghahn, 2003).
[34] Ibid., 409.
[35] Marcel Van Der Linden, 'Labour History: The Old, the New and the Global', *African Studies*, 66, no. 2–3 (2007): 169–80.

supply and demand. The latter instead mattered in the preindustrial labour market for the 'dishonourable trade' of the unskilled workers, 'the non-society men', who were not protected by customary tradition and institutional regulation. For them earnings were decided by competition and a period of a sectorial full employment could even raise their wages above those of skilled workers. Unskilled and skilled workers were not two completely different distinct worlds: 'Skilled trades are like islands threatened on every side by technological innovation and by the inrush of unskilled or juvenile labour', he wrote.[36] The implications of this were not fully explored as the focus of Thompson largely remained on artisans rather than on 'the others',[37] but also because qualitative sources on unskilled workers are extremely rare. Thompson would partially address their culture and agency later in his work about the moral economy of the English crowd.[38] But he recognized that this new concept did not help the understanding of wages.

Yet, heuristically, the social history of wages has proved extremely fruitful, and it will continue to be so as long as we want to appreciate its complexity. Michael Sonenscher, influenced by the linguistic turn, analysed the urban trades of eighteenth-century France by moving beyond the Marxist analysis of the working-class experience and consciousness.[39] Sonenscher analysed the multiple labour relations of workers outside the protection of guilds, through the language of legal institutions, which both reflected and transformed local and trade custom, the working of the economy of workshop, the role of markets, of prices and profits, the mobility and adaptability of labour force, the fluidity of relationship between generations, and between masters and journeymen. These factors shaped the functioning of a bazaar economy, based on 'evanescent arrangements and fluid transactions' at odds with the supposed rigidity of past labour markets. Nevertheless, the role of politics, law and custom in shaping work and wages was central. Customs associated with different statuses, sometimes belonging to an informal oral culture of local and universal character, contributed to determine different levels of wages, payment in kind, perquisites, room, board, privileges, entitlements, and festivities of patron saints' days which regulate the time of work. The intersection between economics and politics resided in the 'quasi-institutional stability' that custom conferred to the labour market, despite and perhaps because of the instability which characterized the economy of the bazaar. Just as Carlo Poni's study on the Italian case,[40] Sonenscher threw new light on the fragility of past labour relations and on the presence of conflict within the world of artisans, which permanently interpreted, rediscussed, and by then legitimized the customary practices involved in the definition of the product and remuneration of work.

---

[36] Thompson, *The Making*, 269.
[37] See the title of chapter 8, Ibid., 234.
[38] Edward Thompson, 'The Moral Economy of the English Crowd in the Eighteenth Century', *Past & Present*, 50 no. 1 (1971): 76–136.
[39] Michael Sonenscher, *Work and Wages. Natural Law, Politics and the Eighteenth-Century French Trades* (Cambridge: Cambridge University Press, 1989).
[40] Carlo Poni, 'Misura Contro Misura: Come il Filo di Seta Divenne Sottile e Rotondo', *Quaderni Storici*, 47, no. 2 (1981): 385–422; Id., Cimona Cerrutti (eds), 'Conflitti nel mondo del lavoro', *Quaderni Storici*, 80, no. 2 (1992).

Innovative studies have broadened the scope of the field and provided new insights. By analysing the role of money and credit in early modern England, Craig Muldrew rethought Thompson's categories.[41] He argued that before the nineteenth century the labour market itself formed a moral economy, not just in a regulatory and conjunctural manner. Early modern labour markets were composed of 'individualistic contractual relations', whose norms and values were shared by both labourers and tradesmen alike. Workers did not behave in accordance with the Smithian self-interest. Why? Firstly, 'most buying, and selling was done on trust, or credit, without specific legally binding instruments, in which an individual's creditworthiness in their community was vital'. Secondly, 'this network of credit was so extensive and intertwined that it introduced moral factors which provided strong reasons for stressing co-operation within the marketing structures of the period'.[42] Mutuality interlinked with the market. Mutual labour, as other studies have shown, existed all over the world, particularly in rural areas in Europe as well as in China *(huangong)*,[43] and the Caribbean *(saam)*.[44] Credit practices intervene to complicate the nature of wages, as in in the lower Yangtze delta during the early Ming, where the payment of cash loans by delayed fixed quantities of rice was strictly customarily regulated.[45]

Scholars like Reinhold Reith, Leonard Rosenband, Henny Gooren, Hans Heger and Michael Huberman working on cases as diverse as the early modern German labour market, the Montgolfier Mill in France Annonay and Vidalon-le Haut in the Upper Langue d'Oc, the nineteenth- and twentieth-centuries Groningen's agriculture or the Lancashire cotton industry, have shown how the different relevance of time-rates and piece-rates depended on local social, cultural and political settings, and conversely on how technology, entrepreneurial innovation and productivity reinvented and superseded previous customary forms of wages and systems of payment.[46] Reith in particular has linked the emergence of the task rates and the spread of the monetary payment in central Europe to the intensification of strikes which put previous relations between masters and apprentices under pressure.[47] These dynamics also occurred outside Europe. In early twentieth-century China, cotton mill pay systems were clearly

---

[41] Craig Muldrew, *The Economy of Obligation: The Culture of Credit and Social Relations in Early Modern England* (London: Macmillan, 1998).
[42] Id., 'Interpreting the Market: The Ethics of Credit and Community Relations in Early Modern England', *Social History*, 18, no. 2 (1993): 163–83.
[43] Akinobu Kuroda, *A Global History of Money* (London: Routledge, 2020), 21.
[44] Nicolas van Meeteren, *Volkskunde van Curaçao* (Willemstad: Drukkerij Scherpenheuvel, 1947).
[45] James C. Shih, *Chinese Rural Society in Transition. A Case Study of the Lake Tai Area y 1368-1800* (Berkeley: Institute of East Asian studies, 1992). On mutuality in labour history see Marcel van der Linden, *Workers of the World. Essays toward a Global Labor History* (Leiden: Brill, 2008), chapter 5 to 8.
[46] Reinhold Reith, *Lohn und Leistung. Lohnformen im Gewerbe, 1450-1900* (Stuttgart: F. Steiner, 1999); Leonard Rosenband, *Papermaking in Eighteenth-Century France: Management, Labor, and Revolution at the Montgolfier Mill, 1761-1805* (Baltimore: Johns Hopkins University Press, 2000); Michael Huberman, *Escape from the market: negotiating work in Lancashire* (Cambridge: Cambridge University Press, 1996); Henny Gooren and Hans Heger, *Per Mud of Bij de Week Gewonnen. De Ontwikkeling van Beloningsystemen in de Groningse Landbouw, 1800-1914* (Groningen: Nederlands Agronomisch-Historisch Instituut, 1993).
[47] Reinhold Reith, 'Wage Forms, Wage Systems and Wage Conflicts in German Crafts during the Eighteenth and Earlier Nineteenth Centuries', in *Experiencing Wages*, eds Scholliers, Schwarz, chapter 6.

gendered: the time rate was exclusively for men, piece rate for women.[48] Weavers in Southern India explicitly mentioned the violation of custom (*mamool*) when denouncing the practices of the East India Company, which upset pre-existing labour relations[49] based on the decision of workers collective bodies and their ability to bargain.[50] The case of the migrant workers from Lancashire at the American Fall River company analysed by Mary Blewett, is a good example of how productivity, industrial revolution and new forms of exploitation increased work hours and effort, and how a new management systematically challenged customary ways to measure and evaluate skills and exertion.[51] In a longer-term perspective, the relations between effort, discipline, leisure, workers' perception of task-time, time-obedience and sense-time, as embedded in a larger history of labour entangled with the advent of capitalist modernity, the spread of mechanical timekeepers, its relation to religion and to rhythms of nature, changed over time[52] and complicate trans-epochal comparisons.

The search for the role of custom in setting wages has shaped the studies on gendered work, above all on the questions of the female–male wage gap and occupational segregation. Pamela Sharpe's work on eighteenth- and nineteenth-century England gathered empirical material for assessing non-market determinants of highly inelastic women's wages, concluding that custom outweighs 'rational economic decision-making'.[53] More recently Jane Whittle has brought substantial arguments to tackle the limits implied both in the ahistorical application of modern neoclassical theory to understand the past role of women in the labour market and the setting of their remuneration.[54] These

---

[48] Peter Scholliers, 'Work floor under tension: working conditions and international competition in textiles', in *The Ashgate Companion to the History of Textile Workers, 1650-2000*, eds Lex Heerma van Voss, Els Hiemstra-Kuperus and Elise van Nederveen Meerkerk (Farnham, Surrey, Burlington, VT: Ashgate, 2010), 695.

[49] Prasannan Parthasarathi, *The Transition to a Colonial Economy. Weavers, Merchants and Kings in South India, 1720-1800* (Cambridge: Cambridge University Press, 2001), 31–4.

[50] Prasannan Parthasarathi, 'Rethinking Wages and Competitiveness in the Eighteenth Century: Britain and South India,' *Past and Present*, 158, no. 1 (1998): 79–109.

[51] Mary H. Blewett, *Constant Turmoil: The Politics of Industrial Life in Nineteenth Century New England* (Manchester: Manchester university Press, 1990).

[52] Edward P. Thompson, 'Time, Work-Discipline, and Industrial Capitalism', *Past & Present*, 38, no. December (1967): 56–97; Douglas A. Reid, 'The Decline of Saint Monday, 1766-1876', *Past & Present*, 71, no. May (1976): 76–101; Moishe Postone, *Time, Labor and Social Domination: A Reinterpretation of Marx's Critical Theory* (New York and Cambridge, Cambridge University Press, 1993); Mark M. Smith, 'Time, Slavery and Plantation Capitalism in the Ante-Bellum American South', *Past & Present*, 150, no. 1 (1996): 142–68; John Hatcher, 'Labour, leisure and economic thought before the nineteenth century', *Past and Present*, 160 (August 1998): 64–115; Hans-Joachim Voth, *Time and Work in England, 1750-1830* (Oxford: Oxford University Press, 2000); Mathieu Arnoux, *Le Temps des Laboureurs. Travail, Ordre Social et Croissance en Europe (XIe-XIVe Siècle)* (Paris: Albin Michel, 2009) ; Didier Terrier, Corinne Maitte (eds), *Les Temps du Travail. Normes, Pratiques, Évolutions (XIVe-XIXe Siècle)* (Rennes: Presses Universitaires de Rennes, 2014).

[53] Pamela Sharpe, *Adapting to Capitalism: Working Women in the English Economy, 1700-1850* (New York: St. Martin's Press, 1996). For a similar conclusion see Gertjan de Groot, *Fabricage van Verschillen. Mannenwerk, vrouwenwerk in de Nederlandse industrie*, (Amsterdam: Aksant, 2001).

[54] Jane C. Whittle, 'A Critique of Approaches to 'Domestic Work': Women, Work and the Preindustrial Economy', *Past & Present*, 243, no. 1 (2019): 35–70. See also Id., Mark Hailwood, 'The Gender Division of Labour in Early Modern England', *Economic History Review*, 73, no. 1 (2020): 3–32, and Penelope Lane, 'A Customary or Market Wage? Women and Work in the East Midlands, c.1700 - 1840' in *Women, Work and Wages in England, 1600 - 1850*, eds Id., Neil Raven and K. D. M. Snell (Woodbridge: The Boydell Press, 2004), 102–18.

include the need to reinsert unpaid work (housework and care) in the economy. This was achieved by redefining work in preindustrial economy as largely unpaid and mostly aimed to the maintenance and survival of the family, by observing that such work was in turn largely connected to the market and commercialized, challenging the common conception about the supposed rigid occupational segregation between men and women, and about women's shorter working daily hours. In the same line of thought, although Joyce Burnett claimed that her work on the eighteenth and first half of the nineteenth century[55] supported a marginal productivity explanation based on the lower strength of women and the existence of a perfect competitive labour market, her results could also be read as meaning that custom was simply less important in determining women's pay, as one would expect. Burnett's thesis has been supported by other scholars, but often with important nuances: a marginal or inexistent gap for piece rate or hourly rate, but unequal monthly salaries because men produce more, work on higher quality products, and are more mobile in the labour market.[56] Peter Scholliers' study of Ghent cotton weaving in the nineteenth century showed a different perspective, stressing how a marginal gap in the long run can hide important gendered differences. Wages are in reality structurally unequal, as the access to the labour market privileged men, as good economic conjunctures favoured more men than women, and as men were assigned to the more valuable products. But women were successful in filling the gap by increasing their productivity, which was in the end higher than that of men, and by profiting from waves of labour conflict.[57]

As Jane Humphries claimed, in opposition to both neoclassical and simplified cultural viewpoints on male–female wage gap, the lack of alternative employment opportunities and insufficient labour mobility, initial endowments, monopsonist employers, and weakness of female bargaining are all structural elements of past labour markets, and not just imperfections of an ideal-typical competitive market. And they explain why women were the losers of the hierarchy in social status and hierarchy of wages. 'Bodily weakness and family responsibilities meant that many women were worthless to employers, but undervaluation extended to that (large) minority of women who did not share these drawbacks. The underrepresentation of exceptional (but commonly encountered) women in wage distributions and employment schedules surely implies the extension of cultural demarcations to all women, and employers, who could segment labour supplies and bargain from positions of strength, may well

---

[55] Joyce Burnett, *Gender, Work and Wages in Industrial Revolution Britain* (Cambridge: Cambridge University Press, 2008).

[56] Elise van Nederveen Meerkerk, 'Market Wage or Discrimination? The Remuneration of Male and Female Wool Spinners in the Seventeenth-Century Dutch Republic', *The Economic History* review, 63, no. 1 (2010): 165–86; Maria Stanfors, Tim Leunig, Björn Eriksson, Tobias Karlsson, 'Gender, Productivity, and the Nature of Work and Pay: Evidence from the Late Nineteenth-Century Tobacco Industry', *The Economic History Review*, 67, no. 1 (2013): 48–65; Maria Stanfors and Joyce Burnett, 'Understanding the Gender Gap Further. The Case of Turn-of-the-Century Swedish Compositors', *The Journal of Economic History*, 80, no. 1 (2020): 175–206; L. Papastefanaki, 'Salaires, Division Sexuée du Travail et Hiérarchies Sociales dans l'Industrie Textile Grecque, 1912 -1936', *Cahiers Balkaniques*, 45, no. December (2018): 101–20.

[57] Peter Scholliers, L'écart Salarial entre Femmes et Hommes dans un Tissage de Coton Gantois au XIXe Siècle', *Le Mouvement Social*, 276, no. 3 (2021) : 93–106.

have been able to pay wages below marginal productivity'.[58] Breadwinner ideologies, where the salary of women is perceived only as a complement to the household budget, have historically been considered a given.[59] Across the world, in the Netherlands, Russia, Japan, Uruguay and China in the textile sector women replaced men from the nineteenth century, clearly not to give employers a labour force with a lower productivity rate, but to resist international competition by lowering the cost of labour.[60] In addition, gender discrimination has been combined with racial discrimination. Such intersectionality in setting wages was patently visible in white settlement South Africa, where white men were remunerated twice as much as white women, and the latter earned twice as much as black men and four times as much as black women and children.[61] As pointed out by Gareth Austin 'in white-ruled settler economies of late nineteenth- and twentieth-century southern and eastern Africa, the mode of repression was different, but the basic effect was the same: land seizures and bans or restrictions on tenancy were intended to drive Africans out of the produce and into the labour market, where they received wages far less than their marginal product'.[62]

Custom and conflict are necessarily neglected and often ignored by most long-run quantitative studies. In this volume we consider them as two key dimensions (alongside the role of labour economic theory and measurement) in the political economy of wages. We interpret custom as binding rules defined as such by workers and employers or whose existence can be inferred by the observation of regular behavioural patterns, whether they convey moral norms or consist in mere repetition of beliefs and acts. We adopt it as a pertinent category for the analysis of preindustrial and industrial economies, as well as both the contemporary wealthy capitalist countries and developing countries. We do not circumscribe the meaning of custom to an equivalent of tradition and want to avoid the implicit assumption of its disappearance in advanced capitalism, or its supposed permanence in developing countries on the basis of a Western-centric narrative of modernity. Conversely, ignoring custom means bringing the illusion of a ubiquitous rational maximizer *homo economicus*, which is at odds with our conception of the working of past (and current) labour market as a social institution, to borrow the words of Robert Solow.[63] By drawing on classical and heterodox economics approaches, firstly we argue that custom is essential to labour market, and embedded in it, firstly as the latter is not able to function without a culturally and socially, as well as biologically, constructed wage floor, which in turn is mutually linked to the setting of other layers of the hierarchical structure of wages. Secondly, custom's direct relevance to the labour market consists in providing, as the law does, stability and predictability (both to workers and employers) in order to cope

---

[58] Jane Humphries, 'The Gender Gap in Wages: Productivity or Prejudice or Market Power in Pursuit of Profits', *Social Science History*, 33, no. 4 (2009): 487–8.
[59] Scholliers, 'Work floor under tension', 698.
[60] Ibid.
[61] Iris Berger, *Threads of Solidarity: Women in South African Industry, 1900–1980* (Bloomington, IN: Indiana University Press, 1992), 20–9.
[62] Gareth Austin and Sugihara Kaoru (eds), *Labour-Intensive Industrialization in Global History* (New York: Routledge, 2013), 294.
[63] Robert Solow, *The Labor Market as a Social Institution* (Oxford: Blackwell, 1990).

with the extreme uncertainty which is inherent to the exchange of this unique commodity. As Marx claimed, 'what the working man sells is not directly his labour, but his labouring power, the temporary disposal of which he makes over to the capitalist'.[64] Even formal written work agreements are necessarily incomplete as cannot guarantee all the expectations of both contractual parties.[65] Thirdly, custom exist because employers and workers reproduce it, appropriate it, bargain and struggle over it. Conflict reveals the existence of customs, as all social historians of labour know, no more than customs exist also through conflict. Productivity alone does not determine the level of wages; if anything, it provides the potential range within which custom, bargaining and capital-labour power relations set it.

Therefore, custom has a degree of inertia, and is usually subject to slow mutation. A relatively long time, often a few decades, appears necessary to make new customs socially binding, at least within a single generation of workers. In a quantitative analytical perspective, stability and stickiness of the level and differential of wages by sector, skills, age, race and gender, regardless of price movements, productivity, change in labour force composition and size, often represent the most important evidence for understanding the impact of customs, but also that of conflict. Nevertheless, this aspect cannot be interpreted in a simplistic way. Customs may go through phases of relatively rapid destabilization, and processes of innovation induced by technological change, the re-organization of work, but also by politics and ideology. The role of custom and bargaining in wage setting also does not disappear if remuneration changes because of other economic factors, nor if wages remain static because of the stability of prices of essential goods. As Leonard Schwarz argued, 'to a large extent the explanation for stability is obvious. Productivity in many trades grew slowly, so when inflation was low it is not surprising if wages changed little, and certain rates of pay came to be seen as "customary"'.[66] Conversely, describing the rigidity of wages only by the stability of essential goods' prices means not taking into account that market forces, bargaining and custom can operate in the same direction. The price driven wage explanation cannot offer any clue for understanding the tendency of wages to stay sticky-down despite periods of inflation, or sticky-up during periods of deflation. Opposing market to custom, customary wages to market wages, is more an analytical tool than an always empirically valid proposition, as custom, bargaining and economic factors recurrently combine to shape the level of wages. Custom, in particular, can have the function of legitimizing the level and differential of wages, and embedding status hierarchies. However, in specific conjunctures determined by events such as environmental, political, and economic shocks custom can also create tensions within the labour market and come into visible contradiction with the forces of supply and demand. Contrasting market and customary forces could certainly be useful to evaluate in the

---

[64] Karl Marx, *Value, Price and Profit. Addressed to Working Men*, (Workers' Intelligence Bureau, 1931 [1898]), 63.
[65] In economic sociology this role is stressed in Bénédicte Reynaud, *Le Salaire, la Règle et le Marché*, Paris, Christian Bourgois, 1992.
[66] Leonard Schwarz, 'Custom, Wages and Workload in England during Industrialization', *Past & Present*, 197, November (2007), 151.

short run the stickiness of wages, and understand the impact of custom and bargaining, as long as the sources are satisfactorily complete to clear the fog of the statistical illusion concerning the impact of all the other pertinent economic factors.[67]

Even seeing wage dispersions at the local level or in a single firm does not necessarily contradict the operation of custom, especially when there is sufficient room for bargaining between the parties. Micro approaches to the history of a single worksite or company, as Thomas Max Safley has convincingly stressed,[68] can make clearer what aggregate studies miss. It is not only a problem of the theoretical model used to engage with historical analysis of the labour market, but a question of scale of observation. Corinne Maitte claims, at the end of her study on the workers in seventeenth-century Medici buildings, that customary stratification of wages was not incompatible with a certain dispersion resulting from a 'constant personalization of the amounts negotiated by each worker'.[69] Manuela Martini on the Lyon weavers' disputes regulated by the councils of *Prod'hommes* in the second half of the nineteenth century has shown how the payment of workers was determined by a sophisticated customary knowledge used as a reference in permanent negotiation occurring from the initial oral agreement until the final actual remuneration of the workers.[70] Conversely, when wages appeared extremely dependent on differentiated rank of skills, products and individual rates of productivity, conflict may intervene to forge new customary practices, as occurred with the glass workers of the seventeenth and eighteenth centuries studied by Francesca Trivellato. By petitioning, these high skilled workers obtained the establishment of a local minimum salary by which they reduced the previously large dispersion in the level of earnings.[71] Remaining in early modern Italy, Andrea Caracausi showed how the 'just wage', according to the scholastic tradition and the following juridical doctrine, was interpreted as a *quasi quoddam pretium* (almost a price), depending on the worker's personal quality, and local customs, as enshrined by mediaeval traditions. There, the evaluation of the 'quality' of the individual was embedded both in skills and social position.[72]

Even taking into account these multiple factors and differentiated outcomes, Phelps Brown and Hopkins' findings about the astounding customary stability of nominal (and even real) preindustrial wage and wage ratio between skilled and unskilled workers have been confirmed by other studies and noticed elsewhere in the world. In

---

[67] See for example Andrew Seltzer, 'Did Firms Cut Nominal Wages in a Deflationary Environment?: Micro-Level Evidence from the Late 19th and early 20th Century Banking Industry', *Explorations in Economic History*, 47, no. 1 (2010): 112–25, and Christopher Hanes, 'The development of nominal wage rigidity in the late 19th century', *The American Economic Review*, 83, no. 4 (1993): 732–56.

[68] Thomas Max Safley, 'The Economy of Work', in *A Cultural History of Work in the Early Modern Age*, eds Id. and Bert De Munck (London, Bloomsbury, 2020), chapter 1.

[69] Corine Maitte, 'Rémunérer et Compter le Travail sur les Chantiers Médicis (fin XVIe Siècle-Début XVIIe Siècle)', *Histoire & Mesure*, 36, no. 1 (2021), 36.

[70] Manuela Martini, 'Pratiques de la Réclamation du Prix du Travail : Différends autour des Rémunérations des Tisseurs et des Tisseuses en Soie de Lyon au Début des Années 1830', *Parlement(s). Revue d'histoire politique*, 33, no. 3 (2020): 63–78.

[71] Francesca Trivellato, *Fondamenta dei Vetrai. Lavoro, Tecnologia e Mercato a Venezia tra Sei e Settecento* (Roma: Donzelli, 2000), chapter 2.

[72] Andrea Caracausi, 'The Just Wage in Early Modern Italy: A Reflection on Zacchia's De Salario seu Operariorum Mercede', *International Review of Social History*, 56, no. S19 (2011): 107–24.

China, throughout the northern and southern Song dynasty until the Ming, it is difficult to find significant changes in real wages measured in units of rice.[73] In India, unskilled wages from 1700 until the late nineteenth century, and agricultural sector wages from 1700 until very recently, have been predominantly characterized by stagnant stable subsistence rates.[74] Wages of builders, as in London and Madrid, show a striking stability over the seventeenth and eighteenth centuries.[75] Such stability can also be found in the intra-industrial ratio between skilled and unskilled workers wages. 5:2 was the ratio for kiln workers in Jingdezhen and carpenters in Huizhou, across the sixteenth century up until the early twentieth century;[76] 3:2 was the ratio in British building trade in 1412 when craftsmen earned 6d per day and labourers 4d per day, and in 1914 when the former earned 10,5d per day and the latter 7d per day (as stressed by Ian Gazeley, this only changed during the interwar years and in the aftermath of the Second World War to about 5:4.)[77] The gender wage gap also decreased in the same period, even if less dramatically.[78] In the interwar years, countries such as Italy and Spain show an opposite trend. The US and France went in the same direction of the British compression of wage differential.[79] Different causes have been highlighted, but at least in the case of the UK the unionization of unskilled workers in amalgamated centralized trade unions and the unions' strategy which spread the adoption of flat-rate bonuses could be the principal explanatory factors.[80] During the 'Golden Age' of the postwar period the exact role of trade unions and labour conflict on the increase of real wage is also disputed. Wages increased in western Europe slightly less than productivity.

---

[73] Zhiwu Chen and Kaixiang Peng, 'Production, Consumption, and Living Standards', in *The Cambridge Economic History of China, Part II 100 to 1800*, eds Debin Ma and Richard von Glahn (Cambridge: Cambridge University Press, 2022), 686.

[74] Jan Lucassen and Radhika Seshan, *Wages earners in India 1500-1900. Regional Approaches in an International Context* (New Delhi: Sage, 2022), Introduction, and chapter 6.

[75] For London see in this volume the chapter of Judy Stephenson. For Madrid see Mario García-Zúñiga and Ernesto López Losa, 'Skills and Human Capital in Eighteenth-Century Spain: Wages and Working Lives in the Construction of the Royal Palace of Madrid (1737–1805)', *The Economic History Review*, 74, no. 3 (2021): 691–720.

[76] Chen, Peng, *Production, Consumption*, 687; Christine Moll-Murata, *State and Crafts in the Qing Dynasty (1644-1911)* (Amsterdam: Amsterdam University Press, 2018), 91.

[77] Ian Gazeley, 'Manual Work and Pay, 1900–70', in *Work and Pay in 20th Century Britain*, eds Nicholas Crafts, Ian Gazeley, and Andrew Newell (Oxford, Oxford University Press, 2007), 77.

[78] Ibid.

[79] Concha Betràn and Maria A. Pons, 'Skilled and Unskilled Wage Differentials and Economic Integration, 1870-1930', *European Review of Economic History*, 8, no. 1 (2004): 29–60. See also Ian Gazeley, 'The levelling of pay in Britain during the Second World War', *European Review of Economic History*, 10, no. 2 (2006): 175–204. For contemporary economic analysis, on the trade union's ability to compress wage differential see S. Rosen, 'Trade Union Power, Threat Effects and the Extent of Organization', *Review of Economic Studies*, 36, no. 2 (1969): 185–96; Richard B. Freeman and James L. Medoff, 'The Impact of the Percentage Organized on Union and Nonunion Wages', *Review of Economics and Statistics*, 63, no. 4 (1981), 561–72; Henry S. Farber, 'Nonunion Wage Rates and the Threat of Unionization', *ILR Review*, 58, no. 3 (2005): 335–52. See also the economics of trade unions Alison Booth, *The Economics of the Trade Union* (Cambridge: Cambridge University Press, 1994), chapter 6; Alex Bryson, Harald Dale-Olsen, Kristine Nergaard, 'Gender differences in the union wage premium? A comparative case study', *European Journal of Industrial Relations*, 26, no. 2 (2020): 173–90.

[80] Roger Penn, 'The Course of Wage Differentials between Skilled and Non-Skilled Manual Workers in Britain between 1856 and 1964', *British Journal of Industrial Relations*, 21, no. 1 (1983): 69–90.

For Gunnar Myrdal trade unions allowed wages to rise by taking advantage of the full employment policies.[81] For Barry Eichengreen, instead, trade unions agreed to install a wage moderation, which in turn favoured investment and growth.[82] Both these theses imply that there was no automatic transfer of labour productivity growth into the level of wages, and that the role of the agency of workers and their organizations cannot be neglected. This reading is confirmed by the observation that the start of the large pay-productivity gap increase in the 1970s is simultaneous with the decline of labour movement (and labour share). Institutional approaches encompassing both bargaining positions within the firm and labour-capital power relations at macro scale seem necessary to grasp the problem. Roberto Franzosi has suggested interpreting the frequency of labour mobilization, strikes in particular, not only as a dependent variable from other factors (business cycles, economic hardship, political-exchange, and the institutionalization of collective bargaining), but as an independent variable. Strikes explain strikes, as they deeply impact the economy, institutions, and politics of society, and by then the ability of workers to bargain for higher wages.[83]

The embeddedness of conflict in the labour market is at the core of Beverly Silver's theory of work. Capital permanently struggles to maintain its profitability by adopting different tactics: i) the 'spatial fix', by delocalizing production; ii) the 'technological/organisational fix', by changing labour processes; iii) the 'product fix', by putting in place new product lines; iv) the 'financial fix', by moving from the real to the financial one.[84] These strategies, which are taken by capital in order to counteract the power of workers, undermine 'established customs and livelihoods', but simultaneously create the conditions for new bargaining positions, 'producing Polanyi-type of movements of self-protection among craftworkers and peasants'.[85] Marcel van der Linden suggested adding a fifth strategy, the 'labour mode fix', that is the substitution of 'one form of labour commodification for another' for example, 'by replacing "free" wage labour with debt bondage or self-employment'.[86] To this, we may add the 'labour force fix', through which capital shifts to employ cheap labour among migrants, women and racial minorities. These dynamics induce us to consider the cyclical nature of conflict within the relation between capital and labour, and fully include non-Western labour

---

[81] Gunnar Myrdal, *Beyond the Welfare State. Economic planning and its international implications* (New Haven, Yale University Press, 1960), 32–3.

[82] Torben Iversen, Barry Eichengreen, 'Institutions and Economic Performance in the 20th Century. Evidence from the Labor Market', *Oxford Review of Economic Policy*, 15 (1) (1999): 121–38. See also Chris Minns and Marian Rizov, 'Institutions, history and wage bargaining outcomes: international evidence from the post-World War Two era', *Business History*, 57, no. 3 (2015): 358–75, which undermine the role of tripartite governance in wage moderation.

[83] Robert Franzosi, 'One Hundred Years of Strike Statistics: Methodological and Theoretical Issues in Quantitative Strike Research', *ILR*, 42, no. 3 (1989): 348–62, and Id., *The Puzzle of Strikes: Class and State Strategies in Postwar Italy*, (Cambridge: Cambridge, University Press, 1994), 10–12. For a similar conclusion about the wave of strikes on the 1880 and 1890s in France, Germany and United Kingdom see Friedhelm Boll, *Arbeitskämpfe und Gewerkschaften in Deutschland, England und Frankreich* (Bonn: Verlag G. H. V. Dietz, 1992).

[84] Beverly Silver, *Forces of Labor*.

[85] Ibid., 131.

[86] Marcel van der Linden, 'Labour History Goes Global', in *The Practice of Global History. European Perspectives* (London: Bloomsbury 2019), 143.

mobilizations, which rose from the 1980s, just when in Europe they abruptly declined. This is a challenge for Western-centric theories and narratives of the end of labour and the agency of workers, as well demonstrated by the strikes triggered since the 1990s in the People's Republic of China, which have contributed to rising wages; the unprecedented Arab world cycle of strikes in Egypt from 1998 to 2010; the 2014 general strike in Argentina; or the huge public sector strike against privatizations which occurred in India in 2016;[87] and in Europe as in UK and in France in 2022–23.

IV

The chapters of the first section of this book tackle the role of custom in setting wage by adopting different perspectives. In the first chapter Craig Muldrew looks at the earnings of wool spinners in England and offers deep insights into the complexity of the nature of wage in the preindustrial period. It intervenes directly in the topical debate on the 'high wages' economy proposed by Jane Humphries and Robert Allen. By relying upon contemporary observers (such as the well-known Arthur Young), and close reading of the available account books for the seventeenth and eighteenth centuries, Muldrew shows the misunderstandings implied in the statistical procedure which translates spinner's earnings into daily monetary wage in order to make them comparable across place and time. He also challenges the reliability of the database constructed by Schneider and Humphries, which mainly uses sources from workhouses, whose employees represented a marginal minority of the whole labour force in this sector. He concludes that the remuneration of spinners worked in a very different way from what we consider a modern wage. Piece rates dominated this sector as a means to cope with the wide range of different qualities of cloth and the volatility of its market. Custom presided over the definition of the complex systems of reels and counts which in turn determined working time required per piece and its remuneration, even in different ways according to prevailing economic conditions. Shortage of small coins made remuneration mainly customary and subject to constant negotiation by payment in kind. Food, lodging and other perquisites represented the bulk of these remunerations. Payment in kind was emphasized by the patriarchal structure of families and the gendered occupational segregation, which were likely to enhance the importance of local supply networks for household necessities (normally purchased by women in the form of payment). Not only the fragmentary character of the sources and poor accounting techniques are at odds with a reliable statistical extraction of data, but as the chapter suggests the exceptional rarity of account books compared to their availability for other trades can reasonably be explained as a result of the informal nature of payments in this sector. The consequence is that spinners' remuneration likely provided a considerable contribution to the household budget, but its poor

---

[87] Sjaak van der Velden, 'Strikes, Lockouts, and Informal Resistance', in *Handbook The Global*, ed. Marcel van der Linden, Berlin: De Gruyter, 2017, 521–50. See also Andreas Bieler and Jörg Nowak (eds), *Labour Conflicts in the Global South* (London: Routledge, 2022).

monetization contributed to maintaining the patriarchal family structure. Therefore its impact on the mobility of labour market and the emancipation of women must be evaluated as marginal.

Peter Scholliers' chapter in this volume analyses the life of a socialist co-operative bakery in Ghent, *Vooruit* ('Forward'), showing the heuristic potential of the micro approach. Labour relations and wages within co-operatives still constitute a rare topic in the historiography. The hand-written minutes of *Vooruit*'s board of administration allow Scholliers to investigate a range of essential elements for understanding wages, such as fixing of tariffs, measurement of output, structure of payments and share of profit. Scholliers sheds light on how workers perceived wages and reacted to technological change as well as on the attitudes of managers and workers about crucial points such as fairness and workload. At *Vooruit*, amidst the rise of the socialist movement between 1880 and the First World War, the combination of new technology and socialist ideology gave rise to a novel wage system characterized by payment per task, a level of wages higher than the usual adopted by other bakeries, but also frequent tariff-cutting and difficult labour relations, which encompassed strikes and dismissals. Scholliers interprets *Vooruit* as a microcosm of a mixed economy driven by conflicting norms – capitalist and socialist. If the use of more and bigger kneading machines and hot-air ovens resulted in an increase of productivity, the culture and agency of workers allowed them to transform it into a system of equal pay, where wage gaps and working hours were reduced. The co-operative was also able to finance a pension fund, provide additional remuneration to compensate the work on Sundays and at night, and to guarantee the workers an income during bad times.

Nevertheless, custom is not always as positive for workers. Seeing custom, in the wake of a Thompsonian approach, solely as a source of workers' counter-hegemony to the market, neglects how custom is also embedded in labour relations which imply a degree of coercion and exploitation. Sigrid Wadauer analyses the role of booklets, *Arbeitsbücher*, (workman's passports or labour booklets), and *Dienstbotenbücher* (servants' certificates or employment booklets) in the Austrian part of the Habsburg Empire across the nineteenth and early twentieth centuries. The topic has been rarely studied by itself. In Austria-Hungary these documents – which in contrast to countries like Germany or France, were not eliminated but extended after the abolition of guilds to include more categories of workers – offer a unique prism to study the evolution of the labour market. Wadauer argues that the development of this policy of categorization remained ambivalent. The initial purpose was the control and repression of dangerous classes and single turbulent workers, as well as the attempt to enforce discipline in the workplace by both the state and by employers. A booklet showing many short-lived jobs or periods of unemployment was sufficient to ruin the worker's reputation. Even if these documents were criticized by workers and trade unions as symbols of coercion and humiliation, their use seem to have reflected and reinforced existing custom and regulations, including those about the form, composition and level of wages. Their correct use became a matter of conflict between employees and employers. Violations occurred by both parties, but the harshest consequences in case of abuses were reserved for workers. In any case, the statistics from trade court records and reports of trade inspectors analysed in this chapter indicate that the most controversial issues concerned the start and termination of work, and to a lesser extent wages.

The extent to which custom protected workers is also questioned by Stephenson, who revisits Hobsbawm's 1960 article on custom and workload, and its relevance for the historiography on early modern labour markets. Stephenson's chapter analyses some of the long-run evidence on the formation of nominal wages and its relationship to income in the building sector, extracted from the reliable and exhaustive records of St Paul's Cathedral and Bridge House in London during the eighteenth century. The figures show an extreme stability of nominal wages, suggesting the presence of custom. That wages recorded over decades, during a period characterized by price volatility and labour conflict, should show such rigidity goes against the conception of custom as solely a benign protective shield for workers. But nor does it support the idea of a perfect competitive labour market, nor Sonenscher's bazaar economy. Instead, the duration and tenure of employment mattered greatly. Stephenson emphasizes that, while wages remained constant, reductions in the number and certainty of days worked reveal a more precarious job market than scholars had recognized. As a result, income for workers in this sector appears lower than the current pessimistic estimates, suggesting a market with an unlimited supply of labour and weak workers' power, or at least insufficient to allow them to sustain sufficient work and pay. Stephenson thus calls for the uncovering of more data on eighteenth-century work, in order to explore the dynamics behind the extraordinarily static nature of nominal wages in the period, which remains unintelligible to modern mainstream economics.

The chapters by Samita Sen, Tobias Karlsson and Limin Teh all focus more directly but in different ways on wage-related labour conflicts and their outcomes. Sen's chapter on the minimum wage in present-day Indian domestic labour sector is at the intersection of gender, custom, conflict and policy. In a labour market where 95 per cent of workers are in the informal sector, the categorization of domestic workers is still debated, and there is no consensus on whether to understand them as precarious workers, 'wageless', or servants. Only indirect legislation (such as the Protection of Women from Domestic Violence Act of 2005, the Unorganised Workers' Social Security Act of 2008, and the Sexual Harassment of Women at Workplace Prevention, Prohibition and Redressal Act of 2013) contributed to their formalization, which is far from being universal and still subject to continuous bargaining and conflict between the parties. Sen provides a fascinating view on West Bengal, based on two qualitative surveys conducted in Kolkata in 2006–7 and 2013–15, including 334 semi-structured interviews with domestic labourers and thirty-four with employers, aiming to understand their opinions on unionization and legislation. Sen's chapter explores the challenges in measuring market wages, as well of setting and implementing a minimum wage within an almost completely informal system of labour relations. The task is complicated by the impact of the separation and the tensions between different social classes, castes and religions. Sen shows that wages are determined by strong local customs and conventions; that despite the flexibility and heterogeneity of arrangements wages dispersion is less significant than could be expected; and that the minimum wage proposed does not meet the requirements of a fair wage or living wage. The struggle for the realization of basic rights and the adoption of wage regulation has been greatly propelled by trade unions, which have successfully influenced the government's attitude and acted as guarantor of the implementation of the minimum wage policy. Nevertheless, for labourers in this sector, which has gone through an important process of feminization during the last four decades, unionization is not easy, and they remain largely marginalized by the main trade unions, leading to the adoption of new conflict strategies by Indian domestic workers seeking to advance their cause.

In a chapter devoted to the analysis of strike patterns in Sweden during the nineteenth and twentieth centuries, Karlsson uses two extraordinarily rich newly digitized micro-level datasets on strikes. These cover data on claims, number of workers, duration and outcome of all recorded Swedish work stoppages between 1863 and 1927. He combines this data with evidence from two case-studies, the shipyards of Götaverken in Gothenburg and of Kockums in Malmö, and the tobacco industry. Karlsson is interested in understanding the frequency of strikes initiated around wage systems, establishing whether some were more associated with strikes than others, and questioning the pertinence of available strikes statistics. He finds that the wage system is not a significant issue for strikers until the end of the nineteenth century, but in particular after 1903 either hourly pay or piece rates became central matters of conflict. Stoppages against piece rates, but above all in favour of them, and of hybrid systems became more frequent. The evidence presented in this chapter, as the author highlights, cannot establish how new Taylorist wage systems influenced the frequency of strikes. Nevertheless, very interestingly the qualitative analysis of shipbuilders and tobacco workers supports the evidence from the statistical series about a shift in union policy, from the initial rejection of piece rate to open advocacy. This is not to be neglected, as strike statistics remain often ambiguous about the claim of the workers involved in the strikes. The chapter provides an intelligent approach for looking at how workers experienced the diffusion of labour management techniques and offers a replicable framework with which to empirically measure Hobsbawm's thesis about the acceptance of 'rules of the game'.

In chapter six of this volume, Teh scrutinizes the conflicts and public discourse of trade unions against the practice of subcontracting in pre-communist China. Her purpose is to understand the progressive loss of importance and legitimacy of this kind of labour relation, in advance of its full eradication in the mid-1950s. Contract labour in this period has been extensively treated in other areas such as India, but rarely studied in China. This chapter helps to fill the gap. Teh interprets the persistence of contractors not as a result of a custom deeply rooted in a feudalist economy, but as functional to the necessity of adaptation to the rapid changes brought into China in the context of imperialism by a rapid flux of foreign investment and the impact of late industrial revolution. Nevertheless, this labour institution soon turned out to be incompatible with further capitalist expansion and mechanization. This premise seems necessary to grasp the fragility of subcontracting as social practice during the China interwar years. On one hand, contractors were progressively absorbed and recruited by the management of big companies. On the other hand, the conflicts led by contract labourers (slowdowns and strikes), which had dock workers and miners as leading forces, challenged the supposed inevitability of subcontracting in the labour market and rediscussed the meaning of fairness in employment relations. As the domestic workers in India analysed by Sen, Chinese contract workers drew on different sources of power. Workers put forward a different conception of wages, which was not the compensation imposed by or negotiated with the contractor anymore, but the remuneration they expected for the commodified labour (time and effort) sold in the labour market, according to the 'rules of game', and the price of labour sufficient to cover the cost of living. These conflicts triggered the production of a public discourse, which directly denounced contractors as the embodiment of backwards labour customs and conflated the practice of subcontracting (*baogong*) with that of indentured labour (*baoshengong*). The decline of contract labour which overlapped with some forms of coerced labour was only a question of time.

V

This volume also aims to bring a further aspect into the discussion of the role of social relations influencing wages. As surveyed above, norms and conflict have been a central plank of the discussion on custom and wages since the earliest days of economic history. But seldom has this interacted with a different strand, that of the history of measurement. We propose that taking the politics of measurement into account can help us understand the social dimension of the wage relation, particularly as earnings become integrated into a modern capitalistic system, where relations are increasingly de-individualized and norms abstracted into rules that are dependent on measurement and quantification. These two aspects are of course linked: at first sight the 'rationalization' of wage relations by their integration into systems of indices, automatic adjustments to the cost of living, etc. can be seen as forms of de-politicization, as argued by Theodore Porter.[88] However, although abstracted and depersonalized, the historical sociology of measurement has shown how the claims of the 'objectivity' of numbers obscure the fundamentally social and political processes that produce them.

Over the past decade different scholarly traditions have come together around an increased attention to the processes through which social objects are (and have been) measured and quantified, and their consequences.[89] These processes are shaped by available technologies of measurement, including the capacity of states to collate data, statistical techniques, and the ability to disseminate numbers. But they are also shaped by political and normative factors which influence what is measured, how it is measured and quantified, and with what consequences.

Labour historians are by now well familiar with the challenges of reconstructing time series from data that were not necessarily quantified at the time it was produced;

---

[88] For Porter, quantification is part of an attempt to produce the ideal (or illusion) of a politically-neutral 'mechanical objectivity': Theodore M. Porter, *Trust in Numbers: The Pursuit of Objectivity in Science and Public Life* (Princeton, N.J.: Princeton University Press, 1995), 4–8.

[89] For recent reviews see: Rainer Diaz-Bone, and Emmanuel Didier, 'Introduction: The Sociology of Quantification - Perspectives on an Emerging Field in the Social Sciences', *Historical Social Research / Historische Sozialforschung*, 41, no. 2 (2016): 7–26; Andrea Mennicken, and Wendy Nelson Espeland, 'What's New with Numbers? Sociological Approaches to the Study of Quantification', *Annual Review of Sociology*, 45 (2019): 223–45.

or regarding the silences in the data created by contemporary norms and ideologies.[90] For instance, reviewing two centuries of European data on work and wages, Humphries and Sarasúa have argued against the long-held assumption that the increases in wages led to an increase in women's participation in paid labour. Instead, they point to as systematic undercounting of women's work across several centuries and different types of data – sometimes because women's work differed in nature (at times less regular or specialized), but principally because 'ideas, cultural norms, and stereotypes acted as filters between the reality of labour markets and their historical images as reflected in official documentation'.[91] Making women's work invisible contributed to its devaluation, as did framing reproductive work as 'unskilled', but there are many other examples of how measurement choices shape considerations of value. For instance, even before the rise of the statistical state, different work contexts in Britain and Germany lead to the dissemination of significantly distinct piece rate systems in the two nations' textile industries, as argued by Biernacki.[92] In Britain, where open markets had emerged from a world of artisanal production, the factory system adopted piece rate systems where pay was measured by quantity of finished output (e.g. a given quantity of cloth), seeing the labour value as embodied in the commodity produced. In contrast, in Germany, given the survival of the guild system until the early nineteenth century, measurement was instead focused on the expense of labour power itself, expressed in the number of shots worked by the shuttle in the loom, i.e. the basic movement undertaken by the labourer. These distinct modes of measurement reflected diverse political settlements about the nature of the labour market and could lead to large differences in the relation between effort and pay, between factory rules and in the nature of labour conflict.

As this example shows, the supposed objectivity of numbers since the nineteenth century and the growing use of quantification – by states, firms and other actors – whilst often seen as a stripping away of custom and its replacement by market-enabling neutral data, can instead be seen as attempt to depoliticize the work relation, most often in favour of those who can and do set measurement conventions. Often, but not always. Workers and their representatives could also engage in their own battles over measures which inscribed values in measures and sought to set floors to wages: modern ideas about a 'living wage' were forged in the moral debates among turn of the century Catholics in the US and Ireland, from whence they made their way into the standards set by the International Labour Organisation (ILO) in the interwar and postwar periods.[93]

Nonetheless, 'living' or 'family wages' often entailed their own exclusionary assumptions, nor was the new age of global standards to have universal application.

---

[90] Hatcher, Stephenson (eds), *Seven Centuries of Unreal Wages*.
[91] Jane Humphries, and Carmen Sarasúa, 'Off the Record: Reconstructing Women's Labor Force Participation in the European Past', *Feminist Economics*, 18, no. 4 (2012): 39–67: 45.
[92] Richard Biernacki, 'Labor as an Imagined Commodity', *Politics & Society*, 29, no. 2 (2001): 173–206.
[93] Lawrence B. Glickman, *A Living Wage: American Workers and the Making of Consumer Society* (Ithaca, NY: Cornell University Press, 1997); Patrick Doyle, 'Irish Social Catholicism and the Development of the Living Wage Doctrine', *Radical History Review*, 143, no. May (2022): 177–193; Emmanuel Reynaud, 'The International Labour Organization and the Living Wage: A Historical Perspective', *Conditions of Work and Employment Series* No. 90 (International Labour Office, Geneva, 2017).

Such issues appear writ large in the three chapters devoted to measurement in this volume. Historians working on parts of the world colonized by European powers have shown how inequalities of power, racial ideologies and infrastructural constraints shaped labour relations. In attempting to transpose modern forms of measurement into colonial contexts, assumptions about the nature of work (such as the existence of written contracts, or the nature of the reward for work, encompassing payments in kind, money, or reciprocal work) or the unit of measurement (the idealized household as a nuclear family) influenced the production of numbers on wages and the colonial economy as a whole, and became sites of contestation.[94]

Focusing on French sub-Saharan Africa and the Belgian Congo between 1919 and independence, Béatrice Touchelay (chapter 9 in this volume) charts the transition from forced or coerced labour to supposedly free waged work. In the context of a chronic shortage of willing workers, the persistence of forced labour resisted the transposition of frames of reference focused on the wage relation as a contract between equals. The 'contractualization' of work, promoted by some colonial officials and by the pressure of newly created international organizations such as the ILO were strongly resisted by both colonizers and colonized. Often recruited through local chieftains, the pay and working conditions of African labourers went uncounted – an exclusion that abetted the discretionary power of employers. Touchelay also notes the different modes of management (and measurement) of labour in the French and Belgian colonies in the interwar period. In the latter, the close alliance between mining interests and the colonial state made for both an increase in the proportion of waged labour, but also the enforcement of limits on alternative employment and a suppression of wages through legal means. Yet Belgian colonial administrators were also known to intervene in criticizing the non-monetary components of the work relation – particularly overly expensive and poor quality goods made available in company stores. In French-controlled areas there was less of an incentive to corral labour into specific industries, forms of employment varied more widely, and there was not such a concern for wage counterparts. However, as the population grew and urban migration with it, the number of formal employees grew through the interwar period, and colonial officials increasingly sought to measure the quantity and the cost of labour. As Touchelay shows, even then racial hierarchies determined the boundaries of measurement – workers were not abstract providers of labour power, but first and foremost grouped in racial categories. Baskets of goods used to determine appropriate wages and taxable capacity were racially differentiated, with European baskets including higher quality and imported goods, while African ones expected cheap foodstuffs and used clothing. Attempts to survey living conditions and wages of the African workforce were underfunded, limited, and often not followed through. The postwar period brought

---

[94] Mary S. Morgan, 'Seeking Parts, Looking for Wholes' in *Histories of Scientific Observation*, eds Lorraine Daston and Elizabeth Lunbeck (Chicago: Chicago University Press, 2011), 303–25; Gerardo Serra, 'An Uneven Statistical Topography: The Political Economy of Household Budget Surveys in Late Colonial Ghana, 1951–1957', *Canadian Journal of Development Studies / Revue Canadienne d'études du développement*, 35, no. 1 (2014): 9–27; Aaron Benanav, 'The Origins of Informality: The ILO at the Limit of the Concept of Unemployment', *Journal of Global History*, 14, no. 1 (2019): 1–19.

significant changes. From the 1940s onwards, Thouchelay notes the influence of ILO standards (as well as of new international discourses of universal equality and plans for 'development' of the colonies) in attempting to impose European models of work relations, an 'ideology of free labour' and a ramping of campaigns against coerced labour. Such ambitions were hampered by the lack of consistent knowledge about working conditions, pay and cost of living of African colonial populations. Gradually, however, the colonial authorities adopted international standards of measurement and a swathe of legislative reforms looked to regulate and protect African workers. Yet, Touchelay also reveals the persistent knowledge deficit on pay and labour conditions which undermined those who sought to capitalize on promises of equality, and the endurance of racialized categories and hierarchies defining labour relations.[95]

Grace Davie's chapter in this volume turns our attention to South Africa in order to explore what Davie terms 'commensuration struggles', or conflicts over the comparability of objects of measurement. In this case, the objects are people and Davie traces the debate about commensurability across racial lines, how 'natives' and 'whites' were considered to have lives and needs which were not comparable, and how over a span of fifty years activists sought to legitimize modes of measurement that did so, and which would expose persistent inequalities. As in the French and Belgian colonies, 1930s South Africa had seen the development of the first attempts to scientifically assess living standards of the population, and the chapter focuses on the pioneering work of Edward Batson's Social Survey of Cape Town. A graduate of the LSE, Batson had been influenced by Arthur Bowley, a statistician who had reconstructed wage series for nineteenth-century Britain and pioneered sample surveying in his *New Survey of London Life and Labour*, conducted in the early 1930s. From his chair at the University of Cape Town, Batson transposed Bowley's methods to South Africa, and used the same assumptions for the needs of Cape Townians as those used for Londoners. The data collected was used to construct the Poverty Datum Line (PDL), a minimum subsistence indicator. Even as it deployed racial categories, separating the population into four 'race' groups, Batson's survey introduced the idea of commensurability of white and non-white workers, and was used by South Africa liberals to argue against discriminatory policies such as race-based wage scales. As Davie shows, this claim to commensurability (and by extension equality of regard), was opposed by white political parties whose greatest concern was the fate of 'the poor white'. It also went against the well-established practices of job reservations for whites and differential wages. Batson's was not in fact the first attempt to chart a poverty line in South Africa, but predecessors had been white-only studies, such as that produced by the 1929 Carnegie Inquiry into the Poor White Problem. In this context, for all the legitimacy bestowed on Batson's survey by the use of the latest surveying methods, the PDL had little impact on South Africa, which after 1948 found itself controlled by a white minority developing the apartheid system. In 1950, National Party initiated plans for 'separate development', which involved re-ruralizing black Africans. The PDL and its methods survived

---

[95] Cf. Frederick Cooper, *Decolonization and African Society: the Labor Question in French and British Africa* (Cambridge: Cambridge University Press, 1996).

amongst opposition circles, and would occasionally be invoked in struggles over pay and rights at the local level. This meant that, while rejected as a tool by the national government, the PDL was adopted by activists and campaigners seeking to highlight the prevalent inequality and injustice. Organizations such as the South African Council of Trade Unions, a Black labour organization, began drawing on statistics using these methods in the 1950s and, despite their suppression in the 1960s, the issue was passed on to a new generation of activists and unions. They also found allies and expertise in academic circles, and a wave of strikes and labour conflict in the 1970s brought the PDL's successors to the attention of employers under pressure from workers, as well as from a growing international boycott movement. Gradually and reluctantly the government ceded ground on differential wages and admitted commensurability, accepting the principle of 'equal pay for equal work'. In Davie's account, measurement of wages and living conditions appears entangled with social relations and political conflict at every point. Racial ideologies made black Africans invisible, or at least incomparable with whites, a factor supporting discriminatory employment practices. Yet measurement also became both object and content of political struggles and as the commensurability of people across racial lines became established, it formed the basis of institutional changes that affected wages and conditions.

The politics behind measurement choices are also in evidence in Massimo Asta's chapter for this volume. Asta highlights the political and normative dimensions of cost of living statistics in Italy through the late liberal period and the rise of Fascism. The idea and measure of the cost of living became a live issue in Italy at the start of the twentieth century. Economists and statisticians began tracing the movement of prices, spurred by the arrival of inflation following a long period of stable prices. Working-class mobilization was also on the ascendancy and the *caro-vita* (expensive living) became a mobilizing banner for labour movements, which added to the pressure on public authorities to collate and publish data on wages and prices. Under the Giolitti government of 1911–14 the state began publishing national retail price series, but these were based on a limited sample of goods and did not take into account significant regional differences. At a time when statistical techniques were developing and spreading rapidly, Italy lagged behind in the development of its official data production. It would remain so for some time: the First World War, the significant inflation it caused, and the need to placate a restive labour movement led to the development of more complex and encompassing methods to measure prices and index wages in many belligerent countries. Yet in Italy the liberal state shied away from the kinds of wartime intervention and economic management seen elsewhere. In its place, unions, employers and municipalities (especially those led by left-wing administrations) stepped in to develop ad hoc cost of living indices and systems of wage indexation at the local level, with Milan at the forefront. After the war and in the context of the heightened social conflict of the *Biennio Rosso*, the Milan model was adopted by other areas but, despite a commitment to do so in 1921, the state did not provide standardized and reliable data upon which to base a national system to measure prices and wages. Yet Italian statisticians and experts were in no way behind the times, and Asta shows how the profession – and particularly its most well-known statistician, Corrado Gini – was deeply involved in the transnational discussion of techniques and standards of measurement of the cost of living. Gini in particular had been involved in wartime inter-allied studies about calorific minima and food rations. This expertise was drawn on by the Fascist state, which created the first national statistical agency – the Central Institute of Statistics (CIS) – in 1926, under Gini's direction. By 1930 the CIS was producing Italy's first national cost of living index. As Asta shows, under fascism and Gini, Italy's cost of living index was developed in the interests of the state, used to 'depoliticise' the cost of living debate and support wage cuts: while individually each technical decision on choice of measurement, sample or weights might be justifiable, the combined effect was to consistently overvalue wages. Amongst other things, the choice of products and retail outlets sampled systematically underplayed actual prices paid by workers. In this regard, the index was part of Fascism's deflationist strategy – to maintain Italian international competitiveness and company profits and was deployed alongside the state's coercive power to reduce wage costs.

In these examples, custom and values; measurement; and conflict combine in different ways to produce wage relations where wages are not solely determined by the price mechanism. Custom, understood broadly, endures in multiple ways – in the arguments of labour for a 'decent' or 'fair' wage now backed by struggles over how to define it statistically; in the social norms influencing what is counted (and what remained uncounted), and how it is valued; or even in the choices of statistical technique or index that draw society's attention to the 'average' worker, or to extremes of poverty and wealth. Seen in this light, rather than operating a fundamental rupture between the worlds of custom and market, measurement and quantification represent more a transformation of the language in which struggles over norms, values and worth are conducted, albeit one with its own particularities and dynamics.

VI

Seeing measurement as socially constructed can also lead us to explore similar questions around economic theory. This need not mean assuming an extreme relativist take on economic ideas, seeing them simply as reflections of political and social contexts. Yet it allows us to ask how economic thought has interacted with them, and why certain approaches (in this case to the wage question) have achieved ascendancy over others. It also allows us to expand the range of ideas we can use to explore the political economy of wages, drawing on the wider classical tradition, and on heterodox schools of thought, including Marxist, institutionalist, Sraffian, Keynesian and feminist economic theory. Since the question of the value of labour is a running thread through the history of modern economic thought, these approaches are also a central part of the history of wages.[96]

---

[96] Antonella Stirati, 'Labour and Employment' in *Handbook on the History of Economic Analysis, Volume III: Development in Major Fields of Economics*, eds Gilbert Faccarello and Heinz D. Kurtz (Cheltenham: Edward Elgar 2016), 357.

Mercantilists and other pre-classical authors tended to defend wage regulation that would keep wages at subsistence level – preserving an incentive to work. Adam Smith crystallized a change in the perspective of political economists by defending high wages as a means to increase productivity, even as others who followed him (including Malthus) held a pessimistic view that high wages would lead to idleness and, ultimately, widespread misery. In none of these perspectives was, however, the wage relation considered to be defined solely by the market for labour.[97] It was the capitalist system, Marx would argue, that created the abstraction of labour. Under capitalism, to a much greater extent than any previous economic system, the worker was alienated from the means and relations of production their labour was applied to, as well as of course from the surplus value produced by it.[98] Yet, in Marx, the reproduction of capital, and the construction of wage relations in it, are imminently social and political processes belonging to a particular moment in historical evolution.

The shift away from theories of wages that sought to take into account custom, politics, values and power was built on the foundations laid by the marginalist revolution and the spread of the marginal productivity theory of wages. According to this model, in a free market wages will depend on the marginal productivity of labour i.e. that the wage will be determined by the efficiency and productivity of workers, to the exclusion of other factors (at least in the long run). As Pullen notes, this becomes a monocausal explanation of wages, and one that carries an implicit productivist morality.[99] Despite the shift in focus operated by the marginalists neither Jevons nor Marshall, two of its early leading lights, sought to detach wages completely from their broader contexts. While modelling labour supply through a utility function, Jevons conceded that the conditions of work, its quality, and considerations of race and class mattered in shaping the work relation.[100] Marshall in turn, although laying the foundations for a more abstracted view of wages, hoped that the 'decorous and chivalrous' behaviour of capitalists, would moderate the consequences of modern industry.[101]

In the United States at least, until the middle of the twentieth century the marginalist view of wages shared the stage with another school of thought which paid considerable attention to their political and social dimensions. The institutionalist school of economics, particularly in its labour economics slant, inherited from the social reform movement of the turn of the century a concern for labour relations as an object of study.[102] In terms of a theory of wages, the institutionalist ambition was to go beyond a narrow vision that saw the competitive market as the only regulating mechanism.[103]

---

[97] Spencer, *The Political Economy of Work*, 17–21
[98] Paul J. McNulty, *The Origins and Development of Labour Economics: a Chapter in the History of Social Thought* (Cambridge, MA: MIT Press, 1980), 95–107.
[99] John Pullen, *The Marginal Productivity Theory of Distribution: a critical history* (Abingdon: Routledge, 2010), 5.
[100] However, as Spencer points out Jevons' views on race and work were fundamentally racist, and he also held typically Victorian views about the English working class: Spencer, *The Political Economy of Work*, 72–4.
[101] Spencer, *The Political Economy of Work*, 85–6.
[102] McNulty, *The Origins and Development of Labour Economics*, 163–4.
[103] McNulty, *The Origins and Development of Labour Economics*, 173–4; George Boyer and Robert Smith, 'The Neoclassical Tradition, 203–5.

However, the institutionalist school failed to develop a method and a set of theories in a manner that would satisfy neoclassical economics, which evolved in other directions, in particular incorporating human capital theory to explain wage differentials within a broader marginal productivity model.[104] Moreover, as noted by David Spencer, 'with the move to embrace the Austrian approach, neoclassical economists came to view the supply of labour as a simple trade-off between income and leisure and as a result ignored the role and impact of work itself'.[105] The advent of the choice of the free agent framed within a purely subjective theory of value discarded the classical problem of cost. Work began to be interpreted 'as a means only', denying 'that it had any wider significance in the understanding of individual welfare'.[106] As a result, and to the extent that the neoclassical marginalist view on wage underpins modern economic theory, it has helped mask the importance of values, norms and social factors that contextualize and underpin the wage relation.

The last three chapters in this volume engage with classical and heterodox economic approaches on wages in different ways. Antonella Stirati builds on her extensive work on classical political economy to revisit the discussion on the nature of wages in Adam Smith. Tiago Mata takes us to another moment in the history of economic thought to explore an attempt by young radical economists to build an understanding of labour markets in alternative and critique to neoclassical theory. In a slightly different, but equally important, register, Zoe Adams explores 'everyday' understandings of wages in two debates about the living wage in Britain a century apart, and how their different assumptions lead to very different understandings of the economy and the value of work. In their different ways, these chapters show us not only that there have been, or potentially were, different ways to conceptualize the wage relation in the discipline of economics, but also how, given the right conditions, such theories inform historical enquiry and political action.

Stirati opens her chapter by summarizing the now mainstream view of wages first outlined, as we have seen, by the pioneers of the marginalist revolution. This theory posits, fundamentally, that there is an inverse relation between real wages and unemployment because of a perfect competition between workers and given that profit-maximizing firms will seek to employ less labour when its cost rises, and conversely use labour-intensive modes of production when its price falls. In this process, the interplay of supply and demand (of labour, commodities and capital) is seen as 'the only causes of income distribution'. In spite of multiple critiques from alternative and heterodox voices in economics, this abstract model continues to dominate analysis and policy to the extent that calls to introduce wage floors or employment protections are seen as interferences in the market that would lead to worse outcomes. Yet, Stirati argues, whilst often claiming descent from Adam Smith, proponents of the mainstream view misrepresent his economic theory, particularly with regards to wages – there is much more 'discontinuity' between classical and

---

[104] McNulty, *The Origins and Development of Labour Economics*, 192–7; Boyer and Smith, 'The Neoclassical Tradition', 207.
[105] Spencer, *The Political Economy of Work*, 70.
[106] Ibid.

neoclassical economics than is acknowledged. In her chapter, Stirati argues that Adam Smith proposed three main determinants of wages: historically-specific understandings of subsistence that place a customary floor on the wage rate; the power imbalance between employers and workers; and the rate of growth of the population. While some viewed these as contradictory, Stirati suggests they can be seen as part of a coherent explanation where the wage level is determined by bargaining within the constraints of customary expectations. One significant feature of this view in Smith is the extent to which social norms are involved in setting the lower limit for wages independent of other factors. This concern is consistent with the views expressed by Smith in *The Theory of Moral Sentiments*. By drawing upon Denis O'Brian's interpretation, Stirati argues that the *Theory of Moral Sentiments* provides a theoretical framework in which public and private laws are able to restrain the individual interest if this conflicts with society. In turn, *The Wealth of Nations*, provides a theory in which individual interests, thus regulated by laws, obtain optimal resource allocation. For Smith, this optimal allocation is not understood in the later neoclassical sense of efficiency, but as an 'appropriate' allocation, as a coordination between production and consumption. Smith sees the 'minimum consistent with common humanity' as barrier to the lowering of wages and, contrary to neoclassical economics, does not seem to envisage this as generating inefficiencies or a decrease in overall wealth. In fact, Stirati argues that for Smith, if this customary floor on wages were absent, unlimited competition would lead to social dislocation and have a negative effect on accumulation. What then, of the famous metaphor of the 'invisible hand'? It only means that by pursuing their own interest, the capitalists will invest and produce to meet the existing demands, a view not dissimilar to Marx's, and does not imply any market optimality. Only in the neoclassical general equilibrium terms will the invisible hand become something very different from Smith's original theory, implying the decreasing demand curves for labour and capital, full employment, simultaneous determination of relative prices, income distribution and quantities demanded. This, Stirati stresses, was simply not present in classical theory.

If Adam Smith is an unavoidable reference, Tiago Mata's contribution to this volume may at first sight appear to focus on less well-known attempts by left-wing economists to challenge dominant assumptions in neoclassical labour economics. However, exploring the segmented labour market theories of the late 1960s and early 1970s takes us to the heart of important debates about the nature of work, poverty and labour that defined that moment, and which also have a resounding echo today. Mata's chapter follows the emergence in the late 1960s and early 1970s of a group of young economists attempting to develop a new theory of labour markets that would explain exploitation and wage differentials across different work sectors, as well as racial and gender lines. As Lyndon Johnson's war on poverty struggled to make an impact, and the US economy continued to splutter, Mata argues that labour economists came to the fore in attempting to explain the value of work in mature economies. Assumptions that market mechanisms determined the price of labour in an efficient way were challenged by the observation of 'sticky wages', layoffs and the uncovering of significant wage differentials. Labour economists in the institutionalist tradition, such as Michael Piore and Peter Doeringer developed new theories to take into account the practices of firms in hiring and employment, arguing for a dual job market divided between primary jobs characterized by higher wages, higher skill and stability; and a secondary market defined by low wages and job precarity. Centred around Harvard and MIT, a group of young economists influenced by the ideas of the New Left criticized and expanded the dual labour market theory, proposing that there were further modes of segmentation and inserting the idea of racial and gender categories as important mechanisms channelling workers to different job roles (and wages). Segmented labour market theories, spearheaded by Richard Edwards, David Gordon and Michael Reich, argued that the age of free markets and competition that had characterized earlier industrial capitalism had given way to forms of cartelization and employer co-operation which used segmentation to undermine workers' collective action and increase the rate of profit. Just as Gary Becker's idea of human capital was in the ascendancy as the solution to questions of productivity and unemployment, the radical labour economists studied by Mata pointed to the educational system as one of the key instruments driving workers into different labour market segments – a view echoed by contemporary critiques of the educational system in Europe, such as Bourdieu and Passeron's *The Inheritors* (1964) or Willis' *Learning to Labour* (1977).[107] One of Mata's important contributions is to place these debates in labour economics against the wider background of political debates about poverty, welfare, race and gender in this period. The attempts by various economists, from Michael Piore and Peter Doeringer to the radical PhD students gathered around Harvard and MIT, to re-evaluate the theory of wages through a political and social lens have to be understood in the context of the rediscovery of poverty amidst affluence exemplified by the success of Michael Harrington's *The Other America*, published in 1962; Lyndon Johnson's 'war on poverty'; the civil rights movement and second-wave feminism, as well as emerging conservative arguments linking race to ideas of welfare dependency.[108] And, especially as industrial economies experienced the end of the postwar boom, debates about the nature of wages and the value of work also have to be linked to the process of de-industrialization, rising unemployment and a critique of the welfare state as expensive and inefficient. While Edwards, Reich, Gordon and their colleagues struggled to develop a theory of how capital used segmentation to drive down wages, other strands of economic theory looked elsewhere. It is at this stage that Milton Friedman's critique of welfare inefficiencies and market distortions began to gain traction amongst conservatives, and his negative income tax proposals (and libertarian versions of guaranteed income) are a market-first response to the challenges of the era. For its proponents, a negative income tax represents the most minimal intervention in the price mechanism possible and envisages a withering away of non-market institutions such as welfare systems.[109]

---

[107] Pierre Bourdieu and Jean-Claude Passeron, *The Inheritors: French Students and their Relation to Culture* (Chicago: Chicago University Press, 1979 [1964]); Paul Willis, *Learning to labor: how working class kids get working class jobs* (New York: Columbia University Press, 1981 [1979]).
[108] Alice O'Connor, *Poverty Knowledge: Social Science, Social Policy and the Poor in Twentieth-Century U.S. History* (Princeton: Princeton University Press, 2001).
[109] Daniel Zamora Vargas, 'Basic Income in the United States, 1940-1972: How the "fiscal revolution" reshaped social policy' in *Universal Basic Income in Historical Perspective*, eds Peter Sloman, Daniel Zamora Vargas and Pedro Ramos Pinto (Chm: Palgrave Macmillan, 2021)

In the end, neither the New Left's call for a coming together of the labour movement nor the neoliberal attempt to dismantle the welfare state won over, although the latter has arguably won more momentous victories along the way. Instead, it was neoclassical labour economics, reinforced by Gary Becker's concept of human capital that would have greater influence in both economic theory and welfare policy, as welfare states were reformed to deliver 'active labour market policies' (i.e. welfare support conditional on job searching and training) and targeted, means-tested transfers of declining generosity to those excluded from employment markets.[110]

Two centuries apart, the debates of classical political economists about custom and wage; and late twentieth-century discussions of guaranteed incomes and the politics of distribution serve to remind us of how much neoclassical wage theories leave out of their models accounting for the price of labour. In her chapter in this volume, Zoe Adams addresses these issues through the perspective of legal scholarship, comparing the underlying framings and jurisprudence around two living wage campaigns that arose in Britain a century apart. In the 1910s, parliamentarians for the Independent Labour Party (ILP) (at the time part of the broader coalition that would later become the modern Labour Party) started a campaign for legislation that would ensure a living wage for workers aimed at countering the widespread practice of 'sweating', i.e. the payment of wages below subsistence level. In the 2010s, in turn, the Living Wage campaign was the result of a broad-based coalition of labour unions, anti-poverty charities and campaigning group, and it set a recommended living wage to be adopted voluntarily by employers. Exploring the underlying understanding of wages in these campaigns, Adams draws on Marxist theory to highlight the distinction between the social category of the Wage (the combination of the social costs of reproduction of the labour force), and workers' wages (the contractual money renumeration by an employer to a worker for the performance of labour). In doing so Adams reminds us that the labour market does not exist in a world separate to the transfers and benefits paid from general taxation and other levies or the regulation of employment contracts and conditions but is enmeshed with the politics and values of redistribution. Presenting the ILP's living wage campaigns of the 1910s and 1930s, Adams reminds us that most late nineteenth- and early twentieth-century social reformers did little to challenge dominant beliefs about the ability of the market to deliver wages at the subsistence rate and above for all. Adams argues that factors such as underpaid female work and child labour were seen as market distortions, not principally as systemic forms of exploitation. If such evils were successfully combatted, the thinking went, men's wages would naturally rise. While not the first proposal for a 'living wage', the ILP's 1913 plans were innovative for their framing of the policy not as an end in itself, but as stepping-stone for a broader and more radical change in the control over the means of production and seeing sufficient wages as the 'first charge' on industry, taking priority over profit.

---

[110] Jamie Peck, *Workfare States* (New York: Guilford Press, 2001). For an insightful account of interplay between arguments for guaranteed income, market solutions and welfare reform in Britain see Peter Sloman, *Transfer State: the Idea of a Guaranteed Income and the Politics of Redistribution in Modern Britain* (Oxford: Oxford University Press, 2019).

Ultimately, the ILPs proposals in both moments would amount to little, but they prove a useful lens with which to consider the re-emergence of the living wage campaign in the early twenty-first century.

The re-emergence of liberal ideas about market efficiency, materialized in the reforms of the Thatcher governments, led to the roll back of the institution of the wage council. Part of the wider postwar settlement between capital and labour, wage councils brought together labour and employer representatives to consider the question of sufficient wages holistically, taking into account profits, investment and the wider range of benefits and decommodified services available to workers. By the 1990s, as it took on the reins of government, New Labour also embraced the idea of human capital investment and 'active labour markets' as the main solution to low wages – but set up a minimum wage commission to propose a floor on wages. However, the minimum wage was framed in terms of what was possible in relation to market conditions and the competitiveness of firms: what businesses wanted to afford gained precedence over the needs of waged workers. When various alliances of grassroots groups, charities and institutions began promoting the idea of a living wage, they argued for an increase in the minimum wage that took more into account than the cost of living. More recently these have been complemented by a campaign for 'living hours', fighting casualization and precarity by demanding a right to contracts that stipulate a minimum of 16 hours' work a week. Yet, unlike the ILPs vision of the living wage in the early twentieth century, these campaigns continue to frame adequate rewards to work as secondary to the profit rate and efficiency. In this way, and despite powerful normative arguments about the need for wages that allow workers to live well and participate fully in society, such political struggles over wages are conducted on a limited terrain shaped by the widespread acceptance of neoclassical theories concerning the value of work.

Taken together, the range of themes and perspectives put forward by the chapters in this volume point to the need to revisit the history of the wage relation broadly understood, taking into account how custom, workers' agency, and economics shaped and continue to shape labour relations. They point to how a more historical understanding of economic theory, of the discipline of economics itself, and how the data used by economists (and others) is produced, is fundamental to opening up the questions we ask of the past, and to a more plural take on the problems of the present. This volume cannot be but a sample of some ways to do this, but we hope one that sparks productive conversations with such aims in mind.

Part One

Custom and Conflict

1

Conceptualizing the Earnings of Wool Spinners in England before Industrialization

Craig Muldrew

The remuneration of spinners has received much attention recently in the continuing debate between Jane Humphries and Benjamin Schneider with Robert Allen over the concept of the 'high wage economy' in the *Economic History Review*.[1] The latter argued that high wages in spinning acted as an impetus towards technical innovation motivated by the desire to save on the cost of this very labour-intensive job. Humphries and Schneider, in reply, have argued that spinner's remuneration was much lower through the eighteenth century, and that technical innovation was actually motivated by profit-seeking clothiers in a desire to employ the even cheaper labour of children.[2] In this debate both Allen and Humphries/Schneider generally attempt to turn the spinner's earnings into a daily wage expressed in pence per day in order that they can be compared to other forms of earnings in place and time.[3] But while Allen relied on examples taken from secondary literature including my own, Humphries and Schneider constructed a new and impressive database which combined estimates of spinning rates together with earnings from account books and other indirect references. However, they prioritized the latter, arguing that 'the subjective judgements of non-spinning passers-by were likely to overstate rather than understate spinners' wages.... [we] remain suspicious of examples provided by commentators with particular agendas or limited direct knowledge.'[4] From these they then constructed an estimated nominal daily wage rate and presented change over time in their Figure 6.[5] The average

---

[1] Jane Humphries and Benjamin Schneider (2019), 'Spinning the Industrial Revolution', *The Economic History Review*, 72, no. 1 (2019): 126–55. I would like to thank John Styles for his helpful comments on this article.
[2] Ibid., 153.
[3] Subsequently, in a more recent series of articles written with Jacob Weisdorf, Humphries has abandoned the idea of trying to formulate day wages and has instead moved to measuring long term earnings by the year rather than the day. Jane Humphries and Jacob Weisdorf (2'15), 'The Wages of Women in England, 1260-1850', *The Journal of Economic History*, 75, no. 2 (2105): 405–47; Jane Humphries and Jacob Weisdorf, 'Unreal Wages? Real Income and Economic Growth in England, 1260-1850', *The Economic Journal*, 623, October (2019) : 2867–87.
[4] Humphries and Schneider, 'Spinning', 133, 144.
[5] Ibid., 143.

remuneration remains at about 2d. per day until 1670, which then sees a rather rapid rise to 6d. a day which lasts until 1750, where there is another rapid drop to about 3d. a day which persists right through the industrialization of spinning. No explanation is given as to why wages collapsed so much earlier than industrialization, and incidentally when exports were continually rising.

I also attempted to measure the earnings of spinners in my article 'Th'ancient Distaff' and 'Whirling Spindle', published in 2011.[6] In the article I was mainly concerned with estimating the level of employment needed to spin enough yarn for the output of the cloth industry, and possible contribution of spinning to the household income of the poor. I claimed that the amount of possible remuneration which could be obtained by spinners had gone up after the Restoration, largely driven by the increasing demand for new draperies which required stronger and thinner yarn for the weft as well as warp, than the old draperies. The new draperies, or worsteds, were thinner cloth with a visible weave, while the old draperies used looser spun yarn to make a heavier felted cloth also known as a broadcloth or a woollen. Here the yarn was pressed together into a felt by the process of fulling with a large hammer driven by a water mill. Because of this, the fineness of the yarn was not as important, although warp yarn still needed to be strong enough to be stretched on the loom. I used the terms wages and earnings pretty interchangeably, but tried to emphasize that earnings were based on piece rates which had many variables, and that work was done by both children and adults, most of which was part time. Thus, any estimates based on production could be indicative only. I also made some estimates of how earnings for spinning could have contributed to a family income over the course of a week and year. But because of the problems stated above, I relied mostly on reports of earnings made by contemporaries, especially Arthur Young. These showed that they went up from the late seventeenth century until the American Revolutionary period, driven by exports of high-quality new draperies.[7]

Although I will return briefly to a discussion as to whether earnings from spinning were rising or falling after 1750, what I wish to focus on most in this article is the complexity of how earnings for spinning, and to some extent other cloth working processes, were arranged within the industry. Because both yarn and woven cloth were manufactured to a truly huge range of different qualities and specifications for different types of cloth, within volatile market conditions of supply and demand, piece rates dominated the industry. In addition, since the demand for labour was so high in an economy chronically short of small coins for payment, we must be careful when we speak of a 'waged' labour force in this regard. This was also a period when the centre of gravity of the industry moved from the south to Northern England as it expanded,

---

[6] Craig Muldrew, 'Th'ancient Distaff' and 'Whirling Spindle': measuring the contribution of spinning to household earnings and the national economy in England, 1550–1770', *Economic History Review*, 65, no. 2 (2012): 126–55.

[7] In the conclusion, however, I did state that the huge demand for labour needed to spin yarn was an incentive for technical innovation, and that I thought that this generally supported Allen's thesis.

where patterns of employment were different as small rather than large capitalist farms were the norm.[8]

* * *

By the eighteenth century the organization of wool preparation, and the production of cloth came to be controlled by clothiers who bought the fleeces, organized the preparation, and sent the prepared wool out to be spun for wages. They then collected it for weaving and various finishing processes. Independent small workers did not disappear, however. A pamphlet of 1741 noted that there were poor families in Hampshire, Wiltshire and Dorsetshire who bought 40–50 pounds of wool at a time for carding and spinning, which they then sold at market rather than working for wages.[9] In addition, as John Styles has emphasized, farm accounts showing local 'home' production of cloth still took place in the eighteenth century.[10] But, it is probable that most of the industry by this time was based on different variations of the putting-out system, and had been for some time. This was more professional and efficient since one clothier could organize the purchase, sorting and preparation of the different staples [length] of wool needed for the yarns which would be spun and woven into the bewildering and ever-changing types of cloth demanded by changing fashion every year.

In spinning, payment was almost always by the piece, as it was based on the fineness and twist, or strength of two basic types of yarn – the warp and the weft. Generally, the quality of the yarn was measured by its fineness, although clothiers also certainly looked out for consistency in the thread. This was done by specifying the length of yarn to be spun from a pound of wool, which was measured by the number of times it could be wound around a reel returned by a spinner. Each revolution was termed a thread, and the number of revolutions was generally termed either a hank or skein, with the subdivision of a lea of half a skein. In different branches of the industry the reel could be of different circumferences. In Yorkshire, as well as the Norfolk worsted industry, a reel was one yard in circumference, and 560 threads (yards) constituted a hank. In the West Country rates of spinning were paid by the score of skeins, in which there was only 360 yards.[11] The number of hanks or skeins spun from a pound of wool constituted the 'count' which was the key measurement of the fineness of the yarn.[12] In the production of woollens, or old draperies, where the wool was carded rather than

---

[8] Keith Sugden, 'Clapham Revisited: The Decline of the Norwich Worsted Industry (c. 1700–1820)', *Continuity and Change*, 33, no. 2 (2018): 203–24.

[9] Michael Zell, *Industry in the Countryside: Wealden Society in the Sixteenth Century*, (Cambridge: Cambridge University Press, 1994), 153–5, 164–5; Julia de Lacy Mann, *The Cloth Industry in the West of England: From 1640 to 1880*, (Oxford: Clarendon Press, 1971), 89–91; Alice Clark, *Working Life of Women in the Seventeenth Century*, (London: Routledge, 1982), 108–9; Pat Hudson and Steeve King, 'Two Textile Townships, c. 1660-1820: A Comparative Demographic Analysis', *The Economic History Review*, 53, no. 4 (2000), 711–12.

[10] John Styles, 'Clothing in the north: the supply of non-élite clothing in the eighteenth-century north of England', *Textile History* 25, no. 2 (1994), 139–66

[11] Mann, *Cloth Industry in the West of England*, 324.

[12] John Styles, 'Spinners and the Law: Regulating Yarn Standards in the English Worsted Industries, 1550-1800', *Textile History*, 44, no. 2 (2013): 145–70; Norman Biggs (2004), 'A tale untangled: measuring the fineness of yarn', *Textile History*, 35, no. 1 (2004): 120–9.

combed, this was often done in the spinner's household, often by children, and this process could be included in the rate of spinning.[13] In addition there were other processes which were remunerated, such as quilling and winding, usually done by children.

In her definitive work on the cloth industry in the west of England Julia de Lacy Mann has provided some rates of spinning remuneration she worked out from two sets of West Country accounts which include some yarn for superfine Spanish Cloths made in 1713–18. This was a type of very high-quality new drapery made from a majority of merino wool. For these the warp was paid at 1s. to 1s. 3d. per score or 1s. 3d. to 1s. 7d. a pound., while the weft was paid at 9d. a pound. In comparison, course cloth from the 1650s paid only 2d to 5d. a pound.[14] Thus, more skilled spinning was paid at much higher rates per pound. However, it also took more time, which makes it very difficult to work out what the skill premium was for better work, assuming that there must have been one to incentivize spinners.

How much time it took to spin yarn is one thing we have learned much more about since I wrote in 2012. Humphries and Schneider found a number of sources which made it possible to measure rates of spinning per week, and subsequently John Styles has provided further examples from spinning contests and workhouses.[15] These examples show that the estimate of Frederick Eden, that a single hard-working woman could spin 6 lbs. of wool in a week, or 1 lb. per day was much too high. Styles has stated 'for worsted yarn, … we might conclude that, for modelling purposes at least, 0.5 lbs. per day might be a reasonable output estimate for Allen's notional "full-time" spinner of worsted, spinning to about 20 worsted count.'[16] And again, the rate would vary according to the fineness required, and the skill of the spinner. These new estimates also imply that Eden's estimate that a married spinner could spin 2.5 lbs. a week would probably be lower as well. If women were paid by the pound for spinning this means that weekly household earnings would be lower. However, it also means that the labour force required to produce the same amount of cloth would have had to have been almost twice as large as what I estimated in my 2012 article using Eden's rates. Indeed, Schneider has made an estimate of possibly as many as 1.38 million spinners by the 1770s using his and Humphries supply side calculations, and by my demand side calculations this might have been as high as 1.7 million in wool alone by the 1770s of married women equivalents.[17]

Although, as we shall see, payment varied greatly, if we assume that there were 1.5 million women spinning earning 6d. a day this would have required payment of £37,500 pounds each day, or £225,000 for a six-day week. However, for most of the

---

[13] Styles, 'Spinners and the law', 152–3.
[14] Mann, *Cloth Industry in the West of England*, 324.
[15] Humphries and Schneider, 'Spinning', 135–40.
[16] http://spinning-wheel.org/2016/12/spinning-little-stories-about-the-high-wage-economy/
[17] Humphries and Schneider, 'Spinning', no. 59, 139; Muldrew, 'Th'ancient Distaff', 518–19. My calculations were based on Eden's married women spinning rate of 2.5 lbs a week, on the assumption that children spinning less and single women spinning more would balance out at the married women's rate. However, this is probably an overestimate since young unmarried women between the ages of 14–28 formed about 24% of the female population in 1751, Edward A. Wrigley and Roger S. Schofield, *The Population History of England*, (Cambridge: Cambridge University Press, 1989), 528.

eighteenth century England's currency had become almost entirely based on gold. The undervaluing of the Mint price of silver in England by Sir Isaac Newton meant that most good quality silver coins had left the country by 1720. Subsequently, in most years before 1750, less than £5,000 was minted, and much less after this date.[18]. The recoinage in 1774 produced only about £800,000 in silver against £18.2 million in gold, demonstrating how low the amount in circulation was.[19] If all the silver in the country was used simply to pay spinning wages it would have had to circulate from the clothiers to the spinners to shopkeepers and to their suppliers and somehow back to the spinners every single month. But, of course, silver coins were needed in even larger numbers for all other economic activities as well, and in the cloth industry coins were more often used to pay male woolcombers and weavers who demanded payment in cash.[20]

But the amounts of bullion available do not tell the whole story of the availability of coins. As has been noted by many authors, there was an especial shortage of small coins because they were expensive to produce. Tradesmen and merchants preferred to see minted into coins that could be used for larger transactions and overseas trade.[21] By the 1670s only one half of one per cent of coins produced were of small denominations, and the lowest denomination minted during the recoinage of 1696 was the sixpence. This was an acute problem for the poor. Because of seasonality and the high elasticity of demand, work, especially industrial work, was often irregular, which damaged the credit of the poor and lowered their ability to buy on credit.[22] Clothiers' probate accounts from Kent show that payments were frequently in arrears for quite long periods of time. One Clothier owed a number of spinners for over 50 days' work each, while another was owed £2 10s.[23] John Styles has shown how an acute local shortage of specie in an area of North Yorkshire in the eighteenth century led to a tacit local acceptance of coining as a means of providing the poor with enough coins until possession of the counterfeit coins became a hindrance to merchants wishing to trade in distant areas where the coins were not accepted.[24]

To deal with this problem it seems that spinning remuneration evolved over time as a system of remuneration based on exchange at local shops where the putting out of

---

[18] C. D. Challis (ed.), *A New History of the Royal Mint* (Cambridge: Cambridge University Press, 1992): 434, 691–3.
[19] A. E. Feavearyear, *The Pound Sterling: A History of English Money* (Oxford: Oxford University Press, 1931), 153–4; Nicholas Mayhew, *Sterling, the History of a Currency*. (New York: Wiley, 2000), 106 7. For the English undervaluation of silver to gold compared to their prices in the rest of Europe, see Thomas Sargent and François Velde, *The Big Problem of Small Change* (Princeton: Princeton University Press, 2003), 296–8.
[20] See below, 31–2.
[21] Sargent and Velde, *Big Problem*, Ch.4
[22] Craig Muldrew, 'Wages and the Problem of Monetary Scarcity in Early Modern England,' in Jan Lucassen (ed.), *Wages and Currency: Global Comparisons from Antiquity to the Twentieth Century*, (Bern: Peter Lang, 2007).
[23] See Zell, *Industry in the Countryside*, 167 and Centre for Kentish Studies, CKS PRC2/34/295, 20/10/165, 20/9/452, 20/6/214, 20/3/507, 20/3/294, 20/2/85, 19/4/59.
[24] John Styles, '"Our traitorous money makers": the Yorkshire coiners and the law, 1760-83 (London: Hutchison, 1980), 176–8, 180. But popular acceptance of counterfeiting was also a feature of the late sixteenth and seventeenth centuries as well. Malcolm Gaskill, *Crime and Mentalities in Early Modern England* (Cambridge: Cambridge University Press, 2002), 123–200.

the wool, to be spun was organized, or on payment in cloth which could be sold locally. As Richard Soderlund has noted, manufacturers often made payments to workers in the form of goods, typically yarn or cloth which were called 'pokey', in reference to the sacking used to transport textile materials. Such materials could be used by workers to make their own clothes, or just as likely, they could be traded on local markets, such as the one held at Dewsbury in Yorkshire.[25] But, what was probably even more common was the practice of using shopkeepers as agents for organizing local spinning. The huge number of spinners most clothiers employed meant they had to turn to various agents to dispense and collect the wool they had prepared for spinning. Such people were usually shopkeepers who had the resources to pay for the wool they were distributed and who could then in turn pay the spinners with goods from their shop, or perhaps with paper receipts for the work done which could circulate within their neighbourhood.

A good example of how this worked can be found in a series of account books of the clothier Thomas Griggs of Ballingdon in the 1740s and 1750s. These survived by accident because of the failure of an executor of his estate to provide proper accounts, leading one of the principal legatees to initiate a Chancery suit in which all documents relating to the estate were delivered to the court as evidence, but which were subsequently never reclaimed.[26] Griggs produced two types of cloth; bunting for naval flags which was strong but coarse, and much finer says for home sales. He acted as a yarn master, purchasing wool, and then sorting, washing and combing it, before delivering it to spinners to be spun, and then collecting the yarn and delivering it to weavers and then dyers for finishing. He employed about 500 people in the various stages of manufacture, of which the largest number by far, 400, were spinners. The sorters and combers worked in Griggs' own premises, but all the spinners and weavers worked in their own homes. To obtain enough labour for spinning Griggs had to employ women from twenty-two different parishes in a fifteen-mile radius around Sudbury.[27] Griggs had actually started his career as a yarn dealer, buying in bulk and retailing it to independent craftsmen or to small masters. At this time his account books reveal that he accepted woven fabrics in lieu of cash for the yarn. Although this business was unsuccessful, leading to his bankruptcy in 1730, he subsequently opened a grocer' shop in Ballingdon, and by 1736 had re-entered the textile industry as a yarn master and was subsequently much more successful. This was because he was able to use his shop goods to both pay the wages of his spinners, and to raise cash for payment from other shop sales.[28] As his business grew, though, he left off shopkeeping to become a full-time clothier organizing all stages of the production of the clothes mentioned above.

---

[25] Richard J. Soderlund, '"Intended as a Terror to the Idle and Profligate": Embezzlement and the Origins of Policing in the Yorkshire Worsted Industry, c. 1750–1777', *Journal of Social History*, 31, no. 3 (1998), 652 and *Leeds Intelligencer*, 26 April 1791.

[26] K. H. Burley, 'Some Accounting Records of an Eighteenth-Century Clothier', *Accounting Research*, 9, January (1958) 50–1.

[27] K. H. Burley, 'An Essex Clothier of the Eighteenth Century', *The Economic History Review*, vol. 11, no. 2 (1958): 290–2. Weaving, of course, was also highly skilled, but being trained through apprenticeship quality here was controlled in a different way. Weaver's were paid according to the number of skeins of woof yarn woven at different rates for each sort of fabric and then were fined if the quality was poorer than set down by various statutes. Ibid., 294.

[28] Burley, 'Essex Clothier', 290–1.

From the late 1740s onwards an agent, Peter Bowers, was employed to assist in the organization of spinning work from a shop in Waldingfield, a parish to the north of Sudbury. One set of accounts survives, but in poor condition which seem to be intended to be a record of all of the wool he put out for spinning every four months, and the amount of yarn returned for the same period. For instance, in the four months from February to May 1755 he put out 2,973 lbs. of wool to be spun and received in 2,197 tops in return – a top being the local word for a skein weighing a pound.[29] This works out to about 18 lbs of yarn per day being delivered back. The yarn was valued by the score and was said to be spun to a certain total value, for which a usually smaller payment was made. This was a result of the practice common in some cloth producing areas of making a deduction from a set rate per reel or pound when demand was lower, which will be discussed in more detail below. This was worth £78 which was delivered in fifteen deliveries of 5–12 scores each.[30] These deliveries are matched on the credit side of the accounts with what are usually listed as just cash payments for slightly different amounts but usually for around £5 to £7, and which add up to totals which are within £2 to £3 of the total value of the yarn delivered. On a few occasions however, shop goods are listed as payment instead of cash. In the entries for January to April 1751 there are nine payments in cash and 4 tea, 4 sugar, one piece of cloth and one cheese. Most of the goods purchased are large amounts such as a pound of tea or 35–50 lbs of cheese, or 14 lbs of sugar. Significantly, they are all luxury items being exchanged for spinning work. Interestingly, inserted into the accounts there is also a loose poem called a grace before tea written by the accountant:

> I Grant That we by drinking Tea
> With Bread and Butter Plenty
> Good Sugar store and water more
> To fill the Pot when empty
> Grant the Cake wich we Do eate
> May make us strong to Leabour
> And that we may our visits
> Pay this Day unto our Naighbour

Although this presents a rather rosy view of what was hard repetitive work, it does show why tea became considered a reward for labour in this period.

However, the payments for goods are mostly confined to a few occasions.[31] The book is also odd, in that no names are ever given for either the debits or credits. Presumably these must have been listed in other books together with the goods sold at the shop, with the cash payments listed here being transferred to the shop book. The main purpose of this book is to keep track of the amount of wool put out and the amount returned. Why some sales of goods ended up being directly recorded in this

---

[29] TNA, C104/19, Book 23, 200. Slide 62–3
[30] Ibid.
[31] For instance, Ibid., the entries for February, March and April 1751, 221. Slide 25.

book is unknown but could have been the result of the accountant needing to do something directly and perhaps quickly. But it is evidence that goods were being used instead of cash payments. Individual spinners, or more often their husbands (named instead of their wives because of the rules of coverture), and their places of residence are named in another book titled 'An account of the spinning brought out of the Ballingdon spinning book July 20, 1750' shown in Fig. 1.1.[32]

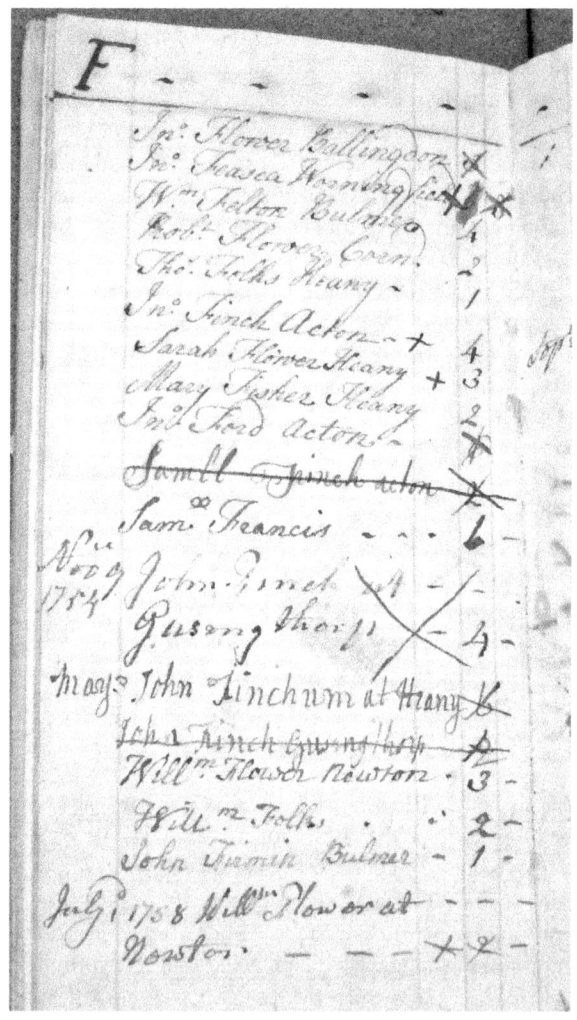

Figure 1.1 Thomas Griggs' Ballingdon Spinning Book, The National Archives (TNA), TNA, C104/19, Book 31.[33]

---

[32] TNA, C104/19, Book 31.
[33] TNA, C104/19, Book 31.

This book consists of an alphabetical listing of probably all of the spinners employed by Griggs listed on the left-hand side of the page together with three columns on the right. These columns contain numbers only in the centre column, with a few x's in the first column or crossing out the number in the second. The numbers are mostly 1–6 but some as high as 12, and some of the names are crossed out. What these figures mean is unclear.

Yet another book exists called cash paid to the work people, from 1758 presented in Fig. 1.2. This book is a list of daily payments of usually 10–20 individuals per day. A small number of the entries are explicitly stated to be payments for spinning winding or scouring, the others have no indication of what they are for. But, given that so many

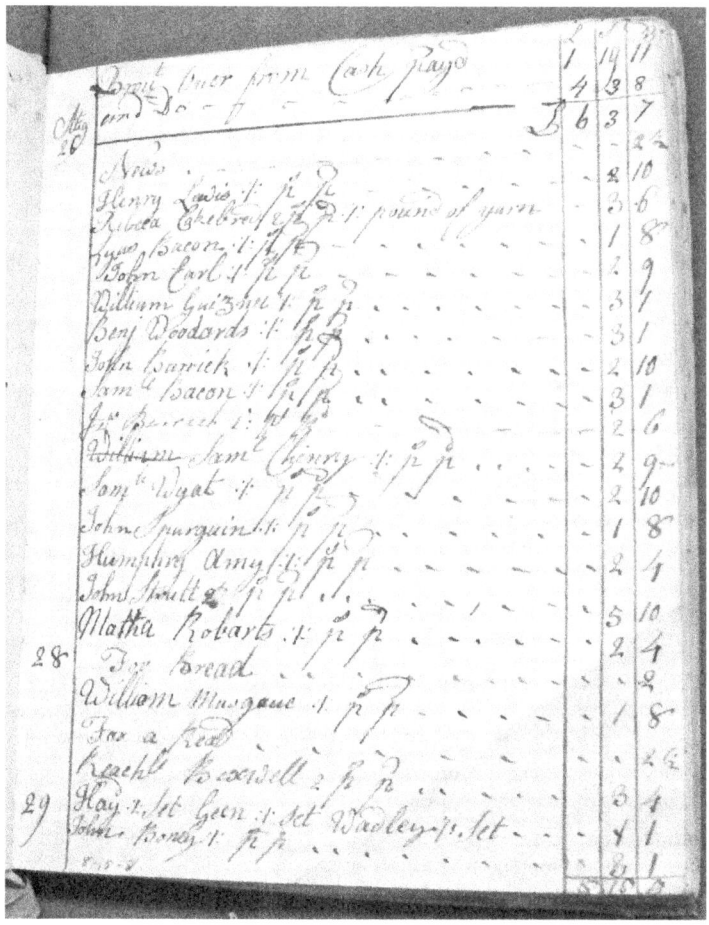

Figure 1.2 Thomas Griggs' Payment Book from 1758, TNA, C104/19, Book 30.[34]

---

[34] TNA, C104/19, Book 30.

of the names are women it is most likely a book of payments for spinning. The payments for individual pounds of yarn range from 6d to 15 d., but the most common payment, however, is simply listed as being for 1 or 2 p^o p^d or 1 or more Do. p^d and Sets, with payments for one being between 2s. 11d. and 3s. It is not clear what these measurements might be. There are also payments for winding sets of warp p^d. The most obvious interpretation would be that p^o is an abbreviation for lb and p^d for paid. Why some spinning is listed by the pound of yarn spelled out is not specified, but in such cases the amount paid is much lower, and some is noted as being obtained from the parish workhouse.[35] It could be that they are designations for different sorts of yarn, and if so this implies that what Griggs had to pay for fine yarn in 1758 was considerably higher than the examples of costs he made in 1752, where fine yarn generally was paid at 1s. 3d. per lb.

Griggs certainly used ready cash, but as his main series of cash books demonstrate he was much more dependent on bills of exchange for his trade with London and especially notes of hand for both local and longer distance payments.[36] Like most early modern account survivals, what has survived of Grigg's records is a hodgepodge of a more complete system of accounting. But even so we can see that it used a mixture of some elements of double entry bookkeeping with traditional methods.

Such methods are even more in evidence in the few other earlier surviving accounts of clothiers. The following examples come from a series of pattern books and accompanying cloth making books which survive for Thomas Long of Melksham, Wiltshire from 1699–1729. He was a maker of medleys, a type of high-quality old drapery. Fig. 1.3 shows a page from a cloth making book for 1700–10 which lists the costs of manufacture for superfine cloths numbers 492–4.

On the left-hand side we can see pounds of wool spun by each spinner and the number of leas this produced. The term lea is not given here, but it is for some other cloths. Then we see monetary amounts after this. These figures were used by Julia de Lacy Mann, to work out the cost per pound of spinning cited above. However, the inclusion of monetary amounts for the spinning in these books is quite rare, and only occurred for superfines.

Fig. 1.4 presents a more typical sort of entry in Long's book, with a lot of numbers. What it seems to be showing is the spinning of different sorts of yarn – each number is probably a score of skeins, although in the bottom right-hand corner we can see that Sarah Pelinnger has been lent 2s. 6d. So, pounds, reels and money can be all mixed up in a system the accountant and the workers must have known how to understand. Since there are many such 'lent' entries I think we can assume this was something the spinners understood, not just the writer of the accounts. Fig. 1.5 is a similar type of entry from Cloth Making Book of John Jeffries and John Usher of Wiltshire, 1721–45 who also made Spanish cloth.[37]

---

[35] This was also the case with Widow Watson cited in Humphries and Schneider, 'Spinning', 136.
[36] Burley, 'Essex Clothier', 298–301.
[37] WRO 927-1 Picture 33.

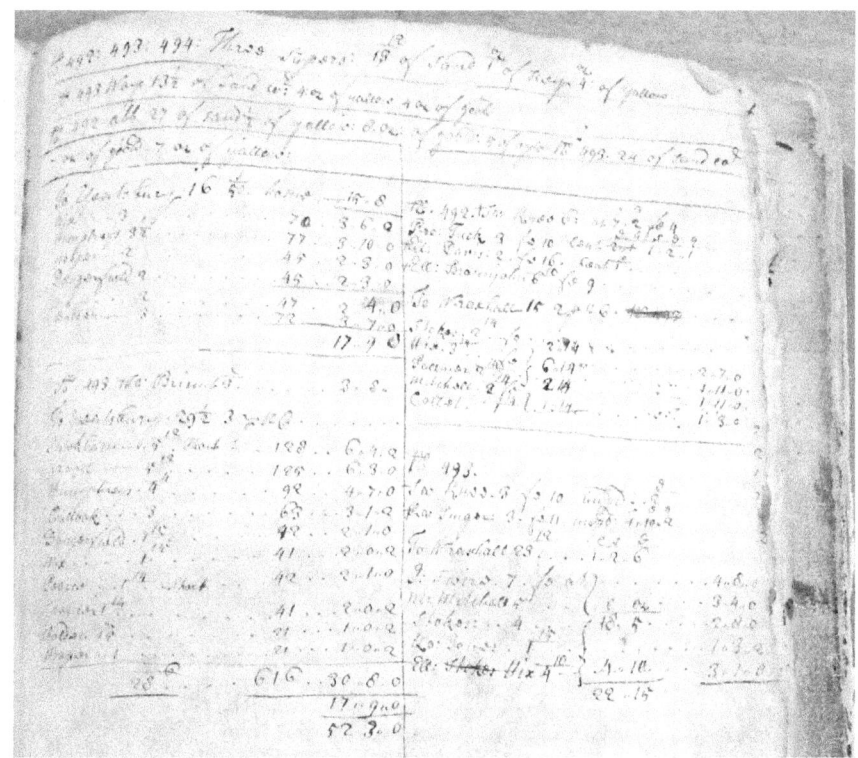

Figure 1.3 Cloth Making Book of Thomas Long of Melksham 1700–10, Wiltshire and Swindon History Centre, WRO 947, 803-2.[38]

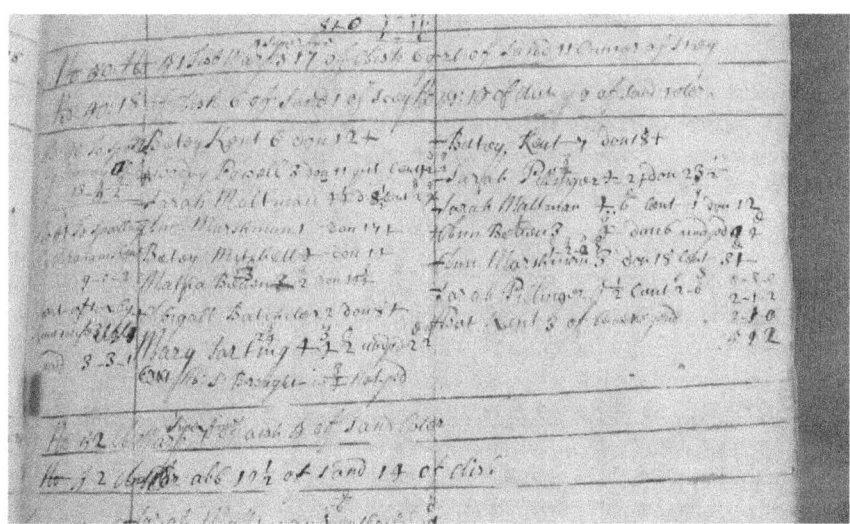

Figure 1.4 Cloth Making Book of Thomas Long of Melksham 1700–10, Wiltshire and Swindon History Centre, WRO 947, 803-1.

[38] WRO 947, 803-2, Picture 561.

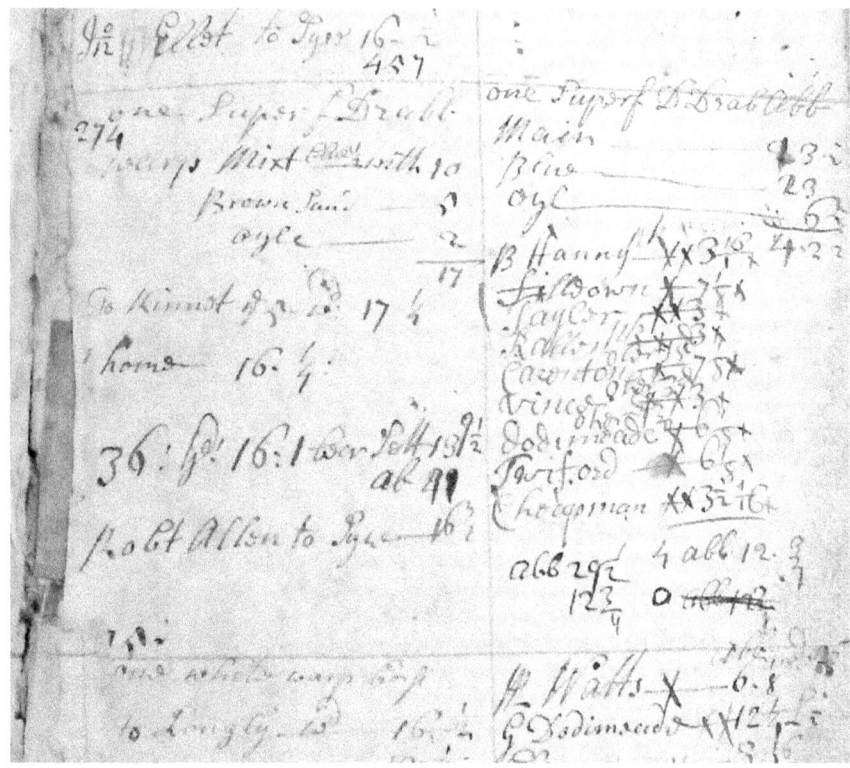

Figure 1.5 Cloth Making Book of John Jeffries and John Usher of Wiltshire, 1721–45.

Fig. 1.6 is a page from a pocket account book of the well-known worsted clothier Jonathan Akroyd of Halifax from the 1770s. Like the Long book, this account has separate sections for yarn spun and payments made in different sections of the books, which can be matched by date. Most of the first entries are divided into fine warp, common, twenties and bagin, although from 1777–87 the yarn is divided up into columns of 30, 24, 20, 18 and 16 count yarn. During these ten years 1,737 lbs of 30 count, 4,418 lbs of 24 count, 2,982 lbs of 20 count and only 85 lbs of 18 and 19 lbs of 16 count yarn (presumably for bags), or 77 lbs per month on average was delivered to Akroyd's agents. Again, most entries are not listed with a name, although Mary Taylor is sometimes mentioned as both receiving wool and delivering yarn. The payment's pages are divided into debtor and creditor sides with payments made on the debtor side to named individuals, most often Mary Taylor or Joseph Taylor, for values of usually of £5 or more. The credit side lists the value of yarn received, and sometimes the payment is less than its value, indicating some form of credit was being used.[39] Also

---

[39] This is not an example of payment being less because of market conditions, since the difference between the value of the yarn and the payment is inconsistent between entries and is most often the same.

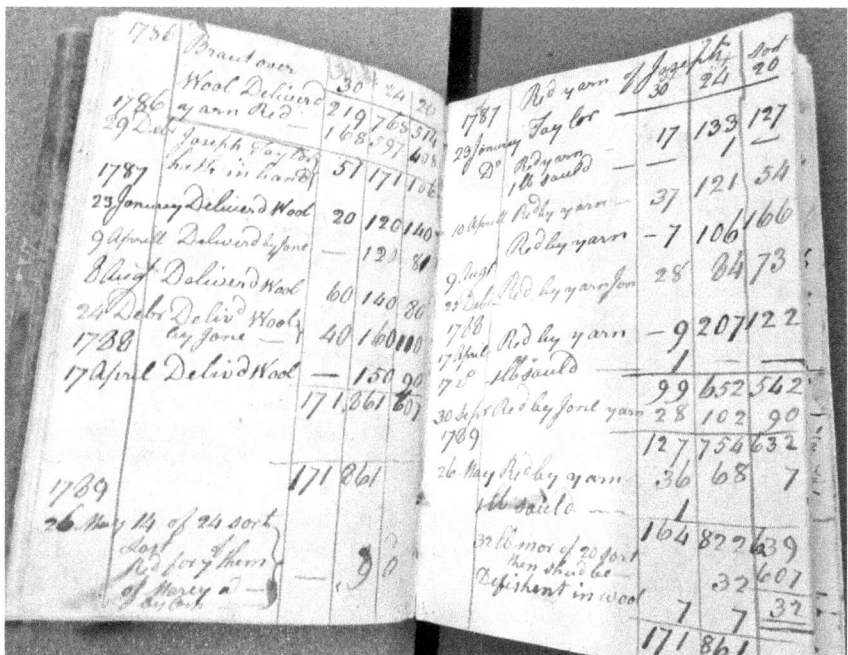

Figure 1.6 Spinning Account Book of Jonathan Akroyd of Halifax, 1770s, Leeds University Library Archives, Ackroyd Accounts, 158-1.[40]

the payments are not divided by count, but are for all yarn delivered by single dates. However, from this we can work out that the average payments per pound for 30–20 count yarn ranged from 12.6 d. to 14.8 d. Again, it seems probable that at this date more advanced accounts existed for Akroyd's business, but what we can learn from these pocketbooks is how day to day payments would have been worked out. In this case Mary Taylor, if she had enough daughters, could have been spinning 2 pounds within her family, but they would have had to have been working all out. But she and her husband might have been sub-putting out wool to other spinners and looking after the payment somehow.

Another striking feature about these accounts is their rarity. Although business accounts in general from before c.1800 are rare, clothier's accounts are rarer than most. I have gone through the catalogues of record offices for the major cloth producing regions, and have visited the archives in search of accounts or payment records, but in the end found only four main series of records which detailed payments for spinning:

1. A series of pattern books and accompanying cloth making books which survive for Thomas Long of Melksham, Wiltshire from 1699–1729

---

[40] Leeds University Library Archives, Ackroyd Accounts, 158-1.

2. The same for John Jeffries and John Usher, also of Wiltshire from 1721–45
3. A series of account books for Thomas Grigg of Ballingdon, Essex from 1740–60
4. An account book of Jonathan Akroyd of Halifax from the 1770s
5. William Heaton of West Yorkshire's Spinning Book, 1771.

This begs the question as to why more account books of a more sophisticated nature have not survived, when it had become England's biggest industry. In comparison, many more accounts of eighteenth-century local banks which eventually merged, have survived in the archives of Lloyds and Barclays and NatWest.[41] Further, although it is difficult to measure with any great accuracy, searching the National Archives Discovery catalogue for the term business accounts from 1600–99 produces 76 hits, while searching the period from 1700–99 produces 3,107 hits! Enough accounts exist for large scale industrial employers like coal mines or brewers to have enabled histories to be written about them.[42] But a search for anything similar in the cloth industry before the establishment of the first silk and cotton factories turns up very little indeed. This seems to further attest to the informal nature of payment systems in the industry.

Although accounts are rare, some important information on the subject was collected by Arthur Young, first as part of the information on earnings and wages which he collected during his various tours of the country along with prices and other wages, and then in his journal the *Annals of Agriculture*. In my previous article I used some of his estimates of earnings from the *Tours*, but by no means all of them.[43] However, in their critique of Allen, Humphries and Schneider were sceptical of reporters like Young, arguing that 'the subjective judgements of non-spinning passers-by were likely to overstate rather than understate spinners' wages.... [we] remain suspicious of examples provided by commentators with particular agendas or limited direct knowledge.'[44] I think there is evidence to suggest he was not just an ignorant outsider willing to swallow the exaggerated reports of local manufacturers.[45] In the mid-1780s, around sixteen years after providing the collections of earnings he published in his various tours, he became actively involved in the political economy of wool, defending what had become known as the landed interest, in opposition to the manufacturing interest. This debate is described by Julian Hoppit in his book *Britain's Political Economies*.[46] It concerned the enforcement of the long-standing ban on the export of English wool abroad. Simplified, this was specifically directed at France to prevent them from competing with English exports. But by the 1780s, farmers latched onto the argument for freer trade in the recently published *Wealth of Nations*, to

---

[41] John Orbell and Alison Turton, *British Banking: A Guide to Historical Records* (London: Routledge, 2001).
[42] John Hatcher, *The History of the British Coal Industry before 1700: Towards the Age of Coal*, I, (Oxford: Oxford University Press, 1992); Peter Mathias, *The Brewing Industry in England 1700-1830*, (Cambridge: Cambridge University Press, 1959).
[43] Muldrew, *Distaff*, 510.
[44] Humphries and Schneider, 'Spinning', 133, 144.
[45] John Styles, 'Fashion, Textiles and the Origins of Industrial Revolution', *East Asian Journal of British History*, 5, March (2016), 166–8.
[46] Julian Hoppit, *Britain's Political Economies: Parliament and Economic Life, 1660-1800*. (Cambridge: Cambridge University Press, 2017), chapter 7.

contend that they should be allowed to sell their wool abroad, and the ban was in reality a corrupt wheeze by cloth manufacturers to keep the price of wool down. This was certainly Young's position, but he went further to accuse the woollen manufacturers of also keeping rates of remuneration of spinners artificially low by maintaining the deductions put in place when exports fell during the American war. As Young correctly noted, exports had been rising again since 1780. He was sympathetic enough to the plight of spinners at the time that he nicknamed his youngest daughter, born in 1783, Bobbin.

This was all done in his periodical the *Annals of Agriculture*, and to find out more about what spinners remuneration was he sent out a questionnaire and invited replies, which he published in 1788 in volume nine. These included the questions: what does a woman earn at present in a day spinning of wool in your neighbourhood?; Are they paid by weight, or skein, or how?; Is there any deduction from their earnings on account of bad times, or are they in such cases out of employment altogether? The replies supply a great deal of evidence about earnings, albeit at a more depressed level than around 1770. Some of the commentators admit their knowledge is second hand, while others defend their accuracy. But I think what is most interesting for my purposes here is the complexity of systems of remuneration they all describe. This extended discussion in the *Annals of Agriculture* shows that the remuneration within the spinning economy worked in a very different fashion than what we generally consider a 'day wage'.[47] We can begin with a description given by Young himself of his home village of Bradfield in Sussex, only ten miles north of Griggs' village of Ballingdon:

> Wool here is combed into tops of a pound weight, which is spun into various lengths, at various prices, which give the denomination of twelve-penny work,, fourteen-penny, eighteen-penny, or two shillings work; that is to say, the nominal price of spinning a pound of the worst wool is a shilling; and, of spinning a pound of the finest, wool is 2s. This nominal price was a real one, and its being real gave the denomination; but, the yarn makers, under the pretence or the fact of bad times, came to make deductions upon an arbitrary principle; himself the judge and jury of his conduct. In some sorts of spinning, 160 yards in length make a single; 2 singles a double; and 6 doubles a skein. A pound of wool for twelve-penny work, is spun into 6 skeins, or to the length of 11,520 yards.
>
> A pound of wool for fourteen-penny work, is spun into 7 skeins, or 13,440 yards.
>
> A pound of wool for eighteen-penny work, is spun into 9 skeins, or 17,280 yards.
>
> A pound of wool for two-shilling work, is wound upon a reel 7 quarters round, 80 of which rounds make a single, 2 singles a double, 6 doubles a skein, and 12 skeins to the pound, or 20,160 yards.
>
> The deductions are,

---

[47] Arthur Young (ed.), *Annals of Agriculture and other Useful Arts*, vol. 9, (London: Bury St. Edmunds, 1788).

1. Instead of paying, 1s. for twelve-penny work, they· pay 7d.
2. Instead. of I4d. for fourteen-penny work, they pay 8d.
3. Instead of 18d. for eighteen-penny work, they pay 11d.
4. Instead of 2s. for two-shilling-work, they pay 15d.

> If the spinner spins a pound of wool into a greater length than stipulated, she is paid double price in fine work, for what she exceeds; and if she falls short of the length, she allows double price for the deficiency. In coarse work, the allowance is 1 1/2d. for one penny-worth of work.[48]

Here we can see the same deductions for bad times in operation which Griggs was applying in the 1750s. It is also very useful in that it gives the lengths of yarn spun. Even with the cheapest 12 penny work, if a woman could spin half a pound in a day this would have amounted to about three miles of yarn, and for the finest spinning a half pound would have equalled 5.7 miles. We can also work out the price paid per yard, which only went up for the finest 2s. yarn. However, with no estimate of how long such spinning took it is impossible to say how much more could be made from spinning fine yarn. However, we can get some indication of this in some of the other reports. That of the Rev. Holmes of Scorton, Yorkshire (Jan. 1, 1788), notes that earnings per day were definitely higher, the higher the count:

> The woolcombers divide it into three sorts; the superfine, as they call it, they have spun into thirty-fix hanks of five hundred and sixty rounds of a yard reel; and for this they pay the Spinner one shilling and ten-pence a pound; for the second twenty-four hanks, eleven-pence half-penny; and for the third, eighteen hanks, eight-pence halfpenny. In spinning the superfine, a good, industrious work-woman will earn a shilling a-day; in the second nine-pence; and in the third nine-pence; the wool-combers make occasional deductions from the spinners wages, but if we may credit their own account – not unreasonable nor arbitrary. Their conduct in this respect is, in the turf-language, give and take; they sometimes pay, for instance, eleven-pence for a shilling, and some – times thirteen-pence, according to their selling prices.[49]

In this example to earn a shilling a day the 'industrious' spinner would have to have spun just over half a pound of the 36 count. Another account noted that in Chichester a woman spinning for 10–12 hours could earn 8-10d a day, which gives an idea that the earnings related by Holmes were certainly full-time work.[50] The Report of Charles Hall of Daventry, Northamptonshire (Jan. 23, 1788), also notes how renumeration went up by the count for finer yarn:

---

[48] Ibid., 347–8.
[49] Young, *Annals*, vol. 9, 280.
[50] Ibid., 319.

The spinners are paid by the pound – but the work cannot be very easily understood, except you are first told in what form the work is carried home. After spinning the wool, it is wound off the spindles on a reel, the circumference of which is just a yard – 80 times round this, makes a knock or leg-six legs are a skein; for every one of which, provided they are so fine as to go either 28, 30, 32, or 34 to the pound, the spinner receives an half-penny; if finer than that, they are paid a penny for every skein, above the number 34, that goes to the pound: for instance, if 35, they charge 18d. per pound; if 36, 19d. – if 37, 20d. – and so on in proportion, as the fineness of the thread gives more skeins to the pound – But if the thread is so coarse as to have only 26 skeins to the pound, they receive only 1s.-if 24, 10d. – if 22, 8d. – if 20, 7d. The goods chiefly made in this neighbourhood, are tammies, wide and narrow.... The spinners at present do not make any abatement for bad times.[51]

Another set of earnings, reported by one John Heigham of Huston, Sussex were said to be taken directly from the account books of someone the author described as a 'considerable manufacturer'. From this, he provided a table of the deductions this manufacturer had imposed for the last 15 years, which show just how much they had increased since 1779, especially for the finer spinning, which had reduced earnings from an average of 1s. 9d. between 1775–8 to 1s. 5.3d. after 1780. However, the same reporter also noted that daily earnings were only between 3.5d. to 4.5d. in 1788 implying that only about 1/3 of a lb was being spun per day here. The reporter also notes that spinning was done by women, children and infirm people, so probably he was reporting rates for married women if there were few independent spinners.[52]

Table 1.1 Deductions in Pence per lb. From Spinning Rates for Market Conditions in Sussex over Time.

	2s.	1s.6d.	1s.
1775	4	1	1
1776	3	2	2
1777	1	0	0
1778	3	2	2
1779	5	4	3
1780	6	3	3
1781	9	6	5
1782	9	6	5
1783	6	4	3
1784	5	3	3
1785	4	3	3
1786	4	3	3
1787	8	6	3
1789	9	7	5

---

[51] Ibid., 292.
[52] Ibid., 327–38.

Apart from the complexity of measuring both quality and volume of such great lengths of wound-up yarn, another report of the Rev. Onley of Stistead, Essex, (December 14, 1787) demonstrates how complex the system of reels and counts could be. He also explicitly notes the role of custom in establishing this system:

> The baize wool in this neighbourhood, which varies as to length, pliancy, and softness, according to the fort into which it is to be wove, is delivered out to the spinner; who always too cards it, to be returned in nearly an equal weight of yarn. This is reeled off into skeins; eighty turns of the reel, by a little index in the lower wheel, marks a knot, and such a number of those knots is spun for a 1d. as the state of the trade, and demand for baize can afford. Five knots in the best, and eight knots in the worst times, are nearly the allowance. But the reel can be expanded or contrasted; and sometimes the spinner, with the same number of turns, to make a knot for the 1d. is obligated to wind off the spinning spindle, by the long reel, one yard and a half in circumference; at others, by the short reel, one yard and a quarter; thus, betwixt the two reels, there is the difference of a quarter of a yard to the spinner. I cannot learn the reason for this distinction, the wool for both is spun into yarn, of the fame degree of fineness and consistency, and no deception could be meant from such a palpable variation, as arises from reeling off the same number of rounds at the same price, by a different circumference. Custom has established it, with eighty rounds of the reel, under this variation to the knot; and, at five knots to the 1d. a grown, skilful and industrious person, can. earn up to 10d. a-day; at eight knots, up to 6d. an aged person about 5d. at five; and 3d. at eight; a child, at nine years of age, about 3d. at five; and 2d. at eight knots. A pound of baize wool may be spun into 15 or 16 knots; the cards are frequently supplied to the spinner, and sometimes a deduction of a penny in the shilling is made from the spinning, on this account; the carding· and spinning this wool, often very coarse, and saturated with oil, equally so, is very troublesome; and from the latter circumstance, and for children especially, probably unwholesome (p. 316)

One characteristic which is immediately noticeable in these examples, which I haven't encountered in male wage rates, is the practice of making a deduction from a set rate per reel or pound in bad times, and also in some rarer cases an addition when demand was high and labour scarcer. Fifteen of Young's respondents stated such deductions were used in their area as compared to only three places where it was not practised. It was one of the main arguments of Young in the *Annals of Agriculture* that the wool manufacturers, through combinations and their monopoly power, were using such deductions illegitimately to keep spinning wages down. Both he and a number of his correspondents argued that by 1788 overseas markets had recovered enough that there was no need for such large reductions as those reported by John Heigham above. Indeed, the customs figures for exports show that after a steep decline from over £5 million worth of cloth exported in 1775 to around £3 million in 1780, exports began recovering and stood at just under £5 million by 1788.[53] The reason Young gives for the

---

[53] Muldrew, 'Distaff', 513.

practice was a desire on the spinner's side to prioritize a continuity of earnings through bad times over stop/start employment at a set 'wage'.[54]

If this is true, it implies a very different strategy to other forms of wage earning where a reduction in demand meant unemployment and no earnings. Since the practice was customary we have no idea how it evolved, or who it was originally most advantageous to, but there must have been a good reason for spinners to have maintained it in the early part of the eighteenth century when almost all accounts note that there was more demand for yarn than labour supply.[55] This might have been linked to family maintenance, since it was the role of the housewife to look after family expenses. In a system of stop/start wage earning, it is possible that credit, which could only have been saved through the husband under coverture might well have been spent at the alehouse. Steady earnings would have been less vulnerable to being consumed by husbands in drink. In fact, Young makes a typically moralistic point about this, noting that most of the much higher pay awarded to woolcombers was spent in the alehouse.[56] A system of continued remuneration in the form of household necessities or clothing might have given the women more control over their earnings. Certainly, this was the case with the daughters of the Latham family who were able to use what they earned spinning flax and cotton to purchase new gowns for themselves.[57] In good times, when there was pressure on employment in worsted spinning, it would also have made sense from the clothier's point of view to have kept a sufficient force of labour employed to meet demand. However, when demand fell, as Young points out, the asymmetry of information meant that the spinners had to rely on the clothiers to apply a realistic reduction, and this could easily be abused.[58]

All of this brings us back to the question of how we can measure the earnings of spinners in any meaningful way. But before looking at spinning remuneration itself, it is useful to re-examine the use of the word wage itself in reference to remuneration. As I wrote in an article I did with Steve King, 'Cash, Wages and the Economy of Makeshifts in England, 1650-1800', the word 'wage' itself, seems to have been derived from 'gage' (a pledge to do something), but the meaning evolved from making a pledge to constituting a reward to someone for a service after it was performed.[59] This understanding seems initially to have been used to refer to the payment of soldiers, as was salary, which came from the Roman payment to soldiers for salt.[60] Tracing the development of the term 'wages' to refer to a cash payment for a day's work is much more difficult. For most of the period before the late eighteenth-century 'servant' was generally used as a catchall term referring to both day labourers and servants in husbandry hired for the year or a

---

[54] Young, *Annals*, vol. 9, 273.
[55] Soderlund, 'Intended as a Terror', 654; Muldrew, 'Distaff', 520–1.
[56] Young, *Annals*, vol. 9, 271.
[57] John Styles, 'Custom or Consumption? Plebeian Fashion in Eighteenth-Century England', in Maxine Berg and Elizabeth Eger (eds.) *Luxury in the Eighteenth Century: Debates, Desires and Delectable goods* (Basingstoke: Palgrave Macmillan, 2003), 108–9.
[58] Humphries and Schneider, 'Spinning', 133.
[59] In *Experiencing Wages*, edited by Scholliers and Schwarz, chapter 10.
[60] *Oxford English Dictionary. Unemancipated - Wau-wau*, vol. XIX, (Oxford: Clarendon Press, 1989), vol. XIX, 803.

part thereof. Wages could refer to the contracted yearly payment, or to a day rate. In their farm accounts both Henry Best (1616–41) and Robert Loader (1610–20) tended to use the term 'wages' only to refer to yearly servant's wages or for harvest wages, while daily labour is referred to by the job done.[61]

However, it was probably an act of Parliament which had the most effect in popularizing the word wage as a monetary measure of earnings. This was William Cecil's Statute of Artificers of 1563, which was an attempt to update the original Statute of Labourers, which in turn had been a political effort to limit the ability of peasants to ask for higher earnings in the period of labour shortage after the black death. After this legislation, well into the eighteenth century, the JPs of every county drew up lists at regular intervals of the maximum wages for various tasks. The majority of these were measured by the day, although yearly wages for servants were also included, as was piece work, which was termed 'work by the great'. There has been much debate about the meaning of these documents, and the degree to which they were enforced, as the rates provided could vary greatly from place to place.[62] But what I wish to stress here is that, from a very early date, the word 'wage' is a top-down conceptualization. To use the phrase of James C. Scott it is a way of seeing earnings 'like a state'.[63]

In contrast, Arthur Young in his *Tours* from the 1770s uses the term 'earnings' much more often than 'wage'. In these tours around the country Young collected masses of data on the prices of provisions and earnings as part of his attempt to assess the general state of the kingdom and 'the people it maintains'.[64] Young was one of the first people to be really interested in the monetary measurement of standards of living through a comparison of prices and earnings in different places. When he used the word wage it was generally to refer to a farming labourer's daily earnings, but he was well aware that earnings were composed of much more than this, and generally had to rely on estimates.

Looking at earnings from the bottom up, so to speak, is to adopt a different perspective – that of negotiation between the worker and employer involving a multitude of factors such as skill, labour supply and demand for the work being done, credit and character, and of course gender, age, status and local custom. This is illustrated very well by the farmer Henry Best of Elmswell of the East Riding in Yorkshire, when describing the negotiations involved in the hiring of farm servants, noted that 'some servants will condition to have soe many sheepe wintered and sommered with theire maisters . . . we account that equall to so many eighteene pences'. In 1622, he recorded paying one servant '6 L. in money, 8 bushells of barley, 2 bushells of oates, and a pecke of oatmeale, and a fries coate, and a stoke of strawe every weeke

---

[61] George E. Fussell (ed.), *Robert Loader's Farm Accounts 1610-1620* (London: Royal Historical Society, 1936), i.e. 100, 146, 152, 154, 166; *Rural Economy in Yorkshire in 1641, Being the Farming and Account Books of Henry Best, of Elmswell, in the East Riding of the County of York*, Surtees Society, vol. 33 (Durham: G. Andrews, 1857), 154.

[62] Craig Muldrew, *Food, Energy and the Creation of Industriousness* (Cambridge: Cambridge University Press, 2011), 267–73.

[63] James C. Scott, *Seeing Like a State How Certain Schemes to Improve the Human Condition Have Failed* (New Haven: Yale University Press, 1998).

[64] Arthur Young, *The Farmer's Tour Through the North of England* (London: printed for W. Strahan, 1771), vol. I, viii.

from Crissmass to Lady Day in Lent', and another 'to have 5 L. in money, and 10 sheep wintered, and the rent of his house and garth the next yeare; and I to pay for his cows cost on the Greets next somer'. We might want to call this 'negotiated earnings', although we must always consider that this was a negotiation within a very asymmetrical power relationship, where the employer generally had the advantage of much greater wealth and status.[65]

Such practices make life very difficult for economic historians who wish to numerically measure things, just as it was difficult for government attempts to regulate earnings. But it was also problematic for those wealthier yeomen farmers who were expanding production into larger estates. They wished to use labour more efficiently by hiring more workers by the day when required, and to do so they needed to understand their enterprise in terms of profit and loss accounting. Hiring labour by the day, for a simple cash wage without any prerequisites was also preferable from an accounting standpoint, although in reality food perquisites were often offered and accounted for separately, as they did not require any form of currency to be 'paid'.[66] Leigh Shaw Taylor has shown capitalist agriculture began in the south in the seventeenth century, and even earlier in some places, but as numerous historians have noted, large scale accounts for farms, which can match the great mediaeval estate records do not begin to reappear in England until the period after 1680.[67] I think these are enough reasons to support a plea to be much more careful when using the term 'wage' rather than earnings. If there is one uncontested thing post-modernism has taught us it is, words matter. If we use the term wage this references the desire to measure from outside, and eventually a desire to standardize a value for accounting purposes. This could be both a liberation, or a gateway to the cash nexus, but it was different than customary arrangements.

Another institution for which accounting was necessary was the eighteenth-century workhouse. Although these institutions developed out of a number of different ideas including industrial education, one main motivation was the idea that expenditure could be reduced by centralizing the costs of out-relief payments for food, fuel and rent by putting the impotent poor under one roof with centralized meal preparation. In order to achieve such savings, cost accounting was necessary, and practised by all institutions. As one of Arthur Young's respondents put it.

> The poor keep no accounts: with them sufficient to the day, is the evil thereof. – For a regular detail, therefore, of the variations in their wages, you must, I apprehend, resort to houses of industry, or such like institutions, where the earnings of the people who inhabit those houses, constitute a part of the public fund, which supports them, and consequently must be regularly noted in the accounts kept by the acting managers.[68]

---

[65] *The Farming and Memorandum Books of Henry Best of Elmswell, 1642*, edited by Donald Woodward (Oxford: Oxford University Press, 1984), 134.
[66] Muldrew, *Food, Energy*, 226–33.
[67] Leigh Shaw-Taylor, 'The Rise of Agrarian Capitalism and the Decline of Family Farming in England' *The Economic History Review*, 65, no. 1 (2012): 26–60; Michal E. Turner, John V. Beckett, and Bethanie Afton, *Farm Production in England 1700-1914* (Oxford: Oxford University Press, 2001), 43–65.
[68] Young, *Annals*, vol. 9, 327–8.

Humphries and Schneider, when constructing their database of daily spinning wages, relied heavily on workhouses for a considerable number of their examples. They then combined such estimates together with earnings from account books and other indirect references. But because there are only a handful of accounts from actual business-oriented clothiers, these provide many fewer data points. From these, they then constructed an estimated nominal daily wage rate, and presented change over time in their Figure 6.[69] This presents, I think, some rather odd results. The average remains at about 2d. per day until 1670, which then sees a rather rapid rise to 6d. a day which lasts until 1750, where there is another rapid drop to about 3d. a day which persists right through the industrialization of spinning. No explanation is given as to why wages collapsed so much earlier than industrialization, and incidentally when exports were continually rising. However, the answer might lie on Figure 5 which shows that it was around 1730 when accounts started being included in large numbers of observations. The online appendix shows that for most decades before 1730 less than 10 observations were found, compared to 751 for 1730–39, 378 for 1740–49, and 703 for 1750–59. In total there were 2,158 data points for accounts or 84 per cent, compared to 401 other types of observation. Although the numbers from each source are not given, many of these observations will be from workhouse accounts.[70]

Certainly, workhouses are an important source, and provide invaluable research into an important sector of the industry. But here I would question whether they can simply be taken as indicative of overall earnings in the commercial sector. Clothiers definitely used yarn produced in workhouses, but not for their best quality material, and the yarn produced there could not have formed a very large part of the market. John Cary, was one of the founders of the concept of the workhouse as a source of yarn production in Bristol. In the early eighteenth century, he noted his direct experience of clothiers only offering low rates of remuneration per pound of spun yarn from his workhouse because they assumed that the quality would be less than what they bought from home spinners.[71] To counter this, as Cary related it,

> the Committee voted, that they would give Employment to all the Poor of the City, who would make Application to them, at the Rates we offered to work, and pay them ready Money for their Labour. We soon found we had taken the right Course, for in a few Weeks we had Sale for our fine Yarn as fast as we could make it, and they [the clothiers] gave us from Eight-pence to Two Shillings per Pound for Spinning the same Goods, for which a little before they paid but Eight-pence, and were very well pleased with it, because they were now able to distinguish between the fine and the coarse Yarn, and to apply each Sort to the Use for which it was most proper: Since which, they have given us Two Shillings and Six-pence per Pound for a great many Pounds, and we spin some, worth Three Shillings and Six-pence per Pound Spinning.[72]

---

[69] Ibid., 143.
[70] Most of the references in the Bibliography are for parish records.
[71] John Cary, *A Discourse on Trade*, (London: printed for T. Osborne, 1745 [2nd edition]), 160–3.
[72] Ibid.

Using the Parliamentary reports on the Relief and Settlement of the Poor from 1776-7, Peter Higgenbotham counted 1,978 workhouses with a *capacity* of 90,000 places. However detailed information from the same report, supplied on workhouses in a number of major towns and cities, including London, shows that not every workhouse, or everyone in a workhouse was engaged in spinning. The average earnings per person engaged in all sorts of work was generally only 10s. to £1 a year. Using Schneider's estimate of an upper bound of 1.38 million workers, this means that workhouse employment could have contributed at most 7 per cent of the workforce, and probably much less.[73]

Workhouses do offer well-kept account books, but these present earnings in the form of a day wage which can easily be put into a longitudinal series, but this is not how most spinners earned their remuneration. Certainly, though, much of the home market would have been for cheaper clothing made with lower count yarn, but this does not account for either exports or more expensive clothes for middling sort and elite consumers in the home market.[74]

For this reason, I would argue that the estimates of *earnings* presented by Arthur Young and his correspondents represent possibly the best sense of potential earnings for the third quarter of the eighteenth century. As I noted above, unlike pamphleteers writing to argue a point, he had no reason to exaggerate earnings. Also, as John Styles has pointed out, in his earlier tours between 1768 to 1771 he prepared them in advance, chose those places he visited carefully and made a very considered collection of cross-sectional evidence of a great range of prices, wages and other things. He was interested in the work of women, children and men as well as both industrial and agricultural earnings.[75] Some of Young's estimates from this period were presented in Table One in my 2012 article. For the woollen producing areas, the average works out to 7.5 pence a day for a six-day week, which is consistent with some of the payments in the clothiers accounts and of those reported by Young's correspondents. By 1788, when Young summarized the various earnings for the reports he published, the average of cloth producing counties was about 8d. a day. This is higher than the previous estimate, which is surprising given the deductions which had taken place, but for all counties, including Suffolk, where the wages reported were probably for married women, the average was 6.25d a day.[76] But we must remember that they could vary greatly by place, in some places being as high as 1s. and others below 5d., as well as many places where Young reported no spinning was available.[77] The highest earnings reported were in some branches of the Manchester cotton industry. For instance, in check handkerchiefs, cotton hollands, furniture cloth and goods for the African market, women and men were stated both to be able to earn 7s. a week or 14d. a day.[78]

---

[73] Humphries and Schneider, 'Spinning', 139.
[74] John Styles, *The Dress of the People: Everyday Fashion in Eighteenth-Century England*, (New Haven: Yale University Press, 2008), 195–212; 257–76.
[75] Styles, 'Spinning with Arthur Young, 1789-1790: The Employment of Women and Children in Rural England', Paper presented at the 2016 ESSHC conference Valencia, 8–9; Styles, 'Fashion', 166–8.
[76] Young, *Annals* vol. 9, 353.
[77] Young, *Annals*, vol. 9, 349–52. Styles, 'Spinning with Arthur Young,' 12.
[78] Arthur Young, *A Six-Month Tour Through the North of England* (London, 1771), vol. 3, 187–91.

However, one thing which Young, nor as far as I can tell, any of his respondents did, was to distinguish between the work of married or single women. Since he distinguished between children and adults and often gave earnings by ages of girls and boys, this is a very curious omission. It seems that the vast majority of earnings were conceived of as for full-time work of 10–12 hours a day as we saw above. But since spinning took place in the home, this could probably only have been realistically achieved by daughters between ages 12 to the age of marriage around 28, in households where cooking and childcare could have been done by their mother or another sister. Some was also done, of course, by children and older women and some men, especially in the workhouses. As Amy Froide has pointed out, a quite large percentage of the population would have been composed of such young single women at all times.[79] Also, as we know the years from c. 1680–1750 saw a large cohort of women who never got married and could have worked independently for much longer.[80] So, perhaps thinking of spinning as a part-time married women's occupation is missing a demographic point, and that it was seen as a young woman's occupation for finer spinning and an older women's occupation for lower counts, and a wife's part time occupation and perhaps organizational task.

Returning to the debate which was addressed at the very beginning of the article, whether or not earnings averaging 7d. to 8d. a day represent a 'high wage' is a question of what perspective the historian wants to take. I would argue that Young's evidence is good enough to say that they had risen *over time* compared to the early seventeenth century, which added to household earnings.[81] However, from the perspective of gender, they were anything but, considering the skill involved. One only has to make a comparison with woolcomber's earnings to see this. In John Haynes' example of the cost of producing new draperies such as 'Fine Stuffs, Serges, Sagathies, Calamancoes', the earnings of woolcombers were listed as being 10s a week, while the spinners were only 1.5 shillings. In this example a weaver's earnings were even more at 16.8 shillings.[82] Richard Soderlund has also found examples of woolcombers earning 12s. a week.[83] Arthur Young compared frugal underpaid female spinners with wasteful overpaid hard-drinking woolcombers.[84] Also in an example from the pamphlet *A State of the Case* (see below) weavers were cited as earning between 13s. to 18s. a week.[85] Without question both woolcombers and weavers were able to earn more because, as men, they were able to organize, strike and lobby Parliament.

An example of this occurred in the 1730s when the weavers in Gloucestershire successfully managed to have a bill passed in Parliament to regulate their wages according to set amounts by the density of the weave.[86] Before this, it seems that the

---

[79] Amy M. Froide, *Never Married. Singlewomen in Early Modern England* (Oxford: Oxford University Press, 2005), 2–5.
[80] Muldrew, 'Distaff', 520.
[81] Ibid., Figure 2, 522; Soderlund, 'Intended as a Terror', 655, 658.
[82] Weavers could also be women, but there is little work, as far as I know, on whether payments were the same for male and female weavers.
[83] Soderlund, 'Intended as a Terror', 658.
[84] Young, *Annals*, vol. 9, 271,
[85] *A State of the Case and A Narrative of the Facts Relating to the Late Commotions and Rising of the Weavers in the County of Gloucestershire* (London: printed for R. Griffiths, 1757), 15.
[86] Ibid., 5–9.

rates paid weavers had been adjusted and negotiated by the clothiers in a similar way to those of spinners, albeit at a higher level.[87] The means by which they influenced Parliament would be fascinating to know, but it seems they were supported by agricultural rate payers who were worried about poor rates. This outraged a number of local Clothiers who refused to abide by the new rates, which led to a riot of weavers in Gloucester in 1738.[88] The Clothiers organized and lobbied to have the law repealed, presenting a petition to Parliament, and writing a number of pamphlets arguing their case. On such, entitled *A State of the Case and A Narrative of the Facts Relating to the late Commotions and Rising of the Weavers in the County of Gloucestershire* argued that set rates were impractical for weaving:

> The other point which arose for the consideration of the court, and to which the clothiers evidence principally tended, was, that the fettling of the wages to be paid to weavers by the hundred, was impracticable to be done, in an equitable manner; because the clothier, or weaver, must frequently be injured by it. It was proved that the highest hundred, or number of threads in the chain, could not ascertain the value of weaving, nor did always deserve the greatest wages. Instances were given, wherein very different prices were paid for cloths of the fame hundred, by the fame mailer; and yet the lowest prices often were the best wages: this difference very frequently amounted to twenty or twenty-five per cent upon the value of weaving, and in some particular instances to forty per cent. since no regard is had to the fort of cloth intended to be made, whether thicker or thinner, narrower or wider; whether the spinning of the abb or shoot is larger or smaller, finer or coarser, what breadth the chain is fet'upon the loom, or what.[89]

One of these, who signed himself Philalethes, wrote a long pamphlet in defence of the Clothiers and their practices, complaining that the landed gentleman who sat as JPs to enforce wages knew nothing of the business. But, his attack on the nature of the weavers as lazy and unskilled is so exaggerated that it is hard to take seriously.

However, when he describes the way a family might combine its earnings the amounts given are not out of line with those provided by Young, with the important caveat that it is quite unlikely that a married woman could earn 3s. a week while also doing all of her household tasks, but if we were to replace her with a twenty-year-old daughter it is perhaps plausible. But what is more relevant is that it shows how family earnings were put together:

> WHILST the Weaver and his Apprentice-Boy are employ'd in the Loom, if the Weaver has a Family, a Child of four Years of Age shall perhaps quill to the Loom, and earn 5 d. per Week; another of fix Years of Age shall acquire perhaps 1 s. 6 d. per Week by spinning; whilst the Wife makes her Wages 2 s. 6d. or 3 s. a Week by the Spinning-wheel also; and at the same time performs all necessary Offices in the

---

[87] Ibid., 26–30.
[88] 'Essay on Riots', *The Daily Post*, nos. 6017–18 (22–23 December 1738).
[89] *The State of the Case*, 21

Family. Many Instances might be given of Weavers, who in this manner have acquired Fortunes from *100 l. to 500 l*. I would be understood to speak here of the *Industrious Poor*, not of the *idle* and *debauch'd* , not of the drunken *Punk*, the tailing *Gossip*, or of the idle vociferous *Fuddle-Cup* such will be always poor, in spite of Providence. Whether there are starving Wages, or the Weavers may be supposed from this, to be in distressed Circumstances, we must leave the candid Reader to judge. If upon considering all these Things, the Weavers should be pronounced in a starving Condition, and the Clothiers Oppressors, I am afraid such Judges will be found to have but little Sense, and lets Honesty; yea, less than the Clothiers themselves.

IT may be observ'd, that their Wives and Families at home often earn 6 or 7 s. per Week more, which added to their Husbands Acquisitions abroad, makes not only a comfortable, but an almost extravagant Sum, when compared with the Wages of the Husbandman and his Family, in many Parts of this Kingdom.[90]

There is also evidence to suggest that in times of high demand weavers and combers also demanded to be paid in cash. This can be seen in the letter book of Joseph Symson from 1711–20. He was a mercer from Kendal, and his main business was the marketing of Kendal's cotton and linsey woolsey cloths. During the time period of the letter book, demand was generally greater than supply so the weavers had considerable power, and preferred to produce the finer sort of cloth for more profit.[91] The weavers could also use the situation to demand ready money instead of credit when selling their work.[92] In 1711 Symson claimed in one letter that paying ready money was the usual way for purchasing linseys.[93] Another reason why clothiers were willing to pay more to combers and weavers was that they were much fewer in number. There were generally eight or nine spinners to every weaver and woolcomber.

The use of scarce cash to pay male workers would have left even less for the spinners. But one way they could supplement their wage discrepancy was, through the practice of 'false reeling'. This was basically a way to earn more by falsifying the counts on a reel to provide less yards of yarn per pound. Given the great lengths of yarn involved this was a fraud, which was easy to implement. Styles has estimated that this might have been on average worth 6 per cent of a spinner's earnings, although it could be much higher than this in some cases. He stressed that for long periods this practice was tolerated by employers as 'customary' because it was a way in which earnings could be made without the need for using cash.[94] Also when demand for cloth was high and

---

[90] Philalethes, *The Case as it now stands between the Clothiers and the Weavers and other Manufacturers* (London: printed for the author, 1739), 15–16.

[91] *An Exact and Industrious Tradesman: The Letter Book of Joseph Symson of Kendal, 1711-1720*, edited by S. D. Smith (Oxford: Oxford University Press for the British Academy, 2002), 27–8. Letter 86 clearly refers to weavers seeking the highest price through competition between cloth purchasers.

[92] Ibid., 41, 45, 60, 134.

[93] Ibid., 500–501, Letter 1616.

[94] John Styles, 'Embezzlement, industry and the law in England, 1500–1800', in *Manufacture in Town and Country Before the Factory*, edited by Maxine Berg, Pat Hudson, and Michael Sonenscher (Cambridge: Cambridge University Press, 1983), 175–7.

competition for spinning labour acute it was tolerated.⁹⁵ However, as Richard Soderlund has argued, the woollen manufacturers in Yorkshire took advantage of the 42 per cent decline in exports during the American war between 1774 and 1780 to crack down on the practice. As we saw, Arthur Young argued vociferously that cloth masters had combined together during these years of declining demand to reduce spinners wages by the means of deductions from payments described above, and as a result false reeling increased as a means to maintain earnings in the face of this. But in Yorkshire they also went further and had a law passed to criminalize false reeling.⁹⁶ This resulted in a dramatic rising in prosecutions and was certainly an attempt to enforce regulation by policing while keeping earnings down.

The clothiers, of course, never tired of arguing that they were in a competitive business, and that lower labour costs in France and elsewhere put them at a competitive disadvantage in non-colonial foreign markets.⁹⁷ It is hard to judge the degree to which this was true, but there is some evidence that the trade was more competitive than some other comparative manufacturing occupations. Julian Hoppit has shown that rates of bankruptcy in the textile sector were much higher than any other, and consisted of about 25 per cent of all bankruptcies over the course of the eighteenth century – much higher than either metal or wood working, both less than 5 per cent.⁹⁸ However, although the number of all bankruptcies went up after 1760, the percentage of textile bankruptcies did not increase during the period of the American war, when the clothiers complained the most of bad times. Also, in a database of probate accounts which have survived from all over the country from an earlier period between 1600–1710, we can compare the wealth of clothiers with other occupations for which sufficient numbers have survived. Probate accounts were a more advanced stage in the

Table 1.2 Probate Accounts from National Probate Account Database: 1600–1710.

	Number	Charge	Balance
Clothiers	120	£204 9s.	£60 14s.
Mercers	63	£345 4s.	£55 15s.
Grocers	48	£868 10s.	£470 6s.

⁹⁵ Styles, 'Spinners and the Law,' 157–8.
⁹⁶ Ivy Pinchbeck, *Women workers and the industrial revolution 1750-1850* (London: George Routledge & Sons, 1930 [reprinted 1969]), 142–4.
⁹⁷ Whether this was true or not is a moot point here, but the difference between French and English spinning remuneration has been debated. John Styles, 'The Rise and Fall of the Spinning Jenny: Domestic Mechanisation in Eighteenth-Century Cotton Spinning' *Textile History*, 51, no. 2 (2020): 195–236. Philalethes, *The Case between the Clothiers and the Weavers*, 54; Julia de Lacy Mann, *Documents Illustrating the Wiltshire Textile Trades in the Eighteenth Century* (Devizes: Wiltshire Archaeological Society, 1964), Introduction, xxi, xxv.
⁹⁸ Julian Hoppit, *Risk and failure in English business 1700-1800* (Cambridge: Cambridge University Press, 1987), 57, 75-8-87. If both food and drink are combined, they reach about 25 per cent, but alehouses were notoriously risky business. We do not have information on the numbers in different occupations and while there were probably more clothiers, metalwork in Birmingham and Sheffield was certainly expanding.

probate process, and here any debts owed by the deceased together with funeral costs and any costs of orphaned children were subtracted from the assets listed in the inventories.[99] This comparison shows that grocers died with more assets and fewer debts than either clothiers or mercers (sellers of woollen goods).

To give a specific example, K. H. Burley calculated Griggs' annual profit in the years between 1742 and 1759. This varied from £167 to £416 but had quite high seasonal variation, of around 25 per cent. Obviously, understanding more about the state of the industry over time would help to explain how exploitative the system of deductions was.[100]

But as it stands, we can venture some general conclusions. First, that the cloth industry developed in the sixteenth and seventeenth centuries before the financial innovations of the eighteenth century, which saw the increased use of local paper credit currency such as bills.[101] It did so by bringing the labour of women and children, which had previously been employed in the non-market production of household clothing, into the marketplace. Since a marketplace required prices, this meant creating some form of monetarily valued remuneration for work. But since there was not enough small change, various 'customary' forms of remuneration involving payment with goods from shops developed. This was not in any way unique. Payment using a monetary system based on tobacco remained common in Virginia well into the eighteenth century, and other commodities such as silk in China or rice in Japan were commonly used as currency.[102] Also, as I have shown elsewhere, in the case of farm labour, probably the majority of remuneration took the form of food and lodging together with other perquisites well into the eighteenth century, with the wage being a form of monetary measurement. Certainly, the system of shop remuneration could have been exploited as a truck system, but it does not seem to have evolved that way since it seems that wages were not being paid and then being forced to be spent at one place with controlled prices, but rather that the payment and exchange system for goods was one of constant negotiation. But importantly this does not mean that it was any more advantageous to the spinners.[103] It was done out of necessity, and change came very rapidly once factories were established and sophisticated accounting systems introduced monetary payments which could be used more widely.[104]

---

[99] This sample is taken from a national database of 28,989 probate accounts surviving from before 1710 collected by Professor Peter Spufford. I would like to thank professor Spufford and Rosemary Rod for helping me with this database. This database is discussed in Peter Spufford, Matthew Brett and Amy Louise Erickson (eds.), *Guide to the Probate Accounts of England and Wales* (The British Record Society, 1999). Also see, Amy Louise Erickson, 'An introduction to probate accounts', in *The records of the Nation*, edited by Geoffrey H. Martin and Peter Spufford (London: Boydell, 1990), 273–86.

[100] Burley (1958), 'Some Accounting Records'.

[101] Craig Muldrew, 'The Social Acceptance of Paper Credit as Currency in Eighteenth Century England: A Case Study of Glastonbury c.1720-1742', in *Financing in Europe: Evolution, Coexistence and Complementarity of Lending Practices from the Middle Ages to Modern Times*, edited by Marcella Lorenzini, Cinzia Lorandini, D'Maris Coffman (London: Palgrave, 2018).

[102] Farley Grubb, 'Creating Maryland's Paper Money Economy, 1720-1740: The Confluence of Political Constituencies, Economic Forces, Transatlantic Markets, and Law', *Journal of Early American History*, 9, no. 1 (2019): 42–58.

[103] Philalethes, *The Case between the Clothiers and the Weavers*, 61

[104] Derbyshire Record Office, W.G. and J. Strutt Ltd of Belper D6948/5/3 Reelers and Pickers Wage Book 1784–87; D6948/5/17, Spinners Wages 1801–1805.

Spinners were also a labour force of which, the majority were embedded within the patriarchal family, and as a result probably much less mobile compared to male labourers before the rise of the factory. It was also a labourer force banned by its gender and age from organizing in a guild to educate and regulate the skill of its practitioners. Because of this it was perhaps easier for payment methods to become intertwined within local supply networks of household necessities which would have been normally purchased by the wife. In spinning the local form of reel was probably as important a means of measurement as money, and it is not impossible that the need to convert into cash was not always necessary for shop purchases.

Also, there was certainly a very wide gender difference in levels of enumeration, with the woolcombers being the most insulated from market fluctuations. But if we look backwards one could say that it was *relatively* less exploitative than other household work most of which women had to, and still have to, perform for free. Looking over the very long term it was an instance of work formerly being done without recompense to gaining some control over the fruits of labour. In this sense it represents a rare instance of women's and children's household work escaping from the patriarchal devaluation of housework to actually being rewarded financially. However, the means of payment were impossible to fully monetize, and certainly undervalued compared to male workers such as woolcombers. But in terms of contributions to *family earnings*, as the example cited above shows, the extra market earnings could have been a considerable addition to poor families' standards of living in the early eighteenth century in comparison to earlier periods.

2

Wage Practices at a Red Bread Factory (Ghent, 1880–1914)[1]

Peter Scholliers

In Ghent in 1880, the socialist co-operative Vooruit ('Forward') installed a modest artisanal bakery that by 1900 had evolved into one of the most modern bread factories in Europe. Not only did foreigners praise the functioning of Vooruit, but they also applauded the hygienic work conditions, the democratic organization, the advantageous working hours, and the generous wages. This chapter focuses on the latter. It does not highlight so much the wage level but considers the co-operative's pay system. How did it emerge? Did it include the common co-operative idea of 'collective remuneration divided among all members of the group in such a manner as shall be arranged upon principles recognised as equitable by the associates themselves'?[2] How were tariffs fixed, how was output measured, did fines and premiums exist, and was profit sharing applied? Related questions tackle the issue of management and work conditions: how was the co-operative run, how did the workers view technological changes, did they adhere to the union, did strikes occur, was the eight-hour day applied, did bakers toil on Sunday, and did a pension or sick fund exist? Not only earnings and labour relations thus come into view, but also attitudes of managers and workers regarding fairness, workload or commitment. This connects to historiographical attention that gained weight after the Second World War and emphasizes the social and cultural dimension of the wage.[3] This approach is now increasingly accepted, to which testifies, for example, the comprehensive interest in gender wage gaps.[4] Moreover, it leads to revise long-established and widely used wage series.[5]

---

[1] This chapter benefited from discussions with the participants of the meeting in May 2021. All translations of Dutch and French quotes are done by the author. Up to 1914, one Belgian franc equalled 9 d. or 19.3 $ cents.
[2] David Schloss, *Methods of industrial remuneration* (London: Williams-Norgate, 1894), 142.
[3] Peter Scholliers, Leonard Schwarz, 'The Wage in Europe since the Sixteenth Century', in *Experiencing Wages. Social and Cultural Aspects of Wage Forms in Europe since 1500*, ed. Peter Scholliers and Leonard Schwarz (New York & Oxford: Berghahn Books, 2003), 8–16.
[4] Jane Humphries, 'The Gender Gap in Wages. Productivity or Prejudice or Market Power in Pursuits of Profits', *Social Science History*, 33, no. 4 (2009): 481–8.
[5] Particularly in Great Britain: John Hatcher and Judy Stephenson (eds.), *Seven Centuries of Unreal Wages* (London: Palgrave, 2019), 2.

This chapter presents a case study of a company that lived through swift mechanization and ardent socialism. The former exemplifies the so-called second industrial revolution. In Belgium, the first commercial bread factories appeared around 1850, using simple kneading machines, small stone ovens, and hardly any steam power. Vooruit revolutionized the baking process by installing big kneading machines, hot-air ovens, steam engines and electronic devices, paving the way for large bread factories in and out Belgium. An observer confidently wrote, 'Vooruit opened the era of mechanical bakeries',[6] while the co-operative claimed, 'The founding of bread factories has formed a new proletariat, that of the bakery workers'.[7] The focus on this bread factory allows insight in the direct effect on wage formation, which reaches beyond Vooruit and Belgium.[8] The same goes for the effect of socialist ideology on work conditions.[9] In general, co-operatives saw themselves as first-rate employers, foreshadowing an equal and fair society. They applied distinct management strategies such as democratic work organization and, in general, they paid high wages. Yet, according to David Schloss's broad survey of wage systems around 1890, co-operatives failed to introduce alternative payment systems.[10] Did Vooruit, an overtly socialist institution that claimed to fervently defend the workers, confirm this? Was the co-operative caught in the contradiction between its socialist ideals and concerns about the production cost? One of the founders of Vooruit unequivocally wrote, 'Companies, also those managed by socialists, have a capitalistic core',[11] and labour leaders in Belgium, France and Holland backed up this view.[12] So, which wage system emerged that embraced the mix of socialism and swift mechanization?

---

[6] Jules Buse, 'La boulangerie à Gand et dans les environs de 1879 à 1905', *Commission nationale de la petite bourgeoisie. Volume III* (Ghent, Plantijn, 1905) 80. See, too, *The Lancet*, 4 January 1890, 43; *Science*, 10, no. 243 (1887), 162.

[7] *Vooruit*, 22 December 1887, 1.

[8] Wage systems in relation to mechanization are rarely studied in an empirical way; notorious exceptions are William Reddy, 'Modes de paiement et contrôle du travail dans les filatures de coton en France, 1750-1848', *Revue du Nord*, 63 (1981): 135–46; Michael Sonenscher, *Work and wages* (Cambridge: Cambridge University Press, 1989) chapter 6; Reinhold Reith, *Lohn und Leistung. Lohnformen im Gewerbe 1450-1900* (Stuttgart: Steiner, 1999); Widukind De Ridder, *Loonsystemen, arbeidsorganisaties en arbeidsverhoudingen in de Belgische glas- en textielnijverheid, 1886-1914* (Brussels: VUB Press, 2010).

[9] Attention to labour relations at co-operatives is present in Ellen Furlough, *Consumer Cooperation in France. The Politics of Consumption, 1834-1914* (Ithaca: Cornell University Press, 1991), 139–43, 229–34; Rachael Vorberg-Rugh, 'Employers and Workers: Conflicting Identities over Women's Wages in the Co-operative Movement, 1906-1918', in *Consumerism and the Co-operative Movement in Modern British History*, ed. Lawrence Black and Nicole Robertson (Manchester: Manchester University Press, 2009) 121–37; Nicole Robertson, *The Co-operative Movement and Communities in Britain, 1914-1960* (Farnham: Ashgate, 2010), 181–208.

[10] Schloss, *Methods*, 9, 214–19.

[11] Paul De Witte, *De geschiedenis van Vooruit en de Gentsche socialistische werkersbeweging* (Ghent, 1898), 118–19.

[12] E.g. Dutch labour leader Henri Polak (*Het Volk. Dagblad voor de arbeiderspartij*, 27 September 1907, 1); French co-operative leader Charles Gide, *Les sociétés coopératives de consommation* (Paris: Colin, 1910), 238, and Belgian party leaders Jules Destrée and Emile Vandervelde, *Le socialisme en Belgique* (Paris: Giard & Brière, 1898), 283.

The history of Vooruit has been largely studied with only marginal attention to working conditions, labour relations or wage formation.[13] An asset when studying Vooruit is its rich documentation. There are brochures and articles in newspapers and magazines by relatively neutral observers, by Vooruit, and by its supporters and opponents. Particularly, the handwritten minutes of the board of administrators of Vooruit allow the study of the wage formation from within. I read these sources not only for what was written but also how it was written, to be able to fully interpret the relationships between employer and employees. Section one considers the background of the wage: Vooruit's organization, labour relations, mechanization and working hours. Section two tackles the wage itself: the tariff, the wage form and system, the fines and premiums, the pay for night work, the negotiations, and the weekly earnings. The conclusion stresses the friction between two lines that characterized Vooruit's labour relations, work conditions and wages: the capitalist and the socialist.

The bakery

In November 1880, a couple of socialists left the co-operative bakery De Vrije Bakkers ('Free Bakers') to found Vooruit, wishing to sell pure bread at a fair price to reach as many workers as possible. The goal was to win them over to socialism.[14] In May 1883 a kneading machine, two hot-air ovens and a steam engine were installed to save on cost of labour and energy and to produce more and better bread. The daring initiative had huge consequences: one oven of about 100 loaves was ready within 35 minutes, whereas a stone oven took two hours, producing 70 loaves.[15] In 1886, 1889 and 1902 more and bigger machines, ovens and tools were installed, and new buildings were erected. By 1910, the bakery had four big kneading machines, eight ovens and a steam engine of 20 horsepower.[16] The bread production skyrocketed, although not linearly, from 4,000 loaves per week in 1881 to 103,000 in 1900. Profit was huge. The number of co-operators rose to 9,000 in 1914, which was close to 20 per cent of the total number of Ghent households. The bakery became the core of a vast commercial enterprise with grocery and garment shops and apothecaries, while it subsidized a successful newspaper (also named *Vooruit*), brass bands, a library, gymnastic clubs and political campaigns. Vooruit supported strikers throughout the country by organizing the supply of bread, a very efficient propaganda tool.

---

[13] Hendrik Defoort, *Werklieden, bemint uw profijt. De Belgische sociaaldemocratie in Europa,* (Leuven: Lannoocampus, 2006); Geert Van Goethem, 'The Belgian Co-operative Model: Elements of Success and Failure', in *A Global History of Consumer Co-operatives since 1850,* ed. Mary Hilson, Silke Neunsinger and Greg Patmore (Leiden: Brill, 2017), 78–98; Guy Vanschoenbeek, *Novecento in Gent. De wortels van de sociaal-democratie in Vlaanderen* (Ghent: Amsab, 1995).
[14] Alfred Micha, 'Belgium', in *Report of the first international co-operative congress* (London: King, 1895), 273.
[15] *De Toekomst,* 10 January 1883, 1.
[16] *The Lancet,* 4 January 1890, 3. In 1910, the Belgian average reached 4.1 horsepower per bread factory, which highlights the position of Vooruit. See, *Recensement de l'industrie et du commerce [31 décembre 1910]. Volume 5* (Brussels : Office de Publicité & Dewit, 1919), 191, 194.

Vooruit was run by the general assembly, according to common co-operative principles.[17] Initially, all co-operators met weekly, applying the one-(wo)man, one-vote concept, but because of the growth of membership these meetings later occurred only twice a year and with relatively modest attendances, despite absentees being fined. Sometimes children were sent to the general assembly, which was not to the board's liking. The general assembly appointed annually the executive committee of five people, but in fact it merely validated this committee. These five selected some 25 reliable co-operators to assist with the daily management. This board of administrators, rather than the general assembly, had all the power: it enlisted and fired workers, fixed the bread price, discussed wage levels and working hours, decided about investments, controlled the accounts, organized all sorts of celebrations, and supervised every single aspect of the co-operative.[18] Its composition changed by co-optation, which was not confirmed by the general assembly. The board met weekly. At these meetings the bakers were regularly invited to discuss the production process and the work conditions. Also, although less frequently, the bakers sent representatives to the meeting or wrote letters to raise a particular issue. Every so often, exceptional meetings with the bakers were organized to discuss specific matters. Negotiations, thus, were institutionalized since the onset of Vooruit, but the co-operative had no democratic functioning in the sense of co-operative ideology.

Vooruit's hierarchical functioning appeared in the way the enterprise was managed. Some administrators had a very permanent commitment. Among them was Edouard Anseele (1856–1938). He was a self-made journalist, a co-founder of the socialist party in Ghent in 1877, and he was elected as one of the first socialist members of Parliament in 1894. He was among the founders of Vooruit, became its general manager and indisputable leader: *un vrai patron*, who impressed everybody.[19] He was obsessed by bread baking as he became aware of the importance of selling good, pure bread as a condition of the smooth performance of the enterprise. He negotiated with millers, ordered baking tests, tasted flour, visited machine builders in Germany and pastry bakeries in Paris, regularly met with the bakers on the work floor, and suggested big and small improvements (for example, a new way of stacking the loaves).

Bakers were enlisted after being tested on accomplishing the whole baking process,[20] but recruitment was smoother if one was member of the socialist party or was introduced by an administrator.[21] Being a devoted co-operator was compulsory but being a union member was not required (the Ghent socialist bakers' union started in

---

[17] Schloss, *Methods*, 228.
[18] 'Le Vooruit. La coopération et l'organisation socialiste en Belgique', *Le Musée Social*. Série A, circulaire 20, 1897, 472–3.
[19] 'Edouard Anseele', in *Dictionnaire des patrons en Belgique*, ed. Ginette Kurgan-van Hentenryck, Serge Jaumain and Valérie Montens (Brussels : De Boeck, 1996), 20–2.
[20] Defoort, *Werklieden*, 254; *Notulen. Raad van Beheer. Samenwerkende Maatschappij Vooruit nr 1*; Archives, AMSAB – ISG (https://www.amsab.be/en/). The minutes can be viewed via http://hdl.handle.net/ 10796/E6D72B8D-5940-4BA7-8D70-D2E1771E9D8F (further referred to as *Notulen*), 22 June 1893.
[21] *Notulen*, 7 March 1884; 26 June 1885 ('We should try to enlist as many party members as possible').

1886, but without much success).²² The board regularly discussed spontaneous work solicitations, which showed enthusiasm for working at Vooruit. As a rule, these were rejected. Good workers were not only praised because of their efforts or skill, but also for their support of the party.²³ Vooruit never had difficulties in recruiting staff.

There were two bakers in 1881 and six in late 1882. Each baker performed all the baking tasks (kneading, dividing the dough, handling the oven,...), although some did specialize (for example, occasionally producing viennoiseries). With the installation of machines in 1883, the number of bakers was reduced to five. In 1884, a second team of five bakers joined the first one.²⁴ A couple of years later, the teams shrunk to four workers each, but when more kneading machines and ovens were used and night work was introduced, the number of bakers per team rose to twelve, while a third team was added.²⁵ By 1900 there were 36 bakers who worked in various units for nine hours during six days, so the bakery could produce seven days a week.²⁶ It was a thoroughly masculine world. Night work began in May 1885, and work on Sunday in 1888, to which the bakers did not oppose.²⁷ One baker led his team, but he had no privileges: he was the go-between with the foreman of the bakery. The latter was the head baker, but in 1893 a supervisor without baking skills was appointed 'to do nothing else than to observe and control everything'.²⁸ Every step of the baking process implied teamwork that required close attention. Hence, the rather severe hierarchy on the work floor, which included three levels: the team leader, the supervisor of the bakery, and the general manager (Anseele).

The co-operative now and then produced mediocre bread. This led to vivid exchanges during the board meetings, which reveals the top-bottom nature of management.²⁹ According to the administrators, the bakers were responsible for producing inferior bread and not the flour, the machines, bad weather or anything else. The quantity of loaves per oven in particular caused many disputes. 'Pulling' more loaves out of 100 kilogrammes of dough increased the co-operative's profit but lowered the bread quality, an essential feature for Vooruit's success.³⁰ The chair of the meetings often used strong language, and for example Anseele said that 'the bakers don't know how to bake' and that 'they are totally incompetent'.³¹ In general, the bakers were distrusted. Anseele again: 'Our bakers do not work with love of our company', 'They never did anything for the party [...] and they should work two hours more to learn

---

[22] Defoort, *Werklieden*, 217. The relationship between co-operatives and unions was delicate: Schloss, *Methods*, 141; Vorberg-Rugh, 'Employers and workers', 123–4.
[23] The bakers of Vooruit were expected to attend political meetings, diffuse brochures and posters, and promote the newspaper (*Notulen*, 9 January 1885).
[24] *Notulen*, 5 June 1885.
[25] *Notulen*, 21 March 1884.
[26] 'Le Vooruit. La coopération', 468. In 1896, the average number of workers in the Ghent bread factories was 22, and in Belgium 18: *Recensement général des industries et métiers [31 octobre 1896], volume 1* (Brussels: Hayez, 1900) 42.
[27] *Notulen*, 4 April 1884, 28 May 1885; 15 March 1888.
[28] *Notulen*, 15 February 1884; 6 April 1893.
[29] Peter Scholliers, 'Quality in the Eye of the Storm. The Bread of the Ghent Co-operative Vooruit, 1880 to 1914', *Cultural and Social History*, 18, no. 1 (2021): 79–96.
[30] *Notulen*, 5 October 1883.
[31] *Notulen*, 8 February 1894; 26 July 1894.

how to bake well.'³² Yet another time, the bakers were accused of 'criminal negligence' and of 'showing a spirit of malignancy'.³³ Often, the bakers protested against the allegations by sending a letter to the board of administrators which, however, was hardly ever discussed. When bakers were present at meetings, their voices were only faintly registered, lest they were intimidated by Anseele and did not dare to speak up. Discussions with the supervisor were aggressive: authority was at stake. Head baker Jan De Hollander, for example, exclaimed 'I never have followed the recommendations of the board. The bread is good because I say so.'³⁴ Conflicts occurred regularly and showed harsh and hierarchical relationships that were miles away from democratic principles. This inspired a Dutch social-democrat paper the following comment, 'Unfortunately, many workers of a co-operative expect to find heaven on earth, but they soon learn that a co-operative involves serious work, that one must arrive on time, and that there are supervisors and bosses.'³⁵

The board reprimanded, fined and, eventually, dismissed workers when the bread was unsatisfactory. An incident in 1884 illustrates this. A board member suggested deducting the 'price of the oven with the bad bread' from the wages of the bakers, but another member proposed subtracting this sum only from the supervisor's wage. The board accepted the latter solution.³⁶ The bread quality did not improve, and neither did the relationship between the board and the supervisor. Anseele suggested firing the supervisor, but this did not happen.³⁷ In early January 1885, the supervisor was invited to a board meeting to hear all grievances against him.³⁸ He defended himself and convinced the board. But the conflict was not over. In spring 1885, the bread was still unsatisfactory, and Anseele again suggested fining all bakers. Nothing happened, except the reprimanding, once more, of the bakers.³⁹ Finally, in May 1885 the head baker was fired by general consent of the board.⁴⁰ No baker had been fined or fired during this episode. Of course, other reasons for fining and firing existed. Two examples: a baker came to work half drunk and was suspended for three days. If this would happen again, he would be fired.⁴¹ Another baker made fun of the supervisor, which led to his dismissal.⁴² All in all, fines and firings were frequently used as a threat, but only rarely applied. When a worker was ultimately fined or fired, he was exhaustively informed and, eventually, could be heard by the board of administrators.

Many observers applauded the exemplary working hours that Vooruit claimed to apply: eight-hour day, six days a week.⁴³ But others stressed that the co-operative was

---

32 *Notulen*, 31 May 1889; 7 February 1890; 26 July 1894.
33 *Notulen*, 3 July 1885; 5 May 1914.
34 *Notulen*, 11 January 1884.
35 *Het Volk. Dagblad voor de arbeiderspartij* (Amsterdam), 27 September 1907, 1.
36 *Notulen*, 5 December 1884.
37 *Notulen*, 26 December 1884.
38 *Notulen*, 2 January 1885.
39 *Notulen*, 10 April 1885.
40 *Notulen*, 8 May 1885.
41 *Notulen*, 6 July 1893.
42 *Notulen*, 7 December 1893.
43 E.g. Buse, 'La boulangerie ', 160 ; 'Le Vooruit. La coopération', 468; Auguste De Winne, *Le Vooruit et ses détracteurs* (Brussels : Brismée, 1906), 7.

not able to keep the eight-hours principle. In 1901, one wrote that 'Vooruit was forced to renounce the minimum wage and the eight-hours day, which it previously had applied'.[44] Actually, work was irregular, experiencing quiet moments with 'idle bakers', according to the administration, followed by overwork. In general, the bakery's working day diminished from above 11 hours in the early 1880s to 9 hours in 1914. What about this eight-hour working day that had particular significance in Europe's labour movement? In the 1880s, there is no trace of it in the bakery. In May 1889, the national bakers' union wrote a letter to Vooruit, asking to introduce the eight hours. Vooruit's bakers approved the demand, adding that their wage should be maintained.[45] The administrators reacted with bewilderment. One board member was shocked because only a short while ago the bakers had wished to work for 12 hours and more (which would generate more wage). Anseele exclaimed that the bakers showed too little commitment to the co-operative and that the work hours could not change. The bakers were present at this meeting, and they replied that 'they had been forced to introduce the demand because Vooruit should give the example', to which Anseele answered that the union should first try to obtain better work conditions in other bakeries. The administrators and the rather tamed bakers agreed that the working time should not change. Four years later the eight-hour day reappeared (there is no indication about who took the initiative), but 'The test by the bakers to work 8 hours did not work. There was too much stale bread, which would cause the loss of members.'[46] This argument lacked any social or ideological consideration. The eight-hour day was only introduced after the First World War.[47] The unsuccessful test with the eight-hour day in June 1893 ended nonetheless by the agreement of extra pay for night work.

Vooruit introduced night work in 1885. During a couple of days one team started work at 4.00 am and stopped at 12.00 am. The test was successful and night work was kept until 1914 (and beyond).[48] The reason for working at night was to 'always provide fresh bread', following the customers' wishes.[49] Seemingly, Vooruit's bakers did not mind working at night. Other bakeries criticized the co-op for this, but Vooruit argued, 'It is true, our bakers work late but they earn more than in any other bakery.'[50] The socialist party and the bakers' union were highly opposed to night work, though. In 1898, the union submitted to the annual congress of the socialist party the proposal to prohibit it.[51] There, a discussion emerged between the party and the union on the one

---

[44] Hubert Bourgin, 'Régime coopératif', *L'Année sociologique* (1901), 508. The board of administrators never discussed the minimum wage, but it claimed that Vooruit applied the wage rate of the bakers' union. See, too, Helge Zoitl, 'Gegen den Brotwucher! Die Gründung der Wiener Hammerbrotwerke', *Zeitgeschichte*, 16, no. 3 (1988), 87.
[45] *Notulen*, 31 May 1889.
[46] *Notulen*, 22 June 1893.
[47] *Notulen*, 14 May 1914 ('There are many demands, such as the eight hours, which we could not yet grant').
[48] Bernardus Heldt, *Instellingen op sociaal en coöperatief gebied in België* (Leeuwarden: Coöperatieve handelsdrukkerij, 1892), 100.
[49] *Notulen*, 28 May 1885; 15 March 1888.
[50] *Vooruit*, 4 July 1887, 3.
[51] *Compte rendu du XIVe congrès annuel. Parti ouvrier belge* (Brussels : Brismée 1898), 72–3.

hand, and the co-operatives on the other (in which, quite surprisingly, Vooruit did not participate). Some delegates argued that co-operative bakeries could show the way, but many others said that this would damage their commercial position. It was finally agreed that co-op bakeries could apply night work, introduce rotating shifts for the bakers, and pay an additional sum for night labour. Noticeably, five years earlier Vooruit had compensated for night work. In the 1900s and 1910s, night work became a very controversial and much debated issue. In 1902, for example, the newspaper *Vooruit* was resolutely opposed to night work in bakeries but found it impossible to abolish it in only one enterprise, i.e. the Vooruit bakery.[52]

Vooruit, thus, was not organized according to co-operative principles. It displayed features of a capitalistic enterprise, although there were some socialist values such as the extra pay for night work and the attempt to introduce the eight hours. It is to be expected that the wage system did not concur with co-operative principles, but how, then, was it arranged?

The wage

The Belgian industrial census of 1896 contains unique information about the wage system, revealing that no less than 88 per cent of the 8,398 Belgian bakery workers got a time wage, overwhelmingly by the week; almost 1 per cent were paid by output; 5.8 per cent were unpaid (apprentices or family members); for 5.4 per cent the pay system was imprecise. These data were not specified by size or legal status of the enterprise. Of all bakery workers, 53 per cent obtained in-kind payment (food and/or lodging).[53]

This information may serve as reference to Vooruit's remuneration system. Little is known about the payment mode of the two workers when the bakery started in November 1880. Democratic management and a form of profit sharing, like co-operative theory would have it,[54] was not applied: the board of administrators directed the co-op, and profit was used for supplying cheaper bread and supporting socialism. Whether workers obtained wages by time or output is unknown. They surely did not get board or lodging. From 1882 onward, the wage system was clear. Vooruit practised a collective task wage for its six bakers, that was calculated by multiplying the tariff rate per oven by the total number of ovens achieved in one week, and this sum was then equally divided between the workers.[55] Collective task wages and linking the team's wage to output were common in some industries, such as paper trade or coal mining, but these were extremely rare in the food trade.[56] Vooruit's linking of the wage to output was a form of bonus, although the output changed but little in the short run. This system was advantageous when business boomed, but unfavourable in times of

---

[52] *Vooruit*, 14 February 1902, 1.
[53] *Recensement général des industries et des métiers. 31 octobre 1896. Volume XVIII. Exposé général des méthodes et des résultats* (Brussels : Weissenbruch, 1902), 340–1.
[54] Schloss, *Methods*, 87, 146.
[55] De Witte, *Geschiedenis*, 119.
[56] De Ridder, *Loonsystemen*, 51.

low production (while weekly wages would guarantee steady income). This collective task wage existed in very few trades and can be considered as utterly innovative in the food trade.[57] It remained until 1914. It was miles away from the co-operative ideal, although one crucial element was present: equal pay. In 1882, Vooruit paid 1.25 francs per oven, and so each of the six bakers got 0.21 francs. If a maximum of thirteen ovens could be prepared per day (each oven required two hours; two ovens in operation; thirteen-hour day, six days a week), this would yield 2.7 francs per day and per baker, or 16.25 francs per week.

The installation of the kneading machine, the hot-air ovens and the steam engine in May 1883 immediately initiated changes in the tariff, followed by conflict. Vooruit proposed to pay the workers a daily wage.[58] This initiative is shrouded in darkness. In some cases, employers preferred time wages when reliable, honest workmen were needed.[59] This could apply to Vooruit's bakers who were mostly party members. Did the proposal refer to the previous practice at the bakery? Which amount was suggested? Did Vooruit anticipate booming sales and, hence, rising wage cost? In any case, Vooruit expected to save on labour costs now that machines had been introduced.[60] But the bakers refused the offer, maybe out of fear of losing money in prosperous times to come.[61] Then, the bakers were offered 1.10 francs per oven, or 12 per cent less than the previous tariff. This rate-cutting was rationalized by the fact that production would rise because of mechanization, which would yield higher earnings.[62] But again, the bakers declined the proposal. Further negotiations failed, and the bakers went on strike, which was a dreadful experience within the context of a socialist co-operative. The six bakers were fired and immediately replaced.[63] This is a textbook capitalist scenario: replacement of recalcitrant workers when new technology arrived, implying lower tariff.[64]

Vooruit swiftly started with a new team of five bakers who, seemingly, had been recruited without difficulty. The new technology allowed them to produce more bread than the six artisanal bakers. The price for one oven was settled at 1 franc, a quarter less than a couple of weeks earlier and 10 per cent less than offered to the six artisanal bakers. Because there were only five bakers, each had 0.20 francs per oven, which was the same amount as each of the six bakers got. But more ovens were produced in one week, which yielded 22 francs a week per baker, or about one-third more than before the mechanization.[65] In 1884, a second team of bakers started work, and more ovens were operated. At that occasion, Anseele suggested paying 0.85 francs per oven, another

---

[57] De Ridder, *Loonsystemen*, 239.
[58] De Witte, *Geschiedenis*, 119.
[59] Schloss, *Methods*, 16.
[60] *De Toekomst*, 6 January 1883, 2; 10 January 1883, 1; 31 March 1883, 3.
[61] Generally, workers feared wage cuts or huge unemployment when the production was mechanized (Vinçard, *Les ouvriers*, 34).
[62] Maurice Dobb, *Wages* (Cambridge, Nisbet, 1966), 58–60.
[63] De Witte, *Geschiedenis*, 120. There is no further information about this strike. The *Notulen* only start in October 1883, and newspapers did not mention it.
[64] Paul Leroy-Beaulieu, *Essai sur la répartition des richesses* (Paris: Guillaumin, 1881), 449–50.
[65] *Notulen*, 11 January 1884.

severe drop of the tariff, which illustrates the direct link between the factory's overall output, the tariff and the individual wage. One administrator proposed paying 0.80 francs, saying 'our company is not doing very well right now, and we have raised wages in the past. The bakers should empathise.'[66] After a long discussion and two rounds of voting, 0.85 francs was accepted. The bakers were not involved in the discussion. An administrator commented, 'One will probably say that this is a wage cut and this might scare off workers. We shall say they will be paid 0.33 francs per hour.'[67]

In January 1885 the bakers' weekly wages had seriously diminished and they demanded a rise of the tariff. This led to vivid discussions among the administrators but not so much between administrators and workers.[68] Anseele explained the diminishing of the weekly wages by the fact that fewer ovens had been produced because of lower sales, which, he argued, was due to the poor bread quality. Another administrator stated that other bakeries paid higher wages than Vooruit and that a rise of 0.10 francs per oven should be given. Yet another said that a pay rise would cost Vooruit a lot of money, that the bakers are aware of the fierce competition, and that they ought to do more for the co-operative. Also, it was suggested to give the bakers part of the profit. No decision was taken, and the idea of giving a share in the profit disappeared for a couple of years.[69] In May of the same year, several administrators suggested to yet increase the tariff to 0.90 francs,[70] and a month later the issue of the tariff imposed a special meeting.[71] The board met without the bakers. The administrators scrutinized the whole baking process and suggested a new tariff: 1 franc per oven, which equalled the price of late 1883. No reasons for this increase were given. Did the introduction of night work in that period play a role? Was bad bread and the ensuing conflict with the head baker relevant? The end of this episode revealed the power relations in the bakery. The bakers, waiting respectfully outside the meeting room, first refused the offer, which may surprise given the rise of the tariff by 25 per cent (no reason for their refusal was noted), but then Anseele went to see them, arguing that in the end they would earn more money, whereafter the bakers accepted the proposal.

In December 1887, the newspaper *Vooruit* provided unique data about the wage form: 'Each day Vooruit produces 50 ovens, using two furnaces. At Vooruit, the bakers are paid 1 franc per oven, and so 50 francs a day are earned by 15 men who work in three teams of five for 24 hours.'[72] Thus, one baker obtained 3.33 francs per day (50 francs divided by 15) or, for six working days, 20.0 francs per week, which was 13 per cent less than in 1885. The time to finish one oven fluctuated around 30 minutes, and so per hour 0.40 francs were earned (1 franc per oven divided by 5 bakers equals 0.20 francs, earned in 30 minutes). This hourly wage of 40 centimes appeared in

---

[66] *Notulen*, 14 March 1884.
[67] *Notulen*, 21 March 1884.
[68] *Notulen*, 9 January 1885.
[69] *Vooruit*, 20 February 1885, 3.
[70] *Notulen*, 8 May 1885.
[71] *Notulen*, 19 June 1885.
[72] *Vooruit*, 20 December 1887, 3.

Vooruit's propaganda,[73] which was exactly double of the hourly wage of the bakers who worked at Vooruit prior to the mechanization. Higher output counteracted the rate cuts.

The opening of the wholly new bakery in April 1889, with larger kneading machines and more and bigger ovens, led to the reconsideration of the work and wage calculation, which caused new confrontations between the bakers and the management. Vooruit proposed diminishing the tariff to 0.90 francs per oven. In a letter, the bakers protested, arguing that Vooruit has 'duped them with the calculations, and they propose 0.98 francs per oven. This is a wage cut, while they work harder for less money'.[74] After hearing the arguments of the bakers, it was decided to impose 0.90 francs per oven. The new bakery of 1889 not only meant the lowering of the tariff, but also the diminishing of the number of workers per team (from five to four), which resulted in 'longer working hours and more work effort [which] allowed each baker to earn 24 to 26 francs per week'.[75] This tariff of 0.90 francs remained for twenty years. During this period, I did not find a claim for higher rates by the bakers, nor an attempt by the management for lowering them. Around 1910 the tariff rose to 1.08 francs and in 1914 to 1.23 francs, which almost equalled the price per oven in 1882.[76] Reasons for both increases were not given.

Changes in the working time, the output, the number of ovens and the composition of the teams led to the increase of the hourly wage to 0.45 francs in 1894 and 0.60 francs in 1914.[77] These changes influenced the weekly wage in contrasting ways: rising hourly wages conflicted with temporally low activity and ensuing diminishing working hours. Anseele testified to this when he mentioned an average weekly wage of 26.6 francs in 1891 and 28.1 francs in 1892, years with both satisfactory sales, while it had been 24 francs in 1893.[78] In 1914, the weekly wage at Vooruit attained 29.7 francs. These amounts will reappear below within context.

The continuous distrust of the administrators about the skills of the bakers not only led to reprimands, fines and firing, but also to a new approach of the wage. Already in October 1883, at a special meeting with the bakers, Anseele mentioned to apply the 'participation principle', a form of profit sharing that would engage the bakers much more in the production process and the bakery's goals. Giving them a bonus would probably lead to better bread. This was accepted.[79] It was not clear how this profit sharing functioned, but most likely it was applied only to the supervisor.[80] This form of premium was very different from the initial concept of co-operative reward.[81] Anseele relaunched his idea in July 1889: 'To force the bakers to work more in favour of the bakery, they would receive a share of the profit above the normal wage.'[82] Anseele

---

[73] E.g. *Vooruit*, 13 June 1888, 3 ('Our bakery workers earn 40 centimes per hour for a job that is far easier than in the days of handwork; no other boss pays more').
[74] *Notulen*, 22 March 1889.
[75] De Witte, *Geschiedenis*, 470.
[76] *Notulen*, 28 May 1914.
[77] *Notulen*, 30 August 1894; 5 March 1914.
[78] *Notulen*, 2 February 1893; De Witte, *Geschiedenis*, 472.
[79] *Notulen*, 20 October 1883.
[80] *Notulen*, 1 February 1884.
[81] Schloss, *Methods*, 9–10.
[82] *Notulen*, 5 July 1889.

calculated the average number of loaves per oven, which was 134; if the bakers would produce more than 134, they would get 50 per cent more per extra bread. Of course, the quality of the bread must remain good.[83] The board accepted to apply this to all bakers. However, 'The bakers were pleased to be able to augment their income and they diluted the dough more and more, so to obtain 140 loaves, but the bread was too limp, and the complaints about the bread augmented.'[84] So, the exact opposite occurred of what was aimed at. In 1893 the participation concept was done with, while the quantity of loaves was limited to 136. The bonus system had hardly influenced the wage. Remarkably, in 1892 the newspaper *Vooruit* sternly condemned the participation principle in general, arguing it rushed the worker, making him constantly watch his co-workers with his mind on the output, leading to greed and divisions amongst workers.[85]

In general, the level of the bakers' wages at Vooruit enjoyed a good reputation. In 1886, The *Pall Mall Gazette* (London) published a piece on Vooruit, that concluded, 'The workmen naturally receive the very highest wages paid in the trade, while they enjoy equal rights with all the other members of the enterprise.'[86] In 1888, a Dutch union leader wrote, 'The wage is 40 centimes per hour, which is much higher than in other bakeries of the town', adding that the bakers worked only eight hours per day and that the head baker obtained an extra 2 francs per week.[87] In 1890, *The Lancet* (London) noted, '[the bakers] earn wages averaging 25 per cent more than is generally paid in this trade at Ghent'.[88] Three years later, *The Citizen* (Gloucester) echoed the 25 per cent difference, mentioning the eight-hour work day.[89] In 1895, *Le Monde Illustré* (Paris) wrote that the bakers' weekly wage reached a comfortable 24 francs.[90] In 1897, *Le Musée Social* (Paris) specified the daily rate: 'At Volksbelang and Vooruit the daily wages of the workers are generally between 3.5 and 4 francs, and some even at 4.5 francs', and the weekly wage reached 24 francs for each baker.[91] In 1905, social investigator J. Buse mentioned a weekly wage at Vooruit of 26.8 francs for six days, adding that a supplement was given for nightwork.[92] And in 1906, an activist of Vooruit wrote, 'Gradually, the eight-hour day has been introduced in the various services of the co-operative. The bakers earn 50 centimes per hour.'[93] The wage system was not mentioned, except briefly in 1890 by *The Lancet* that spoke of a premium system.

The idea of the bakers' high wages and eight-hour day was buoyed by Vooruit. As in other red co-operatives, Vooruit wished to display exemplary labour relations, among

---

[83] *Notulen*, 21 July 1889.
[84] De Witte, *Geschiedenis*, 470–1; *The Lancet*, 4 January 1890, 43.
[85] *Vooruit*, 5 February 1892, 1; see too Gide, *Les sociétés coopératives*, 242–3.
[86] *Pall Mall Gazette*, 28 June 1886, 14.
[87] Bernardus Heldt, *Over coöperatie. Instellingen en uitkomsten van de S.M. Vooruit in Gent en de Coöperatieve bakkerij 'De Volharding' te s'Gravenhage* (Amsterdam: Brinkman, 1888), 12–13.
[88] *The Lancet*, 4 January 1890, 44; 29 March 1890, 719.
[89] *The Citizen*, 14 January 1893, 3.
[90] *Le Monde Illustré*, 13 April 1895, 227.
[91] 'Le Vooruit. La coopération', 455.
[92] Buse, 'La boulangerie', 160.
[93] De Winne, *Le Vooruit et ses détracteurs*, 7, 10.

which high wages were central.⁹⁴ The guiding principle was, 'Our bakers and bread carriers earn more than anywhere else.'⁹⁵ Arguments were not only to be found in fair wages, but also in the fact that these wages were beneficial to the co-operative: 'The co-operative has an interest in paying high salaries to increase the purchasing power of its workers who, at the same time, are its customers.'⁹⁶ The claim of high wages particularly appeared in December 1887 when a strike occurred in Volksbelang. This company was established in May 1887, a large, modern bread factory and was direct challenger of Vooruit. The bakers of Volksbelang demanded the same wages as paid by Vooruit. The newspaper *Vooruit* eagerly exploited this claim: 'The socialist co-operative pays the highest wage of the city, 40 CENTIMES PER HOUR, it allows the bakers to work freely, invites them to the board meetings where they discuss and vote. Vooruit does not wish to make profit out of salaries, and it strives at providing a decent wage and dignity of the workers.'⁹⁷ The illusion that workers effectively decided about their pay, was particularly emphasized. Volksbelang retorted, whereupon Vooruit argued that its bakers earned 4.08 francs per day of 10 hours, but the bakers of Volksbelang had 4.08 francs per day of 12 hours, or 15 per cent less per hour.⁹⁸ After a couple of days, the strike at Volksbelang ended. The strikers were replaced.

Graph 2.1 shows the data of the weekly wages of the bakers, as mentioned in the discussions of the board meetings, the newspaper *Vooruit* and by well-informed

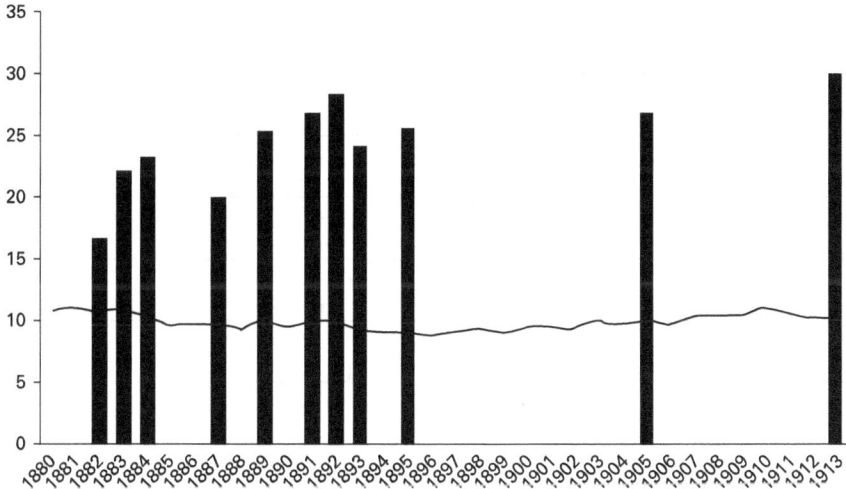

Graph 2.1 Weekly wages of bakers at Vooruit, and cost-of-living index (1913=10), 1880–1913.⁹⁹

---

⁹⁴ Furlough, *Consumer cooperation*, 140; Robertson, *The Co-operative Movement*, 186, Gide, *Les sociétés cooperatives*, 240.
⁹⁵ *Vooruit*, 20 February 1885, 3.
⁹⁶ Charles Andler, 'Le rôle social des coopératives', *Revue de métaphysique et de morale*, 8, no. 1 (1900) : 131.
⁹⁷ *Vooruit*, 20 December 1887, 1.
⁹⁸ *Vooruit*, 21 December 1887, 1.
⁹⁹ See references to the weekly wages in: Peter Scholliers, 'A century of real industrial wages in Belgium, 1840-1939', in *Labour's Reward*, ed. Peter Scholliers, Vera Zamagni (Aldershot: E. Elgar, 1995), 204.

observers. The 34 per cent growth after the mechanization of 1883 was spectacular, just as the 22 per cent increase between 1884 and 1892. Both rises were caused by the specific wage system that stressed increasing production after intensive mechanization. In 1887 and 1893, however, the weekly wage declined, which was due to diminishing sales. Most likely, the weekly wage stagnated between 1895 and 1904, which contrasted to the slightly increasing cost of living of those years (+ 11 per cent). The stagnation might have had several causes: the tariff remained stable, the premium was abolished, the working time diminished slightly, less new machinery was installed, and the rapid growth rate of bread sales had stopped. The bakers never reacted to the stagnating wages and the ensuing loss of purchasing power. By 1913, the weekly wage had risen by 10 per cent compared to 1905, which was caused by the tariff increase of the 1910s. The cost of living first rose by 8 per cent between 1905 and 1910, and then declined by 8 per cent up to 1913, which resulted in a moderately rising buying power in the two decades before 1914.

The 1896 industrial census puts Vooruit's wages in perspective. It shows that artisanal master-bakers paid their adult male workers on average 1.85 francs per day, which was among the lowest of the kingdom (the overall average for adult male workers in industry reached 3.26 francs).[100] This average included wage earners who also had food and/or lodging, which was the case of 53 per cent of the artisanal bakery workers. To disregard this in-kind payment and obtain day wages that are comparable to the national average and wages of factory bakers, I removed the two lowest wage categories (who most probably included the workers with in-kind payment), which led to an average of 3.12 francs, or close to the national average of 3.26 francs. In the *boulangeries mécaniques,* however, the daily wage attained 4.08 francs, or 30 per cent above the 3.12 francs of artisanal bakers without in-kind pay. In 1895, Vooruit paid 4.25 francs per day, or 4 per cent more than the average daily wage of the bread factories and no less than 36 per cent above the 3.12 francs of artisanal bakers. In those days, the co-operative claimed that Vooruit worked 9 hours per day, whereas other bread factories in town worked 10 hours. Vooruit's hourly wage would then exceed that in the other factories by 15 per cent. So, Vooruit's claim of high wages was fair.

Other bakery workers at Vooruit were all paid by the week, about which little is known. The bread carriers not only delivered bread but also functioned as propagandists and contacts between the management, Vooruit's members and the public. They earned 22.5 francs (1897) and 25 francs (1905 and 1912).[101] In 1887, the accountant earned 22.5 francs per week, and the general manager 28 francs.[102] The latter was mentioned during the 'pamphlet war' between Vooruit and Volksbelang, stressing the socialist character of Vooruit.[103] In 1897, the *gérant* earned 40 francs per week, the accountant and the

---

[100] *Recensement général 1896*, 292–3, 302–3. For the national average, see: Peter Scholliers, 'Industrial wage differentials in nineteenth-century Belgium', *Income distribution in historical perspective*, ed. Y. S. Brenner, Hartmut Kaelble, Mark Thomas (Cambridge: Cambridge University Press, 1991), 106.
[101] 'Le Vooruit. La coopération', 467; Buse, 'La boulangerie', 160; *Notulen*, 6 July 1912.
[102] *Vooruit*, 16 June 1887, 1; 21 December 1887, 1. Bourgin ('Régime coopératif', 508) stressed the small wage differentials.
[103] *Vooruit*, 4 July 1887, 3; 21 December 1887, 2–3.

controller 30 francs, and the white-collar workers between 20 and 24 francs.[104] Around 1910, the accountant earned 35 francs.[105] The wage of the supervisor of the bakery was discussed somewhat more frequently. In October 1883, he had 30 francs per week, but various board members pleaded for an increase. Anseele argued that this would force Vooruit to raise the wage of the bread carriers too, which was impossible. He proposed to give the supervisor a share in the profit, but no decision was taken.[106] In February 1884 the supervisor sent a letter to the board of administrators asking for a wage increase because of his many working hours. 'After an altercation it is suggested to give him 32 francs fixed wage and his part of the profit, this is accepted by 13 against 7 and 2 abstentions.'[107] It is not clear what was meant by 'part of the profit'. Later, the minutes of the board mentioned the following wages of the supervisors: 34 francs (February 1884), 35 francs (January 1885 and March 1895) and 40 francs (1911).[108] All in all, small wage differentials were part of the policy of the co-operative, as one of the administrators emphasized: 'We don't wish to have a large gap between wages of white- and blue-collar workers, which is why we pay our bakers well.'[109] The wage difference between the bakers and the accountants reached 12 per cent in 1883 and 18 per cent in 1895 and 1913.

Alongside this striving for small wage gaps and other abovementioned socialist features, Vooruit applied a specific social policy. In 1884, a baker was badly injured by the driving belt of the kneading machine. The board of administrators voted for a payment of 40 francs, or two weeks' wages.[110] This initiative replicated an earlier instance, but I did not find similar examples in later periods. It is possible that all workers of Vooruit adhered to the sickness fund, Bond Moyson (established in 1887), that was supported by Vooruit.[111] In 1897 the co-op launched a pension fund for its workers. Most remarkable was the fact that Vooruit guaranteed a minimum weekly wage in periods of momentary diminishing sales (like the carnival feast in February or the *kermess* in August). In February 1893, the actual pay of the bakers was low, but Vooruit guaranteed a wage of 24 francs.[112] A similar supplement occurred in September of the same year. I did not find other examples of this initiative. Work at night (starting in 1885) was paid an extra franc per week from 1893 onward.[113] Work on Sundays (starting in 1888) was paid an extra 2.5 francs in 1912, but it remains unknown when this started.[114]

Conclusion

The mix of socialist ideas, new technology and, to lesser extent, artisanal concepts about work, led to innovations in Vooruit's labour relations, among which the wage

---

[104] 'Le Vooruit. La coopération', 466.
[105] *Notulen*, 15 May 1911.
[106] *Notulen*, 29 and 30 October 1883.
[107] *Notulen*, 1 February 1884.
[108] *Notulen*, 15 February 1884, 2 January 1885, 21 March 1895; 6 May 1911.
[109] *Notulen*, 14 May 1914.
[110] *Notulen*, 4 January 1884.
[111] Heldt, *Instellingen*, 105.
[112] *Notulen*, 2 February 1893; De Witte, *Geschiedenis*, 472.
[113] *Notulen*, 22 June 1893.
[114] *Notulen*, 28 September 1912.

system was most radical and far-reaching. In the 'formative years' 1881–5, the labour relations and norms were vehemently debated, which led to new practices. Gradually, Vooruit adopted the customs of other enterprises about hierarchy, control and sanctions (i.e. reprimands and fines), which lasted until 1914. Co-operative ideals of democratic decision-making and absence of hierarchy were lacking. Prior to the mechanization of the bakery in 1883, a collective task wage system was introduced, whereas time wages were the rule in the bakery trade. In late 1883, a tariff per oven was settled which was multiplied by the number of ovens per week, and this amount was equally divided among the bakers to set the weekly wage. As more machinery was installed, the tariff per oven was lowered, which angered the bakers who nonetheless never questioned the overall wage system or went on strike. In the long run, the weekly wage did well thanks to the increasing output. Sporadically stagnating sales led now and then to declining earnings. In this respect, Vooruit did not differ from other enterprises, and it offers a telling example of a modern enterprise with a capitalistic pay system, particularly of the way wages were discussed among board members, negotiated with the workers, and, finally, applied.

However, socialist ideology added many features: negotiations were frequent, wage disparities were small, the bakers were treated equally (including the team leader), and work at night and on Sundays was paid extra. Alongside these elements, more socialist accents were added. Attempts were made to introduce the eight-work day (it failed), a pension fund was installed, and additions to the regular wage were granted in times of low production. Finally, and crucially, weekly wages were above the average of wages of modern bread factories and certainly of artisanal bakers. These were new and atypical features. Vooruit was *not* a capitalist enterprise, although it applied many of its principles. On a broader level, it could be argued that Vooruit applied a capitalistic model with corrections, which anticipated general social-democrat policies of the post-1945 era.

3

Papers and Wages: Identity Documents and Work in Habsburg Austria During the Late Nineteenth and Early Twentieth Century[1]

Sigrid Wadauer

Introduction

Global labour history emphasizes the fact that there is no universal, linear and unquestioned tendency towards 'free', documented wage labour in the modern world. There are and have always been various ways in which people made a living in the course of their lives, by alternating and combining jobs and forms of income as well as by performing formal and informal, waged and unwaged, remunerated and unremunerated forms of work and livelihood practices – and doing so more or less voluntarily or by force.[2] This in turn raises issues: how can we capture and measure the diversity of labour relations and forms of livelihood in a global or long-term historical perspective? And how can we determine and evaluate the importance of waged labour in a certain historical context?[3] Data used for describing developments of work relations, wages and living standards raise many questions.[4] Such evidence has been challenged by historical studies which investigate in detail the actual amount of wage

---

[1] This chapter is based on research which was initially funded by the Gerda-Henkel-Stiftung (AZ 52/V/18) and is now funded by the Austrian Science Fund FWF (P32226-G29).

[2] See, just for example, Marcel van der Linden, *Workers of the World. Essays toward a Global Labour History* (Leiden: Brill, 2008); Andreas Eckert (2017),'Von der "freien Lohnarbeit" zum "informellen Sektor"?', *Geschichte und Gesellschaft* 43, no. 2: 297–307; Robert J. Steinfeld and Stanley L. Engermann, 'Labour – Free or Coerced? A Historical Reassessment of Differences and Similarities', in *Free and Unfree Labour. The Debate Continues*, eds. Tom Brass and Marcel van der Linden (Bern et al.: Peter Lang, 1997), 107–26.

[3] See, for example: Karin Hofmeester, Gijs Kessler and Christine Moll-Murata (2016), 'Conquerors, Employers, and Arbiters: States and Shifts in Labour Relations 1500–2000', *International Review of Social History*, 61, Special Issue: 1–26.

[4] In respect to the Habsburg Empire, see for example: Tomas Cvrcek (2013), 'Wages, Prices, and Living Standards in the Habsburg Empire, 1827-1910', *The Journal of Economic History* 73, no. 1: 1–37.

workers received[5] and how they made ends meet.[6] In this framework, questions of categorization, distinction and hierarchization of the variety of practices and resources are likewise attracting increased interest (beginning with and often focusing on legal, scholarly and statistical categories).[7] For it is obvious that in many interactions the differences between occupations or forms of income, between wage work and self-employment, or between work and other practices not acknowledged as work are often blurred and/or contested. Categories and distinctions are subject to, and the historical product of, consensus and conflict. Integrating both perspectives in a satisfying way, however, seems a problem that has not yet been solved.

My chapter takes identity- and work-documents for workers and servants (*Arbeits- und Dienstbotenbücher*) in the Austrian part of the Habsburg Empire (Cisleithania) as a starting point for discussing the relation between the formal categorization and the documentation of work and the forms of wages or livelihood. I will describe how categorization of work-relations and livelihood practices – as manifested in such documents – are reflected in different wages (amount, form, modes of payment or remuneration), in different options for action, in rights and (customary or formally granted) entitlements beyond actual work and wage and in different possibilities for claiming these rights. Wages are, after all, just one form of remuneration and one element in a person's or household's overall livelihood and status, even in the lives of wage workers.[8] In order to assess variations and contrasts in the standards of living or the acknowledged value of work, it seems necessary to take the variety of available resources into consideration. I will sketch out the regulations and official reasoning behind such identity- and work-documents while also illustrating how they could be used practically (in accordance with or in violation to such regulations) in interactions of authorities, employers and workers/servants for establishing and negotiating wages, as well as the terms and conditions of work and any entitlements beyond wages.[9] These identity papers manifest a formalization

---

[5] See, for example: John Hatcher, 'Seven Centuries of Unreal Wages' in *Seven Centuries of Unreal Wages. The Unreliable Data, Sources and Methods that Have Been Used for Measuring Standards of Living in the Past*, eds. John Hatcher and Judy Z. Stephenson. (Cham: Palgrave Macmillan, 2018) 15–70; Peter Scholliers and Vera Zamagni, 'Introduction' in *Labour's Reward. Real Wages and Economic Change in 19th- and 20th-century Europe*, eds. Peter Scholliers and Vera Zamagni (Aldershot: Edward Elgar, 1995), ix–xvii.

[6] Craig Muldrew and Steven King, 'Cash, Wages and the Economy of Makeshifts in England, 1650-1800' in *Experiencing Wages. Social and Cultural Aspects of Wage Forms in Europe since 1500*, eds. Peter Scholliers and Leonard Schwarz (New York: Berghahn Books, 2003), 155–82.

[7] A few examples of this are: Christian Topalov (2001), 'A Revolution in Representations of Work. The Emergence over the 19th Century of the Statistical Category "Occupied Population", in France, Great Britain and the United States,' *Revue Française de Sociologie* 42, Supplement: 79–106; Theresa Wobbe (2012), 'Making up People. Berufsstatistische Klassifikation, geschlechtliche Kategorisierung und wirtschaftliche Inklusion um 1900 in Deutschland,' *Zeitschrift für Soziologie* 41, no. 1: 41–57.

[8] Today, the ILO speaks of 'decent work' and 'social protection floor'. See, for example the *World Social Protection Report 2020-22* (Geneva: ILO, 2021); *Report of the Director-General: Decent Work* (Geneva: ILO, 1999). It would be anachronistic to use these concepts in respect to the period which is in the focus of this paper. Nevertheless, workers and servants were well aware of differences in the rights attached to different labour relations.

[9] On such questions, see for example Eric Hobsbawm, 'Custom, Wages and Work-Load', in *Labouring Men: Studies in the History of Labour* (London: Weidenfeld & Nicolson, 1964), 405–36; Leonard Schwarz (2007), 'Custom, Wages and Workload in England during Industrialization,' *Past & Present*, no. 197: 143–75; Scholliers et al., *Experiencing Wages*.

of labour relations and in this respect an emerging new state policy. Yet, as I will show, neither were those new regulations and forms of identification enforced consequently, nor did they necessarily contradict (what might be perceived as) custom.

Papers

Written documents as a proof of identity, of occupation and of an orderly termination of employment were in use and a topic of regulations already in early modernity.[10] Eighteenth-century writings portrayed them as a necessary means to fight breach of contract, to reduce job-mobility and lack of labour, to regulate wages and to suppress vagrancy.[11] In the nineteenth-century Habsburg Empire – in contrast to other countries like Germany[12] or France[13] – the obligation to possess such papers was not abolished but extended to include ever more categories of wage labour and service.[14] (These documents were in use in both parts of the empire; however, I am here exclusively addressing the kingdoms and lands represented in the Imperial Council.) Whereas the eighteenth century's *Kundschaften* (large one-page certificates issued by guilds) and *Wanderbücher* (booklets which replaced them from the 1830s on) had been mandatory only for journeymen on the tramp,[15] the Trade Law of 1859, with which guilds were

---

[10] Hugo Morgenstern, *Gesindewesen und Gesinderecht in Österreich* (Wien: Alfred Hölder, 1902), 22ff; Klaus Stopp, *Die Handwerkskundschaften mit Ortsansichten*. (Stuttgart: Anton Hiersemann, 1982), vol. 1; on the history of identification in general, see Waltraud Heindl and Edith Saurer, eds. *Grenze und Staat. Paßwesen, Staatsbürgerschaft, Heimatrecht und Fremdengesetzgebung in der österreichischen Monarchie (1750-1867)* (Wien: Böhlau, 2000); Valentin Groebner, *Der Schein der Person. Steckbrief, Ausweis und Kontrolle im Europa des Mittelalters*. (München: C.H. Beck, 2004); Jane Caplan and John Torpey, 'Introduction,' in *Documenting Individual Identity. The Development of State Practices in the Modern World*, eds. Jane Caplan and John Torpey (Princeton: Princeton University Press, 2001), 1–12; Edward Higgs, *Identifying the English. A History of Personal Identification 1500 to the Present* (London: Continuum, 2011); Hilde Greefs and Anne Winter, eds. *Migration Policies and Materialities of Identification in European Cities. Papers and Gates, 1500s to 1930s* (London: Routledge, 2019); Keith Breckenridge and Simon Szreter, *Registration and Recognition. Documenting the Person in World History* (Oxford: British Academy and Oxford University Press, 2012); Ilsen About, James Brown and Gayle Lonergan, eds. *Identification and Registration Practices in Transnational Perspective. People, Papers and Practices*, (London: Palgrave Macmillan, 2013).
[11] Morgenstern, *Gesindewesen*, 22ff.
[12] The Norddeutsche Bund abolished labour books in 1869 but reintroduced them 1878 for juvenile workers under the age of 21. Thorsten Keiser, *Vertragszwang und Vertragsfreiheit im Recht der Arbeit von der frühen Neuzeit bis in die Moderne*. (Frankfurt am Main: Klostermann, 2013), 328.
[13] Wilhelm Stieda, 'Arbeitsbuch,' in *Handwörterbuch der Staatswissenschaften*, eds. J. Conrad, C. Elster, W. Lexis and Edg. Loening, vol. 1. (Jena: Gustav Fischer, 1890), 598–604; Martino Sacchi Landriani (2019), 'Rethinking the Livret d'ouvriers: Time, Space and "Free" Labor in Nineteenth Century France', *Labour History* 60, no. 6: 854–64; Alessandro Stanziani (2009), 'The Legal Status of Labour from the Seventeenth to the Nineteenth Century: Russia in a Comparative European Perspective,' *International Review of Social History* 54, no. 3: 359–89.
[14] They were abolished in the first years for the Republic of Austria. StGBl. 1919/106; the abolition of servants' booklets was slower and step by step, though. StGBl. 1920/101; BGBl. 1926/72.
[15] 'Patent vom 24. Februar 1827. Aufhebung der Kundschaften, Zeugnisse, Wanderpässe für Handwerksgesellen und Arbeiter; Einführung der Wanderbücher', in *Seiner k. k. Majestät Franz des Ersten politische Gesetze und Verordnungen für sämmtliche Provinzen des Österreichischen Kaiserstaates, mit Ausnahme von Ungarn und Siebenbürgen* (Wien: k. k. Hof- u. Staats-Aerarial-Druckerei, 1829), 231f; Kundmachung 231, in: *Politische Gesetze und Verordnungen 1828*, 283–9.

abolished, stipulated *Arbeitsbücher* (workman's passports or labour booklets) for all skilled workers in workshops and factories, both men and women, whether travelling or not.[16] In 1866 labour booklets were introduced for miners.[17] The trade law reform of 1885[18] extended the obligation to include all regularly employed workers, juvenile workers and apprentices (except higher employees), and a law of 1902[19] added workers in railway construction. Servants' laws prescribed *Dienstbotenbücher* (servants' certificates or employment booklets) – similar in design and many aspects of usage – for both agricultural servants and domestic ones (almost exclusively women at the turn of the century).[20] Hence, in the course of the nineteenth century, these papers became more clearly regulated by authorities while they were also being generalized; they equated and at the same time distinguished multiple highly heterogeneous occupations, positions and labour relations, in both rural and urban areas.

These attempts to enforce such documents were understood as a continuation of repressive attitudes[21] towards working or 'dangerous' classes, as well as attempts to control, discipline[22] and closely monitor certain forms of mobility. This aspect of surveillance was openly articulated by public representatives and employers at the time. It was strongly criticized by workers' and servants' organizations in the late nineteenth century; they regarded these papers as mere instruments of coercion and as symbolizing inequality and humiliation.[23] In this spirit, historical research has interpreted such regulations predominantly as contradicting liberal tendencies in the late nineteenth-century migration regime.[24] In this chapter, however, I will highlight the ambivalence of this policy and show that these documents also displayed the commodification of labour (an aspect which became stronger during the nineteenth century, as Keiser has argued)[25] and the formalization of employment in the course of an emerging new state social policy.[26] It was

---

[16] RGBl. 1859/227, §74 and appendix.
[17] RGBl. 1866/72.
[18] RGBl 1885/22.
[19] RGBl. 1902/156.
[20] Edm. O. Ehrenfreund and Franz Mráz, *Wiener Dienstrecht* (Wien: Manz, 1908); Morgenstern, *Gesindewesen*; Hugo Morgenstern, *Österreichisches Gesinderecht* (Wien: Manz, 1912).
[21] Rudolf Brichta (1906), 'Das Dienstzeugnis. Eine gewerbepolitische Studie', *Juristische Blätter* XXXV, no. 10: 109–12; Isidor Ingwer, *Der sogenannte Arbeitsvertrag. Eine sozialpolitische Studie* (Wien: Verl. d. 'Österreichischen Metallarbeiter', 1895), 25.
[22] Ehrenfreund, Mráz, Dienstrecht, 33; 'Die Abschaffung des Arbeitsbuches auf Grund des §14', *Allgemeiner Tiroler Anzeiger* 18.7.1914, 17.
[23] On the reasoning in favour of or against such regulations, see Alfred Ebenhoch and Engelbert Pernerstorfer, eds. *Stenographisches Protokoll der Gewerbe-Enquête im österreichischen Abgeordnetenhause sammt geschichtlicher Einleitung und Anhang* (Wien: Kaiserlich-königliche Hof- und Staatsdruckerei, 1893); 'Antrag des Abgeordneten Smitka, Palme und Genossen, betreffend die Beseitigung der Arbeitsbücher (Entlaßscheine, Seedienstbücher)', *Stenographische Protokolle über die Sitzungen des Hauses der Abgeordneten des österreichischen Reichsrathes*, XXI Session, 1911, Beilage 70.
[24] For example Leo Lucassen, 'A many-Headed Monster: The Evolution of the Passport System in the Netherlands and Germany in the Long Nineteenth Century' in Caplan et al., eds. *Identity*, 235–55; Katrin Lehnert, *Die Un-Ordnung der Grenze. Mobiler Alltag zwischen Sachsen und Böhmen und die Produktion von Migration im 19. Jahrhundert* (Leipzig: Leipziger Universitätsverlag, 2017), 207, 216.
[25] Keiser, *Vertragszwang*; on servants, see Thomas Pierson, *Das Gesinde und die Herausbildung moderner Privatrechtsprinzipien* (Frankfurt am Main: Klostermann, 2016); Thomas Vormbaum, *Politik und Gesinderecht im 19. Jahrhundert (vornehmlich in Preußen 1810–1918)* (Berlin: Duncker & Humblot, 1980).
[26] Writings on the *livret d'ouvrier* point out the ambivalent character of this paper. E.g. Simona Cerutti (2010), 'Travail, mobilité et légitimité. Suppliques au roi dans un société d'Ancien Régime (Turin, XVIIIe siècle)', *Annales. Histoire, Sciences Sociales* 65, no. 3: 571–611.

a development which went along with new social rights, but it was one which was certainly not linear and uncontested. Nor did it suggest an absence of coercion. The enforcement of regulations was slow and remained patchy until the papers were temporarily abolished in interwar Austria.[27] Graph 3.1 demonstrates how slow the issuing of labour booklets was to gain momentum, even in Vienna. I could not find similar complete statistics of servants' booklets.[28] Although labour booklets and servants' ones show many similarities, they were differently administered, monitored and discussed. When artisans and workers protested and argued that it was a violation of their dignity to own and carry around such booklets like servants or prostitutes,[29] they were referring to differences in status and therefore substantial differences in rights and entitlements.

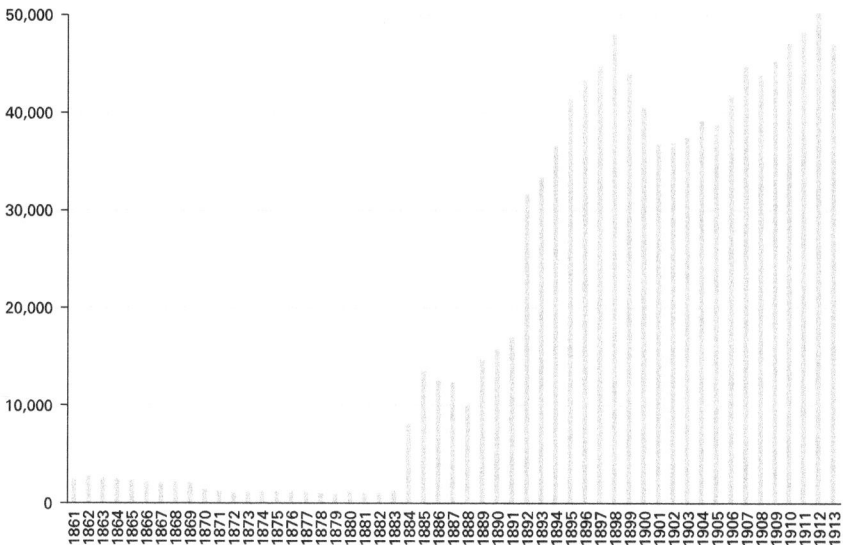

Graph 3.1 Labour booklets issued in Vienna, 1861–1913.[30]

---

[27] This is a similarity to France and Germany, see Stieda, *Arbeitsbuch*. Labour booklets were reintroduced during the Nazi regime: Karsten Linne, 'Von der Arbeitsvermittlung zum "Arbeitseinsatz". Zum Wandel der Arbeitsverwaltung 1933-1945' in *Arbeit im Nationalsozialismus*, eds. Marc Buggeln and Michael Wildt (Berlin: De Gruyter/Oldenbourg, 2014), 53–70.

[28] Between 1876 and 1892 between 10,000 and 5,800 servants' booklets (on average 6,800) were issued every year. Präsidium der k. k. Polizei-Direction, ed., *Die Polizeiverwaltung Wiens 1867-1892*.

[29] *Bericht der k. k. Gewerbe-Inspectoren über ihre Amtstätigkeit* 1886, 22; 1888, 56; 1909, CXXff. The annual reports *Bericht der k. k. Gewerbe-Inspectoren über ihre Amtsthätigkeit* (Wien, Druck und Verlag der kaiserlich-königlichen Staatsdruckerei 1884–1916) are available on https://anno.onb.ac.at/cgi-content/anno-plus?aid=bga&size=45&qid=8NOW3Q7BTUJP10L74FMHIS1OMFOKF8); 'Das Arbeitsbuch', *Salzburger Wacht* 16.8.1911, 1.

[30] Source: *Administrations-Bericht des Wiener Bürgermeisters (Wien 1861-1866)* (available on https://www.digital.wienbibliothek.at/wbrobv/periodical/titleinfo/2041987); *Die Gemeindeverwaltung der Reichs-Haupt und Residenzstadt Wien (Wien 1889-1919)* (available on https://www.digital.wienbibliothek.at/Drucke/periodical/titleinfo/609853). Around 1870 there were about 130,000 workers in Vienna requiring a labour booklet; around 1900, there were approximately 455,000: Josef Ehmer, *Soziale Traditionen in Zeiten des Wandels. Arbeiter und Handwerker im 19. Jahrhundert* (Frankfurt: Campus, 1994), 255; *Statistisches Jahrbuch der Stadt Wien für das Jahr 1901* (Wien: Verlag des Wiener Magistrates, 1903), 68 (available on https://www.digital.wienbibliothek.at/wbrobv/periodical/titleinfo/2057276).

Non-work, Job Search and Wages

Labour or servants' booklets – in theory – allowed an individual to be identified. In addition, these defined the type of work or employment and specified the occupation as well as certifying a person's professional training, work experiences and behaviour. Every post and employment had to be registered in the booklet, which also included work references (or summaries of work references, to be verified by the authorities, police or trade association). Apart from control and order, the official rationale emphasized that labour/servants' booklets in this specific form also served workers/servants because they conveniently combined all the necessary documents enabling them to move freely and search for work.[31] I will start with this aspect, discussing how papers and documentation of employment were related to job search and how the ways of coping with periods of joblessness were related to wages. In which ways did papers predetermine the chances to find an appropriate post or just any job at all? To what extent did work seekers have the possibility to choose, be picky or negotiate the terms of employment?

Different types of papers enabled different modes of job search. They granted access to various different locations and facilities in which people on the move found shelter and support, and in which they received and exchanged information on open vacancies and work conditions, whether accurate or not. Certainly, there were always multiple ways to find employment and get information on open situations, depending on one's occupation and social context. In the nineteenth and early twentieth century, however, searching for employment quite often included mobility on a local level (looking around – *Umschau*) or in a greater area (tramping – or *Wanderschaft, Walz*, as it was called in the context of crafts in the German-speaking area). Job fluctuation was high, the demand for labour variable. Neither roaming nor the problem of vagrancy lost importance in the course of industrialization.[32] Such practices went along with a frequent need for and use of documents in various interactions with police, potential employers, innkeepers or local residents etc. Identity- and work-documents equipped with the necessary entries and permits to travel indicated that it was legitimate for an individual to be on the move. Proper papers evidenced a status and distinguished their holders from vagabonds and vagrants without decent work records – or without papers at all. The policy specified that individuals regarded as unreliable, work-shy or unemployable were not supposed to receive papers or travel permits in the first place.[33]

Even if a person had no employment and no money in his/her pockets, entitlements linked to certain occupations could make a difference: unlike (formally) unskilled workers and servants, journeymen and (formally) skilled workers tramping in search

---

[31] Moriz Ertl (1886), 'Bericht der k. k. Gewerbeinspektoren über ihre Amtsthätigkeit im Jahre 1884. Wien 1885,' *Statistische Monatschrift*, no. 12: 54–9.

[32] See Sigrid Wadauer (2011), 'Establishing Distinctions: Unemployment Versus Vagrancy in Austria from the Late Nineteenth Century to 1938,' *International Review of Social History* 56, no. 1: 31–70; Beate Althammer, *Vagabunden. Eine Geschichte von Armut, Bettel und Mobilität im Zeitalter der Industrialisierung (1815-1933)* (Essen: Klartext, 2017).

[33] '22. Zur Hintanhaltung des Vagabunden-Unwesens' (1900), *Amtsblatt der k. und k. Reichshaupt- und Residenzstadt Wien*, no. 9: 5.

of work could still potentially rely on customary and/or statutory support from local shopkeepers or colleagues, trade associations, occupational organizations or unions.[34] Such support could comprise a stay in the trade association's lodge, an invitation for a drink or a meal, or money. The amount and binding character of such support varied substantially from trade to trade. Some trades allowed for more sedentariness whereas other, less common trades went along with a greater amount of mobility. Some trades were better organized than others. We can find considerable changes and even more diversification of trades throughout the nineteenth century.[35] Yet tramping was and remained a culturally and socially institutionalized practice in the life and 'career' of an artisan up to the twentieth century. A trade law reform of 1883 re-established a certificate of competence more broadly. A record of waged-work as a journeyman for some years – usually connected with mobility – remained a legal precondition for obtaining a permit to establish oneself as a self-employed master artisan.[36] The chances for becoming a master craftsman certainly varied, but overall the share of small workshops and companies remained high.

From a legal perspective a person with entitlement to such support, even in the most rudimentary amount, was not without subsistence and was not to be treated as a vagabond. A *viaticum* (or *Geschenk*) was thus not considered the same as alms. This distinction could be contested and was probably not always acknowledged by the police in practice, yet we can still find references to it even in interwar court records. Apart from these rather traditional and apparently often insufficient resources, identity documents and proof of previous, regular employment were also a prerequisite for getting access to new forms of support that had been established by authorities since the 1880s in the most industrialized lands of Cisleithania.[37] A network of wayfarers' relief stations (*Naturalverpflegsstationen* or *Herbergen*) provided board and shelter for one night as well as information on open positions for work seeking wayfarers.[38] (Similar facilities can be found in German countries and Switzerland.) Distinguishing and separating people who were considered out of work through no fault of their own from vagabonds was supposed to combat vagrancy and begging[39] and to reduce the

---

[34] *Die Arbeitsvermittlung in Österreich, verfasst und herausgegeben vom statistischen Departement im k. k. Handelsministerium* (Wien: Hölder, 1898), 120, 224.
[35] Ehmer, *Soziale Traditionen*, 1994.
[36] Magdalena Pöschl (2010), 'Beständiges und Veränderliches im Gewerberecht – Entwicklung der GewO 1859 bis 2009,' *Österreichische Zeitschrift für Wirtschaftsrecht*, no. 2: 64–74.
[37] Sigrid Wadauer, 'Tramping in Search of Work. Practices of Wayfarers and of Authorities (Austria 1880-1938)', in *The History of Labour Intermediation. Institutions and Finding Employment in the Nineteenth and Early Twentieth Centuries*, eds. Sigrid Wadauer, Thomas Buchner and Alexander Mejstrik (New York: Berghahn, 2015), 286–334.
[38] Sigrid Wadauer, Thomas Buchner and Alexander Mejstrik, 'Introduction: Finding Work and Organizing Placement in the Nineteenth and Twentieth Centuries', in *The History of Labour Intermeditation,* eds. Wadauer, Buchner and Mejstrik, 1–22; Irina Vana, *Gebrauchsweisen der öffentlichen Arbeitsvermittlung (Österreich 1889-1938)*. Unpublished PhD Thesis, University of Vienna (2013).
[39] It seems unlikely that penniless wayfarers could get along without additional support from residents. Nevertheless, in my work on vagrancy in the interwar period I could hardly find cases of travellers with decent papers and entitlement to relief stations arrested by the police. Sigrid Wadauer, *Der Arbeit nachgehen? Auseinandersetzungen um Lebensunterhalt und Mobilität (Österreich 1880-1938)* (Köln: Böhlau, 2021).

costs of forced removals. This policy can also be understood as a step towards formalizing the status of a work-seeker in a more universal sense, independently of their age, gender, religious confession and occupation. It illustrates the beginning of a process of inventing and institutionalizing 'unemployment'.[40] It was also one step towards organizing a territorial, state-wide labour market, which included efforts to collect data on work seekers, job vacancies and placements; however, that knowledge at the time was rudimentary and patchy.

In practice, this policy still mainly involved formally trained, skilled labourers. Thus they tended to be younger, unmarried workers who travelled this way in search of work. Unskilled labourers, agricultural labourers and women were explicitly excluded from admission to the wayfarers' relief stations in most provinces. They supposedly were able to find posts more easily and unselectively without longer periods of search and travelling. This does not mean that these labourers or servants were not at all mobile; rather, they moved in distinctive ways, using different facilities, networks and forms of intermediation, like private placement services.[41] In a local context, papers were apparently less relevant for job search and placement and less indispensable despite the regulations.[42] Up to the twentieth century one can find frequent complaints about servants and workers – quite often local residents, women and juveniles – who did not possess the required documents or could not obtain them from the local authorities.[43]

As a result, these first efforts to establish public labour intermediation indicated a hierarchy of work, either implicitly or explicitly evoking an interrelation between the acknowledged status of unemployment and vocation.[44] Yet these efforts were of limited

---

[40] Wadauer, 'Establishing Distinctions'; Christian Topalov, 'The Invention of Unemployment. Language, Classification and Social Reform 1880-1910', in *Comparing Social Welfare Systems in Europe, vol. 1, Oxford Conference, France – United Kingdom*, ed. Bruno Palier (N.p., 1994), 493–507; Paul T. Ringenbach, *Tramps and Reformers 1873-1916. The Discovery of Unemployment in New York*. (Westport, Conn.: Greenwood Press, 1973).

[41] Jessica Richter, *Die Produktion besonderer Arbeitskräfte. Auseinandersetzungen um den häuslichen Dienst in Österreich (Ende des 19. Jahrhunderts bis 1938)*. Unpublished PhD Thesis, University of Vienna (2017); Raffaella Sarti (2014), 'Historians, Social Scientists, Servants, and Domestic Workers: Fifty Years of Research on Domestic Care Work', *International Review of Social History* 59, no. 2: 279–314; Dirk Hoerder, Elise van Nederveen Meerkerk and Silke Neunsinger, eds. *Towards a Global History of Domestic and Caregiving Workers* (Leiden: Brill, 2015).

[42] Licht emphasizes the importance of personal networks: Walter Licht, *Getting Work. Philadelphia, 1840-1950* (Cambridge, Ma.: Harvard University Press, 1992).

[43] These problems are mentioned year for year in the annual trade inspectors' reports. *Bericht der k. k. Gewerbe-Inspectoren über Ihre Amtstätigkeit im Jahr 1884-1916* (Wien: Kaiserlich und Königliche Staatsdruckerei, 1885-1919) (available on https://anno.onb.ac.at/cgi-content/anno-plus?aid=bga). Problems are also summarized in Bericht des sozialpolitischen Ausschusses betreffend eine über Antrag des Abgeordneten Dr. Freißler im Sinne des §33 G.O. an das Haus zu stellende Vorfrage, "ob die Regierung aufzufordern sei, eine Vorlage einzubringen, welche den Erlaß des Arbeitsbuches für erwachsene Arbeiter durch eine geeignete Legitimation vorsieht", *Stenographische Protokolle über die Sitzungen des Hauses der Abgeordneten des österreichischen Reichsrathes*, XXI Session, 1913, Beilage 1860.

[44] See Bénédicte Zimmermann, *Arbeitslosigkeit in Deutschland. Zur Entstehung einer sozialen Kategorie* (Frankfurt am Main: Campus, 2006). Even after unemployment insurance was established in the interwar period, predominantly rural areas remained excluded from this policy. Vana, *Gebrauchsweisen*, 129.

range and efficiency. Even for the main target group, wayfarer's relief stations and public labour intermediation were not their first choices if better alternatives were available, such as inns or lodges of the Catholic journeymen's association. And such public interventions were not unreservedly welcomed by organized workers. After all, support and labour intermediation had an impact on wages and work conditions.[45] It could strengthen ones' (market) position[46]: collectively, because intermediation and support could be used to set or enforce standards with selective placement, requests for mobility, strikes or boycotts; and individually, because support and intermediation enabled and directed mobility.[47] It allowed searching for work, travelling to places with better work conditions and accepting work selectively, within one's occupation – and not just any work, under any terms and conditions.[48]

Public labour policy intervened and regulated but did not replace either informal networks or labour intermediation by trade associations, unions or workers associations (which requested their members using their placement).[49] Although identity- and work-documents issued by authorities were required and used in these contexts,[50] they were not the sole way to identify and be identified. As we can conclude from cases of conflict, fellow journeymen were identified in interactions and by appropriate behaviour.[51] Trade and labourer's associations, which replaced the guilds and were obliged to provide labour intermediation, continued using their own documents and forms of registration, though not always in accordance with the regulations.[52]

---

[45] Ad Knotter, 'From Placement Control to Control of the Unemployed. Trade Unions and Labour Market Intermediation in Western Europe in the Nineteenth and Early Twentieth Centuries,' in *Labour Intermediation* eds. Wadauer et al., 117–50.

[46] Hobsbawm, 'Custom', 413.

[47] Autobiographical accounts indicate that workers had some knowledge about wage levels in different towns and places: Sigrid Wadauer, *Die Tour der Gesellen. Mobilität und Biographie im Handwerk vom 18. bis zum 20. Jahrhundert* (Frankfurt am Main: Campus, 2005), 268.

[48] Mohl put this in a nutshell: 'It is even worse – at least in respect to moral questions – for one who has to travel without money, and whose parents or relatives no longer care. He is forced to accept work in the very next place and has to accept any weekly wage he is offered. His few possessions get used up, he has no possibility to replace them, the wage is barely enough for basic needs, and he is forced either to beg to be able to move again or to return where he came from – after years without having seen or learned anything. In most occupations the weekly wage is so low that even with greatest thriftiness one can barely survive, much less save money to travel further.' Hugo von Mohl, 'Gekrönte Preisschrift. Wie können die Vortheile, welche durch das Wandern der Handwerksgesellen möglich sind, befördert und die dabey vorkommenden Nachtheile verhütet werden?' in *Kurze Darstellung einiger Handwerks-Mißbräuche, und Vorschläge, wie solche zu verbessern seyn könnten.* (Halle: Curtsche Buchhandlung, 1800), 67–147, 81f. The quotes of German sources are translated by the author.

[49] *Die Arbeitsvermittlung in Österreich*, chapters 'Arbeitsvermittlung bei den gewerblichen Genossenschaften in moderner Zeit' and 'Gewerkschaften und Arbeiterbildungsvereine'; Hans Hülber, *Weg und Ziel der Arbeitsvermittlung. Studie über das Arbeitsmarktgeschehen in Österreich von 1848 bis 1934* (Wien: Verlag des Österreichischen Gewerkschaftsbundes, 1965), 12.

[50] 'Was bei den Unternehmern Frechheit ist', *Arbeiter-Zeitung* 14.1.1902, 7f.

[51] See, for example: Ludwig Funder, *Aus meinem Burschenleben. Gesellenwanderung und Brautwerbung eines Grazer Zuckerbäckers 1862-1869*, ed. Ernst Bruckmüller (Wien: Böhlau, 2000), 72. Sigrid Wadauer, 'Journeymen's Mobility and the Guild System: A Space of Possibilities Based on Central European Cases', in *Guilds and Association in Europe, 900–1900*, eds. Ian A. Gadd and Patrick Wallis, (London: University of London Press, 2007), 169–86.

[52] *Die Arbeitsvermittlung in Österreich*, 126f, 129, 130, 133; *Bericht der k. k. Gewerbe-Inspectoren 1884*, 67f.

'The most important travel document,' the book printer Karl Steinhardt (a Social Democrat and later a Communist politician) wrote in his autobiographical account, 'was the *Quittungsbuch* [a booklet with receipts, S.W.] in which all support received [from the book printers' organization, S.W.] was documented. Vis-à-vis the authorities, this booklet served as legitimation, in order not to be treated as a vagabond.'[53] In this context, the author also pointed out another aspect, relevant for job search and wages: 'The organisation of book printers,' he wrote, 'cared well for its travelling members [...] But the organization's regulations required that the traveller had to accept a job offer. If he refused, he lost travel support.'[54] Neither public, professional nor private support for workers without employment was unconditional and unlimited. It was tied to a legal, statutory or moral and customary obligation not to quit or reject work without good reason.[55] In order not to lose support and the status of a work-seeker, one had to accept work eventually, either by consent or unwillingly.

Josef Jodlbauer – a Social Democratic baker journeymen – depicted these 'rules of the game'[56] in his autobiographical account. He presented himself as combative and insubordinate. Yet, after a (much too) long period of travelling, there was no possibility for negotiation; he was only left with the choice between an undesirable position and criminalization. The relief station's warden was explicitly threatening him with forced removal and the workhouse:

> Rejecting [the job, S.W.] went along with the risk of losing the *Verpflegschein* [certificate necessary for admission at a relief station, S.W.] and – because this was noted in the booklet – he would not get a new one if he could not prove that he was employed in the meantime. He therefore asked what kind of dough was being produced and what amount of work was to be performed. The answer [of the master craftsman, S.W.] was: 'Well, in my workshop, nobody has killed himself by working too much.' The question concerning the wage was also answered in a revolting manner: the agreement would be made on Saturday, after a week and everybody had been satisfied with their wage up to that point. As Josef tried to ask something particular, the warden of the relief station interrupted him. 'You – young man – you have not been working hard enough this year. Let's go, quick.'[57]

The author, while wanting to work, nonetheless emphasized how he was compelled to do so. In the same spirit, Julius Deutsch, a book printer who like Jodlbauer later became a Social Democratic politician, described the conflict between his desire to travel[58] and

---

[53] Karl Steinhardt, *Lebenserinnerungen eines Wiener Arbeiters*, ed. Manfred Mugrauer (Wien: Alfred Klahr Gesellschaft, 2013), 110.
[54] Steinhardt, *Lebenserinnerungen*, 110 and 111.
[55] Wadauer, *Die Tour der Gesellen*.
[56] Eric Hobsbawm: 'Custom, Wages and Work-Load', 405–36, 406.
[57] Jodlbauer writes of himself in third person: Josef Jodlbauer, *Ein Mensch zieht in die Welt. Selbstbiographie eines Altösterreichers*, unpublished Typoskript, 1947–1948 (Dokumentation Lebensgeschichtlicher Aufzeichnungen, University of Vienna), 118.
[58] Julius Deutsch, *Ein weiter Weg. Lebenserinnerungen.* (Zürich: Amalthea, 1960), 45.

his fear of being arrested and expelled from Germany to the Austrian Lands. He found a different solution to this dilemma:

> I was happy when an old fellow journeyman offered to produce me a work certificate. He did it at a cheap rate. [...] Now I could present myself with more confidence. Additionally, I could find occasional work with farmers. When I could stay somewhere, I tried to make myself useful.[59]

This narrative exemplifies further aspects of this topic: the author emphasized that the journeymen were not willing to work at any price. Nor did they like to work just anywhere. People did not move exclusively to work or merely out of necessity owing to joblessness, low wages, poor working conditions or other material motives. Getting around, working at the right places, and seeing the world could serve the reputation and status of a journeyman. Avoiding work in order to keep travelling, finding a way around the necessity to accept work – at least temporary, but not too long – was not generally stigmatized.[60] It could be even idealized,[61] as part of a rite of passage for young men.[62] This is visible even in accounts of politically organized writers, who depicted themselves as workers rather than as journeymen and who explicitly challenged any traditional or romantic notion of tramping.[63] 'Every older locksmith knows what it counted at that time to have been in Hamburg,' one German locksmith wrote:

> Not because one could earn much more than elsewhere. No, the wages were not very high, but it was well-known that in Hamburg good work was done, custom and tradition was held in honour. There was no tolerance for dilletantes, [*Pfuscher*: an incompetent person, not formally trained or not belonging to the guild, S.W.] [...] flatterers or bootlickers. [...] Upright guild journeymen were trained there. [...] The spirit which today honours Hamburg's labourers, the solidarity, was pronounced in old forms and ties; everywhere a locksmith was acknowledged as a real journeyman if he had been in Hamburg, even if he had been mainly hanging around at his digs than working at his vise.[64]

Another aspect illustrated by these accounts is that not every temporary, occasional earning was relevant and registered in the booklet. Casual workers of the 'lowest', most ordinary kind, like day labourers etc., did not need a labour booklet at all.[65] Hence,

---

[59] Deutsch, *Ein weiter Weg*, 49; see also Jodlbauer, *Ein Mensch* 115.
[60] This might not apply to behaviour at the workplace. As Hobsbawm emphasizes, slacking was stigmatized. Hobsbawm, 'Custom, Wages and Work-Load', 411.
[61] In some anarchists' writings, vagrancy is evoked as voluntary avoidance of exploitation, e.g. in Erich Mühsam: 'Boheme', in *Ich bin verdammt zu warten in einem Bürgergarten, vol. 2: Literarische und politische Aufsätze*, ed. Wolfgang Haug (Darmstadt: Luchterhand, 1983), 30–5, 31.
[62] Wadauer, *Die Tour der Gesellen*.
[63] On the different possibilities for practicing and representing journeymen's travelling and work, see Wadauer, *Die Tour der Gesellen*.
[64] [Grillenberger Karl:] 'Des Wanderburschen Freud und Leid. Von einem alten "Katzenkopf"', *Der Wahre Jacob. Illustrierte humoristisch-satirische Zeitschrift*, no. 285, 22.6.1897: 2474–6, 2475f.
[65] Ebenhoch and Pernerstorfer, *Stenographisches Protokoll*, 144.

Graph 3.2 Formal charges (*Anzeigen*) filed by trade inspectors concerning labour booklets, 1894–1916.[66]

these papers and the related obligatory forms of registration in companies and with local authorities foretell a difference, which nowadays is designated and established as a distinction of formal/informal work.[67] In this historical setting, however, it seems more appropriate to speak of regular and irregular work relations.[68]

Contracts and Wages

Regular work required appropriate papers and registration (in the register of employers or that of local authorities).[69] Papers indicated that a person was in a position to make a contract, that he/she was an adult or was old enough for this type of work and had the consent of a legal caretaker.[70] Handing out the papers to the employer signified an

---

[66] These numbers are low, yet cases on labour booklets still involved up to 28.5 per cent of all formal complaints. Numbers dropped during the war because the regulations were not enforced. *Bericht der k. k. Gewerbe-Inspectoren 1894*, 6f; 1895, 4f; 1896, XXIVf; 1897, XXIIIf; 1898, XXf; 1899, XXXVIf; 1900, XXIVf; 1901, XLVf, LIIf; 1902, 74–79; 1903, Tabelle A, 56f; 1904, Tabelle A, LIV; 1905, Tabelle A, LXVII; 1906, LXXII, LXXVIf; 1907, LXXVIIIf, LXXXIIf; 1908, LXVIII, LXXVf; 1909, Lf, LIVf; 1910, LVI-LIX; 1911, LXXIV-LXXVII; 1912, CII-CV; 1913, XlI,LII-LVI; 1914, LIV-LIX; 1915, XLVI-XLIX, LIIIf; 1916, LX-LIII, LVIIIf; 1919, LXIVff; 1920, XXVIII-XXXI; 1921, XXIV-XXXVII, XXX; 1923, 26–31; 1924, 26–31; 1925, XX-XIII.

[67] The term was coined by Keith Hart (1973), 'Informal Income Opportunities and Urban Employment in Ghana', *The Journal of Modern African Studies* II, no. 1: 61–89.

[68] On this question see also: Thomas Buchner and Philip R. Hoffmann-Rehnitz, 'Introduction: Irregular Work and Shadow Economies as a Topic of Modern History – Problems and Possibilities', in *Shadow Economies and Irregular Work in Urban Europe. 16th to early 20th Centuries*, eds. Thomas Buchner and Philip R. Hoffmann-Rehnitz (Münster: LIT Verlag, 2011), 3–36.

[69] Leo Verkauf, 'Arbeitsvertrag', in *Österreichisches Staatswörterbuch. Handbuch des gesamten österreichischen öffentlichen Rechtes*, eds. Ernst Mischler and Josef Ulbrich, 2nd edn, vol. 1 (Wien: Hölder, 1905), 149–87. Trade inspectors' reports saw the usage of labour booklets as a symbol of respect towards the regulations. *Bericht der k. k. Gewerbe-Inspectoren 1886*, 22.

agreement.⁷¹ The worker's data had to be entered in the company's or workshop's register of workers. (Employment of servants had to be reported to and registered at the municipality.) Demanding papers (and wage amount) or returning papers signified the end of the contract. Papers suggested what the accurate type of contract was, whether the trade law or servants' statutes applied, what the basic conditions of employment were, and which authorities were in charge in case of disputes.⁷² A certificate of formal training, the categorization of occupation, the position in a previous job and the continuity of employment could have an impact on whether one got a job, a specific assignment or payment or whether one's earnings improved at one's position. The documentation of employment was also a legal requirement for a 'career' from an apprentice to becoming a journeyman and – as mentioned above – to becoming a self-employed master artisan.

Numerous complaints reported by trade inspectors and cases at trade courts highlight the practical relevance of papers (see graph 3.2).⁷³ We can find problems and conflicts concerning multiple aspects: having the wrong papers or missing papers; mixing up, losing or destroying papers; incorrect or missing entries regarding occupation or employment, forgeries etc.⁷⁴ At the same time, since it was not permitted to give explicitly bad references, the significance of job references – in respect to the assessment of someone's diligence, faithfulness and reliability – could easily be doubted. Identification and assessment of a worker/servant in the context of hiring was not exclusively based on papers, which had to be interpreted or made plausible and relevant in interactions with employers or foremen. In his autobiographical novel, Alfons Petzold sarcastically portrayed such interaction:

> I quickly obeyed and handed over my papers, again with a deep bow, looking up shyly. [...] The boss took no notice of me; he was exclusively occupied with checking my labour booklet. [...] 'Well, my dear, you do not seem to possess a lot of talent or endurance. You only have two references over a year and have never

---

⁷⁰ Trade inspectors yearly reported violations of these law which varied regionally and according to branches. Trade inspectors mention forged data in order to avoid regulations on child labour. StGBl. 1919/292 stipulated work cards for children under the age of 14 years. On service, see Morgenstern, *Gesinderecht*, 38. Women did not necessarily need their husband's consent for working as servant. Yet, according to this author, it was seen as desirable.

⁷¹ Alois Heilinger, *Österreichisches Gewerberecht. Kommentar der Gewerbeordnung*, 3rd edn, eds. Michael Plachy and Alois Tischler (Wien: Manz, 1909). Emil Heller, *Das österreichische Gewerberecht mit Berücksichtigung der Gewerbenovelle vom 5. Februar 1907, RGBl. Nr. 26. Systematische Darstellung für die Praxis* (Wien: Manz, 1908).

⁷² Verkauf, *Arbeitsvertrag*, 149–87. On servants' contracts see Richter, *Die Produktion*, 41.

⁷³ *Sammlungen der Entscheidungen der k. k. Gewerbegerichte*. (Wien: Österreichische Staatsdruckerei, 1900–1920), e.g.: the decision Nr. 20/1899 concerns a worker who complained that in his certificate he was described as a 'Hilfsarbeiterin' (female unskilled worker) instead of a 'Schlosser' (locksmith). Other examples concerning categorization as skilled/unskilled worker can be found for example in the records of the provincial government of Lower Austria. NÖLA, Statthalterei ÜW – XII, 1909, 2113; XII, 1911, 2488.

⁷⁴ *Aus dem Leben eines Handwerksburschen. Erinnerungen von Karl Ernst. Mit einem Geleitwort von Heinrich Hansjakob*, 3rd edn. (Neustadt im Schwarzwald: Karl Wehrle, 1912), 114ff.

been employed in an establishment like ours.' In my desperation I muttered some possible and impossible assertions of faithfulness, devotion and diligence, my laudable adaptability; I became a poet in listing all my deeds as a worker and ended with the recommendation of the lady who had sent me there. Whereupon the man's face brightened and he said patronisingly, 'Well, I'll give it a try with you.'[75]

Other accounts in different settings, however, indicate that neither applicants nor papers were always checked thoroughly, e.g. when many workers were hired at the same time:

Searching for work took place in a primitive and – in comparison to present day's sentiments – undignified manner. At least an hour before start of work, bunches of male and female construction workers crowded in front of the construction site's offices in order to wait for the foreman, who usually made his way through the crowd or stood at the office door and took the offered labour books of those candidates who suited him. [...] Indeed, it has to be noticed that the year 1900 was a relatively good year for construction and consequently it was easier to find work. [...] Those workers who found mercy in the eyes of the main foreman were invited to the office with the words 'get in here'; there everyone had to sign the work rules presented by the construction site's clerk. One can imagine that at that time work rules were made without any representatives of workers and included only obligations and no rights. Even before we left the office, the main foremen gave us our first dressing down. 'With me, you have to work hard. Whoever I catch loafing will be kicked out of here. I hope you've got that.'[76]

Wages are not addressed here by the author, at the time a fourteen-year-old masonry apprentice and later a president of the construction workers' union, who was apparently aiming to depict general circumstances with his narrative. His hopes of finding better work conditions in Vienna were destroyed. People did not always have an accurate knowledge about their chances to get a job or decent payment in another town.

Getting a certain position and wage was also not automatic, the result of one's documents and references. It was instead an object of negotiation or was even simply stated by the employer, either in advance or after a trial period (like in Jodlbauer's example, quoted before). Most accounts mention a one or two weeks work-period for determining the wage.[77] The workers then seem to have the choice to accept or leave. If there was no alternative to the job that was available, savings or other resources were required. Furthermore, a record of changing jobs too frequently was considered suspicious; it could lower the chances at obtaining a better job.

---

[75] Alfons Petzold, *Das rauhe Leben. Der Roman eines Menschen* [1920] (Berlin, Weimar: Aufbau-Verlag, 1985), 332f; the labour booklet is also mentioned on pages 271, 304, and 307.

[76] Johann Böhm: *Erinnerungen aus meinem Leben* (Wien: Verlag des Österreichischen Gewerkschaftsbundes, 1961), 18f.

[77] *Aus dem Leben eines Handwerksburschen*, 258f; František Kebrdle, 'Meine Lebensgeschichte. Geboren 1825', in *Auf der Walz. Erinnerungen böhmischer Handwerksgesellen*, ed. Pavla Vošhalíková (Wien: Böhlau, 1994), 31–42, 36.

Work contracts and wage agreements could be made orally or in writing. (Legal sources mention the possibility of witnesses.) The availability and importance of written documentation varied according to the type and size of the enterprise, the length of contract and the wage form. Labour booklets for apprentices had to include the basic terms of their contracts: duration, payment, or provision of board and lodging. These long-term agreements were regarded as a specific kind of contract and more clearly a matter of public concern since they included the training of minors and, at least in theory, their education. Apart from that, there was no legal obligation to have written agreements,[78] but if written agreements were made, additional or contradictory oral agreements were regarded as irrelevant. Bigger companies had their own bureaucracy and documentation of wages (*Lohnlisten*), not always in accordance with the law. The lists of employed workers and of juvenile workers, as stipulated by the trade law, were often missing. Some factories handed out their status to the workers – sometimes even for a fee – and made them sign the rules on wages, working hours, possible wage reductions etc. In some factories the wage was noted on the receipt a worker received when he/she handed out the labour booklet. Some employers handed out *Tarif-Zettel*, sheets of paper documenting the wage agreement.[79] Wage booklets[80] documenting actual payment or reduction of wage were used in some factories and in mining. Entries on wages and advances can also be found in the servants'[81] and sometimes in the labour booklets.

Although a work contract was an individual agreement, categorization and documentation of employment and wage agreements mattered because in cases of conflict[82] brought forward to the trade courts the fighting parties needed proof of an agreement (or lack of one).[83] If there was no individual agreement, wage, working hours, terms for quitting or dismissal and other terms of the contract were set according to the law[84] and local custom, as defined by the trade court which included both representatives of employers and workers. The wage defined as customary could vary considerably from region to region and in respect to occupation or gender. It was also the basis for calculating the allowance granted by insurances. Such accident and health insurances were established in the second half of the nineteenth century, mainly

---

[78] This differs from regulations in other countries; on this question at an international level: 'Der XXVIII. Deutsche Juristentag. Kiel, 9. bis 12. September 1906', *Allgemeine österreichische Gerichtszeitung* 57, no. 37–9, 1906: 289–307; Sabine Rudischhauser, *Geregelte Verhältnisse. Eine Geschichte des Tarifvertragsrechts in Deutschland und Frankreich (1890–1918/19)* (Köln: Böhlau, 2016), 44.
[79] *Bericht der k. k. Gewerbe-Inspectoren 1894*, 54.
[80] 'Der erste Delegiertentag der Union aller keramischen Arbeiter Österreich-Ungarns', *Arbeiter-Zeitung* 3.8.1896, 3f, 4.
[81] Therese Meyer, *Dienstboten in Oberkärnten*, (Klagenfurt: Verlag des Kärntner Landesarchivs, 1993) 45; *Landesgesetzblatt Niederösterreich* 1922/141.
[82] 'Wie bei den genossenschaftlichen Schiedsgerichten Recht gesprochen wird', *Arbeiter-Zeitung* 22.4.1898, 8; Ingwer mentions that companies tried to trick workers into signing agreements so that the workers would not understand what they were doing; Isidor Ingwer, *Die Rechtsstreitigkeiten vor dem Gewerbegerichte*, (Wien: Konegen, 1899), 156.
[83] Ingwer mentioned that companies often made no agreement at all. Ingwer, *Die Rechtsstreitigkeiten*, 62.
[84] Heiliger, *Österreichisches Gewerberecht*, 515; Karl Schreiber, 'Der Arbeitsvertrag nach heutigem österreichischem Privatrecht', *Allgemeine österreichische Gerichts-Zeitung* XXXVIII (NF XXIV), no. 7, 15.2.1887: 49–51, 49; Meyer, *Dienstboten in Oberkärnten*, 45.

concerning workers in trades and factories.[85] Servants and agricultural workers were not equally included for a long time thereafter.[86]

An important issue was the amount of the wage. Collective agreements on wages – *Tarifverträge* – can be found in Cisleithania as of the 1890s, and an increasing number of agreements in various branches can be found from the 1900s on.[87] In domestic service, a minimum wage was defined after 1920.[88] At issue might also be the form and composition of remuneration (money, provision, board, bonuses, tips, refund of travel expenses etc.) as well as the frequency of payment. Collective wage agreements show how wages and wage forms varied in different branches or occupations; they also illustrate how time wage and piece rates could coexist and combine.[89] According to the trade law, payment in crafts and factories should principally consist of money, the usual payment period was one week, and the period of notice was two weeks.[90] Individual agreements on accommodation or payment in kind were allowed, yet the truck-system was prohibited. Nevertheless, there were frequent complaints of violations[91]: workers claimed that they had received vouchers instead of money, and that they had to eat at companies' canteens or buy at their shops. The most infamous example for the persistence of these illegal practices was the Viennese brickmakers, as conveyed by Victor Adler.[92] In the late nineteenth century, a general prohibition of obligatory board and lodging in the employer's household was requested by workers, for it was apparently still customary in several branches.[93] In contrast to that, there was no legal objection to lodging and board being a regular part of servants' wages since servants were regarded as part of the household. A small amount of money paid or an advance received demonstrated the binding character of these contracts which were also often made for a longer period of time, at

---

[85] Emmerich Tálos and Karl Wörister, *Soziale Sicherung im Sozialstaat Österreich. Entwicklung – Herausforderungen – Strukturen* (Baden-Baden: Nomos, 1994).

[86] Ernst Bruckmüller, Roman Sandgruber and Hannes Stekl, *Soziale Sicherheit im Nachziehverfahren. Die Einbeziehung der Bauern, Landarbeiter, Gewerbetreibenden und Hausgehilfen in das System der österreichischen Sozialversicherung* (Salzburg: Neugebauer, 1978).

[87] In the 1890s leather workers and book printers already had collective agreements on wages. Bakers, shoemakers and tailors soon followed. From 1904 to 1907 the number of agreements increased from 37 to 727. Julius Deutsch, *Die Tarifverträge in Österreich* (Wien: Hueber, 1908), 11ff, 16.

[88] Richter, *Die Produktion*, 126f.

[89] Hans Bayer, *Die Löhne der Arbeiterschaft in Wien und Niederösterreich* (Wien: Verlag d. Kammer f. Arbeiter u. Angestellte, 1936); Jürgen Kocka: *Arbeitsverhältnisse und Arbeiterexistenzen: Grundlagen der Klassenbildung im 19. Jahrhundert* (Bonn: Dietz, 1990), 489. As Zeitlin pointed out, Biernacki only refers to examples of time and piece wages, which support his hypothesis of a culturally based difference in systems of wages. Richard Biernacki, *The Fabrication of Labor: Germany and Britain, 1640-1914* (Berkeley: University of California Press, 1995); Jonathan Zeitlin (1996), 'Review of The Fabrication of Labor: Germany and Britain, 1640-1914, by Richard Biernacki', *The American Journal of Sociology* 101, no. 6, 1770–1772.

[90] *Bericht der k. k. Gewerbe-Inspectoren 1884*, 143.

[91] Ingwer, *Rechtsstreitigkeiten*, 142, 149.

[92] Victor Adler, 'Die Lage der Ziegelarbeiter', in *Aufsätze, Reden und Briefe*, ed. Parteivorstand der Sozialdemokratischen Arbeiterpartei Deutschösterreichs, vol. 4 (Victor Adler über Arbeiterschutz und Sozialreform) (Wien: Wiener Volksbuchhandlung, 1925), 11–16, 12.

[93] 'Zur Lohnbewegung', *Arbeiter-Zeitung* 1.8.1890: 7; 'Allgemeine Rundschau', *Arbeiterwille* 6.9.1893: 4.

least in respect to agricultural servants.[94] (In trades and factories, long-term agreements are described as the exception rather than the rule.) From a critical perspective, service was described as modern slavery, e.g. by Adelheid Popp, who emphasizes the lack of dignity in this kind of work relation.[95]

However, there was significant job fluctuation and people also often worked in various changing jobs, seasonally or in the course of their lives,[96] without frequently getting new documents appropriate to their work-relations and status as servant or worker. As mentioned before, many had no documents or the wrong kind, while others owned both a labour and a servants' booklet. At the same time, labour relations were not always clearly defined or categorized correctly. This seemed to concern primarily women, who according to trade inspectors' reports often received no papers at all, or servants' booklets instead of labour booklets. Women were also often falsely employed in trades as servants, implying that they had no entitlement to insurance for work accidents or illness. Frequently mentioned examples of contested categorizations are, for example: cooks, maids, laundresses and coachmen, occupations which were found in households or in companies, inns and workshops.[97] In such a case it was not decisive if he/she was equipped with a servants' booklet or labour booklet, as stated by a trade court in 1900. The characteristic of service, as the court decision put it, was to be hired to a humble kind of domestic or agricultural labour which goes along with admission in the employer's household and subordination to his supervision.[98] If a person was employed as a worker or servant had to be established in every individual case.

Another problem, manifest in many trade court cases, was that neither employers nor employees necessarily stuck to the initial agreement on work tasks and payments. Or: there was no consensus on the question of what the initial agreement was. Which leads us to the last issue of the options for quitting or leaving a post.

Wages and Notice

Although labour/servants' booklets were a means to establish, categorize and (in some cases) document a contract, they were also seen as a tool to stabilize and enforce it.[99]

---

[94] 'Andere Dienstboten', *St. Pöltner Bote* 10.5.1877: 154. In the case of agricultural servants, such long-term agreements were rather desirable since they included shelter and board during wintertime: Norbert Ortmayr, 'Ländliches Gesinde in Oberösterreich 1918-1938', in *Familienstruktur und Arbeitsorganisation in ländlichen Gesellschaften*, eds. Josef Ehmer and Michael Mitterauer, (Wien: Böhlau, 1986), 325–416.
[95] Adelheid Popp, *Haussklavinnen. Ein Beitrag zur Lage der Dienstmädchen* (Wien: Brand, 1912).
[96] Albert Randow (1887), 'Versuch einer Arbeiterstatistik für das Deutsche Reich und Oesterreich', *Jahrbuch für Gesetzgebung, Verwaltung und Volkswirtschaft im Deutschen Reich* NF, no. 2, 595–636, 599.
[97] 'Aus Fabriken und Werkstätten' (1892), *Arbeiterinnenzeitung* no. 23: 3; there are manifold examples in the trade inspectors' reports, e.g.: 'Bericht der k. k. Gewerbe-Inspectoren' 1885, 263 and 1913, CLXXVf. Or the 'Sammlungen der Entscheidungen der k. k. Gewerbegerichte' Nr. 128/1900, Nr. 129/1900, Nr. 574/1900, Nr. 1903/1901, Nr. 1847/1911. Wrong documents certainly did not mean that the regulations did not apply, as indicated by decision Nr. 809/1902.
[98] *Sammlungen der Entscheidungen der k. k. Gewerbegerichte* 1900, Nr. 128.
[99] Patricia Van den Eeckhout, 'Giving Notice: the Legitimate Way of Quitting and Firing (Ghent, 1877–1896)' in Scholliers et al., *Experiencing Wages*, 81–109.

'The purpose of labour books is to protect the work contract against arbitrary actions from one side, either from the worker or the employer, as well as to instil in young people the serious character of a work contract and its obligations.'[100] Papers had to be handed out to the employer and kept in order so that workers and servants would be deterred from 'running away' before the period of termination was over, before a task was completed or before an advance was worked off. Employers were not allowed to employ a person who had not properly terminated previous employment. Nor were they supposed to lure away workers or servants from other employees.[101] Options for quitting or dismissing someone before the agreed time were legally limited to a small number of serious reasons both for employers and workers/servants.[102]

There were of course complaints and violations of regulations on both sides here as well. Nonetheless, violations had far more severe consequences for workers or servants than for employers. To settle a dispute required time and resources. A frequent complaint of workers and servants was that employers did not return the papers after termination of employment, as had been requested. Or – as mentioned before – employers provided no references, incorrect or negative ones, thereby ruining one's work record and reputation or even hindering one from finding new regular employment. Court cases and trade inspectors' reports document conflicts on the wording of the termination of employment. It could matter if, according to the job certificates, someone left or was dismissed by his/her own choice, or due to lack of work or other reasons. Another complaint was that employers entered secret marks into the booklets to brand workers as participants in strikes or May Day celebrations.[103] As mentioned above, just a work record of too many short time jobs or discontinuous employment could be enough to raise suspicions.

Nonetheless, many workers and servants simply left behind their documents or destroyed them and applied for new ones.[104] After all, not every employer asked for the obligatory papers and documentation of work experiences was not relevant for all kinds of employment. It was ambitious skilled workers and politically organized ones who had the most to gain or lose in this respect. Hence, labour booklets alone were apparently insufficient to discipline and stabilize employment or to prevent strikes, even in combination with the legal threat of fines, compensation, forced return to the workplace or arrest of up to three months for breach of contract (or, in case of servants, even physical punishment). According to trade inspectors' reports, various forms of wage payment[105] were used to tie workers or servants to their jobs: advances,[106] withholding a share of the

---

[100] Heilinger, *Österreichisches Gewerberecht*, 526.
[101] Alfred Böninger, *Die Bestrafung des Arbeitsvertragsbruchs der Arbeiter. Insbesondere der gewerblichen Arbeiter* (Tübingen: Verlag der H. Laupp'schen Buchhandlung, 1891), 56; Heilinger, *Österreichisches Gewerberecht*, 549.
[102] Heilinger, *Österreichisches Gewerberecht*, 537, 541, 543, 545.
[103] Isidor Ingwer, *Zwei Fesseln des Koalitionsrechtes* (Wien: Verlag des österreichischen Metallarbeiterverbandes, 1912).
[104] For example Wenzel Holek, *Lebensgang eines deutsch-tschechischen Handarbeiter*, ed. Paul Göhre (Jena: Diederichs, 1909), 248; *Bericht der k. k. Gewerbe-Inspectoren 1884*, 217.
[105] On the forms of wages in general see, for example, Reinhold Reith, *Lohn und Leistung. Lohnformen im Gewerbe 1450-1900* (Stuttgart: Franz Steiner, 1999).
[106] *Bericht der k. k. Gewerbe-Inspectoren 1885*, 29; Ebenhoch and Pernerstorfer, *Stenographisches Protokoll*, 211.

payment (*Stehgeld*), deposits (for values and possible damage), or extending periods of payment beyond the usual period of one or two weeks.[107] Agricultural servants were rewarded for staying in a situation for many years.

According to the statistics of complaints and trade court cases, conflicts regarding labour booklets occurred regularly but in smaller numbers, whereas disputes over wages (which often mentioned labour booklets) occurred in higher numbers. Most conflicts at trade court or brought forward to trade inspectors, though, seem to concern start, continuation and termination of work. Given the fact that the most common period of notice was two weeks, this seems remarkable. (See graphs 3.3 and 3.4; cases could concern more than one aspect, and if we look at singular cases, they were often

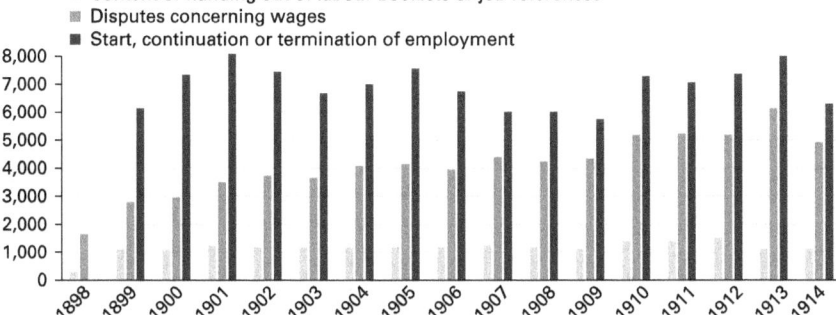

Graph 3.3 Issues at trade courts in Vienna, 1894–1900. (Selected topics. Cases could concern more than one topic.)[108]

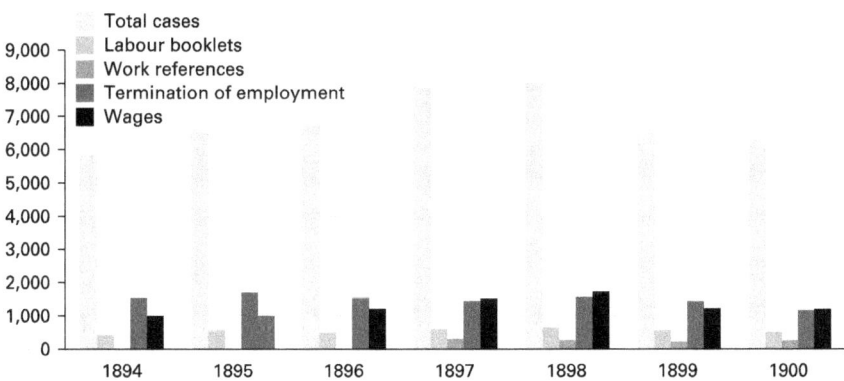

Graph 3.4 Workers' concerns brought forward to trade inspectors, 1894–1900 (Selected topics).[109]

---

[107] *Bericht der k. k. Gewerbe-Inspectoren 1886*, 97, 253, 375,
[108] Source: *Statistisches Jahrbuch der Stadt Wien 1898-1914*.
[109] *Berichte der k. k. Gewerbe-Inspectoren 1894-1900*. Other concerns related to insurance, work conditions, work time, apprenticeship, strike, work regulations etc. In contrast to other countries, trade inspectors could not impose fines or release regulations. They were meant to provide advice and reports. However, they could also file charges with the authorities. Arbeiterschutzgesetzgebung (Oesterreich-Ungarn). In: *Handwörterbuch der Staatswissenschaften*, vol. 1, 422–33, 430.

interrelated.) Unfortunately, it is not possible to tell to what extent these cases involved: dismissals or notice given by the worker, individual termination or collective actions. However, some data suggests that the majority of cases concerned workers' complaints on dismissals.[110] Conflicts in domestic service were also numerous but less well documented, yet it was also more servants than employers who turned to the authorities with their complaints.[111]

Conclusions: were the Papers Worth the Paper?

Work-documents manifested and potentially produced similarities, differences and hierarchies in work and labour relations. They were used to categorize, establish and terminate contracts. They indicated basic terms and conditions of labour relations. They could be used to control, discipline and enforce contracts in respect to wages or other aspects, not always in accordance with the regulations. The obligation to own and carry a labour/servants' booklet was often described as humiliating, and the disciplinary measures as inappropriate or unjust, by workers' and servants' organizations. However, documents also signified various basic – customary or statutory – rights, entitlements and options within and beyond employment. Categorization of work indicated which payment and remuneration (amount, kind, frequency) was regarded customary or appropriate. It also indicated varying options for a livelihood that went beyond wages and actual work, in case of illness or work accidents but also in the situation of joblessness and search for work. These were important options for the ability to negotiate a wage. Documented work experiences could also open up possibilities for better employment and wage or for receiving the permit to establish oneself as a master craftsman.

As I have highlighted, the enforcement of regulations remained fairly patchy throughout the nineteenth and early twentieth centuries. Multiple sources allow us to reconstruct how such papers were used, abused and neglected. Several life accounts which mention such practices are available, but they are predominantly written by male, skilled, travelling and politically organized workers. It was they who, after all, could gain or lose much depending on their booklets and references. It was the politically organized workers who made such documents a symbol of coercion. Reports of trade inspectors and trade court cases permit us to reconstruct considerable variation in practices, regionally and in respect to branches, along with differences in how factories, workshops and households handled such matters. These reports likewise highlight how the distinctions between work and service, skilled and unskilled work – often related to gender – were in flux and often ambiguous, and how those distinctions – given the uneven rights associated with them – were manipulated and contested. Papers and rules did not describe; rather, they were a matter and means of conflict and struggle.[112]

[110] *Statistisches Jahrbuch der Stadt Wien 1889*, 646 and 650.
[111] k. k. Polizei-Direction, ed. *Die Polizeiverwaltung Wiens 1877-1892*.
[112] As argued by Pierre Bourdieu, 'Das Recht und die Umgehung des Rechts', in *Pierre Bourdieu: Neue Perspektiven für die Soziologie der Wirtschaft*, eds. Michael Florian and Frank Hillebrandt (Wiesbaden: VS Verlag für Sozialwissenschaften, 2006), 19–41.

The available reports document multiple violations and conflicts, while at the same time such observations and descriptions are the product of varying attempts to regulate, oversee and to enforce regulations. Status is not only reflected in wage differences.[113] If we are talking about hierarchies and differences in living standards and in the value of work, I maintain that we have to include all these aspects.

---

[113] Hobsbawm, 'Custom, Wages and Work-Load', 408.

4

Custom, Wages, and Hobsbawm's 'Rules of the Game': New Perspectives on Eighteenth-Century Wages

Judy Z. Stephenson

I Introduction

Hobsbawm's famous claim that 'custom' determined wages and workload in the eighteenth century is not quoted much anymore, but for decades it was both a cornerstone and a continuation of substantivist arguments about how industrialized labour markets developed in the industrial revolution.[1] According to the famous 1960 essay, it was only in the mid-nineteenth century that skilled workers and employers adjusted to the use of incentives and price mechanisms in a market system to gauge, measure and agree the wage rate for their work. Before this, wages were set by custom, and were not a 'market calculation'.[2]

Explicit in this narrative of capital and labour's contract in the new transformational productivity of industrialization was that only in the nineteenth century did employers' pursuit of the highest profits necessitate bargaining for lowering of labour costs, against workers looking to expend the least effort for the highest possible wage. The resulting process of discovery of the 'rules of the game' between capital and labour initially gave employers the considerable surplus advantage of 'ultra-cheap wage costs' with customary labour efforts or inputs.[3] As labour moderated effort and output in response, employers turned to scientific management to increase output, and, goes the narrative, it was only at the end of the nineteenth century that the wage bargain could be viewed as a 'fair day's work for a fair day's pay'.[4]

Implicit in this essay and in many associated works of social history, was the idea that preindustrial workers and employers did not transact in such a way, and that the

---

[1] Hobsbawm, Eric. 'Custom, Wages and Work-Load', in *Labouring Men: Studies in the History of Labour* (London: Weidenfeld & Nicolson. 1964), 344.
[2] Ibid., 347.
[3] Ibid., 344, 353.
[4] Schwarz, Leonard D. 'Custom, wages and workload in England during industrialization.' *Past and Present*, 197(1) (2007), 143–75.

price and quantity of labour were fixed by 'non-economic criteria'; that employers were not striving for the lowest labour cost, and that rights, customs and status were respected, or institutionalized.[5] Hobsbawm's thesis about the 'rules of the game' relies on an old notion that in the eighteenth century labour benefited from a 'custom' wage. In some ways this notion of custom in the labour market is long overturned, and in some it persists.

The 'custom' referred to is associated with a 'moral economy' where it was not just money wages that mattered to workers and employers, but where culture, experience, norms, obligations, beliefs, morals were valued in wage setting and payments and the solely commercial exploitation of labour was somehow held off or protected by such institutions.[6, 7] Research on the early modern moral economy once dominated the field of economic and social history concerned with welfare and wages, but has generally receded in the literature on the economic history of eighteenth-century England, since more than thirty years ago historians argued for a 'rejection of the dichotomy [...] between the customary, nonmarket culture of the preindustrial and early industrial working class and the hegemonically imposed market culture of competitive individualism under industrial capitalism'.[8]

Since then, economic history research on labour markets has been more characterized by quantitative evidence of emerging enlightenment and the knowledge economy;[9] of human capital development and structural and occupational development contributing to growth and innovation.[10] Some important work on wage formation has further explored what might be termed the customs of the waged labour market, but crucially, wage formation is not taken into account in calculating average wages, living standards, or their relative comparators.[11]

However, the moral economy as 'an umbrella term for obsolete customary titles and ways of life prior to the "Great Leap" from traditional society to the modern market

---

[5] Hobsbawm, 'Custom, Wages and Work-Load', 344.
[6] See Schwarz, 'Custom', for a full consideration of the practicalities of the thesis; Karl Polanyi, *The Great Transformation* (New York: Rhinehart NY, 1957); John Rule, *The Experience of Labour in Eighteenth Century Industry* (London: Croom Helm, 1981), 194–217. Edward P. Thompson, *Customs in Common* (London: Merlin, 1991), 338, 'where claimants to a commodity can invoke non-monetary rights to that commodity, and where and third parties will act to support these claims, when community membership supersede price as a basis for entitlement'.
[7] Norbert Götz, 'Moral economy': its conceptual history and analytical prospects, *Journal of Global Ethics*, 11, no. 2 (2015): 147–62.
[8] James Jaffe, *The Struggle for Market Power: Industrial Relations in the British Coal Industry, 1800–1840* (Cambridge: Cambridge University Press, 1991), 1–6; John Smail, 'New languages for labour and capital: The transformation of discourse in the early years of the Industrial Revolution', *Social History*, 12, no. 1 (1987): 49–71; Adrian Randall, 'New languages or old? Labour, Capital and discourse in the industrial revolution, *Social History*, 15, no. 2 (1990): 195–216.
[9] Joel Mokyr, *The Enlightened Economy: An Economic History of Britain*, 1700-1850 (New Haven: Yale University Press, 2009).
[10] As indeed has the idea that markets did not operate before. See Mokyr *The Enlightened Economy*; Allen, *The British Industrial Revolution*, for growth and innovation narratives of the eighteenth century. One cannot but think of Cannadine's reference to the mirror of past and present in our view of the industrializing process, David Cannadine, 'The Present and the Past in the English Industrial Revolution 1880-1980', *Past & Present*, 103 no. May (1984), 132.
[11] Scholliers, Peter, and Leonard Schwarz, eds. *Experiencing wages: Social and cultural aspects of wage forms in Europe since 1500*. Berghahn books, 2003.

system', sounds its echoes in a view of capitalism which sees industrialization as the inherently dark and exploitative root of slavery, expropriation, crony capitalism, the allocation of increased risks to labour, and the repeal of the welfare state among other injustices.[12, 13] The idea that status, morality, fairness and custom rather than a 'market calculation' can determine labours' reward before industrialization, or in the twenty-first century, remains attractive.

That markets were not exploitatively commercial before the late eighteenth century or nineteenth century is rooted in a Marxian view of the development of a 'self-regulating' market economy and its subsequent commodification of labour in the process of industrialization or 'transformation'.[14] It was related to and supported by a range of substantivist historical approaches to the preindustrial world, which viewed labour as being socially embedded in social status and relationships, not exchanged in a market or been subject to market or commercial forces. In some versions of this analysis this nonmarket economy is a haven of artisan values and a golden age for labour.[15] Later social historians evaluated these claims as stemming from a sentimental view of preindustrial society. But even John Rule believed that the golden age had some meaning, even if that was that there were brief periods of just over a decade perhaps where 'rates were high and as much work was put out as any man wanted to take'.[16] Such conditions are as far from any definition of custom as has been taken as implied from Hobsbawm's thesis. This begs the question of how custom in eighteenth-century labour markets really worked, and for whom.

A significant and influential strand of economic history over the last three decades has sought to minimize or deny the notion of preindustrial 'custom', largely by advancing evidence of a 'market' for labour, which produced market rates. Although a large body of work uses 'wages' as a proxy for economic growth in this period the accompanying understanding of hiring, supervision and personnel management through contract forms is not matched, and economic historians' current wage scholarship tends towards an assumption that the work that was carried out in the

---

[12] See Eric Hilt, 'Economic History, Historical Analysis, and the "New History of Capitalism"', *The Journal of Economic History*, 77, no. 2 (2017): 511–36, for an economic historian's perspective on the histories of capitalism, referring for the definition of capitalism in some of these works is Geoffrey M. Hodgson, *Conceptualizing capitalism* (Chicago: University of Chicago Press, 2015), where capitalism is conceived as a recent phenomenon, dependant on law and the State, whereas markets have existed for millennia.

[13] Götz, 'Moral economy', 147, writes that the moral economy may offer 'alternative ways of "utility maximisation" through the construction of altruistic meaning for economic transactions'; also , Gabrielle Clark, '"Humbug" or "Human Good?": E.P. Thompson, the Rule of Law and Coercive Labor Relations Under Neoliberal American Capitalism,' *Journal of Social History*, 48, no. 4 (2015): 759–78; Rudi Batzell, Sven Beckert, Andrew Gordon and Gabriel Winant, 'E. P. Thompson, Politics and History: Writing Social History Fifty Years after The Making of the English Working Class', *Journal of Social History*, 48, no. 4 (2015): 753–758.

[14] Polanyi, *Great Transformation*, 43; note that Thompson did not see wages as part of the 'moral economy', see Marc Edelman, 'E.P. Thompson and Moral Economies', in *A companion to moral anthropology*, ed. Didier Fassin (Chichester; Malden, Mass: Wiley-Blackwell, 2012), 49–66.

[15] John Rule. *The Experience of Labour in Eighteenth-Century English Industry*. New York: St. Martin's Press. (1981).

[16] Ibid., 69.

'casual' market can be equated in its value to that in longer-term service contracts.[17] Whilst historians overwhelmingly agree that there was a market for labour over millennia, economists and historians have tended to apply a neoclassical framework of supply and demand to fit that generalized idea of a market rather than considered further what sort of market it was.[18] In practice this has meant adopting the law of one wage, where a 'day wage' earned by one man is representative of the predominant wage for all day wages for equally skilled men, in a world where work is readily available and there are no frictions of search or contract.[19] If custom was at work then wage rates that historian and economist relied on to estimate productivity and GDP per capita would not be able to be used – as they would not be market rates, and so not reflect productivity.

Therefore, how any such moral economy and its customs attributed or bargained the gains from production is rarely articulated. Hobsbawm offers that custom gave the unskilled man merely a subsistence wage, as labour supply meant employers did not have to offer any more to 'attract them away from farm labour', but that the skilled man could expect a premium based on social status of their trade and their place in the hierarchy of that trade.[20] Therefore, a custom wage in the skilled market was one set by social status, where the input of effort or skill input was regulated by task and season and it was this that was challenged and upended by the rules of the new industrialized game, where time was money, and 'factory discipline' brought loss of agency, rights and freedoms of ordinary working men and women.

Schwarz discusses three concepts that form the basis on which the contract for exchange for labour were agreed, entangled in Hobsbawm's thesis. 'The first is the extent to which payment by piece rates became prevalent during the industrial revolution, as many economists advocated and as Marx believed to have occurred. The second is the relationship of piece rates to time rates. This leads to a third question, whether this period saw a new paradigm in the relationship of piece rates to time, of work to effort.'[21] The meaning of these can only be interrogated if assumptions are made about labour costs as being 'wages', and labour time and length or duration of employment. More precisely, Hobsbawm described employment and wages in way that closely represents what we today understand as 'jobs' with a measure of time as the determination of labour input and firms that act as employers to workers, on an ongoing contractual basis. As is becoming increasingly apparent in ongoing scholarship

---

[17] For equation of annual with casual days per year see Humphries and Weisdorf, 'Unreal Wages?', for wages and growth see Allen, 'The Great Divergence in European Wages and Prices'; Gregory Clark, 'The Condition of the Working Class in England, 1209–2004', *The Journal of Political Economy*, 113, no. 6 (2005): 1307–40; van Zanden, 'Wages and the Standard of Living in Europe'.

[18] Lucassen, *The Story of Work*; Peter Scholliers and Leonard Schwarz, 'The Wage in Europe Since the Sixteenth Century', in *Experiencing Wages*, 13, 54–8.

[19] Based on Arthur L. Bowley, *Wages in the United Kingdom* (Cambridge, Cambridge University Press, 1900), 59–60; Gregory Clark and Ysbrand Van Der Werf, 'Work in progress? The industrious revolution', *The Journal of Economic History*, 58, no. 3 (1998): 830–43; for a critique see Hatcher and Stephenson *Seven Centuries of Unreal Wages*.

[20] Hobsbawm, 'Custom', 346–7, that the wages of unskilled labour were fixed around subsistence cost is 'overwhelmingly attested by theorists industrialists and historians' acknowledging that subsistence was not a physiological absolute but varied at different times and in different places.

[21] Schwarz, 'Custom', 145.

on early modern labour markets, and is the experience of many workers today, such a representation can mislead.

The first of the following sections will offer a summary analysis review of this question in the literature on the early modern waged labour markets. Section III gathers some early evidence of preindustrial wage formation and its relationship to income from long-run wage records in London 1700 to 1800. Section IV looks further at the question of time and employment tenure and argues that we should view what has previously been labelled 'custom' in the light of bargaining problems in uncertain conditions, without firms or unions or wage setting institutions. Section IV considers the implications for the long-run study of labour markets and how they distribute labour's share of income from production for today.

II Time, conditions, wages

A significant literature on wage formation and determination, long associated with custom in the preindustrial period tends to vacillate between custom and market, often associating 'custom' with rigidity, or lack of change, and 'market' with flexibility. In probably the key collection of essays on the subject, Scholliers and Schwarz argue that the form of the wage was a key determinant of welfare, but in giving ample evidence of market forces and market flexibility in early modern Europe where many changes in wage levels and wage bargains indicate this, their case studies lean towards the conclusion that the market predominated.[22] (Although they acknowledge there were important elements of 'tradition' in the wage.)[23] Sonenscher, in a very famous work on French journeymen, posited that worker's wages were determined in the 'economy of the bazaar' alongside known regulatory rigidity, and argued that wage rates must have fluctuated beneath. Both works, by focusing on money rates either for piece or time, and their form of bargaining, minimize discussions of time discipline.

E.P. Thompson maintained that the eighteenth-century moral economy did not extend to wages, but operated for the conditions of work and welfare.[24] He was also the author of the classic treatise on 'time discipline' that underpinned one of the key theses about the loss of welfare to workers through industrialization involved in factory discipline.[25] That the measure of working time changed in the industrial revolution is an important and well-wrought strand in the literature on industrialization originating with Thompson. In the nineteenth century this discipline is held to have been an important part of management and productivity – and is a key part of the productivity and fair wage story that Hobsbawm was advancing in 1960.

Working time in the eighteenth century is a far more complex problem. There are far fewer records, and the nature of the many different types of working contract mentioned

---

[22] Scholliers and Schwarz, 'Experiencing Wages'. For an argument about piece rates and time rates on which also see Richard Biernacki, *The Fabrication of Labor: Germany and Britain, 1640-1914* (Berkeley: University of California Press, 1995).
[23] Ibid., 9.
[24] Thompson, *Customs in Common*, 189.
[25] E.P. Thompson, 'Time, Work-Discipline, and Industrial Capitalism,' Past & Present, no.38 (1967): 56–97.

above make generalizations about hours difficult, however, the concomitant thesis for preindustrial productivity is de Vries 'Industrious Revolution' which holds that throughout the eighteenth century skilled and unskilled workers embraced the market both in consumption and production and worked more days per year than they had in previous centuries. The idea is this increased work intensity raised incomes and productivity bringing about economic growth.[26] One of the complexities in substantiating this important thesis has always been that working records give us so little information about working time. To some extent this is because, as Schwarz says, task discipline rather than time discipline, was the means of ensuring output before nineteenth-century factoryization.[27] What mattered was that the task was done, not the length of the working day or the intensity of the hour. So, when we find eighteenth-century wage records it is not always clear how much workload or time they refer to. This makes serious analysis of whether they are evidential of a custom wage or a moral economy very difficult.

III

As Hatcher and Stephenson highlighted in a series of essays recently, the construction of wage series in economic history has been subject to an influential plethora of ideological and methodological agendas around measurement and neoclassical principles. Mostly they are interpreted as the income of a labourer earned for one days' work as if they enjoyed a steady job all year round. This neglects their vital and original context, where such steady work was far from the norm.[28] The 'day wages' so easily found in early modern institutional records, which all wage series from Thorold Rogers and Arthur Bowley onwards rely on are completely out of the all-important social and cultural context when placed in series of the 'average wage'.[29] This is a well-worn point, but the social and cultural context of day wage rates that this essay argues for is not that of class consciousness, or cultural meaning, but of commercial enterprise.[30]

Day wages are not representative of the labour cost, or labour income of a day's work, for a variety of significant reasons. Conditions in early modern labour markets, and the available evidence of wage payments indicate that day wages used in wage series were not steadily paid for regular work.[31] Moreover, they were just one form of

---

[26] Jan de Vries, 'The Industrial Revolution and the Industrious Revolution', *The Journal of Economic History*, 54, no. 2 (1994): 249–70.
[27] Gregory Clark, 'Factory Discipline', *The Journal of Economic History*, 54, no. 1 (1994): 128–163; Schwarz 'Custom', 144–5, for a succinct explanation and exploration of the time discipline concept. Also, Roger Wells, 'E. P. Thompson, customs in common and moral economy', *The Journal of Peasant Studies*, 21, no. 2 (1994): 263–307, 275–7 for custom being a substitute for wage.
[28] Hatcher and Stephenson, *Seven centuries of unreal wages,* chapter 1.
[29] See Craig Calhoun, 'E. P. Thompson and the Discipline of Historical Context', *Social Research*, 61, no. 2 (1994): 223–43, for a discussion of how Thompson viewed the importance of context.
[30] For an expansion of this argument and more information on how the business that produced such day rates were run see Judy Stephenson, *Contracts and Pay. Work in London Construction 1660-1785*, (London: Palgrave Macmillan, 2017), chapters 4 and 5.
[31] Donald Woodward, *Men at Work. Labourers and Building Craftsmen in the Towns of Northern England, 1450-1750* (Cambridge: Cambridge University Press, 1994), 116–19.

payment, and few unskilled workers were actually paid by the day.[32] Less understood until recently was the fact that the recorded rates that appear in wage series were those paid to contractors not workers (where workers received a lower rate from the contractor who took part of the rates paid to him as a margin).[33] A great many workers, many skilled and surprisingly many unskilled, were sole traders or entrepreneurs: they earned payment for intermediate or consumer goods they produced, not 'wages' for their labour power exchanged.[34] Such petty capitalists often, in a rural setting, combined casual work by the day at period of high demand in agriculture for other employers, with subsistence farming, spinning, carting or transport and distribution, and perhaps craft skills.[35]

In all endeavours, production was not continuous. Few, beyond those who served the crown or large estates and aristocrats, had a 'job', and few employers employed the people they did year-round. There was a profound seasonality to employment. Work was far more uncertain than the assumption of steady work or steady by employment giving 250 to 300 days income. Data from building sites and agriculture shows that most workers must have had many employers in any year, but it also shows that large workplaces, such as construction sites, potteries, cutleries and foundries were full of people who were employed by many small masters who rented their fixed assets there rather than by one owner or corporate entity which operated the site.[36] Even famous and old companies people today might be aware of, like the East India Company, or the Bank of England were not 'firms' in the way that today's enterprises have permanent management and employees, until the early nineteenth century.[37]

Thus, early modern wage records are notoriously rare, and where they do present custom in wage rates is not what they show. When wages are found in records they often don't present as what we understand as wages. They are written up as 'worke done', or the prices of goods. Those who have studied wage books and accounts sufficiently generally agree with earlier scholars of wage systems. Work tended to be

---

[32] Day wages were almost overwhelmingly found in construction and shipbuilding. These accounted for less than 15% of the workforce in early eighteenth-century London, A. L. Beier and Roger Finlay, *London 1500-1700. The Making of the Metropolis* (London: Longman, 1986), 141–67.

[33] Judy Stephenson, '"Real" wages? Contractors, Workers, and Pay in London Building Trades, 1650-1800', *The Economic History Review*, 71, no. 1 (2018): 106–132. When the margin is taken into account the real wage may be up to 30% less than previously supposed.

[34] The classic historical essay on this topic is Donald Woodward, 'Wage Rates and Living Standards in Pre-Industrial England', *Past and Present*, 91, no. May (1981): 28–46, ever quoted and long ignored. Also A. Hassel Smith, 'Labourers in Late Sixteenth-Century England: a Case Study from North Norfolk [Part I]', *Continuity and Change*, 4, no. 1 (1989): 23–88; Judy Stephenson, Meredith Paker, Patrick Wallis, 'Day Work, Task Work and Watch Work: Labouring at St Paul's Cathedral 1672-1748', Eighth Annual Conference on Construction History 2021, Department of Architecture, University of Cambridge, Cambridge.

[35] Woodward, 'Wage Rates and Living Standards'.

[36] Meredith Paker, Judy Stephenson, and Patrick Wallis, 'Unskilled labour before the Industrial Revolution', *Economic History Working Papers*, no. 322 (2021), London School of Economics and Political Science, London, UK (http://eprints.lse.ac.uk/108562/); Joyce Burnette, 'Seasonal patterns of agricultural day-labour at eight English farms, 1835–1844' in *Seven Centuries of Unreal wages*, 195–225.

[37] Anne L. Murphy, '"Writes a Fair Hand and Appears to be well Qualified": the Recruitment of Bank of England Clerks, 1800–1815', *Financial History Review*, 22, no. 1 (2015): 19–44.

contracted under any of the following limited systems: work paid by the task; by the day; payment by the piece; salaried positions or positions with allowance, or payment by commission.[38] Each bound the worker and the employer in different ways. Task, day and piece work, which were the way most people exchanged labour, were fleeting, short term contracts, that prioritized employer's flexibility and offered some workers opportunity, but no security. Longer appointments, positions and annual contracts sometimes promised somewhat less in monetary reward but offered tenure and other rights and claims. Payment by the hour was only recorded in the case of overtime – usually at building sites or shipyards – as some kind of perk, and it rarely valued the overtime hours at the same rate as that implied by the day rate. Piece workers were often de-facto subcontractors and supply chain partners who absorbed credit and other risks through high output volatility.

One should note the important distinction between contracts for work, which task, day and piece work dealt with (with some exceptions), and contracts for service, which commission systems and annual contracts were based on. This distinction was socially, legally and economically critical.[39] Moreover, in many contracts (implicit or explicit) the money wage and the work to be carried out were not the sum of the exchange. Apprenticeship, the most well documented type of contract for service usually excluded 'wages' but gave young people board and lodging, clothing, training networks and credit in those networks, in return for a fixed period of service, where the expectation was, they would be at their masters' command.[40] It is now well established that although much in apprenticeship contracts was customary, apprentices experience and their training, workload and responsibility were highly idiosyncratic. Servants in rural husbandry exchanged a year or more continuous service (where they were also expected to submit to their master) for board, lodging, such perquisites as might suit the employer and the promise of a cash lump sum at the year's end.[41] These contractual forms or service contracts can be viewed as 'customary' but they were far *more secure* than that. They had binding legal surety, as attested by the many cases in the sessions and courts.[42] But for casual workers, those who contracted for work by the day with various employers the evidence is that conditions, workload and reward were varied rather than fixed by custom.[43] Whilst those who worked by the day were contracted to submit to their employer's direction solely for those hours of work as agreed on the

---

[38] Schloss, *Methods of Industrial Renumeration*.
[39] Douglas C. Hay, Paul Craven, *Masters, Servants, and Magistrates in Britain and the Empire, 1562-1955* (Chapel Hill, NC: University of North Carolina Press, 2014).
[40] Patrick Wallis, 'Apprenticeship and training in premodern England', *The Journal of Economic History*, 68, no. 3 (2008): 832–61.
[41] Ann Kussmaul, *Servants in husbandry in early modern England* (Cambridge: Cambridge University Press, 1981).
[42] Patrick Wallis, 'Labor, Law, and Training in Early Modern London: Apprenticeship and the City's Institutions', *Journal of British Studies*, 51, no. 4 (2012): 791–819.
[43] See Woodward, *Men at work*; Andrew G. Hann, *Kinship and Exchange Relations within an Estate Economy: Ditchley, 1680–1750* (D.Phil. Thesis, University of Oxford, 1999), 181–4; Jane Humphries, and Jacob Weisdorf (2014), 'The Wages of Women in England, 1260-1850', London: Centre for Economic Policy Research, Discussion paper 9903.

basis that there was no guarantee, expectation nor obligation of future work after those days.

If working time was uncertain for casual workers, it was because the purpose of being able to contract by the day or the piece was generally to protect employers from the expense of paying wages in a demand slump. This meant that the amount of work available to casual workers likely responded to supply and demand in the economy, before any movement in wage rates was necessary. It is relevant therefore that there has always been one aspect of eighteenth-century wage records which has seemed to support the existence of custom wage practices. Wage rates gathered by nineteenth- and twentieth-century historians for the eighteenth century have always exhibited a significant nominal stability. 'Piece rates were as much a matter of custom as market determination and hence exhibited in most trades and amazing stability'.[44] Elizabeth Gilboy, who gathered the largest number of recorded wage rates for eighteenth-century England commented on the stability of her found wages noting the relative lack of movement of wages until after the 1790s.[45] And most famously, Adam Smith noted that customary piece rates remained unchanged for half a century.[46]

These characteristics are observed in London employers wage records in the form of a nominal wage rate stability that is almost absolute in some locations and at some employers. At St Paul's Cathedral the day rate for labourers directly employed by the clerk-of-the-works went unchanged for at least 82 years from 1666 to 1748.[47] The Royal Dockyards notoriously held a day rate for Shipwrights of 2s.1d. from the 1660s to the late 1770's when they attempted to move to task rates (meanwhile 'higher' task rates for those at private yards were notoriously varied and only offered in the short term).[48] At London Bridge the labourers rate per tide for assisting tide carpenters on the water was always 9d. from the 1670s until the early 1720s, then it remained at 12d. until at least the late 1760s. Some carpenters' billing labour by the day at the bridge billed the same rates in 1776 as they did in 1706. Dobson, charting the progression of labour dispute and unrest through the decades of the eighteenth century, noted that despite increasing violence and damage to production, rates generally did not increase after disputes, and the implication of the discussion of the move to task rates at the dockyards in the early 1770s was that a lack of outside options for striking or disputing workers might explain why.[49]

Such entrenched nominal wage stability or rigidity indicates that custom was an important part of wage formation, as it is in the formation of any wage.[50] But a

---

[44] Rule, *Experience*, 61.
[45] Elizabeth W. Gilboy, *Wages in Eighteenth-Century England* (Cambridge, Mass: Harvard University Press, 1934), 20–3.
[46] Adam Smith in *Wealth of Nations*, as quoted by Rule *Experience*, 69.
[47] Meredith Paker, Judy Stephenson and Patrick Wallis, 'Unskilled labour in the industrial revolution', Economic History Working Papers No: 322, London School of Economics, 6, 27.
[48] Roger Knight, 'From Impressment to Task Work: Strikes and Disruption in the Royal Dockyards, 1688-1788' note 11, in *History of Work and Labour Relations in the Royal Dockyards,* eds. Kenneth Lunn and Ann Day (London: Routledge, 1999).
[49] C. R. Dobson, *Masters and Journeymen. A Prehistory of Industrial Relations, 1717-1800,* (London: Croom Helm, 1980).
[50] Michael J. Piore, 'Fragments of a" Sociological" Theory of Wages', *American Economic Review*, 63, no. 2 (1973): 377–84.

presumption that custom is protective of workers' welfare, or beneficial to them is belied by the extremity of the rigidity. The lack of movement in wage rates over such a protracted period where prices were volatile, and particularly through unrest and dispute is at odds with the benign view of custom implied by Hobsbawm and earlier social historians. It suggests instead a market where an almost unlimited supply of labour was available to employers and where workers had little or no bargaining power to enable them to gain or maintain fair pay.[51]

That there was slack in the labour market is almost a trope of eighteenth-century urban social history, filled as it is with descriptions and polemic of the indolence, idleness and drunkenness of a mass of labour on the streets of London.[52] But if some contemporaneous and twentieth-century writers were correct in their observations that 'the condition of life and habits of the people were all against the monotony of regular employment', and employers suffered from a lack of availability of labour due to such idleness one would expect increases in wage enticement.[53] There is no evidence for it.

This question of slack in the labour market is, of course, critical to the idea of an 'industrious revolution' or the idea that labour worked harder and more intensively over the eighteenth century, bringing about growth. There is some limited hard evidence that workers did so. Using court depositions where workers gave their hours of travelling to and from work, or commencing work, Voth found an increase of 19 per cent in working hours between 1750 and 1800 in London.[54] However, if the form of the wage meant that workers were paid no more for those extra hours under a day rate contract where the hours were indeterminate then they would not have benefited their income. Only those working on piece rate contracts could have increased their income or share of income by increasing their *hours* of work. Indeed, even if workers worked longer piecework days (as they reported to the court), if the number of days that they worked in the working year were uncertain or precarious, it would have been hard to sustain raised income from increased hours alone. In other words, if the wage rate for a day or for a piece was constrained by custom, only by working more days, or producing more pieces could workers increase their wages.

Recent close study of the number of days work in the construction and service industries in London have shown that employment relationships were much more widely distributed and varying than previous assumptions of labour market arbitrage might account for. Although work was steady throughout the year for some skilled men and core, trusted workers, only a fraction of any work team held constant work six days a week over more than 48 weeks a year. Stephenson finds the average number of days worked per week at St Paul's by a craftsman's masons' team was 5.2, but that the few men worked all weeks throughout the year, even though the site was open and

---

[51] See Dobson's *Masters and Journeymen* for a fuller description of just how much bargaining power employers had.
[52] See Alfred W. Coats, 'Economic thought and poor law policy in the eighteenth century', *Economic History Review*, 13, no. 1, (1960), 39–61; for example, William Temple, (1758) *A Vindication of commerce and Arts*, 31, quoted by Gilboy *Wages in Eighteenth-century England*, 21. See also Daniel Defoe, *A Tour Thro' the Whole Island of Great Britain, Divided into Circuits or Journies*, vol. II (1724–1727), 95.
[53] Quote from Gilboy, *Wages in Eighteenth-century England*, 21.
[54] Voth, 'Time and Work', 58.

operational throughout the seasons.[55] There was a sharp drop in the availability work in the first quarter of the year. The number of labourers employed in January was about 60 per cent of the number employed in July.[56] Paker et al. find the raw average number of days worked per year for labourers at the same site to be just 145, but labourers who worked at the cathedral for more than a year averaged about 200 days' work per year on average, making an explicit link between employment tenure and a higher number of days worked, and steadier more stable work.

These headline figures for the number of days worked per year are not just much lower than the assumed number of days worked by other authors, they indicate an underlying significantly higher churn in the hiring and separation of workers than workers in construction markets today.[57] Unless search costs were negligible the vast majority of men in the construction industry (and these are all records of working men), could not have worked more than 200 days a year.[58] Therefore, although previous assumptions and calculations of the number of days in a working year based on courts records and assumptions of labour market arbitrage yield high estimates of 270 to 300 days' work, actual working records indicate a much lower number.

Graphic illustrations of these working patterns highlight the fundamental variation and divergence in the experience of waged work. Whilst some workers stayed for a significant length of time with employers and developed a long-term relationship, others experienced fleeting, brief and precarious wage employment. Whether this was by choice as entrepreneurial sole traders searching for and carrying out task work or as underemployed waged labour is hard to discern. What the patterns do not support is a narrative of custom rewarding labour. Working patterns from eighteenth-century account books suggest that those in the construction and service industries in London were constantly making 'market calculations' about the availability of work.

Table 3 shows the distribution of work by tenure, or length of time since hired for men at St 1700 – 1710. Graphs 4.1, 4.2 and 4.3 shows the distribution of tides – or shifts worked – among four teams of 'gin men or tide carpenters' assistants at Bridge house

Table **4.1** Number of days worked by labourers, St Paul's Cathedral, 1676–1709

	No of days per year labouring at St Paul's 1672–1710			
decade	mean	Least hired 25% of labourers	Median	Most hired 25% of labourers
1670	98	31	61	166
1680	116	45	100	187
1690	172	83	188	251
1700	222	168	242	283

Source: London Metropolitan Archives CLC/313/I/B/25473. See http://eprints.lse.ac.uk/id/eprint/108562

[55] Judy Stephenson, 'Working Days in a London Construction Team in the Eighteenth Century: Evidence from St Paul's Cathedral', *The Economic History Review*, 73, no. 2 (2020): 409–30.
[56] Paker et al., 'Unskilled labour', 6, 27.
[57] Paker et al., 'Unskilled labour', 37–8.
[58] Stephenson, 'Working days', finds even the most present workers managed 180–224 days per year, at wages 20% to 30% lower than previous estimates.

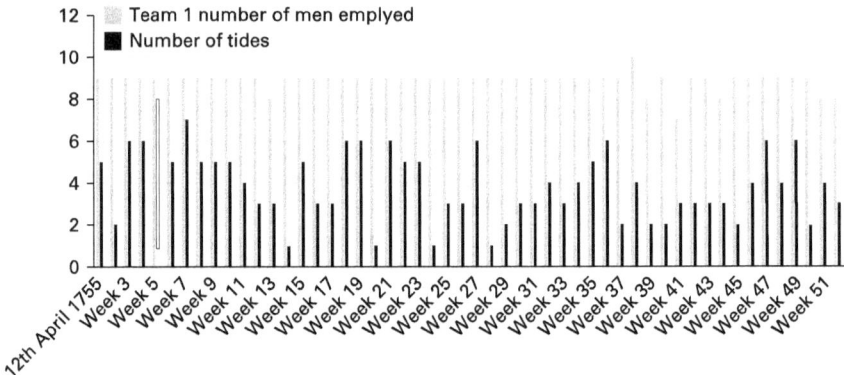

Graph 4.1 Gin men's tide work at Bridge House April 1755 to April 1756. Team 1.

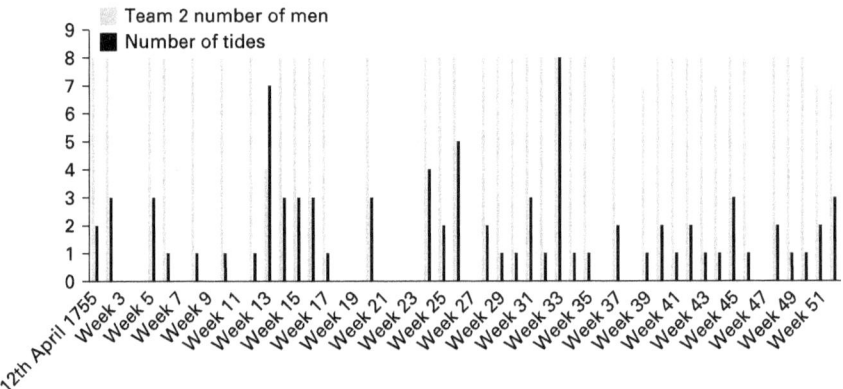

Graph 4.2 Gin men's tide work at Bridge House April 1755 to April 1756. Team 2.

(London Bridge). The fourth team had so little work that it doesn't actually show up chart. These illustrations indicate that even where work was regular for a small core tenured elite, it was unpredictable. Long employment relationships did not guarantee work in any one year – they merely made it more likely that when there was work those who had been around the longest would be hired for it. St Paul's and Bridge House may offer some kind of examples of early 'internal labour markets', certainly that would explain the attraction in making oneself available to work a handful of tides at a shilling each at London Bridge in the 1750s.

Internal or dual labour markets have been speculated on before by eighteenth-century labour historians. Schwarz cites the known work on agricultural labour forces from Yamamoto, and the 'Ditchley estate, [...where there was] a core labour force often employed for 300 days or more per annum existing alongside a casual labour force

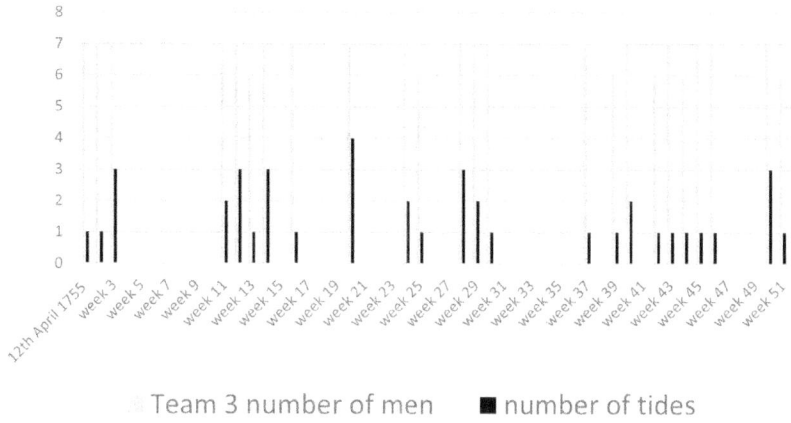

Graph 4.3 Gin men's tide work at Bridge House April 1755 to April 1756. Team 3.

usually working between three weeks and two months in the year and presumably employed elsewhere for most of the year.'[59] The working patterns from London employers seem to bolster the argument that these were a feature of early modern labour markets. That these institutions paid a reliable and stable wage rate is not in doubt. What was in doubt was the availability of work.

Despite a level of nominal wage stability that labour economists today would find jaw dropping, the study of London construction and service labour markets in the long eighteenth century therefore does not support a 'custom' thesis, but nor does it support the flexible, competitive market of the bazaar. Rather, what emerges as a picture of a market of constant bargaining and transactions for work, where despite fixed nominal wage rates incomes were both precarious and unstable.

Leonard Schwarz, writing over a decade ago concluded that the key to understanding custom in the preindustrial labour market was 'entitlements to exchange'. 'Hobsbawm may [...], have overestimated the role and importance of custom in settling wages. Putting the centre of gravity of his study in the second half of the nineteenth century, he did not need to concern himself much with non-monetary entitlements'[60] But in making this case, Schwarz highlighted the role of in-kind subsistence from land and associated rights, that which apply to urban environments. Whilst this conclusion unified much of the previous work on money and non-money reward to labour, it is not borne out by the records of London employers paying day rates in the eighteenth century. Evidence from the building trades is that perquisite was valued in monetary terms and closely guarded by clients and contractors.[61] Evidence from the courts

---

[59] Schwarz, 'Custom', 169, citing Hann, 'Kinship and Exchange'.
[60] Schwarz, 'Custom', 175.
[61] Stephenson, *Contracts and Pay*.

suggests that non-monetary wages substituted no wages, at least for unskilled workers where tasks paid for in kind and sustenance patched over periods waiting to join waged teams. Without further research beyond construction and services we cannot understand what customs governed the non-monetary conditions and pay for work in London in the eighteenth century, the evidence we do have does not support much in the way of custom.

IV

In the twenty-first century as real wages for unskilled workers have fallen in G7 countries since 1994, many have lost faith in the ability of the 'market' rules that Hobsbawm heralded from the mid-nineteenth century to set a fair wage.[62] This essay has sought to use new research on working patterns and hiring records for eighteenth-century London to reconsider ideas about the role of custom wages in the preindustrial economy. What fresh analysis of actual working records has shown is that while there is strong evidence that custom or other social and cultural factors were at work in setting wage rates which stayed almost absolutely rigid over decades, workers did not benefit from stability, or benefits of rights in a 'moral economy', implied by earlier 'custom, wage and workload' literature.

The available records of early modern urban unskilled work in London, at its persistent hiring institutions 1700–1800, present few characteristics of 'custom' other than a rigid wage, but many characteristics of precarity, uncertainty and risk which also are held to distinguish today's unskilled labour market: the commonly found weak-tie (or zero hours) labour contracts where workers were available for employers but not employed; a profound uncertainty of work; a lack of nominal or real wage growth; lastly, a rising inequality and a sharp division between those with and without capital.

That a fair wage could result from the market's 'rules of the game' was both expected and anticipated when Hobsbawm wrote in the 1960s, even if the narrative of the progression to that fair wage since the mid-nineteenth century had not been straightforward or without pain. The 'rules of the game' assumed a progression of modernity in labour markets: a progression of measure of time and effort, and progressive firms and formal institutions. Subsequent developments have overturned these assumptions. The game that Hobsbawm described, which brought large employers, time measures, scientific management, unionization, and the idea of fairness as tied to marginal product revenue was, in historical perspective a short one, perhaps a century from the opening at the Great Reform in 1867 to the mid-1980s. But if what went before industrialization has been assumed to be that of more benign welfare associations, new quantitative analysis of archival records disagrees.

A low and uncertain number of days worked even at stable and persistent institutions suggests a much more precarious labour market than has been taken into account before now. When these working patterns are taken into account likely real and

---

[62] David G. Blanchflower, *Not Working* (Princeton: Princeton University Press, 2019).

nominal income for labour appear even lower than some previously pessimistic estimates. That many workers traded on their own account or had varied sources of income is not under dispute. But in the past these alternative sources of income or entitlements have been assumed to have increased the welfare of wage workers. The new evidence suggests we might also cast the cost of transacting in the market as an aspect of precarity for eighteenth-century workers, and that entitlements did not improve welfare for urban unskilled workers.

More work needs to be done on eighteenth-century records from labour markets, particularly to understand the nominal wage rigidity, which puzzles and astounds modern economists. Another important avenue ahead is to examine the increase in the value of security of tenure in work, by examining the wages and benefits offered in annual or longer-term contracts to see if there was an increasing premium for tenure or a long-term employment relationship. We need much better understanding of the relationship of working days and hours and hiring to output, investment and labour demand, particularly since output volatility has returned with such a vengeance in our new pandemic age. Further, there is significant scope to understand more about the relative power of employers and workers.[63]

Secure jobs and payment or value for workers time are the most basic units of analysis of today's employment in such a fundamental way that we tend to assume they were always intrinsic to labour markets. As they show signs of declining prevalence today as the characteristics of the 'gig' economy become more prevalent and more widely discussed, particularly in unskilled markets, we view precarity as a twenty-first century or late-stage capitalism problem.[64] Archival research demonstrates clearly that secure jobs and payment for time are not universal labour standards that have recently fallen away. Both were mostly absent in London's market for labour in the preindustrial period.

---

[63] Joanna Innes, 'Regulating Wages in Eighteenth and Early Nineteenth-Century England: Arguments in Context', in *Regulating the British Economy 1660-1850*, ed. Perry Gauci (Oxford: Oxford University Press, 2016), 195–215.
[64] Lawrence F. Katz and Alan B. Krueger, 'The Rise and Nature of Alternative Work Arrangements in the United States, 1995–2015', *ILR Review*, 72, no. 2 (2015): 382–416.

5

Regulating Wage, Realizing Rights: Domestic Workers in India

Samita Sen

On 12 July 2017 in Mahagun Moderne, a plush housing estate outside New Delhi, a domestic worker named Zohra Bibi was accused by her employer Mitul Sethi of stealing money. Zohra alleged that she had not been paid her salary; and had been detained in her employer's house. The next morning, led by her husband, hundreds of workers gathered from nearby areas, and forced their way into the complex, armed with rocks and iron rods, to break into her employer's flat. In retaliation, local authorities razed the neighbourhood shanties of the poor; thousands of families in the area locked out their maids. The case was widely discussed in the media and in scholarly and activist circles. What was remarkable was not the nature of the dispute, which was (and is) common, but that it instigated a riot. The fury of the poor and the attack on the housing estate marked for many commentators a signal change in the mistress–maid relationship and a challenge to the exercise of magisterial power wielded by rich employers.[1] In one news story, Mangaldas quotes Manjula, a domestic worker, saying, 'We have no minimum wage, no maximum working hours, no job security, no legal support. If they want to throw us out, they can, any time. If they pay us late or don't pay us at all, it's their choice. And on top of it all, if anything is missing or anything goes wrong, we are the easiest to blame. But what can we do? Nothing.'[2]

Manjula summed up in her short speech the informal employment relationship in domestic work in India. Among the slew of issues she mentioned, the quantum and mode of wage payment has been particularly troublesome and a matter of public controversy in recent years. For instance, Devyani Khobragade, then Indian Deputy Consul General in New York City, was arrested on 12 December 2013 on charges that

---

[1] Maya John, 'Private power, public apathy: labour laws for domestic workers', The Hindu, 7 August 2017, https://www.thehindu.com/opinion/op-ed/private-power-public-apathy-labour-laws-for-domestic-workers/article19439992.ece (accessed 6 February 2021).
[2] Leeza Mangaldas, 'A Conflict Between A Housemaid And Her Employers Exposes India's Dark Side' 28 July 2017. https://www.forbes.com/sites/leezamangaldas/2017/07/28/a-conflict-between-a-housemaid-and-her-employers-exposes-indias-dark-side/?sh=16dde41038ee (accessed 12 January 2021).

included not paying her maid, Sangeeta Richards, the minimum wage.[3] Similar cases were reported about high-profile Indian employers in European countries. These reports underlined the absence of a statutory minimum wage for domestic workers in India and a wide variance in customary combinations of cash and kind. In 2020, during 'lockdown', there were reports from across the country that a significant proportion of employers did not pay their domestic workers, who were not able to come to work. However compelling the cause of non-attendance, in this sector, no work means no pay. The contracts prevailing in domestic service are both informal and asymmetrical.

In India, informal workers are more than 95 per cent of the total workforce. Thus, 'formal' workers comprise a small enclave; informality characterizes a wide range and diversity of occupations. There is no consensus on how these occupations may be classified, but in recent years, the emphasis has been on precarity and the 'wageless'.[4] Such characterizations further complicate our categories, since domestic workers, at an extreme end of the informality spectrum, making a precarious living, are nevertheless 'waged'. Indeed, the regularity of a monthly wage and ease of entry attract poor women to this occupation, even though the rates of wage are low, and workers exercise limited control over working conditions.

One element of extreme informality is the startling discrepancy in available statistics. According to the NSSO (2009–10), there are 2.52 million workers engaged in this occupation; 75 per cent domestic workers are urban; a large majority are women. Some NGO sources estimate 7 million. National Platform of Domestic Workers quotes a much larger figure of 50 million. In one estimate, 92 per cent domestic workers are women, girls and children. In one survey of twelve cities, 78 per cent of domestic workers were found to be women.[5] According to the International Labour Organisation (ILO), Indian homes have witnessed a 120 per cent increase in domestic workers in the decade after liberalization, from 740,000 in 1991 to 1,660,000 in 2001. ILO estimates over 50 million domestic workers in India at present, most of whom are women.[6]

In India (and internationally), the domestic work sector is highly diverse: conditions of employment range from illegal exploitation of children in slave-like conditions to multiple job-sharing arrangements and semi-formal agency-mediated employment.[7]

---

[3] https://www.theguardian.com/world/2014/jan/10/devyani-khobragade-to-leave-us-under-diplomatic-immunity (accessed 7 November 2021). The incident was widely reported and now features in Wikipedia.

[4] Michael Denning, 'Wageless Life', *New Left Review*, 66, November–December (2010): 79–97.

[5] National Commission for Enterprises in the Unorganised Sector, Report on Conditions of Work and Promotion of Livelihoods in the Unorganised Sector, Government of India, August 2007, 86.

[6] International Labour Organisation, India Labour Market Update, Country Office for India. https://www.ilo.org/wcmsp5/groups/public/---asia/---ro-bangkok/---sro new_delhi/documents/publication/wcms_568701.pdf (accessed 10 September 2019). Also see ILO Global Estimates on International Migrant Workers, 2018, https://www.ilo.org/wcmsp5/groups/public/---dgreports/---dcomm/---publ/documents/publication/wcms_652001.pdf (accessed 5 September 2019). For a detailed analysis of some of these numbers, see Introduction in Neetha N. (ed.) *Working in Others' Homes. The Specificities and Challenges of Paid Domestic Work* (New Delhi: Tulika Books, 2019).

[7] In 2006, employment of children under the age of 14 years as domestic workers was prohibited in India. For accounts of these two extremes, see Deepita Chakravarty and Ishita Chakravarty, *Women, Labour and the Economy in India: From migrant manservants to uprooted girl children maids* (Oxon and New York: Routledge, 2016); Shalini Grover, 'English-speaking and Educated Female Domestic Workers in Contemporary India: New Managerial Roles, Social Mobility and Persistent Inequality', *Journal of South Asian Development*, 13, no. 2, (2018): 186–209.

Until very recently, domestic service was wholly outside the ambit of state regulation. There was the possibility of a national law in 2014, a policy framework in 2017 and again in 2019, but successive governments have avoided making any commitment to a national law or even a policy. A large majority of domestic workers remain outside the purview of labour laws.[8] Moreover, contracts are verbal; entry and exit into jobs are not governed by any rules. Usually, these informalities benefit employers; technically, workers too may leave jobs without notice, which they sometimes do. There are, however, no provisions for leave or unemployment benefit. Some of these are characteristics shared across the informal sector. As the Periodic Labour Survey Report of 2017–18 suggests, among informal workers, more than 70 per cent did not have a contract, about 55 per cent were not eligible for paid leave and 50 per cent did not have social security benefits.[9]

In the domestic work sector, however, the principle of a contractual relationship is itself in contest.[10] Do we regard those providing personal services in the private space of the home as servants or as workers?[11] In the only historical monograph on the subject, Swapna Banerjee shows that the employment of domestic servants in colonial Bengal became part of the construction and articulation of a new middle-class identity.[12] Raka Ray and Seemin Qayum argue that these connections linger, and domestic servitude is integral to Indian modernity. Thus, domestic work is not only work, but also an institution.[13] As a result, the terminology of 'care work', used so pervasively in developed countries now, has so far had uneven application in the Indian context.

---

[8] Neetha N. and Rajni Palriwala, 'The Absence of State Law: Domestic Workers in India', *Canadian Journal of Women and the Law*, 23, no.1 (2011): 97–119.

[9] Ravi Srivastava, 'Understanding Circular Migration in India: Its Nature and Dimensions, the Crisis under Lockdown and the Response of the State', WP 04/2020, Centre for Employment Studies Working Paper Series, 2020. http://www.ihdindia.org/working-papers/2020/IHD-CES_WP_04_2020.pdf (downloaded 2 November 2020).

[10] In a survey of employers in four countries – India, Italy, Sweden and Thailand – it was found that 48 per cent did not consider contract necessary for domestic workers, 70 per cent did not wish them to join trade unions, 52 per cent did not approve of minimum wage and 45 per cent did not favour fixed working hours. Bridget Anderson and Julia O'Connell Davidson, 'Is trafficking in human beings demand driven? A multi-country Pilot Study', IOM Migration Research Series, 15, (Geneva: IOM), 2003, 33. https://publications.iom.int/system/files/pdf/mrs_15_2003.pdf accessed 13.11.2020.

[11] International Labour Organisation, 'Persisting Servitude and Gradual Shifts Towards Recognition and Dignity of Labour: A Study of Employers of Domestic Workers in Delhi and Mumbai', 2017, https://www.ilo.org/wcmsp5/groups/public/---asia/---ro-bangkok/---sro-new_delhi/documents/publication/wcms_622812.pdf (accessed 13 November 2020); Pankhuri Tandon, 'Domestic Workers: How to Give Them Their Due', CCS Working Paper No. 278 Summer Research Internship Programme, Centre for Civil Society, 2012, http://ccs.in/internship_papers/2012/278_domestic-workers_pankhuri-tandon.pdf (accessed on 10 August 2014); Bridget Anderson, 'Just another Job? The Commodification of Domestic Labour, in *Global Woman, Nannies, Maids and Sex Workers in the New Economy*, eds. Ehrenreich, B. and Hochschild, A. (London: Granta books, 2002), 104–15. http://isites.harvard.edu/fs/docs/icb.topic1001965.files/Week per cent209 per cent20Readings/Just per cent20Another per cent20Job_104-114_rev.pdf (accessed on 26 October 2014).

[12] Swapna Banerjee, *Men, Women and Domestics: Articulating Middle-Class Identity in Colonial Bengal* (New Delhi: Oxford University Press, 2004).

[13] Raka Ray and Seemin Qayum, *Cultures of Servitude: Modernity, Domesticity, and Class in India* (Stanford: Stanford University Press, 2009).

Given the paucity of research on domestic work in India, we have no clear picture of how the occupation developed in the last two centuries. Prior to British colonial occupation, domestic work was not a distinctive occupational category or a clear-cut social identity. In common with many societies, 'servants' were not necessarily domestic and could refer to grand men within political or religious hierarchies.[14] In the early colonial period, there was continuity in practices of slavery and servitude but the wage-work sector grew apace, particularly in the burgeoning urban centres. The British described Indian slavery as domestic and benign, creating conditions for its continuation in many sectors of the economy. In the case of women and children, familiality, domesticity and slavery were often folded into each other.[15] In the wage economy of domestic work, however, adult men predominated. There was, moreover, a pattern of single men migrating to cities for domestic service, leaving behind families in the countryside. These practices helped cheapen waged domestic labour, individual wages excluding costs of social reproduction. Nevertheless, employers, especially European employers, found the price of labour in a range of domestic and personal services, especially among carriers, much higher than they were willing to pay. They also found it difficult to exercise control over such workers or to enforce contractual obligations. They were particularly anxious about the advance system. They could not obtain workers for some jobs without paying advances but could not prevent them from running away without completing stipulated terms or tasks.

The East India Company state first introduced regulation for domestic 'servants' to protect European employers. There were attempts to limit wage competition among employers, negotiate the bazaar economy, as well as introduce mechanisms of surveillance, with provisions taken piecemeal from the English Masters and Servants law.[16] These measures took a draconian form in section 7, Regulation VII of 1819, which were later repealed by the Indian Penal Code in 1860. There were lengthy discussions about re-introducing regulatory restrictions on domestic servants in the latter decades of the nineteenth century, but no further legislation was undertaken.[17] In 1858, British Indian government enacted the Workmen's Breach of Contract Act, in part to address the advance system, which came to be used in a wide range of occupations (including Assam tea plantations, for which it is best known).[18] Despite

---

[14] Nitin Sinha and Nitin Varma, *Servants' Pasts: Late-Eighteenth to Twentieth-Century South Asia*, vol 1 (Hyderabad: Orient Blackswan, 2019).

[15] Samita Sen, 'Slavery and a History of Domestic Work' in Sinha and Varma, *Servants' Pasts*. Also see 'Slaves, Servants and Concubines: Domestic Workers in Nineteenth-Century Bengal' in Arun Bandopadhyay and Sanjukta Dasgupta (eds), *In Quest of the Historian's Craft: Essays in Honour of Professor B.B. Chaudhuri* (New Delhi: Manohar Publications, 2018).

[16] Nitin Sinha, 'Who Is (Not) a Servant, Anyway? Domestic servants and service in early colonial India', *Modern Asian Studies*, 55, no. 1 (2021): 152–206; 'Genealogies of "Verification": Policing the Master–Servant Relationship in Colonial and Postcolonial India', *International Review of Social History*, 67, no. 1 (2022): 9–41.

[17] Samita Sen, 'Slavery, Servitude and Wage Work: Domestic Work in Bengal', School of Women's Studies (Jadavpur University)-Rosa Luxemburg Stiftung Occasional Paper Series, 1, 2015.

[18] Michael Anderson, 'India, 1858-1930: The Illusion of Free Labour' in Douglas Hay and Paul Craven (eds), *Masters, Servants and Magistrates in Britain and the Empire, 1562-1955* (Chapel Hill and London: University of North Carolina Press, 2004).

repeated demands, however, these measures were not extended to domestic servants. The disinclination of the state to legislate or in any other way interfere with 'domestic' arrangements of the elite continued into the twentieth century and after independence. Domestic workers began to organize in unions and demand legislation from the 1950s. All India Domestic Workers' Union was established in 1953; by 1987, there were 24 domestic workers' unions.[19] These were predominantly men's unions led by men domestic workers. It is only in the new millennium that there has been a feminization of domestic workers' unions.[20]

An overall process of feminization has been the dominant trend in the occupation in the past four decades. More women began to be counted in domestic work jobs from the 1930s; they outstripped men by the 1970s; and their proportion rose steeply between 1983 and 1999.[21] While progress on labour regulation has been slow, women domestic workers have come under the purview of three landmark laws in the new millennium. In 2008, they were included in the Unorganised Workers' Social Security Act in recognition of their social vulnerability. The two other laws to include them were both women-specific legislations but they pulled in opposite directions. Protection of Women from Domestic Violence Act, 2005, included paid women workers, who were in a 'domestic' relationship. By contrast, their inclusion in the Sexual Harassment of Women at Workplace (Prevention, Prohibition and Redressal) Act, 2013, meant recognition as workers, designating the middle-class home as a workplace. There was deep uneasiness in many quarters about such a challenge to class authority, especially in the Ministry of Women and Child, but these were overborne. Moreover, the gender focus of successive legislation has drawn attention to the links between paid and unpaid work, which has helped to underline how workers in the sector suffer devaluation by association with domesticity.[22] The steady increase in women's paid domestic work employment signals a convergence between increased demand from middle-class urban households and increasing supply of cheap migrant workers.[23]

---

[19] For the early post-colonial history of unionization and demand for state intervention, see Nicola Armacost, 'Domestic Workers in India: A Case for Legislative Action', *Journal of the Indian Law Institute*, 36 no. 1 (1994): 53–63.

[20] Rina Agarwala and Shiny Saha, 'The Employment Relationship and Movement Strategies among Domestic Workers in India', *Critical Sociology*, 44, no. 7–8 (2018): 1207–23.

[21] Scholars have charted trends in different periods. See, for instance, Sonal Sharma, 'Of Rasoi ka Kaam/Bathroom ka Kaam Perspectives of Women Domestic Workers,' *Economic and Political Weekly*, 51, no. 7 (2016): 52–61; J. Devika, P.R. Nisha and A.K Rajasree, '"A Tactful Union": Domestic Workers' Unionism, Politics and Citizenship in Kerala, India', *Indian Journal of Gender Studies*, 18, no. 2 (2011) : 185–215; Banerjee, *Men, Women and Domestics*; and Uma Kothari, 'Women's Paid Domestic Work and Rural Transformation: A Study in South Gujarat', *Economic and Political Weekly*, 32, no. 17 (1997), WS5–WS12.

[22] Samita Sen and Nilanjana Sengupta, *Domestic Days: Women, Work and Politics in Contemporary Kolkata* (New Delhi: Oxford University Press, 2016). In April–May 2020, in the run up to the polls, in the states of Tamil Nadu and West Bengal, there were electoral promises of a fixed monthly payment to housewives. In West Bengal, this has been actualized in 2021 as a state government scheme named '*Lakshmir Bhandar*'.

[23] Sharma, 'Of Rasoi ka Kaam/Bathroom ka Kaam'; Kamala Sankaran, "Domestic Work, Unpaid Work and Wage Rates"', *Economic and Political Weekly*, 48, no. 43 (2013): 85–89; Amitava Kundu and Padma Mohanan, 'Employment and Inequality Outcomes in India', OECD paper, 2009, https://www.oecd.org/employment/emp/42546020.pdf (accessed 20 March 2021).

Zohra Bibi, the domestic worker in the eye of the storm in New Delhi in 2017, with whose story this chapter began, is a Bengali. In India, the eastern region – West Bengal, Jharkhand and, increasingly, Assam – are known as source areas. In major cities, such as Delhi, Mumbai and Bengaluru, a large number of domestic workers are migrants from West Bengal. There is also intra-state migration, poor rural women from various districts travelling to Kolkata, the capital city of the state of West Bengal, for domestic work employment. One recent estimate suggests that 23 per cent of women workers in West Bengal are in domestic service.[24] This chapter focuses on West Bengal, drawing comparisons with other regions of India. It is based on two qualitative surveys, both conducted in the region of Kolkata: the first was conducted in 2006–07 and the second in 2013–15. In the first survey, there were 216 interviews in two rounds from two squatter colonies in South Kolkata. In the second project, we interviewed 118 domestic workers across the city and its suburbs. Both were qualitative studies, using semi-structured interviews. Of the 334 interviews, only 26 were of residential workers, all other workers lived in their own households. In the second project, we interviewed 32 employers from different localities, religions, castes, ages, and varying family income. Both workers and employers were asked specifically about their views about legislation and unionization. In addition, we held three focus group discussions in three localities with 80 participants in total and three workshops with activists, workers and employers, each with about 60 participants.[25]

In recent years, one major demand of the domestic workers' movement in India has been for the application of a statutory minimum wage. The Minimum Wages Act of India 1948 provides for 'schedules' of occupations to be maintained both by central and state governments. By a new law in 2019, not yet come into effect, the central schedule has incorporated domestic workers. Meanwhile, state governments began to include domestic workers in their schedules from 2004. This chapter explores demand for, progress on and problems thrown up in the process of extending minimum wage regulation to the domestic work sector. It will discuss wider issues of regulation in the informal sector and problems of definitions of domestic work in the first section. The second section will address modalities of wage fixation, criteria of calculation, institutional mechanisms of wage determination and the relationship between statutory minimum wages and prevailing market rates. In most discussions about minimum wage regulation, a key counterpoint is the trade union: it plays a role in pressuring governments to initiate the process; it is the vehicle through which workers can influence the rates; and it is the chief guarantee of implementation. In all these respects, experiences in the domestic worker sector have been mixed. Despite great strides in recent years, domestic workers' unionization remains patchy and mostly

---

[24] Chakravarty and Chakravarty, *Women, Labour and the Economy in India*.
[25] The first project was conducted with funds received from University Grants Commission, India. The findings have been published in Sen and Sengupta, *Domestic Days*. Some of the findings on wage was published in more detail in Nilanjana Sengupta and Samita Sen, 'Bargaining over Wages: Part-time Domestic Workers in Kolkata', *Economic and Political Weekly*, XLVIII, 43, 26 October 2013. The second project was undertaken in collaboration with Rosa Luxemburg Stiftung, Berlin, 2013–15, coordinated by Nandita Dhawan and Ranjita Biswas for part of the time. I thank them and for their assistance, Srabasti Majumdar, Anindita Ghosh and Somdutta Mukherjee.

outside the ambit of mainstream 'central'[26] trade unions. The third section discusses the difficulties, in such a context, of implementing regulations and realizing basic rights. As Manjula says, in the absence of formal mechanisms, they can do 'nothing' to protect themselves. The Zohra Bibi incident indicates, however, that workers are developing new confrontational strategies. The fourth section shows that workers, with or without support from unions and collectives, are developing their own informal, sometimes combative, strategies of wage negotiation. In response, employers too are devising new discourses and strategies to protect their interests and preserve their control.

Regulating domestic work and the statutory minimum wage

Informal occupations were initially defined by their exclusion from state regulation and were commonly clubbed together as the 'unorganized sector' in India. Broadly speaking, the unregulated occupations are also those not organized in trade unions. In the past decades, however, there have been many shifts and changes in this simple dichotomy. There have been initiatives for both regulation and organization and collective bargaining, and the relationship between these two processes have been many and varied. Analysts have noted that, given the complexity of employment relationships, informal workers' movements tend to appeal directly to the state for security and rights.[27] Domestic workers have not been an exception to this trend.[28] There has been, however, a long and inconclusive debate about how to proceed with state regulation. One school believes that the best way forward is to bring the sector under existing laws; while another group, the majority in the domestic workers' movement, are in favour of new sector-specific legislation, which will cover all aspects of employment, working conditions, and social security. Government has oscillated between these two strategies and some halting developments have been made on both fronts.

These debates reflect wider discussions regarding regulation for the informal sector. Three new processes, including the two mentioned above, which fall short of formalization, but indicate movement in that direction, have been noted by scholars. Kundu and Mohanan have used the term 'formal informalization' to signal decline in casual employment and an increase in regular workers. The greater availability of regular employment, they argue, indicates some amount of formalization of informal activities, a development in some rapidly growing sectors in urban economies, including small-scale manufacturing, trade, commerce, entertainment activities, and paid domestic work.[29] Ritajyoti Bandyopadhyay deploys the term 'un-informalization'

---

[26] Local, firm-level or industry-level trade unions are affiliated to larger federations, which are all affiliated to political parties. The largest federations in the country represent labour at the national and international level and are known as Central Trade Union Organisations (CTU or CTUO). Unionization outside this mainstream also has a long history and has gathered force in the last three decades. In 2002, the New Trade Union Initiative (NTUI) was established, which affiliates many of these so-called 'independent' unions. They are also called labour-NGOs.

[27] Rina Agarwala, *Informal Labor, Formal Politics, and Dignified Discontent in India* (Cambridge: Cambridge University Press, 2014).

[28] Agarwala and Saha, 'The Employment Relationship and Movement Strategies'.

[29] Kundu and Mohanan, 'Employment and Inequality Outcomes in India'.

to describe sector-specific legislation in informal trades. There has been such legislation in *beedi* (indigenous cigarette) and construction industry as well as, more recently, in vending. Bandyopadhyay, observing organization and collective bargaining and regulation in vending, seeks to distinguish these new regulatory processes from the very different formalization undertaken for large-scale industry in late colonial and early independent India.[30] It has been argued that such formalization is mutually beneficial, facilitating governance as well as providing workers with some measure of legal and social protection. Martha Chen makes the point that informal workers can be formalized gradually by bringing them under existing laws, with better contracts, benefits, social security and unionization.[31]

After re-election in 2019, the new BJP-led National Democratic Alliance government has moved ahead with this last strategy – expanding the net of labour regulation to informal workers – but has coupled this, controversially, with a dilution of workers' rights in the formal sector. To consolidate 29 central laws, the Ministry of Labour and Employment introduced four Bills with Codes for Wages, Industrial Relations, Social Security, and Occupational Safety, Health and Working Conditions. The Code on Wages was passed by the Parliament in 2019, but the other three were passed on 22 September 2020, in the middle of the pandemic. The ostensible aim is to simplify labour regulation, a key recommendation of the Second National Commission on Labour in 2002. According to the government, there are over 100 state and 40 more central laws affecting labour, which need rationalization. The Code for Wages (2019) allows for a National Floor Level Minimum Wage, which will apply to all the states and will include domestic workers. In the interim, a draft policy proposes the inclusion of domestic workers under other existing labour laws. Recently, however, the Government of India has postponed the implementation of the new labour codes, since many states are yet to finalize the relevant rules.

Inclusion of domestic workers in the minimum wage schedule has been a long-standing demand. It was recommended by the National Commission on Self-Employed Women and Women in the Informal Sector (Shram Shakti) 1989 and the Second National Commission on Labour 2002. Activists regard this as a symbolic step towards formalization, granting domestic workers visibility and recognition as *workers*. Some states – Karnataka (2004), Andhra Pradesh (2007), Bihar (2007), Rajasthan (2008), Jharkhand (2010), Kerala (2010), Odisha (2012) – have already included domestic workers in their minimum wage schedules. Two other states have done so immediately after the 2019 announcement. For domestic workers, the wage code, the proposed policy, registration, social security and rudimentary unionization have initiated a process, highly limited though it is, of formalization.

---

[30] Ritajyoti Bandyopadhyay, 'The Street Vendors Act and Pedestrianism in India: A Reading of the Archival Politics of the Calcutta Hawker Sangram Committee' in Kristina Graaff and Noa Ha (eds), *Street Vending in the Neoliberal City: A Global Perspective on the Practices* (New York and Oxford: Berghahn, 2015).

[31] Martha Alter Chen, 'Rethinking the Informal Economy: Linkages with the Formal Economy and the Formal Regulatory Environment', DESA Working Paper No. 46 ST/ESA/2007/DWP/46, July, 2007, https://www.un.org/esa/desa/papers/2007/wp46_2007.pdf (accessed 20 March 2021).

For the domestic workers' movement, however, the minimum wage campaign has proved a disappointing success. It took more than half a century after the passing of the Minimum Wage Act of 1948 for it to be extended to domestic workers, but with the central government initiative for the National Floor Level Minimum Wage and with nearly one-third of 37 states and union territories including domestic workers in their minimum wage schedules, there would seem to be cause for celebration. This apparent achievement, however, has yielded little by way of real gains, partly because of the complexities of definitions and calculations.

In the Indian context, the notion of a minimum wages has vacillated between that of a fair wage and a living wage, one referring to the value of the work and the other to the needs of the worker. The Minimum Wage Act of 1948 was passed in relation to the report of the Fair Wages Committee and carries some of that resonance.[32] There have been examples of the courts striking down minimum wages notifications on the grounds that the law did not 'intend' to cover all groups of workers; there have also been court decisions that minimum wage should cover medicines and education.[33] Thus, minimum wage is associated with multiple objectives: as an anti-poverty measure; to ensure social security; or to address inequality. This is in a context where, according to the government's 2004–05 notifications, 42 per cent of wage earners do not receive the minimum wage.[34] Historically, the minimum wage, despite all its rhetorical functions, has had poor coverage.

Most state governments have taken the full-time worker as the model in minimum wage determination, thus continuing exclusionary strategies. Uniquely, in domestic service, there are two kinds of full-time workers. The first group work for 8–12 hours a day but they go to their own homes at the end of the workday. The second category are residential workers, usually on duty 24 hours. They have designated periods of rest, but these can be and are disrupted at the employers' convenience. At present, though this is difficult to support with numbers, most big cities have seen proportionate decline in residential domestic workers and a steep rise in charring arrangements. The 'part-timers' work in several (up to even seven) households every day. There is a great deal of debate about the terminology for this category of workers. Some use the term 'live-out', which seems unnecessarily convoluted; 'part-time' is disputed because these women work longer than a usual workday. I have used the term 'day worker' for this category. The day workers have been the recent focus of attention – for research and activism. They engage much more in bargaining and negotiation; and seek to assert the contractual (rather than personal) element in the employment relationship. They retain flexibility for their own housework; as a result, there is considerable variation in the number of hours they work in a day; and many end up working more than the

---

[32] Ravi Ahuja, 'Beveridge Plan for India? Social Insurance and the Making of the "Formal Sector"', *International Review of Social History*, 64, no. 2 (2019): 207–48.
[33] Vasanthi Nimushakavi, 'Extending Legal Protection to Domestic Workers' in Neetha N. (ed.) *Working in Others' Homes. The Specificities and Challenges of Paid Domestic Work* (New Delhi: Tulika Books, 2019): 250–77.
[34] Report on Extending the coverage of Minimum Wage in India 2010. https://www.ilo.org/wcmsp5/groups/public/---ed_protect/---protrav/---travail/documents/publication/wcms_145336.pdf (accessed 20 August 2020).

8 hours in the day. Moreover, comparatively, charring is the more feminized segment of the workforce.[35] Given that the basket of tasks and time in each household is different, day workers pose a complex problem of wage calculation, which has not been addressed by most state governments.

The gender question is knottier than appears at first sight. Given large-scale feminization, official policy documents often equate domestic service with women. Most state-level regulations in India define domestic work to the exclusion of masculine jobs in the sector. This is in tension with international (especially ILO) definitions, which include, for instance, privately employed drivers and gardeners, who are usually men. Such exclusions narrow the range of tasks covered by minimum wage regulations. The state government initiatives emphasize the 3Cs, viz., cooking, cleaning and care; in the last category, moreover, some minimum wage schedules include childcare but not that of the sick or elderly, which is now an important segment in the market.

The result of exclusions inflicted by definitional choices of state governments is that minimum wage legislation focuses on women domestic workers as typical and 'womanly work' as the norm. First, they exclude the day workers, the largest segment of domestic workers facing complex issues of wage calculation. Second, the work is flattened and homogenized as unskilled. This imparts, argues Neetha, a 'social definition' to domestic work and workers.[36] Apart from these fundamental problems, there are two other debates – first, the determination of wage and, second, the problem of implementation.

Wage determination: diversity, flexibility, and custom

This section will address some of the debates around minimum wage determination, which can be sub-divided further into two separate contentions: the first pertains to the process of fixation and the second is about the actual level at which minimum wage is fixed. We will discuss the first in brief and the second in more detail.

For many activists, minimum wage is a political rather than economic demand. They are concerned less with whether minimum wage notification raises wages and more with its legal implication for their status as workers. In a profession where social subordination and the 'culture of servitude' have been the predominant tropes, the significance of a claim on a 'worker' identity should not be underestimated. Given this political aspect of the demand, there have been contestations about representation and consultation in the fixation process.

The Minimum Wages Act 1948 provides for two methods of fixation – direct notification by government or through a committee. The structure and constitution of the minimum wage committee follows an industrial relations model, with key

---

[35] Ray and Qayum, *Culture of Servitude*; and Sen and Sengupta, *Domestic Days*.
[36] Neetha N., 'Mirroring Devalued Housework? Minimum Wages for Domestic Work' in Neetha N. (ed.) *Working in Others' Homes. The Specificities and Challenges of Paid Domestic Work* (New Delhi: Tulika Books, 2019, 278–97), 281.

involvement of trade unions. These committees are difficult to transplant into the informal sector, where there are no clear-cut channels of representation. There are also Minimum Wage Advisory Boards, but they have contributed little to the process. In the case of domestic workers, even where unions have spearheaded the campaign for minimum wage, as in Karnataka and Andhra Pradesh, they have operated outside mainstream trade unionism. As a result, the committee mode of fixation has been problematic. State governments have responded to pressures from NGOs and civil society organizations, which have led to some recognition of collectivization in the sector,[37] but they have balked at the prospect of involving unrecognized and unregistered collectives/unions in minimum wage committees. On the whole, state governments have opted for direct notification rather than grasp the nettle of institutional representation.

For campaigners, however, the voice and recognition they gain through participation in a minimum wage committee is itself an objective. Unfortunately, the two objectives – getting a minimum wage and playing a role in setting it – have sometimes been at odds. Some states, such as West Bengal, have referred the matter to a committee, and the decision has been pending since 2012. On 10 December 2014, a meeting of trade unions passed a unanimous resolution to demand inclusion of domestic workers in the minimum wage schedule of the state.[38] Ramen Pandey, a leader of Indian National Trade Union Congress (affiliated to the Congress Party), the state's ILO representative in 2013, was fully aware of his responsibilities. As a member of the Minimum Wage Board, he promised, at a public meeting (as well as in the interview he gave us), to further this demand.[39] Moreover, trade unions have been willing to take informal inputs from activists in the domestic workers' movement. One aspect of the impasse has been the highly contradictory position adopted by the West Bengal state government. It has set its face against granting registration to domestic workers' unions but has confounded confusion by making two exceptions. One positive result of the exception has been that one of the two registered unions have been included, officially, in the minimum wage determination process. To no great avail though, since there has been no minimum wage notification so far.

Apart from the process of setting, the calculation of minimum wage has also been controversial. Nimushakavi and Neetha have analysed minimum wage level for domestic workers in five states (Karnataka, Andhra Pradesh, Bihar, Rajasthan and

---

[37] Rajesh Joseph, Roshni Lobo, Balmurli Natrajan, 'Between "Baksheesh" and "Bonus": Precarity, Class, and Collective Action among Domestic Workers in Bengaluru', *EPW*, 53, no. 45 (2018): 38–45; and K.P. Kannan, 'The welfare fund model of social security for informal sector workers: The Kerala experience', Working Paper No. 332 (2002), Centre for Development Studies, Thiruvananthapuram, https://opendocs.ids.ac.uk/opendocs/handle/20.500.12413/3044 (accessed 14 November 2021). Also see Agarwala and Saha, 'The Employment Relationship and Movement Strategies'; and Devika et al., '"A Tactful Union"'.

[38] Prabir Banerjee, Trade Union Co-ordination Centre, affiliated to All-India Forward Bloc, Interview (Kolkata, India), 13 February 2015. Their first union of domestic workers received registration in 2010 and is one of two registered unions in the state. This is the only central trade union in West Bengal to have played a significant role in unionization of domestic workers.

[39] Ramen Pandey, Interview (Kolkata, India), 19 September 2014.

Kerala) and have flagged several issues. First, activists and scholars have accused governments of fixing a minimum rate below the market rate. This has been possible, they argue, because domestic workers' representatives have not been consulted in the process of fixation; but also, it forestalls problems of implementation.[40]

Second, there has been much debate regarding whether to follow a time rate or a task rate in minimum wage determination. If the former, should the rate be per hour (which would help day workers with many jobs) or per day (which would be better for those working full-time in one household). In all these cases, the possibility of a monthly rate has not been considered. This is somewhat surprising because monthly wages are more common in the sector. Indeed, the stability of a monthly wage attracts poor urban women into the occupation.[41]

The impact of minimum wage legislation on real wages has been debated globally, mostly in the Global North and in the context of the formal sector. An emerging scholarship is beginning to explore its role in informal economies in the Global South. There have been a few studies on the impact of minimum wage laws on actual wages in domestic work in South Africa, which has pioneered legislation in this sector.[42] Gudibande and Jacob, in the only study of the impact of minimum wage regulation in domestic work in India (of the four states of Karnataka, Andhra Pradesh, Bihar and Rajasthan), have reached the following conclusions: first, that there was a significant positive impact on wages in the short run (implying that the minimum wage was set above the market rate); second, that this positive impact peters out in the long run (indicating weak monitoring and implementation).[43] These findings agree with the data we collected in West Bengal.

In West Bengal, at a meeting on minimum wage on 14 December 2013, attended by union representatives and the labour minister, it was decided to break down a monthly minimum wage of Rs. 5,000 (£50) to an hourly rate of Rs. 24 (£0.24) because the monthly figure looked too high and was likely to put off ordinary middle-class employers. It was pointed out that it would be helpful for day workers with multiple jobs to have an hourly rate.[44] The proposed rate was higher than those obtaining in at least in some parts of the market at the time. In two rounds of fieldwork in Kolkata (West Bengal) in 2006–07 and 2013–15, we found that wage rates had risen. The highest average hourly rates we had found in 2006–07 was Rs. 6 (£0.06) per hour, which had

---

[40] Nimusakhavi, 'Extending Legal Protection to Domestic Workers'; and Neetha, 'Mirroring Devalued Housework?'
[41] Sen and Sengupta, *Domestic Days*.
[42] H. Bhorat, R. Kanbur, and N. Mayet, 'The impact of sectoral minimum wage laws on employment, wages, and hours of work in South Africa', *IZA Journal of Labor & Development*, no. 2 (2013): 1–27; and T. Dinkelman and V. Ranchhod, 'Evidence on the impact of minimum wage laws in an informal sector: Domestic workers in South Africa', *Journal of Development Economics*, 99, no. 1 (2012): 27–45. For an up-to-date account of studies on impact of minimum wage regulation in the informal sector, see Rohan Ravindra Gudibande and Arun Jacob, 'Minimum wages for domestic workers: impact evaluation of the Indian experience', *World Development*, 130 (2020): 1–19.
[43] Gudibande and Jacob, 'Minimum wages for domestic workers'.
[44] The matter was exhaustively discussed at a workshop on 8 May 2015 at Jadavpur University, held as part of the research project. The meeting included the union representatives, who were negotiating the rates with the government.

risen to Rs. 14.5 (£0.145) per hour in 2013–15. The proposed rate of Rs. 24 was much higher than the wage rates we had found in some areas of the city, and also somewhat higher than in most states that had at that time notified minimum wages, though some states had marginally higher rates. It should be mentioned that in some states the notified rates are divided into a basic pay and allowances, making calculations opaque and comparisons difficult.

There are two more illuminating comparisons that can be made. First, wage rates fixed for domestic work were lower than other unskilled jobs, such as construction, and similar work in non-domestic contexts, such as cleaning in offices. This has led activists to argue that the process of rate-setting is not only arbitrary but also influenced by the low status accorded to domestic work and women workers. One function of state regulation of minimum wage is to raise women's wages, a function not fulfilled if the benchmark is set too low. If successful, regulation of minimum wage can serve as a step towards equitable (if not equal) pay and to build a bridge between the care economy and the wage economy.

Our findings show that there was a 75 to 100 per cent rise in wages across different tasks (cooking, cleaning and care)[45] and categories of workers (part-time and full-time) from 2006 to 2015. This data has to be read with caution for several reasons. First, rates were (and still are) lower in Kolkata than many other major cities of the country. In one trade union survey, it was found that the average wage rates in West Bengal was Rs. 12 per hour, less than half that in Jharkhand, a neighbouring state, at Rs. 25 per hour.[46] Second, there was a particularly low floor in our first survey, which brought

Table 5.1 Rise in average monthly wages of day domestic workers in Kolkata from 2006–07 to 2013–14.

Year	Money wage (Rs.)	Real wage (Rs.)
2006–07	843.27	674.61
2013–14	2810.00	1190.67

Source: Survey of 154 DW (Domestic Days 2016) for 2006–07; Current survey of 118 DW for 2013–14. Real wages calculated on the basis of Consumer Price Index for Industrial Workers (Year 2001=100). See index series in Government of India, Ministry of Labour and Employment, Annual Report, 2015–16, Chapter 17, 169. https://labour.gov.in/sites/default/files/Chapter%20-%2017.pdf (accessed 2 February 2023).

---

[45] There is a caste dimension to task-differentiation in domestic work. The pattern varies considerably according to regions of the country. In the Bengal case, there is a sharp division between cooking and cleaning. Historically, cooking was done by high castes and cleaning by low castes. At present, these divisions do not apply quite so rigidly. However, as a general rule, cooking fetches higher wages and scholars have argued that this follows from the history of caste differentiation. We have very little direct evidence on these issues. See Neetha, 'Mirroring Devalued Housework?', 284; Tanika Sarkar, 'Caste-ing servants in Colonial Kolkata' in Nitin Sinha and Nitin Verma (eds), *Servants' Pasts: Late-Eighteenth to Twentieth-Century South Asia*, Volume 2 (Hyderabad: Orient Blackswan, 2019); Sen and Sengupta, *Domestic Days*, 99–100, 155–57; and Parvati Raghuram, 'Caste and Gender in the Organisation of Paid Domestic Work in India', *Work, Employment and Society*, 15, no. 3 (2001), 607–17.
[46] Prabir Banerjee, Interview (Kolkata, India), 13 February 2015.

down the average; since the two groups in the two surveys are different, the trend captured in the following figures can only be considered broadly illustrative.

We found that the pattern in the average hourly wage was roughly in convergence with variation in monthly income. The lowest rate of wages was among residential workers but that may have been because some of them accepted lower rate of pay in lieu of permission to do part-time work in other households. The workers who entered such flexible arrangements earned more from additional jobs than from the chief residential job, which was supplemented with provision of food and accommodation. Our respondents said repeatedly that day work was more labour-intensive but more lucrative and their perception was borne out by our figures. Additionally, the day workers, who live in families with other earning members, might have earned less because they compromised on wages to work in proximity of their residence to enable them to juggle housework and paid work, another crucial element of flexibility that determines worker preference in the sector.[47]

A vast literature addresses the issue of low wages of women in the informal sector, especially in domestic work; and also emphasizes the variations of wages within the occupation.[48] Our research has shown that though there are no institutional mechanisms for the determination of wage rates, there are in fact strong local customs and conventions governing domestic workers' wages.[49] These typically follow a combination of time and task but there may be other criteria. These standards apply more consistently at the time of the initial contract; there appears to be much less standardization with respect to increments. In the areas we surveyed in 2006–07, there were two chief criteria: by number of tasks, usually Rs. 100 per task, or according to the number of members of employers' households, usually, again, Rs. 100 each.[50] The latter was more common in cooking jobs and the former in cleaning jobs.

There is considerable debate in the domestic work sector over time and task determination of wages, especially in the context of minimum wage setting. Our

---

[47] Sen and Sengupta, *Domestic Days*.
[48] See for instance: Sankaran, 'Domestic Work, Unpaid Work and Wage Rates,'; Martha Alter Chen, "The Informal Economy: Definitions, Theories and Policies", Women in Informal Employment: Globalising and Organising (WEIGO) Working Paper no 1 (2012); Chakravarty and Chakravarty, *Women, Labour and the Economy in India*; C. P. Chandrasekhar and Jayati Ghosh, 'Women Workers in Urban India', *Macroscan*, 6, February (2007); Arup Mitra, 'Women in the Urban Informal Sector: Perpetuation of Meagre Earnings', *Development and Change*, 36, no. 2 (2005): 291–316; U. Kalpagam, 'Globalisation, Liberalisation and Women Workers in the Informal Sector' in Alakh N. Sharma, Amitabh Kundu (eds), *Informal Sector in India: Perspectives and Policies* (New Delhi: Institute for Human Development, Institute of Applied Manpower Research, 2001), 310–30; and Jeemol Unni, 'Gender and Informality in the Labour Market in South Asia', *Economic and Political Weekly*, 36, no. 26 (2001): 2360–77.
[49] In our 2015 findings, we found this to be particularly true of gated estates. Such informal modes of wage determination have been found elsewhere in the country, such as in Mumbai and Delhi NCR. Shraddha Jain and Praveena Kodoth, 'Locality-specific Norms for Wages and Bargaining: "Part-time" Domestic orders in the National Capital Region' in Neetha N. (ed) *Working in Others' Homes. The Specificities and Challenges of Paid Domestic Work* (New Delhi: Tulika Books, 2019), 66–94; ILO, India Labour Market Update, Country Office for India, 2017, https://www.ilo.org/wcmsp5/groups/public/---asia/---ro-bangkok/---sro new_delhi/documents/publication/wcms_568701.pdf (accessed 10 September 2019).
[50] In the area where the survey was conducted the rates nearly doubled by 2018, but in contiguous more affluent areas, the rates have risen even more.

findings indicate that this tussle between time and task rates presumes a clearer boundary between these two criteria than prevails on the ground. In domestic work, wages are often determined by inflexible conventions prevailing in a locality, which constrain both workers and employers. These conventions are not always pegged to either hours or tasks. There are always both considerations involved: task-rates contain a component of time and time-rates include a calculation of output. When neither time nor output is clearly defined, employers take advantage of the resultant flexibility. Thus, as one interviewee, a 'part-time' domestic worker, CH, pointed out, some employers paid for a single shift but demanded the same quantum of cooking as is usual for two shifts. The amount to be cooked is never specified at the time of the negotiation: terms like 'very little cooking' are relative, imprecise and subject to interpretation. SH, another domestic worker we interviewed, resented the fact that her cooking job included errands like buying sweets. Similarly, cleaning jobs can be either fixed by tasks (usually a combination of washing dishes, washing clothes, sweeping and swabbing) or fixed by hours (including in addition fetching and carrying, dropping and picking up children, shopping for food and provisions, dusting, fetching water and helping in the kitchen) or any combination of tasks and hours. Even the content of tasks can vary considerably. The washing of dishes, for instance, may involve squatting on the floor and scrubbing with wood or coal ash, which is physically more demanding than cleaning non-stick pans in kitchen-sinks with nylon scrubs and washing-up liquid. The problem is compounded when issues like floor space, intensity of work, efficiency and speed are taken into account. One domestic worker interviewee, MM, said that while wages are calculated on the size of the area to be cleaned, sometimes by the number of rooms, the nature of the work (heavy/ light) is also taken into consideration. AS, another of our domestic worker interviewees, testified that rates are uniform across their jobs, though the quantum of time and task vary. Most workers in multiple job arrangements agreed with this view.[51]

The discussion in this section has underscored the following: first, institutional modalities of wage fixation, even in case of statutory minimum wages remain weak, even though the sector is characterized by strong local customs and conventions governing wages; despite the complexities of time and task, cash and kind, as well as the extremely flexible and heterogenous arrangements within the occupation, the variation in wages is less than might be expected; second, minimum wage rates already fixed are very low and lower than similar jobs in other sectors or alternative jobs, but there is a closer relationship between market rates and statutory minimum wages than usually argued; third, it could be argued that the low floor of determination met the requirement neither of 'fair wage' nor of 'living wage', neither of value nor of need.

Problems of implementation: unionization outside unionization

A major watershed in the domestic sector has been ILO Convention 189 of 2011, which India (with seven other countries) resisted at first (and has not yet signed). Soon

---

[51] Sen and Sengupta, *Domestic Days*.

after the convention, ILO began an action-research project in Hyderabad (Andhra Pradesh), which included the establishment of a trade union. This explains why Andhra Pradesh has taken a leading role among states in terms of regulatory interventions. The pressure from powerful trade unions makes demand for regulation, including that of minimum wage, more effective. However, matters get complicated when these unions are not, as the Andhra Pradesh State Domestic Workers Union (APSDWU) is not, affiliated to a Central Trade Union.

One major problem with the minimum wage infrastructure is the difficulty of implementation. In the case of factories and establishments, there is provision for inspection. In all state government regulations so far, the domestic worker sector has been exempted from inspection. State governments are hesitant about intrusion into the private realm of middle-class homes. Indeed, they have taken a step further and exempted employers from having to maintain records, which means that the onus of proving violation lies with the worker.

The inspiration for the campaign by the International Federation of Domestic Workers for Convention 189 was domestic work legislation in post-Apartheid South Africa. This was part of the state's new vision of race and class equality, resulting in the most serious effort anywhere in the world to modernize and professionalize domestic work, including a landmark national minimum wage, mandatory formal contracts of employment, extensive leave, formal registration, as well as access to unemployment insurance benefits. Shireen Ally has shown that, despite these pioneering initiatives, cultures of servitude have been resistant to change. The state, positioning itself as the representative and protector, demobilized domestic workers, weakened their unions and muted their voices. Ally describes domestic workers in contemporary South Africa as 'compromised mothers and dehumanized workers'.[52]

These issues resonate strongly in the Indian context. The bulk of workers fear regulation and have little expectation from collective politics. They fear that enforcement of minimum wages, bonus or weekly leave will lead to job loss;[53] and formalization will undermine their ability to negotiate with individual employers.[54] The minimum wage regulation is now nearly two-decades old in Karnataka. Studying its impact, researchers have shown that there has been little or no impact on employment. They admit, however, that this is because of weak implementation.[55] Will more effective formalization impact jobs? Will unionization destroy the accommodation and adjustments achieved with a good employer? Employers often pre-empt bargaining strategies, especially if they are dependent on their workers. Despite these doubts and hesitancy, however, unionization has progressed steadily, though somewhat haltingly.

It is generally agreed that the process of formalization and unionization go together. This is the underlying assumption in regulatory measures, such as minimum wage setting which rely heavily on trade unions to ensure implementation. In India, the twin

---

[52] Shireen Ally, *From Servants to Workers: South African Domestic Workers and the Democratic State* (Ithaca: Cornell University Press, 2009), 182.
[53] Joseph et al., 'Between "Baksheesh" and "Bonus"'.
[54] Sen and Sengupta, *Domestic Days*.
[55] Gudibande and Jacob, 'Minimum wages for domestic workers'.

processes of formalization and unionization have taken also a third dimension – that of masculinization.[56] As a result, women workers have been excluded from labour organization, as leaders as well as members, from above by the state and from below by the unions.[57] This has proved to be a difficult legacy for domestic workers and their struggle for unionization. While there have been rapid strides in unionization, it is a heterogeneous field with the presence of unions led by NGOs, CBOs, feminist collectives, faith-based organizations and radical left groups,[58] often disconnected from mainstream unionism. Many domestic workers' unions were begun not by trade unions or workers' organizations but by NGOs – and these are now being called labour-NGOs. One of the pioneering domestic workers union in India was started in 1980 in Pune by a women's group. Given the neglect of women and informal workers by CTUs, the impetus for creating collectives among domestic workers (and other women workers in the informal sector) has been from the so-called new social movements or women's movements. Much before the CTU initiative for a national platform, the National Domestic Workers' Movement was started by social workers in 1985.[59]

There are now domestic workers' unions in almost all states of the country. In states such as Maharashtra, Karnataka, Kerala and Rajasthan, they have been registered. In Karnataka, labour-NGOs have enhanced self-understanding of domestic workers, lobbied successfully with the state government, and negotiated with employers for leave and bonus.[60] In Kerala, the Self-Employed Women's Association (SEWA), a 'tactful' union, has made enormous gains, also acting as a certifying agency.[61] The Andhra Pradesh union (APSDWU) enabled Renuka Sayola to stand for Lok Sabha elections in 2014. Under the leadership of the Trade Union Coordination Committee (henceforth TUCC), there was an effort to consolidate these unions on a national platform, named National Progressive Domestic Workers' Federation. But in many states, these proliferating unions and/or labour-NGOs remain unregistered. As a result, unions are not a country-wide solution to problems of implementation; and the disconnect between domestic workers unions and CTUs is partly responsible for the nonenforcement of minimum wage notifications.

In West Bengal, which among the states has the largest workforce in this sector, in 2008, under the banner of All-India United Trade Union Centre's (affiliated to the Socialist Unity Centre of India) the Sara Bangla Griha Paricharika Samity (SBGPS) was launched. Soon after, there was the Paschim Banga Agragami Domestic Workers' Union (under the banner of the TUCC, and affiliated to the All-India Forward Bloc),

---

[56] Samita Sen, 'Gender and Class: Women in Indian Industry, 1890-1990', *Modern Asian Studies*, 42, no. 1 (2008): 75–116.
[57] Samita Sen, 'Gender and the Politics of Class: Women in Trade Unions in Bengal', *South Asia: Journal of South Asian Studies*, 44, no. 2 (2021): 362–79.
[58] Agarwala and Saha, 'The Employment Relationship and Movement Strategies'; Joseph et al., 'Between "Baksheesh" and "Bonus"'; Sen and Sengupta, *Domestic Days*; Devika et al., '"A Tactful Union"'.
[59] Lokesh, 'Making the Personal Political: The First Domestic Workers' Strike in Pune, Maharashtra' in Dirk Hoerder, Elise van Nederveen Meerkerk and Silke Neunsinger (eds), *Towards a Global History of Domestic and Caregiving Workers* (Leiden and Boston: Brill, 2015), 202–21; Sen and Sengupta, *Domestic Days*; Agarwala and Saha, 'The Employment Relationship and Movement Strategies'.
[60] Joseph et al., 'Between "Baksheesh" and "Bonus"'.
[61] Devika et al., '"A Tactful Union"'.

and the Sara Bangla Sangrami Paricharika Union [All-India Central Council of Trade Union, affiliated to the Communist Party of India (Marxist Leninist)]. Only one union, however, the Balurghat Agragami Paricharika Union (TUCC) was registered in 2010. Thus, there have been some presence of CTUs in the sector, even though these are comparatively small unions.

There have been labour-NGOs (alternatively designated 'non-political' unions) too in West Bengal. *Paschim Banga Grihaparicharika Samiti* (West Bengal Domestic Workers Association),[62] organized under the joint leadership of Action Aid, *Sramik Sahayata Kendra* (Workers' Aid Centre) and Society for People's Awareness, managed to acquire registration in 2018 in a reversal of the stated policy of the government. Other such aspiring unions, for example, *Durbar Disha Mahila Grihasramik Samanyaya Committee* (Coordinating Committee of Women Domestic Workers)[63], which began work earlier, have not yet been granted registration. Another organization called *Samadhan Dal* (Resolution Group) was started by an NGO called *Parichiti* (Identity), but they have not started a union. The domestic work issue is a challenge not only for working-class politics but also for feminist activism. While women's organizations have been the most active in organizing domestic workers, they are also faced with intractable problems. The class division between the mistress and the maid is one of the few examples of direct exploitation of women by women. Class differences are overlaid with inequalities of caste. These cannot be resolved within the framework of a common or shared exploitation within patriarchy but have to be addressed through the prism of multiple axes of gender, class and caste. Recognition of these complexities and a more sensitive intersectional politics has been a leap forward, unimaginable twenty years ago.

These positive developments notwithstanding, the role of trade unions has been highly ambivalent. Until 2014–15, most CTUs were apathetic about organization of domestic workers.[64] No doubt the large constituency of workers in this sector has been a persuasive argument for many CTUs in recent years. They remain, however, doubtful about whether domestic work is 'productive' work, qualifies as an industry or a trade and how to approach questions of wage setting and implementation of minimum wages in this sector. Neetha has argued that trade unions have been complicit in keeping domestic work categorized as homogeneously unskilled with a low floor rate.[65] It is ironical that while the domestic workers' movement, which has a clear understanding of the critical role trade unions play in negotiating labour laws, have approached, repeatedly, CTUs for affiliation, there has not been enthusiastic reciprocation. Notably, trade union leaders and state government's labour bureaucrats,

---

[62] The literal translation is a little complicated, since the word '*paricharika*' approximates maidservant rather than domestic worker and the reason for adopting this name is a little unclear.

[63] The translation of the name does not contain the words *Durbar Disha*, which means unstoppable horizon and are taken from its sister organization, a pioneering sex workers' collective in the city.

[64] Samita Sen, *Women and Labour in Late Colonial India. The Case of the Bengal Jute Industry* (Cambridge: Cambridge University Press, 1999); Leela Fernandes, *Producing Workers. The Politics of Gender, Class and Culture in the Calcutta Jute Mills* (Philadelphia: University of Pennsylvania Press, 1997).

[65] Neetha N., 'Mirroring Devalued Housework?'

who are responsible for these decisions, and for determining the relationship between the state and unions, are themselves employers of domestic workers. Both groups are cautious about meddling with domestic work arrangements, fearing a middle-class backlash. The Labour Minister of the Government of West Bengal, when we took a petition to him, asked rhetorically, 'Do you want unions to march with flags in middle-class homes?'[66] These attitudes explain the hesitation of successive governments to undertake any serious reform.

On the question of implementation, the other strategy – that of sector-specific legislation – has acquired especial importance. The example of South Africa, notwithstanding Ally's critique, is cited as an example. Similarly, in Brazil, implementation of minimum wage legislation was facilitated by measures such as mandatory registration, issuance of labour cards and basic labour rights.[67] In the Indian context, several attempts at national-level legislation on these lines have failed; some state governments, such as Kerala, Maharashtra and Tamil Nadu, have constituted Welfare Boards for domestic workers. These have provided for registration and, therefore, greater visibility of domestic workers in policy discourses. Such measures of coordinated formalization have been hesitant and at present restricted to small pockets in the country.

In this regulatory void, market-led institutionalization has evolved. There has been a slow spread of 'centres' (as they are called in West Bengal), which are in the main placement agencies. They do not take responsibility for welfare or skill-building. Their chief claim is that they vet the workers to ensure the security of the employer-household, but this is mostly quite cursory. Many workers we interviewed expressed reservations about 'centre'-mediated jobs on the grounds of its de-personalized nature. Though their spread has been slow, some workers said it was getting more difficult to find work without the mediation of the agencies because of employer preference. The agencies operate by eight or twelve-hour shifts; thus, even this rudimentary formality brings rigidity in work conditions. Those with onerous family responsibilities find it impossible to work for a set 'duty' of twelve hours. The loss of flexibility is a major drawback of such formalization.

The formality imparted by agencies, however, helps improve wage rates. Though the rates are higher, agencies cannot guarantee uninterrupted work. In the end, earnings may even out on an annual basis. Moreover, the agencies take a commission from the workers, which may be as high as Rs. 20–30 per day, so employers and workers often mutually agree to cut them out if the arrangement is to their satisfaction. This is often called 'direct'. The chief appeal of agency employment for workers is the element of formality they bring to jobs otherwise defined by erratic contract conditions. Workers feel more secure because there is a precise job definition, negotiated conditions including leave and other facilities. Most importantly, agencies take responsibility for collecting and paying wages, which is a major benefit for workers in highly asymmetric employment and social relationships.

---

[66] A meeting with the Labour Minister, Government of West Bengal, Kolkata, 2015.
[67] Louisa Acciari, 'Decolonising Labour, Reclaiming Subaltern Epistemologies: Brazilian Domestic Workers and the International Struggle for Labour Rights', *Contexto Internacional*, 41, no. 1 (2019), https://doi.org/10.1590/S0102-8529.2019410100003 (accessed 11 February 2021).

Collective conflict: protest, rights and agency

The informality of the domestic work contract and the state's hesitation to interfere with private middle-class households means that workers have little recourse against non-payment of wages or even extra-ordinary degrees of violence. It is only recently that the state and the police have begun to respond to complaints of gross violation of rights. In 2012, the Delhi police made history by arresting a doctor couple who had gone on holiday locking their thirteen-year-old girl domestic worker in their apartment. A year later, the death of Phulmani, a domestic worker aged about sixteen years, who was said to have fallen out of a window when watering a plant, triggered accusations against the Delhi police of trying to cover up a murder. There is public awareness of abuse of domestic workers, a slow shift away from the culture of servitude and a growing consciousness among workers of their rights in employment.

Despite some progress, incidents of abusive and violent behaviour by employers continue to be widespread. The non-payment of wages and/or allegations of theft are the most common forms of employer abuse. It is difficult to ascertain whether there is actual escalation in such incidents or whether the reportage has increased. The official figures have been highest in West Bengal, with 549 cases registered in 2012.[68] Thus, though domestic workers' unions address the state for many of their demands, they cannot avoid conflict with employers. Many unions trace their inception from a single instance of collective confrontation, usually of individual families, but sometimes of a group of employers. In Mumbai, for instance, the current trend of unionization is traced to the mid-1980s, when a young girl was arrested by the local police based on a complaint of theft. A few domestic workers decided not to work for any resident of the housing complex, which became a catalyst for workers' mobilization.[69]

It is relatively unusual for workers to confront employers – they are painfully aware of their vulnerability. They find it easier to leave their jobs even at the cost of foregoing their wages. But they do confront employers when they have some support. Even though domestic workers are dispersed as workers in private spaces of middle-class homes, they also form informal groups, taking on employers. There are always spaces of interaction. This is more apparent in case of workers in gated estates or commuting workers, who spend long hours together in trains. Our respondents have also spoken of neighbourhood spaces, such as streets, shops, markets, tenements, where they speak together. There are at times more than one domestic worker in a household. While, these relationships can sometimes be competitive and conflictual, there is also cooperation and mutuality. They take advantage of these social interactions to discuss the benefits, problems and complexities surrounding their work. They learn from each other and seek collective solutions, which help in the growth of solidarities. For instance as, AS, one of our domestic worker interviewees, who commutes by local train told us, they have their own group of fellow-travellers. When one of them was being fobbed off without payment, they went in a group to retrieve her salary.

---

[68] Daily News and Analysis, February 2014.
[69] Interviews with Sabal Singh, Kranti, and Sujata Ghotoskar, Forum Against Oppression of Women, 14–16 January 2014, Mumbai.

Translating these informal collectives to formal organization is not easy. *Parichiti* has undertaken this task. Shanti Purkayet of *Samadhan Dal* spoke of three cases of injustice, which transformed her into a leader. It began with her own dispute over wages and bonus. She had joined a household seven months before the annual festival of the state. Two days before the holidays began, she was made to clean the entire staircase of a two-storeyed house. This was not part of her contract, but she was unable to refuse. When the time came for payment, the employers gave her half the salary and no extra payment for the extra work. The employers argued that all the domestic workers had voluntarily done some extra work for the festival. 'But I was adamant,' she said. 'I demanded my bonus and salary.' The employers asked her to quit, because they were not ready to pay. She returned the half-salary they had paid her and walked to *Parichiti*'s office. She gathered some of her neighbours as well and they all went in a group to the employer's house. The employer threatened them with the police. When she found that the crowd was unwilling to back down, the mistress succumbed. 'When I was alone, she was not ready to give my money but had to comply in front of a huge gathering,' Shanti says. 'We are just asking for our rights. She called us "low" people.' This event gave her confidence. So, on another occasion, she intervened and was able to extract the bonus money for another domestic worker by mobilizing a group of people. Her sister-in-law was thrown out of her job because she had been absent for two days when she had been bitten by a snake. Shanti went with a group to the residential complex. She was denied entry, but she read out her leaflet to the employers on the speakerphone. The employers tried to browbeat them, but they did not give up. Shanti negotiated. The master was adamant, but the mistress helped them resolve the dispute. In Shanti's words:

> We were successful in this fight because of Parichiti's constant support. I would like to continue this fight till we get our due from the society so that we are not taken for granted. I want to show to people that we are also humans. We also have some dignity. We would also want to walk with our heads held high. I want the government to see to our problems and help us out as much as possible.[70]

Shanti's tactics are now more widely adopted. Neighbourhood-based groups or those affiliated to political parties help domestic workers gather a crowd at the door of an offending employer to shame or intimidate them into paying up. MS has been a member of a *mahila samiti* [affiliated to the CPI(M)] for many years. They have a small neighbourhood group, and they confront employers if workers are wronged. For domestic workers' groups, support in negotiations with employers is a way of recruiting members. Some workers become active members of an association if their interests are successfully defended. KS is a single mother with a small child and makes ends meet working in three houses. A few years ago, she had asked all her employers for a bonus at festival time. One of her employers sacked her over a trifle, avoiding not only the bonus payment but also the wages for the last month she had worked. She appealed to

---

[70] Transcript from Shanti Purkayet's speech at the Workshop on 8 May 2015, School of Women's Studies, Jadavpur University, Kolkata. Author's translation.

the *samiti* (association) of which she is a member; a group visited the employer household and got her the wages though they could not get the bonus. Commenting on this case, the secretary said, employers take advantage if you are shy and modest and that is why the *samiti* is essential.[71]

How do employers respond to these tactics of group confrontation? SJ, who goes out to work and is mother of two young children, resents her dependence: 'it is their world, they are ruling the world'. She feels that she cannot sack her day workers, since they 'threaten to call all the neighbourhood maids'. She has already experienced this once when she sacked a worker, for reasons she thinks entirely justified. ST told us that she sacked a day worker, who had been absent for 15–16 days. She could not pay her the full salary that day because she did not have change and asked her to return the next day. The worker came back with a crowd and created a ruckus. Other employers told similar stories. SG, another working woman, noted the power of informal networks, when domestic workers in her neighbourhood made a concerted demand for four days off in a month. Such groups, she argued, were more effective than unions.

Among our thirty-two employer respondents, opinions are divided about the prospect of legislation and formalization. The majority view is in favour of legislation, which, they argue, is necessary to level the playing-field. Their own dependence on domestic workers, they feel, prevent free competition. The better-off, especially those residing in gated estates, have raised wage rates. TD, IJ and MP, among others, are enthusiastic about minimum wages, because it will result in a 'fair' system. Many employers are enthusiastic about 'regularization' or formal contracts in which both parties will have obligations. This will eliminate problems such as absence without leave, which emerged as the chief grievance of most employers.[72]

This discussion underlines three issues. First, the power asymmetry in domestic work employment is so great that individual workers find it impossible to realize even basic rights such as payment of wages they have earned. Second, domestic workers do not have access to the usual bureaucratic apparatus of the state or trade unions for reporting grievances or for dispute resolution. Third, in this vacuum there has grown modes of 'direct' protest based of neighbourhood or occupational community, which urges a reconsideration of the significance of women's 'spontaneous' protest (in contrast with bureaucratic modes of protests followed by unions). Notably, however, these communities are being mobilized, in a limited way, by NGOs and women's organizations, and sometimes at arm's length, by unions and political parties. Given the nature of domestic work and the difficulty of workplace-centred political mobilization, these alternative collectives, including neighbourhood-based politics of protest, plays an important part in their struggle for rights. Whether and to what extent these can be scaled up or what bureaucratic infrastructure can be imparted remain open questions. It follows, however, that political mobilization has been far more successful among day

---

[71] Interview, TUCC, 13 February 2015.
[72] Of these, only three were men. The monthly family income ranged from Rs. 15,000–85,000 (with only two being above Rs. 60,000). Most of the respondents employ one domestic worker, some of them have two or three workers; only one employer reported five. Most employers did not include drivers when counting domestic workers but three did.

workers, who are struggling between employer paternalism/maternalism and asserting contractual rights.

Conclusion

The chapter has tracked some trajectories of formalization within an occupation that is otherwise characterized by extreme informality. One key demand on which there has been some development in recent years is that of minimum wage fixation, through the national floor level minimum wage by the central government when it comes into effect, and inclusion in their schedules by several state governments. Some states have made this inclusion in ways that have led to a low rate, in part because trade unions and labour officers of state governments have not pursued any systematic analysis of tasks and time rates. In many states, which have not yet made the minimum wage notification, there is considerable fear of a backlash against fixing minimum wage above the market rate. There is fear of alienating a large body of middle-class employers, of causing job loss and creating uncertainty in the market.

There is a wide range of employers within this market. A pervasive 'culture' of paid domestic service is sustained by cheapening costs; hence, there is both feminization in the occupation and increase in part-time hiring. These processes complicate the very notion of a minimum wage; families at the lower end of the market, sometimes those most dependent on hired care, such as those on pensions or diminishing income from savings, or working mothers with small children, may not be able to afford domestic workers if minimum wage regulation raises the market rate. Some campaigners argue that such employers cannot afford a domestic worker; but there is fear both of unemployment and a crisis in social care.

The issue of minimum wage has arisen because of the gathering strength of the domestic workers' movement. First, domestic workers are demanding minimum wage because it is one route to recognition as workers and inclusion in the state's regulatory framework. Second, they realize also that the implementation of such measures depends on their collective strength. There is thus a complementary move towards unionization. Women domestic workers are approaching CTUs for affiliation – but they are finding the road to registration of unions very rocky in some regions. The CTUs have been relatively unenthusiastic about providing leadership to domestic workers' collectives. Instead, women's groups, NGOs and new social movements have been more hospitable for domestic workers' associations. In a sector as vast as this, however, what we have now is a very small beginning.

In cases where workers have been able to build collectives, they have been able to bargain successfully for enforcement of contractual conditions – including such basics as a day off a week, full payment of wages and the festival gifts/bonus (a customary payment), and challenging arbitrary dismissal. There is a greater awareness of rights and a growing assertiveness, but how these efforts can be made more widely effective remains a tricky question, since there remain considerable doubts about the gains from formalization and unionization.

6

Enumerating Fairness: Wages and Labour Contractors in Pre-1949 China

Limin Teh

Contract labour is a stepchild of wage labour in the historiography of labour.[1] Historians often overlook this category of wage labour because they considered contract labour as an extension of free wage labour. Eric Hobsbawm's essay on wages and workload in nineteenth-century England exemplifies the former treatment of contract labour.[2] In this essay, Hobsbawm charted the process of commodifying labour power, pointing to a key moment in the nineteenth century during which workers and employers were impelled to adhere to the market principle, or as Hobsbawm calls it, 'the rules of the game'. In the middle of the nineteenth century, as Hobsbawm observed, 'workers learned to regard labor as a commodity to be sold' and 'employers learned the value of intensive rather than extensive labor utilization'.[3] The commodification process reached its culmination at the end of the nineteenth century when workers began to 'measure effort by payment' and employers turned to 'efficient ways of utilizing their workers' labor time'.[4]

Subcontracting, according to Hobsbawm, was more than compatible with this process of commodification. In fact, Hobsbawm claimed that subcontracting accelerated the process of commodification. Subcontracting began when employers started paying skilled workers by output and allowed these skilled workers to hire their own crew of workers. For skilled workers, payment by output created an incentive to

---

[1] An important exception is the historiography of Indian labour history in which lively and insightful debates over the sardar provided a useful starting point for this chapter. Key works include Tirthankar Roy, 'Sardars, Jobbers, Kanganies: The Labour Contractor and Indian Economic History', *Modern Asian Studies* 42, no. 5 (2008): 971–98; Samita Sen, 'Commercial Recruiting and Informal Intermediation: Debate over the Sardari System in Assam Tea Plantations, 1860–1900', *Modern Asian Studies* 44, no. 1 (2010): 3–28; Crispin Bates and Marina Carter, 'Sirdars as Intermediaries in Nineteenth-Century Indian Ocean Indentured Labour Migration', *Modern Asian Studies* 51, no. 2 (March 2017): 462–84.
[2] Eric J. Hobsbawm, 'Custom, Wages and Work-Load in Nineteenth-Century Industry', in *Essays in Labour History in Memory of G.D.H. Cole, 25 September 1889 - 14 January 1959*, ed. Asa Briggs and John Saville (New York: Palgrave Macmillan, 1967), 113–40.
[3] Ibid., 114.
[4] Ibid., 114.

produce the highest possible output in the least amount of time. Towards this end, skilled workers instead of employers became the agent of intensifying workers' workload, thereby speeding up the process of workers and employers fully learning 'the rules of the game'.[5] But implied in Hobsbawm's argument is that subcontracting would become redundant once the process of commodification was completed. Thereafter, workers themselves would ensure the highest possible price for their labour by forming new unions that restricted the pool of skilled workers and employers would obtain for themselves higher productivity from the workers through the implementation of scientific management. Yet, Hobsbawm conceded that subcontracting did not disappear in 'some countries'.[6]

The persistence of subcontracting in some places and the disappearance of subcontracting in others raises questions about the historical narrative of wage labour presented in Hobsbawm's essay. Assuming that workers and employers in industrialized economies grasped the rules of the game, then why did subcontracting continue in some industrialized economies but not others? In places where subcontracting persisted, what did it tell us about workers' understanding of their labour and wages? Did it mean that workers did not fully regard their labour as a commodity or that workers did not fully utilize their economic position as sellers of labour? In places where subcontracting disappeared, how did it disappear?

This essay attempts to understand how subcontracting disappeared in industrializing societies, paying particular attention to workers' resistance to labour contracting in interwar China. During this period, Chinese workers' resistance to labour contractors challenged the assumed necessity of subcontracting or labour contractors in the labour market. Workers' resistance and an emerging discourse about the parasitic role of labour contractors in this period conflated subcontracting with indentured servitude. By casting all subcontracting in a morally suspicious light in public discourse, the change in workers' attitudes and public discourse, alongside the bureaucratization of labour recruitment and supervision, brought about the decline of labour contracting. The complete elimination of labour contracting occurred in the mid-1950s after the Communist party-state achieved monopoly control over the labour market. I argue that, alongside a new discourse, workers' resistance during the interwar years brought about a fundamental shift in workers' understanding of wage labour and of fairness in employment relations.

Contract labour in Chinese history and historiography

The earliest evidence of using contract labour (*baogong*) in China dates as far back as the twelfth century.[7] The practice of using contract labour seems fairly commonplace by the seventeenth century. Stele inscriptions dating to 1644 describe the punishment

---

[5] Ibid., 125.
[6] Ibid., 131.
[7] Tim Wright, "'A Method of Evading Management'—Contract Labor in Chinese Coal Mines before 1937', *Comparative Studies in Society and History* 23, no. 4 (1981): 656–78.

for contractors in the cloth calendering industry whose workers stole or damaged the cloth.[8] From the seventeenth century onwards, the employment of contract labour is also well-documented in the mining industry. Historians Sun E-Tu Zen and Peter Golas have separately noted the widespread practice of subcontracting in coal and copper mines between the seventeenth and nineteenth centuries.[9] Subcontracting was also the dominant mode of employment in the salt mines in Zigong – a major producer of salt for the Chinese empire in the eighteenth and nineteenth centuries – and small-scale coalmines in Shanxi province during the late nineteenth and early twentieth centuries.[10] It was common practice in these mines for mine owners to pool together their capital to purchase one or multiple shafts, and then contract with skilled miners for the production of a certain amount of extracted resource. These skilled miners, in turn, hired their own family members or native-place kinsmen or women to perform the tasks of extraction, haulage and timbering. In these employment relations, kinship ties – whether blood or fictive – constrained the actions of skilled miners, in that ramifications for killing or injuring a family member or fellow villager would have been more severe than that for a stranger. Where coercion and exploitation of contract workers occurred, the victims were usually destitute migrants with no ties to the local community. But destitute migrants were not ideal workers since they had little incentive to work harder and faced few penalties for not doing so. They could always leave if the terms of employment did not suit them.

When the Chinese state lifted the ban on foreign investment in industrial enterprises in 1895, China's transition to an industrial economy hastened. As the number of industrial sectors – manufacturing, mining and modern transportation – and industrial enterprises grew, the reliance on contract labour deepened. Foreign and Chinese industrial owners in textile manufacturing, mining, construction, steam shipping and harbour cargo handling, and even local government in road building and other civil engineering projects – almost all relied on labour contractors for the supply of labour. Exact figures of total number of labour contractors and contract workers in the Chinese economy in the years 1895–1937 do not exist due to the limited infrastructure of economic statistical data collection.[11] Nevertheless, social surveys, research on Chinese labour, and company documents repeatedly mentioned labour contractors and

---

[8] Mark Elvin, *The Pattern of the Chinese Past* (London: Eyre Methuen, 1973), 281.
[9] E-tu Zen Sun, 'Mining Labor in the Ch'ing Period', in Albert Feuerwerker and Mary Wright (eds), *Approaches to Modern Chinese History* (Berkeley: University of California Press, 1967): 45–67; Peter Golas, *Chemistry and Chemical Technology: Part 13, Mining. Vol. 5. Science and Civilisation in China* (Cambridge: Cambridge University Press, 1999).
[10] Madeleine Zelin, *The Merchants of Zigong: Industrial Entrepreneurship in Early Modern China* (New York, NY: Columbia University Press, 2005); Henrietta Harrison, 'Village Industries and the Making of Rural-Urban Difference in Early Twentieth-Century Shanxi', in Jacob Eyferth (ed.), *How China Works: Perspectives on the Twentieth-century Industrial Workplace* (Abingdon, Oxon: Routledge, 2006), 25–40.
[11] For more on the rise of social surveys and statistics in early twentieth-century China, see Tong Lam, *A Passion for Facts: Social Surveys and the Construction of the Chinese Nation-State, 1900–1949* (Berkeley: University of California Press, 2011) and Arunabh Ghosh, *Making It Count: Statistics and Statecraft in the Early People's Republic of China* (Princeton: Princeton University Press, 2020), chapter 1.

contract labour, especially in relation to labour recruitment. Sociologist Da Chen's 1929 study of Chinese labour, which relied on fragmentary reports of individual workplaces, exemplifies this situation.[12] Despite the absence of standardized statistics, Chen's study revealed widespread use of labour contractors and contractors in both industrial and handicraft workplaces.[13]

During this wave of industrialization, both foreign and Chinese industrial enterprise owners seldom participated in daily operations and labour management, instead relying on independent third-party contractors or powerful foremen who possessed personal connections to recruit and supervise labourers, and technical expertise to run production. The arrangement between owner and contractor on the latter's responsibilities and payment varied by industry, location and workplace. Some contractors were hired exclusively for labour recruitment while others subcontracted entire production processes; some owners paid contractors a lump-sum for fulfilling the terms of their contracts while others paid them a percentage of output. Some contractors provided housing and accommodations while others did not; some contractors used physical violence and indebtedness to bind workers to the contract while others did not. Despite variations in local practices, the contract system granted contractors enormous autonomy over production process and labour relations on the shop floor.

An explanation for the persistence of contract labour in China's first wave of industrialization, commonly found among contemporary observers and Marxist historians, was the endurance of Chinese traditions and customs. Boris Torgasheff, a foreign mining consultant in early twentieth-century China, reasoned that the labour contract system was 'a deep-rooted custom in Chinese mining, handed down from old times', and therefore impossible to eradicate.[14] Torgasheff recounts the story of a Chinese mining engineer's attempt to end this system in the mine under his charge. When this American-trained engineer decided to undertake the task of hiring mine workers on his own, he thought it 'an easy matter' since he saw 'in the neighborhoods many unemployed labourers'. In the course of two months, he was 'able to hire nothing but a limited number of individual miners'.[15] Chinese economic historians in the 1950s and 1960s echo Torgasheff's explanation, though with a notable modification. Working within the paradigm of Marxist historiography, Chinese economic historians attributed labour contracting to the tenacious grip of feudalism, not 'deep-rooted custom'.[16] But attributing the persistence of contract labour to the endurance of Chinese customs or feudalism mistakenly assumed that contract labour did not change.

Contract labour in pre-twentieth-century China was not the same as contract labour in early twentieth-century China. As Mark Elvin described, in the cloth calendering industry between the seventeenth and early nineteenth centuries,

---

[12] Da Chen, *Zhongguo laogong wenti* [China's Labor Question] (Shanghai: Shangwu yinshuguan, 1929).

[13] Ibid., 22–83, 250–380.

[14] Boris Torgasheff, 'Mining Labor in China, Pt. 2,' *Chinese Economic Journal* (1930) v. 6. n. 5, 537.

[15] Ibid., 538–9.

[16] Qidong Zheng, *Dangdai zhongguo jindai jingjishi yanjiu 1949-2019* [Present-day China's Contemporary Economic History] (Beijing: Zhongguo she hui ke xue chu ban she, 2019), chapter 2.

contractors operated calendering workshops to supply cloth merchants. As workshop operators, the contractors owned the equipment and tools in the workshop, recruited contract workers and supervised their work.[17] In the cotton mills of early twentieth-century Shanghai, labour contractors did not own the factory, let alone the equipment and tools. The role of the labour contractors was to recruit workers for the owners of the cotton mills, though some of the labour contractors also worked as supervisors in the mills.[18] In both instances, kinship and native place ties were crucial in the recruitment of workers and even in the formation of the contractor's authority over contract labour, but the role of the early twentieth century contractor was far more proscribed than that of their earlier counterparts. The early twentieth-century labour contractor was more of an entrepreneurial provider of services than a small producer of goods. In this sense, they were similar to the sardars and jobbers in late nineteenth-century Assam plantation and Bombay cotton mills. As Tirthankar Roy explained, sardars and jobbers were traditional authority figures from a premodern economy that became incorporated into the operations of modern industrial enterprises. Their 'incorporation must be understood [...] within the dynamics of late industrialization' and not 'in culturalist terms'.[19] In late industrializing societies, the 'superimposition of a modern sector in the backdrop of largely traditional agriculture and handicrafts' disrupted the existing labour market.[20] Mass worksites of the modern sectors demanded large numbers of workers that the traditional economy could not supply. This 'particular environment' created the need for intermediaries with the knowledge and means of finding, training and retaining workers. Sardars and jobbers filled this need.[21]

Late imperial China bore much resemblance to the 'particular environment' of colonial India that Roy describes. The modern sector in late nineteenth-century China was similarly superimposed on a largely agricultural and handicraft economy, mainly through foreign investment. Foreign investment in this period flowed mainly to light manufacturing (textile and tobacco production, and food processing), mining and railways. The locations where many foreign industrialists established their manufacturing enterprises, mines or railway lines did not have the needed workforce or surplus population. As historian Jean Chesneaux contended, foreign industrialists had to rely on labour brokers, who possessed knowledge and networks needed to recruit seasonal labour from adjacent rural areas.[22] This arrangement profited both foreign investors and labour contractors: the former did not have to employ a dedicated management staff while the latter accrued considerable leverage over workers and owners.

Foreign investors precipitated the emergence of labour contractors in the years 1895–1915, but they did not account for the persistence of labour contractors after

---

[17] Elvin, *The Pattern of the Chinese Past.*, 281.
[18] Emily Honig, 'The Contract Labor System and Women Workers: Pre-Liberation Cotton Mills of Shanghai', *Modern China* 9, no. 4 (1983): 421–54.
[19] Roy, 'Sardars, Jobbers, Kanganies', 977–8.
[20] Ibid., 977.
[21] Ibid., 977.
[22] Jean Chesneaux, *The Chinese Labor Movement, 1919–1927* (Stanford, CA: Stanford University Press, 1968), 49–70.

1915. In the years 1915–27, Chinese investment in the modern sector had caught up and even exceeded foreign investment. In 1920, according to Chesneaux's analysis of coalmines, eleven were Chinese-owned, one partially Chinese-owned, and eight were foreign-owned mines.[23] By 1933, Chinese ownership of industrial enterprises in the modern sector exceeded foreign ownership by 3.5 times.[24] Yet, Tim Wright found that 27 out of the 31 major coalmines in China during the years 1910–37 depended on labour contractors for at least 60 per cent of their workforce.[25] But, as Wright pointed out, these high figures of contract labour in the coalmining industry was comparable to British and Japanese coalmining industries before mechanization and increased management involvement in mining operations.[26] Mine owners, regardless of their nationality, continued relying on labour contractors because of 'the lack of supervisory staff', which was 'a pervasive feature of Chinese industry'.[27] Labour contractors also provided mine owners additional advantages: mine owners had lower business risks since they had 'few obligations to contract workers' and 'the contract system simplified cost calculations and may have kept costs down'.[28]

Traditional customs and foreign imperialism might have lent particular features to the practice of labour contracting at the turn of the twentieth century but it was, as Roy noted, 'the dynamics of late industrialization' that created the conditions for needing labour contracting. Wright concurred with Roy, explaining that labour contracting 'used in order to deal with certain problems in the recruitment and management of labour arising in the early stages of a country's industrialization'.[29] When the solution to these problems proved advantageous to both industrialists and labour contractors alike, the practice of labour contracting continued well into the twentieth century.

Ending contract labour in the workplace

As entrenched as labour contracting in modern workplaces appeared, criticism of labour contracting emerged inside and outside the workplace during the late 1920s. In the workplace, some industrialists and managers discovered the advantages that labour contractors provided had become obstacles to further expansion and mechanization. Outside the workplace, social reformers and public intellectuals wrote denunciations of labour contracting, focusing on the most predatory forms of labour contracting. Below, I examine the concurrent development of both trends.

Fushun coalmine was one of the earliest modern workplaces in which ownership and management found labour contracting incompatible with their production

---

[23] Chesneaux, Ibid., 37–8.
[24] Albert Feuerwerker, 'Economic Trends, 1912-1949' in John K. Fairbank (ed.), *The Cambridge History of China: Volume 12: Republican China, 1912-1949, Part 1* (Cambridge: Cambridge University Press, 1989), 44.
[25] Wright, 'A Method of Evading Management', 660–1.
[26] Ibid., 670–2.
[27] Ibid., 666.
[28] Ibid., 669–70.
[29] Ibid., 677–8.

ambitions. Fushun coalmine in southern Manchuria came under Japanese control in 1907. For the next three decades, Japanese management transformed the mine into one of the largest and modern technologically advanced coalmines in Northeast Asia. Contributing to this transformation was Japanese investment in enlarging the scale of mining operations, and mechanizing coal extraction and haulage in both open and underground pits. Much of this investment occurred in the late 1920s and 1930s. As the pits became larger, deeper and more mechanized, Fushun coalmine was increasingly operated as an underground factory with a uniform mining process, clear division of labour, and greater reliance on skilled labour. By the early 1930s, labour contractors were incorporated into the mine's management structure and despite maintaining their titles as labour contractors, they functioned more as foremen in the pit than labour recruiters. The labour contractors' new function better suited the needs of the recently rationalized mining operations, but the incorporation of labour contractors occurred much earlier.

When the South Manchuria Railway took over the coalfields at Fushun in 1907, the mine had already employed labour contractors for the recruitment, supervision and lodging of mineworkers. Japanese mine management continued this arrangement while also starting its own direct recruitment of mining labour. Mine management compensated these directly recruited mine workers the costs they incurred from travelling to the mine and paid them higher daily wages. Most mine workers in Fushun were migrant workers, who made the seasonal trek from the countryside of northern China to Manchuria for employment in cities, ports and mines. Labour contractors belonged to this broader migration system, enabling about 30–40 million sojourners move between north China and Manchuria in the first half of the twentieth century.[30]

Initially motivating mine management to recruit labour directly was the contractors' demand for more money. But mine management noticed higher levels of labour productivity among directly recruited mine workers.[31] For the next decades, Japanese mine management pursued a two-prong approach towards labour contractors: it deepened its involvement in labour management while bringing labour contractors under the company's control. Japanese management expanded its campaign of direct recruitment into northern China, setting up a network of recruitment centres and agents that Japanese supervisors oversaw. It also provided company housing, stores, canteens and religious and entertainment facilities for directly recruited workers. At the same time, mine management actively curtailed the autonomy of labour contractors. Mine management fixed the commission rate for labour contractors at 3.5 per cent, limited each contractor to a maximum of fifty workers under his supervision, established the authority of mine management to hire and fire contractors, and prohibited contractors from handling the wages of mine workers.

---

[30] Thomas R. Gottschang and Diana Lary, *Swallows and Settlers: The Great Migration from North China to Manchuria* (Ann Arbor: Center for Chinese Studies, The University of Michigan, 2000), chapter 1; Adam McKeown, 'Chinese Emigration in Global Context, 1850–1940', *Journal of Global History* 5, no. 1 (2010): 100.

[31] *Bujuntankō* (1909), 246–50.

In 1924, mine management extended its bureaucratic control over Chinese migrant mining workers with the implementation of a fingerprinting and identity card system that monitored and documented workers' performance and employment history.[32] This system enabled the centralization of all financial transactions and other information on the workers, thereby reducing its reliance on labour contractors to supervise the workforce. Mine management also relied on information stored in this system for firing workers deemed unfit for employment. In doing so, labour contractors were deprived of their ability to fire recruited workers, further diminishing their personal authority. By the 1930s, the labour contractors at Fushun coalmine were completely integrated into the company's management structure. The mine determined how much the contractors earned from the recruited workers, from where and how many workers the contractors recruited, which of their workers were hired or fired, where their recruited workers lived, and how much they ate. Labour contractors retained the title of labour contractors, but their jobs had changed to the point that they functioned more as company employees than as independent contractors. This development of Fushun coalmine anticipated a broader trend of replacing labour contractors with labour unions and middle managers in the rest of China's economy.[33]

Workers' resistance against labour contractors

In the late 1920s, workers also started pushing back against the use of labour contractors. Much of the workers' resistance took place in Shanghai, a centre of Chinese finance, light manufacturing and transportation. Among the earliest attempts at abolishing the use of contract labour was the printworkers' union announcement in 1926 that the union was supplanting the labour contractor in the recruitment and management of printworkers.[34] In the following year, owners of funeral parlours in Shanghai agreed to end the contract labour system and to allow its workers to form unions.[35] In 1928, workers in Shanghai's transport industry began calling for the elimination of labour contractors. The union representing workers in the rail car food service of the Shanghai-Beijing Railway Line petitioned the Shanghai Municipal Government for permission to eradicate the contract labour system. The incident that prompted the union's petition concerned the union's conflict with a labour contractor who had confiscated a worker's deposit. Railway management mediated unsuccessfully between the union and the contractor. When the newly formed Nationalist government expressed support for the workers' resistance against labour contractors, the union began demanding the railway

---

[32] Būjun tankō, *Sakugyō nenpō: Taishō jū yon nendo* [Annual report on operations, 1925], 6; Būjun tankō, *Sakugyō nenpō: Taishō jū san nendo* [Annual report on operations, 1924], 6.
[33] For an account of changes in the Chinese mining industry, see Wright, 'A Method of Evading Management', 671–7.
[34] *Shibao*, 15 July 1926.
[35] *Xinwenbao*, 26 June 1927.

put an end to the contract labour system.[36] The union proposed forming workers' production cooperatives to replace the role of the labour contractor.[37]

The issue gained prominence when Shanghai dockworkers began agitating against the use of contract labour. In October 1928 the Shanghai dockworkers' union discussed modifying the labour contract system with the Port Authorities. The union complained about how labour contractors exploited workers: accusing them of taking a disproportionate share of workers' wages (in the range of 56–80 per cent) and of creating a separate union, which the union insisted was 'not a real workers' organization'. Real unionized dock workers, according to the union, wore frequently repaired cotton clothes, ate coarse feed, lived in grass shacks, walked everywhere and seldom took rickshaws. Those employed by the labour contractors' fake union, the union proceeded to protest, were said to wear fancy clothes, ate luxurious food, lived in foreign homes and went everywhere in automobiles. The union further demanded that workers received their wages directly from shipping and dock warehouse companies, a reduction of labour contractor's share to 10 per cent, a ban on labour contractor's use of thugs.[38]

The newly formed Nationalist government supported the union. The Ministry of Transportation in September 1929 approved the union's call for shipping companies to stop using labour contractors.[39] In the following year, the Nationalist Party included in its industrial labour policy an item on abolishing labour contracting.[40] The party distinguished between piece-work contracting and labour contracting. The latter, according to the party's labour policymakers, was the source of many labour conflicts because labour contractors often 'pocketed the wages of workers and colluded to cheat employers'.[41] Despite support from both government and party of the Nationalist or Guomindang, the practice of using labour contractors in the docks continued among some companies.[42] Labour contractors resorted to the same mobilization strategies – slowdowns and strikes – to defend their position. For instance, the labour contractor Li Hongji had long been contracted by the Pudong Ronglin Docks company to recruit and supervise its dockworkers. But in December 1933 the company decided to take over the tasks of labour recruitment and supervision, which resulted in the dismissal of Li Hongji. Li responded by forcing dockworkers under his supervision and others to stop work for the company. Li's actions brought cargo movement at the busy Pudong docks to a standstill. The dock company appealed to the Nationalist government to

---

[36] *Xinwenbao*, 25 August 1928.
[37] *Shanghai tebieshi shizhengfu shizheng gongbao* (1928) v. 14, 83–6; *Minguo ribao*, 28 July 1929; *Xinwenbao* 2 August 1928.
[38] *Shibao* 22 October 1934; *Xinwenbao*, 26 October 1928.
[39] *Minsheng ribao*, 24 September 1929.
[40] Tingyuan Zhang, *Zhongguo guomindang laogong zhengce de yanjiu* [Research on the Labor Policies of China's Nationalist Party] (Shanghai: Dadong shuju, 1930).
[41] Zhang, Ibid., 62–3.
[42] Brian Martin and Elizabeth Perry attributed the continuation of labor contracting, despite the Nationalist Party's official labour industrial policy, to the party's ties to organized crime. For more on the Green Gang's role in labour contracting, see Brian G. Martin, *The Shanghai Green Gang: Politics and Organized Crime, 1919-1937* (University of California Press, 1996), 82–3 and Elizabeth J. Perry, *Shanghai on Strike: The Politics of Chinese Labor* (Stanford University Press, 1993), 50–8.

intervene. The conflict was finally resolved when Nationalist government officials involved the dockworkers in drafting the settlement, thereby completely marginalizing Li. Under the final agreement, the dockworkers previously hired by Li would be directly employed by the dock company, they would register with the Ministry of Social Affairs, and the Ministry would appoint twelve dock workers to be workers' representatives in charge of recruiting and supervising workers.[43]

Another locus of workers' resistance to labour contractors was the Kailuan Coalmines in Hebei Province, near the major cities of Beijing and Tianjin. Started in 1878 as part of the late imperial Chinese state's modernization project, Kailuan mine became one of the largest coal mines in China during the first half of the twentieth century. Management of the mine varied in this period: it came under British management in the years 1900–12 and joint Sino-British management in 1912–50, with an interim period in 1941–45 under Japanese occupation forces. Kailuan Coalmine, one of the largest coal producers in China during the first half of the twentieth century, relied on a workforce composed of about 66 per cent contract workers.[44] Its reliance on contract labour, as noted in Wright's essay, was not unusual; contract labour featured prominently in the mining industry. What was unusual about Kailuan Coalmine was the mineworkers' organized resistance against the contract labour system. This resistance culminated in two strikes at the mine, one in 1929 and a series of strikes in 1934. It should be noted that strikes occurred with high frequency at Kailuan.

The strike in 1929 began on 11 April 1929 in Majiagou Pit and lasted till early May. The immediate issues that prompted the strike were low wages and long work hours. Mine management had lengthened underground night shift by an hour and underground intermittent shift by half an hour. Contract labour became an issue during the strike because labour contractors started using contract mineworkers to replace the strikers. The strike was called by the mine workers' union, whose membership excluded contract workers. But on 23 April more than 2,000 contract workers convened a general meeting. At this meeting, the contract workers agreed to approach the Kailuan mineworkers' union for permission to join it. The next day, on 24 April, union members at their general meeting voted to allow contract workers into their union. The strike petered out in early May with mixed results. Mineworkers did not get higher wages or the end of the contract labour system, but their gains included shorter shifts and a larger union membership.[45]

Kailuan mineworkers launched a series of strikes against the contract labour system in 1934. The precipitating incident took place on 14 January 1934 when a labour contractor came across a large group of mine workers in Majiagou Pit, who happened to take their break together. The labour contractor mistook the gathering for the start of an industrial action and immediately informed the Majiagou No. 2 Police. The police shot into the crowd of workers to force them to break up, killing two workers and injuring many. Relations between management and workers were already strained

---

[43] *Xinwenbao*, 15 December 1933.
[44] Wright, 'A Method for Evading Management', 660.
[45] *Kuangyezhoubao*, nos. 25–48, 334, 343–4, 355–9.

prior to this incident. In the year before, mine management had fired several thousand employees and contract workers who had been agitating for compensation. Shortly before the incident, the union threatened to strike after learning from an unofficial source that mine management had decided not to pay bonuses to contract workers, an accusation rejected by the mine management. These denials did not defuse the tension in the relationship with the mineworkers, and after the incident, the workers in Majiagou Pit went on strike.

The main grievance of the workers was the contract labour system. In the statement announcing the formation of the Majiagou Post-Tragedy Solidarity Group, workers protested against the excesses of the contract labour system. 'Recently, compensation and benefits are reduced, forcing some workers to become secondary contractors, adding to the number of contractors. One contractor subcontracts the work to three or four contractors to the point that the worker keeps working with an empty belly and sees his monthly wages lowered. The worker's misery is prolonged as he suffers another significant exploitation ....' The workers demanded that contractors maintain their wages and to end the use of secondary contractors. These contractors, as these workers asserted, falsely accused them of planning a strike, sending armed security guards against them, and finally causing the fatal confrontation. These workers called on their fellow comrades to support their struggle, 'for the sake of justice, for the sake of solidarity, for the sake of supporting the trampled-upon legal system, for the sake of securing worker's individual welfare'.

By end of January, about 27,000 workers from three other pits joined out of solidarity in the strike. Among the strikers' demands included punishment for the guilty security guards, compensation for the dead workers' families, and abolition of the contract labour system.[46] On 2 February, the workers finally reached an agreement with mine management, bringing the strike to an end. Under the agreement, all unemployed workers would return to their former positions, the staff who colluded with labour contractors to exploit workers would be dismissed, the workers' representatives at the negotiations in the absence of a proper union were recognized as legal representatives of the workers, the secondary labour contractor system would be abolished, an additional working day would extend the workweek to six days, and mine management would compensate workers for expenses such as travel for talks incurred during the strike.[47] Most importantly, the agreement also stipulated the end of the labour contract system and that the union could nominate workers to become contractors in future.[48]

Nevertheless, despite the agreement to modify the contract labour system and a reorganization of mine management in April, the issue of contract labour remained unresolved.[49] Not all pit supervisors stopped the practice of secondary labour contractors. On 10 December 1934, over one hundred workers at Majiagou Pit No. 3 Underground Tunnel staged a strike during a shift change, carrying placards that

---

[46] *Shenbao* 27 January 1934 and 31 January 1934.
[47] *Shenbao* 2 February 1934.
[48] *Shenbao* 5 February 1934.
[49] *Shenbao* 20 April 1934.

declared 'Oppose secondary contractors'.⁵⁰ The workers demanded that the labour contracting company, Ruisheng Gongsi, end its use of secondary contractors and stop oppressing workers. According to the five elected workers' representative, Ruisheng Gongsi in its greed for profits subcontracted the work in the No. 9 Coalface to secondary contractors, which 'violated the agreement between the Coal Bureau and workers'.⁵¹ After this, although labour contractors remained in use, their numbers and influence declined considerably. More significantly, the mobilization of Kailuan mine workers against labour contractors highlighted changing attitudes towards labour contractors in particular and wage labour in general.

The predatory labour contractor in public discourse

Public discourse turned against labour contractors in the 1930s. This period saw the flourishing of mass media in urban Chinese society: regional and local newspapers enjoyed wide readership, as did periodicals catering to a new readership, such as women, children and workers.⁵² There were at least twenty periodicals by and about labour circulating in this period. In these periodicals and other mass publications, labour contractors emerge as the embodiment of industrial work in factories and mines.

Contract labour became synonymous with indentured labour in the early 1930s. In fairness, contract labour and indentured labour overlapped considerably both in language and in practice. Contract labour in Chinese language was usually called *baogong* while indentured labour *baoshengong*. The additional character *shen* or body distinguished the Chinese word for indentured labour from the Chinese word for contract labour. This distinction aptly captured a key difference in practice: the indentured worker's freedom of movement at and outside work was controlled by the labour contractor while the contract worker's freedom of movement outside work was not necessarily determined by the labour contractor.

Public discourse in the 1930s often elided over this difference and in the process conflated contract labour and indentured labour. Two popular publications on female contract workers in Shanghai textile mills exemplified this discursive move. The first was Sun Yefang's investigative exposé and the second Xia Yan's fictional reportage. The investigation of Sun Yefang, a researcher at the Chinese Academy of Social Science Research, did much to secure the connection between contract labour and indenture labour. In 1932, Sun conducted a three-month long investigation of apprentices or *yangchenggong* in Shanghai's textile mills and published his findings in a popular periodical called *Huanian* [Chinese Youth] under the pseudonym Sun Baoshan. In this two-part exposé, Sun asserted that these female apprentices were 'in reality feudal

---

⁵⁰ *Shenbao* 10 December 1934; *Kuangye zhoubao* no. 315, 33–4.
⁵¹ *Kuangye zhoubao* no. 315, 34.
⁵² S.A. Smith, *Like Cattles and Horses: Nationalist and Labor in Shanghai, 1895-1927* (Durham: Duke University Press, 2002); Eugenia Lean, *Public Passions: The Trial of Shi Jianqiao and the Rise of Popular Sympathy in Republican China* (Berkeley: University of California Press, 2007).

slaves in disguise'.[53] Despite the veneer of legality that the labour contract provided, as Sun argued, these apprentices were really 'indentured workers' because of the coercive conditions under which they had to sell their labour.[54]

According to Sun, these workers were recruited from their homes by recruiters who were either experienced textile workers or professional labour contractors. The recruiters typically identified in their native villages families that were in dire financial straits and had young daughters no more than sixteen *sui* (fifteen years using the Gregorian calendar). In exchange for working three years in the factory, the recruiter agreed to take full responsibility for the worker, transport the worker to the city, and care for the worker in the city. Furthermore, the recruiter agreed to give the worker's family a fixed payment of 30–40 *yuan* as long as the family consented to the contractor pocketing all of the worker's salary. These attractive terms were formalized in a labour contract, which provided the families assurance of their daughters' well-being.

Once the worker arrived in the city, she found herself in horrible living conditions. She was fed plain rice gruel twice a day. Salted vegetables were served on special festival days. For the 12-hour long work shift, she was given six copper pieces to buy a snack during break. She lived in a dormitory that housed 20 to 30 workers. Two workers were assigned to a single bed: both alternated sleeping in the bed during the workday since they worked different shifts, but shared the same bed during rest days. In sum, the labour contractor was careful not to spend more than 5 yuan per worker on their food, lodging and clothing.[55]

It was almost impossible for these workers to stop working before the end of their contracts due to their complete lack of physical freedom and economic autonomy.[56] The worker was not free to move about the city, let alone leave the factory or dormitory. The contractor always escorted the worker to and from the textile factory, and armed guards patrolled the dormitory at all hours. At work, the factory supervisor (or 'Number One') was usually not sympathetic to the worker's plight since the labour contractor regularly bribed the supervisor to monitor his contracted workers. Even if the worker succeeded in running away, she would not have enough money for the transport fare to return to her village. Each month, the factory paid her wages directly to the labour contractor. Some contractors gave the workers small allowances for food snacks, but the allowances were not enough for transport fare. Furthermore, the contractor often fabricated costs to keep the workers and their families indebted to him. These coercive tactics, Sun concluded, kept the workers working for the labour contractor 'like cattle and horses'.[57]

Two years after Sun's two-part story on contract workers in Shanghai textile mills, Chinese writer Xia Yan published his short story, 'Contract Labour', in the inaugural issue of the magazine *Guangming* [Enlightenment].[58] He first learned about contract workers from a student in his evening school. Their plight so moved him that Xia

---

[53] Baoshan Sun, 'Shanghai fangzhichang zhong de baoshenzhi gongren (shang),' *Huanian* 1 (1932) 22: 9.
[54] Ibid., 10.
[55] Ibid., 10–11.
[56] Baoshan Sun, 'Shanghai fangzhichang zhong de baoshenzhi gongren (xia)', *Huanian* 1 (1932) 24: 7–8.
[57] Ibid., 9.
[58] Xia Yan, 'Baoshengong', *Guangming* 1 (1936) 1: 15–23.

decided to write this piece of fictional reportage, using interviews with his student and other contract workers. Like Sun, Xia Yan wanted his writing to expose the dismal living and working conditions of contract workers in Shanghai's textile mills. Most of these contract workers were fifteen- or sixteen-year-old girls from the countryside, where the dire straits of these rural households made extremely appealing the labour contractors' promise of a better life in the city. Once in Shanghai, the girls found themselves shackled to the labour contractor. They lived in cramped quarters, ate rice gruel twice a day, and worked in the humid and noisy silk-reeling factory for twelve hours each day – all under the watchful gaze of the labour contractor who did not hesitate to physically and verbally abuse them. The contractors in Xia Yan's story regularly beat the workers and called them 'pigs', despite sharing ties to the same place of origin. When the workers fell ill or tried to quit, the contractors threatened the workers for violating the three-year labour contract. As Xia Yan explained, 'the bodies of these contract workers belonged to the boss [labour contractor] and thus they had neither the freedom to work or the freedom to not work'.[59] Xia Yan's short story successfully cemented the association of labour contractors with coercive labour customs of 'feudal' China. Even today this story, which remains a part of today's Chinese middle school students' literature curriculum, is celebrated as an important literary representation of labour exploitation in pre-1949 China.[60]

The predatory labour contractor deployed as the embodiment of backwards labour customs was not exclusive to Chinese popular discourse. It was also a familiar metonym in the discourse on labour contractors in the United States during the 1910s and 1920s. A 1921 U.S. government inspector, as Gunther Peck described, considered labour contractors as 'a form of serfdom that had been imported from abroad'.[61] Government inspectors and social reformers consistently portrayed contractors as backwards foreign imports to maintain two intertwined fictions, that the freedom of wage labour could only be secured through the wage labour's ability to directly sell her labour without the interference of third-party mediators, and that only 'free wage labour' existed in post-slavery American workplaces.[62] This discursive move was necessary for Chinese social

---

[59] Ibid., 23.
[60] An example is this online essay: https://www.pinshiwen.com/yuexie/wxjx/20190729162343.html
[61] Gunther Peck, *Reinventing Free Labor: Padrones and Immigrant Workers in the North American West, 1880-1930* (Cambridge: Cambridge University Press, 2000), 18.
[62] Ibid., 15–82. This discursive strategy can also be found in some labor histories of migrant labor. For example, see Jack Masson and Donald Guimary, 'Asian Labor Contractors in the Alaskan Canned Salmon Industry: 1880–1937', *Labor History*, 22, no. 3 (2008), 377–97; Luis F.B. Plascencia, 'State-Sanctioned Coercion and Agricultural Contract Labor: Jamaican and Mexican Workers in Canada and the United States, 1909-2014' in Marcel van der Linden and Magaly Rodriguez Garcia (eds), *On Coerced Labor: Work and Compulsion After Chattel Slavery* (Leiden, NL: Brill, 2016), 225–67. Coercion through extra-economic or nonpecuniary means, such as threat of imprisonment or deportation for breach of contract, functioned to compel migrant workers in North America to accept the terms of employment without negotiation. As Luis Placienca explains, migrant workers in North America are unfree labour because they did not have 'the freedom to bargain for the most advantageous position' and thus 'cannot commodify their labor power and secure the most profitable contract'. By linking the absence of commodification to the conditions of coercion, Placienca seems to be invoking a modernization paradigm that firmly categorized coerced labour as a feature of traditional or feudal economy and free labour as a feature of modern or capitalist economy.

reformers and public intellectuals, though it was animated by a sense of fairness in renumeration, not an anxiety to police the line between free and unfree labour.

This sense of fairness in renumeration must be situated in the context of deteriorating economic conditions for workers. For many workers, the expansion of industrial sectors provided employment opportunities that did not translate into improved living conditions. Social conditions for this group declined in the first three decades of the twentieth century. Pim de Zwart, Bas van Leeuwen and Jieli van Leeuwen-Li used Robert Allen's concept of subsistence baskets to measure real wages globally from 1820s to 2000s.[63] According to these authors, real wages of building labourers in China steadily deteriorated in the period 1900–30. In the 1900s the daily wage of a building labourer in China could buy five subsistence baskets. This number declined to four subsistence baskets in the 1910s and then three by the 1920s and the 1930s. For perspective, the lowest number of subsistence baskets afforded by the building labourer's daily wage across the entire period studied was two, which occurred in the 1850s when the Taiping Rebellion devastated much of the Chinese economy.

Fairness in the discourse on wage labour

Alongside this popular representation of the abusive labour contractor was a growing critique of labour contractors that articulated further the terms of abuse and exploitation. Ling Wu penned an editorial in the newspaper *Zhongyang Ribao*, calling for the end of labour contractors.[64] Ling began the piece by defining the labour contractor as the 'third layer that stands between the industrialist and the worker'. Because of his intermediary position, the labour contractor 'fawns over the industrialist to obtain his private gains' while he 'pushes down the price of labour and exploits the weaknesses of labour to realize his own desires'. For Ling the labour contractor is, more so than the industrialist, a 'direct exploiter of workers and thus a hidden obstacle to the movement to emancipate workers, like a rock blocking the humane movement to liberate working life'. He further detailed the exploitation of workers under labour contractors:

> Labor contractors created pitiful workers who worked long hours for low wages. They give every drop of their blood and tears, from dawn till dusk, to the labor contractor and in return, the labor contractor pays them wages so low they are unable to feed themselves and their wives and children. This should not be allowed to continue in modern society underpinned by the ideologies of human rights and rights to livelihood.[65]

Ling invoked Sun Yatsen's Three People's Principles, the Nationalist government's foundational ideology, in condemning labour contractors. Sun identified nationalism,

---

[63] Pim de Zwart, Bas van Leeuwen, and Jieli van Leeuwen-Li, 'Real Wages since 1820' (Paris: OECD, 2 October 2014), Table 4.6.
[64] *Zhongyang ribao*, 26 November 1929.
[65] *Zhongyang ribao*, 26 November 1929.

democracy and livelihood (sometimes translated as socialism) as the three principles that were fundamental to the construction of the Chinese nation-state. The principle of livelihood broadly promised social equality, though Sun never formulated a detailed programme to achieve this end. Nevertheless, the language of equality and fairness in this principle provided Ling with the moral ground to argue that wages should be commensurate with the length of the workday and sufficient for workers to support their families.

The immorality of labour contractors' imposition of labour discipline and their right to a share of wages came under assault in Gu Zhanran's 1932 essay on labour contracting. Gu, a member of Hu Shi's circle of liberal intellectuals and reformers, penned a polemic against the contract labour system for the first issue of *Duli Pinglun*. In this essay, Gu declares labour contracting a 'major problem' that had been neglected for too long.[66] To illustrate the problems of labour contractors, Gu analysed the work process of Shanghai dockworkers and the wages of contract labour hired at each stage of the process. According to Gu there were four types of work on Shanghai docks: (1) transferring cargo from the ship's cargo hold to its deck; (2) transferring cargo from ship's deck to warehouse; (3) transferring cargo from warehouse to dockside; (4) lightering, or the transfer of cargo from cargo ship to barge.

Shipping companies paid the following rates for each type of work, but contract dock workers seldom received the full amount for their wages. Gu calculates the difference in the following table:[67]

Table 6.1 Workers' earnings of shipping companies in Shanghai, Gu Zhanran, 1932.

Type of work	What shipping company paid per ton (Yuan)	What workers received per ton (Yuan)	Portion of company's payment that reached workers	Workers daily wage (Yuan)	Workers daily wage without labour contractors (Yuan)
(1) Cargo transfer from cargo hold to deck	0.125	0.0297	23.8%	0.833	3.583
(2) Cargo transfer from deck to warehouse	0.347	0.104	30%	0.765	2.597
(3) Cargo transfer from warehouse to dockside	0.291	0.0778	26.6%		
(4) Lightering	0.278	0.0569	20.5%		

As indicated in the table, contract dockworkers received between 20.5 per cent to 30 per cent for each ton of cargo that shipping companies paid. The remaining 70–79.5 per cent went to labour contractors. Because of the high cost of living in Shanghai, contract dockworkers had to work at intensive pace for each nine-hour shift in order

[66] Gu Zhanran, 'Zhongguo de baogong zhi [China's Contract Labor System]', *Duli Pinglun* [Independent Review], 1 (1932): 13–16.
[67] The wages were based on the Shanghai bimetallic currency system. I convert silver to Yuan using the rate, 1 yuan = 7.2 qian of silver.

to earn enough to cover their basic expenses. But as Gu asserted, these workers would see their daily wages triple if labour contractors were removed from the picture.

Gu invoked the idiomatic phrase, '*bulao erhuo* [to gain without labour],' to underscore his moral outrage at the labour contractors' living off labourers. Gainful employment should preclude brokers or middlemen who profited solely from their monopoly over knowledge of labour markets and did not expend energy and time. Underlying his outrage was an understanding that when labour was sold as a commodity, it should receive the full price for what labour had expended and what employers had paid. Moreover, this price should be adequate for the worker to cover basic expenses like food, shelter, rest and relaxation, and healthcare.

Nationalist official Zhang Tiejun also authored an essay analysing labour contractors in Shanghai docks.[68] Zhang traced the origins of the system to the particularities of the labour process.[69] During the early years of the harbour's existence, arrival and departure times of cargo ships were not always predictable. Neither were the size and type of cargo. Moreover, cargo ships were allowed to dock at the harbour for a limited amount of time in which cargo could be unloaded safely and completely. These uncertainties and constraints made it impossible for shipping and warehousing companies to have a permanent workforce for the work of loading and unloading cargo. Instead, companies contracted the work to foremen with the necessary experience and knowledge as well as a ready workforce. The contracting system became more complex over the years. Three more layers of management below the contractors evolved: *dangshou* [managers] oversaw the contractors' overall affairs; *paomatou* [harbour runners] were responsible for estimating the labour needs for each cargo load; and *chaizhangtou* [paymaster] represented the dockworkers in negotiating wage rates with the *dangshou* managers and in collecting wages on behalf of the dockworkers. All three management positions were direct employees of the contractor.

Zhang also looked into the size of the contractor's cut by examining the discrepancy between the amount that the contractor received for the work and the amount that the dockworker received.[70] A total of sixteen shipping companies operated in Shanghai Harbour, eight Chinese-owned and eight foreign-owned. The types of cargo spanned a wide range, from coal and wood to paper and beans. Despite differences in the nationality of ownership and the type of cargo, Zhang discovered that none of the surveyed dockworkers received the full share of what the companies paid the contractors. The size of the contractor's cut ranged from 60 per cent at the lowest to 90 per cent at the highest, making Zhang's calculations higher than the union's. Curiously, contractors at Japanese-owned companies took the smallest cuts at 60–66 per cent while contractors at Chinese-owned companies took the largest cuts at 75–90 per cent. Zhang's calculations of the contractor's cut reinforced Shanghai dockworkers' union's claim of exploitation with the contractor's cut and Gu's assertions.

---

[68] Zhang Tiejun, 'Quxiao baogong zhi de zhipiao zenme duixian [How to honour the commitment to abolish the contract labour system]', *Laogong yuekan* , 1, no. 6 (1932).
[69] Ibid., 23–4.
[70] Ibid., 26–7.

The enumeration of the labour contractor's exploitation is also found in Xia Yan's story. In addition to his poignant portrayal of the dehumanizing abuse that the contract workers endured, he too resorted to numbers to illustrate the workers' exploitation. Citing the example of a contract worker with the nickname 'Reed Stem' [*lúcháibàng*], Xia Yan calculated the earnings from Reed Stem's wages that the labour contractor profited: 'Reed Stem presently earns 38 cents a day, if we take last year's daily wage at an average of 32 cents, after two years' of service, the labour contractor had in reality collected from her body 230 dollars!'

Conclusion

Workers' resistance in the late 1920s and 1930s called into question the relevance of labour contractors in the production process. Workers in the early strikes in the late 1920s demanded unions replace labour contractors in the recruitment and supervision of labour. But the larger strikes in the Shanghai docks and Kailuan Coalmine went further to challenge conventional conception about wages. For these workers, wages should not simply be the price of their labour that the labour contractor was willing to pay, but wages should be the price of labour that reflected the time and effort they had expended, and the price of labour that covered their costs of living. By going on strike for these demands, these workers demonstrated their recognition of their labour as a commodity while also asserting their right as sellers of labour to be compensated on commensurable terms. Popular representations and critiques of labour contractors further turned general attitudes against labour contractors while articulating the immorality and quantifying the unfairness of labour contractors.

Labour contractors did not entirely disappear from pre-1949 Chinese society, but workers' resistance and the emerging discourse in this period underscored the importance of morality and fairness in how wage workers came to learn the 'rules of the game'. For Hobsbawm, the existence of subcontracting indicated an incomplete process of the commodification of labour, in that wage workers who had fully learned 'to measure effort by payment' would not enter into a subcontracting arrangement. But Hobsbawm neglected the significance of moral values about human labour in shaping economic values of wages. When Chinese workers challenged subcontracting, they were not so much exhibiting their awareness of their labour as commodity as they were asserting their right to the full share of what their labour earned. Furthermore, they were also demanding their right to liveable wages, which labour contractors denied them. In this sense, fairness was a critical component in how workers came to embrace and deploy their economic status as sellers of labour. As such, the case of labour contracting in pre-1949 reveals that morality mattered as much as market forces in the commodification of labour.

7

Everywhere but in the Strike Statistics? Wage Systems and Work Stoppages in Sweden, 1863–1927

Tobias Karlsson

Introduction

Labour market institutions and employment relationships underwent dramatic changes in the wake of industrialization. Workers mobilized and put forward their claims collectively in strikes. Most strikes concerned wages, where workers were seeking to either increase their pay or resist wage cuts. Meanwhile employers, inspired by ideas of Frederick W. Taylor and his followers, sought to get better control of the process and intensity of work, for example by introducing new wage systems. Not only did piece rate pay become more common, but various 'bonus plans' were also introduced. The historical introduction and practice of wage systems have been the object of considerable scholarly attention, often in the form of in-depth case studies of individual industries, firms, occupations or conflicts.[1] Less attention has been directed towards wage systems in quantitative strike research. This is unfortunate since contemporary actors as well as some of the case-study literature suggests that the two phenomena – wage systems and strikes – may be related. Listening to early trade union leaders, one would expect an increased use of piece rates being associated with more conflicts. Members of the contemporary rationalization movement would, on the other hand, launch their new systems as ways of sharing the gains of improved efficiency and reducing the antagonism between labour and capital.

In this chapter, I seek to reconcile two strands of research in labour history – quantitative studies of strikes and case-study research on work processes and industrial relations – by focusing on Sweden. The big question concerns the connection between the labour conflicts and the spread of new wage systems. This chapter aims to contribute

---

[1] See for example Wayne Lewchuk, 'Fordism and British Motor Car Employers, 1896–1932', in *Managerial Strategies & Industrial Relations*, ed. Howard F. Gospel and Craig R. Littler (London: Gower, 1983), 82–110 and Ian Smith and Trevor Boyns, 'Scientific Management and the Pursuit of Control in Britain to c. 1960', *Accounting, Business & Financial History* 15, no. 2 (2005): 187–216.

to this bigger discussion by addressing two sets of more specific questions related to the Swedish statistics on work stoppages:

1. To what extent were wage systems mentioned in the official statistics? How common were strikes about wage systems and were some wage systems more associated with conflicts than others were?
2. To what extent can we trust official statistics on work stoppages in this regard? May information related to wage systems have been omitted from the statistics in the process of data compilation and publication?

To approach these questions, I combine evidence from newly digitized micro-level datasets on work stoppages with case-study evidence from two industries. Together, the datasets cover all officially (or semi-officially) recorded strikes and lockouts in Sweden for the period 1863–1927, with information on the claims of the strikers, number of involved workers, conflict duration and outcome. Although often vague, and possibly simplified, the information of immediate strike causes becomes increasingly detailed over time with regard to whether conflicts concerned hourly pay or piece rates. My investigation of the statistics also indicates a shift in workers' position on wage systems – from uniform hostility towards partial acceptance of piece work, which is in line with the conventional narrative. Workers also launched strikes to achieve guaranteed hourly wages in pre-existing piece rate systems. Overall, however, terms related to modern wage systems are not commonly found in Swedish statistics on work stoppages for the period under investigation. To complement the official statistics, I compile case-study evidence from two industries: shipbuilding and tobacco industry. Although these industries differed in character, rationalization measures in general and new wage systems were found in both around the First World War and the years thereafter. Yet, there was only one clear example where workers struck against changed principles for calculating wages. This does not mean that changes of wage systems were uncontroversial, rather that such disagreements were solved through negotiations rather than open conflicts.

Wage forms, wage systems and strikes

According to neoclassical economic theory, labour is paid according to the value of its marginal product. Reality, where the marginal product is not always easily observed, is more complex. First, there are different *wage forms*, with a basic distinction between payment in kind and cash, respectively. Payments in kind have been important in many historical settings and functioned as an insurance to price fluctuations but has restricted the opportunities of independent living arrangements. In addition to kind and cash, wages may be paid as various benefits, such as entitlements to pensions or sickness insurances. Secondly, there are various principles for determining the size of pay, *wage systems*. Here, the most common distinction is between remuneration based on the length of time spent at work and performance-based pay.

Time-based remuneration may, in turn, appear in various forms, such as payment per year, month, week, day or hour. In modern settings, after the introduction of systems of monitoring time and work attendance, hourly pay is the most common for blue-collar workers.² White-collar workers have typically had more flexible arrangements and are more often paid monthly salaries. Within a time-based system, there is often various criteria that may influence the level of pay, such as sex, age, occupation and seniority. Time-based systems are therefore associated with wage discrimination.³

Performance-based remuneration may also appear in various forms, with an important distinction between group payments and sub-contracting arrangements, as often is seen in the building sector, and individual payments, as in the case of piece rate schemes.⁴ Different piece rate schemes may apply to different groups of workers, but typically, schemes are applied to all workers doing the same tasks. Piece rate pay is much associated with industrial production.⁵ Scattered evidence suggests that payment by results became increasingly common over the course of the nineteenth century, and especially so with the advent of mass production and more well-organized labour movements towards the end of the century, pre-dating more elaborated forms of scientific management.⁶ For Taylor, the reason for paying according to performance was to induce workers to increase their effort. Trade unions could, however, be hesitant or hostile towards performance-based pay, as it increased individual competition, increased the risk of fatigue and threatened the solidarity among the workers.

In principle, performance-based pay may be seen as a way to align the interests of employers and workers. If workers keep a high pace, or invent more efficient methods to increase output, workers are rewarded. The problem, however, is that when realizing that work can be done faster or smarter, employers are tempted to reduce piece rates. In the extreme case, the employer recaptures all productivity gains by so-called 'rate busting' to the prevailing market wage.⁷ Workers may then retaliate by withdrawing work effort, abstain from using the most efficient methods or go on strike. The difficulty in setting appropriate piece rates, and the problems associated with adjusting piece rates downwards, was one of the main arguments for combining elements from time- and performance-based wage systems.⁸

---

2   Thompson, 'Time, Work-Discipline'.
3   Claudia Goldin, *Understanding the Gender Gap. An Economic History of American Women* (New York: Oxford University Press, 1990); Maria Stanfors, Tim Leunig, Björn Eriksson and Tobias Karlsson, 'Gender, Productivity, and the Nature of Work and Pay: Evidence from the Late Nineteenth-Century Tobacco Industry', *Economic History Review*, 67, no. 1 (2014): 48–65.
4   Judy Z. Stephenson, 'Real Wages? Contractors'.
5   Georg Styrman, *Verkstadsföreningen 1896–1945* (Stockholm: P. A. Norstedt and Söners Förlag, 1946), 302. However, examples of performance-based pay can be found far back in history and in small-scale craft production. See, Reinhold Reith, 'Wage Forms, Wage systems and Wage Conflicts in German Crafts during the Eighteenth and Earlier Nineteenth Centuries', in *Experiencing Wages: Social and Cultural Aspects of Wage Forms in Europe since 1500*, ed. P. Scholliers and L. D. Schwarz (New York, Berghahn books, 2003), 113–38.
6   E. J. Hobsbawm, *Labouring Men: Studies in the History of Labour*, (Weidenfeld & Nicolson: London, 1964), 356–62.
7   Michael Huberman, 'Piece rates reconsidered: the case of cotton', *Journal of Interdisciplinary History*, 26, no. 3 (1996): 393–417.
8   Horace B. Drury, *Scientific Management: A History and Criticism* (New York: Columbia University, 1915), 34–5; Alf Johansson, *Arbetarrörelsen och taylorismen: Olofström 1895-1925* (Lund, Arkiv, 1990), 89; Lewchuk, 'Fordism and British Motor Car Employers', 84–5.

Various hybrid wage systems, often called 'bonus plans' 'premium plans', or 'premium-bonus plans', have been documented.[9] Typically, these systems meant that workers earnings increased with performance, but at a decreasing rate. Hence, they are sometimes labelled 'progressive wages'.[10] As with straight piece rates, bonuses have long historical roots,[11] but are mainly associated with the rationalization movement.[12] One of Taylor's disciples, H. L. Gantt introduced the 'task and bonus' system,[13] another system, the Towne-Halsey plan was regarded as 'a great invention' by Taylor in *Shop Management*, and described in the following way:

> [...] recording the quickest time in which a job has been done, and fixing this as a standard. If the workman succeeds in doing the job in a shorter time, he is still paid his same wages per hour for the time he works on the job, and in addition is given a premium for having worked faster, consisting of from one-quarter to one-half the difference between the wages earned and the wages originally paid when the job was done in standard time.[14]

Hybrid wage systems are sometimes presented as a kind of 'gain sharing', as employers and workers split the gains of time savings.[15] However, even if hybrid systems have the potential of inducing cooperation between employers and workers, the transition from one wage system to another may give rise to conflicts, as it influences the wage level, the wage distribution between groups and individual workers, work intensity and autonomy of workers. For workers used to straight piece rates, a bonus system could be regarded as a way for employers' to extract the fruits of extra efforts,[16] or an 'automatic price breaker'.[17] Workers also came to associated hybrid wage systems with increased time discipline.[18] In 1909, a committee of the British Trades Union Congress called for the abolishment of bonus plans, the same demand was heard in the wave of craft worker strikes in the 1910s.[19]

---

[9] Drury, *Scientific Management*, 38–52.
[10] David Frederick Schloss, *Methods of Industrial Remuneration* (New York: GP Putnam's Sons, 1892), 55–6.
[11] Reith, 'Wage Forms, Wage systems and Wage Conflicts'.
[12] Hobsbawm, *Labouring Men*, 360–1; Daniel Nelson, 'Scientific Management, Systematic Management, and Labor, 1880-1915', *Business History Review*, 48, no. 4 (1974): 479–500; Peter Scholliers and Leonard Schwartz, 'The Wage in Europe since the Sixteenth Century', in *Experiencing wages: social and cultural aspects of wage forms in Europe since 1500*, ed. Peter Scholliers and Leonard Schwarz (New York, Berghahn books, 2003), 3–24.
[13] Nelson, 'Scientific Management, Systematic Management, and Labor, 1880–1915', 485.
[14] Frederick W. Taylor, *Shop management* (New York: Harper, 1911), 14. Although Taylor saw the Towne-Halsey plan as an improvement, he maintained that this and similar systems should be complemented by systematic time studies.
[15] Drury, *Scientific Management*, 38; Schloss, *Methods of Industrial Remuneration*, 55.
[16] Johansson, *Arbetarrörelsen och taylorismen*, 89.
[17] Jonathan Zeitlin, 'The Labour Strategies of British Engineering Employers, 1890–1922', in *Managerial Strategies & Industrial Relations: An historical and comparative study*, eds Howard F. Gospel and Craig R. Littler (London: Gower, 1983), 39.
[18] Zeitlin, 'The Labour Strategies of British Engineering Employers', 40.
[19] Zeitlin, 'The Labour Strategies of British Engineering Employers', 43–4.

The evolution of labour market institutions and wage systems in Sweden

Although pre-industrial strikes are known from Sweden, this form of labour conflict is essentially a phenomenon that gained prominence with the transformation from an agricultural to an industrial society. As seen in graph 7.1, the absolute strike frequency increased over time until the big showdown between the federation of blue-collar workers (*Landsorganisationen, LO*) and the employers' organizations in 1909. This general strike (*Storstrejken*) weakened, but did not crush, the labour movement. The strike frequency rose to previously unseen levels during the final years of the First World War, towards the backdrop of soaring food prices and pending a major reform of working hours. The absolute peak came in 1918, after which the trend was reversed and strikes became less common. Meanwhile, a new labour market regime took form, where both parties in the labour market were well organized and where the state avoided direct regulation of wages in favour of collective agreements. These features – relative labour peace, organized workers and employers – were further manifested in the famous Saltsjöbaden treaty of 1938 and became cornerstones of the Swedish model of industrial relations that was further developed in the era after the Second World War.[20]

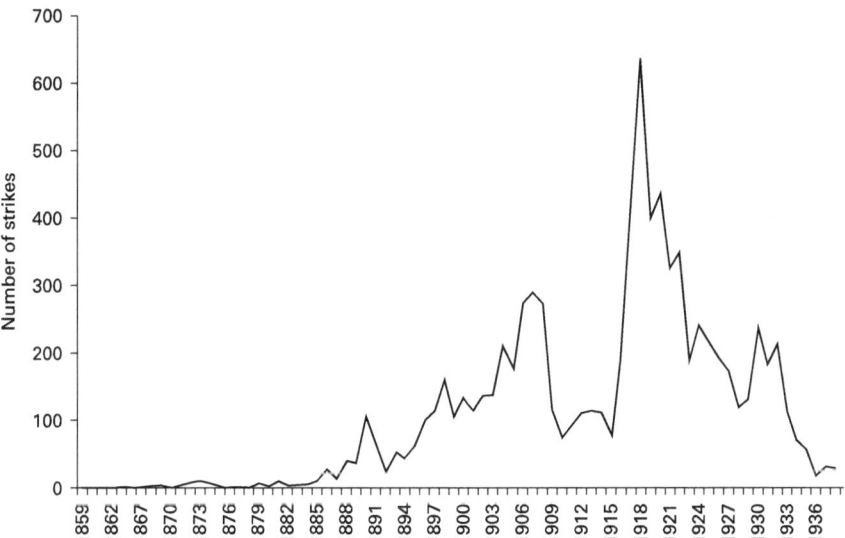

Graph 7.1 Strikes in Sweden, 1859–1938. Source: Kerstin Enflo, Jakob Molinder and Tobias Karlsson, *Från Sundsvall till Saltsjöbaden: ett regionalt perspektiv på strejker på svenska arbetsmarknaden 1859-1938*, Swedish National Data Service (2019). Version 1.0. https://doi.org/10.5878/qqqg-qz51

[20] Christer Lundh, 'Institutional Change in the Swedish Labour Market 1830–1990', in *Wage Formation, Labour Market Institutions and Economic Transformation in Sweden 1860–2000*, ed. Christer Lundh, Jonas Olofsson, Lennart Schön and Lars Svensson (Stockholm: Almqvist & Wiksell International, 2004), 92–142.

Sweden began to industrialize relatively late, but once the transformation began in the 1870s the country rapidly caught up with the technological frontier. Lacking big coal deposits, Sweden soon began to exploit waterpower, building a power grid that connected various parts of the country. This infrastructure contributed to rapid adoption of electricity, changes in the organization of work, the occupational structure and, indeed, the pattern of labour conflicts.[21] Modernization of the economic life also meant organizational changes. In the late 1890s, 'American methods' were advocated in the journals of Swedish engineers and towards the turn of the century these journals brought up new wage systems, aimed at reducing workers' resistance against piece rate cuts.[22] In the mechanical engineering industry, piece rate payments became common practice and a couple of well-known Swedish firms also introduced bonus systems in the beginning of the new century.[23] Taylor's book *Scientific Management* was translated and published in Swedish in 1913 and his ideas actively promoted by the employers' interest organizations.[24] In the 1920s and 1930s, many Swedish firms adopted the use of piece rates and time studies. In the mid-1920s, every other blue-collar worker in the manufacturing sector was paid by the piece. In some industries, such as the mining, metal and wooden industries, the shares on piece rates were even higher.[25] Time studies became increasingly common. In the mid-1920s, such studies had been conducted at every tenth working place in mechanical engineering, representing 40 per cent of the workers in the same industry.[26]

While there was an overall development towards centralization of industrial relations in Sweden in the early twentieth century, the spread of performance-based pay meant that important issues remained to be solved locally. While piece rates and bonus plans could be mentioned in national agreements, detailed price lists and schemes were to be decided in negotiations between management and representatives of union branches.[27]

The early Swedish labour movement had a negative view on performance-based pay. At its very first congress in 1888, the Social Democratic Party adopted a resolution

---

[21] Jakob Molinder, Tobias Karlsson and Kerstin Enflo,' More Power to the People: Electricity Adoption, Technological Change, and Labor Conflict', *Journal of Economic History*, 81, no. 2 (2021): 481–512.
[22] Johansson, *Arbetarrörelsen och taylorismen*, 44.
[23] Alf Johansson, *Den effektiva arbetstiden: verkstäderna och arbetsintensitetens problem 1900–1920* (Uppsala: Uppsala universitet, 1977), 104; Johansson, *Arbetarrörelsen och taylorismen*, 39; Erik August Forsberg, *Industriell ekonomi: allmänna grunder o. principer jämte tillämpningar på praktiskt viktiga fall* (Stockholm: Geber, 1916), 163 ff. In mechanical engineering, straight piece rates were more common in firms with standardized mass-production, whereas firms with a diverse production more often applied bonus systems. Karl Petander, *Arbetsintensiteten inom Sveriges mekaniska verkstadsindustri: en ekonomisk-statistisk undersökning* (Stockholm: Norstedt, 1916).
[24] Frederick W. Taylor, *Rationell arbetsledning: Taylor-systemet* (Stockholm: Sveriges industriförbund, 1913); Hans de Geer, *Rationaliseringsrörelsen i Sverige: effektivitetsidéer och socialt ansvar under mellankrigstiden* (Stockholm: Stockholm University, 1978).
[25] Christer Lundh, *Spelets regler: institutioner och lönebildning på den svenska arbetsmarknaden 1850–2010* (Stockholm: SNS förlag, 2010), 159.
[26] Lundh, *Spelets regler*, 159.
[27] Johansson, *Arbetarrörelsen och taylorismen*, 176 ff; Lars Magnusson, *Arbetet vid en svensk verkstad: Munktells 1900–1920* (Lund: Arkiv förlag, 1987), 219–23.

that condemned piece rates and endorsed hourly pay as 'the basis for wage work'.[28] Over time, outright resistance turned into acceptance.[29] In 1904, for example, the Metal Workers' Union accepted the use of bonus plans in principle.[30] Generally, unions tried to reduce the arbitrariness by which performance-based pay was applied by establishing fixed price lists and guaranteed minimum pay.[31] In contexts where performance-based pay was the norm, minimum hourly pay meant that workers gained the right to switch to time-based remuneration in cases where they were dissatisfied with the piece rates. In the first collective agreement for metal workers, concluded in 1905, this right was reluctantly recognized by the employers and it would remain in agreements for considerable time.

Wage systems in official statistics on work stoppages

In this chapter, I employ two datasets of Swedish work stoppages (strikes, lockouts and mixed conflicts).[32] The first builds on the semi-official statistics that was created by Axel Raphael around 1900, covering the period 1859–1902.[33] The second dataset is based on the official strike statistics that was published in the period 1903–27.[34] The main difference between the datasets is that Raphael collected data retrospectively from newspapers, whereas the official statistical apparatus continuously collected data, using newspaper reports but also questionnaires to involved parties. Both datasets, however, contain information on individual conflicts, such as their immediate (stated) causes, not just aggregate tables and distinguish between strikes and lockouts.[35]

The period 1859–1902

Raphael was an economist and historian who served as the secretary of a public commission on state interference in strikes and lockouts that was appointed in 1899. In

---

[28] Thommy Svensson, *Från ackord till månadslön: en studie av lönepolitiken, fackföreningarna och rationaliseringarna inom svensk varvsindustri under 1900-talet* (Göteborg: Göteborgs universitet, 1983), 165.
[29] Svensson, *Från ackord till månadslön*, 166.
[30] Johansson, *Den effektiva arbetstiden*, 105. See, however, Magnusson, *Arbetet vid en svensk verkstad*, 219–23, for an example of a union branch that opposed bonus plans.
[31] Lars Berggren, *Ångvisslans och brickornas värld: om arbete och facklig organisering vid Kockums mekaniska verkstad och Carl Lunds fabrik i Malmö 1840–1905* (Lund: Lunds universitet, 1991), 243 ff; Johansson, *Den effektiva arbetstiden*, 103; Magnusson, *Arbetet vid en svenska verkstad*, 212 ff.
[32] Both datasets are available upon request through Swedish National Data Service: https://snd.gu.se/en/catalogue/study/snd1088
[33] Described in greater detail in Tobias Karlsson, 'Strikes and Lockouts in Sweden: Reconsidering Raphael's List of Work Stoppages 1859-1902', *Lund Papers in Economic History* 192 (2019).
[34] See Kerstin Enflo and Tobias Karlsson, 'From Conflict to Compromise: The Importance of Mediation in Swedish Work Stoppages 1907–1927', *European Review of Economic History*, 23, no. 3 (2019): 268–98.
[35] On these issues, see Sjaak van der Velden, 'Building a repository for strike data. The search for micro data', in *Striking Numbers: New Approaches to Strike Research*, ed. Sjaak van der Velden, IISH Research Paper 165 (2012) and Jesper Hamark, 'Labour market conflicts in Scandinavia, c. 1900–1938: The scientific need to separate strikes and lockouts', Gothenburg Papers in Economic History 26 (2020).

this position, Raphael went through newspapers retrospectively to get an idea of how the frequency, nature and geographical location of labour conflicts had changed over time. Raphael did a 'complete review of some daily newspapers (mainly *Göteborgs-Posten, Stockholms Dagblad* and *Social-Demokraten*, for some work stoppages also others), at least one for various parts of the period'.[36]

After the publication of the list for the years 1859–1900, Raphael continued collecting data on strikes and lockouts from newspapers until 15 June 1902. Thereafter the staff at the Board of Trade (*Kommerskollegium*) continued his work for the rest of the year 1902. Work stoppages for the years 1901–02 were published in the same way as in the 1901 inquiry.[37]

Historians have pointed out that Raphael's list of 1,449 work stoppages for the period 1859–02 is incomplete, particularly for the 1860s and 1870s.[38] This is not surprising since the only newspaper with connections to the labour movement that Raphael used (*Social-Demokraten*) was not founded until 1885. Raphael himself was aware of this shortcoming and in order to enable later generations of researchers the opportunity to complete the data set he choose to publish all data and not just summary tables. From the 1890s, the data appear to have a better coverage.[39]

For each work stoppage, Raphael tried to include information on when the event began and ended, where it took place, what occupation(s) were involved, the number of participant workers, the workers purpose, and the outcome of the conflict. Since he had to rely on what a couple of newspapers reported many of these columns were left blank. For example, many of the events had a start date but no end date and less than half of the events lacked information on number of participants and the outcome.

However, the workers' purpose (*arbetarnes syfte*) seems to have been mentioned in newspapers. From the 1880s, onwards, Raphael reports the workers' purpose in over 80 per cent of the work stoppages.[40] The vast majority of these events are described as strikes with the purpose of increasing wage levels (or resisting wage cuts). Terms referring to specific wage systems (hourly pay, piece rates etc.) are rare in Raphael's list. The term hourly wage (*timlön*) is mentioned only once in this dataset, namely concerning a lockout of moulders in Borås in 1900. The purpose of this conflict is described very briefly as 'hourly wage, shorter working hours'. Whether this was a conflict over the wage system or basically about the level of pay (and working hours) is unclear.

Piece rates are mentioned 14 times out of a total number of 1,164 events with a recorded purpose (see table 7.1). Two events concern layoffs of piece rate workers, one event the interpretation of an existing agreement on piece rates and another has the vague description 'issue on piece wage' ('*fråga om ackordslön*'). In ten of the cases where piece rates are mentioned, however, it is clearly about workers resisting employers

---

[36] *Förlikmings- och skiljenämndskomiténs betänkande* (Stockholm, 1901), 144.
[37] In *Arbetsstatistik E: Arbetsinställelser i Sverige* (Stockholm, 1909).
[38] Jane Cederqvist, *Arbetare i strejk: studier rörande arbetarnas politiska mobilisering under industrialismens genombrott: Stockholm 1850–1909* (Stockholm: Stockholms universitet, 1980); Ingemar Johansson, *Strejken som vapen: fackföreningar och strejker i Norrköping 1870–1910* (Stockholm: Stockholms universitet, 1982).
[39] Cederqvist, *Arbetare i strejk*; Johansson, *Strejken som vapen*.
[40] Karlsson, *Strikes and Lockouts in Sweden*, 18.

Table 7.1 List of work stoppages where the workers' stated purpose indicates a conflict over piece work in Sweden, 1859–1902.

Year	Ort	Occupation	Participants	Workers' purpose	Outcome
1896	Helsingborg	Weavers	95	Hindering piece work	–
1897	Gunnarsbo	Sawmill workers	30	Abolishing piece work	–
1897	Gefle	Woollen spinners		Abolishing piece work	–
1897	Mohög	Moulders	4	Abolishing piece work etc.	–
1898	Stockholm	Blasters		Abolishing piece work	–
1898	Stockholm	Blasters		Abolishing piece work etc.	Compromise
1899	Malmö	Turners	20	Hindering piece work	–
1901	Yxenhult	Peat factory workers	130	Hindering piece work	–
1901	Södertälje	Glove-cutting workers	13	Hindering piece work	Workers' won
1902	Stockholm	Tailor workers	12	Hindering piece work	Workers' lost

Source: Kerstin Enflo, Jakob Molinder and Tobias Karlsson, *Från Sundsvall till Saltsjöbaden: ett regionalt perspektiv på strejker på svenska arbetsmarknaden 1859-1938*, Swedish National Data Service (2019). Version 1.0. https://doi.org/10.5878/qqqg-qz51

attempts to introduce a new wage system or workers wanting to abolish an existing wage system. Information on the outcome is missing for seven out of the ten wage-system conflicts, including the events that involved most workers, almost 100 weavers in Helsingborg in 1896 and 130 peat factory workers in a Southern village in 1901. Of the remaining three conflicts, one ended with a victory for the workers: in 1901, thirteen glove-cutting workers in Södertälje managed to hinder the introduction of piece work. In the following year, twelve tailor workers failed to achieve the same purpose. A couple of years earlier, an unknown number of blasters (*bergsprängare*) in Stockholm had achieved a compromise solution with employers (although the details are unknown).

The period 1903–27

Interestingly, we observe no dramatic shift in graph 7.1 in the number of recorded work stoppages between 1902 and 1903, when systematic and continuous collection of statistics on work stoppages in Sweden began. The reliability of this branch of the official statistics is generally held in high regard.[41]

The gathering of data was initially based on information in newspapers and trade journals.[42] If a conflict was encountered in a journal, questionnaires were sent out to

---

[41] See Flemming Mikkelsen, *Arbejdskonflikter i Skandinavien 1848-1980* (Copenhagen: University of Copenhagen, 1990), 441 and Christer Thörnqvist, *Arbetarna lämnar fabriken: strejkrörelser i Sverige under efterkrigstiden, deras bakgrund, förlopp och följder* (Göteborg: Göteborgs universitet, 1994), 88–9. However, 'political strikes', such as events during the spring of 1917, may be underreported. Jesper Hamark, *Ports, dock workers and labour market conflicts* (Göteborg: Göteborgs universitet, 2014), 163.
[42] *Arbetsstatistik E*, 9–10.

the involved parties. The response rate was high; in the period 1903–23, responses were gathered from both employer and worker representatives in almost 60 per cent of all work stoppages.[43]

Other informants supplied complementing information. Occasionally annual reports from the trade union confederations and employers' organizations and other sources were consulted. In principle, the statistics should include all conflicts – both small and large. The gathering of information through questionnaires served a twofold purpose: (1) to establish whether a conflict actually had resulted in work stoppages; and (2) to uncover the causes, characteristics and outcomes of the conflict. Cases where the parties supplied contradictory information on whether a conflict-related work stoppage actually had occurred were included in the statistics, but with notes about how the parties had described the events. Until 1927, extensive information was included in the published reports for each individual work stoppage, namely: the beginning and end of a stoppage (dates), nature (strike or lockout), involved occupation(s), location, reason for conflict, number of directly involved employers and workers, whether workers were organized, the outcome of the conflict, the source of information, and additional notes.

In the period when detailed statistics on work stoppages were published (1903–27) about 60 per cent of the 6,367 work stoppages were officially claimed to have concerned wage levels, as seen in graph 7.2.[44] Strikes where workers demanded increased pay were most frequent (about 50 per cent of all work stoppages). Strikes to defend prevailing wage levels, against employers' demands to reduce pay, were less frequent (11 per cent of all work stoppages), except for during the deep economic downturn in 1921–2. Strikes over 'other issues' or 'multiple issues', where disagreements over wage systems are counted constituted about 12 and 8 per cent of all work stoppages, respectively.

Compared to Raphael's data for 1859–1902, explicit references to wage systems are more frequent in the statistics for 1903–27 and there is an increasing trend over time, as shown in graph 7.3. That references to hourly pay, piece rates or similar terms are more common in the official statistics is not surprising since Raphael's colleagues after 1902 had access to much more information. To some extent, the increasing frequency of references to wage systems may simply be due to improved capacity of the statistical apparatus to gather information, but the trend may also reflect an increasing interest in introducing performance-based pay. The spike in 1918 is notable. Looking closer at the conflict causes this particular year reveals considerably that hourly wages in this year often was mentioned in combination with working hours. Many of these conflicts seems to have been closely related to the new regulation of working hours (the 48-hour week) that were about to be passed in 1919. Workers were pushing for higher hourly wages to compensate for the loss of income due to fewer working hours. This reform has been claimed to have encouraged employers' interest in various rationalization measures.[45] The time trend in graph 7.3 is, however, not driven by more mentions of piece rates, but rather by more mentions of *either* hourly pay or piece rates.

---

[43] Mikkelsen 1992, *Arbejdskonflikter i Skandinavien 1848–1980*, 439.
[44] All but three of these events had some kind of information on the cause of the conflict.
[45] Johansson, *Den effektiva arbetstiden*; Erik Bengtsson and Jakob Molinder, 'The economic effects of the 1920 eight-hour working day reform in Sweden', *Scandinavian Economic History Review*, 65, no. 2 (2017): 149–68.

Everywhere but in the Strike Statistics? 173

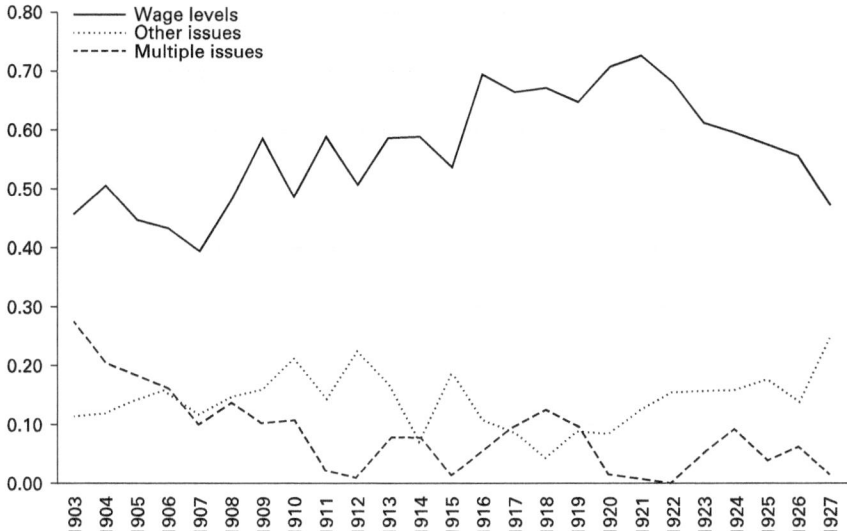

Graph 7.2 Proportions of work stoppages on wage levels, other issues and multiple issues in Sweden, 1903–27. Source: Enflo, Molinder and Karlsson, *Från Sundsvall till Saltsjöbaden*.

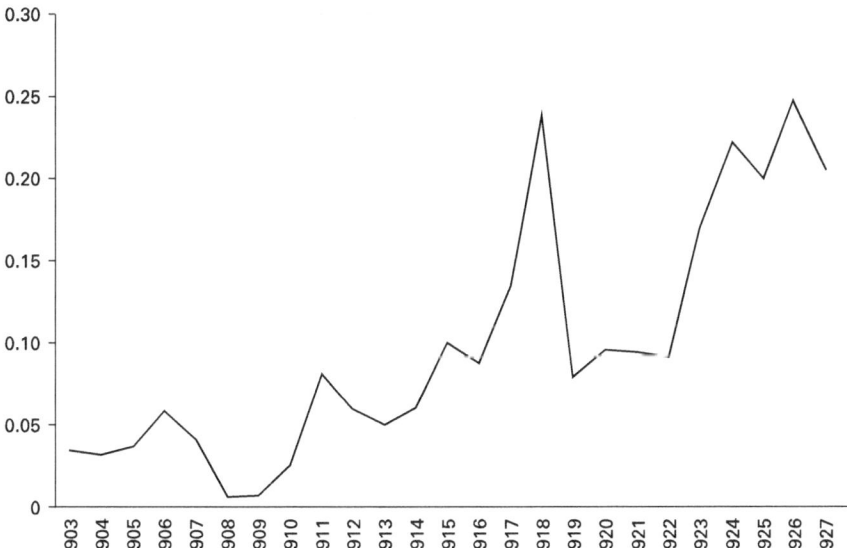

Graph 7.3 Mentions of terms related to specific wage systems (hourly pay, piece rates etc.) in relation to all work stoppages with stated causes in Sweden, 1903–27. Source: Enflo, Molinder and Karlsson, *Från Sundsvall till Saltsjöbaden*.

In total, 'piece rates' (or similar terms) are mentioned in 342 work stoppages in the period 1903–27. Many of these mentions refer to workers demanding higher piece rates (or resisting employers attempts to reduce piece rates), but a significant number (N=77) concerned conflicts related to the wage system. For most of these cases it is possible to get an idea of the workers' (and employers) positions. Table 7.2 presents a simple classification of workers' demands. Here we see that workers were critical of piece rates (either the introduction of piece rates or an existing system) in 31 per cent of the cases. The opposite was true – workers demanding the introduction of piece rates for some or all jobs – in 22 per cent of the cases. The most common type of worker demand in relation to wage-system conflicts in this period was, however, demanding income guarantees within existing system of performance-based pay.

Comparing the evidence from the official statistics after 1902 with the semi-official statistics for the period until 1902 suggests a shift in the workers' attitudes toward performance-based pay. There is still some resistance, but more and more workers seem to have discovered advantages in piece work or reached the conclusion that it is better to reform a piece rate system from within, by introducing income guarantees. Yet, it has to be acknowledged that the evidence is fragmentary. Most officially recorded work stoppages did not mention the wage system and work stoppages that were explicitly concerned wage systems were uncommon. This leads on to the question: can we trust the statistics in this regard?

Immediate causes and deeper causes

The causes of work stoppages that appear in official strike statistics are most often based on the immediate claims of the workers.[46] These claims may, however, have been adjusted to the fact that most labour conflicts arise in connection to negotiations. Workers have reasons to reformulate their claims so that their chances of success increase. If workers are dissatisfied with the wage system but anticipate that the chances of convincing the employers to change the system are small, they may claim higher pay

Table 7.2 Nature of workers' demands in work stoppages related to wage systems in Sweden, 1903–27.

Type of demands	N (work stoppages)	In per cent
Opposing piece work	24	31%
Advocating piece work	17	22%
Demanding guaranteed hourly (or daily) pay for piece work	31	40%
Unclear	5	6%
Total	77	

Source: Enflo, Molinder and Karlsson, *Från Sundsvall till Saltsjöbaden*.

[46] K. G. J. C. Knowles, *Strikes: A Study in Industrial Conflict* (Oxford: Basil Blackwell, 1952), 210, 228–39.

as a more realistic second-best solution. In that case, the conflict will look like an ordinary wage strike in the statistics, but closer investigation will reveal that the deeper cause is discontent with the wage system.[47] Moreover, the causes that shows up in strike statistics may also be simplifications of a more complex set of claims.[48] After all, the whole process of producing statistics is about standardizing and summarizing data.

There are various sources that may be used to reveal the deeper causes – and complexity – of labour conflicts, such as court records, negotiation minutes and correspondence between labour market parties. There is also a substantial amount of existing research on the organization of work in specific industries and workplaces. In the following section, I present case-study evidence from shipbuilding and tobacco production.

Case-study evidence

Shipbuilding

The shipbuilding industry was an offshoot from an older, highly diversified mechanical engineering industry. Mechanical engineering became the backbone of the Swedish economy in the decades around 1900 and served as an example for industrial relations in other industries. Shipbuilding rose to prominence in the former half of the twentieth century and was concentrated to the Western and Southern parts of the country.[49] Gothenburg in the west hosted three of the largest shipyards – Götaverken, Eriksberg and Lindholmen – and Malmö in the south had Kockums. The industry had two main activities – construction of new ships and repairing of old ones. Both construction and repairing involved several occupational groups, including fitters, sheet metal workers, moulders and carpenters.

Industrial relations differed between shipyards.[50] The workers at Kockums in Malmö would form unions in the late nineteenth century and had their level of union density approaching 80 per cent as early as around 1900, after a clash with the employer organization in 1897.[51] During this conflict, many shipbuilding workers in Gothenburg acted as strikebreakers, as Kockums moved some production to the shipyards in that city.

---

[47] On deeper or 'underlying' causes more generally, see Knowles, *Strikes*, 209–24.
[48] Using court records for studying wild strikes in Sweden in the period 1975–9, Thörnqvist finds a clear discrepancy between immediate and deeper causes (*Arbetarna lämnar fabriken*, 152–3). The immediate cause of over three-fourths of the conflicts studied by Thörnqvist were strikes for higher wages, the same motive constituted less than a third of all causes stated in court. Discontent with the wage system constituted 5 per cent of the immediate causes and over 10 per cent of all causes stated in court.
[49] Kent Olsson, *Från pansarbåtsvarv till tankfartygsvarv: de svenska storvarvens utveckling till exportindustri 1880–1936* (Göteborg: Svenska varv, 1983).
[50] Berggren, *Ångvisslans och brickornas värld*; Bo Stråth, *Varvsarbetare i två varvsstäder: en historisk studie av verkstadsklubbarna vid varven i Göteborg och Malmö* (Göteborg: Svenska varv, 1982); Svensson, *Från ackord till månadslön*.
[51] Berggren, *Ångvisslans och brickornas värld*.

The shipbuilding workers in Gothenburg had almost three decades before, in 1870, launched one of the first major strikes in Sweden but did not take significant part in the subsequent upswing of the labour movement more generally in the following decades.[52] This was probably because employers in Gothenburg took early initiatives to forestall unionization. Among other things, these policies included wage differentiation and paternalism. Employers in Gothenburg were ready to reward high-performing and well-behaved workers and would offer its core workers stable terms of employment and social benefits, including company housing. As a consequence, unionization was delayed until the last years of the nineteenth century, when the main part of the labour movement had become associated with the Social Democratic Party. The Metal Workers' Union, which was already strong in Malmö and other parts of the country, approached shipbuilding workers in Gothenburg with demands to raise minimum wages. Hence, when employers tried to differentiate workers, the union tried to create a more homogenous workforce.

The Engineering Employers' Organization (*Verkstadsföreningen*) was initiated in 1896 as a response to the attempts of the Metal Workers' Union to organize the shipbuilding workers in Gothenburg. The conflicts and interactions between the employer and union fostered wage equalization and centralization. This process began in the early years of the twentieth century, first with a general strike for an extension of the franchise that was met by a lockout in 1902, then by strikes for raised minimum wages, which also were followed by a lockout and then again in 1905, with a five-month conflict that resulted in the first national collective agreement in Sweden. So far, scientific management and attempts to rationalize construction and repairing of ships were not in the forefront of disputes.

That would change after the First World War. A severe economic downturn in 1921 was followed by wage cuts and mass layoffs of blue-collar workers. The companies, now endowed with a greater share of white-collar workers, used the crisis as an opportunity to introduce more rational ways of organizing productions. Although the implemented rationalization measures were inspired by Taylor's ideas (a planning department to improve the production flow), this hardly meant far-reaching vertical division of labour where workers lost control over work.[53] Instead, the workers were given stronger economic incentives to increase efficiency and reduce loss of time between various tasks.

Rationalizations at Götaverken had begun even earlier, during the First World War, with an increased focus on shipbuilding and the establishment of new workshops and new machines.[54] In order to facilitate rationalizations, reduce time losses and give workers incentives to cooperate, the management made two moves.[55] First, an extended use of piece rates, with the intention to allow workers to keep parts of the efficiency gains. Second, direct interventions in the process of production, such as standardization

---

[52] Stråth, *Varvsarbetare i två varvsstäder*; Svensson, *Från ackord till månadslön*.
[53] Svensson, *Från ackord till månadslön*, 159. Time and method studies would not take place until the mid-1930s.
[54] Svensson, *Från ackord till månadslön*, 161.
[55] Svensson, *Från ackord till månadslön*, 176.

of material, work tasks and products.⁵⁶ In addition, work teams were gradually divided into smaller units and task specialization increased.

The rationalization measures at Götaverken coincided with increased unionization and general social unrest around the country.⁵⁷ In 1917 the workers at Götaverken struck to achieve compensations for price increases. Simultaneously, however, the union petitioned the management in order to extend the use of piece rates.⁵⁸ As pointed out by Thommy Svensson, this is remarkable in the light of the received wisdom of piece rates being a typical management tool to extract work effort but he observes that the original union resistance towards performance-based pay had been loosened ever since the late nineteenth century. There were differences between occupational groups, as well as between union branches, in this regard. Moulders, which were organized in a craft union, were hostile, whereas the leadership of the Metal Workers' Union had accepted piece rates as 'a necessary evil'.⁵⁹ At about the same time as the union branch at Götaverken sought to increase the use of piece rates, members of the union local at Kockums suggested the total abolishment of piece rates in 1918.

For workers at Götaverken, piece rates were associated with better pay, particularly in the years following the war inflation, namely 1919–20. Thereafter a couple of years with mass layoffs and wage reductions followed. The union local at Götaverken gave notice of a strike in 1922 and again in 1923, when they also executed their threat. Svensson describes the union motives:

> The fight concerned wages and jobs. The actions were not directed towards the rationalizations and the structural changes as such. On the contrary, there are evidence suggesting that the union branch tried to speed up the breakup of so-called long piece rates into smaller units by petitioning the management – in order to increase the weight of the individual performance element.⁶⁰

Moreover, the union wanted to formalize piece rates in collective agreements, which the management accepted as long as the tasks were standardized. By making the piece rates explicit in the agreements, the union hoped to forestall future wage cuts. As pointed out by Svensson, it seems like the union branch gave priority to the members' wages rather than defending their autonomy at work.⁶¹ A possible explanation for this priority is that rationalizations at Götaverken were initiated before the union had gained substantial strength. The union branch's response may have been rational given its limited strength. In a highly complex production process such as shipbuilding with numerous of tasks that could be subject to wage bargaining, the union accepted a great degree of individual negotiations by skilled workers and recognized that these negotiations more often were successful when remuneration was based on performance

---

[56] Svensson, *Från ackord till månadslön*, 177.
[57] Svensson, *Från ackord till månadslön*, 163.
[58] Svensson, *Från ackord till månadslön*, 165.
[59] Svensson, *Från ackord till månadslön*, 166.
[60] Svensson, *Från ackord till månadslön*, 175.
[61] Svensson, *Från ackord till månadslön*, 176.

than when it was based on time. Furthermore, large-scale mechanization of the production process, with a complete loss of autonomy for the workers was in the first decades of the twentieth century a distant scenario in shipbuilding. In this regard, the situation and development in the tobacco industry was quite different.

The tobacco industry

In the late nineteenth and early twentieth century, there were around 100 factories for production of tobacco goods in Sweden, employing over 4,000 workers in total. Cigars was the branch of tobacco production that employed most workers. In this branch, work was essentially manual, and a clear majority of cigar workers were women. Work was divided into three basic stages – preparation, rolling and sorting/packaging. Preparation of leaves mainly employed relatively unskilled labour and almost exclusively women. Rolling and sorting/packaging required more skill and employed both men and women. Whereas remuneration for preparation task largely was time-based, remuneration of rolling and sorting was typically based on performance, with rates related to grade. In the tobacco industry, piece rate pay was established long before scientific management.[62]

Cigar workers were relatively early to unionize. Initially, the organization was de facto a craft union but evolved into a union that encompassed all workers in the tobacco industry. The early history of the Tobacco Workers' Union (1888–97) featured small and big conflicts with employers, often concerning union recognition, wage levels and the behaviour of foremen. The union's prime objective was to raise minimum wages, which also was the immediate cause of the most notable conflict in the industry, a combined strike and lockout in 1896 that involved tobacco workers all around the country. This conflict was successful for the union in the sense that it won recognition, a nation-wide collective agreement and attracted many new members. Industrial relations were further refined some years later with the creation of conciliation boards. There was also a development towards structural rationalization with a decreasing number of individual factories. In 1912 many firms merged into a trust and in 1914, the Swedish parliament decided to create a public–private partnership with monopoly on the production of tobacco goods. This decision was taken in order to boost state revenues and finance rearmament. The Swedish Tobacco Monopoly came into being in 1915. Since existing piece rates were tied to sales prices the existing collective agreement in the industry had to be renegotiated.[63] A partly novel feature in the new agreement was the so-called classification board, a body that had the purpose of forestalling disputes and conflicts concerning pricing of tasks upon the introduction of new tobacco brands.[64]

---

[62] For a more in-depth treatment of labour relations in the Swedish tobacco industry, see Tobias Karlsson, *Downsizing: Personnel Reductions at the Swedish Tobacco Monopoly, 1915–1939* (Lund: Lunds universitet, 2008).
[63] *Minnesskrift utgiven med anledning av Svenska tobaksmonopolets tjugofemåriga verksamhet den 1 juni 1940, 1915–1940* (Stockholm, 1940), 282.
[64] *Minnesskrift*, 383.

The first years of the Tobacco Monopoly were characterized by wartime conditions. Demand for tobacco products soared, while the supply of raw tobacco decreased, in spite of efforts to stimulate domestic growing of tobacco leaves. In the summer of 1918, the Tobacco Monopoly introduced new cigar brands – so-called tip-less cigars – that required smaller amounts of tobacco leaves. Along with the new products, the management also suggested a more widespread application of bonus pay, which had previously been applied for a couple of specific tasks, for example in cigarette production.[65] The management claimed that 'straight piece rates, as little as pure hourly pay, was a successful form of remuneration' and pointed out that the suggested system was applied 'in a number of other industries'.[66] The union leadership was critical of such novelties and recommended the members to turn down the management proposals. The union leadership feared that the bonus plan would cause wage reductions. This fear was based on a belief that the preceding time studies had been biased; the management had estimated the 'average' performance based upon 'a few particularly skilled workers'.[67]

The union branches turned down the proposal in ballots among the members and since the union was bound by an existing agreement, the dispute was to be settled by arbitration.[68] Claiming that the arbitration board's verdict was pro-management and that it would mean wage cuts, cigar workers in Stockholm went on strike anyway. They were soon joined by cigar workers at other locations around the country, and by tobacco workers in other specialties in Stockholm. Essentially, all members of the Tobacco Workers' Union became involved in the conflict, which were named 'the fight over the tip-less cigars'. After two weeks, work was resumed along with negotiations. Reluctantly, the union accepted a compromise where workers transferred to production of tip-less cigars were granted a temporary income amendment. The deal was basically the same as had been suggested by the arbitration board.

In the following year, the bonus plan was established in a new collective agreement as the dominant payment system, along with hourly pay and straight piece rates.[69] Products were divided into various classes, according to the complexity of work. For each class, a normal performance, with an associated level of pay, was established. Workers who exceeded the normal performance were paid a bonus that gradually decreased.

According to the Tobacco Monopoly's official history, the employer's original motive for bonus scheme was to provide incentives to workers to handle raw materials more carefully and maintain high product quality.[70] To the workers, the management

---

[65] Cigarette production began in the late nineteenth century and was from the start highly mechanized, in contrast to cigar production.
[66] Tage Lindbom, *Tobaksarbetarnas förbund i Sverige 1889-1939: en historik* (Stockholm: Svenska tobaksindustriarbetareförbundet, 1940), 247.
[67] Lindbom, *Tobaksarbetarnas förbund i Sverige 1889-1939*, 247.
[68] Lindbom, *Tobaksarbetarnas förbund i Sverige 1889-1939*, 248.
[69] Tage Lindbom, *Tobaksarbetarnas Stockholmsavdelning 1884-1934: historik* (Stockholm: Tiden, 1934), 167.
[70] *Minnesskrift*, 384.

also put forward that the new system of remuneration would reduce wage differences, an argument that won acceptance among some of the workers but not all.[71]

At the congress of the Tobacco Workers' Union in 1923, the bonus system was the object of a lengthy debate.[72] Some speakers argued for the abolishment of the system, others defended it. In between were others who did not object the system as such but thought that the payments for 'normal' performance were too low. One of the union pioneers personally disliked the bonus plan but admitted that 80 per cent of the members benefitted from it. The issue returned again when the congress gathered in 1925.[73] This time, the union board was divided. A majority preferring straight piece rates, and willing to raise strike funds to achieve a return to the old practice, stood against the minority that favoured the existing bonus system. Among the congress delegates, however, the balance of power went the other way. Most of the delegates voted for the continuation of bonus pay as the main form of remuneration. It seems like high-performing workers, which may have been better represented in the union leadership, preferred straight piece rates whereas the average workers had more to gain from a system where remuneration were not linearly related to performance.

From the above description it follows that 'the fight over the tip-less cigars' at least partly concerned a new system of remuneration. This was also indicated in the official statistics.[74] Moreover, this event was the last major strike that the Tobacco Workers' Union fought. Disagreements and disputes over piece rates and hourly pay did not disappear but were solved in the classification board or in collective agreements. Over the following decades, employment in the tobacco industry decreased as labour-saving machines were introduced in cigar production.[75] Securing compensation for redundant or replaced workers became the prime aim of the union, which eventually merged into the Food Workers' Union.

Conclusions

If not the most important form of labour conflict, strikes are the most well documented. For Sweden, semi-official statistics on work stoppages stretches back to the 1860s and are continued by official statistics of high quality for the period 1903 to 1927. This chapter provides a first look at the relationship between new wage systems, for example piece rate schemes and bonus plans, related to scientific management, and labour conflicts. The strike statistics are scrutinized looking for indications of such systems. This exercise shows that while most strikes concerned wages, they did not always mention whether wages were paid by the hour, day or by the piece. In the few pre-1903 events where the wage system was mentioned as an explicit conflict cause, unions were against piece rates. After 1903, wage systems were mentioned more often and from now

[71] Lindbom, *Tobaksarbetarnas Stockholmsavdelning 1884–1934*, 166.
[72] Lindbom, *Tobaksarbetarnas förbund i Sverige 1889–1939*, 260–2.
[73] Lindbom, *Tobaksarbetarnas förbund i Sverige 1889–1939*, 268.
[74] According to the official statistics, the strike was caused by 'Change of piece rates due to reorganization of production' (in Swedish: 'Ändring av ackordslöner med hänsyn till omläggning av tillverkningen').
[75] Karlsson, *Downsizing*.

on, examples where unions advocate piece rates, and in particular hybrid systems, become more frequent. This shift in union policy has also been documented in narrative evidence.

Recognizing the limitations of strike statistics, a closer look at two industries – shipbuilding and production of tobacco goods – follows. These industries differed in many regards. Whereas shipbuilding was a highly complex activity, which involved many occupations and allowed workers a considerable degree of autonomy, tobacco production took place in factories that could be overseen by managers. Both industries had many old-fashioned and manual features but underwent rationalization in various regards, beginning in the early years of the twentieth century and gathering speed in the years around the First World War and thereafter. In shipbuilding, there are clear examples of how union leaders sought to extend the use of piece rates and have it covered by collective agreements. However, this was not done by launching strikes but by negotiations. The case-study evidence suggests that open conflicts in shipbuilding primarily concerned wage levels, rather than wage systems. The same impression applies to the tobacco industry, with one exception: the introduction of a bonus plan, related to other changes in production, caused worker discontent and strike action. This strike failed. So did the union leadership's subsequent attempt to rally workers against the new wage system. Disagreements over wages did not disappear but were solved in negotiations between management and union representatives.

Important changes took place in employment relationships during the Second Industrial Revolution, not the least concerning how workers were remunerated. Performance-based and hybrid wage systems became more common. While the evidence presented in this chapter cannot establish how these new wage systems influenced the frequency of strikes, it is interesting to note that official statistics of work stoppages are aligned with narrative evidence from case studies. There are of course individual examples of conflicts on wage systems that are overlooked in the statistics, but such examples are most likely rare. Future research should look closer into how the adoption of new wage systems was influenced by, and influenced, conflict frequencies and patterns over time, in Sweden and elsewhere. A particularly relevant issue to investigate systematically is also to what extent new wage systems were associated with the creation of institutions where wage disputes played out without open conflict.

Part Two

Measurement and Theory

8

From Poverty Lines to Equal Pay for Equal Work: Commensuration Struggles in Apartheid South Africa

Grace Davie

At a 1977 conference devoted to minimum budgets, Johannesburg's Chamber of Commerce urged employers to 'get away from the idea that Africans don't eat so-called "Western" foods'.[1] Amid labour strikes and the rise of new Black trade unions, business leaders and state officials began to reluctantly concede that wages could be pegged to current prices of basic commodities, as opposed to stereotypes about innate racial and cultural difference. In 1979, the financial press noted the shift. The Poverty Datum Line (PDL), a cost of living indicator 'once scorned by employers', was 'gaining ground – if only in the form of lip-service'.[2] One member of the President's Economic Advisory Council complained: 'Where did all this stuff about the PDL come from? It was orchestrated by people overseas to make South Africa less competitive than them.'[3] For apartheid's defenders, such accusations are perhaps unsurprising given the state's Orwellian policy of 'separate development' resulting in 'independent' tribal homelands located within the Republic's national borders. What still requires explanation and analysis however, are the causal forces and social relations behind this shift in official discourse about the average worker, poverty lines and minimum wages.

Commensuration, the observation and comparison of people and things in relation to one common metric, is a process fundamental to random sampling, opinion polling, climate modelling and other kinds of scientific research.[4] Without commensuration, there could be no population statistics. 'The radical simplification of commensuration,' write Wendy Espeland and Michael Stevens, produce 'decontextualized, depersonalized

---

[1] *Financial Mail*, 27 May 1977 (Press Clippings Collection, South African Labor and Development Research Unit, University of Cape Town (hereafter Saldru Clippings).
[2] *Financial Mail*, 23 March 1979 (Saldru Clippings).
[3] One business leader blamed German trade unions for recent strikes in Port Elizabeth. 'Pay Rises Undermine SA's Competitiveness', *Cape Times*, 20 August 1982 (Saldru Clippings).
[4] The term 'commensuration' evokes some of the concerns of scholars in Science and Technology Studies with the 'translation' of expert knowledge, yet 'commensuration' is a term already familiar to mainstream sociologists and historians. See Wendy N. Espeland and Mitchell L. Stevens, 'Commensuration as a Social Process', *Annual Review of Sociology*, 24 (1998): 313–43.

numbers that are highly portable and easily made public'.[5] In his magisterial history of statistics, Alain Desrosières describes the contingencies of commensuration, including the essential first step in the process, the establishment of a 'space of equivalence'. In Europe and the US, such spaces tended to be 'practical' before they were 'cognitive', fenced off and made governable before vaulted into the realm of language and subjectivity. By mapping plots of land, counting people and governing territories, human and non-human objects of research and regulation were rendered practically and administratively interchangeable.[6] Importantly for this discussion wages and work in South Africa, Desrosières went on to stress the vulnerability of spaces of equivalence to 'disorderly forces'. Rather than representing a fixed 'reality', statistical averages based on the observation of phenomenon within constructed arenas of sameness are 'the provisional and fragile crowning of a series of conventions of equivalence between entities that a host of disorderly forces is continually trying to differentiate and disconnect'.[7]

In South Africa, peasant revolts, workers' movements and anticolonial campaigns challenged, to the point of sometimes successfully disconnecting, colonial conventions of equivalence. With the goal of inviting further analysis of the making and unmaking of spaces of equivalence in the field of labour history, this essay defines *commensuration struggles* as political contests that hinge on the comparability of objects of scientific research, including but not only 'breadwinners' and 'the average household'. Commensuration may be a ubiquitous feature of modernity, yet comparability contests can be uniquely pronounced in the human sciences. As Ian Hacking and others have illustrated, the surveyed can absorb, reject and also redirect expert knowledge imposed on them by surveyors, employers, medical doctors and government agencies.[8] A focus on commensuration struggles lends itself to ongoing interrogation of looping effects in

---

[5] Wendy Nelson Espeland and Michael Sauder, 'Rankings and Reactivity: How Public Measures Recreate Social Worlds', *American Journal of Sociology*, 113, no. 1 (2007): 18. On commensuration also see, Laura Centemeri, 'Reframing Problems of Incommensurability in Environmental Conflicts Through Pragmatic Sociology: From Value Pluralism to the Plurality of Modes of Engagement with the Environment', *Environmental Values*, 24, no. 3 (2015): 299–320. On the making of trust within and across agencies, see Theodore M. Porter, *Trust in Numbers: The Pursuit of Objectivity in Science and Public Life* (Princeton: Princeton University Press, 1995).

[6] Desrosières, like his colleague Thévenot, spoke of 'investments in forms' when describing how conventions in science are made real through their use. Desrosières, *The Politics of Large Numbers* (Cambridge, MA: Harvard University Press, 2002), 10–12. On 'governing through standards', see Laurent Thévenot, 'Certifying the World: Power Infrastructures and Practices in Economies of Conventional Forms', in *Re-Imagining Economic Sociology*, (eds) Patrik Aspers and Nigel Dodd, (Oxford: Oxford University Press, 2015). Also see Søren Jagd, 'Laurent Thévenot and the French Convention School: A Short Introduction', *Economic Sociology: European Electronic Newsletter*, 5, no. 3 (2004): 2–9.

[7] Desrosières, *The Politics of Large Numbers*, 325.

[8] Ian Hacking, *The Social Construction of What?* (Cambridge, MA: Harvard University Press, 1999). For examples of the ways in which the surveyed challenge and redirect survey data, also see Thomas Stapleford, *The Cost of Living in America: A Political History of Economic Statistics, 1880–2000* (New York: Cambridge University Press, 2009); Sarah E. Igo, *The Averaged Americans: Survey, Citizens, and the Making of a Mass Public* (Cambridge, MA: Harvard University Press, 2007); John Carson, *The Measure of Merit: Talents, Intelligence, and Inequality in the French and American Republics, 1750–1940* (Princeton: Princeton University Press, 2007).

the human sciences without returning scholars to the race-class debate that long preoccupied historians of South Africa.[9] By asking how conventions governing minimum wages gain strength through their practical use, it becomes possible to see the value of labor as determined by historically constituted social relations that may be overwhelmingly class-based and somewhat instrumental, or predominantly ideological and culturally layered, or a combination of both.

'Statactivism' is a close cousin to what I am calling commensuration struggles.[10] 'Whether it is anticolonial nationalists in India attempting to estimate per capita incomes in order to expose the effects of British colonial rule, or union workers estimating price rises to negotiate cost of living allowances, numbers can be produced from below as well as from above', note Pedro Ramos Pinto and Poornima Paidipaty. In South Africa, cost of living statistics were sometimes crafted from below. More frequently, poverty and inequality indicators served as 'counter-measurements' mobilized from below, and, indeed, at multiple levels and locations, through interactive dynamics in which the colonized, social reformers, trade unions and anti-apartheid groups deployed statistics strategically. By the 1960s, the PDL stood among several 'insurgent indicators' publicised so as 'to intervene in the politics of distribution', and even to justify armed revolution.[11] Nelson Mandela cited the PDL in his famous 1964 'prepared to die' speech. Revolutionary politics were crucial in rendering previously unthinkable comparisons, not only thinkable in apartheid South Africa, but unavoidable for business leaders such as the Chamber of Commerce representative quoted above. By the late 1970s, 'spaces of equivalence' based on assumptions antithetical to the common sense of racial identity gained acceptance through a highly contentious process. For three decades, companies and officials managed to brush aside Baston's PDL, falling back instead on stereotypes about innate racial and cultural difference. Through commensuration struggles the poverty line gained political traction when multinational corporations and the state responded to a confluence of crises, from labour strikes and sustained township unrest, to sanctions and divestment threats.[12] Without those kinds of pressures, which came from multiple directions, poverty lines and cost of living statistics based on spaces of equivalence that cut across constructed 'race' categories might not have penetrated official discourse.

---

[9] Put differently, empirical analysis of the social relations and shifting conditions that render categories conventional through their use may help to open up generative lines of inquiry into racialized political economies and their transformation. On the dangers of reducing internally contradictory racial ideologies to instrumental materialist readings of class, see Saul Dubow, 'Afrikaner Nationalism, Apartheid and the Conceptualisation of 'Race',' *The Journal of African History* 33, no. 2 (1992): 209–237, 235.

[10] Isabelle Bruno, Emmanuel Didier, and Tommaso Vitale. 'Statactivism: Forms of Action between Disclosure and Affirmation', *Partecipazione e conflictto / Participation and Conflict* 7, no. 2 (2014): 188–220.

[11] Pedro Ramos Pinto and Poornima Paidipaty, 'Introduction: Measuring Matters', Special Issue on 'The Measure of Inequality: Social Knowledge in Historical Perspective', *History of Political Economy*, 52, no. 3 (2020): 214–434, 429.

[12] Grace Davie, *Poverty Knowledge in South Africa: A Social History of Human Science, 1855–2005* (New York: Cambridge University Press, 2015).

Edward Batson and the Social Survey of Cape Town

In the late 1930s, Edward Batson became the first chair of the newly created Department of Social Science at the University of Cape Town. A recent graduate of the London School of Economics, his Social Survey of Cape Town was based on the methods of his mentor, mathematician, and random sampling pioneer Arthur Bowley. Batson's survey insisted on the interchangeableness of London diets and Cape Town diets. He defined the PDL as 'that expenditure which is necessary to procure, at the current prices of the district, those quantities of food, clothing, fuel, lighting, and cleaning materials which are essential for the health and decency of the members of a given household'. A discipline-builder eager to place the social sciences on par with the natural sciences, Batson's sample of 2,000 households equalled 3 per cent of Cape Town's population.[13] As he announced the first results of his multi-year survey, Batson praised his skilled field workers, rejected state commissions of inquiry as overly impressionistic, and deemed household surveys and random sampling essential tools of modern public administration.

In 1939, Prime Minister Jan Smuts led South Africa into the Second World War on the Allied side after debate in Parliament over whether to give Germany access to the country's naval bases. During the war years, Black Africans[14] gained access to jobs

---

[13] This put his findings within the acceptable 5 per cent margin of error, Batson noted. The PDL, which included the cost of rent, varied based on the number of adults and children in the home and relied on the British Medical Association's determination that the average adult male required 3,400 calories per day. See Edward Batson, 'A Further Recalculation of the Poverty Datum Line' in *Reports and Studies of the Social Survey of Cape Town* (Cape Town: University of Cape Town, 1941). On Bowley, see *The Social Survey in Historical Perspective, 1880-1940*, eds Martin Bulmer, Kevin Bales, and Kathryn Kish Sklar (New York: Cambridge University Press, 1991).

[14] This essay uses Black Africans to refer to the indigenous groups Christian missionaries, colonial officials and white settlers deemed 'native'. The phrase implies that white people can be 'African' and that race categories, class identification, and also notions of universal humanness have long and still-unfolding genealogies. Following Mbembe, 'Black' should be seen as shaped by 'transnationalizations'. Slavery and race science produced the category, but also 'the daily work' of 'inventing, telling, repeating and creating variations on the formulas, texts, and rituals whose goal was to produce the Black Man as a racial subject and site of savage exteriority, set up for moral disqualification and practical instrumentalization'. Achille Mbembe, *Critique of Black Reason*, Laurent Dubois, trans. (Durham: Duke University Press, 2017), 15, 27. Beginning in the late 1960s, and inspired by Negritude and Pan-Africanism, Black Consciousness defined 'Black' to include the mixed-race ('Coloureds'), Indians ('Asiatics'), and all the 'tribes' apartheid planners wanted to silo according to high apartheid 'separate development' planning and 'Bantu Education'. A humanizing category meant to counter divide-and-rule tactics, 'Black' for Black Consciousness, as for Black Liberation Theology, imbued the category with new dignity and the promise of political solidarity. In the aftermath of the #RhodesMustFall movement, 'white' is now receiving renewed attention. See Steve Biko, *I Write What I Like: Selected Writings* (Oxford: Heinemann, 1978 [1972]). Also see Deborah Posel, 'What's in a name? Racial Categorisations under Apartheid and their Afterlives', *Transformation* 47 (2001): 50–74; Eric J. Hobsbawm and Terence Ranger (eds), *The Invention of Tradition* (Cambridge: Cambridge University Press, 2014). On tribal identities and 'Indirect Rule', see Mahmood Mamdani, *Citizen and Subject: Contemporary Africa and the Legacy of Late Colonialism* (Princeton: Princeton University Press, 1996). On 'separate development' and 'high apartheid', see Saul Dubow, 'New Approaches to High Apartheid and Anti-Apartheid,' *South African Historical Journal* 69, 2 (2017): 304–29. On whiteness in South Africa, see Danelle van Zyl-Hermann and Jacob Boersman, 'Introduction: The Politics of Whiteness in Africa', *Africa* 87, 4 (2017): 651–61; Tiffany Willoughby-Herard, *Waste of a White Skin: The Carnegie Corporation and the Racial Logic of White Vulnerability* (Berkeley: University of California Press, 2015).

previously reserved for whites workers only.[15] The manufacturing sector expanded and urbanization soared. Facing labour shortages, Smuts temporarily suspended pass laws used to police Black people and to facilitate long-distance labour migration.[16] Overall, historians view the 1940s as a decade of relative openness and optimism in South Africa compared to the apartheid period that began in 1948.[17]

In this context, Batson chastised officials for pleading ignorance about poverty.[18] 'There has been some excuse in the past for our numerous shots in the statistical dark,' Batson wrote in 1943, 'but the excuse is no longer valid.'[19] The Social Survey of Cape Town had quantified the number of households living below minimum levels and found non-Europeans suffered the greatest burden of poverty. Fifty-three per cent were living below the PDL compared to a much smaller percentage of Europeans. Batson illustrated this with a diagram in which Cape Town's four 'race' groups – groups already defined by census-takers – were represented using circles of varied sizes set against one poverty line. The diagram showed 'Europeans' and 'Asiatics' marginally 'submerged' whereas half of all 'Natives' and 'Coloureds' were below the PDL. The South African Institute of Race Relations welcomed the results of the Social Survey of Cape Town and used Batson's findings to reiterate its calls for social welfare reforms. The PDL, based on 'the Rowntree-Bowley method', might not offer the exactitude of the yard measure, but it had definitively shown 'the social conditions of the people', remarked leading liberals. 'If the poverty datum line is a real line below which it is not possible to achieve human living standards, one finds it hard to understand how a standard of three-fifths and still less, a standard two-fifths below it can even be considered.'[20]

Elaborate efforts went into making urban households comparable. Edward Batson and his wife Helen, also an LSE graduate, supervised dozens of fieldworkers, predominantly advanced students of Social Work and Social Science, who trudged across far-flung neighbourhoods to conduct interviews. In marginal notes, they hinted at their troubles classifying people. One boy was reportedly 'very insulted' to be called a Malay. 'These people are real Indians,' noted the fieldworker. Fieldworkers remarked on derelict breadwinners, stingy employers, and one 'household' comprised of four single men.[21] Despite these efforts, lack of political will to tackle Black poverty made Batson's findings – however scientific – irrelevant at the highest levels. When the Smuts

---

[15] William Beinart, *Twentieth-Century South Africa* (New York: Oxford University Press, 2001); Randall M. Packard, *White Plague, Black Labor: Tuberculosis and the Political Economy of Health and Disease in South Africa* (Berkeley: University of California Press, 1989).

[16] Also see Geoffrey C. Bowker and Susan Leigh Star, *Sorting Things Out: Classification and Its Consequences* (Cambridge: The MIT Press, 2000). On the pass system, see Keith Breckenridge, *Biometric State: The Global Politics of Identification and Surveillance in South Africa, 1850 to the Present* (New York: Cambridge University Press, 2014).

[17] Saul Dubow and Alan Jeeves (eds), *South Africa's 1940s: Worlds of Possibility* (Cape Town: Double Storey Books, 2005).

[18] Edward Batson, *Towards Social Security: Collected Papers on the Social Services* (Cape Town: Paul Koston, 1943), 29.

[19] Edward Batson, 'Winning Freedom from Want', *Cape Times*, 5 February 1943.

[20] J. D. Rheinallt-Jones (1942), 'Conclusion', *Race Relations* 9, no. 1: 55–61, 56.

[21] Edward Batson Papers, Social Survey of Cape Town, Card 040, J. S. Gericke Library, University of Stellenbosch, Manuscripts Collection.

government debated social welfare planning, Batson attempted to shape budget proposals. Seventy-five per cent of South Africa's four hundred social welfare organizations currently provided relief to whites only, he complained. South Africa would never achieve 'true social security' without removing these kinds of 'social disservices', including race-based wage scales and 'the entire civilized labour policy' (discussed below). Batson echoed the 1942 Beveridge Report, urging more inclusive welfare provisions: 'We cannot establish an island of security in an ocean of insecurity.' Instead of ethnic discrimination, South Africa needed a social welfare system designed to deal with 'the human claims of all of its members'.[22]

When Baston surveyed Salisbury, Rhodesia (later Harare, Zimbabwe), he rejected the 'dubious indicators' used to govern colonial cities. It was true that indigenous peoples had a 'much simpler diet' than Europeans and Indian women wore 'silk saris, while the Natives often go in rags or barefoot'. Nevertheless, 'the same expenditure for food must be allowed in the Poverty Datum Lines of all members of a given sex and age category, irrespective of their ethnic or cultural categories'. Africans required equal proteins, fats, vitamins and minerals as Westerners, said Batson.[23] Immediately after labour strikes in the East African port of Mombasa, British officials looked to Batson's methods and ideas to advise them in the prevention of more such disturbances.[24] One administrator recommended a wage survey of all of British East Africa.[25] When Batson himself surveyed Zanzibar, he again presented his findings as the kind of 'vital statistics' administrators needed to design a 'properly coordinated program of development'.[26]

The British Colonial Office was by this time embracing economic development in reaction to labour unrest in the colonies, urbanization, 'juvenile delinquency', and postwar budget shortfalls.[27] Batson's PDL was part of this overall elevation of the development concept, even as Batson himself failed to win over South African lawmakers. When Smuts appointed two committees on postwar planning, they shuttled between racially particularistic thinking and Batson's biomedical categories, coming down firmly on neither side. Some members of Smut's United Party heralded the Beveridge Report's vision for a social security code to 'completely and absolutely remove the menace of poverty and want from the life of every citizen by making provision for every contingency of life from birth to death'. In the early 1940s, Smut's Public Health Secretary advocated 'minimum wages capable of meeting the bare cost of living'.[28] However, for the Afrikaner nationalist voting bloc, white poverty was the

---

[22] Batson, *Towards Social Security*, 39, 49, 54.
[23] Edward Batson, *The Poverty Line in Salisbury* (Cape Town: University of Cape Town, 1945), 3, 4, 10–11.
[24] Arthur Phillips, *Report of the Committee of Inquiry into Labor Unrest in Mombasa* (Nairobi: Government Printer, 1945).
[25] He added, there could be no 'importing young South African ladies to Mombasa and letting them work in the native quarters'. Leo Silberman, *Brief Comments on Certain Sections of the Phillips Report on Labor Unrest in Mombasa* (Nairobi: Government Printer, 1946), 31.
[26] Edward Batson, *Report on Proposals for a Social Survey of Zanzibar* (Zanzibar: Government Printer, 1948), 1.
[27] See Cooper, *Decolonization and African Society*.
[28] See Davie, *Poverty Knowledge in South Africa*, chapter Four.

overriding concern. South Africa was 'one of the richest countries in the world with a poor [white] population of over 300,000 who cannot make a decent living in their own country', said one member of the opposition. Rather than calling for social security and minimum wages to meet the basic human needs of all South Africans, this elected leader resorted to racial epithets and prophesized a dire future for the white farmer. The government must help the white farmer to 'live decently like Europeans' rather than 'making a *kaffirland* of South Africa'.[29] It was instrumentally class-based and simultaneously ideological white protectionist arguments like this one that relegated Batson's poverty line the outer margins of official discourse for decades to come.

Colonial Frameworks and Non-Comparability

Making workers comparable in apartheid South Africa required exposing and confronting what Edward Said called the 'dominating frameworks' of colonialism, ways of observing and classifying people inextricably entangled with European justifications for imperialism and racial hierarchy.[30] After the Dutch established a trading station at the Cape in the 1650s, colonial violence and land-grabbing overlaid prompted the classification of native 'tribes', while slavery demarcated free from unfree labour. The 'Cape Coloured' population emerged as a stable colonial category. By the nineteenth century, Christian mission schools were training Black African translators, clerks and native chiefs. Calvinist notions of racial destiny, German social holism, British anti-dependency thinking and indigenous philosophies mixed freely in the nineteenth century, with white settlers continuing to insist on access to indigenous labour, as if by right. In the mid-1850s, when starvation threated some 30,000 isi-Xhosa-speakers in the Eastern Cape after a tragic millenarian cattle-killing episode, the British extended aid to adult men. Xhosa children were compelled to become apprentices.[31] The Cape Colony adopted its own version of the 1834 British Poor Law Amendment whereby native males could access poor relief, but only in exchange for hard labour.[32]

After more than a century of frontier wars in the Cape, the British defeated the Zulu kingdom in 1879. For the colonized, taxation and wage labour became virtually impossible to escape. The discovery of diamonds and gold between the 1860s and 1880s, the emergence of deep-underground mining, and the resulting boom in commercial agriculture pushed white and Black African farmers off the land.[33] By the 1890s, 'the poor white' had become a recognized type. Echoing Victorian discourses,

---

[29] Union of South Africa, Parliamentary Debates, House of Assembly (1943) cols., 3319, 1908 and (1942) cols. 3298, 3347,1848, 3340.
[30] Edward Said, *Orientalism* (New York: Vintage Books, 1979), 40.
[31] Jeff Peires, 'Sir George Grey and the Kaffir Relief Committee', *Journal of Southern African Studies*, 10, 2 (April 1984): 145–69; J. B. Peires, *The Dead Will Arise: Nongqawuse and the Great Xhosa Cattle-Killing Movement, 1856–7* (Bloomington: Indian University Press, 1989).
[32] Stephen Devereux, 'Social Pensions in Southern Africa in the Twentieth Century', *Journal of Southern African Studies*, 33, no. 2 (2007): 539–60; John Iliffe, *The African Poor: A History* (New York: Cambridge University Press, 1987).
[33] Colin Bundy, 'Vagabond Hollanders and Runaway Englishmen: White Poverty in the Cape Before Poor Whiteism' in *Putting a Plough to the Ground: Accumulation and Dispossession in Rural South Africa, 1850–1930*, eds William Beinart, Peter Delius and Stanley Trapido (Johannesburg: Ravan Press, 1986), 120–1, 106.

newspapers decried Cape Town's 'wasteful, indifferent ... filthy' mixed-race 'residuum' into which poorer whites were 'sinking, sinking, sinking'.[34] Public health officials warned of Coloured people mixing with 'the poor white tribe'.[35] When bubonic plague hit Cape Town in the early 1900s, officials blamed 'uncontrolled kaffir hordes' and resolved to relocate Black Africans from the central city.[36] Biological and environmental theories of degeneration and eugenic health became mututally reinforcing.[37]

Concerned to stimulate and also to regulate migrant labour, in 1887, mine owners formed the Chamber of Mines to lobby the nascent Transvaal government for assistance with infrastructure development and long-distance labour recruitment. By the turn of the twentieth century, industry leaders complained of workers who travelled 'only to make enough money to return to their kraals with sufficient money to enable them to marry and live in indolence'.[38] According to a 1904 commission of inquiry on labour, the 'the raw native' came from a world in which 'the mere necessaries of existence are few and obtainable with little exertion'. Deemed equivalent with each other, these newcomers to the Reef did not 'require the ordinary comforts and necessities required by civilized man'.[39] Around the same time, mine owners asked medical doctors to devise minimum nutritional diets for workers living in compounds. In this formative period in the making of South Africa's racialised political economy, the mining industry imposed practical and conceptual 'spaces of equivalence', coupled with definite arenas of non-comparability, as industry managers sought to avoid over-compensating African migrants still enmeshed in rural economies. For it was only in the narrow middle range between material abundance and sickening destitution that 'native labour' could be made reliably productive on the mines but not overly comfortable.

African leaders stridently challenged the dominating frameworks of colonialism. In the last decades of the nineteenth century, the Transvaal Native Congress, the Natal Native Congress, and the Eastern Cape's South African Native Congress were established. Coloured and Indian leaders created similar organizations in this period. M. K. Gandhi pioneered passive resistance tactics in a campaign against the application of the pass laws to Indians of all ages. In 1912, the South African Native National Congress – later renamed the African National Congress (ANC) – became the country's leading mouthpiece for the enunciation of African claims. After the creation of the Union of South Africa in 1910, Solomon Plaatje, a Christianized ANC leader, translator of Shakespeare and novelist, sailed to London in order to appeal to

---

[34] *Cape Times*, 21 January 1896; *Cape Argus*, 21 December 1892, quoted in Vivian Bickford-Smith, *Ethnic Pride and Racial Prejudice in Victorian Cape Town: Group Identity and Social Practice, 1875-1902* (New York: Cambridge University Press, 1995), 118, 119.

[35] Cape Printed Papers, A.10-'06, *Report of Select Committee on the Poor White Question*, 17, quoted in Bundy, 'Vagabond Hollanders', 121.

[36] Maynard Swanson, 'The Sanitation Syndrome: Bubonic Plague and Urban Native Policy in the Cape Colony, 1900-1909', *Journal of African History*, 18, no. 3 (1977): 387-410, 391.

[37] Saul Dubow, *Scientific Racism in Modern South Africa* (Cambridge: Cambridge University Press, 1995).

[38] Hennen Jennings, quoted in Sheila van der Horst, *Native Labor in South Africa* (London: Frank Cass, 1971), 128.

[39] Transvaal Colony, *Report of the Labour Commission* (Johannesburg: Government Printer, 1904), 4, 31–2.

the British public regarding the rights of the 'aboriginal peoples' of South Africa, despite the Union of South Africa's new self-governing status in the Commonwealth.[40] Plaatje's lobbying effort failed. The Union government passed legislation in 1913 that outlawed African land ownership outside the so-called Native Reserves a small fraction of the total territory of the country. As never before, the land issue became a unifying national grievance for native people.

The formalization of race-based job-reservation policies in the Union of South Africa followed from power struggles that doubled as commensurations struggles.[41] When white workers withdrew their labour, or voiced their views at the ballot box, they declared themselves equivalent to one another and not those they feared might 'undercut' them.[42] When jobless whites marched on Johannesburg in the late 1890s, mine owners agreed to hire more unskilled white workers and to create more job-training schemes for whites. During the 1899–1902 South African (Anglo-Boer) War, the Rand Aid Society was established. By 1905, it was alerting employers when additional white poor relief was needed. In 1907, the Chamber of Mines agreed to hire more unemployed white miners, partly to prevent renewed unrest.[43] Historian Shula Marks noted the pattern: 'reform was part of the ruling class response to social unrest and was closely related to a preceding period of popular militancy'.[44] Other scholars agreed: 'fear of insurrection among poorer whites, rather than humanitarian concerns' propelled official studies of white poverty and the outlay of aid to restive landless whites.[45] The 1906–08 Transvaal Indigency Commission fits this pattern of investigation and conciliation.[46] With the stated goal of preventing racial degeneration, this commission called on the church to remain the primary source of relief for 'Europeans,' yet it also envisioned an expanded welfare role for the state.[47]

During the dramatic 1922 Rand Revolt, white mine workers downed tools, took up arms, and occupied several towns along the Reef in a bid to win job protections and higher wages. 'Workers of the World Unite and Fight for a White South Africa' announced one popular slogan. During his first tenure, Prime Minister Jan Smuts, the former war general who colonized South West Africa (Namibia) after the First World

---

[40] Sol. T. Plaatje, *Native Life in South Africa* (Randburg: Raven Press, 1982 [1916]).
[41] See Charles Feinstein, *An Economic History of South Africa: Conquest, Discrimination, Development* (Cambridge: Cambridge University Press, 2005); David Yudelman, *The Emergence of Modern South Africa: State, Capital, and the Incorporation of Organized Labor on the South African Gold Fields, 1902–1939* (Westport: Greenwood Press, 1983).
[42] For one early revisionist analysis, see Robert Davies, 'The White Working-Class in South Africa', *New Left Review*, 1, no. 82 (1973).
[43] Charles van Onselen, *Studies in the Social and Economic History of the Witwatersrand, 1886–1914*, Vol 2: *New Nineveh* (Cape Town: Jonathan Ball, 1982); 132–3.
[44] Shula Marks, *The Ambiguities of Dependence in South Africa: Class, Nationalism, and the State in Twentieth-Century Natal* (Randburg: Raven Press, 1986), 82.
[45] Pieter le Roux, 'Poor Whites', Second Carnegie Inquiry into Poverty and Development in Southern Africa, Carnegie Conference Paper, no. 248 (Cape Town: Saldru, 1982), 6–7.
[46] Transvaal Colony, *Report of the Transvaal Indigency Commission [and Minutes of Evidence], 1906–08* (Pretoria: Government Printer, 1904).
[47] The Transvaal Indigency Commission also relied on two-part definition of indigence, its object of study, similar to Charles Booth's distinction between 'the poor' and 'the very poor'. E. P. Hennock, 'Concepts of Poverty in the British Social Surveys from Charles Booth to Arthur Bowley' in *The Social Survey in Historical Perspective*, 189.

War, imposed martial law and used airplanes to crush the 1922 white miners' revolt, resulting in some two hundred deaths. Immediately after however, Smuts attempted to appease white workers and white voters by promising to investigate economic conditions, and then by extending additional poor relief. Despite these salves, he lost the next election, setting the stage for new investments in white uplift.[48] Capitalizing on anxieties over white poverty, in 1924, Prime Minister J. B. M. Hertzog, having campaigned against *swaartgevaar* (black peril), implemented the 'civilized labour policy'. Hertzog defined civilized labour as labour performed by those 'whose standard of living conforms to the standard generally regarded as tolerable from the European standpoint'. Uncivilized labour was work performed by 'persons whose aim is restricted to the requirements of the necessities of life as understood among barbarous and undeveloped peoples'.[49] In 1926, Hertzog appointed the Commission on Old-Age Pensions and National Insurance. Two years later, white workers gained access to non-contributory means-tested old-age pensions. Coloured workers were included in the new provision, yet their pensions were set at much lower rates. Indian and African workers were excluded.

Why did the colonized not win similar gains through diplomacy and collective protest? Disenfranchisement, police repression and restrictions on public speech made such gains impossible. When Black African and mixed-race workers in urban and rural areas joined the fast-growing Industrial and Commercial Workers Union in the 1920s, the government arrested union leaders and prohibited public gatherings.[50] Meanwhile, in 1924, white workers gained access to collective bargaining rights through new Industrial Councils. The adjudication of minimum wage thresholds for non-European workers fell to the Department of Labour's Wage Boards – employer-dominated committees that met regularly in urban areas to set minimum wages by trade. Taken together, Hertzog's interwar social and economic policies helped establish, in a practical sense, a highly unequal 'distributional regime' that delivered lucrative employment opportunities, relatively generous social grants, and other advantages to white households.[51] In this way, the interwar period cemented the existing conventions that deemed 'the white worker' observable, comparable, and entitled.

The most celebrated interwar social science research project in South Africa endorsed 'the poor white' as a valid category. The 1929–32 Carnegie Inquiry into the Poor White Problem conducted interviews, administered intelligence tests to children, and photographed 'types' of poor white homes.[52] Rejecting British survey methods, this American-funded study embraced local knowledge and idiosyncratic measures. 'Poor

---

[48] David Berger, 'White Poverty and Government Policy in South Africa: 1298–1934', PhD Dissertation, Temple University, 1982, 278.

[49] Pretoria, 31 October 1924, Circular No. 5, *Statutes of the Union of South Africa,* quoted in Gavin Lewis, *Between the Wire and the Wall: A History of South African 'Colored' Politics* (Cape Town: David Philip, 1987), 132.

[50] Helen Bradford, *A Taste of Freedom: The ICU in Rural South Africa, 1924–1930* (New Haven: Yale University Press, 1987).

[51] Nicoli Nattrass and Jeremy Seekings, *Class, Race, and Inequality in South Africa* (New Haven: Yale University Press, 2005).

[52] Willoughby-Herard, *Waste of a White Skin*.

white "statistics" are frequently demanded', noted one commissioner, yet it was just 'not practicable' to set one breadline for all poor whites, especially given variable regional standards.⁵³ What some whites deemed sufficient others deemed lavish. Without constructing a national poverty line, the Carnegie Commission arrived at a rough estimate: 300,000 'very poor whites' nationwide, an electrifying number. The *Afrikannse Vrouevereniging* (Afrikaans Women's Union), the *Volkskongress* (Congress of the People) and the Afrikaans press circulated the Carnegie Commission's findings, as well as its recommendations regarding the need for more high-level solutions to 'the poor white problem'. Some took the occasion to call for compulsory labour colonies to prevent 'the abuse of leisure time' by the 'work-shy'.⁵⁴

By the late 1930s, Afrikaner nationalists were memorializing their frontier history. In this milieu, ending white poverty was tightly linked to Herrenvolk state-building.⁵⁵ One Afrikaner business leader worried that 'too much attention had recently been paid to "this unhealthy section"', meaning poor whites. He wanted the state to 'help the Afrikaner become an entrepreneur'.⁵⁶ The goal should be to 'mobilize the *volk* to capture this foreign capitalist system and to adapt it to our national character'. Hendrik Verwoerd, the future Prime Minister and the architect of apartheid after 1948, described 'poor whites' as the worthy descendants of South Africa's brave frontiersmen' whose 'message to the living was: "Afrikanerize the cities and assume your rightful place in commerce and industry"'.⁵⁷ A psychologist and social work professor – one of dozens of Afrikaner intellectuals who earned his advanced degree in interwar Germany – Verwoerd skillfully popularized the Carnegie Commission's recommendations, building more public support for race-based welfare spending.⁵⁸

In ways that defy easy periodization, in the years before, during, and after the Second World War, the 'civilized labour policy' continued to boost white incomes and to further entrench historically constructed race and class inequities. A state-owned iron and steel corporation was created that provided even more high-paying jobs for whites only. The state funded white labour colonies in forestry and other trades. White workers continued to enjoy access to preferential hiring on the railways. South Africa's manufacturing sector expanded, opening up more 'skilled' jobs. In 1937, a new national Department of Social Welfare was established based on the Carnegie Commission's

---

⁵³ E. G. Malherbe, *Education and the Poor White*, Vol. 3, *The Poor White Problem in South Africa: Report of the Carnegie Commission* (Stellenbosch: Pro Ecclesia, 1932), vii; Ellen Condliffe Lagemann, *The Politics of Knowledge: The Carnegie Corporation Philanthropy, and Public Policy* (Middletown: Wesleyan, 1989).

⁵⁴ Dan O'Meara, *Volkskapitalisme: Class, Capital, and Ideology in the Development of Afrikaner Nationalism, 1934–1948* (Johannesburg: Ravan Press, 1983), 104.

⁵⁵ On the social construction of Afrikaner identity, see Isabelle Hofmeyr, 'Building a Nation from Words: Afrikaans language, literature and ethnic identity, 1902–1924', in *The Politics of Race, Class and Nationalism in Twentieth Century South Africa*, eds Shula Marks and Stanley Trapido (New York: Routledge, 1987); Dunbar Moodie, *The Rise of Afrikanerdom: Power, Apartheid, and the Afrikaner Civil Religion* (Berkeley: University of California Press, 1975).

⁵⁶ E. P. du Plessis and C. G. W. Schumann quoted in O'Meara, *Volkskapitalisme*, 111.

⁵⁷ O'Meara, *Volkskapitalisme*, 108, 111.

⁵⁸ In 1936, Verwoerd became editor of *Die Transvaler*, a newspaper allied with the National Party. See Roberta Balstad Miller, 'Science and Society in the Early Career of H. F. Verwoerd', *Journal of Southern African Studies* 19, no. 4 (1993): 634–61.

recommendations for ending 'the poor white problem'. By the 1940s, district pension officers were administering means tests that qualified white and Coloured retirees for pensions. Through a process propelled in large part by white miners' revolts, but also by culturally flexible Afrikaner nationalism, 'the white worker' became a commensurate object of study, a site of intervention, and a common sense category easily harmonized with long-standing colonial frameworks.

Narrating Injustice: the Poverty Datum Line (PDL) and its Uses

Since the 1980s, historians and anthropologists have explored the afterlives of colonial science and technology, including appropriations of census categories and the development concept.[59] Mary Morgan has commented on this theme, adding that facts travel well 'not just when they are used somewhere else *by* someone else, but when they are used *for* something else', including to create new social patterns and new narratives.[60] Starting in the 1940s, facts about absolute poverty travelled widely in South Africa as anglophone liberals used Batson's indicator to press for reforms. By the 1970s, student activists and the new independent Black trade unions were repurposing the PDL. Through commensuration struggles (which overlapped extensively with struggles for decent pay, national liberation, and democratic freedoms) people classified as non-European in South Africa collectively challenged and eventually dismantled the space of equivalence that once undergirded 'the white worker' as an accepted administrative category.

---

[59] Bernard Cohn, 'The Census, Social Structures and Objectification in South Asia' in *An Anthropologist Among the Historians and other Essays*, ed. Bernard Cohn (Delhi: Oxford University Press, 1987) Also see, Ferguson, *The Anti-Politics Machine: 'Development' Depoliticization, and Bureaucratic Power in Lesotho* (Minneapolis: University of Minnesota Press, 1994); Frederick Cooper, *Decolonization and African Society: The Labor Question in French and British Africa* (New York: Cambridge University Press, 1996); Id. and Randall M. Packard, *International Development and the Social Sciences: Essays on the History and Politics of Knowledge* (Berkeley: University of California Press, 1998); James C. Scott, *Seeing Like a State: How Certain Schemes to Improve the Human Condition have Failed* (New Haven: Yale University Press, 1999); Timothy Mitchell, *Rule of Experts: Egypt, Techno-Politics, Modernity* (Berkeley: University of California Press, 2002); Jane Guyer, *Marginal Gains: Monetary Transactions in Atlantic Africa* (Chicago: Chicago University Press, 2004); Gabrielle Hecht, *Being Nuclear: Africans and the Global Uranium Trade* (Cambridge, MA: The MIT Press, 2012). On the co-creation of official discourse and economic facts, see Sheila Jassanoff (ed.), *States of Knowledge: The Co-Production of Science and Social Order* (New York: Routledge, 2004); Boris Samuel, 'The Shifting Legitimacies of Price Measurements: Official Statistics and the Quantification of *Pwofitasyon* in the 2009 Social Struggle in Guadelope' in *The New Politics of Numbers: Utopia, Evidence and Democracy*, eds Andrea Mennicken and Robert Salais (New York: Palgrave, 2022). On the unreliability of statistics, see Morton Jerven, *Poor Numbers: How We Are Misled by African Development Statistics and What to Do about It* (Ithaca: Cornell University Press, 2013). For a critique of 'the household' an imported concept, see Polly Hill, 'Some Puzzling Spending Habits in Ghana', *The Economic Bulletin of the Economic Society of Ghana*, 11 (1957): 3–7.

[60] Mary S. Morgan, 'Traveling Facts', in *How Well Do Facts Travel? The Dissemination of Reliable Knowledge*, eds Peter Howlett and Mary S. Morgan (New York: Cambridge University Press, 2011), 20 (original emphasis). Also see Madeleine Akrich, 'The Description of Technical Objects' in *Shaping Technology/Building Society: Studies in Sociotechnical Change*, eds Wiebe E. Bijker and John Law (Cambridge, MA: MIT Press, 1992).

It was a lengthy and contingent de-linking process. For many years, PDL statistics circulated among liberal reform groups and critics of apartheid without cutting through the non-comparability described above. In 1943, Smut's Social Security Committee declined to use Batson's poverty line when recommending old-age pensions for Black African workers.[61] Another wartime committee wanted only urbanized natives to qualify for pensions, set at even more austere levels.[62] When Smut's United Party extended old-age pensions to Indians and Africans in 1944, that move had little to do with Batson's arguments about measurable human needs. Most likely, the mining industry feared malnutrition in the country's labour-exporting reserves.[63] The Department of Native Affairs had recently determined that rural households were so impoverished they could not produce healthy migrant workers.[64] Whatever lawmakers' underlying motives, when pensions were extended to African retirees, they were set at one-tenth the level of white pensions (far below the two-fifths ratio suggested by the Social Security Committee).[65]

Ignored at the national level, the PDL had a limited impact at the municipal level during the war. The Cape Town General Board of Aid used it to determine eligibility for poor relief.[66] In 1943, Cape Town's Housing Utility Company began charging reduced rents to those with incomes below the PDL. The PDL also featured in official inquiries into urban protest movements. During the 1943–4 Alexandra Bus Boycotts, the PDL gained some recognition among Johannesburg officials.[67] During this widely supported strike against higher bus fares, the city appointed a Bus Commission that collected testimony from community leaders and experts. Miriam Janish of the Department of Native Affairs reported on her survey of non-European households in the city.[68] Using a version of Batson's methods, Janish interviewed 987 families and found a high percentage living below the PDL. The commission also learned that native households were spending only three-quarters of the amount needed to purchase an adequate minimum diet. Scraping by at that meagre level, African workers could not

---

[61] Union of South Africa, *Report of the Social Security Committee* (Cape Town, Government Printer, 1944), xii; xv–xvi.

[62] Union of South Africa, *Social Services, Their Scope and Cost: A Summary of the Social Security Scheme Recommended by the Social Security Committee and of Report No. 2 of the Social and Economic Planning Council* (Pretoria, Government Printer, 1944), 1.

[63] See Devereux, 'Social Pensions in Southern Africa'.

[64] See F. W. Fox and D. Back, *A Preliminary Survey of the Agricultural and Nutritional Problems of the Ciskei and Transkei Territories* (Johannesburg: Chamber of Mines, 1938); Randall M. Packard, *White Plague, Black Labor: Tuberculosis and the Political Economy of Health and Disease in South Africa* (Berkeley: University of California Press, 1989).

[65] Servaas van der Berg, 'Social Policy to Address Poverty', in *Fighting Poverty: Labor Markets and Inequality in South Africa*, eds Haroon Bhorat, et al. (Cape Town: University of Cape Town Press, 2001), 189; Frances Lund, 'State Social Benefits in South Africa', *International Social Security Review*, 46, no. 1 (1996): 5–25, 10.

[66] Cape Town General Board of Aid, *Report on Causes of Destitution in Cape Town during 1943* (Cape Town: Government Printer, 1944), 8.

[67] Alfred William Stadler, *A Long Way to Walk: Bus Boycotts in Alexandra, 1940–1945* (Johannesburg: University of the Witwatersrand Press, 1979); Baruch Hirson, *Yours for the Union: Class and Community Struggles in South Africa* (London: Zed Books, 1989).

[68] Miriam Janish, *A Study of African Incomes and Expenditure in 987 Families in Johannesburg, January–November 1940* (Johannesburg: Non-European and Native Affairs Department, 1941).

afford higher bus fares, concluded the bus commission.[69] Partly on that basis, this mass-based protest over inflation was deemed justifiable and the company urged to back down.

In these specific cases, local officials accepted the comparability of urban households. When apartheid began in 1948 however, the PDL was more decisively pushed aside.[70] As Minister of Native Affairs, Verwoerd made selective, pragmatic, and seemingly cynical use of survey data. In the early 1950s, he promised that 'separate development' would reverse African urbanization. Behind the scenes, Verwoerd used government-generated statistics on native families living at 'sub-sub-economic' levels in Johannesburg to disqualify more families from rent exemptions, thus making 'native administration' an even smaller overall budget line. At the same time, the Department of Native Affairs invested in expensive 'buffer strips' also described as 'screens' and 'machine-gun belts'.[71] If policing Black areas was deemed a worthy investment, ameliorating Black poverty was not. In regard to rural areas, Verwoerd rejected the idea of major soil-reclamation measures on the basis of their expense, even though some scientists allied with the National Party saw rural development spending as the best alternative to unchecked urban influx. The Tomlinson Commission spent years studying the prospects for economic development in the Native Reserves those scattered and depleted lands carved out by the 1913 Land Act, going so far as to calculate the minimum plots of land the African 'peasant' would need to become self-sufficient. Still, Verwoerd deemed this commission's recommendations on soil reclamation too costly, promoting instead more expedient 'border zone' business development.[72]

'Before drawing lots, one must first compose the urn and the actual balls, and define the terminology and procedures that allow them to be classified,' said Desrosières about the steps involved in the making of people and things statistically comparable.[73] A random sample of households requires an agreed-upon definition of 'the household', as well as a demarcation of the territory to be sampled. Without such agreements, the individual ball, or part, cannot stand in for the whole. Nor can claims be made about averages or exceptions. So it was in apartheid South Africa before disorderly forces pulled apart the social relations and the tacit agreements that previously established 'the white worker' as a stable space of equivalence.

In 1955, the Federation of South African Women cited the PDL when lobbying township authorities for reduced rents in Johannesburg. A year later, women of all races marched on Pretoria in opposition to the pass laws. Living standards stood at

---

[69] 'Memorandum of Evidence Presented by Alexandra Health Committee to the Commission Appointed in Terms of Notice No. 1535', Department of Native Affairs, Secretary of Native Affairs, 9694 717/400 National Archives Repository, Pretoria.

[70] In 1948, D. F. Malan's *Herenigde* (Reunited) National Party won a narrow victory at the polls. Re-election in 1953 cemented the National Party's power.

[71] See Derek Japha, Unpublished manuscript on urban planning in South Africa, University of Cape Town Student Congress Paper, 1986; Ivan Evans, *Bureaucracy and Race: Native Administration in South Africa* (Berkeley: University of California Press, 1997), 137; 129–30.

[72] On apartheid 'purists' compared to Verwoerd and other apartheid 'pragmatists', see John Lazar, 'Conformity and Conflict: Afrikaner Nationalist Politics in South Africa, 1948–1961', PhD Dissertation, Oxford University, 1987.

[73] Desrosières, *The Politics of Large Numbers,* 10.

'dangerously low levels' and the government ought not further 'oppress the low-paid African population, already engaged in a desperate struggle for existence', one liberal newspaper concluded.[74] Black African social workers made related arguments about 'lack of income' threatening the 'moral standard of the household'.[75] Journalists cited the PDL after an urban uprising in Durban in 1957. The average urban family of five required £20 a month to survive yet the average unskilled worker in Durban earned just £12 a month, making a healthy family life impossible. Citing surveyors at the University of Natal, reporters stressed these inequities and bemoaned 'appalling living conditions'.[76] *Drum*, an English-language magazine aimed at Black readers, profiled one Indian family said to be living 'below the PDL' and also ran articles vernacularizing cost of living indicators with headlines such as 'Why Our Living's So Tough' and 'What We Buy'. *Drum* journalist Can Themba asked: 'did I hear that somebody in Johannesburg's planning to step up wages, too? Well sure, step 'em up. Let's step up everything – things like decent houses, decent townships, and more decent regulations. Step 'em up'!'[77] In this way, facts about the PDL travelled well in the 1950s.

'Statactivists' appropriated Batson's poverty line when calling for higher African wages.[78] Nevertheless, the assumptions embedded in the PDL made it a kind of stat-*anathema* for apartheid lawmakers seeking to preserve the country's migrant labor system.[79] In the late 1950s, the South African Congress of Trade Unions (SACTU), a Black trade union organization with links to the ANC, demanded for 'a happy life for all ... free from unemployment, insecurity and poverty, free from racial hatred and oppression, a life of vast opportunity for all people'.[80] This expansive vision echoed the 1955 Freedom Charter, a manifesto calling for sharing the nation's resources. When another major bus strike hit Johannesburg in 1957, and tens of thousands of workers stayed away from work and joined beer-hall boycotts, SACTU leaders made their demands more specific by calling for wages equal to one pound per day, close to what household surveyors now said would equal a minimum family budget. The South African Institute of Race Relations once again compared average wages paid to Black African workers and the cost of basic necessities. Johannesburg's Chamber of

---

[74] *Rand Daily Mail*, 6 April 1956.
[75] A. Mokhetle, 'A Description of Life in Orlando East' in Betty Spence, 'How Our Urban Natives Live', National Building Research Institute, Reprinted from *South African Architectural Record*, 35, no. 10 (1950): 11.
[76] Special Correspondent, 'African Earnings and Cost-of-Living in Durban', *Natal Daily News*, 30 June 1959, Reprinted in SAIRR, Natal Region, 'The Cato Manor Framework', 66/59, Hobart Houghton Papers, Cory Library, Grahamstown.
[77] See Riason Naidoo, *The Indian in Drum Magazine in the 1950s* (Cape Town: Bell Roberts, 2009). D. C. Themba, 'Talk o' the Town: Budget Sent 'em Reeling', *Drum*, September 1958, reprinted in Peter Esterhuysen, ed., *Deep Cuts: Graphic Adaptations of Stories by Can Themba, Alex La Guma, and Bessie Head* (Cape Town: Maskew Miller Longman, 1993).
[78] See Bruno, Didier, and Vitale, 'Statactivism: Forms of Action between Disclosure and Affirmation'.
[79] Apartheid "crowded" African workers into "low-skill, low-status jobs by denying them other jobs, denying them bargaining rights, education, and importing unskilled labor from neighboring countries." Joel Bergsman, 'Apartheid, Wages, and Production Costs in South Africa: An Application of the Crowding Hypothesis,' *The Journal of Human Resources* 17, no. 4 (Autumn, 1982), 633–645, 634–635.
[80] Ken Luckhardt and Brenda Wall, *Organize or Starve! The History of the South African Congress of Trade Unions* (New York: International Publishers, 1980), 94.

Commerce expressed concern about depressed consumer spending amid the ongoing bus strike. Some business leaders floated the idea of a national survey of 'wages, living standards and transport costs of all non-European workers in the larger urban areas'.[81] At a SACTU conference in 1959, workers decried poverty wages, adopting the slogan, *Asinamali-Sifun'Imali* (We have no money, we want more money). Delegates passed a minimum wage resolution. Still, the answer from the Deputy Minister of Labour was clear: 'To plead that you must pay the Natives … a "civilized wage" means only one thing in this county – White wages. To want to pay Natives White wages fails in the first place to take account of their productivity; in the second place it does not take their living standard into account.'[82] According to this view of the wage issue, the value of labour could never be divorced from race. Parliament did debate minimum wages, yet no new legislation was passed. Instead, as in the past, the state relied on repression, policing, banning orders, and the pass laws to quash dissent. Thirty-six SACTU leaders were arrested and banned in this period, barring them from publishing, social gatherings, and public speaking. By 1964, forty-five SACTU leaders had been banned.[83]

When the South African police shot and killed sixty-nine peaceful anti-pass protestors in Sharpeville in 1960, activists in London and elsewhere publicized the killings, solicited support for existing boycott campaigns, and called for trade embargos. After years of discussions about the need to prepare for armed revolution, Mandela and others in the ANC created a new organization, *Umkonto we Sizwe* (MK, the Spear of the Nation). The MK studied revolutionary guerilla movements and carried out sabotage attacks on infrastructure with the goal of causing economic shockwaves and sparking a popular movement to overthrow the state. When Mandela, a lawyer by training, faced a life sentence for his role in these activities in 1964, he defended the ANC's abandonment of non-violent tactics using many arguments, including claims about inescapable poverty. Forty-six per cent of all African households in Johannesburg were living below the PDL, said Mandela during the Rivonia Trial.[84]

The 1973 Durban Strikes and International Employment Codes

After the repression of SACTU in the 1960s, Black African workers remained connected to one another through mutual aid societies, as well as religious and personal networks that spanned home and workplace.[85] Those ties proved crucial to the formation of new independent trade unions in the 1970s. The Black Consciousness Movement began at the same moment Marxist scholars were developing revisionist histories that

---

[81] Alex Hepple, *Poverty Wages* (Johannesburg: Wages Committee, 1959), 4.
[82] Mr. M. Viljoen, 21 May 1959, quoted in Hepple, *Poverty Wages*, back cover.
[83] See Luckhardt and Wall, *Organize or Starve!*, 165, 425, 429.
[84] 'I am Prepared to Die', Nelson Mandela's statement from the dock at the opening of the defense case in the Rivonia Trial, 20 April 1964. https://www.nelsonmandela.org/news/entry/i-am-prepared-to-die (accessed 14 November 2021).
[85] M. Sakhela Buhlungu, 'Democracy and Modernization in the Making of the South African Labor Movement: The Dilemma of Leadership' (Ph.D. diss, University of the Witwatersrand, 2001).

convincingly defined apartheid as a 'cheap-labour system' that used peasant production to supplement the ultra-low wages paid to migrant workers.[86] In 1971, white student activists in the National Union of South African Students (NUSAS) established Student Wages Commissions at the University of Natal and other campuses. In October 1972, some of these students convinced Black African dockworkers in Cape Town and in Durban to attend meetings of the Wage Board, and to make the case for wages above the PDL.[87] By 1974, a government commission had accused NUSAS, the University Christian Movement, and Biko's South African (Black) Students Organization of communist agitation. By that time however, striking factory workers and the international press were putting employers on the defensive.

Labour unrest created the conditions in which cost of living statistics could finally be connected, in a practical sense, to the question of acceptable minimum wages for the average urban worker. In early January 1973, brick workers in Durban walked off the job, sparking an extended general strike. Newspapers blamed sub-subsistence wages. As one striker put it: 'Nowadays money is indispensable. Everything is dear. With our low wages we cannot satisfy our needs.'[88] Following the 1973 Durban Strikes, Harriet Bolton, a white textile union leader, suggested workers fearful of government repression establish a new (neutral-sounding) General Factory Workers Benefit Fund.[89] The next year, it evolved into the Trade Union Advisory Coordinating Council which soon spun off into four proto-unions. In 1979, the Federation of South African Trade Unions (FOSATU) was formed. In the mid-1980s, FOSATU partnered with the United Democratic Front, an umbrella coalition of churches, youth associations, street committees, and civic groups. In 1985, FOSATU became the Congress of South African Trade Unions (COSATU).[90] By that time, South Africa faced massive international pressure, sports boycotts, and a foreign debt crisis brought on partly by transnational anti-apartheid 'bank campaigns'. F.W. de Klerk unbanned political organizations in early 1990. COSATU joined with the ANC and the South African Communist Party (SACP) and, following complex negotiations accompanied by unprecedented political violence in the streets, elections were held and the ANC-COSATU-SACP alliance took power in 1994.

A comparison of wage-setting debates before and after this event reveals how pressure from below enabled commensuration; previously marginalized spaces of equivalence moved to the center of official discourse. In the early 1970s, Johann

---

[86] Harold Wolpe, 'Capitalism and Cheap Labour-Power in South Africa: From Segregation to Apartheid', *Economy and Society* 1, no. 4 (1971): 425–56.
[87] 'Stevedores on Strike', *Daily News*, 23 October 1972.
[88] Institute for Industrial Education, 'African Workers Interview', 1973 Strikes File, Alan Paton Centre, University of Natal, Pietermaritzburg.
[89] This essay does not explore how women's wages were made comparable to male breadwinner wages, but readers should note that women were centrally involved in trade union activities in South Africa. See Malehoko Tshoaedi, 'Women in the Forefront of Workplace Struggles in South Africa: From Invisibility to Mobilization', *Labour, Capital and Society* 45, no. 2 (2012): 58–83. Also see Iris Berger, *Threads of Solidarity: Women in South African Industry, 1900–1980* (Bloomington: Indiana University Press, 1992).
[90] Sakhela Buhlungu, *A Paradox of Victory: COSATU and the Democratic Transformation in South Africa* (Durban: University of KwaZulu-Natal Press, 2010).

Potgieter, a surveyor who had previously worked extensively with Batson, was leading the University of Port Elizabeth's Institute for Planning Research. Before the 1973 Durban Strikes, most companies ignored his findings. After those factory shutdowns, Potgieter was flooded with requests for information on his version of the PDL, the Household Subsistence Level.[91] Managers were now under unprecedented scrutiny and needed cost of living statistics. As South Africa's Bureau of Market Research noted: 'South African firms have begun to view non-White wage levels from a different angle ... the financial position of their employees is gaining increasing prominence in their wage policies.' Publicity overseas since the beginning of the year had raised the minimum wage issue to new levels of prominence, experts noted in mid-1973.[92]

With South Africa's employment practices in the spotlight, multinationals began signing employment codes promising to improve workplace standards. The British Code of Practice required firms to pay adult males above the PDL, and to publish plans for reaching the Effective Minimum Level (EML), set at one and a half times the PDL. American firms signed voluntary agreements. Some went a step further when publicly condemning South Africa's race-based job-reservation policies. Reverend Leon Sullivan, a prominent civil rights leader and African American Baptist minister from Philadelphia, joined the board of directors of General Motors. When he visited South Africa, he met with Potgieter and developed the Sullivan Principles.[93] Signatories pledged to pay minimum wages that reached or exceeded Potgieter's poverty line. South Africa's economy had boomed in the 1960s and early 1970s. Foreign investors did want to divest their assets. By 1977, the European Economic Community had endorsed a British proposal calling on all European companies still operating in South Africa to pay workers above minimum levels and endorsing their right to legalized collective bargaining. Canada and Australia adopted similar codes with wage floors pegged to measures of the average urban household's basic needs.

With these acknowledgements of the validity of Batson's methods, old assertions about non-comparability crumbled, at least at the level of overt company polices. The average worker became a space of equivalence at a time when poverty lines offered something politically useful to multinational companies looking for benchmarks of progress toward 'corporate social responsibility'. Racial capitalism evolved to accommodate these challenges. Meanwhile, survey statistics were tied to radical, reformist, and emergent neoliberal arguments. For some, the PDL continued to explain the youth-led township unrest. During the 1976–7 Soweto Student Uprisings, African clergy in Cape Town used the PDL to decry inequality. 'Far too many of our people are receiving wages below the Poverty Datum Line let alone the Effective Minimum Level,'

---

[91] Johann Potgieter, interview by the author, East London, 9 April 2002.
[92] P. A. Nel, M. Loubser, and J. J. A. Steenkamp, 'The Minimum Subsistence Level and the Minimum Humane Standard of Living of Non-Whites Living in the Main Urban Areas of the Republic of South Africa, May 1973', Bureau of Market Research, Research Report, no. 33, vi.
[93] See Gay Seidman, 'Monitoring Multinationals: Lessons from the Anti-Apartheid Era', *Politics and Society*, 31, no. 3 (2003): 381–406; Robert Massie, *Loosing the Bonds: The United States and South Africa in the Apartheid Years* (New York: Doubleday, 1997).

they wrote. 'The present huge wage gap between rich and poor is totally unjust and a major source of deep dissatisfaction.'[94] For their part, researchers working with business groups looked at 'expectations of the future' among 'average blacks'.[95]

Marking a departure from the past, in 1977, the Prime Minister announced that wages for public sector workers would soon reflect the principle of 'equal pay for equal work'.[96] Simultaneously, in what remained a highly contradictory phase, homeland independence rendered vast numbers of people uncountable and invisible. The Republic of South Africa stopped collecting statistics on income, spending and employment in the Transkei, Ciskei, Bophuthatswana, and Venda after those territories were declared self-governing between 1976 and 1981.[97] In 1982, the *Afrikaanse Handelsinstituut*, a research group allied with the National Party, raised alarm bells about overpopulation. Despite the state's 'laudable efforts and incentives at decentralization and homeland development', population growth meant 'separate development' was an impossible dream. 'Economic integration of the Blacks is inevitable and unstoppable if work and welfare are to be created and maintained.'[98]

Marking another departure, the 1979 Wiehahn Commission recommended the legalization of the new independent trade unions as well as the end of white job-reservation policies in core sectors of the economy. Black workers could now unionize openly. The new Black trade unions were soon pressing even harder for fair pay and national liberation.[99] That year, another state commission recommended the abolition of the urban pass system on the grounds that a stabilized workforce was more productive than a migratory one.[100] By the early 1980s, old-age pensions for Black Africans had been raised to levels close to white pensions, another major shift in comparability practices. The minimum economic needs of 'the average worker' had become commensurate across constructed 'race' lines in ways apartheid leaders had long deemed unthinkable. Collective action by striking workers, sustained unrest among township youth, progress toward comprehensive international sanctions, and transnational advocacy networks had altered the fundamental terrain of economic thinking and statistical comparison. Through a process that included commensuration

---

[94] The Ministers' Fraternal of Langa, Guguletu and Nyanga, 'Message for 1977', Cape Town, January 1977, reprinted in Thomas G. Karis and Gail M. Gerhart (eds), *Nadir and Resurgence, 1964–1979*, Vol. 5, *From Protest to Challenge: A Documentary History of African Politics in South Africa, 1882–1990* (Bloomington: Indiana University Press, 1997), 593.

[95] Mari Harris, 'Monitoring Optimism in South Africa', in *Quality of Life in South Africa*, ed. Valerie Møller (Boston: Kluwer Academic Publishers, 1997), 302.

[96] Nattrass and Seekings, *Class, Race, and Inequality in South Africa*, 259.

[97] Francis Wilson and Dudley Horner, 'Lessons from the Project for Statistics on Living Standards and Development: The South African Story', Washington DC, The World Bank, March 1996.

[98] *Volkshandel*, May 1982 quoted in Stanley B. Greenberg, Legitimating the Illegitimate: State, Markets, and Resistance in South Africa (Berkeley: University of California Press, 1987), 150.

[99] Republic of South Africa, *Report of the Commission of Inquiry into Labour Legislation* (Pretoria: Government Printer, 1979). Also see, Alex Lictenstein, '"We feel that our strength is on the factory floor": Dualism, Shop-Floor Power, and Labor Law Reform in Late Apartheid South Africa', *Labor History* 60, no. 6 (2019): 606–25; Owen Crankshaw, *Race, Class and the Changing Divisions of Labour Under Apartheid* (London: Routledge, 1997).

[100] Republic of South Africa, *Commission of Inquiry into Legislation Affecting Utilisation of Manpower* (Pretoria: Government Printer, 1979).

struggles, the average worker in South Africa was redefined, and with that came the possibility of linking the poverty line to minimum wage laws as well as the provision of de-racialised and expanded social grants after 1994 that have had important redistributive effects.[101]

Conclusion

During the Second World War, Edward Batson's Social Survey of Cape Town challenged established conventions in South Africa that deemed whites deserving of 'civilized standards of living'. Settler colonialism, slavery, the mining industry, and white job-reservation, as well as the provision of pensions to white retirees, had transformed white work into something widely recognized and staunchly defended. By the interwar period, the non-comparability of workers across constructed 'race' lines stood as a bulwark against biomedical appeals to universal human needs. Batson's survey had only a limited impact at the local level in this context. By the 1950s, relief agencies in Cape Town were using the PDL to make rent exceptions and allocate aid. Liberal reformers relied on PDL statistics to explain bus boycotts in wartime Johannesburg and following urban uprisings. For their part, in the 1950s and 1960s, Verwoerd and other National Party leaders dismissed the premise of the PDL. Having ended the so-called 'poor white problem', and having crafted the cheapest possible approaches to 'native administration' and homeland decentralization, apartheid economics meant that business leaders showed interest in raising wages above the PDL only when concerned about depressed consumer spending. Until the 1970s, 'the average urban household' remained only an unofficial space of comparability.

The 1973 Durban Strikes broke that stalemate. After this working-class mobilisation and the trade union activity that followed, multinational businesses abandoned 'the white worker' as a category. International employment codes turned cost of living indicators into controversial yet widely recognized corporate monitoring tools. 'The average worker' was made comparable, even as male 'breadwinners' remained sharply differentiated from female wage-earners. The urban household became a recognized object of study in apartheid South Africa, not as the result of networks built by experts themselves, but rather because industry leaders, as well as the white-minority government, were forced to make concessions in the face of popular demonstrations and external pressures. Through complex dynamics involving strikes, threats of sanctions and transnational south-south solidarity boycotts, the PDL moved from the position of marginal concept to widely used decision-making device closely linked to the principle of 'equal pay for equal work'. Commensuration struggles, defined here as contests over the comparability and non-comparability of objects of scientific research, were clearly an essential feature of this historical process.

---

[101] Iliffe, *The African Poor*, 272. Also see Devereux, 'Social Pensions in Southern Africa'.

By the 1990s, the nation's new leaders were debating redistributive post-Keynesian policies meant to ameliorate poverty and reduce inequality.[102] Democracy created new opportunities for facts to travel, for conflictual and mutually constitutive interactions between observers and the observed, and for social movements and their leaders to weaponize poverty statistics, the Gini coefficient, and insurgent 'countermeasures'. Focused on the postwar and apartheid years, this essay has shown how specific forces primarily 'from below', transformed the PDL from a fringe indicator easily ignored by the state into an accepted non-racial 'space of equivalence'. For scholars interested in how agreements are established that determine the value of labour in the global world, the setting of minimum wages, budget allocations, the provision of social welfare grants, and other policy-relevant questions, a focus on commensuration struggles may help to elucidate the unpredictable ways in which 'workers', and other subjects of governance, are made statistically equivalent, while also shedding light on the kinds of 'disorderly forces' that can open the door to expanded and dramatically reconceptualized social and economic rights.

---

[102] There is a large literature on inequality and lack of access to wages through the labor market in post-apartheid South Africa. See, for example, Murray Leibbrandt, Vimal Ranchhod, and Pippa Green, 'South Africa: The Top End, Labour Markets, Fiscal Redistribution, and the Persistence of Very High Inequality', in Carlos Gradín, Murray Leibbrandt, and Finn Tarp (eds), *Inequality in the Developing World* (New York: Oxford University Press 2022).

9

Wages Measurement in the Belgian Congo and French Sub-Saharan Africa from 1919 to Independence: a Challenge?

Béatrice Touchelay

If we consider that wages are the price of labour, that they are the subject of a contract, written or verbal, between the employer or an intermediary and the employee, and that they are negotiated in the same way as the conditions of work, to what extent does this situation apply to the colonized world? How did the colonists intend to value and pay for the work of the populations of these territories? The persistence of forced forms of labour after the abolition of slavery attests to the difficulties of labour mobilization in the colonies. It posed specific problems that racist considerations about the 'laziness' of the colonized populations are not enough to explain. The difficulties of putting people to work are particularly visible in the Belgian and French colonies of sub-Saharan Africa, where the low demographic density, the small number of colonists and the strength of local customs hindered the appropriation of wealth by the colonial minority.[1] These difficulties led to the definition of a particular form of colonial wage employment: the use of local intermediaries for recruitment, the 'nest egg' kept by employers to 'retain' the employees,[2] the nature of the contract, which was often verbal and not very well adhered to, the duration of recruitment, which could be very long,[3] the marked inequalities in wages between colonists and colonized or according to

---

[1] See Béatrice Touchelay, 'Le Drainage des Ressources' in *La France et l'Afrique 1830 1960*, eds. Isabelle Surun (Paris: Atlande, 2020), 113–18.
[2] The 'nest egg' is the *pécule* in French. Officially, this sum is intended to inculcate in the natives a taste for thrift (a reference to the civilizing mission of colonization) but in fact to fix the workforce and limit desertions.
[3] 'The duration of the contracts is such (about five years) that it often exceeds the "average understanding" of the natives and its breach leads to penal sanctions for the latter, thus including "an indisputable element of constraint". This is a practice that dates to the end of the 19th century when in several colonial territories [...] a kind of "regulated immigration" was used [...]. These immigrant workers entered into long-term contracts [...] which could be turned into disguised forms of forced labour because of default (often the inability to repay the debt incurred by the immigrant during the journey)', Ferruccio Ricciardi, 'Le Salariat au Miroir du 'Travail Indigène': Sociohistoire d'une Catégorisation Occidentale', in *Crise(s) et Mondes du Travail*, eds Anne-Marie Arborio, Paul Bouffartigue et Annie Lamanthe (Toulouse: Octarès, 2019), 30.

location (town/country) and economic situation, the distance between the place of origin and living and the place of work, etc. The resistance of the actors, both colonists and colonized, to the individualization and 'contractualization' of work and the question of the family wage raised by the International Labour Organisation (ILO) at the end of the 1930s attest to the difficulties of transplanting the European wage model into a colonial situation.

Nevertheless, the introduction of wage labour progressed between the two wars. It was accompanied by the rudiments of social legislation, encouraged by the internationalization of debates on colonization at the League of Nations (LoN) and the ILO. Wage employment increased between 1945 and independence (the 1960s), but the conditions of wage employment, its measurement and its counterparts, which bear witness to the difficulties of wage acculturation in French-speaking sub-Saharan Africa, remain unknown.

A comparison of the two French-speaking colonial areas, the Belgian Congo and French sub-Saharan Africa, shows that the spread of wage labour was part of the process of colonial domination and that it was the result of political and racially biased choices and not of 'natural' determinisms. This chapter aims to analyse the colonial wage as a reflection of a more general process of subjugation of the colonized populations.

The period selected is that of the transition from forced or coerced labour to 'contractualized' 'free labour'. Wage labour imposed a model of growth, individualizing the relationship to work, distancing the wage earner from the customary economy, and reproducing in the twentieth century the violence of labour in Western societies of the eighteenth and nineteenth centuries.[4] In both cases, the work performed preceded both its measurement and the rights or rules governing its remuneration. This was followed by the introduction of contracts, which took into account the duration of employment, the arduousness of the tasks and the qualifications and the performance of the employee, whose basic needs it would in principle cover. In the colonies, this wage contract spread from the inter-war period, preceding statistical studies on lifestyles, the cost of living, purchasing power and employees' attributes (qualifications, productivity, etc.). In the absence of an extensive statistical apparatus, labour contracts and consequently wage determination was based on vague criteria. Their forms and amounts were left to the arbitrariness of colonial employers, especially in France, with a framed empire, even more than Belgium, with a better funded and more centralized colonial administration. France was slow to finance the development of colonial statistics and therefore to impose wage arrangements in the colonies. In both cases the priority was to get people to accept the individual contract and to impose a fixed-term commitment without any prospect of promotion or career. The arbitrary nature of the

---

[4] See Jean-Pierre Le Crom, 'Conclusion' in Jean-Pierre Le Crom, Philippe Auvergnon, Katia Barragan, Dominique Blonz-Colombo, Marc Boninchi, et al. *Histoire du droit du travail dans les colonies françaises (1848–1960)*. [Rapport] Law and Justice Research Mission. 2017, 195–6. The author reminds us of the extent to which the employment contract is contrary to the aspirations of workers and refers to the article by Alain Cottereau, 'Droit et bon droit. Un droit des ouvriers instauré puis évincé par le droit du travail (France XIXe s)', *Annales. Histoires sciences sociales*, 57, no. 6 (2002): 1521–57

system did not require statistics, but their existence makes it possible to know, denounce and limit the most blatant abuses.

The chapter draws on colonial archive material located in Belgium (ACB, Ministry of Foreign Affairs, Brussels),[5] France (*Archives Nationales d'Outre-mer* – ANOM, Aix-en-Provence) and the ILO in Geneva and aims to shed light on the specific conditions of wage labour in the sub-Saharan African territories colonized by Belgium and France. There follows an analysis of the role of international organizations in this process and an account of the changes introduced between the Second World War and independence. We will also see that, at least on paper, the Belgians were better informed about the content, the counterparts and the limits of the wage system in the Belgian Congo than were the authorities in Equatorial Africa or French West Africa (AEF, AOF). We will try to explain this difference and analyse its effects. We hypothesize that wage statistics are not only pieces of information but that their existence and dissemination are in themselves real pressures on employers to either conceal or limit abuse. Their perception of the interest of the political authorities in labour compensation, which is reflected in the frequency of surveys and the quality of the available statistics, influences their behaviour and thus the level of wages.

1) The specificities of labour in the Belgian and French colonies of sub-Saharan Africa

With the exception of the crisis period of the 1930s and the slowdown in infrastructure development projects, there was a chronic shortage of available labour in the colonized territories of sub-Saharan Africa.[6] Settlers relied on the administration to recruit workers, and the administration in turn relied on traditional chiefs. Local wage earners were migrants, usually temporary, who returned to their communities after the work period. They were found in urban areas (service activities, banks and the colonial administrations, which employed local skilled labour or labourers), in companies, firms and plantations run by the colonists. Wage employment based on negotiation and reciprocal commitment, as practised in the West, was the exception. Necessary for the payment of taxes, and even for the payment of a dowry in case of surplus, the passage through the wage system was a colonial constraint. Compared to slavery, it certainly represented a notable improvement, but it was not liberation. Its conditions were not negotiated and were not guaranteed by any legal or regulatory framework. The length (duration), the content (nature of the service) and the payment of the employee (accommodation, cash) and its counterparts (standard of living) depended on the goodwill of the employer. The absence of regular statistical surveys and the lack of knowledge of local living conditions prevented any rational determination of wages.

---

[5] These archives are currently being transferred to the Archives of the Kingdom of Belgium (Brussels).
[6] See Hélène d'Almeida-Topor, 'Recherches sur l'Évolution du Travail Salarié en AOF pendant la Crise Économique 1930–1936', *Cahiers d'études africaines*, 16, no. 61–62 (1976): 103–17. These archives are currently being transferred to the Archives of the Kingdom of Belgium (Brussels).

The demographic weakness of the French-speaking colonies in sub-Saharan Africa, the very unequal distribution of wealth, the frequency of famines, the dispersion of populations and the intense competition between the British, Belgian and French colonists as they sought to attract labour all played a role in favour of improving working conditions. They also reinforced the pressure exerted by employers on the colonial administrations to have cheap labour and to tighten the constraints. The links that the employee retained with his or her community of origin worked in employers' favour, since it relieved them of the non-wage costs incurred for 'social protection'.

The forms of labour mobilization adopted by the Belgian and French colonial administrations were similar in that they shared a lack of regard for local labour and made use of traditional chiefs. They also agreed on the low productivity of local labour. The regulation of 1 March 1930 for the use of the staff of the Office central de travail du Katanga (OCTK)[7] states in this respect that 'efforts must be made to overcome the dislike of the natives for work' and to make work 'friendly' to them to eliminate their 'instinctive aversion to working for European companies'.[8] Some considerations followed on the 'good morale of the native', 'a thinking being, who has his affections and a moral personality which must be considered as much as his aspirations in the family and social order'. Because 'the inferior development of the Congolese black man undoubtedly impinges upon his duties of guardianship', the text invites us to treat him 'with humanity, equity and benevolence', to respect 'his rights' and 'his legitimate interests'. The contradiction between these recommendations and the length of the commitments, 'of 390, 570, 750 or 951 working days', which explains 'the flight of personnel', goes unremarked upon.[9]

Despite these conditions, in the two French-speaking colonies of sub-Saharan Africa, the number of employees increased sharply during the inter-war period. In French West Africa, for example, it rose from 60,000 in 1927 to 243,518 in 1936 (1.63 per cent of the total population).[10] Even if it only represented a small part of the total population, the wage-earning sector had a strong influence on the colonial labour world. It was very vulnerable to the vagaries of the economic situation and very unequal.

The economic performance of the Belgian Congo was particularly strong on the eve of the Second World War. All industrial production, electrical engineering, cement and soap production, as well as textiles, reached record levels.[11] Industrialization affected several regions of the four provinces of the Belgian Congo and the situation was closely monitored by the colonial power.

---

[7] Archives coloniales belges (ACB), ministère des Affaires étrangères (Bruxelles) Main-d'œuvre indigène (MOI) (3552) Office central de travail du Katanga (OCTK), statuts, 1926, 257 pages. Office central of Work of Katanga (OCTK), a Congolese limited liability company formed in 1910 by the Railway Company of the Bas Congo of Katanga, the *Union inière du Haut Katanga*, the Railway Company of Katanga, and the *Compagnie foncière agricole et pastorale* du Congo.
[8] Introduction of the regulation of 1st March 1930 for the use of staff.
[9] ACB MOI (native workers) (3552) Office central de travail du Katanga (OCTK) 1926. Regulation OCTK 1st March 1930 for the staff of the OCTK, Introduction, 1–7.
[10] Ibid., Table 1, 105, not including migrants who go to work abroad.
[11] See M. Masoin, 'La Structure *Économique* du Congo Belge', *Bulletin de l'Institut de Recherches Économiques et Sociales*, 15, no. 1 (1949): 153–72. See Ibid., the Table 1, 105, not including migrants who go to work abroad.

Every year, the Minister for the Colonies presented a summary of the colonial administrators' reports to the legislative chambers, which presupposes that the information is centralized beforehand. Data were gathered at all geographical levels of the territories and the results obtained were often checked.[12] The tables on the recruitment of labour had to be very detailed in order to provide information to firms established outside the territory. In principle, they presented 'data from the chiefdoms listing the male population, the number of recruits, the destinations and employers, the date of recruitment, the duration of the engagement and its conditions (cash or in-kind rations and average wage) and information from the police court on convictions for desertion'.[13] Most often, 'only the information on the male population employed in the territory classified by chiefdom and village and the number of recruits, the employer, the place, the duration of the recruitment, its conditions (rations and average salary) and the mentions of convictions for desertion at the police court' were filled in. The list of headings for the information to be provided on economic activity was regularly extended.

From 1930 onwards, the section devoted to work also sheds light on the cost of goods in various urban centres, which comes from a survey organized at the end of 1929. The marked differences in the baskets of goods used for Europeans and 'natives' give a measure of the inequalities in lifestyles and the stereotypes that governed the construction of the indices. The European basket includes, for example, imported butter, ordinary bottled Bordeaux wine, one packet of Albert cigarettes, the cost of the boy cooks and his weekly ration, and housing. The 'native' basket includes, for example, corn on the cob, lower quality rice, accommodation, oil, blankets, used trousers and jackets and shoes.[14] This assessment of the expenses of 'coloured employees and workers in the various native employment centres' was used to determine the wages paid and the weekly rations distributed.[15] The cost-of-living surveys were also to be used in calculating the amount of tax to be paid.[16]

Information at industry level was also being expanded.[17] One section of the annual reports was given over to 'personnel censuses'. It listed the number of 'indigenous and non-indigenous workers', their wages and the list of establishments by province and sector. These reports contain pre-printed tables which were often commented on.[18] The

[12] ACB, Affaires indigènes et main-d'œuvre (AIMO), Annual reports kept by the second directorate. An investigation into how the annual reports were drawn up was carried out in the provinces and districts of the Belgian Congo in 1922, and the production of the annual reports of the districts was again checked in 1930.
[13] ACB RACCB-719 Boende (District Tshuapa-Équateur), Economic Report of the territorial on the 1st (manuscript) and 2nd semester (mimeographed) 1921.
[14] ACB RACCB-719, Economic Report, list of firms and headings (1929), 31 December 1929.
[15] ACB RACCB-719, Economic report Bakutu (1930).
[16] ACB RACCB 719/Mitwaba (1933–1950). District du Haut Katanga Élisabethville, Letter from District Commissioner Zieglet de Ziegler to the Territorial Administrator of Sampwe: 'I have the honor to ask you to send me urgently the annual economic report for 1933 in triplicate', 20 March 1934. The report is sent to the District Commissioner on 14 April. It is handwritten, 'the work being urgently required of me having left my typewriter at the post office, I apologize for not having been able to take all the care required', signed by the territorial administrator second class.
[17] ACB AIMO (85) Kigali (Affaires économiques) industrial statistics, 1930.
[18] ACB RACCB/719/Inongo, Annual economic reports (1932). Report of the Territorial Administrator of 15 January 1933.

turnover of the factories is mentioned and, in some cases, maps were drawn by the district commissioners to locate them.[19] The centralization of Belgian statistics was reinforced by the Royal Decree of 27 October 1934, which entrusted the Central Statistical Office, attached to the Ministry of Economic Affairs, with periodic censuses, the mechanical processing of statistics and surveys and the dissemination of their results.

The instructions for drafting these annual reports became clearer in 1934.[20] The numerous reminders attest both to the cumbersome nature of the task and the lack of enthusiasm on the part of certain administrators.[21] From 1935 onwards, the provinces' annual reports were no longer published.[22] The model report remained the same until it was simplified in October 1950.[23]

The concentration of enterprises made it easier to collect information on colonial labour conditions.[24] Despite their imperfections and the reluctance of companies to fill in the questionnaires, the statistics from the annual economic reports from the Belgian colonies have no equivalent in sub-Saharan French Africa. The reports by the colonial inspectorate and the Labour Inspectorate created in 1932 are full of details, but they rarely concern the private sector and are neither regular nor statistical in nature. The production of French colonial statistics was the responsibility of the territorial administrations, and their results were centralized by various ministries (Ministry of the Colonies, of Labour, etc.) and by agencies that received little funding. Colonial administrators' lack of interest in statistics was exacerbated by their heavy workload and by the freedom of companies to decide whether or not to respond to surveys. Official publications provide little information on employees' work and wages.

The *Annuaire Statistique de l'AOF*, which provided information on the railway's workforce, distinguishing between 'Europeans' and 'natives' by line and service (general

---

[19] ACB RACCB/719/Inongo, Annual economic reports (1933). The Tumba District Report of 1933, for example, presents the economic map of part of the territory submitted by the Tshuapa District Commissioner at the request of the Tumba District Commissioner, 26 February 1934.

[20] ACB RACCB 1 Instruction on economic reports, General Administration, 1st office to the 5th Directorate-General which is 'requested to make the necessary changes in red ink before sending to the publisher', Brussels, 24 May 1935.

[21] ACB RACCB 1 Report on the administration of the Belgian Congo for 1934: 'I would be obliged to the department to examine carefully and without delay the documents listed above and to send them back to the General Administrator as soon as possible', signed by Governor-General Ryckmans who reminds the heads of department of the General Government that the annual report should have been received by the department at the beginning of June and asks for it to be transmitted without delay, 5 June 1935. It is specified that 'statistical and other tables which are not to be included in the report should be marked in red ink "not to be published"'.

[22] ACB RACCB 1 Office of Governor-General Ryckmans. Notes for the Commander-in-Chief of the Police Force and the Heads of Service of the General Government: 'Proposals will have to be submitted to me as a matter of urgency concerning the repercussions of this decision for the drawing up of the report of the provinces, both to reduce the size of this report and to speeding up its dispatch to the Governor General', Leopoldville 7 December 1935.

[23] ACB RACCB 1 Report on the administration of the Belgian Congo. Letter from the Governor-General No. 911/32/6.367, 8 May 1950 concerning the simplifications of the new model annual report approved by the Minister.

[24] ACB 3DG (1693)2 Hygiene (transport) International Office of Public Hygiene, Africa, the special situation for certain indigenous people (1936).

services, tracks, police, etc.) and the related expenses, is an exception.[25] Little is known about wage labour in French-dominated territories. Several workforce surveys were, nevertheless, carried out in accordance with the circulars of 1909 and 1912. They included around a hundred questions concerning the organization of work and workers' living conditions. A special commission was charged with examining the question of labour at the Ministry of the Colonies, but it did not put forward any proposals until 1926. A vast enquiry into the workforce was then conducted among the colonial authorities at the request of the Minister of the Colonies, Léon Perrier.[26] An ad hoc commission was set up to follow up the survey within the *Conseil supérieur des colonies*.[27] The survey remained subject to the goodwill and budget of the territories and did not fill in the gaps.

No survey on industrial production was carried out before the Second World War, except for Togo and AOF in 1939.[28] This survey provided information on cost prices, each company's production capacity, the number of workers and their distribution between 'specialist or non-specialist', 'European' or 'native' for the year 1938. Organized by the Ministry of the Colonies, the survey was to be conducted throughout the French empire, but it was criticized by the Directorate of Economic Affairs for giving 'an enormous amount of space' to foreign trade statistics and for neglecting 'a lot of information of great interest', such as working conditions: 'we are only entitled to two figures for average hourly wages, which are not defined in the instruction or the questionnaire, and we don't even know the nature of the drive forces used'.

However, the survey provides information on the name and head office of each company, its legal status, its capital, its location, the nature of its activity, its production capacity in 1938, the number of its workers and its 'European' and 'indigenous' specialists.[29] Its results were not analysed until later.[30] The inadequacy and dispersion of documentation on work in the territories colonized by France testify to the indifference of the French political majority to colonial issues and internal quarrels within the management.

Two distinct modes of management

The differences between the official statistics for the Belgian Congo and French Africa reflect the differences in colonial management methods. The alliance between the

---

[25] Nothing similar can be found for the AEF, nor other sectors of activity, whereas the annual reports of the territories of the Belgian Congo present these numbers for each of the major companies.

[26] See Marc Boninchi, 'La genèse des règles de protection. Les dynamiques de la réforme sociale aux colonies', in *La Chicotte et le Pécule. Les Travailleurs à l'Épreuve du Droit Colonial Français (XIX-XXe siècles)*, eds Jean-Pierre Le Crom and Marc Boninchi (Rennes, PUR, 2021), 21–70, 32.

[27] Jean-Pierre Le Crom, 'Conclusion' in Le Crom, Auvergnon, Barragan, Blonz-Colombo, Boninchi, et al. *Histoire du droit du travail*, 195–6.

[28] ANOM 1 AFFECO/59 Economic Affairs 1930- ... Statistical results of the 1939 survey on industrial production in AOF and Togo. Note from Economic Affairs for the Ministry of the Colonies, 1 February 1942.

[29] Ibid., Industrial production AOF and Togo.

[30] Ibid., Dossier 2. Inventory concerning industrial production in the African colonies, 1942. Organization committee of the colonial industrial production, food industry sector, sent to the Economic Affairs Department, Ministry of Colonies, 21 August 1942.

colonial administration and the business community in the Belgian Congo was formed between the two wars, at a time when the governors were all-powerful in French sub-Saharan Africa and were not really answerable to the colonial power of the parent state.

In the Belgian Congo, from the beginning of the twentieth century, 'the state's collection of the economic surplus made it possible to finance the administrative occupation and to set up the minimal infrastructure necessary for the exploration of new exportable resources that attracted Belgian financial capital'.[31] The administration was strengthened and mobilized 'peasant labour and the agricultural surplus for the world market'.[32] It 'justified the use of coercion by 'the behaviour of the African peasant, who was sometimes short-sighted and sometimes reluctant to work'.[33]

The strong economic expansion of the Belgian Congo between 1920 and 1930 (mining exports increased sixfold, agricultural exports tripled) attracted financial capital and stimulated concentration. At the beginning of the 1930s, four Belgian financial groups controlled 75 per cent of the capital invested in the Congo, with the main one (the Société Générale) alone controlling 60 per cent of the capital.[34] The 'quite privileged relationship' that was established 'between financial capital and the colonial administration' aimed to meet the 'considerable' need for wage labour, which quadrupled between 1918 and 1930. The administration 'formed itself into a diversified and hierarchical body' and undertook to 'administer the African world'. It controlled trade by limiting the customary power of the chieftainship. To address the major problem of labour mobilization, it limited 'trading activities', avoiding any increase in the price of labour. 'The 'convergence of interests' with financial capital 'to supply the mining and urban centres with labour was reinforced'. To avoid emptying the countryside and 'to continue to have cheap food', the administration 'limited migration to the city and the mines to 25 per cent of able-bodied adult men'. Mechanization developed and the large companies attracted and stabilized the workforce by attracting families and 'offering better housing and food'.[35]

The crisis of the 1930s re-established the demographic balance between the cities and the countryside, but the administration increased its pressure on the countryside to compensate for the fall in mineral exports with that of agricultural products. The Belgian economist J.-P. Peemans wrote that 'the colonial system creates a cultural alienation that seems much greater than in the English or French systems'.[36] In the longer term, this process of establishing wage labour in the colonies explains the difficulties experienced in the agricultural sector and the persistence of famines after independence.

In contrast, the management of the French colonies in sub-Saharan Africa was characterized by the larger degree of autonomy enjoyed by governors and

---

[31] See Jean-Philippe Peemans, 'Le Modèle Spécifique de Développement Hérité du Système Colonial Belge' in *Accumulation et sous-développement au Zaïre. 1960–1980,* eds Fernand Bezy, Jean-Philippe Peemans and Jean-Marie Wautelet (Louvain-la-Neuve: 1981), 15.
[32] Ibid., 16.
[33] Ibid., 19.
[34] Ibid., 20–3.
[35] Ibid., 27.
[36] Ibid., 36.

administrations and by the weakness of their resources, budgetary self-sufficiency being the rule from 1909 onwards. General regulations were promulgated in each colony at the beginning of the 1920s, but most governors did not legislate much on labour matters.[37] Work was carried out in various forms, ranging from forced labour to free labour, short-term work and contractual work, governed by a few laws and regulations specific to each territory. In AOF and AEF, the regulations applied only to indigenous people. They governed the health and safety conditions of women and children, but they were seldom complied with. The number of employment contracts remained low, the protection of the workforce and the means of control were very limited.[38] Many administrators justified the weakness of the regulations by the 'reluctance of workers to sign written contracts'.[39] In fact, in 1935, this number reached 178,908 people in French West Africa – 315 in Dahomey, 209 in Senegal, 7 in Niger, 74 in Sudan, 1,236 in Guinea, 21,367 in Côte d'Ivoire (with 38,320 employed by the public services and 140,588 by private companies), out of a total population of 14 million inhabitants.

Colonial working conditions were of little concern. Governor Jean-Victor Augagneur was an exception, introducing several restrictive rules, first in Madagascar and then in the AEF.[40] He had the decree of 11 February 1923 on the regulation of work adopted, which subjected employers to a whole series of obligations and made recruitment by private companies subject to an authorization procedure. Article 9, the most innovative, introduced a minimum wage, which was generalized in the colonies of sub-Saharan Africa in 1926. It also obliged employers to specify the weight of any rations provided as a complement to wages paid, as well as the surface area of the dwellings intended for the workers, which says a lot about previous abuses, and limits the working time to 10 hours a day.[41] In 1926, Augagneur, who had become an honorary governor-general, wrote a report on indigenous labour in the French colonies of AOF, AEF and Madagascar.[42] He indicated that the 'indigenous policy' of the 'colonial administration' consisted of 'encouraging the natives to collaborate with us' by regulating 'work in such a way as to ensure' their rights 'as well as those of their employers'.[43] Specifying that 'the native' did not 'go to look for the white man' to 'toil on roads under construction, on tracks in the savannah of the forest, to transport at great distances the equipment and food of the occupying troops', he demands compensation.[44] The 'taste for work' will be stimulated by the 'desire to obtain objects of which the European will have demonstrated the use and the advantage' [...] 'laziness will only diminish if the native feels the need

---

[37] See Le Crom and Boninchi, eds, *La Chicotte et le Pécule*, 16.
[38] Ibid.
[39] See Jean-Pierre Le Crom, 'Conclusion' in Le Crom, Auvergnon, Barragan, Blonz-Colombo, Boninchi, et al. *Histoire du droit du travail*, 195–6, 111.
[40] See Boninchi, 'La Genèse des Règles de Protection', 34–6.
[41] See d'Almeira-Topor, 'Recherches sur l'Évolution du Travail Salarié'.
[42] ANOM 4 Affaires économiques (AFFECO) /73 Economic Department, 1st Office. Economic sections of the High Council of the colonies, sessions from 1926 to 1933. Report on the indigenous workforce in the French colonies of the AOF, AEF and Madagascar presented by Augagneur, honorary Governor-General, at the Economic Council meeting of 16 December 1926.
[43] Ibid., 24–5.
[44] Ibid., 8.

...to enrich himself by earning money'.⁴⁵ Augagneur concludes: 'The question of labour dominates the whole colonial question in black countries where the white man, because of the climate, cannot do any hard work and is limited to the role of leader.' This observation was also made at the 1944 Brazzaville conference, which noted the failure of labour policies that had not succeeded in instilling 'a taste for work' by creating 'new needs' in the French colonies of Africa.⁴⁶ The low pay levels were cited as one of the reasons for this failure. Another was the poor quality of the goods offered in the colonized territories, which was mentioned by several administrators in the Belgian Congo between the two world wars.

A leitmotif of the criticisms addressed by Belgian colonial administrators to the colonial companies in charge of importing the goods offered to employees was their poor quality and cost. This reproach appears as early as 1921 in the half-yearly report on the economic conditions in the territories by the Itoko administrator, who levelled his criticism at the SAB, a large commercial company.⁴⁷ It appears in other reports criticizing the high cost of 'imported fabrics' which are 'of such poor quality that their importation should be prohibited'.⁴⁸ The directors warned against the dangers of these abuses, stating that 'the fact of selling very expensive [European] articles of no value make people lose confidence in Europeans in general [...] moreover [it] creates an ever-growing antipathy against us'. Considering that 'the natives are children for whom we are the guardians', the rapporteur refuses to 'force [the native] to work and to procure by his labour the pitiful articles offered to him', considering that 'he has some nobler mission to fulfil'.

This approach to one of the components of wage practices is complemented by a call for better remuneration for the copal harvest, which was also organized by the SAB and which served to 'pay the tax'. The low level of remuneration was one of the explanations for the 'bad spirit of the workers' for whom resignation was 'an entertainment' and he called for 'stricter regulations'.⁴⁹ The next year's report showed that the situation had not improved; the price of iron and copper remained high, intensifying the discontent of the population, and preventing any improvement in the copal harvest.⁵⁰ Recruitment conditions had even deteriorated, 'despite the reinforcement of constraints introduced by the 1922 decree on employment contracts, which introduced the procedure of the Police Court for certain minor offences'. The writer of the report wonders 'whether the system of punishment by whipping for defaulting workers, just as is done for state workers by a state agent, would not suffice'.

---

⁴⁵ Ibid., 6.
⁴⁶ ANOM 1 AFFECO 101 French African Conference of Brazzaville. Minutes of the plenary session, Tuesday 1 February 1944. Noted 'Secret'. In a very different spirit, René Pleven states that 'in French Black Africa' demography and 'the question of manpower dominate everything since the general demographic density is less than 3 inhabitants per square kilometer', 9.
⁴⁷ ACB RACCB-719 Boende (District Tshuapa-Ecuador) Economic report Itoko 1st semester 1921. Economic affairs. Manuscript of the territorial administrator. The profit made by the SAB is also denounced. For example, the axes and machetes put on sale by the SAB firm: selling price to the natives' machete 6.50 francs and axe 5 francs whereas the SAB bought them 3.50 francs each
⁴⁸ ACB RACCB-719 Boende (District Tshuapa-Équateur), Economic report Itoko 2nd semester 1921, 14 January 1922.
⁴⁹ Ibid.
⁵⁰ ACB RACCB-719, Economic report of 4 June 1923, tables by districts of Equator and by territory.

These six-monthly economic reports show the weak incentive to engage in wage labour, apart from the tax constraint. This incentive was all the weaker because 'our currency has not aroused the enthusiasm of the natives who continue to count among themselves' in traditional units.[51]

The archives consulted to shed light on the positions of the French colonial administrations in the territories of sub-Saharan Africa do not show the same attention to the counterparts of wage labour (food rations, accommodation, medical aid) before the changes of 1936. The appointment of the socialist Marius Moutet to the Ministry of the Colonies by the Popular Front made it possible to introduce some rudimentary legislation in six months, to introduce collective agreements in Senegal and to organize a commission of enquiry in the overseas territories (law of 30 January 1937) 'responsible for researching the needs and legitimate aspirations of the populations living in the colonies, protectorate countries and countries under mandate'.[52] Even if they did not survive Léon Blum's government, these changes testify to an awareness that Louis Mérat, Marius Moutet's advisor, summarized in a book published in 1936: 'the infatuation with the colonies is very recent in France' and 'is nothing more than the pursuit of a solution to the crisis according to barely renewed methods (the search for foreign or colonial clients)'.[53] Mérat called for the development and diversification of the economies of the colonized territories, for the populations to be 'protected from famine' and for the 'native' to be provided with other incentives 'than the replacement of his traditional life by a miserable wage-earning system [...]', deeming inevitable 'the industrialization of the colonies' and the 'satisfaction of the population's less limited needs'[54]. He concludes that a 'destitute and hopeless wage-earning system will not be enough to win over the indigenous populations', nor to 'accommodate a system of exploitation for the benefit of a few'.[55] He called for 'the constant raising of the standard of living of the masses' to 'achieve the unity of the French empire'.[56] The change of perspective is important: 'Above all, it is advisable to ensure that the insufficiently nourished populations are satisfied with their essential food needs by increasing production on the spot, rather than thinking about the progression of exports, which is the almost constant goal of any development or even of domestic trade.'[57]

These ideas were taken up again during the occupation, as shown by the lecture given by Robert Lemaignen, president of the colonial industrial grouping, at the colonial high school on 19 January 1944.[58] Lemaignen invited people to think about industrialization in French West Africa 'to improve the standard of living of the overseas populations'.[59]

---

[51] ACB RACCB-719 Boende (District Tshuapa-Equator), Economic report Itoko 2nd semester 1921, 14 January 1922.
[52] ANOM 1 AFFECO//9 Gernut committee. Formation, historic.
[53] Louis Mérat, *L'Heure de l'Économie Dirigée d'Intérêt Général aux Colonies*, prefaced by Marius Petit, Minister of Colonies (Paris: Recueil Sirey, 1936), 24–32.
[54] Ibid., 40–4.
[55] Ibid., 47.
[56] Ibid., 51.
[57] Ibid., 58.
[58] See ANOM Librairy Robert Lemaignen, 'L'Industrialisation des Colonies, Action Administrative en Matière Économique', conference of 19 January, 27 pages.
[59] Ibid., 11–12.

The increase in public capital allocated in the central state budget and in private capital and the formation of local capital from savings, as well as the development of 'basic information without which the creation of important companies cannot be seriously envisaged' and which were to be the responsibility of the public authorities were the recommended remedies.[60]

The Brazzaville conference organized by the French Committee for National Liberation from 30 January to 6 February 1944 illustrates this change in approach to the colonial world.[61] On 1 February 1944, at the plenary session, René Pleven 'strongly advocated the principle of serious control of private initiative' and invited proposals for a plan aimed 'essentially at increasing the purchasing power of the colonial populations' and at developing information 'on the effects of industrialization on the social condition of the natives'. He deplored the weakness of statistics from the 'colonies, apart from the AOF', which forced him to look for information 'in foreign colonial statistics, mainly English'.

To what extent did the pressure exerted by the ILO between the two wars contribute to this awareness and what were the major changes in the post-Second World War period?

2) International pressures, the ILO and the transformations of the 1950s

Headed by the French socialist Albert Thomas at the time it was founded, the ILO denounced the excesses of colonization and the exploitation of indigenous labour,[62] but it had few resources and its pressure had little effect.[63] The institution at least had the merit of raising questions and provoking reactions. After the Slavery Convention was signed by the LoN in 1926, the ILO organized three important conferences on labour in the colonies, one on forced labour in 1930 (No. 29),[64] the second on the recruitment of indigenous workers in 1936 (No. 50) and the last on labour contracts and penal sanctions for these workers in 1939 (No. 64). Adopted during these plenary conferences, the conventions were prepared over several years and gave rise to

---

[60] Ibid., 20.
[61] ANOM 1 AFFECO 101 Conférence africaine française de Brazzaville. Procès-verbaux des séances. Séance du 7 février 1944, 3. See Sandrine Kott and Joëlle Droux, eds, *Globalizing social rights: the International Labour Organization and beyond* (London: Palgrave Macmillan, 2013), and Aaron Benanav, 'The origins of informality: the ILO at the limit of the concept of unemployment', *Journal of Global History*, 14, no. 1 (2019): 1–19.
[62] For an analysis of the role of the institution see Kott and Droux, eds, *Globalizing Social Rights*; on the difficulties of classifications at the time of decolorizations see: Benanav, 'The Origins of Informality'.
[63] 'The influence of the ILO ultimately proved to be rather weak for the French colonies. Forced labour continued until the end of the Second World War [...]. While in the texts it should only be used for work in the public interest [...] it very largely concerns "natives" who work for private companies, the employers being helped by the local administration and by the native village chiefs', See Le Crom and Boninchi, eds, *La Chicotte et le Pécule*, 15
[64] This convention was not ratified by France before the decree of 17 June 1937, and it was little respected since a new convention on the same subject was adopted in 1957 (no105).

numerous discussions between the representatives of the member states. The preliminary reports were discussed in committees and the member states undertook to ratify and respect the conventions adopted. Regional conferences extended these discussions. The Santiago Conference in 1936, for example, raised awareness of racial problems at work.[65] No conference directly addressed the issue of labour remuneration.

The French governments, often supported by their Belgian counterparts, were suspicious of the ILO's attempts to regulate 'indigenous' labour. This distrust was manifested in the refusal to respond to its requests for information on working conditions in the colonized territories.[66] Thus, the Minister of the Colonies authorized the Governor-General of French West Africa to transmit the results of the 1926 labour survey, but he forbade it to the other colonies.[67] The projects for 'regulation of indigenous labour', discussed since 1927, worried the government more as they thought that the ILO was not very favourable to 'France's colonizing action'. They considered that there was 'no point in providing the organization, whose international character must never be forgotten, with documents' that could be modified 'for special views'. The risk that the issues raised in Geneva would have political repercussions led to the centralization of all information on 'indigenous labour at the Ministry of Colonies and to limit its dissemination'. This did little to encourage any expansion of knowledge on wage labour in the colonial situation.

This mistrust seems excessive, since even in the West, knowledge of working conditions and salaries, as well as studies on family budgets and the cost of living, was embryonic.[68] The Ford-Filene survey, the first comparative study on the cost of living conducted by the ILO, dates from the 1930s and concerned only a few large cities in Europe and the United States.[69] Colonized territories were not mentioned at the first conferences of ILO labour statisticians.[70] Indigenous labour issues were entrusted to a Committee of Experts set up by the ILO Governing Body in 1926, which participated in the preparation of conferences on forced labour and

---

[65] This convention was not ratified by France before the decree of 17 June 1937, and it was little respected since a new convention on the same subject was adopted in 1957 (no 105), see Luis Rodriguez-Pinero, *Indigenous Peoples, Postcolonialism, and International Law. The ILO Regime (1919-1989)* (Oxford, New York: Oxford University Press, 2005), 6.

[66] ANOM 7 AFFECO/39 Economic Affairs – Labour. Ministry of the Colonies, note for the Directorate of Economic Affairs, 2nd office, concerning the request for documentation on working conditions in the colonies of the group addressed by the Director of the ILO to the Governor of the AOF, 20 March 1928. In the margin, in pencil, 'to send a letter of refusal to Thomas'.

[67] ANOM 7 AFFECO/39 Economic and labour affairs. Ministry of the Colonies. Report on the work of the 1927 Committee of Experts which 'gives the ILO's trends in the field of indigenous labour'. Signed Besson, State Councillor, Director of Political Affairs.

[68] BIT T 127/1003 Correspondance on methods of conducting family living studies nutritional surveys (1937–1938) débuts des études sur les budgets familiaux, Genève, ILO, 1926.

[69] BIT T 101/0/1/0/1/2 Inquiry into International Cost of living (Ford-Filene): circular to governments, replies, report, observations (1929–1933).

[70] ILO T 105/1/1 Labor statistics: 1st international conference of labour statisticians (1923–1928); ILO T 127/1003 Correspondence on methods of conducting family living studies nutritional surveys (1937–1938); ILO T 1000/5 Labour statistics technical conference of official labour statistician's 5th session 1937. The harmonization of methods for comparing wages in different countries and the progress of family budget studies was welcomed at this conference, but it did not concern colonized territories.

contracts.⁷¹ The Committee launched a survey on the 'organisation, working conditions and forms of classification' of 'indigenous workers' to 'identify the main features of a labour market' that was poorly regulated and monitored.⁷² The questionnaire aimed at shedding light on 'the conditions of employment, the typology of contracts (remuneration, duration, number of hours worked per day, compensation provided by the employer – food, transport to the workplace, housing, medical care, etc.)' and 'the use of the "pécule" (deduction from the daily wage to build up a sum paid at the end of the contract) or of advances on remuneration (the legitimacy of which was often contested)'.⁷³ The issue of contract labour in the colonies was put on the agenda of the 1935 International Labour Conference. By making 'the labour contract the cornerstone of policies for the integration of wage earners', the ILO subjected colonial areas to 'the ideology of free labour', to the detriment of 'traditional activities (agriculture and crafts)'.⁷⁴ It forced the construction of 'a sort of colonial labour code' for 'indigenous labour indexed on criteria of racial differentiation'.⁷⁵

The ILO thus imposed on colonial societies a 'Eurocentric' conception of work, perceived as 'a subordinate activity in exchange for a series of counterparts (wages and social rights)'. The lack of consideration for the amount and measurement of wages and the lack of understanding of the cost of living and purchasing power limited these ambitions until the social laws of the colonial powers linked wages and the cost of living in the colonies after 1950. This late linkage led the ILO to renew its approach to wages on the eve of independence and to question the capacity of territories to offer decent wages to their populations. The analysis of these capacities required increased statistical knowledge of the various wage components, which is part of the profound changes in colonial policies introduced by the Second World War.

The Second World War accelerated the introduction of wage labour in the colonized territories.⁷⁶ In the Belgian Congo, there were 800,000 men in paid employment in 1945, compared to 480,000 in 1938 and 1929.⁷⁷ The increase in pressure on the workforce and the extension of compulsory cultivation led to strong social tensions that were gradually reduced by the increase in urban purchasing power linked to the development of public employment, rationalization efforts and productivity gains. The political orientations of the colonial powers had changed.

The 1944 Philadelphia International Conference attested to the awareness of the urgency of social reforms. It affirmed the international community's commitment to genuine equality of rights and condemned the differences in legislation between the

---

⁷¹ ILO N 206/2/0/0 42 Committee of experts for Colored Labour; ILO N 206/2/3-4-5/0 Native Labor. Meeting of the Committee, Geneva, 1930. The first meeting of the Committee in 1927 discussed the draft report on forced labour, the second in 1928 dealt with the question of contract labour [...], the sixth session in 1936 dealt with contract labour and a seventh in 1937 with recruitment, health, and wage problems; ILO N 206/7/28/1 Native Labour. Correspondance on Professional workers in the colonies (1936).
⁷² F. Ricciardi, 'Le Salariat au Miroir', 25.
⁷³ Ibid.
⁷⁴ Ibid., 25–6.
⁷⁵ Ibid., 30–3.
⁷⁶ See J. P. Peemans, 'Le Modèle Spécifique de Développement', 11.
⁷⁷ Ibid., 37.

colonial powers and their colonies. The ILO undertook to promote universal social rights, while the UN had new monitoring powers that the LoN had not had. These positions were reflected in the Brazzaville conference in early 1944.[78] Even if the measures introduced 'were not revolutionary, since trade unions were still not recognized everywhere and the end of forced labour was not planned until five years later', the conference 'marked a turning point in the awareness of the damage caused by colonization, particularly in the field of labour'. The change of mindset became apparent as soon as France was liberated. 'Laws or decrees were henceforth promulgated for all the overseas territories, eliminating the "omnipotence of governors and governors-general".'[79] Three important laws were adopted: the first officially abolished forced labour; the second recognized trade union rights, 'thus moving labour law from a purely individual to a collective dimension'; the third created a 'genuine labour inspectorate in the overseas territories, organized vertically from Paris and in theory independent of local colonial authorities'.[80] The French constitution of 1946 laid down the principle of equality for all citizens in French West Africa, but 'in fact, only 5 to 10 per cent of the population was concerned, i.e. 297,303 native employees, out of a native population of 15,955,000 people according to a parliamentary information report of 1954'.[81]

A further step was taken with the adoption and promulgation of the Labour Code for the territories and associated territories under the Ministry of Overseas France in the Act of 15 December 1952.[82] Its 241 articles were largely inspired by the metropolitan code, 'following the wishes of the African parliamentarians and all the trade unionists'. Even if 'social protection was reduced to a trickle' before 1956 and although workplace accidents were not included before 1957, 'the Code regulates collective relations (collective agreements, conciliation and arbitration of labour disputes, staff delegates) and individual relations (formal equal pay, daily and weekly working hours, paid holidays, etc.)'.[83] Its article 91 specifies that 'for equal conditions of work, professional qualification and performance, wages are equal for all workers, regardless of their origin, sex, age and status'.[84] On the ground, conditions remained very unequal. In 1951 in Dakar, the range of European wages was 23,100 to 54,500 CFA francs per month in manufacturing industry, compared to 3,955 to 18,800 CFA francs for Africans, not including trade.[85] Differences in qualifications and geographical disparities reinforced these inequalities since 70 to 75 per cent of employees were paid the minimum wage, and an out-of-class employee in Dakar earned 800 francs a day, i.e. forty times the

---

[78] Le Crom and Boninchi, eds, *La Chicotte et le Pécule*, 17.
[79] Ibid.
[80] Ibid.
[81] Florence Renucci (2006), 'L'Élaboration du Code du Travail Outre-Mer et la Réduction du Temps de Travail en AOF', in *Les Politiques du Travail (1906-2006), Acteurs, Institutions, Réseaux*, eds Odile Join-Lambert, Alain Chatriot and Vincent Viet (Rennes: PUR, 2006), 59–68.
[82] See Boninchi, 'La Genèse des Règles de Protection', 51.
[83] Katia Barragan, 'Le Droit du Travail des Européens dans les Colonies Françaises d'Exploitation entre Différenciation et Assimilation', in *La Chicotte et le Pécule*, 311.
[84] See Le Crom, Barragan, Blonz-Colombo, Boninchi, et al., *Histoire du Droit du Travail*.
[85] K. Barragan, 'Le Droit du Travail', 311.

minimum wage of a labourer in northern Cameroon (20 francs).[86] In these conditions, the legal limitation of working hours, which had to be accompanied by a reduction in wages, triggered strikes.[87] Protests about low wages were endemic in AEF and forced an increase in the minimum wage in the 1950s.[88] Inequalities between the wages of Europeans and Africans also remained high in the Belgian Congo.[89] The same applied to the concentration of wealth.[90]

This 'extreme polarisation' had a lasting influence on the colonized territories. In the Belgian Congo after 1960, for example, 'when the state power goes into crisis, nothing prevents the brutal collapse of urban real wages'.[91] In the longer term, the dynamics of colonial society become an essentially urban phenomenon, the growth of agriculture remains exclusively extensive while the rural world, which includes most of the active population, 'sinks into stagnation'.[92]

For the post-war period, more information about the situation is available thanks to the development of labour statistics in accordance with UN requirements.[93] Progress was more marked in the Belgian Congo than in the French overseas territories. From July 1944 onwards, the cost-of-living indices in the Belgian Congo and Ruanda Urundi were published quarterly for Europeans and half-yearly for the 'advanced natives'.[94] The Belgian colonial statistics service was supervised by 'four Europeans of university standing who had worked in Belgium in public or private statistics offices'. Population statistics became more precise. From 1949 onwards, triennial demographic censuses of the 'non-indigenous population' were organized using individual and then household bulletins, which supplemented the use of registration certificates issued by the immigration service.[95] For the indigenous population, the population statistics were based on the continuous recording of compulsory registrations in the territory of

---

[86] Ibid.
[87] Ibid.
[88] See Boninchi, 'La Genèse des Règles de Protection', 69.
[89] Table 11. Evolution of African and European average wages in the transport sector. Annual wages report: in 1927 for example, the European wages is 220 when the African wages is 6. The differences increase with the Second World War when the European wages growth (260 and 5 in 1945). The wages of Africans increase after 1955 from 10 to 18 and the European one from 320 to 450. See Peemans, 'Le Modèle Spécifique de Développement', 38.
[90] Ibid., 10.
[91] Ibid., 37.
[92] Ibid., 38.
[93] ACB RACCB 719/Mitwaba (1951–1959). Economic Report 1952, two annexed tables added to those of 1951: Distribution of the indigenous working population by type of activity (indigenous and foreign, male and female) as at 31 December 1952 and wages and rations paid in the various employment centres, signed the territorial administrator, 14 January 1952.
[94] ACB RACCB/719/Inongo Renseignements statistiques sur le Congo Belge.
[95] ACB CP407 Report to the Minister of Colonies on statistics in the Belgian Congo, mission report (July–September 1956), J.-P. Lamouche, head of the department at the Central Bank of the Belgian Congo and Ruanda-Urundi, 96 pages. This mission followed two others: the first in August 1947 when Mr Dufrasne, Director General of the Belgian National Institute of Statistics, was to 'examine the possibility of establishing statistics in the colony on a rational basis and to seek the most appropriate material to ensure their rapid publication', and the second when Mr De Reymaeker Loeys and Mr Carbonnelle were to 'assess the studies of the Commissariat for the Ten-Year Plan on the national income of the colony and to put forward suggestions for improving the estimates' in October 1953.

residence, from which departures and deaths were subtracted. The annual count of these records shows the registered population by province and territory, its distribution by sex and major age groups and its economic and social location. The file was to be updated every year by agents visiting the villages, but omissions were frequent.[96] The gradual organization of the civil registry and the formation of a specialized office (two agents and eighty 'suitably trained' indigenous investigators) which relieved the territorial framework of statistical work from 1954 onwards, and then 'mechanography' improved the situation.

Labour statistics were also developed from the use of monthly processing sheets, annual statistics from the mining department and the three-yearly censuses for European workers. Statistics on the indigenous workforce were much less clear until the ordinance of 31 August 1956, which prescribed quarterly surveys on the number, origin and composition of workers' families.

Cost-of-living indices and wage statistics were still more developed for Europeans than for Africans, although there is no data on the wages of private-sector employees before 1957. From 1952 onwards, monthly statistics on the wages paid to indigenous workers in the administration and a biannual index of the cost of indigenous labour in enterprises with more than 500 employees were established.

The organization of annual industrial censuses specified by the ordinance of 20 September 1955, which made it 'compulsory to communicate a whole series of information on the activity of enterprises for statistical purposes', gradually filled the gaps.[97] From 1957 onwards, it was planned that this information would be extended to include staff salaries. Thus, even if the Belgian Congo's statistical apparatus was still in its infancy and required additional expenditure, 'the reforms that it would allow to be carried out would contribute to relieving an overworked territorial staff that could not today fulfil the educational and political mission that it was entitled to'.[98] The lack of knowledge of the conditions of employment of the indigenous population, which represented most of the working population, can be interpreted as a sign of the persistence of very marked inequalities, but unlike in the pre-war period, this lack of knowledge was no longer the result of general indifference.

Conclusion

The history of wage measurement in French-speaking colonial sub-Saharan Africa is that of a failure: that of the forced export of a mode of work based on the individual contract in societies driven by collective bargaining. Until 1945, this failure was largely based on stereotypes. Despite the efforts of international organizations, and even if the Belgians were more a question of different arrangements and economic contexts than the French in developing statistics on the components of wages in the Congo in order to understand the reasons for the lack of attractiveness of wage work, most colonists

[96] Ibid., 14.
[97] Ibid., 43.
[98] Ibid., 86.

remained convinced of their superiority and did not intend to evaluate or pay a fair price for the labour of the colonized. The focus of the debates in the colonial metropolises and international organizations on the nature of the labour contract (duration of the contract and conditions of the worker) was at the expense of any analysis of its monetary counterparts. It was as if the remuneration of the 'colonized employee' was secondary. Under these conditions, the statistics that are essential for determining wages (cost of living and lifestyle assessments, qualification grids) were not considered necessary. These stereotypes were swept away from the end of the 1930s by the assertion of colonial elites and by workers' protests in major colonial industrial centres, and they did not survive the Second World War.

The Philadelphia and Brazzaville conferences reaffirmed the principle of equality between men, overturning the foundations of colonial management. Association was to replace domination. The development of work measurement and statistics was slower in the territories colonized by France because of the delay accumulated before the war, but it was progressing in the Belgian Congo. Better knowledge of the conditions of paid work confirmed the presence of very pronounced inequalities. The persistence of low wages, accentuated by the reduction in legal working hours, the inadequacy of the training offered to the colonized populations and the lack of prospects for social advancement through work had left a lasting mark on colonial wage labour. These limitations of wage labour based on a contract whose forms were imported from the colonial power persisted after independence.

The inadequacy of statistics on wage work prevented it from being remunerated fairly and from creating the conditions for its improvement. It condemned us to prolong the colonial wage contract. Taking up Marc Boninchi's words, who wondered 'whether the very expression "colonial labour law" is not somewhat antinomic' we can ask ourselves whether the wage as a 'fair remuneration for work' is not incompatible with 'the very principles of a colonization founded on a logic of exploitation'.[99] The unwillingness of the colonial authorities to improve statistics on the conditions of wage labour suggests that Boninchi's question can be answered in the negative: is it possible to protect workers effectively in a system naturally designed to dominate ?[100] The 1958 ILO report on labour problems in Africa denounced the persistent lack of knowledge about the working conditions, nature and wages of colonized populations.[101] It also shows that labour in Africa was still approached as a problem whose terms had hardly changed since the inter-war period. Is the lack of interest in measuring labour in the colonial situation not due to the efforts made to develop 'contractualization'?

In the end, the question of wages and their measurement, which determined work organization and relations – and even the social hierarchy – and the sharing of benefits in the colonized world, was considered of secondary importance by the regulators, who confined the 'natives' to low-paid subordinate roles. The development of the wage

---

[99] Boninchi, 'Conclusion. Le sort des travailleurs', in *La chicotte*, 320.
[100] Ibid., 'The impression of a comprehensive protective text left by the 1952 Overseas Territories Labour Code is an illusion', 320.
[101] See BIT, Les Problèmes du Travail en Afrique, Études et Document, no. 48, Genève, 1958.

economy in the newly independent countries of sub-Saharan Africa inherited the categories and inequalities of colonization, distinguishing between urban and rural and skilled and unskilled labourers, and is still marked by racist conceptions – classifying people according to their 'ethnic' (geographical) origin and their 'capacities' for work – that define the wage hierarchy and contribute to the 'creation' of racial categories and hierarchies. These conceptions in turn influenced the situation of workers from former colonies who immigrated to Belgian and French territories. As Ferruccio Ricciardi points out, these dynamics are part of another history of wage labour, which is irreducible to the single dimension of the submission of the worker to the employer.[102] In the colonial context, the absence or insufficiency of statistics on wages testifies to the disinterest of the political authorities in the question and gives free rein to the unlimited exploitation of workers. This is not to claim that these statistics play any role in determining wages. This is of course only standardized information on the counterparts of the work. However, because they presuppose surveys, because they create a relationship between their sponsors (political authorities), the surveyors (administrative and auxiliary services), the respondents (employers, businesses), because they are the tools of government, which have a cost and presuppose funding, these conventions create links, 'make things stand together'[103] and make it possible to know, compare or even standardize and regulate very heterogeneous situations. These tools bear witness to the will and capacity of political authorities to govern.

---

[102] Ricciardi, 'Le Salariat au Miroir', 33.
[103] Alain Desrosières, 'Comment faire des choses qui tiennent: histoire sociale et statistique', *Histoire & Mesure*, 4, no. 3/4 (1989): 225-2–42.

10

Down with the *Caro-vita*! A Social and Intellectual History of the Cost-of-Living Statistics in Italy, 1910s–1930s[1]

Massimo Asta

The history of cost-of-living statistics deals with surveys on consumption, the definition of household budgets and living standards, the measurement of retail prices, and mechanisms of indexation of wages. Cost-of-living indexes have been considered key statistical indicators ever since they began to be regularly calculated and published at the start of the twentieth century in the USA and European countries such as Great Britain, Germany, France, Italy and Russia. The actors involved in its production and adoption have attributed to it an important performative power, capable of affecting the wellbeing of workers and the functioning of the relations between employees and employers. Yet, such numbers were controversial: they generated disputes between trade unions, employers and states, bringing into question their effectiveness in understanding social reality. Critics also questioned the legitimacy of the administrative structures and statisticians in charge of the calculation and the publication of these numbers.

This chapter aims to chart the intellectual history of the emergence in Italy of cost-of-living statistics, and how this was embedded in the country's social and political history. In the wake of the works of scholars such as Alain Derosières, Béatrice Touchelay, Simon Sretzer, Emily Berman, Sally Engle Merry and Daniel Hirschamn, it sees statistics as a co-constructed social technique, resulting from the interaction between the internal procedures of science with institutional and political dimensions, which give rise to priorities, interests and interventions that shape how statisticians construct their questions and techniques of measurement.[2] It also suggests going

---

[1] I would like to thank Pedro Ramos Pinto and Béatrice Touchelay for their comments on earlier versions of this chapter.
[2] See, Alain Desrosières, *La Politique des Grands Nombres. Histoire de la Raison Statistique* (Paris : La Découverte, 1993) ; Id., *Pour une Sociologie Historique de la Quantification. L'Argument Statistique I* (Paris : Presses de l'École des Mines de Paris, 2008) ; Id., *Gouverner par les Nombres. L'Argument Statistique II* (Paris : Presses de l'École des Mines de Paris, 2008) ; Id., *Prouver et gouverner. Une Analyse Politique des Statistiques Publiques*, (Paris : La Découverte, 2014) ; Béatrice Touchelay, Isabelle Bruno, Florence Jany-Catrice (eds), *The Social Sciences of Quantification. From Politics of*

beyond the role of the state, by arguing that, at least in the Italian case, industrial relations and relations between labour and capital were constitutive elements of the genesis and evolution of this statistical technique. These social dynamics should be taken into account not only as a field of intervention of the state, of its experts and specific goal-oriented knowledge aiming to govern through numbers, but also as a sphere which influences both the production of statistical knowledge and the institutionalization of its administrative practice. This is what happened in Italy during the 1910s and the 1930s, where statistical authorities struggled to generate trust in their work, and whose cost-of-living numbers were not able to be fully translated into accepted conventions and technical artefacts.

Italy, from the start of the twentieth century up until the advent of fascism, represents a useful case study. This was a period characterized by important historical breaks, whose analysis can contribute to understanding how the intellectual history of the cost-of-living statistics is influenced by evolving institutional, political and social dimensions. Despite the presence of elements of continuity between the statistics of the liberal period and those of the fascist period at the academic level (institutions, networks and practices),[3] there were important changes in the cost-of-living measurement.

In a Weberian perspective, cost-of-living statistics can represent a rationalizing tool for mediating between capital and labour, used by a state conceived as an institution above divergent and conflicting interests. The application of this 'rational' tool of quantitative calculation is meant to limit the room for manoeuvre of working-class movements within a set of rules.[4] Historical accounts stressing this framework emphasize the Great War, as well as the 1930s, as critical junctures that explain the emergence of cost-of-living statistics, as they triggered the creation of new administrative structures, the ascendancy of state experts, and the beginning of state intervention in the economy. I argue that this argument in the case of Italy tends to backdate the emergence of the state as mediator in industrial relations to the beginning of the twentieth century, i.e. to give the state a role that it would only fully have after the

---

Large Numbers to Target-Driven Policies (Cham: Springer, 2016); Emmanuel Didier, *America by the Numbers. Quantification, Democracy, and the Birth of National Statistics* (Cambridge, Massachusetts: MIT Press, 2020); Béatrice Touchelay, and Philippe Verheyde (eds), *La Genèse de la Décision. Chiffres Publics, chiffres Privés dans la France du XXe siècle* (Pompignac-près-Bordeaux : éditions Bière, 2009); Emily Barman, *Caring Capitalism. The Meaning and Measure of Social Value* (Cambridge: Cambridge University Press, 2016); Sally Engle Merry, *The Seductions of Quantification: Measuring Human Rights, Gender Violence, and Sex Trafficking* (Chicago: University of Chicago Press, 2016). See also the special issue on the history of the measurement of inequality, *History of Political Economy*, 52, no. 3 (2020): 413–34 eds Pedro Ramos Pinto and Poornima Paidipaty; Ann Rudinow Sætnan, Heidi Mork Lomell, and Svein Hammer (eds), *The Mutual Construction of Statistics and Society* (London: Routledge, 2012).

[3] Jean-Guy Prévost, *A Total Science. Statistics in Liberal and Fascist Italy* (Montreal-Kingston: McGill-Queen's University Press, 2009).

[4] For this perspective see Thomas Stapleford, *The Cost of Living in America. A Political History of Economic Statistics, 1880–2000* (Cambridge: Cambridge University Press, 2009); Cecilia Lanata Briones, 'Constructing Cost of Living Indices: Ideas and Individuals, Argentina, 1918–1935', *History of Political Economy*, 53, no. (2021): 57–87.

Second World War. State involvement in this kind of expertise instead was slow in coming. Other factors primarily matter.

How did a decentralized and pluralistic production of retail price statistics made by municipalities, state, and even trade unions evolve into a centralized technique under fascism that was used to compress salaries rather than regulate relations between labour and capital? Was the Great War or instead the rise of social conflict during Italy's *Biennio Rosso* of 1919-20 [the Red Two Years] the turning point for both the technical production of such indexes and their adoption as a tool for the regulation of wages? To what extent did the rise in prices, and its contemporary perception, matter? And in a transnational perspective, what was the role of the International Institute of Statistics (IIS) and the International Labour Organisation (ILO) in spreading the use of these techniques? By tackling these issues, this chapter analyses the politics of numbers, the role of experts and their political engagement, and power relations. Even if it also questions the performative power of the cost-of-living figures, the focus is on the making and the socio-political concern of the production of these statistics.

The emergence of a new statistical tool in liberal Italy

After a long period of stability and deflation during the nineteenth century, prices began to rise in 1896 and shaped a period of lasting moderate inflation until the outbreak of the First World War. If seen through the lens of the inflationist twentieth century, these years may appear as a period of low inflation: an average of 0.6 per cent between 1896 and 1914, 1.3 per cent in the time of more persistent inflation between 1903 and 1912. All the indicators of the Italian wellbeing, such as life expectancy, mortality rate, available calories, height, per capita income and real wages continued to show progressive though very slow improvements until the outbreak of the war.[5] Nevertheless, the general level of Italian wages in comparative perspective remained extremely low, in particular that of unskilled workers, which was close to subsistence.[6] This can help explain the social and political anxiety surrounding the modest pre-war inflation.

Contemporary experts showed their concern. The *Giornale degli Economisti e Rivista di Statistica*, the most important Italian economic and statistical journal of the time, offers a vantage point to understand this change of mood with regards to prices. From the early 1910s, the inflationist shift was interpreted by its contributors as an important and structural change. At that point, economists and statisticians such as Giorgio Mortara, who was initially interested in demography, and Gustavo del Vecchio,[7] an expert in monetary

---

[5] See the data of annual inflation in Giovanni Vecchi, *Measuring Wellbeing. A History of Italian Living Standards* (Oxford: Oxford University Press, 2019). For the data of the annual inflation see Ibid., 589-90.

[6] Giovanni Federico, Alessandro Nuvolari and Michelangelo Vasta, 'The Origins of the Italian Regional Divide. Evidence from Real Wages, 1861-1913', *The Journal of Economic History*, 79, no. 1 (2019): 63-98.

[7] *Omaggio a Giorgio Mortara. A Tribute to Giorgio Mortara, 1885-1967. Vita e Opere. His Life and Works* (Roma: Università degli studi di Roma 'La Sapienza', 1985); and Gianfranco Tusset, *Money as Organization, Gustavo Del Vecchio's Theory* (London: Routledge, 2014).

theory, started to investigate prices and calculate index numbers: synthetic economic indexes to describe 'economic progress', but also price and cost-of-living indexes, and household budgets.[8] In 1913, Del Vecchio used the data of a survey on the prices paid by National Boarding Schools for the supplies necessary for boarders during the years 1890–1912 and wrote of a 'very remarkable increase' of retail and wholesale prices since 1896–7. He identified international causes to explain the new inflation and concluded that this 'rising movement of food prices does not in any way seem destined to stop'.[9]

Given the Italian level of wages, the problem of prices necessarily had to become a social and political matter, particularly from 1909, after the slowdown of the economic growth of 1907–08 and concurrently with the moderate resumption of the working-class mobilization, visible by an increase in the numbers of strikes and strikers.[10] On 22 January 1911, the Italian General Confederation of Labour organized 'the day against the *caro-vita* (expensive life) and for universal suffrage'.[11] *Caro-vita* represented a useful subject to activate interest around the electoral reforms, but the event was also meant to prepare activists and public opinion for the discussion in parliament of the Italian Socialist Party's (ISP) motion against price increases.[12] The Socialist members of parliament were aware of the international nature of the phenomenon but highlighted two factors of economic policy which had an impact on inflation: tariffs, in particular the duty on wheat, and the role of intermediaries between production and consumption. They proposed as a solution to the former, the abolition of tariffs; and to the latter, the development of consumer cooperatives and municipal stores.

This strategy was combined with, and for the most ardent supporters of free trade (within and outside the ISP) driven by, the claim for a state withdrawal in economy and for lower tax burden on consumption in order to defend the economic interests of northern industrial workers and industries, as conceived as opposed to those of farmers and the agrarian South, who benefited from tariffs on food imports. Socialists were initially more interested in denouncing the protectionist policy of the state, than in proposing statistical techniques for understanding the impact of inflation on workers' life and to regulate industrial relations. Their discourse was in line with the ideas of moderate liberals who supported industrial development through free trade, and who had criticized Italy's protectionist stance since the 1880s.[13] In turn, some

---

[8] See Giorgio Mortara, 'Numeri Indici delle Condizioni Economiche d'Italia', *Giornale degli Economisti e Rivista di Statistica*, 47, no. 9 (1913): 193–204; Id., 'Costo della Vita e Salari a Trieste dal 1885 al 1911', *Giornale degli Economisti e Rivista di Statistica*, 45 no. 11/12 (1912): 515–16; Gustavo del Vecchio, 'Relazioni fra Entrata e Consumo', *Giornale degli Economisti e Rivista di Statistica*, 44, no. 2 (1912): 111–42; Id., 'Continuazione', 44, no. 3 (1912): 228–54; Id., 'Continuazione e Fine', 44, no. 4/5 (1912): 389–439; Id., 'Nuovi Dati sul Costo della Vita', *Giornale degli Economisti e Rivista di Statistica*, 46, no. 6 (1913): 612–18.

[9] Ibid.

[10] Adolfo Pepe, *Storia del Sindacato in Italia nel '900*, vol. 1, *La CGdL e l'Età Liberale* (Roma, Ediesse, 1997), chapter 5.

[11] 'Caro Vivere e Suffragio Universale', *Avanti!*, 16 January 1911.

[12] Chamber, proceedings, XIII Kingdom legislature, 27 and 28 January 1911, 11530–53 and 11573–95.

[13] Luca Tedesco, *L'Alternativa Liberista in Italia. Crisi di Fine Secolo, Antiprotezionismo* (Soveria Mannelli: Rubbettino, 2003); Germano Maifreda, 'La panificazione e i prezzi del pane a Milano tra Otto e Novecento', in *Le Vie del Cibo. Italia Settentrionale (secc. XVI–XX)*, eds Marina Cavallera, Silvia A. Conca Messina and Blythe Alice Raviola (Roma: Carocci, 2019), 191–221; Antonio Cardini, *Stato Liberale e Protezionismo in Italia, 1890–1900* (Bologna: Il Mulino, 1981).

liberals, such as the economist and Radical Party MP Antonio De Viti de Marco, welcomed the emergence of the working classes movement and accepted strikes as a necessary tool to adjust wages distorted by rising prices.[14] The protectionist government line was defended by Francesco Saverio Nitti, who denied in parliament the social impact of price rises. Rather, he criticized the socialist motion and attributed inflation exclusively to international causes and the recent increase of the level of wages and rising consumption from the working class.

This attitude of the government was consistent with its lack of interest in economic statistical techniques. Alain Desrosières suggested that statistical forms and their uses are related to the forms of state.[15] Italy was a young Liberal state, built on tax-based manhood suffrage, and with a long pre-unitarian history of municipal autonomy.[16] At the beginning of the twentieth century, instead of the emergence of the big state, Italy experienced a crisis of statistics and a disinvestment of the state in this branch of the civil service. From 1901 to 1910 the staff of the Department of Statistics decreased from 81 units to 45; the budget decreased from 219,430 lire to 160,300 lire. The Department of Statistics dealt only with vital records, emigration and judicial statistics. Only three volumes of the Statistical Yearbook were published (1900, 1904 and 1905–07). The weakness of Italian statistics was compounded by the fragmentation of its production, as important statistical tasks were divided between different ministers and departments.[17] Conversely, in 1905 the Statistical Union of Italian Towns was founded with the aim to unify the criteria for the publication of statistical data, demonstrating the municipalities' desire to maintain an autonomous role, not only a delegated one by the state, with regard to the production of statistics.[18]

At the national level, innovations in cost-of-living statistics only occurred under the new cabinet led by Giovanni Giolitti (March 1911–March 1914), which was more concerned with the social question and open to dialogue with the socialist opposition. The Bureau of Labour of the Ministry of Agriculture, Industry and Trade started producing series of national retail prices of nineteen food items (plus petrol, coking coal, and firewood) from July 1913.[19] There are a number of interesting links between the 1911 debates in parliament and these innovations. The natural scientist Luigi Montemartini was among the signatories of the socialist parliamentary motion against the *caro-vita*. His brother, Giovanni Montemartini, a socialist engaged economist, had been the head of the Bureau of Labour since its establishment in 1903, and in 1912 had taken the initiative of an important survey on the agricultural wholesale prices, carried out by the mathematician and economist Luigi Amoroso. The purpose was to

---

[14] See the speech of Antonio De Viti de Marco Antonio, Chamber proceedings, XXIII Kingdom legislature, 1 February 1911, 11692–7.
[15] Alain Desrosières, 'L'État, le Marché et les Statistiques. Cinq Façons d'Agir sur l'Économie', *Courrier des Statistiques*, 95–6 (2000): 3–10.
[16] See for instance, Maria Letizia D'Autilia, *Il Cittadino senza Burocrazia. Società Umanitaria e Amministrazione Pubblica nell'Italia Liberale* (Torino: Giuffré, 1995).
[17] Dora Marucco, *L'Amministrazione della Statistica nell'Italia Unita* (Roma-Bari: Laterza, 1996), chapter 5.
[18] It is no coincidence that the foreign institutional reference of this municipal movement was the German federal model, and the statistical materials produced by its towns.
[19] *Bollettino dell'Ufficio del Lavoro*, 20, no. July (1913), 68–77.

understand the impact of wholesale prices on retail prices.[20] The measurement of this relationship, which could prove the usefulness of an abandonment of the protectionist tariffs, had already been a matter of debate during the parliamentary discussion.

The first series of retail price index numbers were directed by the economist and statistician Riccardo Bachi, called to head the Bureau of Labour after Montemartini's death. Bachi belonged to the same progressive, and often socialist, intellectual and political network as Montemartini, which included other neoclassical economists, namely from the Laboratory of Political Economy at the University of Turin (such as Attilio Cabiati and Luigi Einaudi).[21] Bachi had been working extensively on index numbers.[22] He was the author of a theoretical contribution on this topic in 1913,[23] which shows his engagement with the international statistical debate on index numbers. As editor of *L'Italia Economica*, a statistical yearbook published as a supplement to the journal *La Riforma Sociale*, he created the Bachi index, partly drawing on the wholesale prices index of the British *Economist*.[24] The data of the retail price index adopted under his leadership by the national Bureau of Labour since March 1913 were collected by municipal authorities, cooperatives, trade unions' chambers of labour, and chambers of commerce of forty-two towns. It included the prices of seven items of food: wheaten bread, wheaten flour, macaroni, beef, bacon, oil and milk. It was calculated on the prices per unit of weight or unit of capacity (a kilogram for the first five articles, a litre for the other two), according to Laspeyres' method and used as base the year 1912. Relative prices were calculated separately for each of the seven articles, taking as monthly average price the arithmetical average of the local prices. The final index number resulted from the geometric average of these seven index numbers, as the Bureau of Labour stated, because it deals with 'prices of different goods, and therefore the average is done between heterogeneous quantities, and is analogous to an estimation price'.[25] Nevertheless, the geometric average provided (with one hypothetical mathematical exception) a lower result than what can be obtained by using an arithmetic average. This method also made it possible to generate a smoother curve, minimizing the wide

---

[20] *Consiglio Superiore di Statistica*, proceedings, session post meridian of the 3 March 1914, series 5, vol. 8, 77–94.

[21] Marco E. L. Guidi and Luca Michelini (eds), 'Marginalismo e Socialismo nell'Italia Liberale, 1870–1925', *Annali della Fondazione Giangiacomo Feltrinelli*, 35 (2001).

[22] Francesco Cassata, 'La «Dura Fatica» dei Numeri: Riccardo Bachi e la Statistica Economica', *Scuola di Economia di Torino: Co-protagonisti ed Epigoni*, ed. Roberto Marchionatti (Firenze: L.S. Olschki, 2009), 85–126.

[23] He created a model for statistical economic forecasting intermediate between the analytical index of the American Roger W. Babson and the synthetic index of the *Business Prospects Yearbook* by the British Joseph Davies and C. P. Hailey, see Ibid., 115.

[24] The Bachi index was based on forty goods, aggregated through a simple arithmetical average and used the average price for these goods over the five-year period from 1901 to 1905 as the base period. He started to collect the data in 1914 and published the series in *Supplemento Statistico del Corriere Economico* from 1916. After the war, he changed the method of calculation, adopting a chain-based index, and constructing two series obtained by the geometric and arithmetic average, see Riccardo Bachi, 'Nuova Serie di Numeri Indici per il Movimento dei Prezzi delle Merci in Italia nel Commercio all'Ingrosso', *L'Economista*, 24 April 1921 and Lisa Sella, Roberto Marchionatti, 'On the Cyclical Variability of Economic Growth in Italy, 1881–1913: a Critical Note', *Cliometrica*, 6 (2012): 307–328.

[25] *Bollettino dell'Ufficio del Lavoro*, 1, March (1913), 32.

price oscillations of the war period. Starting from December 1915, the Bureau of Labour added the publication of a local index of retail prices for seventeen towns by adopting a different base period, the first semester of 1914.[26]

This first retail price index had some limitations. The simultaneous and autonomous publication by the statistical bureaus of the principal Italian municipalities of their local retail prices index, which followed a different method of calculation, could raise doubts about the reliability and relevance of figures coming from the Bureau of Labour. The national index took into account only food items, but did not consider any green vegetables and fruit, which represented a fundamental part of workers' daily nutrition. The collection of data was not standardized across the country. Above all, the index was not weighted according to the different importance of items in the composition of the household budgets. It was a retail cost of goods index, not a cost-of-living index. Nevertheless, it represented an important innovation. It was used as a measurement for the cost of living, and consequently for assessing the value of wages. Starting from 1913, the state also started to hold new and more reliable statistical series for wages, produced by the National Fund for Labour Accidents, which gathered the data on workers injured at work. Both were necessary steps to making possible the implementation of a wage-setting policy.

In reaction to the global rise in prices, as well as the presence of dynamics of emulation and circulation of ideas among states and statisticians, the years 1913–14 were a pivotal moment in the development of cost-of-living statistics in Europe. The USA had been the leading country in the production of series of retail prices at the beginning of the twentieth century, as was the United Kingdom, for its empire and its role in global trade, in that of the series of wholesale prices. The USA published a series of retail prices indexes from 1904 to 1907, and again starting from 1913, and a cost-of-living index from 1919.[27] The UK started enquiries into prices and rents in 1905 and 1912, and several international studies were conducted between 1908 and 1912. The UK began in 1910 a series of food retail prices index and introduced a cost-of-living index in 1914.[28] France, Russia and Portugal adopted series of retail prices indexes with a base period 1913.[29] According to Adam Tooze, the first official demand for calculating a cost-of-living index in Prussia dates back to 1912, but it was put into practice only by the Weimar Republic, in 1919.[30] Spain and Switzerland started in 1914.

The IIS, headed by the Italian Luigi Bodio from 1902, played a role in spreading the belief in the necessity of the production of cost-of-living indexes. At the 13th session of

---

[26] *Bollettino dell'Ufficio del Lavoro*, 28, December (1915), 296.
[27] Stapleford, *The Cost of Living in America*, 51–8.
[28] On the British case see, Rebecca Searle, 'Is There Anything Real about Real Wages? A History of the Official British Cost of Living Index, 1914–62', *Economic History Review*, 68, no. 1 (2015): 145–66; and Robert O'Neill, Jeff Ralph, and Paul A. Smith, *Inflation: History and Measurement* (London: Palgrave Macmillan, 2017).
[29] On the French case Béatrice Touchelay, 'Les Ordres de la Mesure des Prix. Luttes Politiques, Bureaucratiques et Sociales Autour de l'Indice des Prix à la Consommation (1911–2012)', *Politix*, 105, no. 1 (2014) : 117–38. On the Russian case, Institut national de la statistique et des études économiques, 'Les Fluctuations des Prix de Détail en Union Soviétique', *Etudes et Conjoncture*, 10, no. 4 (1955) : 329–84.
[30] On the German case, Adam Tooze, *Statistics and the German State, 1900–1945: The Making of Modern Economic Knowledge* (Cambridge: Cambridge University Press, 2001).

IIS held at The Hague in September 1911, the delegates discussed retail prices statistics for the first time. On the agenda were the presentation of the study by Émile Waxweiler on the movement of the prices of ten food articles of prevalent consumption in Brussels from 1880 to 1910, and the results of materials on price index numbers from different countries collected by the Frenchman Alfred de Foville. The winter before the meeting, each IIS member had received a circular inviting them to fill out a form on annual variations in the level of prices. Twenty-two statisticians, belonging to twelve European and non-European countries, had responded to the call, including Achille Necco for Italy. At the section devoted to the topic of index numbers, the participants also discussed a communication by Irving Fisher, who was independently developing an international survey on the cost of living, and was asking for the IIS's cooperation in the project.[31] On the eve of the First World War, Italy was trying to catch up with the other industrialized countries in this field of knowledge and government technique.

The Great War: a missed turning point

Cost-of-living statistics were a sensitive issue during the First World War, since they concerned the maintenance of the wage–price relation and productive capacity, the regimentation of the population and, ultimately, the stability of public order in the home front. In Italy their use for the indexation of wages was extensive on industrial workers of the massive Industrial Mobilisation (IM) programme of the Ministry of Armaments and Munitions. By the end of the war, the IM involved 1,926 factories, which employed about 900,000 workers.[32]

Under this regime the indexation of wages occurred in a different way throughout the country, varying according to sector, region, but also factory. The IM metallurgical and mechanical sector was the most receptive to the adoption of cost-of-living compensation. Piedmont was the region where negotiations were comparatively resolved more favourably for workers; Liguria constituted the opposite case. In Florence, a bi-monthly reviewed cost-of-living indemnity was set up in April 1918, based on an ad hoc index weighted according to percentages of food items agreed by workers and employers, different from that produced by the statistical bureau of the local municipality. Half of the cost-of-living indemnity was not calculated as a percentage, but in absolute value, corresponding to the updated cost for the purchase of the goods of the basket.[33]

---

[31] See the proceedings of the meeting of 5 September, *Bulletin de l'Institut International de Statistique*, Tome 19, 1ère livraison, La Haye, W. P Van Stockum and Fils, 65–73.

[32] 35.7 per cent were military exempted and military workers, 33 per cent were civilian workers, 28.6 per cent were women and teenagers, 2.1 per cent were prisoners and refugees, and 0.6 per cent came from the Libyan colony, see Fabio degli Esposti, 'The Industrial and Agricultural Mobilization of Italy', *Italy in the Era of the Great War*, ed. Vanda Wilcox (Leiden: Brill, 2018), 309–28.

[33] Luigi Tomassini, 'Intervento dello Stato e Politica Salariale durante la Prima Guerra Mondiale: Esperimenti e Studi per la Determinazione di una "Scala Mobile" delle Retribuzioni Operaie', *Annali della Fondazione Giangiacomo Feltrinelli*, 22 (1983): 87–184.

Two factors are relevant to explaining the diffusion of these practices: firstly, high inflation – from 1914 to 1917, retail prices rose by 89 per cent; and secondly conflict in industrial relations, which the war regulated by suspending trade union freedoms, but did not prevent or completely exclude. Starting from the second half of 1916 wage indexation spread without national coordination or regulation in the wake of the multiplication of factory disputes, which rose from 115 in 1916 to 504 in the following year. As pointed out by Luigi Tomassini, after the first two years of war industrialists accepted indexation as a rationalizing way to decide on the level of wages. The galloping inflation and the practice of workers to present claims at very short intervals in the same factory suggested to them the need to adopt a technique to restore stability, ensure the level of productivity, and give back the capacity to predict labour cost within a reasonable time frame. In 1917, some industry representatives at the central committee of the IM proposed to generalize a cost-of-living wage escalator, as long as it did not bring into question the freezing of underlying base wages; it was zero or minimal for the highest wages; and did not change the internal hierarchy of wages due to skills, gender or age. The setting of cost-of-living compensation directly questioned the conceptions of the multiple nature of wage and the social practice linked to the remuneration of labour. One industrialist proposal envisaged a compensation for women equal to 60 per cent, and for boys equal to 50 per cent, of that granted to men. This suggested a conception of cost-of-living indexation linked to a subsistence wage, which also customarily discriminated by gender.[34] It is hard to link these figures to the different marginal productivity of categories of workers, particularly given the important part of salary paid for piecework.[35]

The attitude of trade unions to indexation was ambiguous. Grassroots workers' representatives and internal factory committees drove the use of the escalator, contradicting the stance of national trade union leaders. The Italian Metalworker Federation (IMF) had preferred to end the freeze on base wages, to keep the part of the wages rewarding piecework high, and to link salaries more to productivity through piecework bonuses. When the proposal of a national mechanism on indexation of wages within the IM was under discussion in the Central Committee, the IMF, together with industrialists, advocated for its abandonment. The IMF stressed the limited reliability of the available cost-of-living indexes. It showed concern about the risk that the cost-of-living indemnity devalued the base wages. And it did not hide its fear that automatic wage indexation could reduce workers' conflict and, therefore, diminish the bargaining power of trade unions.[36]

The late interest of industrialists in wage-setting mechanisms, the suspicions of the trade unions, and a lack of willingness on the part of the state to enforce them largely

---

[34] On the working women in Italy, see Barbara Curli, *Italiane al Lavoro, 1914–1920* (Venezia: Marsilio, 1998), and Alessandra Pescarolo, *Il Lavoro delle Donne nell'Italia Contemporanea* (Roma: Viella, 2019). This customary-based proportion was re-proposed after the war in 1920 by the Italian Federation of Metalworkers (Federazione italiana dei metalmeccanici-FIOM), see Maurizio Antonioli and Bruno Bezza (eds), *La Fiom dalle Origini al Fascismo* (Bari: De Donato, 1978), 119.

[35] On this theoretical issue see the introduction and the chapters of Antonella Stirati, Zoe Adams and Craig Muldrew, *infra*.

[36] See Luigi Tomassini, 'Intervento dello Stato'.

explain the absence of advances in statistical measurement of wages in this period. The wage indexation of the war period continued to be largely anchored in the statistical production of municipal authorities. The national Bureau of Labour continued to publish the unweighted index number of retail prices with base year 1913. What innovation there was came from the locality.

The first series of cost-of-living indexes, calculated on the price trend of a weighted consumption basket of a typical household, was produced by the municipality of Milan from April 1916 with the first half of 1914 as a base period.[37] The Milanese basket was taken from a survey conducted by Angelo Pugliese in 1913 on the food consumption of 51 families in Milan, inspired by the 1910 Belgian study of Auguste Slosse and Émile Waxweiler.[38] The survey was carried out on behalf of the Milanese Humanitarian Society, a leading institution of social reform, which had been led by Giovanni Montemartini, among others. Drawing on the figures produced by Max Rubner and Wilbur O. Atwater, Pugliese set the caloric values of daily food rations for relative rest or light work at 2,400, and those needed by the worker performing normal work (10 hours a day) at 3,500. He noted that out of 51 families surveyed, only two exceeded the minimum number of calories of the normal work ration; four barely reached them; and all others were below this quota. Eight families did not obtain the minimum calories required even for light work. Moreover, a considerable part of the daily caloric intake came from wine, which in some cases provided between one-quarter and one-fifth of the total. Pugliese concluded in the study that 'the energy intake of our working families was almost always characterized by a shortage of albumin, fats and carbohydrates. [...] The deficient nutrition became evident in the proletarian woman, whose body weight was often well below the average normal weight of the woman.'[39] By using this survey, the local statistical bureau matched the daily consumption of a typical family for the calculation of the cost-of-living index with the caloric amount below which it would not be possible to fall without a deterioration of the 'normal physiological conditions'.[40] It therefore calculated the number of calories necessary for a typical family of workers of five members to 3.5 units (Atwater), i.e. 9,900 calories, without wine (2,825 calories per Atwater unit of consumption).[41] It produced two types of monthly cost-of-living index series: an unchanged consumption index, which resulted from the calculation on the same quality and quantity of foodstuffs of the pre-war period, and a modified monthly updated consumption index, which took into account the shortage of food produced by the war. For its food part, the modified consumption index calculated a basket which had to guarantee the

---

[37] Città di Milano, *Bollettino Mensile di Cronaca Amministrativa e Statistica*, 4 (1916), 224. See also Giuseppe Galletti, *L'Alimentazione ed il suo Costo* (Milano: Grafica cooperativa degli operai, 1923) and Ugo Giusti, 'Methods of Recording Retail Prices and Measuring the Cost of Living in Italy', *International Labour Review*, 4, no. 2 (1921): 45–62, which nevertheless contains some imprecisions.

[38] Angelo Pugliese, *Il Bilancio Alimentare di 51 Famiglie Operaie Milanesi* (Milano: Tipografia degli operai – Soc. coop., 1914).

[39] Ibid., 28.

[40] Ufficio del lavoro e della statistica del Comune di Milano, Alessandro Schiavi, *Le Variazioni dei Salari in Rapporto al Rincaro della Vita* (Milano: Tipografia municipale, 1920 [1918]), 60.

[41] See Città di Milano, *Bollettino Mensile di Cronaca Amministrativa e Statistica*, no. 1 (1927): 33.

grams of albumin, fats and carbohydrates necessary to produce the minimum caloric intake[42].

The reliability of this index could be questionable. It could penalize workers. The food expenses of the basket of the typical family could be adopted by employers in absolute value as a reference for setting salaries. In Great Britain, according to the Sumner Committee set up by the government in 1918 to inquire into the increase in the cost of living, the average caloric intake of the typical family corresponded to 4.57 units Atwater, 1,07 more than that proposed by the Milanese statistical bureau. The problem of the statistical representativeness of the sample of 51 families was not addressed by Pugliese. As a medical physiologist his primary aim was not to gather data for the calculation of cost-of-living statistics, but to understand the quality and quantity of the human alimentary regime within a specific social and working setting. That was coherent with the purpose of the Humanitarian Society, which commissioned the survey, and intended to prove how deficient the nutrition of the working class was, in order to campaign for social improvements. The method for the choice of the composition of the sample was neither a random sampling nor a set of stratified cases, as the analysed families all lived in the Humanitarian Society's housing. The typical family could not be considered as the average family. The workers included in the survey did thirty-three different jobs and, as Pugliese recognized, probably belonged to the 'less poor' Milanese working class. The calculation of housing costs was penalizing, since a two-room apartment was attributed to a family of five people. Finally, the cost-of-living index ended up reproducing the misery of the working class. But it at least provided a statistical reference for adjusting wages to the cost of living.

The Milan municipality, led by socialists since 1914, sparked statistical innovation and favoured indexation practices compensating for the inertia of the state.[43] It set up an indexation mechanism on the base of its retail price statistical series to calculate the local allowance of the families of soldiers, which integrated the national allowance.[44] Outside the industries covered by the IM, the first indexation of wages in Italy was that of the typographers of Milan in December 1916.[45] The mediation of the municipal labour and statistical bureau, headed by the socialist intellectual and social reformer Alessandro Schiavi, was important to define the agreement between strikers and employers. They approved that if the retail prices index varied by 5 per cent from the price index of November 1916, the cost-of-living compensation should be correspondingly adjusted for the following quarter. This indexation was inversely proportional to the level of wages: for weekly salaries of up to L. 30, a 20 per cent salary increase; from L. 31 to L. 60 half a cent less of the increase for each extra lira above

---

[42] The caloric intake used for the weekly basket of a typical worker family was based on the data of a second inquiry led by Pugliese, Angelo Pugliese, *L'Alimentazione della Famiglia Operaia Milanese Durante la Guerra. Risultati di due Inchieste Indette dal Museo Sociale dell'Umanitaria nel Marzo 1916 e nel Febbraio 1917* (Milano, Scuola del libro, 1918).

[43] On the socialist municipalism economic culture see, Giulio Sapelli, *Comunità e Mercato. Socialisti, Cattolici e "Governo Economico Municipale" agli Inizi del XX Secolo* (Bologna: Il Mulino, 1986).

[44] Maurizio Punzo, *La Giunta Caldara. L'Amministrazione Comunale di Milano negli Anni 1914–1920* (Bari-Roma: Laterza, 1986), 109.

[45] 'I tipografi', *Avanti!*, Milanese edition, 13 December 1916.

L. 30; and 5 per cent for wages over L. 60. This suggests the existence of a customary floor for lowest salaries. Half of the compensation was not calculated in percentage terms, but in absolute value as compensation for gas bills, clothes and shoes. The cost-of-living indemnity was to be paid for a period of up to three months after the cessation of the war. The rates could be revised every three months by a joint commission of employers and workers chaired by a municipal labour consultant.[46] This model of agreement with few amendments was soon adopted by the workers of the municipal tramway enterprise and the bakers of Milan, as well as by other Milanese industries of the IM, such as Pirelli, between October and November 1917.[47] The spread of the indexation practices was local, followed a bottom-up dynamic, and was driven by trade unions.

At the national level the state did not act as mediator between capital and labour. It intervened instead using military force when the discipline in the factories was at stake. We know that the labour share of national income collapsed during the Great War, to an extent mostly not seen in other countries.[48] Wages in metal engineering sector lost less than textile and construction sectors,[49] but in the first two years of the war the labour share lost almost 12 percentage points. Private consumption dropped even more dramatically than labour shares between 1914 and 1919.[50] Only as an employer did the state generalize the indexation of wages. By 1916 the only category of workers to enjoy a uniform protection of the purchasing power throughout the national territory were civil servants. With the royal decree of 26 July 1917 (n. 1181), a similar treatment was extended to the employees of municipalities and provincial authorities.

The ephemeral *Biennio Rosso*

From the aftermath of the First World War up until the *fascistissime* laws (1925–6), the production of state-level statistics on the cost of living did not change substantially. From April 1919, the Department of Labour started publishing an updated retail price index, increasing the number of food items to twenty-one. The calculation method remained unchanged, except for the average of the final index which was arithmetic instead of geometric.[51] Municipalities continued to make up for the weakness of central state statistics. Twenty-five Italian cities agreed to adopt new cost-of-living index series using the same approach in July 1920.[52] These indexes calculated the variation of prices

---

[46] Schiavi, *Le Variazioni dei Salari*, 7–29.
[47] Ibid., 33–4.
[48] Giacomo Gabbuti, 'Labour Shares and Inequality: Insights from Italian Economic History, 1895–1970', *European Review of Economic History*, 25, no. 2 (2021): 355–78.
[49] Vera Zamagni in *Labour's Reward. Real Wages and Economic Change in 19th and 20th Century Europe*, eds Id. and Peter Scholliers, Aldershot, Edward Elgar, 1995, 231.
[50] Alberto Baffigi, *Il PIL per la Storia d'Italia. Istruzioni per l'Uso* (Venezia: Marsilio, 2015), 27.
[51] *Bollettino del Lavoro e della Previdenza Sociale*, 22, no. 1 (1919): 42.
[52] The decision was made at the Statistical Union of Italian Cities conference held in Milan in March 1920. It was after approved by the Congress of municipal statistical and labour bureaus (Milan, 6–8 July 1920), see Oscar Gaspari, *Storia dell'Usci. Unione Statistica delle Città Italiane. 1905–1987. La Rete degli Statistici Comunali* (Gavardo: Liberedizioni, 2022).

through the budget of a typical working-class family, weighted according to local consumption patterns: food (including green vegetable), rent, lighting, heating, clothing and miscellaneous items.

Between 1919 and 1920, the *Biennio Rosso*, Italy experienced intense social conflict. The ISP was led by revolutionaries influenced by the soviet model. Strikes, protests against the *caro-vita*, occupations of land and factories, and the electoral success of the socialists in 1919 determined the advancement of the social legislation, the improvement of labour rights and a rise in wages. In 1921 and 1922, labour shares of national income reached 55 per cent: the peak for the interwar period.[53] Wage indexation to face inflation, which rose to 31.4 per cent in 1920, was generalized thanks to collective bargaining by sector on an inter-regional and national basis. The state finally tried to make its debut as a mediator in industrial relations. The collective agreement of September 1919 for metallurgists of Lombardy and Emilia established a 5-cent increase of the indemnity (L. 1.20 per day for men), for each increase of two points of the cost-of-living index. This mechanism was adopted by the national agreement of September 1920 with slight modifications (7 cents for every two points of increase in the cost-of-living index, instead of 5, to be adjusted every two months).[54] Both agreements were based for its food part on the household budget calculated by the statistical bureau of Milan.

In February 1921, the Ministry of Labour expressed the aim of regulating and co-ordinating investigations into the cost of living of the working classes. The project included the creation in each provincial capital of a special consultative committee on cost of living and variations of wages matters, to which public authorities, industrial, merchants' and workers' organizations could have recourse to (Decree, 26 February 1921). The decision did not have any practical application. From summer 1921, encouraged by the successes of the fascist campaign of violence against the labour movement, industrialists began to reduce wages and denounce the validity of previous collective agreements. The polarization of Italian politics prevented any stabilization of this crucial statistical measurement. In Milan, during the second half of 1923, the statistical bureau of the trade union chamber of labour started to produce its own cost-of-living index, collecting the prices data directly from the workers in order to challenge the legitimacy of the figures produced by the municipality of Milan, which was by then led by a coalition of liberals, fascists and the Popular Party.

The convergence of opinion between neoclassical economists, free-trade supporters, reformist socialists and the labour movement which had fostered the emergence of the cost-of-living problem in the 1910s had quickly dissolved due to the acuity of the post-war social conflict. The stance expressed on the *caro-vita* since 1919 in *Corriere della Sera* by Luigi Einaudi, who was at the turn of the century close to the socialists, are indicative of this social and intellectual laceration.[55]

---

[53] See Gabbuti, 'Labour Shares and Inequality', 14.
[54] See Antonioli, Bezza (eds), *La Fiom dalle Origini al Fascismo,* 752–4.
[55] Luigi Einaudi in *Corriere della Sera* of 12 and 18 January 1919; 3, 6, 8, 12 and 16 July 1919, reprinted in id. *Cronache Economiche e Politiche di un Trentennio (1893-1925),* vol. V (Torino: Einaudi, 1961), 258–93.

By going on strike, interrupting the work of the factories, the tramways and trains, the problem is not solved. It gets worse. The government is incapable of providing its support, which in any case would be very limited, in solving the problem of expensive living; but the strikes do not facilitate its action and only exacerbate the problem. This is a time when industrialists would have gotten lucky if they could run their factories without losses; which means that for the moment labour absorbs all the net product of industry. To grow this net product, to grow the part of the worker, to gradually create that abundance of products from which the reduction in food will eventually emerge, the only solution is social tranquillity [...] Therefore we invoke above all that the popular masses be reasonable again. The bad is in us; in our expectation of the new and the impossible.

Riccardo Bachi, the father of the retail index number of the national Bureau of Labour, came to have a similar opinion. From 1919, he assumed a new militant tone, taking a firm stand in favour of laissez-faire and against the economic policy of the first post-war period and the political economy of the revolutionary left.[56] In the introduction to *Il Fallimento della Politica Annonaria* of 1921, which reproduces the course he taught at Bocconi University in 1919, the right-wing liberal statistician and economist Umberto Ricci expressed a judgement that was shared by many left-wing intellectuals and experts: 'It is the fate of all socialism. [...] Since, as soon as an administration, with the intention of saving the people from poverty and inequality, starts producing and distributing economic goods, or regulating the economic activity of humans, it becomes a cause of collective impoverishment.'[57] The ideas of the economist Aldo Contento were not common. In 1921 he still defended that the state should carry out a vast survey on the consumption of the popular classes and considered unreasonable any attempt to set real wages back to the pre-war level.[58] In the aftermath of the Great War, only the civil servants working for the municipal statistical bureaus, such as Lanfranco Maroi, Giuseppe Galletti, Francesco Repaci, Alessandro Molinari and Ugo Giusti, continued to publish on technical matters around the cost-of-living indexes. Moreover, with few exceptions such as Galletti and Repaci, most of them put their expertise at the service of the fascist regime.

A fascist cost-of-living index?

Albeit in an indirect way, the question of a cost-of-living index again arose interest among economists and experts with the publication of Irving Fisher's book *The Making of Index Numbers* of 1922. Fisher's research was funded by the Pollak Foundation for

---

[56] See Cassata, 'La Dura Fatica dei Numeri', 97.
[57] Umberto Ricci, *Il Fallimento della Politica Annonaria. Lezioni Tenute all'Università Commerciale Bocconi* (Firenze: Soc. An. Ed. La Voce, 1921), IV. On the stances of Ricci and other liberal economists see Clara Mattei, *The Capital Order. How Economists Invented Austerity and Paved the Way to Fascism* (Chicago: University of Chicago Press, 2022).
[58] Aldo Contento, 'Sulla Misura delle Variazioni del Costo della Vita', *Giornale degli Economisti e Rivista di Statistica*, 61, no. 1 (1921): 1–27.

Economic Research and was part of the widespread international movement towards the standardization of mathematical methods in economics and statistics.[59] In an essay published in the Italian progressive journal *La Riforma Sociale,* the economist Pasquale Jannaccone endorsed the spirit of the book, supporting 'the opportunity to unify the methods of construction of the number-indexes of prices' so that 'an embarrassing diversity of procedures and incompatibility of results' did not 'continue to dominate'. But he criticized the specific perfect formula proposed by Fisher for the calculation of index numbers both on a theoretical and practical level.[60] The work of Jannaccone influenced the technicians of the statistical local bureaus, who used it to support the thesis of the substantial equivalence and effectiveness of the constant goods index with that of the chain system, leading them to continue to defend the usefulness of the former, and criticize the unnecessary complexity of the latter.[61]

The other important impetus to the discussion came from the second conference of labour statisticians of the ILO, held at Geneva in April 1925. The reliability of the cost-of-living statistics and the international comparison of real wages were on the delegates' agenda.[62] They debated a survey carried out in 1921 in Belgium on household budgets, exploring whether the same standard budget could be used for purposes of international comparison of real wages, as well as for the calculation of cost-of-living indexes in the other countries. On that occasion, the Italian statistician Corrado Gini stated that the best standard was the theoretical subsistence minimum. He proposed that the ILO should define a minimum budget by cooperating with statisticians and physiologists, allowing for differences in habits of consumption in different countries due to climate and race. The German Ernst Wagemann and the Austrian Felix Klezl supported Gini's stance. Conversely, the British E. C. Ramsbottom and John Hilton emphatically opposed the Italian proposal, as the construction of a minimum subsistence budget would have involved a far too large arbitrary element in wage policies. For them a government should not be empowered to give official sanction to a minimum of consumption necessary to support life.[63]

Gini had already dealt with the subject during the war. As a member of the inter-allied scientific food commission, he was called to negotiate and coordinate the quantity of food to be assigned to the various countries of the Entente. In the search for a scientifically based distribution criterion, Gini had worked together with other Italian

---

[59] Robert W. Dimand, 'The Cowles Commission and Foundation on the Functioning of Financial Markets. From Irving Fisher and Alfred Cowles to Harry Markowitz and James Tobin', *Revue d'Histoire des Sciences Humaines,* 20, no. 1 (2009): 79–100.

[60] Pasquale Jannaccone, 'Sulla Misura delle Variazioni dei Prezzi', *La Riforma Sociale,* 34, no. 3–4 (1923): 241–65.

[61] Alessandro Molinari, 'I Numeri Indici del Costo della Vita in Italia', *La Riforma Sociale,* 35, no. 1–2 (1924): 10–37.

[62] The previous conference of 1923 had decided that 'detailed statistics of rates of wages, of actual earnings, and of normal and actual hours of labour should be collected and published in each country'. These statistics had to include a real wage index, International Labour Office, *Studies and Reports,* Series N (Statistics), 4, International Conference of Labour Statisticians, 'Report on the International Conference of Representatives of Labour Statistical Departments, held at Geneva, 29 October to 2 November 1923', March 1924, Geneva, 72–3.

[63] 'The Second International Conference of Labour Statisticians', *International Labour Review,* vol. XII., 1 July 1925, 2–5.

statisticians to define the minimum caloric requirement of the average man, who weighs 70 kg, works 8 hours a day in climatic conditions equivalent to average temperature of England, Italy and France.[64] To these negotiations were linked the first statistical analyses on the economic-commercial, chemical (as calculated for carbohydrates, fats, and proteins) and physiological (caloric) food balance in the different countries. For physiologists and statisticians, the Great War had therefore constituted a huge social engineering experiment with which to measure the endurance of people to shortages of foodstuffs. The results of these studies were further fine-tuned after the war. Gini supervised Mario Balestrieri's research on the trend of Italian consumption between 1910 and 1921, conducted thanks to a grant from the University of Padua, funded by the Industrialists' Confederation.[65] The study showed how the calorific value per quintal of the country's food balance had increased during the war, remained stable during the following three years, and then decreased starting from 1921. According to the author of this study, and to Gini, who prefaced the publication, this proved a law of consumer's behaviour which could be considered as complementary to Engel's law: that food shortages induce consumers to prefer foods which have, for the same weight, greater calorific value. This pattern tended to persist for a certain period even when the shortage disappeared. The industrialists' request of a generalized wage cut had found a further scientific basis in this study, which added to that of the wage–price spiral theory. Besides, Balestrieri–Gini's thesis, helped transforming the eighteenth-century polemic on luxury based on moral discourse about corruption, coming from manufacturing sector's interests as opposed to the rentiers', into a modern political depiction of a working class enriched by industrial development, and whose standard of living was well beyond of mere subsistence.

Gini's positions about consumer behaviour and minimum caloric intake for the average man must have deeply impacted the construction of the cost-of-living index series produced by the new Central Statistics Institute (CSI), created in 1926. Mussolini wanted Gini himself for the leadership of the institute, and he became its first president.[66] The CSI was placed under the direct responsibility of the head of state and took over the different statistical departments and structures of the Italian liberal state. From July 1927, it published in *Bollettino dei Prezzi* an initially fortnightly, then monthly retail prices index with 1913 as the basis period. These series continued those of the Bureau of Labour but expanded the number of cities to eighty-four. From 1930, the CSI started to publish the first national index of cost of living (with a base in June 1927). This index was obtained by calculating i) first, the index of cost of living for each compartment[67] obtained by the weighted arithmetic average of the index of its

---

[64] It equaled 3,300 calories. On this work see Corrado Gini, *Problemi Sociologici della Guerra* (Roma: Zanichelli, 1921), chapters 7 and 8.
[65] Mario Balestrieri, *I Consumi Alimentari della Popolazione Italiana dal 1910 al 1921* (Padova: Biblioteca del Metron, 1925).
[66] On Corrado Gini and fascist statistic, Francesco Cassata, *Il Fascismo Razionale: Corrado Gini fra Scienza e Politica* (Roma: Carocci, Roma, 2006); Giovanni Favero, 'A Reciprocal Legitimation: Corrado Gini and Statistics in Fascist Italy', *Management & Organizational History*, 12, no. 3 (2017): 261–84. See also Carl Ipsen, *Dictating Demography. The Problem of Population in Fascist Italy* (Cambridge: Cambridge University Press, 1996), and Prévost, *A Total Science*.
[67] A compartment was a pure statistical geographical unit similar to current Italian regions.

provincial capital towns, and by using as weight the local population working in the industrial and commercial sectors; ii) secondly, the weighted arithmetic average of the so calculated compartment index, by using as weight the population working in the industrial and commercial sectors in each compartment.[68]

The series of the national index represented more the price movements of the industrial areas of the country (as desired by Gini), and less those of southern and rural areas that a weighted calculation on the importance of the urban population would have partially provided.[69] The last option had been proposed by Alessandro Molinari, a statistician of socialist and anarchist sympathies, who became director of the CSI in 1929.[70] Molinari was responsible for the studies on the calculation of the weekly local basket of major cities which constituted the fundamental data for the elaboration of the national index. Nevertheless, despite the recognized importance of his work, it would be Gini's approach that shaped the method by which the cost of living was calculated during the fascist period.

The operation consisted in depoliticizing the matter of cost-of-living statistics, and in defending the full neutrality of the meaning of the index. The goal was achieved first of all by hiding a part of the calculation procedure. The weights of the various groups of items of consumption (food, clothing, heating, housing and miscellaneous for a total of 58 items), and in particular the weighting of the foodstuffs basket were not publicly known, given that the CSI did not provide any information on these issues and that many cities did not publish the quantities and food items of their local basket.

The CSI had made public that Molinari built the basket 'on the basis of the number of calories developed by the individual nutritional elements, taking into account the normal calories requirement of the members of the typical family, also in relation to the physical characteristics – particularly the climate – of the individual territorial units considered'.[71] It was a conception of a typical budget compatible with Gini's proposal for the determination of the theoretical subsistence minimum, which had been the subject of tense debates at the ILO's second conference of statisticians. The CSI did not conduct any official new surveys into working-class household consumption budgets as the ILO's second conference of labour statisticians in Geneva had recommended. Italy lagged behind countries which had first developed government-led inquiries into household budgets such as Switzerland, Belgium,[72] Denmark, Norway, Japan and the UK,[73] and the other thirty-five countries which did so before the end of the 1930s.[74]

---

[68] *Annali di Statistica. Atti del Consiglio di Statistica*, Ordinary session, 9 10 January 1931, Minutes of Meetings and Reports of the CSI, 287.

[69] 'Report on the Activity of the Departments of the Central Statistical Institute from July 1927 to November 1929' in *Annali di Statistica. Atti del Consiglio superiore di Statistica*, Series VII, vol. VII, 1930, 80.

[70] On the figure of Alessandro Molinari see, Simone Misiani, *I Numeri e la Politica. Statistica, Programmazione e Mezzogiorno nell'Impegno di Alessandro Molinari* (Bologna: Il Mulino, 2007).

[71] CSI, *Decennale, 1926-IV-1936-XIV*, (Rome: Istituto Poligrafico dello Stato, 1936), 103.

[72] Peter Scholliers, 'Index Linked Wages, Purchasing Power and Social Conflict Between Wars. The Belgian Approach (Internationally Compared)', *Journal of European Economic History*, 20, no. 2 (1991): 407–39.

[73] Ian Gazeley, Rose Holmes and Andrew Newell, *The Household Budget Survey in Western Europe, 1795–1965*, IZA Discussion Papers, n. 11429, Bonn, Institute of Labour Economics (IZA), 2008.

[74] Robert M. Woodbury, *Méthodes d'Enquête sur les Conditions de Vie des Familles* (Genève : BIT, 1941), 147.

The construction of the food budget of the typical family was then partially based on the series with July 1920 as a base, as adopted in the main cities following the instructions of the conference held in Milan by the Statistical Union of Italian Municipalities. The fascist basket also brought about some substantial changes, which resulted in a decrease, in some cases drastic, in the weekly caloric requirement for a typical family of five individuals. In the local baskets of the six largest Italian cities built by the CSI for the calculation of the national index based on June 1927, the importance of starch food increased in Milan (+ 17%), Turin (+ 14.2%) and Bologna (+ 41%) but decreased in the cities of Venice (− 8.5%), Rome (− 4.5%), and Naples (− 17%). Foods of animal origin remained substantially unchanged in Milan and Rome, but significantly decreased in Venice (− 30%), Bologna (− 18.9%), and Naples (− 44.8%). Milk and eggs decreased almost everywhere.[75]

Moreover, the technical justification of the CSI for the choice to adopt the calculation method of the unchanged consumption was aimed at putting an end to the public debate arose during the war years and the *Biennio Rosso*, which had involved trade unions, industrialists, municipalities, statisticians and the government regarding the determination of the cost of living as well as their use to setting wages:

> But it would frustrate the intentions of the Government if, as has sometimes happened and especially in the past, one wanted to attribute to these indexes a meaning they do not have. They are not a measuring instrument for determining the size of wages, but only a means for measuring the fluctuations of certain economic phenomena on the basis of which wage changes can also be made. What counts in the formation of the indexes is not the amount of expenditure taken by base but its subsequent variations. When the list of consumptions is put together taking into account, at least approximately, the way in which their distribution usually occurs in life, it sufficiently meets the necessary conditions for the starting point of a good index. Whoever lingers in wanting to increase the basic budget does not benefit from his assumption; on the contrary, perhaps it introduces elements into the calculation intended to weaken the fluctuations.[76]

---

[75] The percentages are calculated taking into account the variations in terms of weight between the local typical budgets with base July 1920 and those with base June 1927 of the cities of Milan, Rome, Naples, Venice, Bologna and Turin of bread, pasta, potatoes, rice (plus corn flour for the cities of Bologna and Venice) as foods rich in carbohydrates; and meat, cheese, cod, butter, lard, fresh fish, salted cold cuts as foods of animal origin. The calculation adopted gives only an indirect assessment of the variation of the caloric intake. The January 1920 typical budget has been used only for Rome where the composition of the basket was periodically changed. The city of Genoa is not included because its municipal bulletin did not publish the data relating to the budget of the typical family for the series based on June 1927. For the data of the local typical budget see Roma Municipal Labour Bureau's *Bollettino Mensile*; *Capitolium. Rassegna di Attività Municipale*; *Bollettino del Comune di Napoli*; City of Milan's *Bollettino Municipale Mensile di Cronaca Amministrativa e di Statistica*; *Rivista Mensile della Città di Venezia*; Bureau of Statistics of the Municipality of Venice's *Bollettino Mensile di Statistica*; *Torino. Rivista Mensile Municipale*; Bologna's municipality, *Rassegna mensile di cronaca amministrativa e di statistica*; *Bollettino del Comune di Napoli. Rassegna illustrata di storia, arte, topografia e statistica napoletana.*
[76] Presidenza del Consiglio dei Ministri, Istituto Centrale di Statistica, *Norme per la Formazione dei Numeri Indici del Costo della Vita* (Roma: Tipografia Failli, 1927), 7.

A similar tone could be found in the CSI's surreptitious criticism of the chain-index, which echoed the scepticism expressed by Jannaccone about the perfect index of Fisher:

> To construct a good index, a choice of items is required which excludes any uncertainty in the surveys and justifies as much as possible the reliability of the continuity of consumption. Once the items have been chosen, they must remain unchanged quantitatively and qualitatively. Those who deem it appropriate to vary the composition of the budget on which the calculation is based because some commodities more or less abound on the markets and have the virtue of attracting consumers more or less, no longer calculate the variations in the cost of living, but the modifications of the diet or lifestyle in relation to an alleged case. The indexes are calculated keeping the quantities and qualities unchanged.[77]

The CSI could maintain a partial opacity of the method of calculating the cost-of-living index as the government had conferred to it the monopoly on the production and publication of index numbers for the cost of living. The decree of 20 February 1927, established that 'no public administration, parastate body, trade union organization, private body in any case subject to protection, supervision or control by the state, other than the Municipalities appointed by the Central Institute of Statistics, may publish cost of living indexes, even if in the past it has made such calculations'.[78]

This raises a central question. Did this centralization of the procedure for the calculation and publication of the cost-of-living index allow the regime to manipulate the statistical figures for political and industrial lobbying purposes? The method of calculation had aroused contemporary criticism, particularly from the outlawed leftist organizations.[79] Later historians would also cast doubt on the reliability of the index, suggesting the possibility of a deliberate manipulation of data without fully proving it.[80] Rather the fascist statistical series of the cost of living were the result of a legitimate technical construction socially aimed to justify the achievement of a rapid and generalized wage cut; and by then the success of the deflationary policies undertaken since 1926 on whose success Mussolini relied on to consolidate the fate of the regime.

From the outset, politics mattered. The framework for the construction of the index of cost of living was not solely provided by the CSI technicians. At the time of the creation of the CSI, Mussolini had intervened directly on this issue, and above all so did the industrialists. They, better than the other components of the corporatist powers, had openly managed to set the tone of the committee appointed by the Minister of

---

[77] Ibid., 8–9.
[78] Royal Decree-Law 20 February 1927, no. 222, art. 3, paragraph 3.
[79] Girolamo Li Causi, 'I Numeri Indici e la Classe Operaia Italiana', *Lo Stato Operaio*, 2, no. 4 (1928): 161–72; Ibid., 2, no. 6: 337–43.
[80] Gaetano Salvemini, *Under the Axe of Fascism* (New York: The. Viking Press, 1936), chapter 11; Anthony Lyttelton, *The Seizure of Power. Fascim in Italy, 1919–1929* (Princeton: Princeton University Press, 1973), 503. For a different hypothesis which mentions the problem of the collection of data and the importance of company stores, see Giovanni Favero, 'Le Statistiche dei Salari Industriali in Periodo Fascista', *Quaderni Storici*, 134, no. 2 (2010): 319–57.

National Economy, Belluzzo, for the creation and spread of company stores destined to supply basic necessities at cost prices to workers. The committee proposal supported by the representatives of the industrialists of Antonio Stefano Benni and Gino Olivetti to give maximum impetus to the creation of company stores, given that the cost-of-living indexes adopted by the government would be calculated on their prices and serve as a basis for reviewing work agreements.[81] Equally eminently political was the composition of the CSI central advisory commission responsible to evaluate eventual changes to the rules for the construction of the cost-of-living index.[82]

The CSI had established that the prices for the calculation of the indexes had to be collected by provincial commissions chaired by the *podestà* from company stores, consumers' cooperatives and marketplaces proportionally to the relative importance of each of them in the retail local structure. At stake was above all the percentage to be granted locally to company stores. But some categories of shops, those where the highest prices were generally offered to consumers, were thus excluded from the surveys. That was likely to include systematic reductions in price surveys, bringing them closer to cost prices.

The new local baskets built by the CSI also included a greater portion of ceiling price food items than previously used by municipalities before 1927. In particular, the generalized increase in the quantity of rice in the weekly expenditure of the typical family led to a further fall in the estimated weekly expenditure, given the downward trend in the price of that item. But this more important presence of the rice in the basket reflected the will of the regime to facilitate the economic self-sufficiency of the country, rather than a real change in the consumption habits of the popular classes.

As Molinari himself admitted the year after the start of the series of the new index of cost of living,

> retail prices and wages therefore offered, on the whole, a sensitive resistance to revaluation, a resistance which for some items has even turned into immobility. Unfortunately, the analytical examination of the different prices – which reacted very differently to the deflationary wave – would show that in reality the aforementioned resistance is even more remarkable than that resulting from the official figures and this mainly due to the fact that about 70% of the elements considered by the official statistics (food and rents) consists of political prices that

---

[81] 'La Campagna contro il Caro Vita. Come Verranno Creati gli Spacci', *Corriere della Sera*, 24 July 1926.
[82] The members of the committee were Bruno Biagi president of National Consumers' Cooperative Federation, Filippo Carli theorist of the corporatist economy, Francesco Coppola d'Anna linked with the Public Companies Association, Bramante Cucini sansepolcrista and fascist member of parliament fully engaged in the corporatist reconstruction of labour relations, Riccardo del Giudice, professor of labour law who belonged to the left-wing of fascism, Ettore Lolini civil servant of the minister of finance, Mario Mammoli of the National Fascist Confederation of Credit and Insurance, Gino Olivetti general secretary of Confindustria. And economists and statisticians fully involved in the politics of fascism as Giuseppe Tassinari, Pietro Sitta and Arrigo Serpieri. Only Ugo Giusti and Livio Livi exclusively showed expert status, see *Annali di Statistica. Consiglio Superiore di Statistica*, Ordinary session of the 7 December 1929, Minute of the meeting e report of the activity of the CSI from July 1927 to November 1929, 137.

either do not always find confirmation in reality or that seem destined in the near future to rise above the current level.[83]

Moreover, the publication of the concatenation of the statistical series of the new cost-of-living index based on June 1927 with the pre-war series based on the first half of 1914 raises perplexity about its reliability, given the uneven practices used to collect prices in the two periods. On the whole, the CSI index provided the statistical representation of a process of deflation greater than that perceived by consumers, which endorsed the decisions of a salary cut.

The anti-worker image of Gini's CSI, and therefore the doubts about the neutrality of his statistical production, probably mitigated by the involvement and hiring of the heads of the municipal statistical offices both in the National Statistics Council and in the CSI structures, was fanned by his controversy with Giorgio Mortara about wages. In 1923, Gini had adopted a controversial stance about wage statistics, attacking the reliability of the series developed by Mortara, who based his calculations on the data produced by the National Fund for Work Accidents. As Giovanni Favero pointed out, Gini had thus provided to the Industrial Confederation the necessary technical arguments to dismantle Mortara's work. In the view of Confindustria, Mortara was guilty of having overestimated recent wage reductions. In 1928, the CSI began to calculate a new index of industrial wages by using the series produced by the organization of the industrialists. Since 1930, the CSI's *Bollettino Statistico* started to publish only the wage series based on the Industrial Confederation data on the hourly earnings of industrial workers, thus giving the statistical series produced by the organization of industrialists an official public legitimation. These series (as the series of the cost-of-living index did about the movement of retail prices) were more useful to understand the variation of wages than to measure the value of wages in absolute terms.[84]

Conclusion

Cost-of-living statistics emerged in Italy through the impulse of a diverse range of social and institutional actors: i) the labour movement and its engaged economists and statisticians; ii) the supporters of free trade; iii) municipal reformers; and iv) transnational institutions which favoured the circulation of statistical knowledge and practices. Nevertheless, these intertwined factors did not translate into wage indexation until the beginning of the First World War. The war represented a selective and fragile turning point. The dissemination of wage indexation practices mainly followed a bottom-up development. The state did not innovate in the production of cost-of-living statistics and refused to acquire a role of mediator and direction between capital and labour. This contributes – along with other factors, such as the Italian weaker economic

---

[83] Alessandro Molinari, 'La Rivalutazione della Lira, i Prezzi al Minuto ed i Salari', *Giornale degli Economisti e Rivista di Statistica*, 68, no. 4 (1928): 334–9.
[84] Favero, 'Le Statistiche dei Salari Industriali'.

power than those of other belligerent countries – to understanding why the war's productive effort and the elimination of unemployment during the war years failed to improve the bargaining power of labour and to raise salaries, as occurred in other European countries such as France and the United Kingdom. During the *Biennio Rosso* the use of cost-of-living statistics for setting wages spread thanks to the power conquered by the labour movement and the change of attitude of the state, which finally recognized the necessity of mediating industrial relations. Nevertheless, this favourable phase for workers was an ephemeral interlude. Fascism rapidly put an end to it, demonstrating how the cost-of-living statistics could be used for a policy of wage compression.

The degree of the performative power of this crucial statistical index is hard to evaluate. Rather than the manipulation of statistical data, the establishment of the monopoly of the fascist state on the production of cost-of-living indexes served the interests of the regime and the industrialists. The creation of the CSI in 1926, and the calculation of cost-of-living indexes coincided with the start of Mussolini's deflationary policy. In 1927, the government decided by decree two wage reductions for a total of 20 per cent. The decrease in the cost of living measured by the indexes of the CSI was higher than the wage reductions that had been decided by each sector in 1929. This gap was used as an argument by the Industrial Confederation in May 1930 to call for another general wage cut.[85] The government granted it in November 1930, bringing a further reduction of 8 per cent. Another cut of 7 per cent was approved in 1934. It was only the sustained rise in prices after 1936, which the regime was not able to avoid, that forced it to consider the possibility of new wage increases.[86] Already in 1927, fascism had abolished the cost-of-living indemnity for workers and progressively reduced it for civil servants. The requests of industrialists to reduce wages had provoked resistances, even if in some cases, such as in Fiat the cut was implemented in agreement with the fascist trade unions and the workers. The dramatic decline of conflict in the factories, and outside them, as well as the statistical retail prices numbers of the CSI, were then insufficient, as the intervention of the government proved necessary to establish by decree the reduction of wages.

---

[85] Vera Zamagni, 'Una Ricostruzione dell'Andamento Mensile dei Salari Industriali e dell'Occupazione 1919-1939', *Ricerche per la Storia della Banca d'Italia* (Bari: Laterza, 1994), 351–2.
[86] Ornella Bianchi, *Il Sindacato di Stato (1930–1940)*, in *Storia del Sindacato in Italia nel '900*, vol. I, *La CGdL e lo Stato Autoritario*, ed. Adolfo Pepe (Roma: Ediesse, 1997), 173–9.

11

Adam Smith on Wages and Labour: Social Norm and Institutions as Necessary Limits to Competition

Antonella Stirati

1. Introduction

In the course of the history of economic thought different economic theories have been developed, with profound implications for the interpretation of the forces determining wages and employment. Concerning these subjects, one often overlooked different analytical framework and general perspective with respect to the contemporary mainstream can be found in the Classical economists,[1] including Adam Smith, all too often regarded instead as the forerunner of contemporary neoclassical economics and its neoliberal implications.

Of course, the interpretations of Adam Smith have been ever since very varied and controversial.[2] It is outside the scope of this chapter to analyse in detail such controversies. The much narrower purpose will be to offer an additional, somewhat unusual, angle from which to look at such controversies and, more important, to focus on a specific terrain – the analysis of wages and the labour market – to compare Smith's views and contemporary economics and discuss the relationship between *Wealth of Nations* and *Theory of Moral Sentiments*.

Adam Smith's views on wages, quite paradigmatic of Classical and pre-Classical ones on the matter, can be of interest to modern economists, historians and social scientists for three intertwined reasons. First, they show that the development of economic theory has not proceeded in a straightforward manner along a line of progress within a given unifying general framework, still shared by contemporary

---

[1] By 'Classical economists' I mean here (as in Marx) the economists from Petty to Ricardo, including the French Phisiocrats. The term is today often used in a different manner, to indicate all economists from Ricardo to Marshall and Pigou as well as their modern epigones such as Friedman. This second use of the term was made popular by Keynes who (wrongly) saw the 'Classics' in the latter sense as encompassing all the economists believing in the tendency of market economies to full-employment equilibria (for a survey of different approaches to labour and income distribution in the history of economic thought see Antonella Stirati, in *Handbook on the History of Economic Analysis Volume III*, eds Gilbert Faccarello and Heinz D. Kurz (Cheltenham, Edward Elgar, 2016): 356–71.

[2] Emma Rothschild, 'Adam Smith and Conservative Economics', *Economic History Review*, 45, no 1 (1992): 74–96.

mainstream economists. Accordingly, the history of economic theories and debates can be a source of inspiration and alternative perspectives. Second, the critical and constructive contribution initiated by Piero Sraffa has on the one hand exposed serious analytical flaws in the still dominant marginalist (neoclassical) approach and on the other hand contributed to the revival and development of the Classical surplus approach as an alternative and sound theoretical framework. Third, several recent empirical and historical analyses of income distribution and the labour market are again bringing to light the importance of the set of factors (power relations, institutions and social norms) that were highlighted in Classical Political Economy, thus confirming that old theories may indeed provide a useful alternative framework for the understanding of contemporary economic phenomena.

In the exposition below I shall proceed as follows. First, I shall briefly summarize the main tenets of mainstream views of the functioning of labour markets and the determination of income distribution – this is particularly for the benefit of readers who are not academic economists, so that they can better understand the difference with Smith's approach outlined in the rest of the chapter (section 2). Second, I will present a brief discussion of the interpretations of Adam Smith and the Classical approach in general and highlight some inner contradictions, even among the readings of prominent representatives of the currently dominant approach (section 3). Third, I will present the main features of Smith's analysis of what determines wages (section 4) and highlight the fundamental role of social norms and institutions in the labour market (section 5). Finally, I shall discuss the well-known passages in the *Wealth of Nations* about the role of self-interest and how they are not in contrast with the views on human behaviour found in the *Theory of Moral Sentiments* (section 6) and reconsider the meaning and implications of the 'invisible hand' in the light of Smith's analysis of the labour market (section 7).

2. Currently prevailing views of wages and the labour market

The marginalist or neoclassical analytical framework that still today represents the background of all strands in mainstream economics was systematized and became dominant with the works of Alfred Marshall and Leon Walras at the end of the nineteenth century,[3] after a long phase of transition and gestation of new ideas that began already in the first half of that century, after Ricardo's death.

[3] Actually, it was mainly the Marshallian approach, characterized by partial equilibrium analysis (that is, the analysis of changes in specific markets under a *ceteris paribus* assumption) and limited use of mathematical formal tools that was originally dominant in the profession, and still is in most textbooks and applied and economic policy analyses. The Walrasian general equilibrium, highly formalized, approach became the dominant one in 'high theory' only later, in the belief it could overcome the theoretical difficulties emerged both concerning the '*ceteris paribus*' assumption (Piero Sraffa, 'Sulle relazioni fra costo e quantità prodotta', *Annali di economia*, 2 (1925): 277–328; Piero Sraffa, 'The Laws of Returns under Competitive Conditions', *The Economic Journal*, 36, no. 144 (1926): 535–50), and capital theory, (Piero Sraffa, *Production of Commodities by means of Commodities. Prelude to a Critique of Economic Theory* (Cambridge: Cambridge University Press: 1960); Luigi Pasinetti, 'Paradoxes in Capital Theory: A Symposium: Changes in the Rate of Profit and Switches of Techniques', *The Quarterly Journal of Economics*, 80, no. 4 (1966): 503–17; Pierangelo Garegnani, 'Heterogeneous Capital, the Production Function and the Theory of Distribution', *The Review of Economic Studies*, 37, no. 3 (1970): 407–436). Despite their differences however Marshallian and Walrasian approaches share the theoretical foundations discussed in this paragraph.

The main feature of this approach is the notion that there are demand functions for the so-called factors of production – labour, capital and land – such that there is an inverse relation between their remunerations (wages, interest and rent) and their employment. On this basis, it can be argued that, if there is competition and no obstacles to changes in those remunerations, the system will spontaneously tend towards the full utilization of the 'factors of production' and hence, given the technical knowledge and the endowments of resources, towards the highest possible level of output. Looking specifically at wages, the theory would maintain that whenever there is unemployment, competition among workers in the labour market will determine a fall in real wages and lead to full employment (or its equivalent, the so-called natural or equilibrium unemployment rate caused by unavoidable frictions and market imperfections that exist in the real world).

This fundamental notion that there is an inverse relation between the real wage and employment (and symmetrically between interest rate and demand for capital – hence, productive investment) is not based on (more or less sophisticated) observation of facts but on a complex *deductive* analytical construction. It is maintained that if real wages fall profit maximizing firms will look to use production techniques that require a higher labour to capital ratio, i.e. those that use more labour per unit of output. At the same time, it is supposed that the relative prices of commodities produced with higher labour intensity will fall, thus inducing consumers to modify the composition of their consumption baskets in favour of the more labour-intensive commodities. Both processes (factor substitution in production and, indirectly, in consumption) lead to higher demand for labour in the economy, for given endowments and use of the other factors of production (capital and land). The decreasing relation between wages and employment therefore requires changes in production techniques within each industry and in the composition of consumption in the economy as a whole as a consequence of the changes in income distribution.

The view that derives from the neoclassical theory is that not only is there a tendency to full utilization of labour, capital and land (hence efficiency of the system) but also that their remuneration reflects (given technical knowledge) the scarcity of these factors of production vis-à-vis the needs and tastes of consumers. A change in the latter in favour of more labour-intensive goods for example would cause (other things given) an increase in wages, and vice versa. Also, the traditional view implies that, in a flexible and competitive economy, supply and demand curves (which in turn reflect endowments of resources, consumer preferences and technical knowledge) *are the only causes of income distribution*. The same logic fully applies to wage differentials, when the existence of different types of labour (professional skills) is taken into account: they will reflect their relative scarcity vis-à-vis consumer demands.

Various contributions in the 1960s and 1970s challenged the analytical foundations of this theory by showing that, under the same assumptions usually made by the theory itself, a change in income distribution causes very complex changes in relative prices of all commodities, including capital goods, and this in turn leads to apparently 'paradoxical' results such that it is not possible to demonstrate that if wages fall, changes in the profitability of techniques or in relative prices of consumption goods will lead to higher demand for labour in the economic system (or, symmetrically, lower interest rates will lead to higher investments).[4]

Despite these analytical flaws, the theory still dominates textbooks and academic research and represents the hallmark of mainstream analyses. This is true even for those more recent versions of mainstream theory that acknowledge the role of institutions in persistently affecting wages. Although apparently more realistic, even in these versions the underlying theoretical framework is unchanged. Accordingly, labour market institutions such as minimum wages or employment protection are regarded as 'interferences' with otherwise efficient market mechanisms. They represent obstacles to competition and price flexibility that hinder the tendency of the system towards full employment (or 'natural unemployment') thus causing high and persistent ('structural') unemployment rates and inefficient use of resources.

3. Readings of Adam Smith and the Classics

As mentioned in the introduction, nowadays Adam Smith is most often claimed to be the father and forerunner of neoclassical theory and neoliberal economic policies, with their emphasis on the virtues of unfettered market forces.

One example among many can be found in the following statement by Olivier Blanchard, an internationally renowned economist, and former chief economist at IMF:

> More than two hundred years ago Adam Smith explained that, in a market economy, individualistic egoisms combined in such a way as *to bring about the best possible collective outcome*. The proposition was so striking and so heavily loaded with consequences that understanding its nature and its limits became paramount. Thanks to Walras, at the beginning of the twentieth century and, 50 years later, thanks to economists like Arrow or Debreu, and above all, thanks to an enormous effort of abstraction and to the utilisation of powerful mathematical tools, the conditions underlying Adam Smith's theorem have been clarified.[5]

Of course, this reading of Adam Smith has been challenged by several scholars, mostly on the basis of his views on human behaviour expounded in the *Theory of Moral Sentiments*. A view rightly regarded as quite far from the atomistic and selfish individual behaviour usually assumed in contemporary economics.

My perspective in this chapter however will be somewhat different: I will claim that Adam Smith's *economic theory*, not just his view of human behaviour, is profoundly different from modern neoclassical theory, and this is particularly evident, and with

---

[4] Sraffa *Production of Commodities*; Pasinetti, Paradoxes in Capital Theory; Garegnani (1970), 'Heterogeneous Capital'.
[5] Olivier Blanchard, quoted in Jospeh Halevi, 'Teaching Economic Theory Based on the History of Economic Thought', *Teaching the History of Economic Thought*, eds Daniela Tavasci and Luigi Ventimiglia (Cheltenham: Edward Elgar, 2018), 34, emphasis added.

profound consequences, in his theory concerning wages and employment determination.

Indeed, some clues running against the 'continuity' view expressed in Blanchard's passage can be found in the texts of important scholars in economics and history of economic thought who fully endorsed neoclassical theory. Scholars like Edwin Cannan, Frank Knight or Joseph Schumpeter, expressed quite a lot of disconcert in the face of Smith's chapter on wages. Knight for example wrote that Classical theory: 'sheds no light whatever on the economic principles of distribution, and is an amazing tissue of inconsistency and irrelevance.'[6]

Thus, quite in contrast with the widespread view expressed in Blanchard's statement, these very important scholars saw Smith's discussion of wages as completely detached from and at variance with neoclassical principles, which they understood as the only possible foundations of the theory of distribution. Recently, it has been argued that the readings of Smith by various generations of 'Chicago' scholars (among them Knight) are the product of diverse emphases reflecting the changes in their own approaches to free market advocacy and more generally the scope of economics. But perhaps there have been other factors at play, generally neglected, that I would like to bring to attention. Except for Marshall, who tended to suggest continuity and progress between his contribution and the Classical tradition, with the aim of preserving the prestige and credibility of the discipline, most of the early interpretations tended to point out differences rather than similarity, and to emphasize the superiority of the marginalist approach. Things appear to have changed when the contributions by Sraffa[7] and other economists have shown the flaws of the 'new' theory and suggested that the Classical surplus approach could be amended and developed to represent a consistent alternative framework: several contributions have since then emphasized continuity.[8]

It can be maintained that scholars like Knight and Cannan were right concerning the distance between Smith's discussion of wages and neoclassical theory; however, as I shall argue, Smith's views were not inconsistent, but rather representative of a *different and internally coherent theory*, which was the *prevailing one* at his time and up to Ricardo's death. In this regard, it is useful to remind of the nature of Smith's *Wealth of Nations* as a work assembling in a broad coherent body ideas that had often been already advanced by his contemporaries and predecessors. It is so with regards to his treatment of wages and labour, since many of the ideas presented by Smith can be found, sometimes even with very similar wordings, in other economists of the time. It should also be recollected that in his *preface* to the *Principles*, Ricardo characterizes his own contribution as dealing with his (narrow, but analytically very important) points

---

[6] Frank H. Knight, *On the History and Method in Economics*, (Chicago: Chicago University Press, 1963 [1956]), 75. For similar views see also Edwin Cannan, *A History of the Theories of Production and Distribution in English Political Economy from 1776 to 1848* (London: Percival and co. 1893), 235, 379–83; and Joseph Schumpeter, *History of Economic Analysis*, (London: Allen and Unwin, 1982 [1954]), 82, 268–9.

[7] Piero Sraffa, 'Introduction' to David Ricardo, *Works and Correspondence*, edited by Piero Sraffa, vol. I (Cambridge: Cambridge University Press 1951), XIII–LXII; Sraffa, *Production of Commodities*.

[8] A most prominent example is Paul Samuelson, 'The Canonical Classical Model of Political Economy', *Journal of Economic Literature*, 16, no. December (1978): 1415–35.

of disagreement with Adam Smith concerning the theory of relative prices and profit rate, while substantially accepting his contribution on all other matters.

4. Smith's theory of wages

4.1 Main themes

Smith's discussion in the chapter *Of the Wages of Labour* in Book I of the *Wealth of Nations* highlights three major influences on the general level of wages (for unskilled, adult male labour, with wage differentials conceived to remain rather stable over time, so that the wages of all types of labour would normally move in step with the compensation of unskilled workers):

1. the customary living standard of workers which determines 'subsistence consumption' regarded as a floor for the natural (normal) wage rate;
2. the bargaining advantage enjoyed by the masters with respect to the workers;
3. the respective rates of growth of employment and population.

This led some interpreters to attribute three different theories to Adam Smith, and to maintain that all are actually present in his writings, even if they are not consistent with one another.[9] These three theories would be: i) a subsistence theory in which wages are taken as a social datum;[10] (ii) a monopsony theory in which wages are arbitrarily determined by a 'fiat' of the employers;[11] and (iii) the wage fund doctrine according to which the course of wages over time depends on the ratio between the wage fund and (working-class) population.[12]

However, the various factors described by Smith can by contrast be regarded as part of a consistent explanation of the natural or normal wage level as determined essentially by the bargaining position of the parties, within boundaries determined by custom and social rules. But this reading requires understanding that in Smith's (and his contemporaries) there was no notion of a systematic decreasing relationship between the real wage and the employment level (i.e. a decreasing demand for labour as a function of the real wage). Such relationship, as described in section 2, is a theoretical construct (not an observed, self-evident fact) that was developed only later on, and brings with it the idea of a 'spontaneous' (i.e. brought about by market forces alone) tendency of the economy towards full employment under the assumption of

---

[9] Marc Blaug *Economic Theory in Retrospect* (Cambridge: Cambridge University Press, 4th edition 1985), 44;
Cannan, *A History of the Theories of Production and Distribution*, 235, 379–83; Samuel Hollander *The Economics of Adam Smith* (London: Heineman, 1973), 185–6; Knight, *On the History and Method*, 80–3; Schumpeter, *History of Economic Analysis*, 268–9
[10] Schumpeter, *History of Economic Analysis*, 665.
[11] Frank H. Knight, *On the History and Method*, 81; Samuel Hollander, *The Economics of Adam Smith* (London: Heineman, 1973), 185.
[12] Cannan, *A History of the Theories of Production and Distribution*, 235–7.

competitive conditions and real wage flexibility or, as become more fashionable, a spontaneous tendency towards the maximum level of employment consistent with the given market imperfections and rigidities, corresponding to an equilibrium unemployment rate labelled natural unemployment or non-accelerating-inflation unemployment rate.

In what follows I will look more closely at these propositions in Smith and provide some references to similar views expressed by his contemporaries.

4.2 The customary nature of the subsistence minimum

For Smith, subsistence consumption represents a minimum floor below which the natural or normal wage rate for unskilled labour cannot fall: the 'rate below which it is impossible to reduce, for any considerable time, the ordinary wages even of the lowest species of labour'.[13] This however is not a biological but a customary, socially determined minimum:[14]

> by necessaries I understand not only the commodities which are indispensably necessary for the support of life, but whatever the custom of the country renders it indecent for creditable people, even of the lowest order, to be without [. . .]. Under necessaries therefore I comprehend not only those things which nature, but those things which the established rules of decency have rendered necessary to the lowest rank of people.[15]

4.3 The tendency of wages towards the subsistence minimum, and counter circumstances

It was the general view at the time that the workers are the weakest party in the bargaining over wages (where 'bargaining' does not mean necessarily that there are 'organizations' on either side, but even when the wage rate is established by an agreement between individual worker and employer, it results from a negotiation between them), and because of this are generally not in a position to obtain more than the customary subsistence minimum – yet no less than that, despite the masters' advantage. This is very clearly articulated by Smith in his chapter *On Wages*.

---

[13] Adam Smith *An Inquiry into the Nature and Causes of the Wealth of Nations*, two vols, in Roy H. Campbell and Andrew S. Skinner (eds), *The Glasgow edition of The Works and Correspondence of Adam Smith* (OUP and Liberty Classics (1776 [1976]), Book I, Chapter viii, Par. 14. From now on: WN I.viii.14.

[14] For an example of an entirely similar definition of subsistence as a floor for wages, which is not however a biological minimum see Anne Robert Jaques Turgot, 'Lettres sur le commerce des grains' in Gustave Schelle (ed.) *Oevres de Turgot et documents le concernant*, vol. III (Librairie Felix Alcan, Paris, 1913–23), 288. Steuart also had clearly referred to habit and custom: "The nature of man furnishes him with some desires [. . .] which [. . .] are formed by habit and education, and when once *regularly established*, create another kind of necessary, which [. . .] I shall call *political* (James Steuart (1766a) *An Inquiry into the Principles of Political Oeconomy*, abridged edition, Andrew S. Skinner (ed.) (Edinburgh and London : Oliver & Boyd for the Scottish Economic Society 1966), 270–7, emphasis in the original.

[15] WN V.ii.k.3.

What are the common wages of labour, depends everywhere upon the contract usually made between those two parties, whose interests are by no means the same.[...]. It is not, however, difficult to foresee which of the two parties must, upon all ordinary occasions, have the advantage in the dispute, and force the other into a compliance with their terms. The masters, being fewer in number, can combine much more easily: and the law, besides, authorises, or at least does not prohibit, their combinations, while it prohibits those of the workmen.[...]. In all such disputes, the masters can hold out much longer. A landlord, a farmer, a master manufacturer, or merchant, though they did not employ a single workman, could generally live a year or two upon the stocks, which they have already acquired. Many workmen could not subsist a week, few could subsist a month, and scarce any a year, without employment. [...] Masters are always and everywhere in a sort of tacit, but constant and uniform, combination, not to raise the wages of labour above their actual rate. To violate this combination is everywhere a most unpopular action, and a sort of reproach to a master among his neighbours and equals. [...]. But though, in disputes with their workmen, masters must generally have the advantage, there is, however, a certain rate, below which it seems impossible to reduce, for any considerable time, the ordinary wages even of the lowest species of labour. A man must always live by his work, and his wages must at least be sufficient to maintain him. They must even upon most occasions be somewhat more, otherwise it would be impossible for him to bring up a family, and the race of such workmen could not last beyond the first generation.[16]

Thus, wage-fixing is understood as the result of negotiations going on between two parties with opposite interests and very unequal bargaining power.[17] In turn the advantage of the masters is explained by various factors. One is the institutional set-up, such that the law (and the police) prohibits the 'combinations' of the workers while 'silent' combinations of the masters, that is, a generalized attitude not to raise wages, supported by social norms within the employers' community, is most usual. Social rules play an important role in the 'combinations' of the masters. What Smith describes here is not a 'monopsony' or a 'cartel', but a rather subtler 'tacit agreement' (elsewhere, he describes monopsonies proper with much clearer and different terms).

It is important to emphasize that Smith here does not have in mind a 'cartel' or monopsony whereby masters can arbitrarily set wages in a non-competitive environment, since Smith on the contrary emphasizes the role of free competition in

---

[16] WN; I.viii.11–12.
[17] The themes of the 'great number of workers' competing with one another, and that of workers' urgent need to work in order to survive as reasons for the tendency of wages to be at the subsistence minimum are in Anne Robert Jaques Turgot 'Reflections on the formation and distribution of wealth' (1766), in Roland L. Meek (ed.), *Turgot on Progress, Sociology and Economics* (Cambridge: Cambridge University Press, 1973), paragraph VI, 122 and Turgot 'Lettres sur le commerce des grains, 336–7; similar expressions also in Jaques Necker (1775) *Sur la législation et le commerce des grains*, in Id. *Oevres Complètes*, edited by M. le Baron de Stael, vol I, (Paris: Treuttel and Wurtz: 1820–1), 137–8; for a discussion see Antonella Stirati *The Theory of Wages in Classical Economics* (Cheltenham: Elgar, 1994), 37–8; 45–7.

income distribution: in bringing about uniformity of profit rates across different employment of capital and of wages of workers with the same characteristics, and also, as we shall see, in causing rising wages in tight labour markets.

Another factor in masters' advantage is the separation between labour and ownership of the means of production, along with the enormous differences in wealth, so that the workers have no other means of survival than selling their labour, while the 'masters' can hold on for a long time without employing labourers.

Thus, the causes of the tendency of wages to the socially determined subsistence floor are social and institutional, which also implies that institutional changes might raise them above that minimum (as implied, for example by Hume's and Necker's reference to the 'forms of government' as a cause of higher wages in countries were the people can enjoy some rights and political representation).[18]

Another circumstance that might raise wages is a buoyant labour market, while the existence of ample labour reserves, regarded as a normal feature of economies that are not fast-growing, is among the factors determining the masters' advantage. According to Smith, in stagnant or declining economies, the 'constant scarcity of employment' contributes to keeping wages at subsistence. In a stationary economy:

> the number of labourers employed every year could easily supply, and even more than supply, the number wanted the following year. There could seldom be any scarcity of hands, nor could the masters be obliged to bid against one another in order to get them. The hands, on the contrary, would, in this case, naturally multiply beyond their employment. *There would be a constant scarcity of employment*, and the labourers would be obliged to bid against one another in order to get it. If in such a country the wages of labour had ever been more than sufficient to maintain the labourer, and to enable him to bring up a family, the competition of the labourers and the interest of the masters would soon reduce them to the lowest rate which is consistent with common humanity.[19]

In a declining economy the persistent lack of jobs would be even worse, would be felt in all professions, but would be particularly severe in the market for unskilled labour, since this section of the labour market would be overcrowded also as a result of the inflow of skilled workers that in different circumstances could have access to better, more qualified employments. Adam Smith also describes how a condition of persistent unemployment eventually pushes people at the margin of society:

> Every year the demand for servants and labourers would, in all the different classes of employments, be less than it had been the year before. Many who had been bred

---

[18] While Smith mentions the laws prohibiting workers' combinations, others among his contemporaries provide a broader picture of the relevant institutions, including the 'form of government' and the political rights enjoyed by the people (Jaques Necker, *De l'administration des finances de la France* (1785) in Id. *Oevres Complètes*, edited by M. le Baron de Stael, vol I, (Paris: Treuttel and Wurtz 1820–1), 326–9; David Hume, *Of Commerce* (1752), in *Writings on Economics* edited by Eugene Rotwein (Edinburgh: Nelson, 1955), 16.

[19] WN I.viii.24, emphasis added.

in the superior classes, not being able to find employment in their own business, would be glad to seek it in the lowest. The lowest class being not only overstocked with its own workmen, but with the overflowings of all the other classes, the competition for employment would be so great in it, as to reduce the wages of labour to the most miserable and scanty subsistence of the labourer. *Many would not be able to find employment* even upon these hard terms, but would either starve, or be driven to seek a subsistence, either by begging, or by the perpetration perhaps, of the greatest enormities.[20]

Thus, in such economies there is a *persistent* excess of labourers with respect to employment – no tendency to full employment can be detected in Smith's description – and this situation contributes significantly to the differences in bargaining power that are at the core of Smith's discussion of wage determination. On the other hand, in a fast-growing economy, the continuous increase in employment leads the masters to compete with each other to attract the workers they want to hire by increasing wages – in such economic circumstances the employers break their 'tacit agreement' or social rule not to raise wages for the sake of their individual interest in obtaining the number of workmen necessary to allow the desired level of production in their own enterprise:[21]

There are certain circumstances, however, which sometimes give the labourers an advantage, and enable them to raise their wages considerably above this [subsistence] rate, evidently the lowest which is consistent with common humanity. When in any country the demand for those who live by wages, labourers, journeymen, servants of every kind, is continually increasing; when every year furnishes employment for a greater number than had been employed the year before, the workmen have no occasion to combine in order to raise their wages. The scarcity of hands occasions a competition among masters, who bid against one another in order to get workmen, and thus voluntarily break through the natural combination of masters not to raise wages.[22]

Thus, in those circumstances, i.e. in conditions of persistently tight labour market (as, according to Smith, happens in North America, where 'there is a *continual complaint of the scarcity of hands*')[23], the natural wage rises above the subsistence minimum. It is important to note that the normal or natural wage rate can persistently settle above what is regarded at a particular time and place as the subsistence minimum, since this also provides a key to understanding how and why the subsistence minimum itself can evolve over time, and therefore give rise to the changes that admittedly the subsistence floor can undergo over time or in different places: given the social/customary definition of such minimum, some ratchet effect from the normal wage rate and habitual living standard to what is socially regarded as a minimum floor cannot be

---

[20] WN; I.viii.26.
[21] Similarly in Turgot, 'Lettres sur le commerce des grains', 321.
[22] WN I.viii.16–17.
[23] WN I.viii.22, emphasis added.

ruled out on logical grounds and was actually spelt out clearly by some of Smith's contemporaries.[24]

Persistent labour market conditions associated to the pace of accumulation cause lasting changes in what was called the 'natural' i.e. normal wage rate and have to be kept distinct from temporary fluctuations in actual wages determined by short term, transitory changes in economic conditions, such as those typically caused at the time by good or bad harvests, that are clearly indicated as causing fluctuations *around* the natural wage rate.

5. Why not below the minimum? Competition and social norms

A remarkable difference between the views expressed at Smith's time and current economic theory is that despite large unemployment and underemployment, as described for the cases of stagnant and declining economy, and despite the other sources of advantage of the masters in wage determination, the natural wage cannot be squeezed by competition below the subsistence floor, with the latter, as we have seen, *not* regarded as a merely biological datum. Contemporary theory by contrast would predict that under competitive conditions, wages would, under such circumstances, keep falling as a result of competition among the labourers to obtain a job.

In Smith this is not the case, since competition operates in many ways, but within boundaries that are determined by social norms – in this case by norms concerning what is the minimum 'consistent with common humanity' – that affect both workers' and employers' behaviour. Customary living standards determine what is regarded as a floor and this stands as an anchor for natural wages: they cannot fall below it, they can rise above it at a higher *level*, as described for fast-growing economies, but they will not keep rising, even in a tight labour market.

The influence of contemporary economic theory and ways of thinking have led some interpreters to see the downward 'rigidity' of the wage rate in Classical theory as the *cause* of the presence of unemployment in their analysis of the labour market.

However, there are no indications whatsoever that in Smith there was the notion of an inverse relation between wage level and employment level (a decreasing demand curve for labour as the one we would find in any contemporary economic textbook). In the passages quoted above, Smith always discusses the relative sizes of employment and labour force in the economy, with no hints at a systematic relation between wages and employment. In addition, Smith writes that: 'The demand for those who live by wages, therefore, naturally increases with the increase of national wealth, and *cannot*

---

[24] See for example James Steuart, 'because the workmen, having long enjoyed [higher incomes] will have bettered their way of living: and as they are many, and live uniformly, anything which obliges them to retrench a part of their habitual expense, is supposed to deprive them of necessaries' (James Steuart (1766b) *An Inquiry into the Principles of Political Oeconomy*, in *The Works. Political, Metaphysical, and Chronological of the late Sir James Staeuart* collected by Sir J. Steuart Bart, his son, vol. III (Cadell and Davies: London, 1805), 11.

possibly increase without it',[25] thus clearly indicating that the increase in employment is the result of accumulation and economic growth, while excluding other possible causes, such as wage reductions.[26]

Indeed, the decreasing labour demand curve is very far from being a 'fact' under everybody's eyes, which Smith and other economists could not fail to see. Quite the opposite: it is the result of a rather complex theoretical and deductive construct, which has been found to be flawed on these same grounds, and which has proven very difficult to confirm empirically, even with current data and techniques for their analysis. Hence, the decreasing relationship between wage levels and employment is not now and was not at Smith's time a self-evident fact that could not be ignored; while at the same time its abstract, theoretical derivation cannot be detected in his writings or those of his contemporaries.

Thus, there is indeed a connection between the acknowledgement of unemployment and underemployment as a common, normal feature of economic reality, and the notion of a downward floor for wages, *but it runs in the opposite direction* than the one supposed in the light of contemporary ways of thinking. In the absence of an inverse relation between the wage level and employment, unlimited competition over wages when there is unemployment would soon disrupt the lives of the workers and their families and unsettle the economy and society at large, with no beneficial effect on employment. Hence, in an economy functioning in the way the Classics describe it, some downward wage 'rigidity' *must* be there to ensure economic and social stability and viability. Should it not exist, it would have to be established. Similarly, unlimited competition among masters in the event of an excess demand for labour would cause (according to modern conception of competition) a continuous increase in wages that, in the absence of a negative effect on employment (as in the Classic's framework), would encounter no limit. Again, this would be a very implausible conclusion.

Put in other terms: an unlimited competition over wages is plausible and, in addition, can be described as a *beneficial* market mechanism *only if* it goes hand in hand with a systematic inverse relation between real wage and employment levels, so that changes in wages cause a change in employment in the opposite direction, which in turn closes the gap between labour force and employment levels (i.e. establishes a full employment equilibrium) and sets an end to the fall or rise in wage levels.

But in an economy, as was understood by Smith, in which such a systematic relation between wages and employment simply is not envisaged, it must be the case that although wages are affected by competition and labour market slack or tightness, this occurs *within boundaries*. There must be customary and institutional anchors to set limits to wage changes. This is necessary both in the sense that otherwise the theory would predict unrealistic, non-observed phenomena, and in the sense that they are

---

[25] WN I.viii.21, emphasis added.
[26] It may be of interest to note here that according to Turgot, real wage reductions might even be damaging, since consumption of agricultural products would be negatively affected: '[...] if the worker earns less, he consumes less, ad if he consumes less the money value of agricultural production is lower' (Anne Robert Jaques Turgot, *Memoire Graslin* (1767), in Gustave Schelle (ed.) *Oevres de Turgot et documents le concernant*, vol II (Librairie Felix Alcan, Paris, 1913–23), 634, my translation.

necessary in the real world to prevent destabilizing economic and social outcomes. Actually, it has been shown that in the history of economic thought the notion of *unlimited* competition over wages that would occur when there is unemployment appears only after Ricardo's death, in combination with the emergence of the notion that changes in the wage rate would cause changes in the employment level in the opposite direction, as it is the case in the wage fund theory – a view that was highly controversial at the time of its introduction.[27]

6. The relationship between *Theory of Moral Sentiments* and *Wealth of Nations* in the light of the explanation of wages

The role of social norms described above, defining the boundaries within which competition can operate, is quite consistent with Smith's views on human behaviour developed in the *Theory of Moral Sentiments*, thus overcoming the often-claimed contradiction between this work and the *Wealth of Nations*.[28] Even in the economic sphere humans are seen as social beings, keen on social approval and sensitive to social norms of behaviour: 'What is the end of avarice and ambition, of the pursuit of wealth, of power, and pre-eminence? [...] to be taken notice of with sympathy, complacency, and approbation.'[29] Although: 'It is not from the benevolence of the butcher, the brewer, or the baker, that we expect our dinner, but from their regard to their own interest'[30] – that is, the butcher only needs to rely on his self-interest in order to put on sale a quantity of meat that matches the requests from his customers – this does not prevent that in negotiating the wages he pays to his employees he may be quite sensitive to social norms concerning a 'decent pay' on the one hand and loyalty to the interests of his fellow employers on the other.

I believe that a correct view about the connections between the *Theory of Moral Sentiments* and *Wealth of Nations* was put forward by O'Brien, in whose opinion the first 'offers a theory of the way in which both public and private laws limit the operation of individual interests *where those may conflict with social interests*'; and the second

---

[27] Enrico Sergio Levrero, 'Some notes on Wages and Competition in the Labour Market', in Roberto Ciccone, Christian Gehrke, Gary Mongiovi (eds), *Sraffa and Modern Economics* (London: Routledge, 2011), 361–83; Antonella Stirati, 'Classical Roots of the Criticisms of John Stuart Mill's Wage-Fund Theory', in eds Ghislain Deleplace, Cristina Marcuzzo and Paolo Paesani, *New Perspectives on Political Economy and Its History* (London: Routledge: 2020), 149–69.
[28] An immediate indication that Smith did not see the two works as contradictory can be seen in the fact that the last edition of the *Theory of Moral Sentiments* is subsequent to the publication of the *Wealth of Nations*, and yet it does not contain revisions that might be interpreted as changes of opinion or emphasis in the light of the latter (Alec L. Macfie and David D. Raphael, 'Introduction' to *The Theory of Moral Sentiments* (6th edition, 1790), in Roy H Campbell. and Andrew S. Skinner (eds), *The Glasgow edition of The Works and Correspondence of Adam Smith* (Oxford: Clarendon and Liberty Classics, 1976), 20.
[29] Adam Smith, *The Theory of Moral Sentiments*, in Campbell Roy H. and Andrew S. Skinner (eds) The *Glasgow edition of The Works and Correspondence of Adam Smith* (Oxford: Clarendon and Liberty Classics (6th edition 1790 [1976]) Book I. Chapter iii, section 2 par. 1. From now on: TMS I.iii.2.1.
[30] WN I.ii.2.

'offers a theory of the way in which individual interests thus limited produce optimal resource allocation'.[31] Actually, I do not subscribe to the notion that in Smith there is an 'optimal' resource allocation in the modern sense (more on this below) and would rather refer to an 'appropriate' allocation, in the more limited sense of the coordination between production and consumption. But the point to be emphasized here in connection with O'Brien's suggestion, is that the realm of income distribution, owing to the absence of a systematic inverse relation between real wage and employment levels, is precisely a field in which *unlimited competition and pursuit of self-interest would be socially detrimental*, and hence the emergence of private or public norms limiting it is necessary.

7. Markets, efficiency and the 'invisible hand'

Adam Smith was certainly in favour of some liberalization of the economy, particularly in opposition to constraints that derived from the feudal order and appeared to favour the landed classes. One case in point was his opposition to the poor laws combined with the law of settlements prevailing at the time, which tended to limit workers mobility and tie them to the parish of origin. He also opposed the limitations imposed by rules concerning apprenticeship which were used to limit access to particular jobs and professions, which he regarded as favouring some sections of the workers at the expense of others. But what does all this mean? Would his views imply, as maintained by many modern economists, that unfettered market forces, in competitive conditions, would deliver the best possible outcome – at least on efficiency grounds? Certainly not, since in the first place, this is fully denied by the normal existence of unemployment and underemployment that are not only a cause of social distress, but also involve a major economic inefficiency, i.e. a lower output and income level than could be reached if all were employed. In addition, as we have seen, his theory of distribution does not entail any 'allocative efficiency' whatsoever: wages at large reflect bargaining power, social norms acquired through history and habit, institutional set-up, inequality of wealth and property rights. Even with regards to wage differentials – to be understood relative to the wages of unskilled adult male workers – Smith saw them as only to a limited extent related to ability and effort. To a large extent, differences across professions were regarded as depending, besides the costs of acquiring the skills, on social hierarchies, and differences related to age and gender as depending on family roles (an adult male pay comprising the support of his family, which was not the case for female and child labour).

What then should we do with the invisible hand? The meaning of the famous passages is, I believe, of less (or at any rate different) import than usually thought in the light of modern economic theory. Consider the following famous statement:

> Every individual necessarily labours to render the annual revenue of society as great as he can. He generally neither intends to promote the public interest, nor

---

[31] Denis P. O'Brien, *The Classical Economists* (Oxford: Clarendon, 1975), 31, emphasis added.

knows how much he is promoting it [...] He intends only his own gain, and he is, in this, as in many other cases, led by an invisible hand to promote an end which was no part of his intention.[32]

It only implies that by pursuing their own interests, the capitalists/entrepreneurs will invest and increase production and will also direct it towards meeting the existing demands. Something that was also fully recognized by Marx, but does not entail any 'optimality' of the market mechanism.[33] In Adam Smith and all the Classical economists, self-interested economic action in the market is what brings about, besides the accumulation of means of production, a coordination between the *composition* of demand and the *composition* of production, since the (transitory) changes in relative profitability of various activities in response to changes in the quantity demanded, can ensure such coordination, that is, ensure that 'the butcher' will normally have enough meat to satisfy his customers. This is a very important statement about the role of competition and market forces, which is quite realistic and very important for the development of economic theory – and involves a change in perspective with regard to much of the earlier mercantilist literature, that had a normative attitude and a view of the economic system as (mostly) a 'command' economy. However, Smith's views about the coordinating properties of market forces (essentially: free capital mobility across industries) do not necessarily imply that self-interest is the *only* motivation of human behaviour, even in the economic sphere, nor do they entail an optimality of the outcome in the modern sense. The passage on the 'invisible hand' has no implication – in his theoretical framework – of full employment, or 'utility maximization'. It is only in modern neoclassical general equilibrium theory that all these things are supposed to go together, with a simultaneous determination of relative prices, quantities demanded, income distribution, all determined at full employment, through complex interdependencies – where the decreasing demand curves for labour and capital have a prominent role – that simply did not exist, or had quite different nature and forms, in the Classical theoretical framework.[34]

Thus, in all strands of modern mainstream economic theory, institutions affecting income distribution are seen as interferences with market forces, which always have drawbacks in terms of efficiency of the system and in terms of its ability to produce full employment of labour – drawbacks that are generally admitted even by those who, despite adhering to the theory, claim that such interferences may nevertheless be desirable on principles of social justice and equality in opportunities. By contrast, in the old Classical framework, social norms and institutions, along with persistent conditions of labour market slack or tightness, are *the* forces normally determining

---

[32] WN IV.ii.9.
[33] Rather, it did imply for Marx, as for many Classical economists, the progressive and disruptive nature of the then rising capitalist industrialization vis-à-vis the earlier order dominated by the landed aristocracy.
[34] Antonella Stirati, 'On Hollander on Sraffa and the "Marxian Dimension"', in Roberto Ciccone, Christian Gehrke and Gary Mongiovi (eds), *Sraffa and Modern Economics* (London: Routledge 2011), 318–34.

income distribution – *no other market mechanisms being around*. In this theoretical framework there are no general, a priori implications concerning the greater or lesser 'efficiency' of different arrangements; not only in terms of allocative efficiency of given resources, but even in terms of their effects on the accumulation of capital. Indeed, although productive investments were seen as financed by profit incomes (a proposition no longer to be regarded as acceptable in modern economies and after Keynes' contribution), it was also clearly maintained that although high profits *may* have favoured accumulation, it was not *necessarily* so, since much would depend, for example, on the attitudes of the wealthier classes towards productive investment vis-à-vis luxury consumption or accumulation of wealth rather than capital

A return to the Classics' theory of distribution – as supported by recent research on economic theory and facts – would have profound implications for the interpretations of the forces behind income distribution and wage formation as well as for the design of policies affecting it.

12

Devaluing Labour and Radical Theories of Worker Discrimination in North America in the Late Twentieth Century

Tiago Mata

Devaluing labour

Writing about nineteenth-century British capitalism, Eric Hobsbawn remarked that 'wage calculation remained for long, …, largely a customary and not a market calculation'.[1] Hobsbawn was surprised by how long it took before employers and workers came to grips with the rules of the (market) game.[2] In other words, Hobsbawn was telling us that wages, with their intricate human geographies and occupational gradations, have histories that markets could not easily erase.

A decade on from the publication of Hobsbawn's essay, a group of early career economists came to a very similar insight. Their subject was not nineteenth-century Britain but rather the unevenness of mature capitalism in twentieth-century America. The self-identified radical economists were, like Hobsbawn, drawn to unruly workers, who were disrupting orderly union politics with wildcat strikes over issues of supervision and workplace culture. With the anodyne title of 'segmented labour market theory', radicals argued that a key element in calculating the value of labour was the sorting of workers into kinds and that supply and demand and collective arbitration were significant only in segments of the labour market.[3]

The radicals were not trying to impress their academic peers, rather they wanted their research to be a resource for political mobilization, circulated and understood beyond academia. The political lesson they were teaching was that employers encouraged difference to weaken workers' political resolve, in their phrase 'to divide

---

[1] E.J. Hobsbawn, 'Custom, Wages and Work Load', in *Labouring Men: Studies in the History of Labour* (New York: Basic Books, 1964), 409.
[2] The view of rupture is in my view epitomized in Karl Polanyi's classic, *The Great Transformation* (New York: Farrar & Rinehart, 1944).
[3] Although it begins in the work of labour economists, sociologists and cultural anthropologists also contributed to this literature. As the attention of the American economics profession drifted elsewhere, as it often does, forgetting unfinished business, the subject was picked up by institutional sociology. For a survey, see David B. Bills, Valentina Di Stasio, Klarita Gërxhani, 'The Demand Side of Hiring: Employers in the Labor Market', *Annual Review of Sociology*, 43, no. 1 (2007): 291–310.

and conquer'. Radicals hoped this insight would ignite socialist sentiment in America. It was not to be so.

Segmented labour market theory deserves our attention because it prompts us to think about value alongside devaluing. The indexical of wage and the scalar logics freighted by that conception are replaced by value as qualities, such as the autonomy of the work, stability of employment and opportunities for advancement and enrichment. To conduct our analysis this way is to look for sets of qualities arranged in stable constellations, asking how those constellations came into being and what holds them in place.

In what follows I will not attempt to reckon whether radical economics, or indeed Hobsbawn's account, give us a true and complete description of wage calculation in the 1960s or today, that must remain the subject of important and ongoing debate.[4] I want to take a few steps back from the question of value to address some framing concerns. I want to look for the conditions of knowledge that supported the radicals' investigations into the qualities of labour. And I want to ask what did scholars hope to accomplish from their insights onto markets' discriminating logics. I put to one side the questions that interest economic and social historians, what was the value of labour and how was it changing, to ask questions about the epistemology of value and its politics.

I was drawn to this record because it speaks to the entanglements between social science and the American social state.[5] A central feature of American social policy in this period was the disputed status of its programmes. Many of these programmes were designed, monitored and evaluated by social scientists. Seen from today's vantage point these appear to us as experiments that left far more enduring imprints on social knowledge than on national policy.[6] Segmented labour market theory developed from a conjunction of this type: sourced with data generated by public policy, asking questions of policy effectiveness, federally funded. Radical theory would not exist without the social state and its contested policies. Another intriguing feature of this record was the tension between the elitism of standard economics and the radicals' ambition to build a participatory politics of social movements. Radicals had hoped that the 1970s would be a decade of insurgent labour militancy. Scholars must be forgiven when they fail to divine the future of the American polity but radicals also failed in the

---

[4] For an early survey, see Glein G. Cain, 'The Challenge of Segmented Labor Market Theories to Orthodox Theory: A Survey', *Journal of Economic Literature*, 14, no. 4 (1976): 1215-57; for more recent contributions that continue to update this discussion see for instance, Charles Tilly and Chris Tilly, *Work Under Capitalism* (London: Routledge, 1998); Arne L. Kalleberg, *Good Jobs, Bad Jobs: The Rise of Polarized and Precarious Employment Systems in the United States, 1970s-2000s* (New York: Russell Sage Foundation, 2011).

[5] My understanding of these issues was informed by two exceptional books, Alice O'Connor, *Poverty Knowledge: Social Science, Social Policy, and the Poor in Twentieth-Century U.S. History* (Princeton: Princeton University Press, 2001); and Romain Huret, *The Experts' War on Poverty: Social Research and the Welfare Agenda in Postwar America* (Ithaca, NY : Cornell University Press, 2018).

[6] See for instance Robert A. Levine, Harold Watts, Robinson Hollister, Walter Williams, Alice O'Connor, and Karl Widerquist, 'A Retrospective on the Negative Income Tax Experiments: Looking Back at the Most Innovative Field Studies in Social Policy', in *The Ethics and Economics of the Basic Income Guarantee*, eds Karl Widerquist and Michael Anthony Lewis (Aldershot: Ashgate, 2005). Arguably, the experimental character of social policy became more acute after Richard Nixon became President.

terms they set for themselves: they were unable to articulate goals that would animate labour movements.

The starting point of my account is the emergence, circa 1960, of the 'working poor' as a subject of concern in American political life. Policy action on poverty was locked in place by a set of early conceptual choices, notably talk of a 'culture of poverty'. It is only after we are acquainted with the trajectory of these policies, known collectively as the 'war on poverty', and the partnered social science, that the main actors of my account are introduced. I look at how the dual labour market hypothesis developed into segmented labour market theory in efforts to evaluate programmes of the 'war on poverty'. Pausing on the fine distinctions between economics texts gives us clues on what political lessons radicals were aiming for. I conclude by finding my way back to this introduction and to Hobsbawn's 1960 essay, noting how segmented labour market theory was reinterpreted in the early 1980s with diminished political ambitions, as an historical account.

Working poor

The poor were out of place in the public culture of the 1950s United States. Although public opinion was startled by news of a Soviet satellite hovering the globe in 1957 and its hints at a science and technology gap, when it came to consumer goods, recreation and life's conveniences the USA's superiority was unquestioned. Vice President Richard Nixon was delighted to debate Premier Nikita Khrushchev on the view of a model (idealized) American kitchen, on occasion of the American National Exhibition in the summer of 1959. America was a post-scarcity society like no other in human history and proud of it.

Apologists of the American way and social critics agreed. John Kenneth Galbraith in his 1958 best-selling *The Affluent Society* saw an imbalance in the provision of public goods compared to private wares but he did not doubt that the basic necessities of life had been met for all. To the Beats, the Greenwich Village bohemia or the New Left, the deluge of consumption goods was doing injury to the human spirit. More mainstream figures like John Updike, ironized consumerism's ubiquity, like in his short poem 'Superman', when he wrote of 'Supercilious men and women / Call me superficial – me! / Who so superbly learned to swim in / Supercolossality.' In this collective view, the greatest threats to American society were banality and alienation not deprivation.[7]

Since the 1930s the American state was supporting millions of individuals in need but the conventional wisdom of high journalism and of campaigning conservatives was that these welfare recipients had placed themselves in situations of need because they knew they would get support. The corollary was a belief that welfare policies dating back to the Great Depression were inadequate for post-scarcity America and

---

[7] John Kenneth Galbraith, *The Affluent Society* (New York: Houghton Mifflin, 1958); John Updike, 'Superman', *The New Yorker*, 12 November 1955: 56. Herbert Marcuse, *One-Dimensional Man: Studies in the Ideology of Advanced Industrial Society* (Boston: Beacon Press, 1964).

were encouraging poverty. Galbraith, in his *Affluent Society* book, asserted that poverty would be eradicated if the poor were willing to travel to places with jobs. This too was another conventional wisdom, sourced from textbook economics. Social workers, civil rights activists and many others knew that America's postwar boom had not eliminated need but their knowledge did not make poverty into a live political priority. What it took to change this state of affairs was a book review in the *New Yorker*.

At the turn of the 1960s, several studies backed by University research institutes and foundations turned to the problem of poverty.[8] The scale and severity of deprivation in the United States began to come into focus and one contribution above all became the icon of this shift in the civic consciousness, Michael Harrington's 1962 book, *The Other America: Poverty in the United States*. Like a handful of books of that period, Rachel Carson's *Silent Spring* and a little later Alex Haley's *Autobiography of Malcolm X*, *The Other America*, holds the status of a landmark in storytelling about the 'sixties' and is mentioned in numerous genres of historical writing, political, cultural and autobiographical.[9] At the time of writing *Other America*, Harrington was a contributor to the literate magazine *Dissent* and editor of the Socialist Party's biweekly *New America*, he therefore did not have a reputation that would recommend him for the best-seller lists. One explanation for the success of the book was that when he asked the question of why poverty in America could be so extensive and yet so invisible, Harrington's answer was compelling. He told his middle-class readers that they were enjoying an unprecedented period of prosperity and that same prosperity had removed them from encountering the other Americans of inner city and southern deprivation and neglect. Harrington approached his suburbanite readers with a Christian moral mission.

The influence of *Other America* may have also been independent of its sales record. One of the repeated myths about the book was that Ted Sorensen read a book review of *Other America* in the *New Yorker* and shared it with the President (JF Kennedy) animating a will to make poverty a focus of policy. However bright, well informed and witty, Dwight MacDonald's review of *Other America* is not a plausible force to move politics. During the election Kennedy had campaigned in West Virginia where the closure of mines and steel mills had left a trail of economic devastation. One of his campaign pledges was to break from the orthodoxy of the Eisenhower administration of relying on policies directed at national prosperity (and aggregate demand management) and rejecting measures that might steer business into certain regions and industries or to train the unemployed for jobs.

As early as the 1920s, American public policy had been concerned with unemployment trailing economic progress, the obsolescence of those trained for an earlier technological age.[10] The rising unemployment of the late 1950s seemed to fit

---

[8] See Huret's *Experts War on Poverty* for an itinerary of these contributions and discussions. For a near contemporary review see Cowell Gallaway, 'The Foundations of the War on Poverty', *American Economic Review*, 55, no 1 (1965): 122–31.

[9] On Harrington and the book's influence see Maurice Isserman, *The Other American: The Life of Michael Harrington* (New York: PublicAffairs, 2000).

[10] *Recent Economic Changes in the United States: Report of the Committee on Recent Economic Changes of the President's Conference on Unemployment, Herbert Hoover, Chairman*. Two volumes, (New York: McGraw-Hill Book Company, 1929). William Fielding Ogburn, leading sociologist at the University of Chicago is the best-known author speaking about the phenomena of 'cultural lag'.

that picture since it was concentrated in industrial fields facing automation. After a protracted negotiation in Congress, the Manpower Development and Training Act of 1962 became law on 15 March. The Secretary of Labour was made responsible for researching the nation's skill development and providing regular updates through an annual 'Manpower Report' submitted to Congress. The Secretary was authorized to plan and coordinate occupational job training programmes for the unemployed but also for the part-time employed, for individuals who had exhausted unemployment benefits, and for those without prior work experience. Trainees were given generous allowances of up to 52 weeks to conduct their training.[11]

To make poverty a moral and political concern was well aligned with the Kennedy's administration's policy preferences: rather than regulate business which would be criticized as undermining free enterprise, the government offered more services and better support to workers and their families. Training and education was not a route to immediate results but it was easier to defend against an oppositional Congress.

In *Other America*, Harrington cautioned that no piecemeal policy would measure up to the task. Changes to minimum wage, job training programmes or redesigns of the welfare safety net would fail because poverty was a 'culture, a way of life and feeling'. Poverty was a totalizing experience arising from a 'web of disabilities', afflicting people who at once lacked education and skill, had poor physical and mental health, bad housing, and no prospects or ambitions. If Harrington was right then fixes to markets or state infrastructure would not free individuals and communities from the web, it would take a whole programme of actions.

Other America elevated poverty to the nation's attention. Harrington was not carried with his cause to the halls of power, his preferred policy response was guaranteed income which was trialled but never widely implemented.[12] Social scientists in the White House, in particular economists and statisticians at the Council of Economic Advisers, were ready and willing to frame poverty into a set of policies that matched Kennedy's wider policy agenda. In their reports they gave figures to the number of poor and characterized their needs and set out the programs that the President would bring to Congress. The President was assassinated in Dallas on 22 November 1963, but surprisingly little changed in the course that had been drawn. As he took up the Presidency, Lyndon B. Johnson saw eradicating poverty as a political goal he could make his own.

---

[11] Gladys Roth Kremen, 'MTDA: The Origins of the Manpower Development and Training Act of 1962', Department of Labor Historical Office, 1974. https://www.dol.gov/general/aboutdol/history/mono-mdtatext#:~:text=The%20Manpower%20Development%20and%20Training%20Act%20of%201962%20endeavored%20to,of%20automation%20and%20technological%20change (accessed 5 April 2022). The longer story is fascinating. It involves Senator Paul Douglas and his campaign over many years to introduce a bill on job training. Douglas was also instigator to some of those early studies on poverty.

[12] Harrington alongside Gunnar Myrdal, Dwight MacDonald, Todd Gitlin and Tom Hayden, to name only a few of the names, signed the Triple Revolution report which was issued as the Economic Opportunity Act was becoming law.

War on poverty

When in 1964 President Johnson declared 'war on poverty' he did not expect poverty to fight back.[13] There were skirmishes with anti-welfare advocates that obstructed the plans of the White House. The deadlock was resolved when Johnson appointed Sargent Shriver to lead the effort. The brother-in-law of the assassinated President and originator of the Peace Corps put together by compromise policies that reinforced the welfare safety net with loans, legal aid, and education to the most disadvantaged and that empowered community groups with grants and volunteers.

Less consequential, but indicative of the tide of conservative opinion, were the assaults by intellectuals over the numbers of the poor, their types and location. *Other America* claimed that about 40 to 50 million Americans, one-quarter of the population, lived in poverty. MacDonald in the *New Yorker* working with a poverty line of 4,000 dollars of income for families, and 2,000 dollars of income for individuals, settled on 42,5 million. The Council of Economic Advisers, adopting a 3,000 dollar poverty line, estimated 9.3 million families in need, about a fifth of the population, more than 30 million persons. Countering those estimates, Rose Friedman argued that 3,000 was too high a poverty line and settled on a much lower figure of 2,200 per family and halving the estimate of the White House economists.[14]

Despite its name, the Economic Opportunity Act was not primarily economic. Its emblematic Job Corps programme was under funded, and like its Neighbourhood Youth Corps was directed at the young. The most distinctive work of the Office of Economic Opportunity (OEO) was its community action programmes, including preschool education, legal services and health programmes.

Shriver led the negotiation, rollout and administration of the OEO but another figure in the intellectual history of the policies stands out as ally and antagonist. Daniel Patrick Moynihan was Assistant Secretary of Labour for Policy, Planning and Research in Johnson's administration. In 1965 as he was about to leave that role, Moynihan published *The Negro Family: The Case For National Action*, a report that ignited a controversy of national proportions. Like Harrington, Moynihan wrote about a culture of poverty. He noted that many African American families were led by women, often single, divorced or unmarried, and these women were too busy earning a meagre income to emotionally nurture their children. Matriarchy was a 'social disorganization', a legacy of slavery and discrimination, that fostered pathological behavioural traits,

---

[13] 'War' was the unifying metaphor of Johnson's presidency and this social policy diverted attention only briefly from another unpopular and escalating conflict. Many at the time and since, argued that Johnson's war in Vietnam received far more support than the war on poverty as attention and resources were concentrated on the former in detriment of the latter.

[14] Council of Economic Advisers, *Economic Report of the President* (Washington: United States Government Printing Office, 1964). Rose Friedman, *Poverty: Definition and Perspectives* (Washington: American Enterprise Institute, 1965). The last word should go to Mollie Orshansky, one of the most significant and not sufficiently celebrated experts of inequality within the US administration, 'Counting the Poor: Another Look at the Poverty Profile', *Social Security Bulletin*, 28, no. 1 (1965): 3–29. Working from four definitions, Orshansky arrived at a fairly consistent number of between 33.4 to 34.6 million Americans in poverty, out of a population of 187,2 million.

such as the search for instant gratification of young black youths, the common euphemism for complaints over petty crime, truancy and absenteeism. Moynihan had intended the report to press the Johnson administration to go beyond civil rights and heed the call of African American leaders towards economic rights, but his description of African American families proved toxic. Very quickly the President disowned the report, as Moynihan was accused of being a racist and of blaming the victim.[15] As Moynihan's report was read in a myriad of ways, then and now, it signalled a key moment in the war on poverty, when after only one year of activity the focus shifted to African Americans and their communities.

Moynihan called attention to a culture of poverty but his conception, of 'social organization', was different from Harrington's 'web of disabilities'. Harrington was posing the problem of why poverty was so difficult to eradicate, anticipating that the best designed interventions would be disabled by the combined pull of other registers of deprivation, i.e. to offer someone a job without healthcare, or healthcare without a job, or both without adequate housing. Moynihan placed the difficulties deep within family structures where a past of oppression had left a damaging imprint. To him, it was morally and politically right to reorganize African American communities and families and it was eminently achievable, the first and most important task was to give employment, and a family wage, to black males. Moynihan brought the poverty discussion back to jobs and their quality.

Alongside these two conceptions there was a third meaning to the phrase culture of poverty, bound to the writings of anthropologist Oscar Lewis. In a series of related studies of Puerto Rican and Mexican families, Lewis argued that behaviours by the poor that appeared morally flawed or civically injurious were adaptations to circumstances of want and uncertainty.[16] The choices of the poor made sense for Lewis and the poor were neither restive nor helpless when facing chains of deprivation or legacies of a colonial past. The culture of poverty was therefore not an enemy combatant, a causal chain to be broken.

Differences on how to conceive the culture of poverty did not develop into open disagreement. The opposite is closer to the truth, the conceptions intermingled in use.[17]

---

[15] Daniel Geary, *Beyond Civil Rights: The Moynihan Report and Its Legacy* (Philadelphia: University of Pennsylvania Press, 2015). The Moynihan report and its immediate critical readings can be found in *The Moynihan Report and the politics of controversy*, eds. Lee Rainwater and William Yancey. (Boston: Massachusetts Institute of Technology Press, 1967).

[16] For Lewis, the culture of poverty was not disorganization, not deprivation, or absence of something, it was a positive, without which the poor could hardly carry on. The key features of the culture for Lewis were: strong feelings of marginality, of helplessness, of dependency and inferiority, high incidence of material deprivation, of orality, and of weak ego structure, confusion of sexual identification, lack of impulse control, strong present time orientation, with little ability to defer gratification and to plan for the future, sense of resignation and fatalism, belief in male superiority, high tolerance for psychological pathologies of all sorts. These features often appeared in clusters. Oscar Lewis, 'The culture of poverty', in *On Understanding Poverty* ed. Daniel P. Moynihan (New York. Basic Books, 1968-9), 187-200.

[17] Moynihan in 1968 published a collection of essays that hinted at a genealogy for his ideas, with mentions to Oscar Lewis, and included some of its critics such as Herbert Gans and Otis Dudley Duncan, *On understanding poverty*. Further supporters of the idea were Edward Banfield, *The Unheavenly City* (Boston: Little, Brown, and Company, 1970); Ben Baruch Seligman, *Permanent poverty: An American syndrome* (Chicago: Quadrangle Books, 1968).

They had much in common. Neither overtly blamed the victim, the focus on culture allowed these authors to look past the usual complaints over vice, unruliness and various other personal failings. And yet, events in 1966–8 seemed to suggest the poor were unwilling to accept the opportunities offered to them and were not without blame for their predicament. Counter to the assumptions of liberal elites, aiding and empowering deprived communities did not usher appreciation for authority or a declaration of loyalty to conventional American values. The press reporting on the race riots of 1967 found that Job Corps and OEO-connected persons had joined in the looting. The undeserving poor had returned into public discourse. The outcome was another round of compromises with conservatives in Congress and more constraints to working in the field.[18] Shriver resigned in defeat on 12 April 1968 (his penance was to become Ambassador to France).

It was against these cultural readings that economists contributed rival explanations for the deep rooting of poverty. Rather than looking at the once 'invisible' sites of squalor, urban ghettos, 'broken' families, and dysfunctional communities, economists turned to another opaque site, firms and their labour politics.

Economists were involved in those early studies that brought the problem of poverty into the open and economists shaped the design of the 'war on poverty' policies[19] but when speaking for their discipline their answer to poverty was Keynesian styled, aggregate demand management. That campaign for countercyclical fiscal policy culminated in the tax cuts that in 1964–5 rapidly reduced unemployment.[20] It was labour economists not macroeconomists that entered the scene in the late 1960s, as the war on poverty floundered in its public image and in its self-confidence. It is at this juncture that the poverty question is reframed as a question over the value of labour. But at the same time that labour economists spoke to social policy, social policy changed labour economics and the question of value of labour expanded beyond how wages were set to include the devaluing of labour and the engineering of labour types.

Race, segment and gender

Academic economics of the 1950s was gripped by dualism, between nations and within them. The Cold War provided a stark geopolitical binary that gave life to the fields of comparative economic systems and international relations. Mature industrial nations were themselves dual in that private and public enterprises coexisted. And one influential model of economic growth described developing economies as made up of two sectors, one advanced and one traditional (usually described as industrial and agricultural) operating in distinct logics.

---

[18] David Zarefsky, *President Johnson's War on Poverty* (Tuscaloosa: University of Alabama Press, 1986).
[19] See Huret, *Experts War on Poverty*.
[20] Tiago Mata, 'Trust in Independence: The identities of Economists in Business Magazines, 1945–1970', *Journal of the History of the Behavioral Sciences*, 47, no. 4 January (2011): 359–79; Beatrice Cherrier, 'How to Write a Memo to Convince a President: Walter Heller, Policy-Advising, and the Kennedy Tax Cut', *Œconomia*, 9, no. 2 (2019): 315–35.

The discovery of dualism in the labour market coincided with this appetite for binary models. The earliest distinction was between internal and external markets for labour. The markets described by neoclassical/conventional economics were external to firms: supply and demand determined wages in the marketplace and individual worker characteristics were matched to jobs. Labour economists in the early 1950s noted that within firms another set of rules regulated labour. Those rules were administrative and independent of movements in supply and demand. One of the earlier formulations of this idea was by a scholar at the University of California, Berkeley.[21] A decade later, as these ideas took a new form, Clark Kerr had risen to the office of President of the University of California system and was known across the nation as the antagonist of the 1964 Free Speech Movement. Those that would rework this distinction were on the other corner of the country, the former students of Harvard Professor John T. Dunlop.[22]

In 1970, Michael Piore and Peter Doeringer wrote an influential report for the Office of Manpower Policy, Evaluation and Research of the U.S. Department of Labour.[23] The Office was a creation of the 1962 Manpower Development and Training Act. In their report Piore and Doeringer remade the internal/external distinction into a primary/secondary dichotomy. *Primary* jobs required and developed stable working habits, with skills acquired on the job, wages were high and there were opportunities for advancement. *Secondary* jobs were characterized by high turnover, no learning and low wages. Doeringer and Piore observed that those secondary jobs were filled by those drawn from the ranks of the poor. The report offered no causal story for how or why such stark distinctions had emerged.

A widely accepted view among economists, associated with the writings of Gary Becker, was that the market economy was remedial of discrimination.[24] Competition would over time bankrupt the racists who would incur higher costs by not hiring the best person for the job, or by refusing to pay them a wage matching their productivity. But what if jobs made workers? Doeringer and Piore documented that income differentials did not match pre-existing skill differences, or workers' investment in education (the common proxy to human capital). Their alternative explanation was that training happened on the job and therefore employers' recruitment policies were the best explanation for the gaps in income.

---

[21] Clark Kerr, 'Balkanization of Labor Markets', in *Labor mobility and economic opportunity*, eds. E. W. Bakke et al. (Cambridge: M.I.T. Press, 1954), 92–110, somewhat prefigured in his Clark Kerr, 'Labor Markets: Their Character and Consequences', *American Economic Review*, 40, no. 2 (1950): 278–91.
[22] Dunlop alongside Kerr was a seminal contributor to this study of administrative labor markets, first in John T. Dunlop 'The Task of Contemporary Wage Theory', in *New Concepts in Wage Discrimination*, eds George W. Taylor and Frank C. Pierson (New York: McGraw-Hill, 1957), 117–39, and later expanded in his *Industrial relations systems* (New York: Holt, 1958). Dunlop was Professor at Harvard from 1938 to 1984 and served as Gerald Ford's Secretary of Labour in 1975–6 and resigned when his work as arbitrator in wages disputes floundered.
[23] The report was published the following year as Peter B. Doeringer and Michael J. Piore, *Internal labor markets and manpower analysis* (Lexington, Mass.: Heath, 1971).
[24] The so called 'new labour economics' was the work of many scholars but University of Chicago Gary S. Becker is often presented as the intellectual leader, largely out of the bold contributions, Gary S Becker, *Human Capital* (New York: National Bureau of Economic Research, 1964) and Id., *The economics of discrimination* (Chicago: University of Chicago Press, 1957).

The report offered a depressing lesson to the Department of Labour. The Office of Manpower Research was charged to evaluate what educational programmes might reskill the long-term unemployed for employability. Doeringer and Piore concluded that those programmes were futile. Instead, they proposed a negative income tax for those stuck in the secondary markets. Their preferred long-term policies would focus on the 'demand for labour' targeting racial and other discriminations in job searches, encouraging union organization and collective bargaining in the secondary markets and using public jobs as a way to lift people from their labour market trap.

The internal market argument of the 1950s had cautioned that capitalism was more administrative than the picture provided in standard economics and in Cold War propaganda. The dual labour market hypothesis of the 1960s took that notion further suggesting that even external markets were not a sphere of liberty where workers would receive what they were due. These markets rather than correcting prejudice were possibly the source of discrimination.

The dual labour market proposal was linked to the war on poverty in telling ways. It originated in a report directed at the failure of the labour training policies started in 1962, expanded with the 1964 OEO, and by 1969 ran by the Department of Labour. The report's description of how markets enabled discrimination built upon arguments of poverty as a culture. The secondary markets for labour recruited those that had no choice but to accept heavy work discipline and precarity and reinforced those cultural traits that prevented those workers from seeking better alternatives. But the labour economists did not believe that culture was to blame or that changing culture by empowerment, education or training would help. Oversight on employers and their practices with stronger unions or creating public jobs, were the ways to improve the lives and incomes of those in-and-out of work and the working poor.

With labour market discrimination replacing the culture of poverty, the politics of how to eradicate poverty changed. It was this reorientation that drew in radical economists.

Academic and labour militants

In 1970 radical social science was a novel invention. Although the term 'radical' has a distinguished genealogy in North American and Western thought, its meaning was rescripted by the campus-based New Left. One organization, leader of the national student movement, was responsible for these changes: the Students for Democratic Society (SDS). It was within SDS, and the initiatives it engendered, that the ideals of radical professionals and also of radical social scientists were forged.[25]

Radical economics was becoming a viable identity when SDS was breaking apart. In 1969, the more agitational wings of the campus Left adopted Third World socialism as political strategy, groups like Progressive Labour and the Revolutionary Youth

---

[25] Kirkpatrick Sale, *SDS* (New York: Vintage Books, 1974).

Movement.[26] These small would-be parties or 'revolutionary party formations', chose as main priorities labour organizing, and seizing the leadership of key activist unions.[27] The engagement with labour I am interested in this essay draws me not to the New Leftists who turned to Mao Tse-Tung and fantasies of armed revolution, but to those more conventionally holding academic appointments and who served as advisers to unions and social movements. They too looked to labour with bold ambitions but they organized through learned societies like the Union for Radical Political Economics, and scholarly publications, like *Radical America*.

The group that radically reinterpreted the dual labour market hypothesis was made up by junior professors and graduate students at Harvard and at MIT.[28] Some of them had worked with Doeringer and Piore as research staff for the 1970 report. They travelled to OEO employment offices to interview applicants, to businesses running training programmes, and to the poorer neighbourhoods in Boston to collect and later code employment histories. Several of them later received further funding from the Department of Labour to work on their PhDs.[29] Their research was embedded in the social state and its bureaucracy. They too were workers in training funded by the public purse and the label they chose for their contribution, segmented labour market theory, hints at a technocratic orientation befitting the statist framing.[30]

In 1973, as a capstone to their grant and PhDs, radicals hosted a conference at Harvard and later published the proceedings as a volume. Although there are other source writings, this volume best captures the early formulation of their theory.[31] Radicals adopted the distinction between primary and secondary markets but added further segments. Primary markets in their schema were also split between subordinate and independent. Independent primary markets were those that prized problem-solving, creativity and initiative from workers, often adopting professional standards of work. These workers could choose their employment and its terms. Subordinate primary markets were not so free and the work life was strictly disciplined and patterned, encouraging personality characteristics of dependability, responsiveness to rules and authority, and acceptance of a firm's goals. All along the three-step hierarchy of markets (primary independent, primary subordinate, secondary) there were further

---

[26] Max Elbaum, *Revolution in the Air: Sixties Radicals turn to Lenin, Mao and Che* (London: Verso Books, 2002). The other major group was the Weather Underground who went on an ultimately self-destructive campaign of terror which they hoped would trigger a popular uprising.

[27] Kieran W. Taylor, *Turn to the Working Class: the New Left, Black Liberation, and the U.S. Labor Movement, 1967-1981*, PhD Dissertation (Chapel Hill: University of North Carolina, 2017).

[28] Glen Cain, 'The Challenge of Dual and Radical Theories of the Labor Market to Orthodox Theory', *American Economic Review*, 65, no. 2 (1975): 16–22.

[29] On the data collection, personal communication with Michael Reich, 2 December 2021. The grant from the Office of Manpower Research had reference 21-25-73-18, and concluded in 1973.

[30] Their argument was honed while teaching a popular course for Harvard's general education programme, 'Social Sciences 125. The Capitalist Economy: Conflict and Power'. See Richard C. Edwards, Arthur MacEwan and Staff of Social Sciences 125, 'A Radical Approach to Economics: Basis for a New Curriculum', *The American Economic Review*, 60, no. 2 (1970): 352–63; Tiago Mata, 'Migrations and Boundary Work: Harvard, Radical Economists, and the Committee on Political Discrimination', *Science in Context*, 22, no. 1 (2009): 115–43.

[31] Richard Edwards, Michael Reich and David M. Gordon (eds), *Labor Market Segmentation* (Lexington, Mass.: Heath, 1975).

segments by 'race-types' and by 'gender-types'. These later refinements were the most consequential. Race and gender were moved to the heart of the analysis and one-third of the contributions to the 1975 collected volume were on women's work.

The Harvard/MIT group was not the first to research labour markets from a New Left perspective. It was readily acknowledged that Barry Bluestone and others had noted the play of hierarchy a couple of years earlier.[32] Bluestone was the son of a United Auto Workers chief economist, and was a serial organizer, involved at a very young age with SDS, founder of the Union for Radical Political Economics and its first secretary. Bluestone would earn his reputation with the influential book *The deindustrialisation of America*, co-authored with Bennett Harrison in 1982. In the early 1970s as he looked at labour markets, Bluestone borrowed the language of core and periphery made famous by Immanuel Wallerstein's world systems approach. The Harvard/MIT outlook had many advantages over the Michigan one, it had links to ongoing labour economics discussions, it involved more scholars, it had better backing, organizationally and in funding, and was as a result more visible. Finally, and as I have wanted to highlight, the research of the Cambridge radicals spoke to the puzzles of social policy.

The spokespersons for segmented labour market theory were Richard Edwards, David Gordon and Michael Reich. The title of theory they claimed for their contribution, had to be earned. Doeringer and Piore had no account of how the duality of labour markets had formed. The radical economists' explanation in 1973/5 relied on a simple historical narrative. They contrasted an earlier nineteenth-century age of free market capitalism to an oligopolistic age, from the Gilded Age to the Great Depression. In that half century, big corporations gained extensive reach into product and factor markets and stopped fearing competition against one another. The relations between capitalists became patterned by concentration and coordination. The most significant threat to the long-run stability of capitalism in the age of big business became organized labour and a socialist alternative. To forestall that threat, the captains of industry differentiated the experiences of workers to undermine community of interests and identity in opposition to capitalism. It was not a complete and satisfactory explanation, and Edwards, Gordon and Reich promised to return to the topic in later works. Taking a phrase from military strategy, they summarized their intuitions as organized business's strategy of 'divide and conquer'.

Education had been at the heart of the 'new labour economics' of human capital and it was a pillar of public policy both for cushioning the disruptions of modernity and for levelling economic opportunity. By contrast, for radicals education was a servant in a regime of discrimination and inequality. The critique of education was an enduring theme of the New Left: it was in the Port Huron Statement and at the moment of creation of SDS and it was implicit and explicit in the anti-war teach-ins, in the Free

---

[32] See for instance, Bluestone, Barry; William M. Murphy and Mary Stevenson, *Low wages and the working poor* (Ann Arbor, Mich.: Institute of Labor and Industrial Relations, The University of Michigan-Wayne State University, 1973); Howard M. Wachtel, 'Capitalism and Poverty in America: Paradox or Contradiction?', *American Economic Review*, 62, no. 2 (1972): 187–94; Francine Blau Weisskoff, 'Women's Place' in the Labor Market', *American Economic Review*, 62, no. 2 (1972): 161–6. See also Harry Braverman, *Labor and Monopoly Capital: The Degradation of Work in the Twentieth Century* (New York: Monthly Review Press, 1974).

University movement, and the New University Conference initiative of the mid-1960s. The radical economists transformed that criticism into a research agenda. Instead of picturing educational institutions as grey sites of boredom and irrelevance, they described them as ante-chambers preparing workers for a life in capitalism, formatting subjectivities for obedience, and fostering perceptions of difference in abilities and skills where there were none. Educational credentials determined job prospects by regularizing skill requirements for jobs, and employers were active architects of educational reform to ensure institutions served these channelling functions.[33] Turning the argument of public education on its head, radicals believed that the segmented labour markets reached upstream to mould educational institutions to their image.

In their labour theory radicals attempted to synthesize various concerns of the New Left. Educational reform, feminism, civil rights and ultimately labour militancy were joined together into a stage theory of American capitalism. Intellectual historian Dan Rodgers described the long 1970s as an age where the American polity fractured into diverging identities. If we accept that picture then radicals were trying to rework the pieces onto a new whole, one where differences could be erased because they were historical artefacts and a calculated deception. Their political imagination was old fashioned, willing to reveal and undermine one of the 'principal barriers to united anticapitalist opposition among workers'.[34]

In their explanation of how labour markets had segmented, Edwards, Gordon and Reich portrayed race and gender as instruments for fostering dissension amongst workers, and therefore subordinate to the dynamics of class politics. The primacy given to labour as the privileged historical agent of social change has deep roots in socialist doctrine, with the belief that strength in numbers ensured clarity of purpose. Even in those early writings hopeful for unity, the prospect of a unified labour movement must have seemed implausible. But if that horizon may have seemed far removed, their theory still offered them a powerful critique of social policy and an alternative origin story for the culture of poverty. And it offered a new language to make sense of an unruly labour movement that like the radical economists, was confronting authority and convention.

The crisis of organized labour in the United States in the last quarter of the twentieth century has been chronicled many times. Union activists, political scientists, historians and economists (including the radical cohort I have been discussing) have disagreed over the causes of the contraction in membership, militancy and political influence. Some have paid attention to shifts in the political economy, the triad of deindustrialization, financialization and stagflation, paired with changes to the coalitions of voters that sustained the Democratic and Republican parties.[35] Others

---

[33] See Gintis Herbert, 'Education, Technology, and Characteristics of Worker Productivity', *American Economic Review*, 61 no. 2 (1971): 266–79 and in particular Samuel Bowles and Herbert Gintis, *Schooling in Capitalist America* (New York: Basic Books, 1975).

[34] Michael Reich, David M. Gordon and Richard C. Edwards , 'Dual Labor Markets: A Theory of Labor Market Segmentation', *American Economic Review*, 63, no. 2 (1973): 359–65.

[35] See Judith Stein, *Pivotal Decade: How the United States Traded Factories for Finance in the Seventies* (New Haven: Yale Press, 2010). Radical economists themselves have looked back at this moment and sought to understand what they had missed, that impulse originated the literature known as Social Structures of Accumulation.

noted a cultural shift happening at mid-decade, a move away from a time of optimism and collective ambition to one of disenchantment and individualism.[36] Those are the views from today. In the 1960s the data on union membership was unequivocal about a trend of decline but there was also evidence of greater militancy and political ambition.

In the late 1960s and early 1970s, the American trade union movement remained a political force to be reckoned with. In 1970, after five years of boycotts and strikes, the United Farmworkers led by Cesar Chavez won recognition and collective contracts from twenty-six major grape growers. The year of 1970 saw about 400 major work stoppages involving two and a half million workers, a record in labour activity in the postwar era. These included a nationwide strike against General Electric, a Post Office walkout that required US troops to sort the mail and the longest walkout since 1946 at General Motors. This was in part a global phenomenon, in Europe similar records were being set and the examples of alliances between youths and workers there helped energize a younger and more combative generation of organizers (several Vietnam war vets) in the USA. These organizers led a string of wildcat strikes, many focused on issues of control and supervision on the shop floor rather than 'bread and butter' issues.

In 1974 union activity began to decline sharply. Economic calamities washed through the USA in quick succession: the collapse of the Bretton Woods system and the devaluation of the dollar, inflation and price controls, the oil crisis and a food price crisis, recession and more inflation, a political scandal that led the President to resign. These events plagued those that radicals had described as being most vulnerable, those in the secondary labour markets, but also the youngest agitators, the rank-and-file of 1969–73 union insurgencies.

Radical scholars were animated with the ambition of creating a more inclusive and egalitarian democracy in America. They were primed to look with suspicion at the discourses guiding public policy. When they encountered the beneficiaries of employment policies, of Job Corps and manpower training programmes, they saw hopelessness, individuals who regardless of their efforts in personal improvement were given no chance at a better job. Radicals' attention and theoretical imagination went to study business power which they saw as creating labour kinds and then elevating or diminishing them. In that early 1970s work the focus of their research went to a proof of existence, attempting statistical analyses and industry narratives that demonstrated the breakup of class into segments.[37] It took Edwards, Gordon and Reich a decade before they published a fuller theoretical account.

---

[36] Jefferson R. Cowie. *Stayin Alive. The 1970s and the Last Days of the Working Class* (New York: The New Press, 2010). Cowie's views build on many of the media commentary and some of the popular sociology of the period describing the 1970s as half 1960s and half 1980s, and Ronald Reagan's election as identifying of a new mood.

[37] Class did not disappear from the segmented market analysis, but it was muted. In 1972 David Gordon attempted to work out a reconciliation of the radical outlook and the Marxist one. To achieve this, he introduced the term 'strata', the approach did not catch on. David Gordon, *Theories of Poverty and Unemployment: Orthodox, Radical and Dual Labor Market Perspectives* (Lanham: Lexington Books, 1972).

Questions of political value

I began this essay noticing an echo of Hobsbawn's 1960 essay on the role of custom and institutions in the valuing of labour in the theories of radical economists of the 1970s. One reasonably expects that when economists get to work on a theory, custom and institutions are dropped in favour of a mathematical model of a toy economy. What Edwards, Gordon and Reich meant by theory was an expansion of their 1973/75 historical teaser. In a book of 1982, *Segmented Work, Divided Workers*, they adopted the idiom of 'social structures of accumulation', a perspective that Gordon was developing with others and had kinship to Marxist-inspired work by French economists, known as the regulationist school. They constructed a periodization of the regulation of labour and the structure of labour markets that was tied to long wave theory, an idea that circulated on the left of economics thanks to the writings of another European Marxist, Ernest Mandel. While the radical economists had fleshed out their argument about the past and reached for yet another synthesis of intuitions and concepts on the left of economics, their explanatory achievement earned them no greater insight on the present or the future.[38] The contrary was true.

In the early 1970s writings they were optimistic for labour unity. In 1972 they equivocated on the political strategy, the recommendation was wait and see. Acknowledging that a socialist future for America was nowhere in sight, they argued that the future politics would emerge on the shop floor in interstitial battles over control of labour. After several hundred pages detailing the construction of a system of power and discrimination, operating at multiple levels, – what they now called a social structure of accumulation – it seemed implausible to expect it to suddenly reset into a blank slate. The future would have to be built from those discriminating market structures in the unpredictable interplay of power between firms, markets, unions and the unruly.

Although they did not phrase it as such, radicals had miscalculated. They had predicted a labour insurgency in times of accelerated social dislocation that had drained the resources of unions and of community groups. The miscalculation was political and analytical. The political miscalculation was to believe that the labour movement could federate the causes of the New Left. The demands of working women and working minorities because of the structures and traditions of discriminating markets and workplaces, could not be reconciled with those of the relatively more privileged, white male workers. Contemporary social science calls this intersectionality and it implies that unity must be achieved by a coalition of distinct agendas, none taking precedence over the others. Radicals would adopt that outlook but only after a decade resisting the idea. But there was also an analytical miscalculation. Radicals had shown that neither profit nor efficiency explained the career of American capitalism beyond the 1890s, it was instead the pursuit of safety against existential threat that led captains of industry to reshape markets and educational institutions. In the terms

---

[38] David Gordon, Richard Edwards, and Michael Reich, *Segmented Work, Divided Workers: The historical transformation of labor in the United States* (Cambridge, Mass.: Cambridge University Press, 1972).

made famous a decade later by two economic sociologists, it was the management of uncertainty that shaped institutional design.[39] Yet, radicals expected workers in the face of growing uncertainty to pick the most uncertain path of all, that of social revolution. Radicals were right that for economic rationality managing uncertainty is more important than maximizing gain, and if so then the labour movement in the middle years of the 1970s held ever more tightly to what it had, segmented markets and all, becoming in the literal sense of the word, conservative.

The legacy of segmented labour market theory for radicals' political imagination was to first place labour unity as a central political goal and then to replace it with a politics of alliance between movements. It was coalitions, the rainbow of race, class and gender that followed the disappointment of the mid-1970s. The writings on labour are a record of change in the political strategies of New Left intellectuals but this record also speaks to continuities. Perhaps the most significant, because it sets radicals apart from their conventional peers, was their interest in studying the lived experience of capitalism and how it shaped subjects. The kernel of their interest in labour markets was a desire to understand power and control.[40]

The question of the value of labour was posed in the 1960s as a puzzle of policy failure. The high rhetoric of the 'war on poverty' quickly unravelled into recrimination against the poor and their ways of being. The most important dimension of that value question was why there were so many mediocre jobs. Labour economists rejected the argument that the mediocre jobs existed because of the mediocre workers that filled them. The alternative, radical outlook was to counter the tradition of public policy that looked to workers and their skills or education and pay closer attention to institutions and custom of labour markets.

---

[39] Paul J. DiMaggio and Walter W. Powell, 'The Iron Cage Revisited: Institutional Isomorphism and Collective Rationality in Organizational Fields', *American Sociological Review*, 48, no. 2 (1983): 147–60. DiMaggio and Powell refer to institutional economics and the work of radicals on the economics of education.

[40] The economics of hierarchical control, a reading of bureaucratic practices, was the subject of the most significant essay published in radical economists' house journal, *Review of Radical Political Economics*, in its early years. As it so happens by another Harvard-based economist, Stephen A. Marglin, 'What Do Bosses Do? The Origins and Functions of Hierarchy in Capitalist Production', *Review of Radical Political Economics*, 6, Summer, no. 2 (1974): 60–112.

13

Rethinking the Concept of the Living Wage: Ontological Presuppositions of Emancipatory Action

Zoe Adams

1. Introduction

Inspired by a Marxian understanding of the nature, and dynamics, of capitalist labour markets, this chapter argues that underlying conceptions of the wage and implicit ontologies of capitalism have shaped not only the way in which questions of wage regulation have been framed and conceived, but also, how the concept of the *living wage* has been conceptualized, and deployed, in legal and political practice. To illustrate this argument and focusing the analysis on historical approaches to wage regulation in the UK, this article contrasts the Living Wage Policy that emerged in the late nineteenth and early twentieth century, with the modern, twenty-first century revival of that policy, in the form of the Living Wage Campaign associated with Citizens UK. It shows that, while the living wage concept was harnessed in the early twentieth century in a way that not only problematized the way in which wages were conceived but sought to link proposals for living wages with wider mobilizations oriented towards structural change; in the twenty-first century, the modern Living Wage Campaign has harnessed the concept for very different purposes, with very different implications. Seeing living wage policies as ends in themselves and failing to embed their justifications in a *structural* understanding of capitalism and the causes of low pay, the modern Living Wage Campaign risks reinforcing the causes of low pay, while undermining broader attempts to bring about the sort of changes that will be required to overcome it. This chapter concludes by arguing that only a political conception of the wage that expressly situates itself in a structural understanding of capitalism is capable of realizing the living wage's emancipatory potential; its potential to not merely improve life and work *in* capitalism; to *sustain* capitalism and its exploitative practices, but to do so in a way that actively contributes to wider attempts to *transcend* it.

The chapter will be structured as follows: section two introduces two conceptions of the wage, an economic and a political conception, and explains the ontological assumptions underpinning each. It then explores the implications of these understandings for conceptions and approaches to the *Living Wage,* teasing out their normative implications. Section three then contrasts the Living Wage Policy developed by the Independent Labour Party (ILP) in the early twentieth century with the modern reincarnation of that policy in the form of the Living Wage Campaign. Section four concludes.

2. The Wage

2.1: Preliminary definitions

For the purposes of this chapter, the concept of the Wage refers to a social category that is unique, and integral to capitalism. It is, on the one hand, an expression of the monetary form assumed by workers' (collective) subsistence, and, on the other hand, an expression of the cost, to Capital (collectively), of reproducing the labour power of those workers in existing conditions. The gap between the Wage – the value advanced to purchase workers' labour power – and the value realized when the commodities produced by that labour power are sold in the market, expresses the amount of surplus value produced in a given production period, and which is thereby available for appropriation (as profit, rent, interest and/or taxation).[1]

The existence of surplus value, and as such, of the Wage itself, presupposes the historical processes through which workers were forcefully separated from access to the non-market means of production and subsistence, a separation in which law, and legal institutions, play a material part. It is this separation that brings into being the labour market, the sphere of interaction in which labour power is exchanged for wages (lower case), where wages express the costs to employers of purchasing the labour power of particular workers in the labour market, and, at the same time, the sum which workers are (contractually) entitled to receive in exchange for the labour power they provide.

While the social category of the Wage presupposes the exchanges of work and wages made between individual employers and workers, the sum total of wages paid by individual employers will often be less than the total value of the Wage. This is because the market is just one of the mechanisms through which the reproduction of labour power is mediated, such that wages are just one element – the market-based element – of workers' subsistence in capitalism. This market-based element is supplemented by various non-market elements, including direct cash transfers, and/or public services, funded out of accumulated capital appropriated by way of taxation, but not by individual employers.

The precise distribution of the Wage as between the market and non-market elements will vary, depending on the institutional and social history of the particular society in question, and on the particular way in which the class struggle has concretely played out: as workers, and employers, react to the way in which capitalism's structural contradictions manifest and are experienced by them in the context of their everyday

---

[1] Karl Marx, *Capital*, vol. I, (Harmondsworth: Penguin/New Left Review, 1967 [1867]), 186.

practices. In the context of these struggles, the concept of the living wage has been harnessed, at various time, to express the normative premise that the non-market element of workers *monetary* income should be kept to a minimum, and that employers ought to bear the bulk of the monetary costs involved in reproducing the labour power of their own workers, their basic costs of living. However much public services, and other forms of collective provisioning might be necessary and/or desirable, then, not least to support and maintain workers, and their dependents, during periods when they are not in work; the living wage concept expresses the premise that employers should pay their own workers' wages that approximate, as far as possible, their basic, and immediate, costs of living.

2.2: The living wage and conceptions of wages

The living wage thus expresses the idea that the *market-based* element of workers' income ought to approximate workers' costs of living. Conclusions about how this normative premise might be realized, however, ultimately depend on how one understands the nature, and constitution, of wages, and thus, the relative 'roles', within that constitution, of the law, and the market. To illustrate this point, I want to distinguish between two competing approaches, or conceptions, of the wage. These two approaches do not refer to generally recognized categories of orthodox or heterodox wage-theories, rather, they are proposed as useful heuristic devices, to distinguish between categories, or groups, of wage theory based on their shared, ontological premises. In this respect, while what I refer to as 'economic' approaches tend to abstract labour markets from their wider socio-historical context, and as a result, implicitly presents wages as if they are independent from wider legal and political structures, other, 'political' approaches develop their conception of wages from an analysis of those structures, and so, are much more self-consciously aware of the labour market's legal, and political, foundations, as well as its historical specificity. The contrast I draw is one which is implicit in a number of chapters in this volume: for example, in the distinction drawn by Antonella Stirati, between the conception of wages often attributed to Adam Smith and other Classical Political Economists ('economic'), and that which can be gleaned from a careful reading of his work capable of taking into account the complexity of wage-bargaining and determination as it necessarily occurs in the context of capitalism ('political').

The economic conception of wages

The 'economic' conception of the wage sees the wage as the price of a particular commodity, labour power, which, like all prices, is determined by the inter-play of supply and demand – market forces.[2] From this perspective, the market is simply an expression of individuals' natural proclivity to engage in exchange, an emergent effect

---

[2] John Hicks, *The Theory of Wages*. (London: Palgrave Macmillan, 1963).

of the free, 'economic' decisions that autonomous actors make about what to buy, sell, and in what quantity.[3] Given that no (economically) rational actor, acting free from coercion, would decide to sell a commodity for less than it cost to (re)produce it; and given that no consumer would purchase a commodity if he/she could purchase it at a lower price elsewhere, we can expect, in a context of competition (i.e. in which all actors can act freely and with perfect information) that prices will converge around average costs of (re)production.

If we apply this analysis to the labour market, then, we can expect wages (conceived as the price of the commodity labour power) to converge, in the long-run, around the costs of living – the costs of reproducing labour power – of the average worker, and this means that if labour power is allocated *purely* by the pricing mechanism, and markets are operating competitively, we can expect an optimum allocation of labour power throughout society: maximum efficiency.

The economic conception of the wage recognizes the possibility that while wages might converge in the long-run around the costs of living of the average worker, this does not mean that the wages of each worker will be sufficient to cover the costs of living of that *particular* worker at a given time: all workers have different circumstances, skill levels and/or health conditions, such that what is appropriate for the average, may not be appropriate, in practice, for particular individuals.[4] This conception also recognizes, moreover, that wages will not necessarily cover the costs of living of even the average worker in the short run, given the scope for short-run fluctuations in supply and demand to temporally depress, and/or raise wages, of particular workers and/or groups. To avoid 'interfering' with the efficient process of market allocation, however, those adhering to an economic conception of the wage tend to argue in favour of non-market mechanisms as a way of solving this problem: as a way to top up wages to subsistence level – whether in the form of means tested cash transfers, and/or public services funded by way of taxation.[5] From this perspective, then, the only justification for directly regulating wages – through, for example, a legislative minimum wage – is in the case of a clearly identified market failure or imperfection, one which can be precisely identified and targeted. Legislation can, from this perspective, be seen to be merely substituting *actual* wage, the market-clearing wage, in place of the 'imperfect' or distorted wage, and so, reinforcing, rather than interfering with, the market.

The political conception of wages

The political conception of the wage, by contrast, agrees that wages *appear* to express the price of a commodity, and that this price *ought* to cover the costs of (re)producing

---

[3] Giulio Palermo, 'The Ontology of Economic Power in Capitalism: Mainstream Economics and Marx', *Cambridge Journal of Economics*, 31, no. 4 (2006): 539–61.
[4] This chapter does not discuss the complex relationship between skill and wage differentials. Here, skill is seen as a factor influencing worker need, rather than as something that potentially explains differences in wage-rates between particular groups, due to short-run fluctuations in the supply and demand of particular types of work.
[5] Zoe Adams, 'Understanding the Minimum Wage: Political Economy and Legal Form', *The Cambridge Law Journal*, 78, no. 1 (2019): 42–69.

labour power, but it argues that not only is this not the outcome of a natural and spontaneous process, but of a process which is brought about, and sustained, through law; but also, in reality, in the context of even a 'perfectly' competitive market, the wage will *systematically* fall short of workers' costs of living (both individual workers, and workers' generally) as a result of the peculiar nature of the labour commodity; *and* as a result of the nature of the structures which explain how the labour market itself comes to be.[6]

The political conception of the wage starts with the observation that the mediation of social relations by markets, and the allocation of society's collective labour time via the pricing mechanism – 'free competition' – is a by-product of the express exclusion of workers from access to the means of production and subsistence. Given that this exclusion is something that is brought about, and reproduced, by law, moreover, the precise nature and constitution of the market is a product of the nature of the legal institutions through which this exclusion is brought about, as well as of any additional mechanisms that may or may not have been introduced at various times with a view to regulating/shaping it. It is, in other words, contingent on legal and political decisions.[7] Different approaches to property and its protection; to contract and its interpretation and enforcement, as well as to the regulation of competition and legal capacity (etc.), all give rise to a different set of market conditions, influencing the *degree* of inequality of bargaining power between capital and labour, fundamentally shaping the competitive process by which a particular wage rate comes to be.

Given this, according to the political conception, the 'wage' that is 'set' by market forces not only presupposes the structural separation (of workers from the means of production) that is immanent and integral to capitalism, and thus, systematic, structural, coercion; but its content, or magnitude, is profoundly influenced by various legal and political decisions that could, within the confines of that structure, have been different.[8] This suggests that the market wage – the *actual* wage set in competitive conditions – can enjoy no privileged status as compared to a wage that is set by any other means – including, by means of a (democratically secured) political agreement. This would imply that a mandatory wage introduced by way of legislation cannot be said, a priori, to be any less efficient, or legitimate, than a wage rate that emerges 'through' the free play of so-called market forces.

The political conception of the wage not only challenges the naturalistic view of the wage and the market, it also offers an explanation for why we might expect the market wage to *systematically* deviate from workers' costs of living in practice – whether the costs of living of workers *generally*, taken as an average, or the costs of living of specific workers: something of which, as Stirati notes elsewhere in this volume, Adam Smith, and many other Classical Political Economists, were only too aware.[9] The first reason

---

[6] See Giulio Palermo, 'Power, Competition and the Free Trader Vulgaris', *Cambridge Journal of Economics*, 40, no. 1 (2016): 259–81.
[7] See Zoe Adams, *Labour and the Wage: A Critical Perspective* (Oxford, New York: Oxford University Press, 2020); Karl Klare, 'On Ruth Dukes, The Labour Constitution: The Enduring Idea of Labour Law', *Jurisprudence. An International Journal of Legal and Political Thought*, 9, no. 2 (2018): 1–6.
[8] Ibid.
[9] Adams, 'Understanding the Minimum Wage'.

relates to the unique nature of the commodity labour power that the exclusion of workers' from access to the means of production brings into being, and, in particular, the fact that the costs of reproducing the labour power purchased in the labour market cannot be identified independently from the costs of reproducing the worker – including, any of his/her dependents.[10] These costs depend not only on market conditions and the costs of purchasing consumption goods and services, moreover, but also, wider familial norms, health, personal circumstances, and a myriad of other factors 'invisible' to the market, and not directly mediated by exchange.[11] The costs of reproducing labour power also necessarily extend over the workers' entire life-course, during which time, there will be a number of periods when he is unable to work, and so, unable to receive any *market-based* income at all. This makes the market, if not inadequate, at least insufficient, to cover the costs of labour power's reproduction, such that *some form* of collectivization of those costs cannot be (sustainably) avoided.

It is not simply, however, that the reproduction of labour power involves costs not directly related to the consumption of that labour power in the production process – the necessity to reproduce the entire worker over time.[12] In addition to, and in part, related to this, the structural context in which decisions about the purchase and sale of labour power are made, prevent considerations about the *real* costs of labour power's immediate reproduction from being incorporated into the wage rate.[13] The assumption that prices converge around costs of (re)production is based on the premise that sellers will not sell at a price that does not cover their production costs; and buyers will not pay more than they have to, given the next best alternative. The problem, however, is that many workers often have little alternative but to accept *whatever wage is offered today*, even if there may, hypothetically, be a wage that better meets their needs available to them if they wait to see if they can get work *tomorrow*. The pressures of immediate survival thus often override workers' capacity to refuse wages that fall short of even their immediate needs, therefore, which means: first, that many workers simply do not have the capacity to meaningfully resist attempts to depress wages, and second, and relatedly, that information about their personal circumstances, and about wider societal conditions (which, as we saw above, influence the value of labour power), are unlikely to become embedded in the wage rate at all.[14] Given that there is a real incentive on employers to reduce wages to a minimum, in the name of their own economic survival,

---

[10] Judy Fudge, 'Labour as a "Fictive Commodity": Radically Reconceptualizing Labour Law', in *The Idea of Labour Law*, ed. Guy Davidov and Brian Langille, 120–36. There is an important gendered dimension to debates over the living wage, given its historical link with the family wage and the breadwinner model of the family. For a preliminary discussion, see: Michelle Barrett and Mary McIntosh, 'The "Family Wage": Some Problems for Socialists and Feminists', *Capital & Class*, 4, no. 2 (1980): 51–72; Anna Clark, 'The New Poor Law and the Breadwinner Wage: Contrasting Assumptions', *Journal of Social History*, 34, no. 2 (2000): 261–81.

[11] See Antonella Picchio, *Social Reproduction: The Political Economy of the Labour Market* (Cambridge: Cambridge University Press, 1992).

[12] See Zoe Adams, 'The EU Minimum Wage Directive: A Missed Opportunity?, *UK Labour Law*, 12 November 2020 [https://uklabourlawblog.com/2020/11/12/the-eu-minimum-wage-directive-a-missed-opportunity-by-zoe-adams/].

[13] See id., *Labour and the Wage*.

[14] See id., 'Understanding The Minimum Wage'.

(and/or short-run profitability) therefore, the result (given a context of competition) is that the wages of all workers will tend to be depressed, with potentially detrimental effects for the labour supply, workers' living standards and productivity – not to mention, potentially, consumer demand.[15]

The political conception of the wage thus generates an understanding of minimum wage regulation that frames the latter as an ontological necessity generated from within capitalism itself, a necessity driven by its structural contradictions, a condition for its sustainable reproduction. If the market cannot by itself guarantee the payment of a 'living wage', in other words, such a wage must be legally compelled. This was the basis of the case advanced by Beatrice Webb in favour of a minimum wage. The purpose of this minimum wage regulation would not, on this view, be to simply correct market failures, to substitute the actual wage rate by some hypothetical 'real' equilibrium wage. Rather, a political conception of the wage would imply that minimum wage regulation must be capable of bringing *into* the market, information about workers' *actual* costs of living, of aligning the wage with what workers actually *need* to survive in a given socio-historical context. Something which, as Stirati has usefully highlighted, Adam Smith himself recognized via his understanding of the 'natural' wage.

The Living Wage: Economic and political conceptualizations

The concept of the Living Wage has different implications depending on whether one subscribes to an economic, or political, conception of wages. For example, economic conceptions of the wage suggest that the competitive market sets the most *efficient* wage in the long-run. Certain articulations of this approach would concede, however, the possibility of market failures, creating inefficiencies, that may well have to be remedied in various ways, including, potentially, by law. But economic conceptions of the wage also do not *necessarily* imply that efficiency is to be elevated over all other values, and so, might accommodate non-economic arguments for a minimum wage set at subsistence level, even if they would tend to assume that such will inevitably imply a trade-off in terms of efficiency. Nor do economic conceptions necessarily imply that, *in the short run*, wages might not deviate from subsistence level; or even, that employers shouldn't voluntarily agree to pay higher wages, whenever they feel able and willing to do so in practice. Not only is a *voluntary* living wage entirely compatible with an economic conception of the wage – as rational employers would only pay such a wage where such is likely to lead to benefits in terms of future efficiency – then, but it is perfectly possible to argue that *as a matter of fairness*, employers ought to pay workers' a living wage whenever they can afford it, as a form of redistribution. The living wage can, and often has, therefore, featured in the normative arguments of even those who subscribe, explicitly or implicitly, to what this chapter would describe as an economic conception of the wage. Where this has been so, however, no attempt tends to be made to explain the structural reasons why a living wage might be a necessity, with the result

---

[15] See John M. Keynes, 'The General Theory of Employment. Quarterly', *Journal of Economics,* 51, no. 2 (1937): 209–23.

that a living wage is implicitly assumed to be something that can only be achieved within existing structures, and thus, in light of prevailing economic constraints.

While an economic conception of the wage cannot explain *why* a living wage might be normatively required/desirable nor offer a structural understanding of the causes of low pay, a political conception of the wage derives the *normative* argument for living wages from an analysis of capitalism and its structural contradictions. It thus identifies the living wage as a normative precondition *required* by capitalism itself, to be guaranteed irrespective of market conditions. From this perspective, then, a living wage policy is not something that requires a 'trade-off' of efficiency against fairness, nor is it something that can only be worked out from within the confines of what 'the market' will allow: it is already presupposed by the particular conception of efficiency that is generated from within capitalism itself – a normative requirement for sustainable accumulation.

Given that the political conception of the wage posits that markets are legally and politically constituted, however, it becomes impossible to hold to the idea that workers' costs of living are in any sense predetermined and un-amenable to alteration – that there is an objective definition of what costs of living actually *are*. Guaranteeing a living wage can no longer be framed as an empirical exercise, therefore, about calculating a predetermined living-cost. Rather it becomes an inherently political and normative exercise; a question of what standard of living workers *ought* to be entitled, in exchange for the social role they play in capitalism, *and* of what role the monetary payment made by employers in the market ought to be. From the perspective of a political conception of the wage, therefore, living wages are not, or need not, *merely* be about 'meeting' objective conditions for capitalism's sustainable reproduction, they might instead form part of a strategy through which we decide what *sort* of capitalism we want to develop: how unequal the bargaining power between capital and labour should be, what sort of working and living standards workers should be entitled to expect, and what role the market *ought* to play in its realization.

A political understanding of the wage thus reveals the contradictions inherent in the living wage concept itself, and actually highlights the possibility, and necessity, of harnessing its inherent emancipatory potential, with a view to reaching beyond it. This means that, from the perspective of a political understanding of the wage, the living wage seeks to respond to a social problem, low pay, without addressing its structural causes. While living wages might be useful for improving life and work *within* capitalism, and sustaining life *as presently constituted*, then, it does little to address (and potentially reinforces) the structural contradictions which give rise to the necessity for living wages in the first place. This suggests that living wages are normatively desirable, and structurally necessary in capitalism, but they are also, to some extent, self-defeating: they reinforce the wage dependence that lies at the heart of the contradictions immanent in the system. This suggests that living wage policies can never be seen as ends in themselves; insofar as they accept as given the existence of the wages system, and the mediation of social relations by the market, they risk becoming as much a part of the problem, as they are part of a strategy towards an eventual solution. While living wages may indeed be a short-term necessity, then, and go some way towards boosting the power of labour, they are not enough. What is required is not merely a mechanism for altering the *rate* at which workers are paid for labour power, but some mechanism, or set of mechanisms, that seek to remove the structural necessity for their being paid *any* such rate in the first place: mechanisms which do not simply reinforce labour power's commodification, but which actually go some way towards challenging its commodity status.[16] This would include, for example, mechanisms that aim at developing the sort of collective provisions, and systems of universal service provision, that might make it possible to transcend the existence of the wages system, and the mediation of social relations by markets, entirely.[17] From this perspective, then, living wages should be seen as one way of building the political capacities, and momentum, that would be required to bring about a socialization, or collectivization, of production.

3. The living wage in the UK: an historical examination

Having demonstrated the potential significance of a political conception of the wage when it comes to realizing the normative ideal, and emancipatory potential, immanent in the living wage concept, the rest of this chapter seeks to explore how far different articulations of the Living Wage concept in the context of particular social movements, have harnessed such a political conception of the wage in practice. To do this, the article contrasts the early twentieth century Living Wage Policy of the ILP, with the modern-day re-articulation of that policy in the form of Citizens UK Living Wage Campaign.

3.1 The Living Wage Policy: The ILP

Early attempts to articulate a concept of the living wage emerged in response to debates about the social problem of sweating towards the end of the nineteenth century.[18] This 'problem', widely recognized to be endemic in a large number of industries, had largely been conceptualized in terms of the receipt, by workers, of wages that were insufficient to maintain them in conditions of basic health and efficiency, something which, however, dominant conceptions of wages failed to adequately explain. According to economic orthodoxy, the market price of labour – the wage rate – expressed the objective value of that labour, such that any attempt to interfere with the setting of that price – such as by way of wage-fixing machinery – would *inevitably* lead to inefficiencies,

---

[16] See Ana Cecilia Dinerstein and Frederick Harry Pitts, 'From Post-Work to Post-Capitalism? Discussing the Basic Income and Struggles for Alternative Forms of Social Reproduction', *Journal of Labor and Society*, 21, no. 4 (2018): 471–91.

[17] See Nate Holdren, 'Capitalism, Law, and Critical Theory: A Reply to Karl Klare', *Legal Form. A Forum for Marxist Analysis and Critique*, 30 November 2020 [https://legalform.blog/2020/11/30/capitalism-law-and-critical-theory-a-reply-to-karl-klare-nate-holdren/].

[18] See Sheila Blackburn, *A Fair Day's Wage for a Fair Day's Work?: Sweated Labour and the Origins of Minimum Wage Legislation in Britain* (Ashgate Publishing, Ltd., 2007); Duncan Bythell, *The Sweated Trades: Outwork in Nineteenth-Century Britain* (New York: St. Martin's Press, 1978). For perhaps the earliest articulation, see: John A. Hobson, 'A Living Wage', *Commonwealth* 1 (1896): 128–9, 165–7. This was then followed by arguments by the Webbs in Sidney Webb and Beatrice Webb, *Industrial Democracy*, 2 vols, (Longmans: Green, and Company, 1897).

and ultimately, to unemployment.¹⁹ The only solution to low wages, then, was to improve the quality of the labour for which wages were paid – and this was something for which individual workers were ultimately responsible. Given growing concerns about the socio-economic, and political, implications of sweating, however, it was clear that a new diagnosis was needed. And it is in this context that the idea behind the living wage concept began to gain currency, as social reformers sought both to *explain* the existence and prevalence of sweating, and to offer certain practical and collective solutions, to help to address it.²⁰

While the debates about sweating certainly provided a platform on which discussions about living wages could take place, these discussions did little to shake the orthodox view of the nature of the wage, and the relationship between the State and the market.²¹ While the normative premise at the heart of the living wage concept, that wages should cover workers' living costs, was widely accepted, explanations of below-subsistence wages tended to focus on the specific characteristics of the industries in which sweating was prevalent – an over-supply of labour, a lack of organization, and the dominance of children, women and immigrants.²² As a result, no structural or systemic explanation for the necessity of living wages emerged, and the requirement for mandatory living wages came to be seen as little more than an argument for a temporary 'palliative', a mechanisms to remedy a short-run 'failure' in the otherwise self-equilibrating mechanism of the market.

While the normative premise at the heart of the living wage concept had been accepted, then, it had not really challenged the basic premise that *provided that markets are operating competitively*, supply and demand would tend towards equilibrium, and workers' living costs would be met.²³ That this is so is particularly clear from the conceptual architecture of the Trade Boards Act, the mechanism introduced in 1909 to address the problem of sweating.²⁴ This Act made no attempt to align wages with costs of living, nor to introduce a mandatory minimum wage. Instead, it simply made provision for the setting up of collective wage-fixing machinery in industries in which sweating was deemed to be a particular problem. The purpose of these mechanisms was not to determine how much workers *should* be paid, moreover, but to substitute for the actual wage rate (the wage that these workers would be paid absent the interference of the Trade Board), the wage rate that was 'normal' for the industry – the union rate.²⁵ The Act thus clearly articulated the premise that, while yes, certain labour market institutions might be required to *facilitate* free competition, to correct for, and mitigate

---

[19] See Sheila Blackburn, 'Ideology and Social Policy: The Origins of the Trade Boards Act', *The Historical Journal*, 34, no. 1 (1991): 43–64.
[20] N. N. Feltes, 'Misery or the Production of Misery: Defining Sweated Labour in 1890', *Social History*, 17, no. 3 (1992): 441–52.
[21] See Adams, *Labour and the Wage*.
[22] See Blackburn, *A Fair Day's Wage for a Fair Day's Work?*; Bythell, *The Sweated Trades*; Schmiechen, *Sweated Industries and Sweated Labor*.
[23] See Adams, *Labour and the Wage*.
[24] Sheila Blackburn, 'Working-Class Attitudes to Social Reform: Black Country Chainmakers and Anti-Sweating Legislation, 1880–1930', *International Review of Social History*, 33, no. 1 (1988): 42–69.
[25] See Adams, *Labour and the Wage*.

against, market failure. But at the end of the day, free competition is the only way to ensure an alignment between wages and workers' costs of living in practice.

In the framework of the Trade Board Act, therefore, below-subsistence wages became something attributable to the immoral and exploitative practices of employers, and of the failure by workers to collectively organize so as to facilitate their capacity for free bargaining, rather than something to be attributed to the structural conditions under which such employers, and workers, *in all* industries, *necessarily* act. True, a greater role for the State had been conceded – not merely protecting private property and enforcing contracts, but also, facilitating free competition – but the basic premise that competitive markets are the most efficient, and normatively desirable mechanism, for mediating social relations, and thus, the allocation and reproduction of labour power, had not been questioned.[26]

Given this, it is perhaps unsurprising that the Trade Board system did little to overcome the problem of sweating, such that, by the early twentieth century, new arguments about the necessity of wage regulation had begun to emerge. This provided an opportunity for a re-articulation of the living wage concept,[27] as can be seen from the speech of Labour MP Will Crooks who invoked the concept in a 1911 speech before the House of Commons. Demanding a Living Wage for all workers, Crooks argued '... that the right of every family of the country to an income sufficient to enable it to maintain its members in decency and comfort should be recognised; [and that] a general minimum wage of 30s. per week for every adult worker should be established by law.'[28]

While little came of Crooks' arguments, the Living Wage concept continued to be harnessed in political debates, particularly within the emerging Labour Party, as the need for some intervention in the setting of wages was becoming increasingly apparent.[29] Accordingly, in 1913, Mr Snowden, a member of the ILP, introduced an Amendment into the House calling for a discussion of a potential Living Wage Bill, placing the question of minimum wage regulation once again upon the political agenda.

Snowden proposed that, 'in the first place, that by legislation every workman shall be guaranteed a minimum wage. By a minimum wage I mean a wage sufficient to maintain a man and his dependents in good physical health and in industrial efficiency, and to give him a fair proportion of the ordinary comforts of civilised existence.'[30] In a move that contrasted, sharply, with Crooks' approach, Snowden went on to emphasize why such a measure could not be an end in itself, that minimum wage regulation could only be seen as something 'in the nature of a temporary palliative' if the underlying causes of low wages and sweating is to be overcome. He thus argued that:

---

[26] See Adams, 'Understanding The Minimum Wage'.
[27] Ian Bullock, *Under Siege: The Independent Labour Party in Interwar Britain* (Athabasca: Athabasca University Press, 2017).
[28] *Hansard*, House of Commons Debates (HC), 26 April 1911, vol 24, cols 881–924.
[29] Bullock, *Under Siege*.
[30] HC Debates 13 March 1913, vol 50, cols 459–573, at 466.

If we are going to secure to the working classes a far juster share of the wealth produced by the workers, manual and brain, we shall have to go down a great deal further. We maintain that the reason for the maldistribution of the wealth to which I have referred is in the fact that a certain number of people, or small classes, have a monopoly of the essentials of life; that land without which men cannot live; that land without, which man cannot labour; the instruments of production and the means of distribution like railways; that these are owned and controlled by a few people. So long as there is private ownership it will be impossible for the great masses of the people to very materially improve their conditions. and combined this proposal with a number of further proposals deemed to follow logically from this, and to be necessary to make it meaningful and effective.[31]

The 1913 articulation of the living wage policy was the first to coherently and consistently emphasize the *systemic* and *structural* causes of low wages, and to take seriously the implications of this observation with a view to embedding proposals for living wages within a broader set of measures aimed not merely to raise wages *within* existing structures, but to pave the way for changing or transcending them. The living wage concept was thus being used to problematize explanations of low wages, to expose the structural underpinnings of those wages, so as to maintain momentum not merely around the need to improve workers' terms and conditions, but also, around the need for wider action aimed towards overthrowing the wages system entirely.

Accordingly, Snowden coupled this wide-ranging structural critique with more moderate arguments that sought to show that mandatory living wages were actually essential for *sustaining* capitalism, that the logic of free competition *itself* implied the internalization, by employers, of the social costs of employing labour power. In this way, he sought to garner support not only of a Labour Party committed to a socialization of production, but also, of the defenders of capitalism who were concerned, first and foremost, with questions of national efficiency, and social and economic stability. Drawing an analogy with the prices of other forms of capital (means of production), he highlighted that:

If it were a case of horses, everybody would recognise that a well-fed, well-groomed, and well-stabled horse is very much more valuable both to his employer and to the community at large than an animal which is indifferently looked after. The same thing applies to every other form of livestock which you can find upon a farm. We are asking the Government to recognise that the same principle applies to our human stock. If you secure to men fair wages, decent homes, decent food, and decent comforts of life, the result will be greater efficiency, more satisfaction to the employer, and greater wealth produced for the benefit of the State. [...] [Equally]if it were a matter of fixed machinery which broke down nobody would suggest that either the working man or the State should be at all called upon to provide a Grant-in-Aid in order to set the machinery working again. To my mind

---

[31] HC Debates 13 March 1913, vol 50, cols 459–573, at 466–7.

exactly the same principle applies to the living machinery. The man who gets the direct benefit is the employer of labour, and he is the man who ought to pay the cost of putting the human machine into a decent and efficient condition.[32]

For the ILP, the Living Wage idea was attractive because it could be framed as a simple, and transparent, appeal to the working classes, that could then be built upon to garner support for more 'radical' proposals in the future.[33] As with Snowden's proposal in 1913, then, the Living Wage Policy (or the Living Income, and Socialism for Our Time policies, as it became known), was not simply an argument for a legislative 'living wage', but was integrated with a broader set of measures designed, on the one hand, to make a Living Wage meaningful and workable, and, on the other, to pave the way for the reorganization of society along non-capitalist lines.[34]

The ILP made another important move. Whereas previously, any measures aimed at securing living wages were implicitly conceptualized as *redistributive*, the Labour Party now took pains to emphasize that the entire intention of the living wage policy was to 'make wages the first charge on industry'. In other words, the living wage policy did not take the profit-rate as given; it sought to make the receipt by workers of living wages a condition for profitability.

Progress on the living wage was hampered by the outbreak of the First World War, and internal divisions within the ILP, most particularly, different visions as to the role of parliamentary politics in the realization of socialism.[35] The election to the ILP in 1922 of a number of Scottish MPs who were highly critical of the parliamentary Labour Party, led to a revival, and elaboration, of the living wage policy, as part of a much broader project oriented towards the structural transformation of society.[36] Led by the newly elected leader of the ILP (in 1926) James Maxton, this ultimately resulted in the introduction of a new Private Members Bill into the House of Commons in 1931, calling for a legislative living wage.

The conceptual move made by the ILP in the 1930s was significant: as a redistributive measure, living wages could be seen as something to be worked out within the confines of existing business, and existing structures. As a pre-distributive or market constituting measure, however, it had to be seen instead as laying down the conditions on which the competition for profits could be *allowed* to proceed in a civilized (and sustainable) society. This helped to reinforce their wider arguments about the link between living wage policies and the necessity for wider, *structural* reform: 'If hon. Members opposite object to this Bill and say that it is impossible for British industry to guarantee a minimum standard of life to the workers *under the present organization of society* they have no reason to complain of those who say that the community should step in and

---

[32] HC Debates 13 March 1913 vol 50, cols 459–573, at 485, Per Mr McCurdy.
[33] See Henry Noel Brailsford, Socialism for Today (New Leader, 1925); Id., John A. Hobson, Arthur Creech Jones, and Edward Frank Wise, 'Living Wage: A Report Submitted to the National Administrative Council of the Independent Labour Party'(London: Independent labour Party Publication Department, 1926); Bullock, *Under Siege*.
[34] See Brailsford et al., 'Living Wage'.
[35] Bullock, *Under Seige*.
[36] A. J. Cook and J. Maxton, *Our Case for a Socialist Revival* (Workers' Publications 1928)

organize the industry upon a better basis [emphasis added]'.[37] The ILP thus suggested that if a legislative living wage was not conceded, not only would the Government face potential political revolt, and thus, a challenge to the existing system; but the existing system would simply cease to sustain itself: socialism would become an inevitability.

There is no doubt that the ILP was plagued by internal disagreements and conflicts.[38] Despite the presentation of the Bill in the House of Commons, the policy itself was mired by uncertainty, and disagreement, not least over the question of what a post-capitalist future might imply.[39] While the ILP were convinced of the necessity of revolutionary action, there was little agreement over what that would actually entail, or require.[40] This prevented them from elaborating exactly how the transition was to be made from a system of guaranteed living wages, to one in which such wages would no longer be required. This situation was not helped, moreover, by the fact that, while the ILP sought to exploit the Labour Party's position in the House of Commons, they also remained highly sceptical when it came to how far structural reform could be achieved via a parliamentary system which presupposed the very structures they sought to change.[41]

3.2 The Living Wage Campaign: Citizens UK

Living Wage campaigns of various sorts have emerged in many industrialized countries, including the US, throughout the twentieth century.[42] In the UK, a clearly articulated Living Wage Campaign did not re-emerge until 2001. The origins of this campaign can be traced back to the 1970s, and the dismantling, by the Conservative Government, of the UK Wages Councils system, established in 1945.[43] While falling short of a mandatory legislative wage based on workers' costs of living, the Wages Councils system had nonetheless sought to guarantee all workers in regulated industries a *reasonable remuneration* in exchange for their employment, a guaranteed weekly or monthly income that would be sufficient to sustain them in a reasonable standard of living. It represented a decisive break with the Trade Boards system, therefore, for it went far beyond setting a minimum rate – or price – for work; it actually sought to ensure workers regularity and sufficiency of income in exchange for their contribution to society.[44] Embedded within a relatively comprehensive system of social security protection, unemployment insurance, and pensions, along with wide-spread provision of public services, the Wages Councils system expressed a political commitment to the *idea* of the Living Wage; a clear recognition of the scope for legal and political institutions to shape and structure the labour market in a way that might ensure that

---

[37] HC Debates 06 February 1931 vol 247 cols2269-354, at 2343.
[38] See Bullock, *Under Siege*.
[39] See Deborah M. Figart, *Living Wage Movements: Global Perspectives* (London: Taylor & Francis Group, 2004).
[40] See Bullock, *Under Siege*.
[41] Ibid.
[42] See Figart, *Living Wage Movements*.
[43] See Adams, *Labour and the Wage*.
[44] See Adams, 'Understanding The Minimum Wage'.

social needs could be met. This was a framework that sought to place a large proportion of workers' living costs onto employers, not only through the levelling up of wages, but also, through the institutions of employment and social security law in which the wages council system was embedded.

In the 1970s, however, against a backdrop of inflation and rising unemployment, the premises underpinning the 'post-war' consensus began to be questioned. The idea that there exists an objective market-clearing wage returned, and a new consensus emerged around the premise that the labour market could operate competitively and efficiently provided that the State did not intervene: any attempt to do so through the setting of wage rates could not but lead to unemployment. This applied as much to 'state support' for collective bargaining as it did to state support for a statutory minimum wage. The logical implication of this policy led to the scaling back, and eventual abolition of the wages council's system, such that the only exception to the principle of 'non-intervention' that had survived by the early 1990s was a limited system of wage supplementation targeting low wage earners with dependent children.[45]

The abolition of the wages councils did not, however, have the effect that the Tory Government had predicted: in place of higher wages and more jobs in wages-council industries, the result was lower wages and rising unemployment.[46] The door had been opened, therefore, for the election of a Labour Government, on a platform of a new commitment to 'making work pay'.[47]

For the 'New' Labour Party, making work pay did not mean making employers pay.[48] Rather, the only way to tackle the problem of below-subsistence wages was to boost the marginal productivity of labour, for this, only investments in skills and training, and the introduction of incentives to work, would suffice.

To tackle the immediate problem of in-work poverty, then, the Labour Government opted not for a statutory minimum wage set by reference to actual living costs; but for a system of tax credits, underpinned by a statutory minimum wage set below subsistence level, and conceived as a form of fiscal protection.[49] While the National Minimum Wage Act (NMWA) was the UK's first example of a statutory minimum wage, and so, in this sense, was historically significant; importantly, it was not framed as a way to align the market wage with workers' costs of living, but rather, as a way of preventing the tax credit system from *distorting* the market, protecting against 'unfair' competition.[50] The NMWA was thus firmly rooted in an economic conception of the wage that remains committed to the idea that the 'efficient' wage is that which is set by the 'free play' of market forces, even if various labour market institutions might be required to

---

[45] See Simon Deakin and Frank Wilkinson, *The Law of the Labour Market Industrialization, Employment, and Legal Evolution* (Oxford: Oxford University Press, 2005), chapter 3.
[46] See Richard Dickens, Paul Gregg, Stephen Machin, Alan Manning, and Jonathan Wadsworth, 'Wages Councils: Was There a Case for Abolition?', *British Journal of Industrial Relations*, 31, no. 4 (1993): 515–29.
[47] See Her Majesty's Treasury, 'Tackling Poverty and Making Work Pay: Tax Credits for the 21st Century', *The Modernisation of Britain's Tax and Benefit System*, no. 6 (2000).
[48] See Adams, *Labour and the Wage*, 198.
[49] Ibid., 199.
[50] Chris Grover, 'Living Wages and the "Making Work Pay" Strategy'. Critical Social Policy', 25, no. 1 (2005): 5–27.

secure that 'free play' in practice.[51] As the Supreme Court has recently reiterated, '[the NMW] clearly helps to redress the law of supply and demand where there may be market failure, and the worker is not able to obtain basic recompense for his labour' but it does [not proceed on the basis that the worker must be paid a living wage].'[52]

Consistently with this, the Low Pay Commission, charged with making recommendations about the appropriate rate, was expressly instructed to have regard to business conditions and competitiveness in making such recommendations. The NMWA thus made the minimum wage rate a function of what industry could *afford*, rather than what workers' need, continuing the basic ontological premises that had underpinned the abolition of the wages councils' system, and the deregulatory policy agenda of the Conservative Government. While the Labour Party did take steps to raise wages by investing in skills and productivity, then, it remained firmly committed to the premise that the 'appropriate' and 'legitimate' wage is that which is 'set' by the market.[53]

By the early 2000s it had become clear that the Labour Government's policy of 'making work pay' was not translating, for the majority of workers, into higher wages and more stable work.[54] Combined with the Government's policy of privatization and out-sourcing, a policy that threatened to usher in further cuts in the wages of the lowest paid, the time was ripe for a re-articulation of the Living Wage concept, a task embraced in 2001 by the community organization, Citizens UK.[55]

Citizens UK is a broad-based, community organization consisting of faith groups, schools, universities, unions, community groups and housing associations. It lacks the clear links with Parliament that the ILP could claim as a result of its affiliation to the Labour Party, and so operates primarily through assemblies and demonstrations, and by targeting individual employers with a view to encouraging them to *voluntarily agree* to pay their workers living wages. Today, the movement is advanced by the Living Wage Foundation, an organization that seeks to convince employers of the reputational harms associated with low wages, placing emphasis on the reputational and productivity advantages to those employers of agreeing to pay living wages. To this end, it offers accreditation to employers that agree to pay living wages to their workers, allowing them to capitalize on the reputational benefits of being seen as a 'Living Wage' employers.

The Living Wage Foundation operates in conjunction with the Resolution Foundation, overseen by the Living Wage Commission, as the body tasked with calculating the living wage rate and publishing that rate every year. This rate is calculated on the basis that the wages received by those in *full-time work* should be sufficient to cover the costs of purchasing a basic basket of goods and services, the

---

[51] See Keith Ewing, John Hendy and Carolyn Jones, 'A Manifesto for Labour Law: Towards a Comprehensive Revision of Workers' Rights' (Liverpool: Institute of Employment Rights, 2016).
[52] *Royal Mencap Society v Tomlinson Blake*, [2021] UKSC 8
[53] See Grover, 'Living Wages and the "Making Work Pay" Strategy'.
[54] See Paul Bunyan, 'The Role of Civil Society in Reducing Poverty and Inequality: A Case Study of the Living Wage Campaign in the UK', *Local Economy: The Journal of the Local Economy Policy Unit*, 31, no. 4 (2016): 489–501.
[55] See Grover, 'Living Wages and the "Making Work Pay" Strategy'.

content of which is calculated by reference to evidence about living standards in London and the UK.

The policy underpinning the Living Wage Campaign is consistent with the normative premise, implicit in the 1930 Living Wage Policy, that wages ought to approximate workers' costs of living and that this is an inherently *political* question, in the sense that it depends on non-market assessments of what workers actually need, and are deemed to be entitled. It differs from the 1930 policy, however, in accepting as given the premise that such a wage can only be paid *insofar* as it is a wage that employers are *willing* to pay, and *insofar* as it is a wage that industry is deemed to be able to afford. Citizens UK's case for the living wage was thus not based on a refutation of the premise that *were* higher wages to produce unemployment, they *ought not* be paid; it was based simply on the premise that, very often, higher wages *would not necessarily* produce unemployment, because the increased costs that might ordinarily lead to job cuts can often be off-set by reduced costs related to lower turnover and increased productivity. This is because 'when workers receive a higher wage a firm benefit in many ways including reduced labour turnover, better quality of work, better cooperation with management, more flexibility in the operation of a business and higher overall morale.'[56] Given that increased wages might mean a wider distribution of disposable income, moreover, employment opportunities might actually *increase* as an indirect result of increasing demand.

This re-articulation of the Living Wage concept stops short, then, of suggesting that living wages should be paid *regardless* of affordability, that employers who refuse, or cannot afford, to pay such wages, ought either be restructured, or allowed to become obsolete. It simply suggests that where profit-rates are sufficiently high, employers should be encouraged to 're-invest' some of those profits by boosting workers' wages, and that, in doing so, they might be surprised to see their profits increase over time.

In 2019, Citizens UK launched the Living Hours Campaign, which was designed to supplement the Living Wage Campaign, calling on employers who already provide a real Living Wage, *and who are able to*, to also provide 'Living Hours'. Living Hours involves providing workers with a right to decent notice periods for shifts, namely, at least four weeks' notice with guaranteed payment if shifts are cancelled within the notice period, and 'A Contract with Living Hours'. This is a right to a contract that reflects actual hours worked, and a guaranteed minimum of 16 hours a week (unless the worker requests otherwise).[57] This campaign is to be underpinned by a new Living Hours accreditation programme, also run by the Living Wage Foundation, coupled with dedicated support for employers.

The rationale behind this new initiative is that while the Living Wage has always focused on asking employers to ensure that full-time workers earn enough to 'make ends meet'; they recognize that expecting employers to provide only full-time work

---

[56] TELCO, 'Mapping Low Pay in East London', September 2021. https://www.york.ac.uk/res/fbu/documents/mlpinel_sep2001.pdf (accessed 38 August 2022).
[57] Rachel McEwen, 'Living Hours: Providing Security of Hours alongside a Real Living Wage', Living Wage Foundation, no. 28 (2019).

runs against the desire of many people for flexibility, as well as not being viable for many businesses. Rather than banning zero or short-hours contracts entirely, therefore, the Living Wage Foundation has instead sought to prescribe measures that would provide additional stability and predictability, so that families can better plan their finances and handle household expenditure. This 'creates an incentive for employers to plan effectively and share the risk of any fluctuations with workers, rather than expecting workers to shoulder the full costs of uncertainty'. In addition, guaranteeing a minimum of 16 hours a week, unless the worker requests otherwise, is designed to align with the requirements on workers to meet the terms of their 'Claimant Commitment' under the new Universal Credit system, and so, to ensure, that Living Hours does not produce negative side-effects in light of the structure of the existing social security system.[58]

The attempt to combine a Living Hours guarantee with a 'real' living wage' recognizes that guaranteeing an *income* sufficient to cover workers' living costs, making the normative ideal of a living wage a reality, cannot be secured unless some guarantee exists as to the amount of work with which individuals would be provided. In this way, the Living Hours initiative addresses the labour market reality that the 'norm' in terms of employment for the majority of low-paid workers is not that of full-time regular work as the Living Wage Campaign presupposed, but irregular, casualized work, where irregularity of income and insufficiency of work is as much a problem when it comes to meeting actual costs of living, as is the amount of pay received per hour of work performed.

In reality, of course, even this new initiative still does not challenge the premise that wages are paid for work, and thus, that the only way to guarantee a living wage in practice, is to ensure that enough work is provided to *earn* a 'living wage' – to ensure, in other words, that employers actually receive sufficient benefit in exchange for the wages that they pay. It falls short, then, of recognizing that individuals ought to be absolutely entitled to receive sufficient income to meet their living costs, merely by reason of the social role they play in capitalism, and thus, their participation in the labour market.[59] Nor, moreover, does it go so far as to compel employers to offer 'Living Hours' (or Living Wages!) where they claim they are unable to do so. The Living Wage, and Living Hours Campaigns, even *reinforce* the premise that the living wage is a good, or generous, concession, made by 'good employers', rather than a social and economic necessity that ought to be legally compelled. It thus reconceptualizes the living wage as something the payment of which is accepted to be conditional upon the private economic advantages that such can bring to individual employers, rather than depending instead on the wider, social benefits, that the payment of living wages brings to society more generally.

Perhaps even more significant than these limitations is the fact that the Living Wage Campaign makes the Living Wage an end to be pursued for its own sake. While Citizens UK do also campaign for social care, affordable housing, street safety etc., and, as we have seen, are not blind to other labour market problems, such as casualization, they do

---

[58] See Keith Puttick, '"21st Century Welfare" and the Wage-Work-Welfare Bargain', *Industrial Law Journal*, 41, no. 1 (2012): 122–31.
[59] See Adams, 'Understanding the Minimum Wage'.

not embed any of these policies in a coherent strategy oriented around a particular understanding of the structural and systemic linkages between the problems they each address.[60] In fact, the Living Wage Campaign simply targets an empirically observed problem, namely, that many workers receive a wage that falls short of their costs of living, and seeks to deploy a moralistic argument to advance certain 'practical' proposals, in the form of redistributive measures, that might help address these empirically observed problems in practice – in a way that might be seen as appealing not just to workers, but to employers as well.

The problem here is that, in contrast with the ILP, Citizens UK never really attempted to embed its campaign in an understanding of the capitalist system, nor the structural forces *explaining* the problem of low pay to which the campaign is directed. Even its discussion of Living Hours tends to focus on surface-level problems, taking labour market casualization and desires for 'flexibility' as given, rather than challenging their underlying ontological premises.[61] The entire campaign has been framed in terms of apparently inevitable economic trends, immoral practices by unenlightened employers, and/or inadequate regulation.[62] Rather than explaining *why* capitalism itself presupposes a living wage, the necessity of covering workers' living costs as a condition for sustainable accumulation, therefore, publications associated with Citizens UK and the Living Wage Foundation tend to simply take for granted that a minimum wage ought to cover workers' living costs, and that the best way to do this is through the wage-packet.[63] Low pay and poverty, and/or precarious work, are taken as the wrongs being targeted, then, rather than these problems being seen as negative side-effects, or surface-level manifestations, of a fundamentally unequal and exploitative socio-economic system.

A by-product of this framing is that the modern Living Wage Campaign implicitly accepts the premise that wages represent a distributed share of the fruits of industry, rather than being the *source* of those fruits, and thus, a legitimate *conditioning* factor on the rate or profit. The overriding premise, then, is that industries *that can afford living wages* should agree to pay them; rather than, as was the case in the 1930s, that the provision of a living wage to all workers should be seen as a condition for firms being allowed to carry on business, a condition which ought to be imposed by law. And because the Living Wage is pursued as an end in itself and is seen as something to be pursued within existing economic constraints, it has not been linked with a wider policy-narrative that recognizes the *additional* reforms which will be necessary if the normative premises at the heart of the Living Wage are to be realized. Instead, the Living Wage has been reduced to a plea to employers to use some of their guaranteed profits to reward their workers, with the hope that they will be rewarded in their own turn as a result of the beneficial effects of higher wages on their workforce and its productivity.

The Living Wage Campaign does not, then, actually challenge the mainstream conception of the wage, and the function of wage regulation at all. Indeed, the

---

[60] See Grover, 'Living Wages and the "Making Work Pay" Strategy'.
[61] See McEwen, 'Living Hours: Providing Security of Hours alongside a Real Living Wage'.
[62] See TELCO, 'Mapping Low Pay in East London'.
[63] See Ibid.; McEwen, 'Living Hours: Providing Security of Hours alongside a Real Living Wage'.

compatibility of the Living Wage Campaign with the Government's conception of wages is evident from the way in which it has been co-opted and distorted by the latter for alternative purposes.[64] Thus, following an announcement in the 2015 budget speech, in 2016, the Government introduced the National Living Wage, harnessing the normative appeal of the campaign, without, however, accepting all of its central premises.[65] Framed *as if it* provides for a living wage, this policy actually reproduces the assumptions built into the NMWA as initially introduced.[66] Not only does the rate still fall far short of a minimum wage set by reference to costs of living, being set instead by reference to a percentage of median income, but it is still intended to operate within a framework in which the gap between the wage and costs of living is made up predominantly by the State through tax credits (now, Universal Credit) – all in a context, moreover, of limited provision of public services.[67] Despite the change in name, the national 'living' wage is still required to have regard to what industry can afford, and as the Low Pay Commission argued in its 2019 report 'a higher NLW must be supported by economic conditions, including strong employment, economic growth, increasing pay, productivity growth [and] the affordability of increases to firms and the quality of jobs for workers.'[68] Even this highly limited articulation of a living wage is, then, constrained by what firms are able, and willing, to pay, circumscribed, therefore, by existing structures.

4. Conclusion

At the end of the day, the Living Wage Campaign does not embrace the political understanding of the wage that enabled early twentieth century social reformers to make convincing policy arguments about the necessity, and possibility, of legislating for a minimum wage set by reference to what workers need, and to what they are normatively deemed to be entitled. Nor does it allow for the much broader, structural critique, that such policy arguments had necessitated. The causes of low pay thus continue to be constructed as if they arise from the unfair, illegal practices of individual firms, failing to uphold their minimum wage (or even, moral) obligations, rather than as being an expression of capitalism's underlying, structural contradictions.

Of course, the 1931 Living Wage Bill was defeated. In this limited sense, the Living Wage Policy failed. However, not only did the idea of the living wage have a lasting impact on policy-making throughout the twentieth century, it was also progressively embedded in the legal and social fabric in a number of ways, only to be dismantled in the 1970s under the aegis of neoliberalism and its unmitigated pursuit of free

---

[64] See Bunyan, 'The Role of Civil Society in Reducing Poverty and Inequality'; Grover, 'Living Wages and the "Making Work Pay" Strategy'.
[65] See Osborne, George. Chancellor George Osborne's Summer Budget 2015 speech – GOV.UK https://www.gov.uk/government/speeches/chancellor-george-osbornes-summer-budget-2015-speech (accessed 7 August 2017).
[66] See Adams, 'Understanding The Minimum Wage'.
[67] Ibid.
[68] Low Pay Commission, 'The National Minimum Wage Beyond 2020', January 2020.

competition.⁶⁹ We must not forget, moreover, that the momentum behind the 1930s campaign was largely stymied by the Second World War even if it was partly experiences during the war that enabled new ideas to emerge about the nature of the market and the role in relation to it of the State and the law.⁷⁰ After all, during the war, the State exercised a much more direct role over the allocation of resources, over prices, and over wages, and many of these principles were continued, albeit partially, in the years after the war was concluded, reflected in the Wages Councils Act 1945.⁷¹

The Wages Councils model embodied the idea that workers were entitled to receive a guaranteed income that was *adequate* – to meet their living standards – and that this was something paid in exchange for the benefit of their employment, and not merely to be paid in proportion with a given quantity of work.⁷² Shifting some of the risks of fluctuating demand onto the employer, and ensuring that the income of workers was not subject to the vagaries of market fluctuation, this helped reduce the extent (if not the existence) of the inequality between labour and capital, enabling a 'partial' decommodification of labour power. This was particularly so given that this framework went hand in hand with a massive expansion in public service provision, and a tax and social security system that sought to provide protection against unemployment and in the event of retirement.⁷³ Of course, there were gaps in coverage; and, of course, casual labour and evasive employment practices were not eliminated. But the guarantee, to workers, of an adequate, stable income, sufficient to cover their costs of living, was deeply embedded in the institutional architecture in a way it had not been before.⁷⁴ While, inevitably, this model operated *within* the framework of capitalism's constitutive structures, and so, did not actually challenge the *existence* of the wages system, nor the necessity for workers to work for wages; it *did* embody a fundamentally different understanding of the conditions in which capitalism is acceptable, making the competitive market something which the State *permitted*, and sought to *constitute* in a way that prioritized the meeting of social needs, over the endless pursuit of profit.

Rooted in a deep, structural understanding of the causes of low pay, and an understanding of capitalism's underlying, systemic logic, the ILP's Living Wage Campaign did more than most to expose the contradictions internal to capitalism in a way that might provide concrete guidance for the formulation and enactment of policy. Unfortunately, the same cannot be said of its modern reincarnation. While the campaign continues to enjoy considerable support amongst a number of employers, and indeed, while many employers do and have agreed to pay a living wage voluntarily (given the social capital that the status of being a 'living wage' employer carries), it has done little to penetrate policy-making circles (or not advantageously so), nor to

---

[69] See Grover, 'Living Wages and the "Making Work Pay" Strategy'; Bunyan, 'The Role of Civil Society in Reducing Poverty and Inequality'; Adams, *Labour and the Wage*.
[70] See Adams, *Labour and the Wage*.
[71] See Adams, 'Understanding The Minimum Wage'.
[72] See Adams, *Labour and the Wage*, 157–58.
[73] See Beveridge, William Henry Beveridge Baron. Full Employment in a Free Society (London: Allen & Unwin, 1944).
[74] See Adams, *Labour and the Wage*.

challenge the basic terms on which the debate about minimum wages takes place. True, it can be credited for its success in maintaining momentum around a normative commitment to the ideal of the living wage, and, more recently, for recognizing the connection between workers' income and the quantity of work to which they have access. But it has done so without embedding that normative idea within a systematic and structural understanding of capitalism, and thus, without any intention to realize the ideal of a living wage in ways that either impede short-term competitiveness and profitability, acting against the subjectively perceived interests of employers, or in ways that seek to lay the groundwork for wider, structural, reform. The living wage concept has today become less a radical critique of capitalism and its internal contradictions, then, and more an argument about how we might secure a redistribution of value in ways which might provide for better living conditions to the worst off group in society, while, ultimately, accepting the inevitability of the wages system, and thus, its associated mode of exploitation.

Selected Bibliography

Acciari, Louisa. 'Decolonising Labour, Reclaiming Subaltern Epistemologies: Brazilian Domestic Workers and the International Struggle for Labour Rights'. *Contexto Internacional*, 41, no. 1 (2019): 39–62.
Adams, Zoe. 'Understanding the Minimum Wage: Political Economy and Legal Form'. *The Cambridge Law Journal*, 78, no. 1 (2019): 42–69.
Adams, Zoe. *Labour and the Wage: A Critical Perspective*. Oxford, New York: Oxford University Press, 2020.
Agarwala, Rina and Shiny Saha. 'The Employment Relationship and Movement Strategies among Domestic Workers in India'. *Critical Sociology*, 44, no. 7–8 (2018): 1207–23.
Agarwala, Rina. *Informal Labor, Formal Politics, and Dignified Discontent in India*. Cambridge: Cambridge University Press, 2014.
Ahuja, Ravi. 'Beveridge Plan for India? Social Insurance and the Making of the "Formal Sector"'. *International Review of Social History*, 64, no. 2 (2019): 207–48.
Allen, Robert et al. 'Wages, Prices and Living Standards in China 1738–1925 in comparison with Europe, Japan and India', *The Economic History Review*, 64, no. S1 (2011): 8–38.
Allen, Robert. 'The Great Divergence in European Wages and Prices from the Middle Ages to the First World War'. *Explorations in Economic History*, 38, no. 4 (2001): 411–47.
Allen, Robert. *The British Industrial Revolution in Global Perspective*. Cambridge: Cambridge University Press, 2009.
Ally, Shireen. *From Servants to Workers: South African Domestic Workers and the Democratic State*. Ithaca: Cornell University Press, 2009.
Althammer, Beate. *Vagabunden. Eine Geschichte von Armut, Bettel und Mobilität im Zeitalter der Industrialisierung (1815–1933)*. Essen: Klartext, 2017.
Anderson, Bridget. eds 'Just another Job? The Commodification of Domestic Labour', in *Global Woman, Nannies, Maids and Sex Workers in the New Economy*, edited by Barbara Ehrenreich and Arlie Russell Hochschild, London: Granta Books, 2002 104–15.
Anderson, Michael. 'India, 1858–1930: The Illusion of Free Labour', in eds Douglas Hay and Paul Craven, *Masters, Servants and Magistrates in Britain and the Empire, 1562–1955*, 127–35. Chapel Hill and London: University of North Carolina Press, 2004.
Antonioli, Maurizio and Bruno Beza (eds). *La Fiom dalle Origini al Fascismo*. Bari: De Donato, 1978.
Arborio, Anne-Marie, Paul Bouffartigue and Annie Lamanthe (eds). *Crise(s) et Mondes du Travail*. Toulouse: Octarès, 2019, 30.
Armacost, Nicola. 'Domestic Workers in India: A Case for Legislative Action'. *Journal of the Indian Law Institute*, 36 no. 1 (1994): 53–63.
Arnoux, Mathieu. *Le Temps des Laboureurs. Travail, Ordre Social et Croissance en Europe (XIe-XIVe Siècle)*. Paris: Albin Michel, 2009.
Austin Gareth and Sugihara Karou (eds). *Labour-Intensive Industrialization in Global History*. New York: Routledge, 2013.

Baccaro, Lucio and Chris Howell. *Trajectories of Neoliberal Transformation: European Industrial Relations Since the 1970s.* Cambridge: Cambridge University Press, 2017.

Balstad Miller, Roberta. 'Science and Society in the Early Career of H. F. Verwoerd'. *Journal of Southern African Studies*, 19, no. 4 (1993): 634–61.

Bandopadhyay, Arun and Sanjukta Dasgupta (eds). *In Quest of the Historian's Craft: Essays in Honour of Professor B.B. Chaudhuri.* New Delhi: Manohar Publications, 2018.

Bandyopadhyay, Ritajyoti. 'The Street Vendors Act and Pedestrianism in India: A Reading of the Archival Politics of the Calcutta Hawker Sangram Committee'. In *Street Vending in the Neoliberal City: A Global Perspective on the Practices* eds Kristina Graaff and Noa Ha. New York and Oxford: Berghahn, 2015.

Banerjee, Swapna. *Men, Women and Domestics: Articulating Middle-Class Identity in Colonial Bengal.* New Delhi: Oxford University Press, 2004.

Banfield, Edward. *The Unheavenly City.* Boston: Little, Brown, and Company, 1970.

Barman, Emily. *Caring Capitalism. The Meaning and Measure of Social Value.* Cambridge: Cambridge University Press, 2016.

Barrett, Michelle and Mary McIntosh. 'The "Family Wage": Some Problems for Socialists and Feminists'. *Capital & Class*, 4, no. 2 (1980): 51–72.

Bates, Crispin and Marina Carter. 'Sirdars as Intermediaries in Nineteenth-Century Indian Ocean Indentured Labour Migration'. *Modern Asian Studies*, 51, no. 2 (2017): 462–84.

Batzell, Rudi Beckert, Andrew Sven Gordon and Gabriel Winant, 'E. P. Thompson, Politics and History: Writing Social History Fifty Years after The Making of the English Working Class'. *Journal of Social History*, 48, no. 4 (2015): 753–8.

Beckert, Sven and Dominic Sachsenmaier (eds). *Global History Globally.* London: Bloomsbury, 2018.

Beier, A. L. and Roger Finlay. *London 1500–1700. The Making of the Metropolis.* London: Longman, 1986.

Beinart, William, Peter Delius and Stanley Trapido (eds). *Putting a Plough to the Ground: Accumulation and Dispossession in Rural South Africa, 1850–1930.* Johannesburg: Ravan Press, 1986.

Beinart, William. *Twentieth-Century South Africa.* New York: Oxford University Press, 2001.

Benanav, Aaron. 'The Origins of Informality: The ILO at the Limit of the Concept of Unemployment', *Journal of Global History*, 14, no. 1 (2019): 1–19.

Bengtsson, Erik and Jakob Molinder. 'The economic effects of the 1920 eight-hour working day reform in Sweden'. *Scandinavian Economic History Review*, 65, no. 2 (2017): 149–68.

Berg, Maxine and Elizabeth Eger (eds). *Luxury in the Eighteenth Century: Debates, Desires and Delectable goods.* Basingstoke: Palgrave Macmillan, 2003.

Berg, Maxine, Pat Hudson and Michael Sonenscher (eds). *Manufacture in Town and Country Before the Factory.* Cambridge: Cambridge University Press, 1983.

Berger, Iris. *Threads of Solidarity: Women in South African Industry, 1900–1980.* Bloomington, IN: Indiana University Press, 1992.

Berggren, Lars. *Ångvisslans och brickornas värld: om arbete och facklig organisering vid Kockums mekaniska verkstad och Carl Lunds fabrik i Malmö 1840–1905.* Lund: Lunds universitet, 1991.

Betràn, Concha and Pons, Maria. 'Skilled and Unskilled Wage Differentials and Economic Integration, 1870–1930'. *European Review of Economic History*, 8, no. 1 (2004): 29–60.

Bezy, Fernand, Jean-Philippe Peemans and Jean-Marie Wautelet. *Accumulation et sous-développement au Zaïre. 1960–1980.* Louvain-la-Neuve: 1981.

Bhorat, Harun, Ravi Kanbur and Natahsa Mayet 'The impact of sectoral minimum wage laws on employment, wages, and hours of work in South Africa', *IZA Journal of Labor & Development*, no. 2 (2013): 1–27.
Bhorat, Haroon et al. (eds). *Fighting Poverty: Labor Markets and Inequality in South Africa*. Cape Town: University of Cape Town Press, 2001.
Bianchi, Ornella. *Il Sindacato di Stato (1930–1940)*, in *Storia del Sindacato in Italia nel '900*. vol. I. *La CGdL e lo Stato Autoritario*. ed. Adolfo Pepe, 173–9. Roma: Ediesse, 1997.
Bickford-Smith, Vivian. *Ethnic Pride and Racial Prejudice in Victorian Cape Town: Group Identity and Social Practice, 1875–1902*. New York: Cambridge University Press, 1995.
Bieler, Andreas and Jörg Nowak (eds). *Labour Conflicts in the Global South*. London: Routledge, 2022.
Biernacki, Richard. 'Labor as an Imagined Commodity'. *Politics & Society* 29, no. 2 (2001): 173–206.
Biernacki, Richard. *The Fabrication of Labor: Germany and Britain, 1640–1914*. Berkeley: University of California Press, 1995.
Biggs, Norman, 'A tale untangled: measuring the fineness of yarn'. *Textile History*, 35, no. 1 (2004): 120–9.
Bijker, Wiebe E. and John Law (eds). *Shaping Technology/Building Society: Studies in Sociotechnical Change*. Cambridge, MA: MIT Press, 1992.
Bills, David B., Valentina Di Stasio and Klarita Gërxhani. 'The Demand Side of Hiring: Employers in the Labor Market'. *Annual Review of Sociology*, 43, no. 1 (2007): 291–310.
Blackburn, Sheila. 'Ideology and Social Policy: The Origins of the Trade Boards Act'. *The Historical Journal*, 34, no. 1 (1991): 43–64.
Blackburn, Sheila. 'Working-Class Attitudes to Social Reform: Black Country Chainmakers and Anti-Sweating Legislation, 1880–1930'. *International Review of Social History*, 33, no. 1 (1988): 42–69.
Blackburn, Sheila. *A Fair Day's Wage for a Fair Day's Work?: Sweated Labour and the Origins of Minimum Wage Legislation in Britain*. Ashgate Publishing, Ltd., 2007.
Blaug, Marc. *Economic Theory in Retrospect*. 4th edition. Cambridge: Cambridge University Press, 1985.
Blewett, Mary. *Constant Turmoil: The Politics of Industrial Life in Nineteenth Century New England*. Manchester: Manchester university Press, 1990.
Boal, William M. and Michael Ransom. 'Monopsony in the Labour Market', *Journal of Economic Literature*, 35, no. 1 (1997): 86–112.
Boll, Friedhelm. *Arbeitskämpfe und Gewerkschaften in Deutschland, England und Frankreich*. Bonn: Verlag G. H. V. Dietz, 1992.
Booth, Alison. *The Economics of the Trade Union*. Cambridge: Cambridge University Press, 1994.
Bourdieu, Pierre and Jean-Claude Passeron. *The Inheritors: French Students and their Relation to Culture*. Chicago: Chicago University Press, 1979 [1964].
Boyer, George and Robert Smith. 'The Neoclassical Tradition in Labor Economics'. *Industrial and Labor Relations Review*, 54, no. 2 (2001): 199–223.
Bradford, Helen. *A Taste of Freedom: The ICU in Rural South Africa, 1924–1930*. New Haven: Yale University Press, 1987.
Breckenridge, Keith. *Biometric State: The Global Politics of Identification and Surveillance in South Africa, 1850 to the Present*. New York: Cambridge University Press, 2014.
Broadberry, Stephen and Gupta Bishnupriya. 'The Early Modern Great Divergence: Wages, Prices and Economic Development in Europe and Asia, 1500–1800'. *The Economic History Review*, 59, no. 1 (2006): 2–31.

Bruckmüller, Ernst (ed.). *Aus meinem Burschenleben. Gesellenwanderung und Brautwerbung eines Grazer Zuckerbäckers 1862–1869*. Wien: Böhlau, 2000.

Bruckmüller, Ernst, Roman Sandgruber and Hannes Stekl. *Soziale Sicherheit im Nachziehverfahren. Die Einbeziehung der Bauern, Landarbeiter, Gewerbetreibenden und Hausgehilfen in das System der österreichischen Sozialversicherung*. Salzburg: Neugebauer, 1978.

Bruno, Isabelle, Emmanuel Didier and Tommaso Vitale. 'Statactivism: Forms of Action between Disclosure and Affirmation'. *Partecipazione e conflictto / Participation and Conflict* 7, no. 2 (2014): 188–220.

Bryson, Alex, Harald Dale-Olsen and Kristine Nergaard. 'Gender differences in the union wage premium? A comparative case study'. *European Journal of Industrial Relations*, 26, no. 2 (2020): 173–90.

Buchner, Thomas and Philip R. Hoffman-Rehnitz (eds). *Shadow Economies and Irregular Work in Urban Europe. 16th to early 20th Centuries*. Münster: LIT Verlag, 2011.

Buhlungu, Sakhela. *A Paradox of Victory: COSATU and the Democratic Transformation in South Africa*. Durban: University of KwaZulu-Natal Press, 2010.

Bullock, Ian. *Under Siege: The Independent Labour Party in Interwar Britain*. Athabasca: Athabasca University Press, 2017.

Bulmer, Martin, Kevin Bales and Kathryn Kish Sklar. *The Social Survey in Historical Perspective, 1880–1940*. New York: Cambridge University Press, 1991.

Bunyan, Paul. 'The Role of Civil Society in Reducing Poverty and Inequality: A Case Study of the Living Wage Campaign in the UK'. *Local Economy: The Journal of the Local Economy Policy Unit*, 31, no. 4 (2016): 489–501.

Burnett, Joyce. *Gender, Work and Wages in Industrial Revolution Britain*. Cambridge: Cambridge University Press, 2008.

Bythell, Duncan. *The Sweated Trades: Outwork in Nineteenth-Century Britain*. New York: St. Martin's Press, 1978.

Cain, Glein G. 'The Challenge of Segmented Labor Market Theories to Orthodox Theory: A Survey'. *Journal of Economic Literature*, 14, no. 4 (1976): 1215–57.

Cannan, Edwin. *A History of the Theories of Production and Distribution in English Political Economy from 1776 to 1848*. London: Percival and co. 1893.

Caracausi, Andrea. 'The Just Wage in Early Modern Italy: A Reflection on Zacchia's De Salario seu Operariorum Mercede'. *International Review of Social History*, 56, no. S19 (2011): 107–24.

Cardini, Antonio. *Stato Liberale e Protezionismo in Italia, 1890–1900*. Bologna: Il Mulino, 1981.

Carson, John. *The Measure of Merit: Talents, Intelligence, and Inequality in the French and American Republics, 1750–1940*. Princeton: Princeton University Press, 2007.

Cassata, Francesco. 'La "Dura Fatica" dei Numeri: Riccardo Bachi e la Statistica Economica' in *Scuola di Economia di Torino: Co-protagonisti ed Epigoni*, edited by Roberto Marchionatti, 85–126. Firenze: L.S. Olschki, 2009.

Cassata, Francesco. *Il Fascismo Razionale: Corrado Gini fra Scienza e Politica*. Roma: Carocci, Roma, 2006.

Cederqvist, Jane. *Arbetare i strejk: studier rörande arbetarnas politiska mobilisering under industrialismens genombrott: Stockholm 1850–1909*. Stockholm: Stockholms universitet, 1980.

Centemeri, Laura. 'Reframing Problems of Incommensurability in Environmental Conflicts Through Pragmatic Sociology: From Value Pluralism to the Plurality of Modes of Engagement with the Environment'. *Environmental Values*, 24, no. 3 (2015): 299–320.

Cerutti, Simona. 'Travail, mobilité et légitimité. Suppliques au roi dans un société d'Ancien Régime (Turin, XVIIIe siècle)'. *Annales. Histoire, Sciences Sociales*, 65, no. 3 (2010): 571–611.
Chakravarty, Deepita and Ishita Chakravarty. *Women, Labour and the Economy in India: From migrant manservants to uprooted girl children maids.* New York: Routledge, 2016.
Chélini, Michel-Pierre. *Histoire des salaires en France des années 1940 aux années 1960 (1944–67). Analyse historique et économique d'un système salarial avancé.* Bern: Peter Lang, 2021.
Chen, Zhiwuand and Kaixing Peng. 'Production, Consumption, and Living Standards', in *The Cambridge Economic History of China, Part II 100 to 1800*, eds Debin Ma and Richard von Glahn. Cambridge: Cambridge University Press, 2022.
Cherrier, Beatrice. 'How to Write a Memo to Convince a President: Walter Heller, Policy-Advising, and the Kennedy Tax Cut'. *Œconomia*, 9, no. 2 (2019): 315–35.
Chesneaux, Jean. *The Chinese Labor Movement, 1919–1927.* Stanford, CA: Stanford University Press, 1968.
Clark, Alice. *Working Life of Women in the Seventeenth Century.* London: Routledge, 1982.
Clark, Anna. 'The New Poor Law and the Breadwinner Wage: Contrasting Assumptions'. *Journal of Social History*, 34, no. 2 (2000): 261–81.
Clark, Gabrielle. '"Humbug" or "Human Good?": E.P. Thompson, the Rule of Law and Coercive Labor Relations Under Neoliberal American Capitalism'. *Journal of Social History*, 48, no. 4 (2015): 759–78.
Clark, Gregory. 'Factory Discipline'. *The Journal of Economic History*, 54, no. 1 (1994): 128–63.
Clark, Gregory. 'The Condition of the Working Class in England, 1209–2004'. *The Journal of Political Economy,* 113, no. 6 (2005): 1307–1340.
Cohn, Bernard. 'The Census, Social Structures and Objectification in South Asia', in *An Anthropologist Among the Historians and other Essays*, edited by Cohn, Bernard 224–54. Delhi: Oxford University Press, 1987.
Condliffe Lagemann, Ellen. *The Politics of Knowledge: The Carnegie Corporation Philanthropy, and Public Policy.* Middletown: Wesleyan, 1989.
Cooper, Frederick and Randall M. Packard. *International Development and the Social Sciences: Essays on the History and Politics of Knowledge.* Berkeley: University of California Press, 1998.
Cooper, Frederick. *Decolonization and African Society: the Labor Question in French and British Africa.* Cambridge: Cambridge University Press, 1996.
Cottereau, Alain. 'Droit et bon droit. Un droit des ouvriers instauré puis évincé par le droit du travail (France XIXe s)'. *Annales. Histoires sciences sociales,* 57, no. 6 (2002): 1521–57
Cowie, Jefferson R. *Stayin Alive. The 1970s and the Last Days of the Working Class.* New York: The New Press, 2010.
Crafts, Nicholas, Ian Gazeley and Andrew Newell (eds). *Work and Pay in 20th Century Britain*, eds Oxford, Oxford University Press, 2007.
Crankshaw, Owen. *Race, Class and the Changing Divisions of Labour Under Apartheid.* London: Routledge, 1997.
Curli, Barbara. *Italiane al Lavoro, 1914–1920.* Venezia: Marsilio, 1998.
Cvrcek, Tomas. 'Wages, Prices, and Living Standards in the Habsburg Empire, 1827–1910'. *The Journal of Economic History* 73, no. 1 (2013): 1–37.
d'Almeida-Topor, Hélène. 'Recherches sur l'Évolution du Travail Salarié en AOF pendant la Crise Économique 1930–1936'. *Cahiers d'études africaines*, 16, no. 61–62 (1976): 103–17.

D'Autilia, Maria Letizia. *Il Cittadino senza Burocrazia. Società Umanitaria e Amministrazione Pubblica nell'Italia Liberale*. Torino: Giuffré, 1995.
Davie, Grace. *Poverty Knowledge in South Africa: A Social History of Human Science, 1855–2005*. New York: Cambridge University Press, 2015.
de Geer, Hans. *Rationaliseringsrörelsen i Sverige: effektivitetsidéer och socialt ansvar under mellankrigstiden*. Stockholm: Stockholm University, 1978.
de Groot, Gertjan *Fabricage van Verschillen. Mannenwerk, vrouwenwerk in de Nederlandse industrie*. Amsterdam: Aksant, 2001.
de Lacy Mann, Julia. *Documents Illustrating the Wiltshire Textile Trades in the Eighteenth Century*. Devizes: Wiltshire Archaeological Society, 1964.
de Lacy Mann, Julia. *The Cloth Industry in the West of England: From 1640 to 1880*. Oxford: Clarendon Press, 1971.
De Ridder, Widukind. *Loonsystemen, arbeidsorganisaties en arbeidsverhoudingen in de Belgische glas- en textielnijverheid, 1886–1914*. Brussels: VUB Press, 2010.
de Vries, Jan. 'The Industrial Revolution and the Industrious Revolution'. *The Journal of Economic History*, 54, no. 2 (1994): 249–270.
de Vries, Jan. *The Industrious Revolution: Consumer Demand and the Household Economy, 1650 to the Present*. Cambridge: Cambridge University Press, 2008.
Deakin, Simon and Frank Wilkinson. *The Law of the Labour Market Industrialization, Employment, and Legal Evolution*. Oxford: Oxford University Press, 2005.
Defoort, Hendrik. *Werklieden, bemint uw profijt. De Belgische sociaaldemocratie in Europa*. Leuven: Lannoocampus, 2006.
degli Esposti, Fabio. 'The Industrial and Agricultural Mobilization of Italy'. *Italy in the Era of the Great War*, ed. Vanda Wilcox, 309–28. Leiden: Brill, 2018.
Desrosières, Alain. 'Comment faire des choses qui tiennent: histoire sociale et statistique'. *Histoire & Mesure*, 1989, Vol. 4, no. 3/4 (1989): 225–42.
Desrosières, Alain. 'L'État, le Marché et les Statistiques. Cinq Façons d'Agir sur l'Économie'. *Courrier des Statistiques*, 95–96 (2000): 3–10.
Desrosières, Alain. *The Politics of Large Numbers*. Cambridge, MA: Harvard University Press, 2002.
Desrosières, Alain. *Gouverner par les Nombres. L'Argument Statistique II*. Paris: Presses de l'École des Mines de Paris, 2008.
Desrosières, Alain. *Pour une Sociologie Historique de la Quantification. L'Argument Statistique I*. Paris: Presses de l'École des Mines de Paris, 2008.
Desrosières, Alain. *Prouver et gouverner. Une Analyse Politique des Statistiques Publiques*. Paris: La Découverte, 2014.
Devereux, Stephen. 'Social Pensions in Southern Africa in the Twentieth Century'. *Journal of Southern African Studies*, 33, no. 2 (2007): 539–60.
Devika, J. P.R. Nisha and A. K. Rajasree. 'A Tactful Union': Domestic Workers' Unionism, Politics and Citizenship in Kerala, India'. *Indian Journal of Gender Studies*, 18, no. 2 (2011): 185–215.
DiMaggio, Paul J. and Walter W. Powell 'The Iron Cage Revisited: Institutional Isomorphism and Collective Rationality in Organizational Fields'. *American Sociological Review*, 48, no. 2 (1983): 147–60.
Diaz-Bone, Rainer and Emmanuel Didier. 'Introduction: The Sociology of Quantification – Perspectives on an Emerging Field in the Social Sciences'. *Historical Social Research / Historische Sozialforschung*, 41, no. 2 (2016): 7–26.
Diaz-Bone, Rainer. 'Convention Theory, Classification and Quantification'. *Historical Social Research / Historische Sozialforschung*, 41, no. 2 (2015): 48–71.

Dickens, Richard, Paul Gregg, Stephen Machin, Alan Manning, and Jonathan Wadsworth. 'Wages Councils: Was There a Case for Abolition?' *British Journal of Industrial Relations*, 31, no. 4 (1993): 515–29.

Didier, Emmanuel. *America by the Numbers. Quantification, Democracy, and the Birth of National Statistics*. Cambridge, Massachusetts: MIT Press, 2020.

Dimand, Robert W. 'The Cowles Commission and Foundation on the Functioning of Financial Markets. From Irving Fisher and Alfred Cowles to Harry Markowitz and James Tobin'. *Revue d'Histoire des Sciences Humaines,* 20, no. 1 (2009): 79–100.

Dinerstein, Ana Cecilia and Frederick Harry Pitts. 'From Post-Work to Post-Capitalism? Discussing the Basic Income and Struggles for Alternative Forms of Social Reproduction'. *Journal of Labor and Society*, 21, no. 4 (2018): 471–91.

Dinkelman, T. and V. Ranchhod, 'Evidence on the impact of minimum wage laws in an informal sector: Domestic workers in South Africa', *Journal of Development Economics*, 99, no. 1 (2012): 27–45.

Dobb, Maurice. *Wages*. London: Nisbet and Co and Cambridge University Press, 1959.

Dobson, C. R. *Masters and Journeymen. A Prehistory of Industrial Relations*, 1717–1800. London: Croom Helm, 1980.

Doyle, Patrick. 'Irish Social Catholicism and the Development of the Living Wage Doctrine'. *Radical History Review*, 143, no. May (2022): 177–193.

Drury, Horace B. *Scientific Management: A History and Criticism*. New York: Columbia University, 1915.

Dubois, Laurent. 'An Enslaved Enlightenment: Rethinking the Intellectual History of the French Atlantic'. *Social History*, 31, no. 1 (2006): 1–14.

Dubow, Saul and Alan Jeeves (eds). *South Africa's 1940s: Worlds of Possibility*. Cape Town: Double Storey Books, 2005.

Dubow, Saul. *Scientific Racism in Modern South Africa*. Cambridge: Cambridge University Press, 1995.

Eckert, Andreas. 'Von der "freien Lohnarbeit" zum "informellen Sektor"?'. *Geschichte und Gesellschaft* 43, no. 2 (2017): 297–307.

Edwards, Richard C. Michael, Reich and David M., Gordon (eds). *Labor Market Segmentation*. Lexington, Mass.: Heath, 1975.

Ehmer, Josef. *Soziale Traditionen in Zeiten des Wandels. Arbeiter und Handwerker im 19. Jahrhundert*. Frankfurt: Campus, 1994.

Elbaum, Max. *Revolution in the Air: Sixties Radicals turn to Lenin, Mao and Che*. London: Verso Books, 2002.

Elvin, Mark. *The Pattern of the Chinese Past*. London: Eyre Methuen, 1973).

Enflo, Kerstin and Tobias Karlsson. 'From Conflict to Compromise: The Importance of Mediation in Swedish Work Stoppages 1907–1927'. *European Review of Economic History*, 23, no. 3 (2019): 268–98.

Engle Merry, Sally. *The Seductions of Quantification: Measuring Human Rights, Gender Violence, and Sex Trafficking*. Chicago: University of Chicago Press, 2016.

Espeland, Wendy N. and Michael Sauder. 'Rankings and Reactivity: How Public Measures Recreate Social Worlds'. *American Journal of Sociology*, 113, no. 1 (2007): 1–40.

Espeland, Wendy N. and Mitchell L. Stevens 'Commensuration as a Social Process'. *Annual Review of Sociology,* 24 (1998): 313–43.

Evans, Ivan. *Bureaucracy and Race: Native Administration in South Africa*. Berkeley: University of California Press, 1997.

Ewing, Keith, John Hendy and Carolyn Jones. 'A Manifesto for Labour Law: Towards a Comprehensive Revision of Workers' Rights'. Liverpool: Institute of Employment Rights, 2016.

Farber, Henry S. 'Nonunion Wage Rates and the Threat of Unionization', *ILR Review*, 58, no. 3 (2005): 335–52.

Fassin, Didier (ed.). *A companion to moral anthropology*. Chichester; Malden, Mass: Wiley-Blackwell, 2012.

Favero, Giovanni. 'A Reciprocal Legitimation: Corrado Gini and Statistics in Fascist Italy'. *Management & Organizational History*, 12, no. 3 (2017): 261–84.

Favero, Giovanni. 'Le Statistiche dei Salari Industriali in Periodo Fascista'. *Quaderni Storici*, 134, no. 2 (2010): 319–57.

Federico, Giovanni, Alessandro Nuvolari and Michaelangelo Vasta. 'The Origins of the Italian Regional Divide. Evidence from Real Wages, 1861–1913'. *The Journal of Economic History*, 79, no. 1 (2019): 63–98.

Feinstein, Charles. *An Economic History of South Africa: Conquest, Discrimination, Development*. Cambridge: Cambridge University Press, 2005.

Feltes, N. N. 'Misery or the Production of Misery: Defining Sweated Labour in 1890'. *Social History*, 17, no. 3 (1992): 441–52.

Ferguson, James. *The Anti-Politics Machine: 'Development' Depoliticization, and Bureaucratic Power in Lesotho*. Minneapolis: University of Minnesota Press, 1994.

Fernandes, Leela. *Producing Workers. The Politics of Gender, Class and Culture in the Calcutta Jute Mills*. Philadelphia: University of Pennsylvania Press, 1997.

Feuerwerker, Albert. 'Economic Trends, 1912–1949' in *The Cambridge History of China: Volume 12: Republican China, 1912–1949,* Part 1, ed. John K. Fairbank chapter 2. Cambridge: Cambridge University Press, 1989.

Franzosi, Roberto. 'One Hundred Years of Strike Statistics: Methodological and Theoretical Issues in Quantitative Strike Research'. *ILR*, 42, no. 3 (1989): 348–62.

Franzosi, Roberto. *The Puzzle of Strikes: Class and State Strategies in Postwar Italy*. Cambridge: Cambridge, University Press, 1994.

Freeman, Richard B. and James L. Medoff. 'The Impact of the Percentage Organized on Union and Nonunion Wages'. *Review of Economics and Statistics*, 63, no. 4 (1981): 561–72.

Froide, Amy M. *Never Married. Singlewomen in Early Modern England*. Oxford: Oxford University Press, 2005).

Fudge, Judy. 'Labour as a "Fictive Commodity": Radically Reconceptualizing Labour Law', in *The Idea of Labour Law*, eds Davidov, Guy and Langille, Brian, 120–36. Oxford: Oxford University Press, 2011.

Furlough, Ellen. *Consumer Cooperation in France. The Politics of Consumption, 1834–1914*. Ithaca: Cornell University Press, 1991.

Fussell George E. (ed.), *Robert Loader's Farm Accounts 1610–1620*. London: Royal Historical Society, 1936.

Gabbuti, Giacomo. 'Labour Shares and Inequality: Insights from Italian Economic History, 1895–1970'. *European Review of Economic History*, 25, no. 2 (2021): 355–78.

Galbraith, John Kenneth. *The Affluent Society*. New York: Houghton Mifflin, 1958.

Gallaway, Cowell. 'The Foundations of the War on Poverty'. *American Economic Review*, 55, no. 1 (1965): 122–31.

García-Zúñiga, Mario and Ernesto López Losa. 'Skills and Human Capital in Eighteenth-Century Spain: Wages and Working Lives in the Construction of the Royal Palace of Madrid (1737–1805)'. *The Economic History Review*, 74, no. 3 (2021): 691–720.

Garegnani, Pierangelo. 'Heterogeneous Capital, the Production Function and the Theory of Distribution'. *The Review of Economic Studies*, 37, no. 3 (1970): 407–436.
Gaspari, Oscar. *Storia dell'Usci. Unione Statistica delle Città Italiane. 1905–1987. La Rete degli Statistici Comunali*. Gavardo: Liberedizioni, 2022.
Gazeley, Ian, Rose Holmes and Andrew Newell. *The Household Budget Survey in Western Europe, 1795–1965*. IZA Discussion Papers, n. 11429, Bonn, Institute of Labour Economics, 2008.
Gazeley, Ian. 'The levelling of pay in Britain during the Second World War'. *European Review of Economic History*, 10, no. 2 (2006): 175–204.
Geary, Daniel. *Beyond Civil Rights: The Moynihan Report and Its Legacy*. Philadelphia: University of Pennsylvania Press, 2015.
Ghosh, Arunabh. *Making It Count: Statistics and Statecraft in the Early People's Republic of China*. Princeton: Princeton University Press, 2020.
Gilboy, Elizabeth W. *Wages in Eighteenth-Century England*. Cambridge, Mass: Harvard University Press, 1934.
Glickman, Lawrence B. *A Living Wage: American Workers and the Making of Consumer Society*. Ithaca, NY: Cornell University Press, 1997.
Golas, Peter. *Chemistry and Chemical Technology: Part 13, Mining. Vol. 5. Science and Civilisation in China*. Cambridge: Cambridge University Press, 1999.
Goldin, Claudia. *Understanding the Gender Gap. An Economic History of American Women*. New York: Oxford University Press, 1990.
Gooren, Henny and Hans Heger. *Per Mud of Bij de Week Gewonnen. De Ontwikkeling van Beloningsystemen in de Groningse Landbouw, 1800–1914*. Groningen: Nederlands Agronomisch-Historisch Instituut, 1993.
Gordon, David, Richard Edwards and Michael Reich. *Segmented Work, Divided Workers: The historical transformation of labor in the United States*. Cambridge, Mass.: Cambridge University Press, 1972.
Gordon, David. *Theories of Poverty and Unemployment: Orthodox, Radical and Dual Labor Market Perspectives*. Lanham: Lexington Books, 1972.
Gottschang, Thomas R. and Diana Lary. *Swallows and Settlers: The Great Migration from North China to Manchuria*. Ann Arbor: Center for Chinese Studies, The University of Michigan, 2000.
Graeber, David. *Bullshit Jobs. A Theory*. London: Penguin 2018.
Griffin, Emma. 'Diets, Hunger and Living Standards During the British Industrial Revolution'. *Past & Present*, 239, no. 1 (2018): 71–111.
Grover, Chris. 'Living Wages and the "Making Work Pay" Strategy'. *Critical Social Policy*, 25, no. 1 (2005): 5–27.
Grover, Shalini. 'English-speaking and Educated Female Domestic Workers in Contemporary India: New Managerial Roles, Social Mobility and Persistent Inequality'. *Journal of South Asian Development*, 13, no. 2, (2018): 186–209.
Grubb, Farley. 'Creating Maryland's Paper Money Economy, 1720–1740: The Confluence of Political Constituencies, Economic Forces, Transatlantic Markets, and Law'. *Journal of Early American History*, 9, no. 1 (2019): 42–58.
Guidi, Marco E. L. and Luca Michelini (eds). 'Marginalismo e Socialismo nell'Italia Liberale, 1870–1925'. *Annali della Fondazione Giangiacomo Feltrinelli*, 35 (2001).
Guyer, Jane *Marginal Gains: Monetary Transactions in Atlantic Africa*. Chicago: Chicago University Press, 2004.
Hacking, Ian. *The Social Construction of What?*. Cambridge, MA: Harvard University Press, 1999.

Hamark, Jesper. 'Labour market conflicts in Scandinavia, c. 1900–1938: The scientific need to separate strikes and lockouts'. *Gothenburg Papers in Economic History*, no. 26 (2020).

Hamark, Jesper. *Ports, dock workers and labour market conflicts*. Göteborg: Göteborgs universitet, 2014.

Hanes, Christopher. 'The development of nominal wage rigidity in the late 19th century'. *The American Economic Review*, 83, no. 4 (1993): 732–56.

Harrison, Henrietta. 'Village Industries and the Making of Rural-Urban Difference in Early Twentieth-Century Shanxi', in *How China Works: Perspectives on the Twentieth-century Industrial Workplace*, ed. Jacob Eyferth, 25–40. Abingdon, Oxon: Routledge, 2006.

Hatcher, John. 'Labour, leisure and economic thought before the nineteenth century'. *Past and Present*, 160 no. August (1998): 64–115.

Hatcher, John. *The History of the British Coal Industry before 1700: Towards the Age of Coal*, I. Oxford: Oxford University Press, 1992.

Hay, Douglas C., and Paul Craven. *Masters, Servants, and Magistrates in Britain and the Empire, 1562–1955*. Chapel Hill, NC: University of North Carolina Press, 2014.

Hecht, Gabrielle. *Being Nuclear: Africans and the Global Uranium Trade*. Cambridge, MA: The MIT Press, 2012.

Hicks, John. *The Theory of Wages*. London: Palgrave Macmillan, 1963.

Hilson, Mary, Silke Neunsinger and Greg Patmore (eds). *A Global History of Consumer Co-operatives since 1850*. Leiden: Brill, 2017.

Hilt, Eric. 'Economic History, Historical Analysis, and the "New History of Capitalism"'. *The Journal of Economic History*, 77, no. 2 (2017): 511–36.

Hirson, Baruch. *Yours for the Union: Class and Community Struggles in South Africa*. London: Zed Books, 1989.

Hobsbawm, Eric J. and Terence Ranger (eds). *The Invention of Tradition*. Cambridge: Cambridge University Press, 2014.

Hobsbawm, Eric J. *Labouring Men: Studies in the History of Labour*. London: Anchor Books, [1964]1968).

Hodgson, Geoffrey M. *Conceptualizing capitalism*. Chicago: University of Chicago Press, 2015.

Hoerder, Dirk, Elise van Nederveen Meerkerk and Silke Neunsinger (eds). *Towards a Global History of Domestic and Caregiving Workers*. Leiden and Boston: Brill, 2015.

Hofmeester, Karin, Gijs Kessler and Christine Moll-Murata. 'Conquerors, Employers, and Arbiters: States and Shifts in Labour Relations 1500–2000'. *International Review of Social History*, 61, Special Issue (2016): 1–26.

Hollander, Samuel. *The Economics of Adam Smith*. London: Heineman, 1973.

Honig, Emily. 'The Contract Labor System and Women Workers: Pre-Liberation Cotton Mills of Shanghai'. *Modern China*, 9, no. 4 (1983): 421–54.

Hoppit Julian. *Risk and failure in English business 1700–1800*. Cambridge: Cambridge University Press, 1987.

Hoppit, Julian. *Britain's Political Economies: Parliament and Economic Life, 1660–1800*. Cambridge: Cambridge University Press, 2017.

Horrell, Sara, Jane Humphries and Jacob Weisdorf. 'Beyond the male breadwinner: Life-cycle living standards of intact and disrupted English working families, 1260–1850'. *The Economic History Review*, 75, no. 2 (2022): 530–60.

Howlett, Peter and Mary S. Morgan (eds). *How Well Do Facts Travel? The Dissemination of Reliable Knowledge*. New York: Cambridge University Press, 2011.

Huberman, Michael. 'Piece rates reconsidered: the case of cotton'. *Journal of Interdisciplinary History*, 26, no. 3 (1996): 393–417.
Huberman, Michael. *Escape from the market: negotiating work in Lancashire*. Cambridge: Cambridge University Press, 1996.
Hudson, Pat and Steve King. 'Two Textile Townships, c. 1660–1820: A Comparative Demographic Analysis'. *The Economic History Review*, 53, no. 4 (2000), 711–12.
Humphries, Jane 'The Gender Gap in Wages: Productivity or Prejudice or Market Power in Pursuit of Profits'. *Social Science History*, 33, no. 4 (2009): 487–8.
Humphries, Jane and Carmen Sarasúa. 'Off the Record: Reconstructing Women's Labor Force Participation in the European Past'. *Feminist Economics*, 18, no. 4 (2012): 39–67.
Humphries, Jane and Jacob Weisdorf. 'Wages of Women in England, 1260–1850'. *The Journal of Economic History*, 75, no. 2 (2015): 405–47.
Humphries, Jane and Benjamin Schneider, 'Spinning the Industrial Revolution', *The Economic History Review*, 72, no. 1 (2019): 126–55.
Humphries, Jane. 'Unreal Wages? Real Income and Economic Growth in England, 1260–1850'. *The Economic Journal*, 623, October (2019): 2867–2887.
Huret, Romain. *The Experts' War on Poverty: Social Research and the Welfare Agenda in Postwar America*. Ithaca, NY: Cornell University Press, 2018.
Igo, Sarah E. *The Averaged Americans: Survey, Citizens, and the Making of a Mass Public*. Cambridge, MA: Harvard University Press, 2007.
Iliffe, John. *The African Poor: A History*. New York: Cambridge University Press, 1987.
Innes, Joanna. 'Regulating Wages in Eighteenth and Early Nineteenth-Century England: Arguments in Context', in *Regulating the British Economy 1660–1850*, edited by Perry, Gauci, 195–215. Oxford: Oxford University Press, 2016.
Ipsen, Carl. *Dictating Demography. The Problem of Population in Fascist Italy*. Cambridge: Cambridge University Press, 1996.
Isserman, Maurice. *The Other American: The Life of Michael Harrington*. New York: PublicAffairs, 2000.
Iversen, Torben and Barry Eichengreen. 'Institutions and Economic Performance in the 20th Century: Evidence from the Labor Market'. *Oxford Review of Economic Policy*, 15, no. 4 (1999): 121–38.
Jaffe, James. *The Struggle for Market Power: Industrial Relations in the British Coal Industry, 1800–1840*. Cambridge: Cambridge University Press, 1991.
Jagd, Søren. 'Laurent Thévenot and the French Convention School: A Short Introduction'. *Economic Sociology: European Electronic Newsletter*, 5, no. 3 (2004): 2–9.
Jain, Shraddha and Praveena Kodoth. 'Locality-specific Norms for Wages and Bargaining: "Part-time" Domestic orders in the National Capital Region', in *Working in Others' Homes. The Specificities and Challenges of Paid Domestic Work* edited by N. Neetha, 66–94. New Delhi: Tulika Books, 2019.
Jassanoff, Sheila (ed.), *States of Knowledge: The Co-Production of Science and Social Order*. New York: Routledge, 2004.
Jerven, Morton. *Poor Numbers: How We Are Misled by African Development Statistics and What to Do about It*. Ithaca: Cornell University Press, 2013.
Johansson, Alf. *Arbetarrörelsen och taylorismen: Olofström 1895–1925*. Lund: Arkiv, 1990.
Johansson, Alf. *Den effektiva arbetstiden: verkstäderna och arbetsintensitetens problem 1900–1920*. Uppsala: Uppsala universitet, 1977.
Johansson, Ingemar. *Strejken som vapen: fackföreningar och strejker i Norrköping 1870–1910*. Stockholm: Stockholms Universitet, 1982.

Join-Lambert, Odile, Alain Chatriot and Vincent Viet (eds). *Les Politiques du Travail (1906-2006), Acteurs, Institutions, Réseaux*. Rennes: PUR, 2006.

Joseph, Rajesh, Lobo, Roshni and Natrajan, Balmurli 'Between "Baksheesh" and "Bonus": Precarity, Class, and Collective Action among Domestic Workers in Bengaluru', *EPW*, 53, no. 45 (2018): 38–45.

Kalleberg, Arne L. *Good Jobs, Bad Jobs: The Rise of Polarized and Precarious Employment Systems in the United States, 1970s-2000s*. New York: Russell Sage Foundation, 2011.

Kalpagam, U. 'Globalisation, Liberalisation and Women Workers in the Informal Sector', in *Informal Sector in India: Perspectives and Policies*, eds Alakh N. Sharma, Amitabh Kundu, 310–30. New Delhi: Institute for Human Development, Institute of Applied Manpower Research, 2001.

Karis, Thomas G. and Gail M. Gerhart (eds). *Nadir and Resurgence, 1964–1979*. Vol. 5. *From Protest to Challenge: A Documentary History of African Politics in South Africa, 1882-1990*. Bloomington: Indiana University Press, 1997.

Karlsson, Tobias. 'Strikes and Lockouts in Sweden: Reconsidering Raphael's List of Work Stoppages 1859-1902'. *Lund Papers in Economic History*, no. 192 (2019).

Karlsson, Tobias. *Downsizing: Personnel Reductions at the Swedish Tobacco Monopoly, 1915-1939*. Lund: Lunds universitet, 2008.

Katz, Lawrence F. and Alan B. Krueger 'The Rise and Nature of Alternative Work Arrangements in the United States, 1995–2015'. *ILR Review*, 72, no. 2 (2015): 382–416.

Keiser, Thorsten. *Vertragszwang und Vertragsfreiheit im Recht der Arbeit von der frühen Neuzeit bis in die Moderne*. Frankfurt am Main: Klostermann 2013.

Klare, Karl. 'On Ruth Dukes, The Labour Constitution: The Enduring Idea of Labour Law'. *Jurisprudence. An International Journal of Legal and Political Thought*, 9, no. 2 (2018): 1–6.

Knight, Frank H. *On the History and Method in Economics*. Chicago: Chicago University Press, 1963 [1956].

Knight, Roger. 'From Impressment to Task Work: Strikes and Disruption in the Royal Dockyards, 1688–1788', in *History of Work and Labour Relations in the Royal Dockyards*, edited by Kenneth Lunn and Ann Day, 1–20. London: Routledge, 1999.

Knowles, K. G. J. C. *Strikes: A Study in Industrial Conflict*. Oxford: Basil Blackwell, 1952.

Kott, Sandrine and Joëlle Droux (eds). *Globalizing social rights: the International Labour Organization and beyond*. London: Palgrave Macmillan, 2013.

Kuroda, Akinobu. *A Global History of Money*. London: Routledge, 2020.

Kussmaul, Ann. *Servants in husbandry in early modern England*. Cambridge: Cambridge University Press, 1981.

Lam, Tong. *A Passion for Facts: Social Surveys and the Construction of the Chinese Nation-State, 1900–1949*. Berkeley: University of California Press, 2011.

Lanata Briones, Cecilia. 'Constructing Cost of Living Indices: Ideas and Individuals, Argentina, 1918–1935'. *History of Political Economy*, 53, no. 1 (2021): 57–87.

Lane, Penelope, Neil Raven and K.D.M. Snell. (eds). *Women, Work and Wages in England, 1600 – 1850*. Woodbridge: The Boydell Press, 2004.

Le Crom, Jean-Pierre and Marc Bonichini (eds). *La Chicotte et le Pécule. Les Travailleurs à l'Épreuve du Droit Colonial Français (XIX-XXe siècles)*. Rennes: PUR, 2021.

Le Crom, Jean-Pierre, Philippe Auvergnon, Katia Barragan, Dominique Blonz-Colombo, Marc Bonichini et al. *Histoire du droit du travail dans les colonies françaises (1848–1960)*. [Rapport] Law and Justice Research Mission, 2017.

Lean, Eugenia. *Public Passions: The Trial of Shi Jianqiao and the Rise of Popular Sympathy in Republican China*. Berkeley: University of California Press, 2007.

Levrero, Enrico Sergio. 'Some notes on Wages and Competition in the Labour Market', in *Sraffa and Modern Economics,* eds Ciccone, Roberto Gehrke, Christian and Mongiovi, Gary, 361–83. London: Routledge, 2011.

Lewchuk, Wayne. 'Fordism and British Motor Car Employers, 1896-1932', in *Managerial Strategies & Industrial Relations,* edited by Howard F. Gospel and Craig R. Littler, 82–110. London: Gower, 1983.

Licht, Walter. *Getting Work. Philadelphia, 1840–1950.* Cambridge, MA.: Harvard University Press, 1992.

Lictenstein, Alex. 'We feel that our strength is on the factory floor': Dualism, Shop-Floor Power, and Labor Law Reform in Late Apartheid South Africa'. *Labor History,* 60, no. 6 (2019): 606-25.

Linne, Karsten. 'Von der Arbeitsvermittlung zum "Arbeitseinsatz". Zum Wandel der Arbeitsverwaltung 1933-1945', in *Arbeit im Nationalsozialismus,* eds Marc Buggeln and Michael Wildt, 53–70. Michael Berlin: De Gruyter/Oldenbourg, 2014.

Lis, Catharina, Jan Lucassen and Hugo Soly (eds). 'Before the Unions: Wage Earners and Collective Action in Europe, 1300-1850'. *International Review of Social History,* 39 no. 2 supplement (1994).

Lucassen, Jan (ed.). *Global Labour History A State of the Art. International and Comparative Social History.* Oxford: Blackwell, 2008.

Lucassen, Jan and Sabyasachi Bhattacharya (eds). *Workers In The Informal Sector: Studies In Labour History 1800–2000.* Delhi: MacMillan, 2006.

Lucassen, Jan and Radhika Seshan. *Wages earners in India 1500–1900. Regional Approaches in an International Context.* New Delhi: Sage, 2022.

Lucassen, Jan. *The Story of Work: A New History of Humankind.* New Haven: Yale University Press, 2021.

Luckhardt, Ken and Brenda Wall. *Organize or Starve! The History of the South African Congress of Trade Unions.* New York: International Publishers, 1980.

Lund, Frances. 'State Social Benefits in South Africa'. *International Social Security Review,* 46, no. 1 (1996): 5-25.

Lundh, Christer. 'Institutional Change in the Swedish Labour Market 1830–1990', in *Wage Formation, Labour Market Institutions and Economic Transformation in Sweden 1860–2000,* eds Christer Lundh, Jonas Olofsson, Lennart Schön and Lars Svensson, 92-142. Stockholm: Almqvist & Wiksell International, 2004.

Lundh, Christer. *Spelets regler: institutioner och lönebildning på den svenska arbetsmarknaden 1850–2010.* Stockholm: SNS förlag, 2010.

Lyttelton, Anthony. *The Seizure of Power. Fascim in Italy, 1919–1929.* Princeton: Princeton University Press, 1973.

Magnusson, Lars. *Arbetet vid en svensk verkstad: Munktells 1900–1920.* Lund: Arkiv förlag, 1987.

Maifreda, Germano. 'La panificazione e i prezzi del pane a Milano tra Otto e Novecento', in *Le Vie del Cibo. Italia Settentrionale (secc. XVI-XX),* edited by Marina Cavallera, Silvia A. Conca Messina and Blythe Alice Raviola, 191–221. Roma: Carocci, 2019.

Maitte, Corine. 'Rémunérer et Compter le Travail sur les Chantiers Médicis (fin XVIe Siècle-Début XVIIe Siècle)'. *Histoire & Mesure,* 36, no. 1 (2021): 3–36.

Mamdani, Mahmood. *Citizen and Subject: Contemporary Africa and the Legacy of Late Colonialism.* Princeton: Princeton University Press, 1996.

Manning, Alan. *Monopsony in Motion. Imperfect Competition in Labor Markets.* Princeton: Princeton University Press, 2003.

Marcuse, Herbert. *One-Dimensional Man: Studies in the Ideology of Advanced Industrial Society*. Boston: Beacon Press, 1964.

Margairaz, Michel and Michel Pigenet (eds). *Le Prix du Travail, France et espaces coloniaux, XIXe XXIe siècle*. Paris: Éditions de la Sorbonne, 2019

Marglin, Stephen A. 'What Do Bosses Do? The Origins and Functions of Hierarchy in Capitalist Production'. *Review of Radical Political Economics*, 6, Summer, no. 2 (1974): 60–112.

Marks, Shula and Stanley Trapido (eds). *The Politics of Race, Class and Nationalism in Twentieth Century South Africa*. New York: Routledge, 1987.

Martin, Brian G. *The Shanghai Green Gang: Politics and Organized Crime, 1919–1937*. University of California Press, 1996.

Martini, Manuela. 'Pratiques de la Réclamation du Prix du Travail: Différends autour des Rémunérations des Tisseurs et des Tisseuses en Soie de Lyon au Début des Années 1830'. *Parlement(s). Revue d'histoire politique*, 33, no. 3 (2020): 63–78.

Marucco, Dora. *L'Amministrazione della Statistica nell'Italia Unita*. Roma-Bari: Laterza, 1996.

Marx, Karl. *Capital. A Critique of Political Economy*. Vol. I. Hamburg: Verlag von Otto Meissner, 1867.

Marx, Karl. *Value, Price and Profit. Addressed to Working Men*. Workers' Intelligence Bureau, 1931 [1898].

Massie, Robert. *Loosing the Bonds: The United States and South Africa in the Apartheid Years*. New York: Doubleday, 1997.

Masson, Jack and Donald Guimary. 'Asian Labor Contractors in the Alaskan Canned Salmon Industry: 1880–1937'. *Labor History*, 22, no. 3 (2008), 377–97.

Mata, Tiago. 'Migrations and Boundary Work: Harvard, Radical Economists, and the Committee on Political Discrimination'. *Science in Context*, 22, no. 1 (2009): 115–43.

Mata, Tiago. 'Trust in Independence: The identities of Economists in Business Magazines, 1945–1970'. *Journal of the History of the Behavioral Sciences*, 47, no. January (2011): 359–79.

Mazzucato Mariana. *The Value of Everything. Making and Taking in the Global Economy*. London: Allen Lane, 2018.

Mbembe, Achille. *Critique of Black Reason*. Durham: Duke University Press, 2017.

McEwen, Rachel. 'Living Hours: Providing Security of Hours alongside a Real Living Wage'. Living Wage Foundation, no. 28 (2019).

McKeown, Adam. 'Chinese Emigration in Global Context, 1850–1940'. *Journal of Global History*, 5, no. 1 (2010): 95–124.

McNulty, Paul. *The Origins and Development of Labour Economics: a Chapter in the History of Social Thought*. Cambridge, MA: MIT Press, 1980.

Mennicken, Andrea and Wendy Nelson Espeland. 'What's New with Numbers? Sociological Approaches to the Study of Quantification'. *Annual Review of Sociology*, 45 (2019): 223–45.

Mennicken, Andrea and Robert Salais (eds). *The New Politics of Numbers: Utopia, Evidence and Democracy*. New York: Palgrave, 2022.

Mikkelsen, Flemming. *Arbejdskonflikter i Skandinavien 1848–1980*. Copenhagen: University of Copenhagen, 1990.

Milanovic, Branko *Global Inequality: A New Approach for the Age of Globalization*. Cambridge: Harvard University Press, 2016.

Minns, Chris and Marian Rizov. 'Institutions, history and wage bargaining outcomes: international evidence from the post-World War Two era'. *Business History*, 57, no. 3 (2015): 358–75.

Misiani, Simone. *I Numeri e la Politica. Statistica, Programmazione e Mezzogiorno nell'Impegno di Alessandro Molinari*. Bologna: Il Mulino, 2007.
Mitra, Arup. 'Women in the Urban Informal Sector: Perpetuation of Meagre Earnings'. *Development and Change*, 36, no. 2 (2005): 291–316.
Mokyr, Joel. *The Enlightened Economy: An Economic History of Britain, 1700–1850*. New Haven: Yale University Press, 2009.
Molinder, Jakob, Tobias Karlsson and Kerstin Enflo. 'More Power to the People: Electricity Adoption, Technological Change, and Labor Conflict'. *Journal of Economic History*, 81, no. 2 (2021): 481–512.
Møller, Valerie (ed.). *Quality of Life in South Africa*. Boston: Kluwer Academic Publishers, 1997.
Moll-Murata, Christine. *State and Crafts in the Qing Dynasty (1644-1911)*. Amsterdam: Amsterdam University Press, 2018.
Moodie, Dunbar. *The Rise of Afrikanerdom: Power, Apartheid, and the Afrikaner Civil Religion*. Berkeley: University of California Press, 1975.
Morgan, Mary S. 'Seeking Parts, Looking for Wholes', in *Histories of Scientific Observation*, edited by Lorraine Daston and Elizabeth Lunbeck, 303–25. Chicago: Chicago University Press, 2011.
Moynihan, Daniel P. (ed.). *On Understanding Poverty*. New York. Basic Books, 1968–9.
Muldrew, Craig. 'Interpreting the Market: The Ethics of Credit and Community Relations in Early Modern England'. *Social History*, 18, no. 2 (1993): 163–83.
Muldrew, Craig. 'Th'ancient Distaff' and 'Whirling Spindle': measuring the contribution of spinning to household earnings and the national economy in England, 1550–1770'. *Economic History Review*, 65, no. 2 (2012): 126–55.
Muldrew, Craig. 'The Social Acceptance of Paper Credit as Currency in Eighteenth Century England: A Case Study of Glastonbury c.1720–1742', in *Financing in Europe: Evolution, Coexistence and Complementarity of Lending Practices from the Middle Ages to Modern Times*, edited by Marcella Lorenzini, Cinzia Lorandini and D'Maris Coffman, London: Palgrave, 2018.
Muldrew, Craig. 'Wages and the Problem of Monetary Scarcity in Early Modern England', in *Wages and Currency: Global Comparisons from Antiquity to the Twentieth Century* edited by Jan Lucassen, Bern: Peter Lang, 2007.
Muldrew, Craig. *Food, Energy and the Creation of Industriousness*. Cambridge: Cambridge University Press, 2011.
Muldrew, Craig. *The Economy of Obligation: The Culture of Credit and Social Relations in Early Modern England*. London: Macmillan, 1998.
Myrdal, Gunnar. *Beyond the Welfare State. Economic planning and its international implications*. New Haven, Yale University Press, 1960.
Neetha, N. (ed.). *Working in Others' Homes. The Specificities and Challenges of Paid Domestic Work*. New Delhi: Tulika Books, 2019.
Neetha, N. and Ranji Palriwala. 'The Absence of State Law: Domestic Workers in India'. *Canadian Journal of Women and the Law*, 23, no.1 (2011): 97–119.
Neetha, N. 'Mirroring Devalued Housework? Minimum Wages for Domestic Work', in *Working in Others' Homes. The Specificities and Challenges of Paid Domestic Work*, edited by N. Neetha. 278–97. New Delhi: Tulika Books, 2019.
Nattrass, Nicoli and Jeremy Seekings. *Class, Race, and Inequality in South Africa*. New Haven: Yale University Press, 2005.
Nelson, Daniel. 'Scientific Management, Systematic Management, and Labor, 1880–1915'. *Business History Review*, 48, no. 4 (1974): 479–500.

Nimushakavi, Vasanthi. 'Extending Legal Protection to Domestic Workers', in *Working in Others' Homes. The Specificities and Challenges of Paid Domestic Work*. edited by N. Neetha. 250–77. New Delhi: Tulika Books, 2019.

O'Connor, Alice. *Poverty Knowledge: Social Science, Social Policy, and the Poor in Twentieth-Century U.S. History*. Princeton: Princeton University Press, 2001.

O'Meara, Dan. *Volkskapitalisme: Class, Capital, and Ideology in the Development of Afrikaner Nationalism, 1934–1948*. Johannesburg: Ravan Press, 1983.

O'Neill, Robert, Jeff Ralph and Paul A. Smith. *Inflation: History and Measurement*. London: Palgrave Macmillan, 2017.

Olsson, Kent. *Från pansarbåtsvarv till tankfartygsvarv: de svenska storvarvens utveckling till exportindustri 1880–1936*. Göteborg: Svenska varv, 1983.

Packard, Randall M. *White Plague. Black Labor: Tuberculosis and the Political Economy of Health and Disease in South Africa*. Berkeley: University of California Press, 1989.

Paker, Meredith, Judy Stephenson and Patrick Wallis. 'Unskilled labour before the Industrial Revolution'. *Economic History Working Papers*, no. 322 (2021), London School of Economics and Political Science, London, UK (http://eprints.lse.ac.uk/108562/).

Palermo, Giulio. 'Power, Competition and the Free Trader Vulgaris'. *Cambridge Journal of Economics*, 40, no. 1 (2016): 259–81.

Palermo, Giulio. 'The Ontology of Economic Power in Capitalism: Mainstream Economics and Marx'. *Cambridge Journal of Economics*, 31, no. 4 (2006): 539–61.

Papastefanaki, L. 'Salaires, Division Sexuée du Travail et Hiérarchies Sociales dans l'Industrie Textile Grecque, 1912–1936', *Cahiers Balkaniques*, 45, no. December (2018): 101–20.

Parthasarathi, Prasannan. 'Rethinking Wages and Competitiveness in the Eighteenth Century: Britain and South India.' *Past and Present*, 158, no. 1 (1998): 79–109.

Parthasarathi, Prasannan. *The Transition to a Colonial Economy. Weavers, Merchants and Kings in South India, 1720–1800*. Cambridge: Cambridge University Press, 2001.

Pasinetti, Luigi. 'Paradoxes in Capital Theory: A Symposium: Changes in the Rate of Profit and Switches of Techniques'. *The Quarterly Journal of Economics*, 80, no. 4 (1966): 503–17.

Peck, Gunther. *Reinventing Free Labor: Padrones and Immigrant Workers in the North American West, 1880–1930*. Cambridge: Cambridge University Press, 2000.

Peck, Jamie. *Workfare States*. New York: Guilford Press, 2001.

Peires, J. B. *The Dead Will Arise: Nongqawuse and the Great Xhosa Cattle-Killing Movement, 1856–7*. Bloomington: Indiana University Press, 1989.

Peires, Jeff. 'Sir George Grey and the Kaffir Relief Committee'. *Journal of Southern African Studies*, 10, no. 2 (1984): 145–69.

Penn, Roger. 'The Course of Wage Differentials between Skilled and Non-Skilled Manual Workers in Britain between 1856 and 1964'. *British Journal of Industrial Relations*, 21, no. 1 (1983): 69–90.

Pepe, Adolfo. *Storia del Sindacato in Italia nel '900*, vol. 1, *La CGdL e l'Età Liberale*. Roma, Ediesse, 1997.

Perry, Elizabeth J. *Shanghai on Strike: The Politics of Chinese Labor*. Stanford University Press, 1993.

Pescarolo, Alessandra. *Il Lavoro delle Donne nell'Italia Contemporanea*. Roma: Viella, 2019.

Phelps Brown, E. H. and Sheila V. Hopkins. 'Seven Centuries of Building Wages'. *Economica*, 87, (1955): 195–206.

Phelps Brown, E. H. and Sheila V. Hopkins 'Seven centuries of the prices of consumables, compared with builders' wage-rates'. *Economica*, 23 (1956): 296–314.

Phelps Brown, E. H. and Sheila V. Hopkins. *A Perspective of Wages and Prices*. London: Routledge, 2013.
Picchio, Antonella. *Social Reproduction: The Political Economy of the Labour Market*. Cambridge: Cambridge University Press, 1992.
Pierson, Thomas. *Das Gesinde und die Herausbildung moderner Privatrechtsprinzipien*. Frankfurt am Main: Klostermann, 2016.
Piketty, Thomas. *Capital in the Twenty-First Century*. Cambridge: Harvard University Press, 2016.
Pinchbeck, Ivy. *Women workers and the industrial revolution 1750-1850*. London: George Routledge & Sons, 1930 [reprinted 1969].
Piore, Michael J. 'Fragments of a "Sociological" Theory of Wages'. *American Economic Review*, 63, no. 2 (1973): 377-84.
Piore, Michael J. *Internal labor markets and manpower analysis*. Lexington, Mass.: Heath, 1971.
Polanyi, Karl, *The Great Transformation*. New York: Farrar & Rinehart, 1944.
Poni, Carlo and Cimona Cerrutti (eds). 'Conflitti nel mondo del lavoro', *Quaderni Storici*, 80, no. 2 (1992).
Poni, Carlo. 'Misura Contro Misura: Come il Filo di Seta Divenne Sottile e Rotondo'. *Quaderni Storici*, 47, no. 2 (1981): 385-422.
Porter, Theodore M. *Trust in Numbers: The Pursuit of Objectivity in Science and Public Life*. Princeton, N.J.: Princeton University Press, 1995.
Pöschl, Magdalena. 'Beständiges und Veränderliches im Gewerberecht - Entwicklung der GewO 1859 bis 2009'. *Österreichische Zeitschrift für Wirtschaftsrecht*, no. 2 (2010): 64-74.
Postone, Moishe. *Time, Labor and Social Domination: A Reinterpretation of Marx's Critical Theory*. New York and Cambridge, Cambridge University Press, 1993.
Prévost, Jean-Guy. *A Total Science. Statistics in Liberal and Fascist Italy*. Montreal-Kingston: McGill-Queen's University Press, 2009.
Pullen, John. *The Marginal Productivity Theory of Distribution: a critical history*. Abingdon: Routledge, 2010.
Punzo, Maurizio. *La Giunta Caldara. L'Amministrazione Comunale di Milano negli Anni 1914-1920*. Bari-Roma: Laterza, 1986.
Puttick, Keith. '"21st Century Welfare" and the Wage-Work-Welfare Bargain'. *Industrial Law Journal*, 41, no. 1 (2012): 122-31.
Raghuram, Parvati. 'Caste and Gender in the Organisation of Paid Domestic Work in India'. *Work, Employment and Society*, 15, no. 3 (2001), 607-17.
Ramos Pinto, Pedro and Poornima Paidipaty. 'Introduction: Measuring Matters' *History of Political Economy*, 52, no. 3 (2020): 413-34.
Randall, Adrian. 'New languages or old? Labour, Capital and discourse in the industrial revolution'. *Social History*, 15, no. 2 (1990): 195-216.
Ravallion, Martin. *The Economics of Poverty: History, Measurement, and Policy*. Oxford: Oxford University Press, 2016.
Ray, Raka and Seemin Qayum. *Cultures of Servitude: Modernity, Domesticity, and Class in India*. Stanford: Stanford University Press, 2009.
Reddy, William. 'Modes de paiement et contrôle du travail dans les filatures de coton en France, 1750-1848'. *Revue du Nord*, 63 (1981): 135-46.
Reich, Michael, David M. Gordon and Richard C. Edwards 'Dual Labor Markets: A Theory of Labor Market Segmentation'. *American Economic Review*, 63, no. 2 (1973): 359-65.

Reid, Douglas A. 'The Decline of Saint Monday, 1766–1876'. *Past & Present*, 71, no. May (1976): 76–101.
Reith, Reinhold. *Lohn und Leistung. Lohnformen im Gewerbe, 1450–1900.* Stuttgart: F. Steiner, 1999.
Reynaud, Bénédicte. *Le Salaire, la Règle et le Marché.* Paris, Christian Bourgois, 1992.
Reynaud, Emmanuel. 'The International Labour Organization and the Living Wage: A Historical Perspective'. *Conditions of Work and Employment Series* no. 90, International Labour Office, Geneva, 2017.
Ringenbach, Paul T. *Tramps and Reformers 1873–1916. The Discovery of Unemployment in New York.* Westport, Conn.: Greenwood Press, 1973.
Robbins, Lionel. *Wages: An Introductory Analysis of the Wage System under Modern Capitalism.* London: Jarrolds, 1926.
Robertson, Nicole. *The Co-operative Movement and Communities in Britain, 1914–1960.* Farnham: Ashgate, 2010.
Rodriguez-Pinero, Luis. *Indigenous Peoples, Postcolonialism, and International Law. The ILO Regime (1919–1989).* Oxford, New York Oxford University Press, 2005.
Rosenband, Leonard. *Papermaking in Eighteenth-Century France: Management, Labor, and Revolution at the Montgolfier Mill, 1761–1805.* Baltimore: Johns Hopkins University Press, 2000.
Rothschild, Emma. 'Adam Smith and Conservative Economics'. *Economic History Review*, 45, no. 1 (1992): 74–96.
Rottenburg, Richard and Sally Engle Merry. 'A World of Indicators: The Making of Governmental Knowledge through Quantification', in *The World of Indicators: The Making of Governmental Knowledge through Quantification*, edited by Johanna Mugler, Richard Rottenburg, Sally E. Merry, and Sung-Joon Park, 1–33. Cambridge: Cambridge University Press, 2015.
Roy, Tirthankar. 'Sardars, Jobbers, Kanganies: The Labour Contractor and Indian Economic History'. *Modern Asian Studies*, 42, no. 5 (2008): 971–98.
Rudinow Sætnan, Ann, Heidi Mork Lomell and Svein Hammer (eds). *The Mutual Construction of Statistics and Society.* London: Routledge, 2012.
Rudischhauser, Sabine. *Geregelte Verhältnisse. Eine Geschichte des Tarifvertragsrechts in Deutschland und Frankreich (1890–1918/19).* Köln: Böhlau, 2016.
Rule, John. *The Experience of Labour in Eighteenth Century Industry.* London: Croom Helm, 1981.
Sacchi Landriani, Martino. 'Rethinking the Livret d'ouvriers: Time, Space and "Free" Labor in Nineteenth Century France'. *Labour History*, 60, no. 6 (2019): 854–64.
Safley Thomas Max and Bert de Munck (eds). *A Cultural History of Work in the Early Modern Age.* London, Bloomsbury, 2020.
Said, Edward. *Orientalism.* New York: Vintage Books, 1979.
Salvemini, Gaetano. *Under the Axe of Fascism.* New York: The Viking Press, 1936.
Sapelli, Giulio. *Comunità e Mercato. Socialisti, Cattolici e "Governo Economico Municipale" agli Inizi del XX Secolo.* Bologna: Il Mulino, 1986.
Sarkar, Tanika. 'Caste-ing servants in Colonial Kolkata', in *Servants' Pasts: Late-Eighteenth to Twentieth-Century South Asia*, vol. 2, edited by Nitin Sinha and Nitin Verma Hyderabad: Orient Blackswan, 2019.
Sarti Raffaella. 'Historians, Social Scientists, Servants, and Domestic Workers: Fifty Years of Research on Domestic Care Work'. *International Review of Social History*, 59, no. 2 (2014): 279–314.

Scholliers Peter and Vera Zamagni. *Labour's Reward. Real Wages and Economic Change in 19th- and 20th-century Europe.* Aldershot: Edward Elgar 1995.

Scholliers, Peter and Leonard Schwarz (eds). *Experiencing Wages. Social and Cultural Aspects of Wage Forms in Europe since 1500.* New York, Oxford: Berghahn, 2003.

Scholliers, Peter. 'Index Linked Wages, Purchasing Power and Social Conflict Between Wars. The Belgian Approach (Internationally Compared)'. *Journal of European Economic History*, 20, no. 2 (1991): 407–39.

Scholliers, Peter. 'Industrial wage differentials in nineteenth-century Belgium.' *Income distribution in historical perspective*, eds Y.S. Brenner, Hartmut Kaelble, Mark Thomas. Cambridge: Cambridge University Press, 1991.

Scholliers, Peter. 'Work floor under tension: working conditions and international competition in textiles', in *The Ashgate Companion to the History of Textile Workers, 1650–2000*, edited by Lex Heerma van Voss, Els Hiemstra-Kuperus and Elise van Nederveen Meerkerk (Farnham, Surrey, Burlington, VT: Ashgate, 2010)

Scholliers, Peter. 'L'écart Salarial entre Femmes et Hommes dans un Tissage de Coton Gantois au XIXe Siècle'. *Le Mouvement Social*, 276, no. 3 (2021): 93–106.

Scholliers, Peter. 'Quality in the Eye of the Storm. The Bread of the Ghent Co-operative Vooruit, 1880 to 1914'. *Cultural and Social History*, 18, no. 1 (2021): 79–96.

Schumpeter, Joseph. *History of Economic Analysis.* London: Allen and Unwin, 1982 [1954].

Schwarz, Leonard. 'Custom, Wages and Workload in England during Industrialization'. *Past & Present*, 197, no. November (2007): 143–175.

Searle, Rebecca. 'Is There Anything Real about Real Wages? A History of the Official British Cost of Living Index, 1914–62'. *Economic History Review*, 68, no. 1 (2015): 145–66.

Seidman, Gay. 'Monitoring Multinationals: Lessons from the Anti-Apartheid Era'. *Politics and Society*, 31, no. 3 (2003): 381–406.

Seligman, Ben Baruch. *Permanent poverty: An American syndrome.* Chicago: Quadrangle Books, 1968.

Sella, Lisa and Roberto Marchionatti. 'On the Cyclical Variability of Economic Growth in Italy, 1881–1913: a Critical Note'. *Cliometrica*, 6 (2012): 307–28.

Seltzer, Andrew. 'Did Firms Cut Nominal Wages in a Deflationary Environment?: Micro-Level Evidence from the Late 19th and early 20th Century Banking Industry'. *Explorations in Economic History*, 47, no. 1 (2010): 112–25.

Sen, Samita 'Gender and Class: Women in Indian Industry, 1890–1990', *Modern Asian Studies*, 42, no. 1 (2008): 75–116.

Sen, Samita. 'Commercial Recruiting and Informal Intermediation: Debate over the Sardari System in Assam Tea Plantations, 1860–1900'. *Modern Asian Studies,* 44, no. 1 (2010): 3–28.

Sen, Samita. 'Gender and the Politics of Class: Women in Trade Unions in Bengal'. *South Asia: Journal of South Asian Studies*, 44, no. 2 (2021): 362–79.

Sen, Samita. 'Slavery, Servitude and Wage Work: Domestic Work in Bengal', School of Women's Studies. Jadavpur University-Rosa Luxemburg Stiftung Occasional Paper Series, 1, 2015.

Sen, Samita. *Women and Labour in Late Colonial India. The Case of the Bengal Jute Industry.* Cambridge: Cambridge University Press, 1999.

Sen, Samita and Nilanjana Sengupta. *Domestic Days: Women, Work and Politics in Contemporary Kolkata.* New Delhi: Oxford University Press, 2016.

Serra, Gerardo. 'An Uneven Statistical Topography: The Political Economy of Household Budget Surveys in Late Colonial Ghana, 1951–1957'. *Canadian Journal of Development Studies / Revue Canadienne d'études du développement*, 35, no. 1 (2014): 9–27.

Sewell, William H. *Work and Revolution in France: The Language of Labor from the Old Regime to 1848*. Cambridge: Cambridge University Press, 1980.

Sharma, Sonal. 'Of Rasoi ka Kaam/Bathroom ka Kaam Perspectives of Women Domestic Workers'. *Economic and Political Weekly*, 51, no. 7 (2016): 52–61.

Sharpe, Pamela. *Adapting to Capitalism: Working Women in the English Economy, 1700–1850*. New York: St. Martin's Press, 1996.

Shaw-Taylor, Leigh. 'The Rise of Agrarian Capitalism and the Decline of Family Farming in England'. *The Economic History Review*, 65, no. 1 (2012): 26–60.

Shih, James C. *Chinese Rural Society in Transition. A Case Study of the Lake Tai Area y 1368–1800*. Berkeley: Institute of East Asian studies, 1992.

Silver, Beverly. *Forces of Labor. Workers' Movements and Globalization since 1870*. Cambridge: Cambridge University Press, 2003.

Simonton, Deborah and Anne Montenach (eds). *A Cultural History of Work in the Age of Enlightenment*. London: Bloomsbury, 2018.

Sinha, Nitin and Nitin Varma *Servants' Pasts: Late-Eighteenth to Twentieth-Century South Asia*. Hyderabad: Orient Blackswan, 2019.

Sinha, Nitin. 'Genealogies of "Verification": Policing the Master–Servant Relationship in Colonial and Postcolonial India'. *International Review of Social History*, 67, no. 1 (2022): 9–41.

Sinha, Nitin. 'Who Is (Not) a Servant, Anyway? Domestic servants and service in early colonial India'. *Modern Asian Studies*, 55, no. 1 (2021): 152–206.

Sloman, Peter, Daniel Zamora Vargas and Pedro Ramos Pinto (eds). *Universal Basic Income in Historical Perspective*. Chm: Palgrave Macmillan, 2021)

Sloman, Peter. *Transfer State: the Idea of a Guaranteed Income and the Politics of Redistribution in Modern Britain*. Oxford: Oxford University Press, 2019.

Smail, John. 'New languages for labour and capital: The transformation of discourse in the early years of the Industrial Revolution'. *Social History*, 12, no. 1 (1987): 49–71

Smith, Ian and Trevor Boyns. 'Scientific Management and the Pursuit of Control in Britain to c. 1960'. *Accounting, Business & Financial History,* 15, no. 2 (2005): 187–216.

Smith, Mark M. 'Time, Slavery and Plantation Capitalism in the Ante-Bellum American South'. *Past & Present*, 150, no. 1 (1996): 142–68.

Smith, S. A. *Like Cattles and Horses: Nationalist and Labor in Shanghai, 1895–1927*. Durham: Duke University Press, 2002.

Smith, Timothy. *Rule of Experts: Egypt, Techno-Politics, Modernity*. Berkeley: University of California Press, 2002.

Soderlund, Richard J. '"Intended as a Terror to the Idle and Profligate": Embezzlement and the Origins of Policing in the Yorkshire Worsted Industry, c. 1750–1777'. *Journal of Social History*, 31, no. 3 (1998): 647–69.

Solow, Robert. *The Labor Market as a Social Institution*. Oxford: Blackwell, 1990.

Sonenscher, Michael *Work and Wages. Natural Law, Politics and the Eighteenth-Century French Trades*. Cambridge: Cambridge University Press, 1989.

Spencer, David. *The Political Economy of Work*. London: Routledge, 2008.

Sraffa, Piero. 'Introduction'. to *David Ricardo, Works and Correspondence*, edited by Piero Sraffa, vol. I. Cambridge: Cambridge University Press 1951.

Sraffa, Piero. 'Sulle relazioni fra costo e quantità prodotta'. *Annali di economia*, 2 (1925): 277–328.

Sraffa, Piero. 'The Laws of Returns under Competitive Conditions'. *The Economic Journal*, 36, no. 144 (1926): 535–550.
Sraffa, Piero. *Production of Commodities by means of Commodities. Prelude to a Critique of Economic Theory*. Cambridge: Cambridge University Press: 1960.
Stadler, Alfred William. *A Long Way to Walk: Bus Boycotts in Alexandra, 1940–1945*. Johannesburg: University of the Witwatersrand Press, 1979.
Stanfors, Maria and Joyce Burnett. 'Understanding the Gender Gap Further. The Case of Turn-of the-Century Swedish Compositors'. *The Journal of Economic History*, 80, no. 1 (2020): 175–206.
Stanfors, Maria Leunig, Björn Tim Eriksson and Tobias Karlsson. 'Gender, Productivity, and the Nature of Work and Pay: Evidence from the Late Nineteenth-Century Tobacco Industry'. *The Economic History Review*, 67, no. 1 (2013): 48–65.
Stanziani, Alessandro. 'The Legal Status of Labour from the Seventeenth to the Nineteenth Century: Russia in a Comparative European Perspective'. *International Review of Social History*, 54, no. 3 (2009): 359–89.
Stapleford, Thomas. *The Cost of Living in America: A Political History of Economic Statistics, 1880–2000*. New York: Cambridge University Press, 2009.
Stein, Judith. *Pivotal Decade: How the United States Traded Factories for Finance in the Seventies*. New Haven: Yale Press, 2010.
Steinfeld Robert J. and Stanley L. Engermann 'Labour – Free or Coerced? A Historical Reassessment of Differences and Similarities', in *Free and Unfree Labour. The Debate Continues*, edited by Brass, Tom and van der Marcel Linden, 107–26. Bern et al.: Peter Lang, 1997.
Stephenson, Judy and John Hatcher (eds). *Seven Centuries of Unreal Wages. The Unreliable Data, Sources and Methods that have been used for Measuring Standards of Living in the Past*, London: Palgrave, 2018.
Stephenson, Judy. '"Real" wages? Contractors, Workers, and Pay in London Building Trades, 1650–1800'. *The Economic History Review*, 71, no. 1 (2018): 106–132.
Stephenson, Judy. 'Working Days in a London Construction Team in the Eighteenth Century: Evidence from St Paul's Cathedral'. *The Economic History Review*, 73, no. 2 (2020): 409–430.
Stirati, Antonella 'Classical Roots of the Criticisms of John Stuart Mill's Wage-Fund Theory', in *New Perspectives on Political Economy and Its History*, edited by Ghilain Marcuzzo Deleplace and Paolo Paesani, 149–69. London: Routledge: 2020.
Stirati, Antonella. 'Labour and employment', in *Handbook on the History of Economic Analysis Volume III*, edited by Gilbert Faccarello and Heinz D. Kurz, 356–71. Cheltenham, Edward Elgar, 2016.
Stirati, Antonella. 'On Hollander on Sraffa and the "Marxian Dimension"', in *Sraffa and Modern Economics*, edited by Ciccone, Roberto Gehrke, Christian and Gary Mongiovi. London: Routledge 2011.
Stirati, Antonella. *The Theory of Wages in Classical Economics*. Cheltenham: Elgar, 1994.
Styles, John. 'Clothing in the north: the supply of non-élite clothing in the eighteenth-century north of England'. *Textile History*, 25, no. 2 (1994), 139–66.
Styles, John. 'Fashion, Textiles and the Origins of Industrial Revolution'. *East Asian Journal of British History*, 5, March (2016), 161–90.
Styles, John. 'Spinners and the Law: Regulating Yarn Standards in the English Worsted Industries, 1550–1800'. *Textile History*, 44, no. 2 (2013): 145–70.
Styles, John. 'The Rise and Fall of the Spinning Jenny: Domestic Mechanisation in Eighteenth-Century Cotton Spinning'. *Textile History*, 51, no. 2 (2020): 195–236.

Styles, John. *The Dress of the People: Everyday Fashion in Eighteenth-Century England*. New Haven: Yale University Press, 2008.

Sugden, Keith. 'Clapham Revisited: The Decline of the Norwich Worsted Industry (c. 1700–1820)'. *Continuity and Change,* 33, no. 2 (2018): 203–24.

Sun, E-tu Zen. 'Mining Labor in the Ch'ing Period', in *Approaches to Modern Chinese History*, edited by Albert Feuerwerker and Mary Wright, 45–67. Berkeley: University of California Press, 1967.

Svensson, Thommy. *Från ackord till månadslön: en studie av lönepolitiken, fackföreningarna och rationaliseringarna inom svensk varvsindustri under 1900-talet.* Göteborg: Göteborgs universitet, 1983.

Swanson, Maynard. 'The Sanitation Syndrome: Bubonic Plague and Urban Native Policy in the Cape Colony, 1900–1909'. *Journal of African History,* 18, no. 3 (1977): 387–410.

Tavasci, Daniela and Luigi Ventimiglia (eds). *Teaching the History of Economic Thought.* Cheltenham: Edward Elgar, 2018.

Tedesco, Luca. *L'Alternativa Liberista in Italia. Crisi di Fine Secolo, Antiprotezionismo.* Soveria Mannelli: Rubbettino, 2003.

Terrier, Didier and Corinne Maitte (eds). *Les Temps du Travail. Normes, Pratiques, Évolutions (XIVe-XIXe Siècle).* Rennes: Presses Universitaires de Rennes, 2014.

The Farming and Memorandum Books of Henry Best of Elmswell, 1642. edited by Donald Woodward, Oxford: Oxford University Press, 1984.

Thévenot, Laurent. 'Certifying the World: Power Infrastructures and Practices in Economies of Conventional Forms', in *Re-Imagining Economic Sociology*, edited by Patrik Aspers and Nigel Dodd, 195–223. Oxford: Oxford University Press, 2015.

Thompson, Edward P. 'The Moral Economy of the English Crowd in the Eighteenth Century'. *Past & Present,* 50, no. 1 (1971): 76–136.

Thompson, Edward P. 'Time, Work-Discipline, and Industrial Capitalism'. *Past & Present,* 38, no. December (1967): 56–97.

Thompson, Edward P. *The Making of the English Working Class*. London: V. Gollancz, 1963.

Thörnqvist, Christer. *Arbetarna lämnar fabriken: strejkrörelser i Sverige under efterkrigstiden, deras bakgrund, förlopp och följder.* Göteborg: Göteborgs universitet, 1994.

Tilly, Charles and Chris Tilly. *Work Under Capitalism.* London: Routledge, 1998.

Tomassini, Luigi. 'Intervento dello Stato e Politica Salariale durante la Prima Guerra Mondiale: Esperimenti e Studi per la Determinazione di una "Scala Mobile" delle Retribuzioni Operaie', *Annali della Fondazione Giangiacomo Feltrinelli*, 22 (1983): 87–184.

Tooze, Adam. *Statistics and the German State, 1900–1945: The Making of Modern Economic Knowledge.* Cambridge: Cambridge University Press, 2001.

Topalov, Christian. 'A Revolution in Representations of Work. The Emergence over the 19th Century of the Statistical Category "Occupied Population", in France, Great Britain and the United States.' *Revue Française de Sociologie,* 42, no. 79 Supplement (2001): 79–106.

Touchelay, Béatrice and Philippe Verheyde (eds). *La Genèse de la Décision. Chiffres Publics, chiffres Privés dans la France du XXe siècle.* Pompignac-près-Bordeaux: Éditions Bière, 2009.

Touchelay, Béatrice, Isabelle Bruno and Florence Jany-Catrice (eds). *The Social Sciences of Quantification. From Politics of Large Numbers to Target-Driven Policies*. Cham: Springer, 2016.

Touchelay, Béatrice. 'Le Drainage des Ressources' in *La France et l'Afrique 1830–1960*, eds, Isabelle Surun, 113–18. Paris: Atlande, 2020.

Touchelay, Béatrice. 'Les Ordres de la Mesure des Prix. Luttes Politiques, Bureaucratiques et Sociales Autour de l'Indice des Prix à la Consommation (1911–2012)'. *Politix*, 105, no. 1 (2014): 117–38.
Trivellato, Francesca. *Fondamenta dei Vetrai. Lavoro, Tecnologia e Mercato a Venezia tra Sei e Settecento*. Roma: Donzelli, 2000.
Tshoaedi, Malehoko. 'Women in the Forefront of Workplace Struggles in South Africa: From Invisibility to Mobilization'. *Labour, Capital and Society* 45, no. 2 (2012): 58–83.
Turner, Michal E., John V. Beckett and Bethanie Afton. *Farm Production in England 1700–1914*. Oxford: Oxford University Press, 2001.
Tusset, Gianfranco. *Money as Organization, Gustavo Del Vecchio's Theory*. London: Routledge, 2014.
Unni, Jeemol. 'Gender and Informality in the Labour Market in South Asia'. *Economic and Political Weekly*, 36, no. 26 (2001): 2360–77.
van der Linden, Marcel and Karin Hofmeester (eds), *Handbook The Global History of Work*. Berlin: Degruyter, 2018.
van der Linden, Marcel and Magaly Rodriguez Garcia (eds). *On Coerced Labor: Work and Compulsion After Chattel Slavery*. Leiden, NL: Brill, 2016.
van der Linden, Marcel. 'Labour History Goes Global', in *The Practice of Global History. European Perspectives*. London: Bloomsbury 2019, chapter 5.
van der Linden, Marcel. 'Labour History: The Old, the New and the Global'. *African Studies*, 66, no. 2–3 (2007): 169–80.
van der Linden, Marcel. 'The Promise and Challenges of Global Labor History'. *International Labor and Working-Class History*, 82, Fortieth Anniversary Issue, (2012): 57–76.
van der Linden, Marcel. *Workers of the World. Essays toward a Global Labor History*. Leiden: Brill, 2008.
van der Velden, Sjaak. 'Building a repository for strike data. The search for micro data', in *Striking Numbers: New Approaches to Strike Research*, ed. Sjaal van der Velden, IISH Research Paper, no. 165 (2012).
van der Velden, Sjaak. 'Strikes, Lockouts, and Informal Resistance', in *Handbook Global History of Work*, ed. Marcel van der Linden, 521–50. Berlin: De Gruyter, 2017.
Van Der Werf, Ysbrand. 'Work in progress? The industrious revolution'. *The Journal of Economic History*, 58, no. 3 (1998): 830–43.
van Meeteren, Nicolas. *Volkskunde van Curaçao*. Willemstad: Drukkerij Scherpenheuvel, 1947.
van Nederveen Meerkerk, Elise. 'Market Wage or Discrimination? The Remuneration of Male and Female Wool Spinners in the Seventeenth-Century Dutch Republic'. *The Economic History review*, 63, no. 1 (2010): 165–86.
Van Zanden, Jan Lun. 'Wages and Standards of Living in Europe, 1500–1800'. *European Review of Economic History*, 3, no. 2 (1999): 175–198
van Zyl-Hermann, Danelle and Jacob Boersman. 'Introduction: The Politics of Whiteness in Africa'. *Africa*, 87, 4 (2017): 651–61.
Vanschoenbeek, Guy. *Novecento in Gent. De wortels van de sociaal-democratie in Vlaanderen*. Ghent: Amsab, 1995.
Vecchi, Giovanni. *Measuring Wellbeing. A History of Italian Living Standards*. Oxford: Oxford University Press, 2019.
Vorberg-Rugh, Rachael. 'Employers and Workers: Conflicting Identities over Women's Wages in the Co-operative Movement, 1906–1918', in *Consumerism and the Co-operative Movement in Modern British History*, edited by Lawrence Black and Nicole Robertson, 121–37. Manchester: Manchester University Press, 2009.

Vormbaum, Thomas. *Politik und Gesinderecht im 19. Jahrhundert (vornehmlich in Preußen 1810-1918)*. Berlin: Duncker & Humblot, 1980.
Voss, Lex Heerma van, Els Hiemstra-Kuperus and Elise van Nederveen Meerkerk (eds). *The Ashgate Companion to the History of Textile Workers, 1650-2000*. Farnham, Surrey, Burlington, VT: Ashgate, 2010.
Voth, Hans-Joachim. *Time and Work in England, 1750-1830*. Oxford: Oxford University Press, 2000.
Wadauer, Sigrid, Thomas Buchner and Alexander Mejstrik (eds). *The History of Labour Intermeditation, Institutions and Finding Employment in the Nineteenth and Early Twentieth Centuries*. New York: Berghahn, 2015.
Wadauer, Sigrid. 'Establishing Distinctions: Unemployment Versus Vagrancy in Austria from the Late Nineteenth Century to 1938.' *International Review of Social History*, 56, no.1 (2011): 31-70.
Wadauer, Sigrid. 'Journeymen's Mobility and the Guild System: A Space of Possibilities Based on Central European Cases', in *Guilds and Association in Europe, 900-1900*, edited by Ian A. Gadd and Patrick Wallis 169-86. London: University of London Press, 2007.
Wadauer, Sigrid. *Der Arbeit nachgehen? Auseinandersetzungen um Lebensunterhalt und Mobilität (Österreich 1880-1938)*. Köln: Böhlau 2021.
Wallis, Patrick. 'Apprenticeship and training in premodern England'. *The Journal of Economic History*, 68, no. 3 (2008): 832-61.
Wallis, Patrick. 'Labor, Law, and Training in Early Modern London: Apprenticeship and the City's Institutions'. *Journal of British Studies*, 51, no. 4 (2012): 791-819.
Whittle, Jane C. 'A Critique of Approaches to "Domestic Work": Women, Work and the Preindustrial Economy'. *Past & Present*, 243, no. 1 (2019): 35-70.
Whittle, Jane C. and Mark Hailwood. 'The Gender Division of Labour in Early Modern England'. *Economic History Review*, 73, no. 1 (2020): 3-32.
Widerquist, Karl and Michael Anthony Lewis (eds). *The Ethics and Economics of the Basic Income Guarantee*. Aldershot: Ashgate, 2005.
Willis, Paul. *Learning to Labor: how working class kids get working class jobs*. New York: Columbia University Press, 1981 [1979])
Willoughby-Herard, Tiffany. *Waste of a White Skin: The Carnegie Corporation and the Racial Logic of White Vulnerability*. Berkeley: University of California Press, 2015.
Wobbe, Theresa. 'Making up People. Berufsstatistische Klassifikation, geschlechtliche Kategorisierung und wirtschaftliche Inklusion um 1900 in Deutschland'. *Zeitschrift für Soziologie*, 41, no.1 (2012): 41-57.
Woodward, Donald. 'Wage Rates and Living Standards in Pre-Industrial England'. *Past and Present*, 91, no. May (1981): 28-46.
Woodward, Donald. *Men at Work. Labourers and Building Craftsmen in the Towns of Northern England, 1450-1750*. Cambridge: Cambridge University Press, 1994.
Wright, Erik Olin. 'Working-class Power, Capitalist-class Interests and Class Compromise'. *American Journal of Sociology*, 105, no. 4 (2000): 957-1002.
Wright, Tim '"A Method of Evading Management"—Contract Labor in Chinese Coal Mines before 1937', *Comparative Studies in Society and History*, 23, no. 4 (1981): 656-78.
Yudelman, David. *The Emergence of Modern South Africa: State, Capital, and the Incorporation of Organized Labor on the South African Gold Fields, 1902-1939*. Westport: Greenwood Press, 1983.
Zamagni, Vera. 'Una Ricostruzione dell'Andamento Mensile dei Salari Industriali e dell'Occupazione 1919-1939', *Ricerche per la Storia della Banca d'Italia*, 351-2. Bari: Laterza, 1994.

Zarefsky, David. *President Johnson's War on Poverty*. Tuscaloosa: University of Alabama Press, 1986.

Zelin, Madeleine. *The Merchants of Zigong: Industrial Entrepreneurship in Early Modern China*. New York, NY: Columbia University Press, 2005.

Zell, Michael. *Industry in the Countryside: Wealden Society in the Sixteenth Century*. Cambridge: Cambridge University Press, 1994.

Zheng, Qidong. *Dangdai zhongguo jindai jingjishi yanjiu 1949–2019* [Present-day China's Contemporary Economic History]. Beijing: Zhongguo she hui ke xue chu ban she, 2019.

Zimmermann, Bénédicte. *Arbeitslosigkeit in Deutschland. Zur Entstehung einer sozialen Kategorie*. Frankfurt am Main: Campus, 2006.

Index

Abbott, Edith 4
Adams, Zoe 29, 32
Adler, Victor 98
Akroyd, Jonathan 48–50
Allen, Robert 5, 6, 18, 37, 38n, 40, 50, 159
Amoroso, Luigi 231
Anseele, Edouard 70-3, 75-7
Arrow, Kenneth 252
Asta, Massimo 1n, 26
Atwater, Wilbur O. 236
Augagneur, Jean-Victor 215, 216
Austin, Gareth 13

Bachi, Riccardo 232, 232n
Balestrieri, Mario 242
Bandyopadhyay, Ritajyoti 127
Banerjee, Swapna 123
Batson, Edward 25, 188–90, 199, 204
Becker Gary 31, 32, 273
Belluzzo, Giuseppe 246
Benni, Antonio Stefano 246
Berman, Emily 227
Best of Elmswell, Henry 56
Biagi, Bruno 246n
Bibi, Zohra 121, 126, 127
Biernacki, Richard 23
Biswas, Ranjita 126n
Blanchard, Olivier 252n, 253
Blewett, Mary 11
Bluestone, Barry 276
Blum, Léon 217
Bodio, Luigi 4, 233
Bolton, Harriet 201
Bourdieu, Pierre 31
Bowers, Peter 43
Bowley, Arthur 4, 189
Broadberry, Stephen 5
Brown, Henry Phelps 5
Burley, K. H. 64
Burnett, Joyce 12
Buse, J. 78

Cabiati, Attilio, 232
Cannadine, Daid 106n
Cannan, Edwin 253
Caracausi, Andrea 15
Carbonnelle 222n
Carli, Filippo 246n
Cary, John 58
Cecil, William 56
Chavez, Cesar 278
Chen, Martha 128
Chesneaux, Jean 149, 150
Coppola d'Anna, Francesco 246n
Cowie, Jefferson R. 278n
Crooks, Will 291
Cucini, Bramante 246n

Davie, Grace 25
de Foville, Alfred 234
De Hollander, Jan 72
de Klerk, Frederik Willem 201
De Reymaeker, Loeys 222n
De Viti de Marco, Antonio 231
de Zwart, Pim 159
Debreu, Gérard 252
del Giudice, Riccardo 246n
Desrosières, Alain 186, 186n, 198, 227, 232
Deutsch, Julius 92
Dhawan, Nandita 126n
Dobb, Maurice 7
Dobson, C. R. 113
Doeringer, Peter 30, 31, 273, 274, 276
Douglas, Paul H. 4
Dufrasne 222n
Dunlop, John T. 273

Edwards, Richard 31, 276–9
Eichengreen, Barry 17
Einaudi, Luigi 239
Elvin, Mark 148
Engle Merry, Sally 227

Fielding Ogburn, William 268n
Fisher, Irving 234, 245
Franzosi, Roberto 17
Friedman, Milton 31, 249n
Friedman, Rose 270
Froide, Amy 60

Galbraith, John Kenneth 267
Galletti, Giuseppe 240
Gandhi, Mohandas Karamchand 192, 200
Gantt, H. L. 166
Gazeley, Ian 16
Ghosh, Anindita 126n
Gilboy, Elizabeth 113
Gini, Corrado, 26, 27, 205, 241, 242, 243, 247
Giolitti, Giovanni 231
Giusti, Ugo 240, 246n
Golas, Peter 147
Gongsi, Ruisheng 156
Gooren, Henny 10
Gordon, David 31, 276–9
Griggs, Thomas 42, 44–6, 50–2, 64

Hacking, Ian 186
Hall of Daventry, Charles 52
Harrington, Michael 31, 268, 269, 271
Harrison, Bennett 276
Hatcher, John 5, 110
Haynes, John 60
Heaton, William 50
Heger, Hans 10
Heigham of Huston, John 53, 54
Helen, Batson 189
Hertzog, J. B. M. 194
Higgenbotham, Peter 59
Hilton, John 241
Hirschamn, Daniel 227
Hobsbawm, Eric 7, 8, 20, 21, 93n, 108, 109, 114, 117, 118, 145, 146, 162
Holmes, of Scorton (Rev.) 52
Hongji, Li 153
Hopkins, Sheila 5
Huberman, Michael 10
Humphries, Jane 12, 18, 23, 37, 37n, 40, 50, 58

Jannaccone, Pasquale 241, 245
Jeffries, John 46, 48, 50

Jevons, William Stanley 28
Jodlbauer, Josef 92
Johnson, Lyndon 30, 31, 269, 270, 270n

Karlsson, Tobias 20, 21
Kennedy, John F. 269
Kerr, Clark 273
Keynes, John Maynard 249n
Khobragade, Devyani 121
Khrushchev, Nikita 267
King, Steve 55
Klezl, Felix 241
Knight, Frank 253
Kuczynski, Robert 4

Lamouche, J.-P. 222n
Laspeyres, Étienne 232
Latham (family) 55
Lemaignen, Robert 217
Levasseur, Émile 4
Lewis, Oscar 271, 271n
Livi, Livio 246n
Loader, Robert 56
Lolini, Ettore 246n
Long of Melksham, Thomas 46, 47, 49

MacDonald, Dwight 268
Maitte, Corinne 15
Majumdar, Srabasti 126n
Malthus, Thomas 1n, 28
Mammoli, Mario 246n
Mandela, Nelson 187, 200
Mann, Julia de Lacy 40
Marks, Shula 193
Maroi, Lanfranco 240
Marshall, Alfred 28, 249n, 250, 253
Martin, Brian 153n
Martini, Manuela 15
Marx, Karl 1n, 7, 14, 28, 30, 108, 249n, 263, 263n
Mata, Tiago 29–31
Maxton, James 293
Mbembe, Achille 188
Mérat, Louis 217
Mitchell, Wesley C. 4
Molinari, Alessandro 240, 243, 246
Montemartini, Giovanni 231, 232, 236
Montemartini, Luigi 231
Morgan, Mary 196

Mortara, Giorgio 247
Moutet, Marius 217
Moynihan, Patrick 270, 271
Mukherjee, Somdutta 126n
Muldrew, Craig 10, 18
Mussolini, Benito 242
Myrdal, Gunnar 17

Nearing, Scott 4
Necco, Achille 234
Neetha, N. 131
Newton, Isaac 41
Nimushakavi, Vasanthi 131
Nitti, Francesco Saverio 231
Nixon, Richard 266n, 267

O'Brien, Denis P. 29, 261, 262
Olivetti, Gino 246, 246n
Onley of Stistead (Rev.) 54
Orshansky, Mollie 270n

Paidipaty, Poornima 187
Paker, Meredith 115
Pandey, Ramen 131
Passeron, Jean-Claude 31
Peck, Gunther 158
Peemans, J.-P. 214
Pelinnger, Sarah 46
Perrier, Léon 213
Perry, Elizabeth 153n
Petty, William 249n
Pigou, Arthur Cecil 249n
Pinto, Pedro Ramos 1n, 187, 227n
Piore, Michael 30, 31, 273, 274, 276
Plaatje, Solomon 192, 193
Placienca, Luis 158n
Pleven, René 216n, 218
Polanyi, Karl 17
Popp, Adelheid 99
Porter, Theodore 22, 22n
Potgieter, Johann 201–2
Pugliese, Angelo 236, 237
Pullen, John 28
Purkayet, Shanti 141, 141n

Qayum, Seemin 123

Ramsbottom, E. C. 241
Raphael, Axel 169, 170, 172

Ray, Raka 123
Reagan, Ronald 378n
Reich, Michael 31, 276–9
Reith, Reinhold 10
Repaci, Francesco 240
Ricardo, David 249n
Ricca Salerno, Giuseppe 4
Ricci, Umberto 240
Ricciardi, Ferruccio 225
Richards, Sangeeta 122
Robbins, Lionel 7
Robinson, Joan 1n
Rod, Rosemary 64n
Rogers, James E. T. 4
Rogers, Thorold 110
Rosenband, Leonard 10
Rowntree, Seebohm 189
Rubner, Max 236
Rule, John 107
Ryckmans, Pierre 212n

Safley, Max 15
Said, Edward 191
Sarasúa, Carmen 23
Sayola, Renuka 137
Schmoller, Gustav 4
Schneider, Benjamin 18, 37, 40, 50, 58, 59
Scholliers, Peter 8, 12, 19, 109
Schumpeter, Joseph 253
Schwarz, Leonard 8, 109, 110, 117
Scott, James C. 56
Sen, Samita 20, 22
Serpieri, Arrigo 246n
Sethi, Mitul 121
Sharpe, Pamela 11
Shaw Taylor, Leigh 57
Shriver, Sargent 270, 272
Silver, Beverly 17
Simiand, François 4
Sitta, Pietro 246n
Slosse, Auguste 236
Smith, Adam 1n, 28–30, 113, 249, 250, 252–3, 283, 285, 287
Smuts, Jan 188, 189, 193
Snowden, Philip 292
Soderlund, Richard 42, 60, 63
Solow, Robert 13
Sonenscher, Michael 20
Song (dynasty) 16

Sorensen, Ted 268
Spencer, David 28n, 29
Spufford, Peter 64n
Sraffa, Piero 250, 253
Sretzer, Simon 227
Steinhardt, Karl 92
Stem, Reed (nickname) 162
Stephenson, Judy 5, 20, 110, 114
Stirati, Antonella 29, 30
Styles, John 40, 41
Sun, Baoshan (pseud. of Sun Yefang) 156
Sun, E-Tu Zen 147
Sun, Yatsen 159
Sun, Yefang 156–8
Symson, Joseph 62

Tassinari, Giuseppe 246n
Taylor, Frederick Winslow 165, 166
Taylor, Joseph 48
Taylor, Mary 48
Teh, Limin 20, 21
Thatcher, Margaret 33
Themba, Can 199
Thévenot, Laurent 186n
Thomas, Albert 218
Thompson, Edward P. 8, 109
Thörnqvist 175n
Tiejun, Zhang 161
Tirthankar, Roy 149, 150
Tomassini, Luigi 235
Tooze, Adam 233

Torgasheff, Boris 148
Touchelay, Béatrice 24, 25, 227, 227n
Trivellato, Francesca 15

Usher of Wiltshire, John 46, 48, 50

Van der Linden, Marcel 17
van Leeuwen, Bas 159
van Leeuwen-Li, Jieli 159
Van Zanden, Jan Luiten 5
Verwoerd, Hendrik 204
von Mohl, Hugo 91

Wadauer, Sigrid 19
Wagemann, Ernst 241
Wallerstein, Immanuel 276
Walras, Leon 250
Watson, Widow 46n
Waxweiler, Émile 234, 236
Webb, Beatrice
Weisdorf, Jacob 37n
Whittle, Jane 11
Willis, Paul 31
Wood, George 4
Wright, Tim 150
Wu, Ling 159

Yan, Xia 156–8, 162
Young, Arthur 18, 38, 50, 51, 54–7, 59–61, 63

Zhanran, Gu 160, 161

www.ingramcontent.com/pod-product-compliance
Lightning Source LLC
Chambersburg PA
CBHW070722020526
44116CB00031B/1145